COMMON USAGE DICTIONARY

SPANISH-ENGLISH
ENGLISH-SPANISH

By Ralph Weiman

FORMERLY CHIEF OF LANGUAGE SECTION,
U.S. WAR DEPARTMENT

AND

O.A. Succar

Revised and enlarged by

Robert E. Hammarstrand, Ph.D.

ASSISTANT PROFESSOR OF EDUCATION, HUNTER COLLEGE

CONTAINING OVER 20,000 BASIC TERMS WITH
MEANINGS ILLUSTRATED BY SENTENCES AND
1000 ESSENTIAL WORDS SPECIALLY INDICATED

Crown Publishers, Inc., New York

Copyright 1946, © 1955, 1968, 1974, 1983, 1985 by Crown Publishers, Inc.
All rights reserved.

THE LIVING LANGUAGE COURSE is a registered trademark, and
CROWN, and LIVING LANGUAGE and colophon are trademarks of
Crown Publishers, Inc., 225 Park Avenue South, New York, New York
10003

Manufactured in the United States of America.

Library of Congress Catalog Card Number: 55-12164

ISBN 0-517-55788-6
1985 Updated Edition

20   19   18   17

TABLE OF CONTENTS

INTRODUCTION

The Spanish Common Usage Dictionary lists the most frequently used Spanish words, gives their most important meanings and illustrates their use.

1. The *basic* words are indicated by capitals. These are the words generally considered essential for any reasonable command of the language.

2. Only the most important meanings are given.

3. These meanings are illustrated, wherever necessary, by means of everyday phrases and sentences. Where there is no close English equivalent for a Spanish word or where the English equivalent has several different meanings, the context of the illustrative sentences helps to make the meanings clear.

4. Each important word is followed by the everyday expression and sentences in which it most frequently occurs. The Common Usage Dictionary serves accordingly as a phrase book or conversation guide: it contains thousands of everyday sentences which are of practical importance (for traveling, correspondence, etc.) or which serve as illustrations of the grammatical features of current written and spoken Spanish. The Common Usage Dictionary should, therefore, prove helpful both to beginners who are building up their vocabulary and to advanced students who want to perfect their command of colloquial Spanish.

5. In translating the Spanish phrases and sentences an attempt has been made to give not a mere translation but an equivalent—that is, what an English speaker would say in the same situation. (Literal translations have been added to help the beginner.) The user is thus furnished with numerous examples of how common Spanish expressions (particularly the very idiomatic and the very colloquial ones) can best be translated into English. This feature makes the Common Usage Dictionary especially useful for translation work.

6. The English-Spanish part contains the most common English words and their Spanish equivalents. By consulting the sentences given under the Spanish word in the Spanish-English part the reader can observe whether the Spanish word always translates the English one or whether it does so only in certain cases.

EXPLANATORY NOTES

Literal translations are in quotation marks.

Very colloquial phrases and sentences are marked *coll.*

Expressions used in Latin America are marked *Amer.*

Expressions used in a particular country are followed by an abbreviation of the name of the country (*Mex.*, *Arg.*, etc.).

SPANISH-ENGLISH

A

A *to, in, at, on, by, for.*

Voy a Barcelona. *I'm going to Barcelona.*

¿A quién quiere Ud. escribir? *Who(m) do you want to write to?*

Dígaselo a él. *Tell it to him.*

A la derecha. *To the right. On the right.*

A las cinco y cuarto. *At a quarter past five.*

A veces. *At times.*

A la vista. *At sight.*

A tiempo. *In time.*

A pie. *On foot.*

Uno a uno. *One by one.*

ABAJO *down, below, under; downstairs.*

Está abajo. *He's downstairs.*

De arriba abajo. *From top to bottom. From top to toe. From head to foot.*

Calle abajo. *Down the street.*

abandonado *adj. abandoned, given up; untidy; careless.*

abandonar *to abandon, to give up, to leave.*

Después de cinco años lo abandonó. *He gave it up after five years.*

abandono *m. abandonment; slovenliness.*

abanico *m. fan.*

abarcar *to embrace, include, contain; to cover (a subject); to reach, extend to.*

La tienda abarca toda la cuadra. *The store occupies the whole block.*

abarrotes *m. groceries; grocery (store).*

Tienda de abarrotes. *Grocery.*

abastecer *to supply, to provide.*

abastecimiento *m. supply.*

abdomen *m. abdomen.*

abecedario *m. the alphabet; primer (book).*

abeja *f. bee.*

abiertamente *openly, frankly, plainly.*

ABIERTO *adj. open; frank.*

¿Hasta qué hora está la tienda abierta? *How late does the store stay open? Till what time does the store stay open?*

Ha dejado Ud. abierta la ventana. *You've left the window open.*

abogado *m. lawyer, attorney; mediator.*

abonado *adj. reliable, rich; m. subscriber; commuter.*

Guía de abonados. *Telephone directory.*

abonar *to credit to; to pay; to fertilize (the soil).*

abonarse *to subscribe to.*

abono *m. allowance; subscription; commutation ticket; fertilizer.*

aborrecer *to despise, to hate, to dislike.*

aborrecimiento *m. hatred, abhorrence.*

abotonar *to button.*

Abotónese el chaleco. *Button your vest.*

abrazar *to embrace, to hug.*

abrazo *m. hug, embrace.*

abrelatas *m. can opener.*

abreviar *to abbreviate.*

abreviatura *f. abbreviation.*

abridor *m. opener.*

abrigar *to shelter, to protect; to make or keep warm.*

abrigarse *to take shelter; to cover oneself; to dress warmly.*

ABRIGO *m. shelter; protection; overcoat.*

ABRIL *m. April.*

ABRIR *to open, to unlock.*

Abra la ventana. *Open the window.*

abrochar *to button; to fasten.*

absceso *m. abscess.*

ABSOLUTAMENTE *absolutely.*

absoluto *adj. absolute.*

absolver *to absolve, to acquit.*

abstenerse *to abstain, to refrain.*

abstinencia *f. abstinence, temperance.*

absuelto *adj. absolved, acquitted.*

absurdo *adj. absurd.*

Es un cuento absurdo. *It's an absurd story.*

abuela *f. grandmother.*

abuelo *m. grandfather.*

abundancia *f. abundance.*

abundante *adj. abundant.*

abundar *to abound.*

aburrido *adj. weary, bored, tiresome.*

aburrimiento *m. weariness, boredom.*

aburrir *to bore; to annoy.*

aburrirse *to be (get) bored.*

abusar *to abuse; to take advantage of.*

Abusa de su bondad. *He's taking advantage of your kindness.*

abuso *m. abuse, misuse.*

¡Esto es un abuso! *That's taking advantage!*

ACÁ *here, this way.*

¡Ven acá! *Come here!*

¿De cuándo acá? *Since when?*

ACABAR *to finish, to complete, to end.*

¿Consiguió Ud. acabar su trabajo? *Did you manage to finish your work?*

Acabar de. *To have just.*

Acabo de comer. *I've just eaten.*

El tren acaba de llegar. *The train has just arrived.*

academia *f. academy.*

acaecer *to happen, to take place.*

acaecimiento *m. event, incident.*

acampar *to camp, to encamp.*

acaparamiento *m. monopoly; hoarding.*

acaparar *to monopolize; to control the market; to hoard.*

acariciar *to caress, to pet; to cherish.*

acarrear *to carry, to transport; to cause.*

acarreo *m. carrying, transportation; carriage, cartage.*

ACASO *by chance, perhaps; m. chance, accident.*

Acaso preferiría usted ir en persona. *Perhaps you would prefer to go in person.*

Por si acaso va Ud. allí. *If you happen to go*

there.

Llevemos paraguas por si acaso llueve. *Let's take umbrellas in case it rains.*

acatarrarse *to catch cold.*

Estoy acatarrado. *I've caught a cold. I have a cold.*

acceder *to accede, to agree, to consent.*

accesorio *adj. accessory, additional.*

accidental *adj. accidental.*

ACCIDENTE *m. accident.*

El accidente ocurrió aquí mismo. *The accident happened right here.*

Fué un accidente. *It was an accident.*

ACCION *f. action, act, deed, feat; share; stock.*

Sus acciones contradicen sus palabras. *His actions contradict his words.*

¿Tiene Ud. acciones de la compañía X.? *Have you any shares of the X company?*

Acciones ferroviarias. *Railway stocks (bonds).*

accionista *m. and f. stockholder, shareholder.*

aceitar *to oil, to lubricate.*

aceite *m. oil.*

Aceite de olivo. *Olive oil.*

aceitera *f. oil cruet (glass bottle set on the table); oil can.*

aceituna *f. olive.*

acelerador *m. accelerator.*

acelerar *to accelerate, to hasten, to hurry.*

ACENTO *m. accent; accent mark.*

Habla con acento español. *He speaks with a Spanish accent.*

acentuar *to accent; to accentuate, to emphasize.*

aceptación *f. acceptance; approval.*

ACEPTAR *to accept.*

¿Aceptan ustedes cheques de viajeros? *Do you accept travelers' checks here?*

acera *f. sidewalk.*

ACERCA *about, concerning, in regard to.*

Le escribimos acerca de su viaje. *We wrote to him concerning your trip.*

¿Qué opina Ud. acerca de eso? *What do you think of (about) that?*

acercar *to approach; to bring near.*

Acerque Ud. esa silla. *Pull up that chair. Bring that chair closer.*

acercarse *to approach, to come near.*

¡Acérquese! *Come nearer!*

El invierno se acerca. *It will soon be winter. ("Winter is approaching.")*

acero *m. steel.*

acertadamente *opportunely, fitly, wisely.*

Lo ha dicho Ud. acertadamente. *That's well said (put).*

acertado *adj. fit, apt, proper, to the point.*

Su observación fué muy acertada. *His remark was to the point.*

Eso es lo más acertado. *That's the best thing to do.*

ACERTAR *to hit the mark, to guess right; to succeed.*

Es difícil acertar quien va a ganar. *It's difficult to guess who's going to win.*

Acertaba a pasar por la casa cuando salía. *I happened to be passing by the house when she came out.*

Acertó con la casa. *He succeeded in finding the house.*

ácido *m. acid.*

ácido *adj. sour.*

acierto *m. good hit; skill; tact.*

Obrar con acierto. *To act wisely.*

aclaración *f. explanation, clarification.*

aclarar *to explain, to make clear; to clear up; to rinse (clothes).*

¿Aclarará hoy el tiempo? *Will the weather clear up today?*

Va aclarando. *It's clearing up.*

aclimater *to acclimatize, to acclimate.*

acoger *to receive, to welcome.*

Le acogieron cordialmente. *They received him cordially.*

Le acogimos como a un familiar. *We gave him a warm welcome. ("We welcomed him as a relative.")*

acogida *f. reception; welcome.*

Una calurosa acogida. *A warm welcome.*

acomodador *m. usher.*

acomodar *to accommodate, to suit; to arrange, to place.*

Haga Ud. lo que le acomode. *Do as you please.*

acompañante *chaperon; companion.*

acompañar *to accompany, to escort, to attend.*

No puedo persuadirla que nos acompañe. *I can't get (persuade) her to come with us.*

Le acompañaré hasta la esquina. *I'll go with you as far as the corner.*

Si Ud. me permite la acompañaré a su casa. *If you don't mind I'll take you home.*

Acompaño a usted en el sentimiento. *I'm very sorry to hear about your loss.*

acongojarse *to become sad, to grieve.*

aconsejable *adj. advisable.*

aconsejar *to advise.*

¿Qué me aconseja Ud. que haga? *What do you advise me to do?*

acontecer *to happen, to take place.*

acontecimiento *m. event, happening.*

acorazado *m. battleship.*

acordar *to agree; to resolve; to remind.*

Tenemos que acordar la hora de salida. *We have to agree on the time of departure.*

ACORDARSE *to come to an agreement; to remember, to keep in mind.*

Se acordó enviarle un telegrama. *It was decided to send him a telegram.*

No me acuerdo de su nombre. *I don't recall*

his name.

acortar *to shorten, to cut short.*

ACOSTARSE *to go to bed, to lie down.*

acostumbrar *to accustom, to be accustomed.*

Estoy acostumbrado a acostarme tarde. *I'm used to going to bed late.*

acreditar *to credit; to accredit.*

acreedor *m. creditor.*

acrobacia *f. acrobatics.*

acróbata *m. and f. acrobat.*

acta *f. minutes, record of proceedings; certificate.*

Acta de matrimonio. *Marriage certificate.*

actitud *f. attitude.*

actividad *f. activity.*

En plena actividad. *In full swing.*

activo *adj. active; m. assets.*

ACTO *m. act, action, deed; meeting.*

En el acto. *At once.*

Acto seguido. *Then. Immediately afterwards.*

Primer acto. *First act.*

actor *m. actor, performer.*

actriz *f. actress.*

actuación *f. way of acting; role; record (of a person); play, work (of a team); pl. proceedings.*

ACTUAL *adj. present, existing. (The equivalent of "actual" is real, verdadero.)*

La moda actual. *The present-day fashion. The fashion now.*

El cinco del actual. *The fifth of this month.*

actualidad *f. present time.*

En la actualidad. *At present.*

actualmente *at present, at the present time, nowadays. ("Actually" is realmente.)*

Está actualmente en Madrid. *He's at present in Madrid.*

actuar *to act, to put into action.*

acuatizar *to land on water (a plane).*

ACUDIR *to rush to, to come to; to turn to; to attend.*

No sé a quién acudir. *I don't know who(m) to turn to.*

Un policía acudió en nuestra ayuda. *A policeman came to our aid.*

acueducto *m. aqueduct.*

ACUERDO *m. agreement, accord, understanding; resolution.*

No estoy de acuerdo con Ud. *I don't agree with you.*

Llegar a un acuerdo. *To come to an understanding. To reach an agreement.*

De común acuerdo. *By mutual consent (agreement).*

De acuerdo. *All right.*

acumulador, *m. battery.*

acusación *f. accusation.*

acusado *m. defendant.*

acusar *to accuse, to prosecute; to acknowledge (receipt).*

Acusar recibo. *To acknowledge receipt.*

adaptable *adj. adaptable.*

adaptar *to adapt, to fit.*

adaptarse *to adapt oneself.*

adecuado *adj. adequate, fit, suited.*

ADELANTADO *adj. anticipated, advance, in advance.*

Pagar adelantado. *To pay in advance.*

Por adelantado. *Beforehand. In advance.*

adelantar *to advance; to pay in advance; to be fast (a watch).*

Mi reloj adelanta. *My watch is fast.*

Poco se adelanta con eso. *Little can be gained by that. That won't get one (you) very far.*

adelantarse *to take the lead, to come forward.*

ADELANTE *ahead, farther on, forward, onward.*

¡Adelante! 1. *Go on!* 2. *Come in!*

De hoy en adelante. *From today on.*

En adelante. *Henceforth. From now on.*

Más adelante se lo explicaré. *I'll explain it to you later on.*

adelanto *m. progress, improvement; advance payment.*

Adelantos modernos. *Modern improvements.*

adelgazar *to make thin; to become slender, to lose weight.*

Me parece que usted ha adelgazado un poco. *I think you've gotten a little thinner.*

ademán *m. gesture, motion.*

ADEMAS *moreover, besides, furthermore, too.*

Además de eso. *Moreover. Besides that.*

ADENTRO *inside, within, inwardly.*

Vaya adentro. *Go in.*

Decir a sus adentros. *To say to oneself.*

adeudar *to owe; to pay (duty or freight).*

adeudarse *to get into debt.*

adherente *m. follower, supporter (of a party, society, etc.).*

adherirse *to become a member, to join.*

adhesión *f. adhesion; belonging to.*

adición *f. addition.*

ADICIONAL *adj. additional.*

adiestramiento *m. training.*

adiestrar *to train, to instruct, to teach.*

adinerado *adj. rich, wealthy.*

ADIOS *m. Goodby.*

adivinanza *f. riddle, puzzle, guess.*

adivinar *to guess, to foretell.*

adjetivo *m. adjective.*

adjuntar *to enclose, to attach.*

adjunto *adj. enclosed, attached, annexed: m. assistant.*

administración *f. administration, management; office of an administrator.*

administrador *m. administrator, manager.*

administrar *to administer, to manage.*

admirable *adj. admirable.*

admirablemente *admirably.*

admiración f. admiration, wonder; exclamation mark.

admirador m. admirer.

admirar to admire.

admirarse to wonder, to be amazed, to be surprised.

admisión f. admission, acceptance.

ADMITIR to admit, to accept, to grant.

ADONDE where, whither.

¿Adónde? Where?

¿Adónde va Ud.? Where are you going?

adopción f. adoption.

adoptar to adopt.

adoquinado m. pavement.

adorable adj. adorable.

adoración f. adoration.

adorar to adore, to worship.

adormecimiento m. drowsiness; numbness.

adornar to trim, to adorn, to decorate.

adquirir to acquire.

adquisición f. acquisition.

adrede purposely, on purpose.

Lo hizo adrede. He did it on purpose.

aduana f. customhouse, customs.

aduanero m. customs official.

adulador m. flatterer.

adular to flatter.

adulón adj. and m. flatterer.

adulterio m. adultery.

adulto adj. and n. adult.

adverbio m. adverb.

adversario m. adversary, enemy.

adversidad f. adversity.

advertencia f. warning, admonition, notice, advice.

advertir to warn, to give notice, to let know; to take notice of.

aéreo adj. aerial, by air, air.

Por correo aéreo. By air mail.

aeródromo m. airdrome, airport.

aeronáutica f. aeronautics.

aeronave f. airship.

aeroplano m. airplane.

aeropuerto m. airport.

afán m. anxiety, eagerness.

afanarse to be uneasy, to be anxious; to act eagerly; to work hard or eagerly, to take pains.

No se afane tanto. Don't work so hard. Take it easy.

afección f. affection, fondness.

afectar to affect, to concern.

afecto m. affection, fondness, love.

Afecto a. Fond of.

En prueba de mi afecto. As a token of my affection (esteem).

afeitado adj. shaven.

afeitar to shave.

Hojas de afeitar. Razor blades.

afeitarse to shave oneself.

afición f. fondness; hobby.

aficionado adj. fond of; m. fan, amateur.

¿Es Ud. un aficionado a los deportes? Are you a sports fan? Are you fond of sports?

afilar to sharpen.

afiliado adj. affiliated; m. member (of a society).

afiliarse to affiliate oneself, to join, to become a member (of a society).

afinidad f. affinity, analogy, resemblance.

afirmación f. affirmation, assertion, statement.

afirmar to affirm, to assert; to fasten, to make fast.

afirmativamente affirmatively.

aflicción f. affliction, sorrow, grief.

afligirse to grieve, to become despondent, to worry.

No hay porque afligirse. There's no reason to worry.

aflojar to loosen; to slacken; to become lax.

afortunadamente fortunately, luckily.

afortunado adj. fortunate, lucky.

¡Qué afortunado es Ud.! How fortunate (lucky) you are!

afrenta f. affront, insult, outrage.

afrontar to confront, to face.

AFUERA out, outside; f. pl. suburbs, outskirts.

Salgamos afuera. Let's go outside.

¡Afuera! Get out of the way!

La fábrica está en las afueras de la ciudad. The factory is on the outskirts of the city.

agacharse to bend down, to stoop.

agarrar to grasp, to seize.

agarrarse to clinch; to grapple, to hold on.

agasajar to entertain, to receive and treat hospitably.

agencia f. agency.

agenda f. notebook, memorandum book.

agente m. agent.

ágil adj. agile, light, fast.

agitación f. agitation, excitement.

agitar to agitate, to stir, to shake up.

Agítese antes de usarse. Shake well before using.

agonía f. agony.

agonizar to be dying; to tantalize.

AGOSTO m. August.

agotamiento m. exhaustion.

AGOTAR to drain, to exhaust, to run out of.

Estoy agotado. I'm exhausted.

Se me agotó la gasolina. I ran out of gas.

Esta edición está agotada. This edition is out of print.

Se han agotado las localidades. All the seats are sold out.

AGRADABLE adj. agreeable, pleasant, pleasing.

Pasamos un rato muy agradable. We had a very pleasant time.

AGRADAR to please, to like.

Esto me agrada más. I like this (one) better.

This (one) pleases me more.

AGRADECER *to give thanks, to be grateful.*

Se lo agradezco mucho. *I appreciate this very much.*

Le estoy muy agredecido. *I'm very much obliged to you.*

agradecimiento *m. gratitude, gratefulness.*

agrado *m. liking, pleasure.*

Ser del agrado de uno. *To be to one's taste (liking).*

agravarse *to grow worse.*

agregar *to add; to aggregate, to heap together; to assign temporarily.*

agresión *f. aggression.*

agresor *m. aggressor.*

agriarse *to turn sour.*

agricultor *m. farmer.*

agricultura *f. farming, agriculture.*

agrietarse *to crack; to chap.*

AGRIO *adj. sour.*

agrupación *f. gathering, crowd; association.*

agrupar *to bring together; to group, to come together in a group.*

AGUA *f. water.*

Agua corriente. *Running water.*

Agua fresca. *Cold water.*

Agua mineral. *Mineral water.*

Agua potable. *Drinking water.*

Agua tibia. *Lukewarm water.*

aguacate *m. alligator pear, avocado.*

aguacero *m. downpour, heavy shower.*

aguantar *to bear, to endure; to resist.*

Lo siento pero no la puedo aguantar. *I'm sorry but I can't stand her.*

AGUARDAR *to expect; to wait for; to allow time for.*

Estoy aguardando a un amigo. *I'm expecting (waiting for) a friend.*

Podemos aguardar en la sala. *We can wait in the living room.*

¡Aguarda un momento! *Wait a minute!*

¡Aguárdame! *Wait for me!*

águila *f. eagle.*

aguinaldo *m. Christmas or New Year's gift.*

AGUJA *f. needle.*

Pasar la hebra por el ojo de la aguja. *To thread a needle.*

agujerear *to bore, to make holes.*

agujero *m. hole.*

¡ah! *ah! oh!*

¡Ah, se me olvidaba! *Oh, I almost forgot!*

ahí *there (near the person addressed).*

¿Qué tiene Ud. ahí? *What have you got there?*

Ponlo ahí. *Put it there.*

¡Ahí viene! *There he comes!*

Por ahí. *Over there. That way.*

De ahí que. *Hence. Therefore. As a consequence.*

ahijado *m. godchild; protégé.*

ahogado *adj. drowned.*

ahogar *to drown; to choke.*

ahogarse *to drown; to be suffocated.*

AHORA *now, at present.*

Vámonos ahora. *Let's go now.*

Ahora me toca a mí. *It's my turn now.*

Ahora mismo. *Right now. This very moment.*

Venga Ud. ahora mismo. *Come right away (this moment).*

ahorcar *to hang (to suspend by the neck).*

ahorita *in a little while, just now, this minute.*

Ahorita mismo. *Right away.*

Ahorita pasará el autobús. *The bus will pass by in a little while.*

Libreta de la Caja de Ahorros. *Bankbook.*

ahorrar *to save, to economize; to spare.*

Ahorrar algo para el día de mañana. *To lay something aside for a rainy day.*

ahorro *m. savings; thrift.*

AIRE *m. air, wind; aspect, look.*

Una corriente de aire. *A draft ("current of air").*

Voy a salir a tomar un poco de aire. *I'm going out for some fresh air.*

¿Qué aires lo traen a Ud. por acá? *"What good wind blows you here?"*

Tiene un aire muy severo. *He has a very severe (stern) look.*

Estar en el aire. *To be up in the air.*

Al aire libre. *In the open. Outdoors.*

Aire popular. *Folk music. Folk song.*

ajedrez *m. chess.*

ajeno *another's, of others, other people's, foreign, strange.*

Estoy completamente ajeno de ello. *I'm completely unaware of it. I know absolutely nothing about it.*

Ajeno al asunto. *Foreign to the subject. Having nothing to do with the subject.*

Lo ajeno. *That which belongs to others.*

Bienes ajenos. *Other people's goods (property).*

ají *m. chili.*

ajo *m. garlic.*

ajustar *to adjust; to fit; to settle (an account, matter, etc.).*

AL *(contraction of a + el) to the, at the; on, when. See also a and el.*

Aviso al público. *Notice to the public.*

Al contrario. *On the contrary.*

Al amanecer. *At dawn (daybreak).*

Al anochecer. *At dusk (nightfall).*

Al fin y al cabo. *At last. In the end. At length. After all. In the long run.*

Al saberlo. *When I learned that.*

Se rieron mucho al oír eso. *They laughed a lot when they heard that.*

ala *f. wing; brim (of a hat).*

alabar *to praise.*

alabarse *to praise oneself, to boast.*

alacena *f. kitchen closet, cupboard.*

alacrán *m. scorpion.*

alambrado *m. wire fence, wire net.*

alambre *m. wire.*

alameda *f. public walk lined with trees.*

alarde *m. ostentation, showing off, boasting.*
>Hacer alarde de. *To boast of (about).*

alargar *to lengthen; to stretch, to extend; to prolong, to drag on; to hand over, to pass.*
>Alargar el paso. *To walk faster.*

alargarse *to become or grow longer.*
>Se alargan los días. *The days are growing (getting) longer.*

alarma *f. alarm.*

alarmarse *to become alarmed; to be alarmed.*

alba *f. dawn.*
>Al rayar el alba. *At daybreak.*

albañil *m. mason, bricklayer.*

albaricoque *m. apricot.*

albóndiga *f. meatball.*

alborotarse *to become excited.*

alboroto *m. excitement; disturbance.*

álbum *m. album.*

alcachofa *f. artichoke.*

alcalde *m. mayor.*

alcance *m. reach, range; scope; ability, intelligence.*
>De gran alcance. *Far-reaching.*
>Estar al alcance de. *To be within the reach of. To be within someone's means.*
>Dar alcance. *To cutch up with. To catch (arrest).*
>Es un hombre de pocos alcances. *He's not very intelligent.*

alcancía *f. money box, a small bank.*

alcanfor *m. camphor.*

alcanzar *to overtake, to catch up with; to catch; to reach; to obtain, to attain, to get; to be enough, to be sufficient; to hand, to pass; to affect.*
>Los alcanzaremos con nuestro coche. *We'll overtake them with our car.*
>¿Pudieron alcanzar el tren? *Were they able to catch the train?*
>No alcanza para todos. *There's not enough for everybody.*
>Tenga la bondad de alcanzarme el salero. *Please pass me the saltshaker.*
>Alcanzar a comprender. *To understand. To make out.*
>Poco se le alcanza. *He doesn't understand it very well. He doesn't care very much about it.*
>Alcanzar con la mano. *To reach with one's hand.*

alcoba *f. bedroom.*

alcohol *m. alcohol.*

aldaba *f. door knocker, latch.*

aldea *f. small village.*

alegrar *to gladden, to make glad, to enliven.*

ALEGRARSE *to rejoice, to be glad, to be happy.*
>Me alegro muchísimo. *I'm very glad. I'm delighted.*
>Me alegro de que esté usted mejor. *I'm very glad you're better.*
>Me alegro de saberlo. *I'm happy to know it.*

alegre *adj. glad, merry, happy.*

alegría *f. merriment, gaiety, delight, rejoicing, joy.*
>Está llena de alegría. *She's very happy.*

alejar *to remove, to take away; to hold off (at a distance).*

alejarse *to go far away; to move away.*

alemán *adj. and n. German.*

alfabeto *m. alphabet.*

alfiler *m. pin.*

alfombra *f. carpet, rug.*

ALGO *some, something, anything, somewhat.*
>Algo que comer. *Something to eat.*
>En algo. *In some way. Somewhat.*
>Por algo. *For some reason.*
>¿Hay algo de particular? *Is there anything special?*
>¿Necesita Ud. algo más? *Do you need anything else?*
>¿Tiene Ud. algo que hacer esta tarde? *Do you have anything to do this afternoon?*
>¿Quiere Ud. tomar algo? *Do you want anything to drink?*
>Quiero comer algo ligero. *I want something light to eat.*
>Tengo algo que decirle. *I have something to tell you.*
>Lo encuentro algo caro. *I find it somewhat expensive.*
>Comprendo algo. *I understand a little.*

algodón *m. cotton.*

alguacil *m. constable.*

ALGUIEN *somebody, someone.*
>Alguien llama a la puerta. *Someone's knocking at the door.*
>¿Aguarda Ud. a alguien? *Are you waiting for someone?*

algún *adj. (used only before a masculine noun) some, any.*
>¿Tiene Ud. algún libro para prestarme? *Have you a (any) book to lend me?*
>Algún día se lo contaré. *I'll tell you some day.*
>Durante algún tiempo. *For some time.*

ALGUNO *adj. some, any.*
>En modo alguno. *In any way.*
>Alguna cosa. *Anything.*
>En alguna parte. *Anywhere.*
>¿Hay alguna farmacia cerca de aquí? *Is there a drugstore near here?*
>Lo habré leído en alguno que otro periódico.

I probably read it in some newspaper or other.

Déjeme ver algunas camisas. *Let me see some shirts.*

Conozco a algunas personas aquí pero no a todas. *I know some (several) people here but not everyone.*

Alguna que otra vez. *Once in a while. Occasionally.*

alhaja *f. jewel.*

alianza *f. alliance.*

alicates *m. pliers, pincers.*

aliento *m. breath; courage.*

Sin aliento. *Out of breath.*

Dar aliento. *To encourage.*

alimentación *f. feeding, food.*

alimentar *to feed, to nourish; to cherish.*

alimento *m. food, nourishment.*

alistar *to enlist; to get ready.*

alistarse *to enlist; to get ready.*

Se estaba alistando para salir. *He was getting ready to go out (leave).*

Se alistó en el ejército. *He enlisted in the army.*

aliviar *to lighten; to make things easier; to get better.*

¡Que se alivie pronto! *I hope you'll get better soon.*

alivio *m. relief, ease.*

¡Qué alivio! *What a relief!*

ALMA *f. soul.*

No hay ningún alma viviente en este lugar. *There's not a living soul in this place.*

Con toda mi alma. *With all my heart.*

Lo siento en el alma. *I deeply regret it. I'm extremely sorry about it.*

almacén *m. warehouse; store, shop.*

Tener en almacén. *To have in stock.*

Almacenes. *Department store.*

almacenar *to store; to hoard.*

almanaque *m. almanac, calendar.*

almeja *f. clam.*

almendra *f. almond.*

almendro *m. almond tree.*

almidón *m. starch.*

almidonar *to starch.*

almirante *m. admiral.*

almohada *f. pillow, bolster.*

almohadón *m. large cushion or pillow.*

almorzar *to lunch; to breakfast (Mex.).*

ALMUERZO *m. lunch.*

alojamiento *m. lodging; billeting (soldiers).*

alojar *to lodge; to billet (soldiers).*

alpargata *f. hemp sandal.*

ALQUILAR *to rent, to hire.*

Se alquila. *To let (a room, a house, etc.). For rent.*

La casa está por alquilar. *The house is for rent.*

ALQUILER *m. rent, rental, the act of hiring or renting.*

¿Cuánto es el alquiler? *How much is the rent?*

ALREDEDOR *around; pl. outskirts, surroundings.*

Tengo alrededor de veinte dólares. *I have about twenty dollars.*

Un viaje alrededor del mundo. *A trip around the world.*

Vive en los alrededores de Madrid. *He lives in the outskirts of Madrid.*

altavoz *m. loudspeaker.*

alterarse *to become angry, to get annoyed.*

altercado *m. quarrel.*

alternar *to alternate.*

alternativa *f. alternative.*

ALTO *adj. high, tall; loud; halt, stop.*

Es muy alto para su edad. *He's very tall for his age.*

Haga el favor de hablar más alto. *Please speak louder.*

No puedo alcanzarlo, está muy alto. *I can't reach it; it's too high.*

Hacer alto. *To halt.*

¡Alto! *Stop!*

¡Alto ahí! *Stop there!*

Se me pasó por alto. *I overlooked it. I didn't notice it.*

A altas horas de la noche. *Late at night.*

altoparlante *m. loudspeaker.*

altura *f. height, altitude.*

aludir *to allude, to refer to.*

alumbrado *m. lighting, illumination.*

alumbrar *to light, to illuminate.*

aluminio *m. aluminum.*

alumno *m. pupil, student.*

alza *f. rise, increase (price, stocks, etc.); sight (on a gun, on instruments).*

ALZAR *to raise, to lift up.*

Alce eso. *Lift that.*

Alzar cabeza. *To get on one's feet again. ("To raise one's head.")*

ALLÁ *there, over there (away from the speaker); in other times, formerly.*

Más allá. *Farther on. Beyond.*

Más allá de. *Beyond.*

Vaya Ud. allá. *Go there.*

¡Allá voy! *I'm coming!*

Allá en España. *Over there in Spain.*

Allá en el sur. *Down South.*

Allá en mis mocedades. *In the days of my youth.*

Eso allá él. *It's his own business.*

ALLÍ *there, in that place.*

De allí. *From there. From that place.*

Allí mismo. *Right there. In that very place.*

Lléveme allí. *Take me there.*

Vive allí, en la casa de la esquina. *He lives in the corner house over there.*

Esté Ud. allí a las nueve. *Be there at nine o'clock.*

Por allí. *That way. Over there.*

ama *f. mistress of the house, landlady.*

Ama de llaves. *Housekeeper.*

AMABILIDAD *f. amiability, affability, kindness.*

¿Tendría Ud. la amabilidad de decirme la hora? *What time is it, please? Can you please tell me the time?*

Le agradezco mucho su amabilidad. *Thanks for your kindness.*

AMABLE *adj. amiable, kind.*

Ud. es muy amable. *You're very kind. That's very kind of you.*

AMANECER *m. daybreak, dawn.*

Al amanecer. *At dawn (daybreak).*

amante *adj. loving; m. and f. lover, sweetheart.*

Ser amante de. *To be fond of.*

AMAR *to love.*

AMARGO *adj. bitter.*

AMARILLO *adj. yellow.*

amarrar *to tie, to fasten; to moor.*

amartillar *to hammer; to cock (a gun).*

amasar *to knead, to mold.*

ambición *f. ambition.*

ambicioso *adj. ambitious; greedy.*

ambiente *m. environment; atmosphere.*

AMBOS *adj. both.*

Ambos hermanos vinieron a la fiesta. *Both brothers came to the party.*

Ambos a dos. *The two together.*

ambulancia *f. ambulance.*

amenaza *f. menace, threat.*

amenazar *to menace, to threaten.*

ameno *adj. pleasant, agreeable, pleasing; light, entertaining (reading).*

americana *f. man's coat, jacket; an American (woman).*

americano *m. American.*

ametralladora *f. machine gun.*

amigablemente *amicably, in a friendly manner.*

amígdala *f. tonsil.*

AMIGO *m. friend.*

Somos amigos íntimos. *We're close friends.*

Vino a vernos con su amiga. *He came to see us with his girl friend.*

Ser amigo de. *To be fond of.*

amistad *f. friendship.*

amistosamente *amicably, in a friendly manner.*

amistoso *adj. friendly.*

amo *m. master, lord; proprietor, owner; boss.*

amontonar *to heap, to pile up.*

AMOR *m. love.*

De mil amores. *With great pleasure.*

amparar *to shelter, to protect, to help.*

ampliación *f. enlargement.*

ampolla *f. blister; ampule.*

amputar *to amputate.*

amueblar *to furnish.*

analfabeto *adj. illiterate.*

análisis *m. analysis.*

anatomía *f. anatomy.*

anciano *m. old man.*

ancla *f. anchor.*

ANCHO *adj. broad, wide; m. width, breadth.*

Estos zapatos me vienen muy anchos. *These shoes are too wide for me.*

Dos pies de ancho. *Two feet wide.*

A todo el ancho. *Full-width.*

Estoy a mis anchas aquí. *I'm very comfortable here.*

anchura *f. width, breadth.*

ANDAR *to walk; to go; to be.*

Andar a pie. *To go on foot.*

Es demasiado lejos para ir andando. *It's too far to walk.*

¿Anda bien su reloj? *Does your watch keep good time?*

Ando mal de dinero. *I'm short of money.*

Andar triste. *To be sad.*

Andar en mangas de camisa. *To go around in one's shirt sleeves.*

Andar en cuerpo. *To go outdoors without an overcoat.*

Andando el tiempo. *In the course of time.*

¡Andando! *Let's get going!*

¡Anda! *Go on! Come on!*

andén *m. platform of a railroad station, track.*

anécdota *f. anecdote.*

anemia *f. anemia.*

anfitrión *m. host.*

ángel *m. angel.*

angosto *adj. narrow.*

anguila *f. eel.*

ángulo *m. angle.*

angustia *f. anguish, distress, affliction.*

anhelar *to long for, to yearn.*

anhelo *m. desire, longing.*

anillo *m. ring, band.*

animal *animal; brute.*

¡No seas animal! *Don't be stupid!*

animar *to animate, to encourage, to cheer up, to enliven.*

animarse *to become lively, to feel encouraged, to cheer up.*

ÁNIMO *m. courage; mind, feeling.*

No me animo a hacerlo, *I wouldn't dare to do it.*

Los ánimos están excitadísimos. *Feeling is running very high.*

¡Ánimo! *Cheer up!*

aniversario *m. anniversary.*

ANOCHE *last night.*

¿Se divirtieron Uds. anoche? *Did you have a good time last night?*

anochecer *to grow dark.*
> Anochecía (se hacía de noche) cuando llegamos a Madrid. *It was getting dark when we arrived in Madrid.*
> Al anochecer. *At dusk (nightfall).*

anormal *adj. abnormal.*

anotar *to annotate, to make notes; to write down.*

ansia *f. anxiety, eagerness, longing.*

ansiedad *f. anxiety.*

ansioso *adj. anxious, eager.*

ANTE *before, in the presence of.*
> Ante todo. *Above all. First of all.*

ante *m. suede.*

ANTEAYER *the day before yesterday.*

antebrazo *m. forearm.*

antecedente *m. antecedent; pl. data, references, record (of a person).*

antecesores *m. ancestors.*

antemano *beforehand.*

antena *f. antenna, aerial.*

ANTENOCHE *night before last.*

anteojos *m. pl. glasses.*

antepasado *adj. past, last; m. pl. ancestors, forefathers.*

anterior *adj. anterior, previous, former, preceding.*

anteriormente *previously.*

ANTES *before.*
> Cuanto antes. *As soon as possible.*
> Hágalo cuanto antes. *Do it as soon as possible.*
> Agítese antes de usarse. *Shake well before using.*
> Haga antes un borrador. *Make a rough copy first.*
> Antes de tiempo. *Ahead of time.*

anticipación *f. anticipation, foretaste.*
> Si vienes, avísame con anticipación. *Let me know in advance if you come.*

anticipar *to anticipate; to advance (money).*
> Me anticipó veinte pesos. *He gave me twenty pesos in advance.*

anticiparse *to anticipate; to act or occur before the regular or expected time.*
> Se anticiparon media hora. *They arrived half an hour earlier.*

anticipo *m. advance payment, advance.*

anticuado *adj. old fashioned.*

anticuario *m. antiques dealer, antiquarian.*

ANTIER *day before yesterday.*

antifaz *m. mask.*

antiguamente *formerly, in ancient times.*

antigüedad *f. antiquity; antique; seniority.*
> Tienda de antigüedades. *Antique shop.*

ANTIGUO *adj. antique, ancient, old.*
> Ese es un dicho muy antiguo. *That's a very old saying.*

antipatía *f. antipathy, dislike, aversion.*

antipático *adj. displeasing, not congenial.*
> Me es muy antipático. *I don't find him at all congenial. I don't like him.*

antiséptico *adj. and n. antiseptic.*

antojarse *to desire, to long for, to crave.*
> Tiene cuanto se le antoja. *She has everything she could wish for.*
> Que haga lo que se le antoje. *Let him do as he pleases.*

antojo *m. desire, caprice, whim.*

anual *adj. yearly, annual.*

anular *to void, to annul, to make void.*

ANUNCIAR *to announce; to advertise.*
> Lo acaban de anunciar en la radio. *They just announced that on the radio.*
> La tienda anuncia un saldo. *The store is advertising a sale.*

ANUNCIO *m. announcement, notice, sign, advertisement.*

anzuelo *m. fishhook; bait.*

AÑADIR *to add.*
> Añádalo a mi cuenta. *Add it to my bill.*

AÑO *m. year.*
> ¿En qué año ocurrió? (In) *What year did it happen?*
> Hace dos años que vivo aquí. *I've been living here for two years.*
> Todo el año. *All year. All year round.*
> El año pasado. *Last year.*
> El año que viene. *Next year.*
> ¡Feliz año nuevo! *Happy New Year!*
> ¿Cuántos años tiene Ud.? *How old are you?* ("How many years do you have?")
> Tengo treinta años. *I am thirty years old.* ("I have thirty years.")

apagar *to quench, to extinguish, to put out.*
> Apague la luz. *Turn off the light. Put out the light.*

apagarse *to go out (of a light, fire, etc.).*
> Se apagaron las luces. *The lights went out.*

aparador *m. sideboard, cupboard.*

aparato *m. apparatus, device; ostentation.*

APARECER *to appear, to show up, to turn up.*
> No apareció en todo el día. *He didn't show up all day.*
> Apareció como por ensalmo. *He appeared as though by magic.*

aparentar *to pretend, to affect.*
> Aparenta ser rico. *He seems to be rich.*

aparentemente *apparently.*
> Aparentemente es así. *Apparently it's so.*

apariencia *f. appearance, looks, aspect.*
> Las apariencias engañan. *Appearances are deceiving.*
> Al juzgar por las apariencias. *To judge by appearances.*

apartado *adj. separated, distant; m. post-office box.*
> Apartado de correos. *Post-office box.*

apartamento m. *apartment. (also written* **aparta-miento**.)

Casa de apartamentos. *Apartment house.*

¿Tienen apartamentos por alquilar? *Do you have any vacancies? Are there any apartments for rent?*

apartamiento m. *separation; a distant place; apartment.*

apartar *to separate, to lay aside.*

apartarse *to keep away, to get out of the way.*

Apártese del fuego. *Get away from the fire.*

Se apartó de nosotros. *He kept away from us.*

APARTE *aside, separately.*

Ponga este paquete aparte. *Put this package aside.*

Esa es una cuestión aparte. *That's another question.*

apearse *to get off.*

Quiero apearme en la próxima parada. *I want to get off at the next stop.*

apellido m. *surname, last name, family name.*

Escriba su nombre y apellido. *Write down your first and last names.*

APENAS *scarcely, hardly; no sooner than, as soon as.*

Apenas puedo creerlo. *I can hardly believe it.*

Apenas podía moverse. *He could scarcely move.*

Las dos apenas. *Not quite two o'clock. A little before two.*

apetecer *to long for, to desire.*

apetito m. *appetite.*

apio m. *celery.*

aplaudir *to applaud.*

aplauso m. *applause, praise; approbation.*

aplazar *to put off, to postpone, to defer, to convene, to adjourn.*

Han aplazado el viaje hasta el mes que viene. *They've put off the trip until next month.*

aplicado adj. *studious, industrious, diligent.*

aplicarse *to apply oneself, to devote oneself to; to study.*

apoderarse *to take possession of.*

apodo m. *nickname.*

apostar *to bet; to post (soldiers, etc.).*

¿Cuánto apuestas? *How much do you bet?*

Apuesto cualquier cosa a que no lo dice. *I'll bet anything he won't say it.*

apoyar *to favor, to back up, to support, to defend, to aid; to lean.*

Apóyalo contra la pared. *Lean it against the wall.*

Apoyar una moción. *To second a motion.*

apreciación f. *estimation, appreciation.*

apreciar *to estimate, to value, to appreciate, to esteem.*

aprecio m. *appreciation, esteem, regard.*

Le tengo mucho aprecio. *I have a high regard for him.*

apremiante adj. *urgent, pressing.*

apremiar *to urge, to press.*

APRENDER *to learn.*

Aprendí solamente un poco de español. *I learned only a little Spanish.*

Apréndaselo de memoria. *Learn it by heart.*

apresurarse *to hurry, to hasten.*

Apresúrese si no quiere perder el tren. *Hurry up if you don't want to miss the train.*

apretado adj. *tight.*

apretar *to tighten, to press, to compress, to squeeze.*

Estos zapatos me aprietan un poco. *These shoes are a little tight for me.*

aprieto m. *difficulty, fix, spot.*

Estoy en un verdadero aprieto. *I'm in a tough spot. I'm in a bad fix.*

Ya saldremos de aprietos. *We'll get out of these difficulties.*

APRISA *fast, swiftly, promptly.*

Vaya lo más aprisa posible. *Go as quickly as you can.*

aprobación f. *approval.*

aprobar *to approve, to approve of; to pass (an examination).*

¿Ha sido aprobado el plan? *Has the plan been approved?*

Apruebo su conducta. *I approve of his conduct.*

No me aprobaron en historia. *I failed in history.*

aprovechar *to be useful or beneficial; to profit; to make use of.*

Hay que aprovechar la ocasión. *We must take advantage of the opportunity.*

Esta cocinera sabe aprovechar los restos. *This cook knows how to make good use of the leftovers.*

Aprovechar el tiempo. *To make good use of one's time.*

No deje que se aprovechen de Ud. *Don't let people take advantage of you.*

¡Que aproveche! *I hope you enjoy it (said when entering a room where people are eating).*

aprovecharse *to take advantage of, to derive profit from, to make use of.*

aprovisionamiento m. *supply.*

aproximadamente *approximately.*

aproximarse *to approach, to come near.*

aptitud f. *aptitude, fitness, ability; pl. qualifications.*

apuesta f. *bet, wager.*

La gané la apuesta. *I won the bet from him.*

apuntar *to aim; to indicate, to point out; to write down.*

Apunte la dirección para que no se le olvide. *Write down the address so you won't forget it.*

Apúntelo en mi cuenta. *Charge it to my account.*

apuñalar *to stab.*

apurarse *to hurry; to worry, to fret; to exert oneself.*

¡Apúrese! *Hurry up!*

No se apure Ud. que ya saldremos de aprietos. *Don't worry, we'll get out of these difficulties.*

apuro m. *want; affliction; plight; fix, difficulty, scrape.*

¿Salió Ud. del apuro? *Did you manage to get out of that difficulty?*

Estar en apuros. *To be in difficulties.*

AQUEL *that, that one; the former.*

Mire aquel avión. *Look at that plane.*

Aquel negocio le arruinó. *That business ruined him.*

En aquel mismo momento llegó. *He arrived at that very moment.*

En aquel entonces. *At that time.*

No quería éste sino aquél. *I didn't want this one but the one over there.*

aquella (f. of aquel) *that, that one.*

Aquella muchacha baila muy bien. *That girl (over there) dances very well.*

Esta silla es más cómoda que aquélla. *This chair is more comfortable than that one.*

aquellas (pl. of aquella) *those.*

Mira aquellas chicas que van allá. *Look at those girls walking over there.*

aquello (neuter) *that (referring to an idea).*

Aquello fué horrible. *That was horrible.*

Ya pasó aquello. *That's gone (past) and forgotten. That's water under the bridge.*

aquellos (pl. of aquel) *those.*

¿Te acuerdas de aquellos tiempos? *Do you remember the good old days?*

¿Cuáles prefieres, éstos o aquéllos? *Which do you prefer, these or those?*

AQUÍ *here, in this place.*

¿Paramos aquí? *Do we stop here?*

¿Vive Ud. aquí? *Do you live here?*

¿Se puede telefonear desde aquí? *Can we phone from here?*

¿Qué demonios hace Ud. aquí? *What on earth are you doing here?*

Venga Ud. por aquí. *Come this way.*

¿Cuánto hay de aquí a Zaragoza? *How far is it from here to Zaragoza?*

Está muy lejos de aquí. *It's quite a distance from here.*

Aquí tiene lo que ha pedido. *Here's what you ordered (asked for).*

De aquí en adelante. *From now on.*

araña f. *spider; chandelier.*

arañazo m. *a long, deep scratch.*

árbol m. *tree; mast; shaft.*

La raíz del árbol. *The root of a tree.*

El tronco del árbol. *The trunk of a tree.*

archipiélago m. *archipelago.*

archivar *to keep in an archive, to file.*

archivo m. *archives; file, files; records.*

arco m. *arch.*

arcón m. *chest.*

arder *to burn.*

ardilla f. *squirrel.*

arena f. *sand; arena.*

argumento m. *reason; argument; plot (of a novel, play, etc.).*

No me convencen sus argumentos. *His arguments don't convince me.*

No me gustó el argumento de la película. *I didn't like the plot of the film.*

aritmética f. *arithmetic.*

arma f. *weapon, arm.*

armamento m. *armament.*

armario m. *closet, cabinet.*

armisticio m. *armistice.*

aroma m. *aroma.*

arquitecto m. *architect.*

arquitectura f. *architecture.*

arrabal m. *suburb.*

arrancar *to tear out by the roots, to tear off; to start (car, etc.).*

arranque (or **arrancador**) m. *starter.*

arrastrar *to drag, to haul.*

arreglar *to arrange; to settle; to regulate; to fix.*

Todo está arreglado. *Everything has been arranged.*

Arreglar una cuenta. *To settle an account.*

¿Cuánto pide Ud. para arreglar una radio? *How much do you charge to fix a radio?*

arreglarse *to make up, to get ready; to manage; to be settled; to come up.*

Arréglate un poco y vámonos al cine. *Get yourself ready and we'll go to the movies.*

arreglárselas *to manage (oneself).*

Me las arreglé para escaparme. *I managed to escape.*

arrendamiento m. *rental, lease, renting.*

arrendar *to rent, to lease, to hire.*

arrepentirse *to repeat, to regret.*

Te arrepentirás de esto. *You'll be sorry for this.*

ARRIBA *up, above, over, overhead, upstairs.*

Vamos arriba. *Let's go upstairs.*

Patas arriba. *Upside down.*

De arriba abajo. *From top to bottom. From head to foot.*

arriendo m. *renting, lease, rental.*

arrimar *to approach, to draw near; to lay aside.*

arrimarse *to lean against; to draw near.*

Arrímese a la estufa. *Draw up (come closer) to the stove.*

arrodillarse *to kneel down.*

arrojar *to throw, to hurl; to show, to leave (a balance).*

arte m. and f. *art; skill.*

Bellas artes. *Fine arts.*

artículo m. *article; clause.*

Artículo de fondo. *Editorial.*

Artículos de tocador. *Toilet articles.*

artificial *adj. artificial.*

artista *m. and f. artist.*

arzobispo *m. archbishop.*

as *m. ace.*

asa *f. handle, haft.*

asado *adj. roasted; m. roast meat.*

asador *m. spit (for roasting meat).*

asalto *m. assault; holdup.*

asamblea *f. assembly.*

asar *to roast.*

ascender *to ascend, to climb; to amount to; to be promoted.*

La cuenta asciende a cien pesos. *The bill amounts to one hundred pesos.*

ascenso *m. promotion.*

ascensor *m. elevator.*

aseado *adj. clean, neat.*

asear *to clean, to make neat.*

asegurar *to insure; to secure, to fasten; to assure; to affirm, to assert.*

Le aseguro que estaré allí dentro de una hora. *I assure you that I'll be there in an hour.*

El equipaje está asegurado. *The baggage is insured.*

aseo *m. cleanliness, neatness.*

aserrar *to saw.*

asesinar *to assassinate, to murder.*

asesinato *m. assassination, murder.*

asesino *m. assassin, murderer.*

asfalto *m. asphalt.*

ASÍ *so, thus, in this manner, therefore, so that.*

Así lo espero. *I hope so.*

Lo debe Ud. hacer así. *You must (have to) do it this way.*

No es así, se lo aseguro. *I assure you that's not so.*

Así, así. *So, so.*

Más vale así. *It's better this way.*

Así que llegue le avisaré. *As soon as I arrive I'll notify you.*

Así que hubo hablado se marchó. *He left as soon as he'd finished speaking.*

asiento *m. seat, chair; entry, registry; bottom.*

¿Está tomado este asiento? *Is this seat taken?*

Tome Ud. asiento. *Take a seat. Have a seat.*

asignar *to assign; to appoint; to allot.*

asignatura *f. subject (in school).*

asilo *m. asylum; refuge.*

asimismo *likewise, exactly so.*

asir *to grasp, to hold, to grip.*

asirse de *to avail oneself of; to hold to; to take hold of.*

asistir *to attend; to assist, to help; to be treated by (a doctor).*

No asistió a clase hoy. *He did not attend class today.*

¿Asistió Ud. a la reunión? *Did you attend the meeting?*

Un médico famoso asiste a mi mujer. *My wife is being treated by a famous doctor.*

asno *m. donkey, ass.*

asociación *f. association.*

asomar *to loom, to become visible, to begin to appear.*

asomarse *to look out of, to lean out (of a window, etc.).*

Asómese Ud. a la ventana. *Look out (lean out) of the window.*

¡Prohibido asomarse! *Don't lean out of the window!*

asombro *m. amazement, astonishment.*

Figúrese mi asombro. *Imagine my amazement.*

No salgo de mi asombro. *I can't get over it.*

aspecto *m. aspect, appearance, look.*

Ud. no tiene mal aspecto. *You don't look ill.*

Trate de mejorar su aspecto. *Try to improve your appearance.*

aspirina *f. aspirin.*

astuto *adj. cunning, sly.*

ASUNTO *m. subject, matter, business.*

Necesito más detalles sobre este asunto. *I need more information on this matter.*

Conozco a fondo el asunto. *I'm thoroughly acquainted with the matter.*

¿Cuál es el asunto de esa comedia? *What's the subject of that play?*

asustar *to frighten.*

asustarse *to be frightened.*

¿De qué te asustas? *What are you afraid of?*

atacar *to attack.*

ataque *m. attack.*

atar *to bind, to tie, to fasten.*

Atese los zapatos. *Tie your shoelaces.*

atardecer *to grow late (toward the end of the afternoon).*

ataúd *m. coffin.*

atemorizar *to frighten, to intimidate.*

ATENCIÓN *f. attention.*

Quisiera llamar la atención de Ud. sobre este punto. *I'd like to bring this point to your attention.*

Muchas gracias por su atención. *Thanks for your attention.*

Le estoy muy reconocido por sus atenciones. *I'm grateful for your kindness.*

En atención a. *Considering. In view of.*

atender *to attend, to pay attention; to look after; to wait on.*

atenta *f. "Your esteemed (letter)."*

Su atenta. *Your ("esteemed") letter.*

atentado *m. attempt.*

atentar *to try, to attempt.*

atento *adj. attentive, courteous.*

Su atento y seguro servidor. *Very truly yours.*

aterrizaje m. *landing (of an airplane).*
aterrizar *to land (an airplane).*
atestado adj. *crowded.*
atestiguar *to depose, to testify.*
atinar *to guess right, to hit on.*
atlántico m. *Atlantic.*
atleta m. and f. *athlete.*
atlético adj. *athletic.*
atmósfera f. *atmosphere.*
átomo m. *atom.*
atornillar *to screw.*
atracar *to dock, to moor; to hold up.*
atraco m. *assault, holdup.*
atractivo adj. *attractive, appealing.*
atraer *to attract.*
ATRÁS *behind, backwards, past; ago.*
    Quedarse atrás. *To remain behind.*
    Volverse atrás. *To go back on one's word. To retract.*
    Hacerse atrás. *To move backward. To back up. To recoil.*
    Tres días atrás. *Three days ago.*
atrasar *to retard, to delay; to be in arrears; to be slow (a watch).*
atrasarse *to remain behind; to be late; to get behind (in payment).*
    Mi reloj atrasa. *My watch is slow.*
    Nos estamos atrasando en el trabajo. *We're getting behind in our work.*
    Esto atrasará mucho mi viaje. *This will delay my trip a long time.*
    Atrasarse en los pagos. *To fall behind in one's payments.*
atravesar *to cross, to move across; to lay a thing across; to pierce.*
    Atravesemos la calle. *Let's cross the street.*
atrayente adj. *attractive.*
atreverse *to dare, to venture.*
atrevido adj. *bold, daring; fresh.*
atribuir *to attribute, to impute.*
atrocidad f. *atrocity.*
    ¡Qué atrocidad! *What a horrible (awful) thing!*
atropellar *to trample, to run over; to abuse, to insult.*
    Fué atropellado por un coche. *He was run over by a car.*
atropello m. *trampling, abuse, outrage.*
atroz adj. *atrocious, outrageous; enormous.*
    Tengo un hambre atroz. *I'm famished. ("I have an enormous hunger.")*
atún *tuna fish.*
aturdido adj. *bewildered, stunned, dizzy.*
aturdir *to stun.*
audición f. *audition.*
auditorio m. *audience.*
aumentar *to augment, to enlarge, to increase.*
aumentarse *to grow larger.*
aumento m. *increase.*

Aumento de precios. *Price increase. Increase in prices.*
Aumento de salario. *Salary increase.*
AUN *yet, still; even (written* aún *when it follows a verb).*
    Aun no lo sabe. *He doesn't know yet.*
    Tengo que escribir aún otra carta. *I've still got another letter to write.*
    Aun cuando. *Although. Even though.*
AUNQUE *though, notwithstanding, even if.*
aurora f. *dawn, daybreak.*
ausencia f. *absence.*
AUSENTARSE *to be absent, to be away.*
AUSENTE adj. *absent.*
auténtico adj. *authentic, genuine.*
auto m. *automobile, motor car; sentence, edict.*
    ¿Le parece a Ud. que demos un paseo en auto? *How would you like to take a ride?*
autobús m. *bus.*
    ¿Dónde para el autobús? *Where does the bus stop?*
    ¿Dónde queda la parada del autobús? *Where's the bus stop?*
autocar m. *bus (in Spain).*
automático adj. *automatic.*
automóvil m. *automobile.*
autor m. *author.*
autoridad f. *authority.*
autorización f. *authorization.*
autorizar *to authorize.*
autorretrato m. *self-portrait.*
auxiliar *to aid, to help;* adj. *auxiliary.*
auxilio m. *help, aid, assistance.*
avance m. *advance, progress.*
avanzar *to advance, to go ahead, to progress.*
ave f. *bird; fowl.*
    Aves de corral. *Fowl. Poultry.*
avena f. *oats.*
avenida f. *avenue.*
aventura f. *adventure.*
aventurarse *to venture, to risk, to take a chance.*
    No se aventure usted. *Don't take the risk. Don't take a chance.*
avergonzarse *to be ashamed.*
avería f. *damage, loss.*
averiguar *to inquire, to find out, to investigate.*
    Averigüe a que hora sale el tren. *Find out (at) what time the train leaves.*
aviación f. *aviation.*
aviador m. *aviator.*
avión m. *airplane.*
avisar *to inform, to notify, to let know; to warn.*
    Avíseme con tiempo. *Notify me in time.*
    Ya le avisaré. *I'll let you know.*
aviso m. *notice; advertisement; warning.*
    Aviso al publico. *Public Notice. Notice to the Public.*
AYER *yesterday.*

Ayer por la tarde. *Yesterday afternoon.*

ayuda *f. help, assistance, aid.*

ayudante *m. and f. assistant; adjutant (in the army).*

AYUDAR *to aid, to assist, to help.*

¿Permítame que le ayude? *May I help you? Allow me to help you.*

ayuntamiento *m. city hall.*

azadón *m. hoe.*

azahar *m. orange or lemon blossom.*

azar *m. chance; hazard.*

Al azar. *At random.*

azotar *to whip.*

azote *m. whip; whipping, spanking.*

azotea *f. flat roof; roof garden.*

AZÚCAR *m. sugar.*

AZUL *adj. blue.*

Azul celeste. *Sky blue.*

Azul marino. *Navy blue.*

B

bacalao *m. codfish.*

bagatela *f. bagatelle, trifle.*

bahía *f. bay, harbor.*

bailar *to dance.*

baile *m. dance, ball.*

baja *f. fall, depreciation (price); casualty.*

BAJAR *to go (come) down; to get (bring) down; to get off; to lower, let down; to drop (fever, temperature, etc.).*

Bajaré dentro de unos minutos. *I'll come (be) down in a few minutes.*

Bajaron del tranvía. *They got off the streetcar.*

Haga Ud. que bajen los baúles. *Have them get (bring) the trunks down.*

BAJO *low; under, below.*

El es algo más bajo que yo. *He's a little bit shorter than I am.*

Hable un poco más bajo. *Speak a little lower.*

Tenemos diez grados bajo cero. *It's ten degrees below zero.*

bala *f. bullet.*

balance *m. balance.*

balde *m. bucket.*

De balde. *Free. For nothing.*

Trabajó de balde. *He worked for nothing. He didn't get paid for his work. He did the work free.*

En balde. *In vain. With no result. To no purpose.*

Trabajó en balde. *He worked in vain.*

ballena *f. whale.*

banana *f. banana.*

banano *m. banana tree.*

banco *m. bench; bank.*

banda *f. band; sash, ribbon; gang.*

bandeja *f. tray.*

bandéra *f. flag, banner.*

bandido *m. bandit, outlaw.*

banquero *m. banker.*

BAÑO *m. bath; bathroom; bathtub.*

BARATO *adj. cheap.*

barba *f. chin; beard.*

En sus barbas. *To his face.*

Por barba. *A head. Apiece.*

barbería *f. barbershop.*

barbero *m. barber.*

barca *f. small boat.*

barco *m. boat, vessel, ship.*

barniz *m. varnish.*

barómetro *m. barometer.*

barranco *m. ravine, gully.*

barrer *to sweep.*

barriada *f. district, ward, suburb.*

barriga *f. belly.*

barril *m. barrel.*

barrio *m. district, ward, suburb.*

barro *m. mud.*

báscula *f. platform scale.*

base *f. base, basis.*

básico *adj. basic.*

basquetbol *m. basketball.*

BASTANTE *enough, sufficient.*

Tiene bastante dinero. *He has enough money.*

Bastante bien. *Pretty well. Rather well.*

BASTAR *to suffice, be enough.*

Eso basta por ahora. *That's enough for now.*

¡Basta, ya! *That's enough!*

bastón *m. cane, walking stick.*

basura *f. refuse, garbage.*

bata *f. robe, gown.*

Bata de baño. *Bathrobe.*

Bata de dormir. *Nightgown.*

batalla *f. battle, combat, fight.*

batallar *to battle, to fight.*

batallón *m. battalion.*

batería *f. battery.*

Batería de cocina. *Kitchen utensils.*

batir *to beat.*

baúl *m. trunk, chest.*

bautizar *to baptize, christen.*

bautizo *m. baptism. christening.*

bebé *m. baby.*

BEBER *to drink.*

¿Le gustaría beber algo? *Would you like something to drink?*

bebida *f. drink, beverage.*

becerro *m. calf; calfskin.*

belleza *f. beauty.*

BELLO *adj. beautiful.*

Una mujer bella. *A beautiful woman.*

Las bellas artes. *The fine arts.*

¡Qué bello! *How beautiful!*

bendecir *to bless.*

¡Dios le bendiga! *God bless you!*

bendición f. blessing; benediction.

bendito adj. blessed; m. simpleton.
> Es un bendito. He's a simpleton.

beneficiar to benefit, to profit.

beneficio m. benefit, profit.

berenjena f. eggplant.

berro m. watercress.

besar to kiss.

beso m. kiss.

bestia f. beast.

betún m. shoepolish.

biberón m. nursing bottle.

bibliografía f. bibliography.

biblioteca f. library; bookcase.

bicarbonato m. bicarbonate.

bicicleta f. bicycle.

bicho m. insect; vermin; a ridiculous person (coll.). (Not to be used in Puerto Rico.)
> Es un mal bicho. He's a bad egg.
> Es un bicho raro. He's very odd. He's a queer person.

BIEN well, right.
> ¿Está Ud. bien? Are you all right?
> Muy bien, gracias. Very well, thank you.
> No muy bien. Not so well.
> ¡Qué lo pase Ud. bien! Good luck to you!
> Está bien. All right. O.K.

bienes m. pl. property, estate, possessions.

bienestar m. well-being, welfare.

bienvenida f. welcome.

BILLETE m. ticket; bank note. (See boleto.)
> ¿Dónde puedo sacar mis billetes? Where can I buy my tickets?
> ¿Puede usted cambiarme un billete de diez dólares? Can you change a ten-dollar bill for me?
> Billete de ida y vuelta. Round-trip ticket.

billetera f. wallet, pocketbook.

biombo m. screen.

blanco adj. white; m. mark, target.
> Dar en el blanco. To hit the mark.

blando adj. soft, smooth.

blondo adj. blond.

bobo adj. foolish, silly; m. fool, simpleton.

boca f. mouth.

bocacalle f. street intersection.

bocadillo m. a snack; sandwich.

bocado m. mouthful, a bite (to eat).
> No he probado bocado desde ayer. I haven't had a bite to eat since yesterday.

bocina f. horn (of a car).

boda f. wedding.

bodega f. wine-cellar; hold (of a ship); storeroom, grocery store.

bofetada f. a slap in the face.
> Soltar una bofetada. To slap in the face.

boina f. beret.

bola f. ball, globe.

BOLETO m. ticket. (See billete.)

bolsa f. purse; bag; stock exchange.

bolsillo m. pocket.

bolso m. change purse; bag.

bomba f. pump; fire engine; bomb.

bombilla f. flashbulb.

bombón m. candy, bonbon.

bombonera f. candy box.

bondad f. goodness, kindness.
> Tenga la bondad de servirse. Please help yourself.
> Tenga Ud. la bondad de sentarse. Please sit down.

bonito adj. pretty, good, graceful; m. bonito (a kind of fish).

bordo, a on board.
> Todo el pasaje estaba a bordo. All the passengers were on board.

borracho adj. drunk, intoxicated; m. drunkard.

borrador m. eraser; rough draft.

borrar to strike or cross out, to erase.

borrón m. blot, stain.

bosque m. wood, forest.

bostezar to yawn, to gape.

botar to launch (a ship); to bounce; to throw (Amer.).

bote m. boat; jar, can, container.
> Bote salvavidas. Lifeboat.
> Un bote de mermelada. A jar of marmalade.

BOTELLA f. bottle.

botica f. drugstore.

boticario m. druggist.

botiquín m. medicine cabinet, medicine chest.

botón m. button; bud.

botones m. hotel page, bellboy.

boxeador m. boxer.

boxear to box.

boxeo m. boxing.

bravo adj. brave.

¡Bravo! Bravo!

brazalete m. bracelet.

BRAZO m. arm.
> Puede llevar el paquete debajo del brazo. You can carry the package under your arm.
> Iban del brazo. They were walking arm in arm.

BREVE adj. brief, short.
> En breve. Shortly. In a little while.

brevedad f. briefness, brevity.

brigada f. brigade.

brillante adj. brilliant, sparkling; m. diamond.

brillar to shine, to sparkle.

brindar to toast; to offer; to invite.

brindis m. toast, drinking someone's health.

brisa f. breeze.

brocha f. brush.
> Brocha para afeitar. Shaving brush.

broche m. clasp; brooch; hook-and-eye.

broma f. joke, jest.

En broma. *As a joke. Jestingly.*

Tomar a broma. *To take as a joke.*

bromear *to joke, to have fun.*

¡Ud. bromea! *You're joking! You're kidding!*

bromista *m. and f. joker.*

bronce *m. bronze, brass.*

bruma *f. fog, mist.*

brusco *adj. brusque, rude, rough.*

brutal *adj. brutal, brutish.*

bruto *adj. brutal; rude.*

En bruto. *In the rough. In a rough state. In the raw state.*

Peso bruto. *Gross weight.*

BUEN *(contraction of bueno; used only before a masculine noun).*

Pasamos un buen rato en el cine. *We had a good time at the movies.*

¡Buen viaje! *Bon voyage! Have a pleasant trip!*

Tuve un buen día. *I spent a pleasant day.*

Hace muy buen tiempo. *The weather's very nice.*

En buen estado. *In good condition.*

Un buen hombre. *A good man.*

BUENO *adj. good; kind; satisfactory; suited; fit; well.*

¡Buenos días! *Good morning!*

¡Buenas tardes! *Good afternoon! Good evening!*

¡Buenas noches! *Good night!*

Esa es una buena idea. *That's a good idea.*

He pasado muy buena noche. *I've had a very good night's rest.*

¿Tiene Ud. algo de bueno? *Have you anything good (to eat)?*

¡Sé buena! *Be good!*

Se pasa de bueno. *He's too good.*

¡Tanto bueno por aquí! *Look who's here! I'm glad to see you.*

¡Eso sí que está bueno! *That's a pretty how-do-you-do!*

De buena gana. *Willingly.*

buho *m. owl.*

buitre *m. vulture.*

bujía *f. candle; spark plug.*

bulla *f. noise, fuss.*

No metan tanta bulla. *Don't make so much noise.*

bullicio *m. noise, bustle, tumult.*

bulto *m. bundle, parcel, package.*

¿Cabrán estos bultos en su coche? *Will these packages fit in your car?*

Compré todos sus muebles a bulto. *I bought all his furniture for a lump sum.*

buñuelo *m. bun, cruller, fritter.*

buque *m. ship, vessel, steamer.*

burla *f. mockery, scoffing, sneering, fun.*

Le hicimos burla de su sombrero. *We made fun of her hat.*

¿Se burla usted de mí? *Are you making fun of me?*

burlón *adj. mocking, bantering; m. mocker, jester, scoffer.*

burro *m. ass, donkey.*

BUSCAR *to seek, look for, search; to fetch, get.*

¿Qué busca Ud.? *What are you looking for?*

¿A quién busca Ud.? *Who(m) do you wish to see? Who(m) are you looking for?*

Está buscando una colocación. *He's looking for a job.*

Voy a buscar mis libros. *I'm going to get my books.*

¿Quién la va a buscar? *Who's going to get her? Who's going after her?*

Enviaron a buscar al médico. *They sent someone for the doctor.*

búsqueda *f. search.*

busto *m. bust.*

butaca *f. easy chair; orchestra seat (in a theater).*

Siéntese Ud. en esta butaca. *Sit down in this armchair.*

Sacaré tres butacas. *I'll buy three orchestra seats.*

butifarra *f. kind of sausage.*

buzón *m. mailbox.*

Eche Ud. la carta en el buzón. *Put the letter in the mailbox.*

C

¡cá! *Oh, no!*

¡Cá! ¡Por supuesto que no! *No, indeed! Nonsense! Of course not!*

cabalgar *to ride on horseback.*

caballa *f. mackerel.*

caballería *f. cavalry; riding horse.*

caballero *m. gentleman; knight; horseman.*

Es todo un caballero. *He's a perfect gentleman.*

caballo *m. horse; knight (in chess); queen (cards).*

cabaña *f. hut, cabin.*

cabaret *m. cabaret, night club.*

cabecera *f. head of a bed or table.*

Sentarse a la cabecera. *To take one's place (to sit) at the head of the table.*

CABELLO *m. hair.*

CABER *to fit into; to have enough room; to contain.*

El libro no cabe en el estante. *The book won't fit on the shelf.*

No cabe más en el baúl. *The trunk won't hold any more. There's no more room in the trunk.*

No me cabe la menor duda. *I haven't the slightest doubt.*

Todo cabe en él. *He's capable of anything.*

Eso cabe en lo posible. *It's possible.*

CABEZA *f. head.*

Me duele la cabeza. *I've a headache.*

¿Le lavo la cabeza? *Do you want a shampoo? ("Shall I wash your hair?")*

Tiene mala cabeza. *He's reckless.*

Pagar a tanto por cabeza. *To pay so much per head.*

De pies a cabeza. *From head to foot.*

cabina f. *cabin, booth.*

Cabina telefónica. *Telephone booth.*

cable m. *cable; rope, line.*

cablegrafiar *to cable.*

CABO m. *tip, extremity, end; cape; rope; corporal.*

Al cabo de día. *At the end of the day.*

Leyó el libro de cabo a rabo. *She read the book from cover to cover.*

Al fin y al cabo. *At last. In the end. At length. After all. In the long run.*

Al cabo y a la postre. *At last. In the end. At length. After all. In the long run.*

Llevar a cabo. *To accomplish. To carry through.*

cabra f. *goat.*

cacahuate m. *peanut.*

cacao m. *cocoa; cocoa tree.*

cacería f. *hunt, hunting.*

cacerola f. *casserole, pan.*

cacharro m. *coarse earthen pot, piece of junk.*

cachetada f. *a slap in the face.*

cachimba f. *pipe (for smoking).*

CADA adj. *every, each.*

Cada hora. *Every hour.*

Cada cual. *Each one.*

Cada vez que viene. *Every time he comes.*

Dar a cada uno lo suyo. *To give everyone his due.*

Cada día se pone más delgada. *She's growing thinner day by day.*

cadáver m. *corpse, cadaver.*

cadena f. *chain.*

cadera f. *hip.*

cadete m. *cadet.*

CAER *to fall; to tumble down; to drop; to become, fit; to realize.*

Por poco me caigo. *I almost (nearly) fell down.*

Cayó enfermo ayer. *He fell ill yesterday. He got sick yesterday.*

¿Qué se le ha caído a Ud.? *What have you dropped?*

Yo caigo en ello. *I catch on. I see. I get it.*

No había caído en cuenta. *I didn't realize what you meant.*

Caer bien con. *To match. To match well with.*

Ese vestido le cae muy bien. *That dress fits her very well.*

La ventana cae al río. *The window overlooks the river.*

La pascua cae en marzo este año. *Easter falls (comes) in March this year.*

caerse *to fall down.*

Me caí. *I fell down.*

café m. *coffee; café.*

Una taza de café. *A cup of coffee.*

Café con leche. *Coffee with cream.*

Café solo. *Black coffee.*

Tomemos una cerveza en este café. *Let's have some beer in this café.*

cafetera f. *coffeepot.*

caída f. *fall, downfall.*

calambre m. *cramp.*

CAJA f. *box, case; coffin; chest; cash.*

Quiero una caja de galletas surtidas. *I want a box of assorted cookies.*

En caja. *Cash. Cash on hand.*

Pague en la caja. *Pay the cashier.*

Caja registradora. *Cash register.*

Caja de ahorros. *Savings bank.*

Caja fuerte. *A safe. ("Strong box.")*

Caja de caudales. *A safe.*

cajero m. *cashier.*

cajón m. *drawer; box, case (made of wood).*

calabaza f. *pumpkin. squash.*

¿Te dieron calabazas? *Didn't you pass (an exam)? Did you fail?*

Ella le dió calabazas. *She refused him (a suitor). She gave him the air.*

calabozo m. *dungeon, prison, cell.*

calamar m. *squid.*

calamidad f. *calamity, misfortune.*

calavera f. *skull; m. madcap.*

Es un calavera. *He leads a wild life.*

calcetín m. *sock.*

calcular *to calculate, estimate.*

cálculo m. *computation; estimate; calculus.*

caldo m. *broth.*

Caldo de gallina. *Chicken broth.*

calefacción f. *heating.*

calendario m. *almanac, calendar.*

calentador m. *heater.*

calentar *to warm, heat.*

calentarse *to grow warm, to warm oneself; to become excited, to get angry.*

No quiero calentarme la cabeza por éso. *I don't want to worry my head about that.*

calentura f. *fever.*

calibre m. *caliber; bore; gauge.*

calidad f. *quality; condition, capacity.*

CALIENTE adj. *warm, hot.*

Prefiero la leche fría a la caliente. *I prefer cold milk to warm.*

El sol está muy caliente. *The sun's very hot.*

calificación f. *qualification; mark (in an examination).*

calificar *to qualify; to rate; to describe; to authorize; to attest.*

caligrafía f. *calligraphy, handwriting.*

calma f. *calm, calmness, slowness.*

Tómelo con calma. *Take it easy.*

Debemos mirar este asunto con más calma. *We must look at this matter more calmly.*

calmante m. *sedative.*

calmar to calm, to quiet.

calmarse to quiet down.

> ¡Cálmese! Calm yourself!

CALOR m. heat, warmth; thick (of a fight).

> Tengo calor. I'm warm. I'm hot.

> Hace mucho calor. It's very hot.

calumniar to calumniate, to slander.

caluroso adj. warm, hot.

> Es un día caluroso. It's a hot day.

calva f. bald head.

calvicie f. baldness.

calvo adj. bald; barren.

calzada f. causeway, highway.

calzado m. footwear.

calzador m. shoe horn.

calzar to put on shoes; to wedge.

calzoncillos m. shorts.

callado adj. quiet; silent; discreet, reserved.

callar to keep quiet, to be silent; to conceal.

> ¡Cállate! Keep quiet!

> En este caso vale más callar. In this case it's better to keep quiet (to say nothing).

callarse to be quiet, to shut up.

CALLE f. street; lane.

> Atravesemos la calle. Let's cross the street.

> ¿Qué calle es ésta? What street is this?

> ¿Cómo se llama esta calle? What's the name of this street?

> ¿Cuál es la calle próxima? What's the street after this? What's the next street?

> Esta calle es de dirección única. This is a one-way street.

> Al otro lado de la calle. Across the street.

> Echar a la calle. To throw out. To put out. ("To throw out into the street.")

> Quedarse en la calle. To be left penniless.

callejón m. alley.

> Callejón sin salida. Blind alley.

callo m. corn, callus.

CAMA f. bed; couch; litter; layer.

> Hacer la cama. To make the bed.

> Guardar cama. To be confined to bed. To stay in bed.

camarada m. and f. comrade.

camarera f. waitress, chambermaid.

camarero m. waiter; steward.

camarote m. cabin, stateroom.

CAMBIAR to barter, to exchange; to change.

> ¿Puede Ud. cambiarme un billete de diez dólares? Can you change a ten-dollar bill for me?

> He cambiado mi reloj por uno nuevo. I've exchanged my watch for a new one.

> ¿En qué estación cambiamos de tren? At what station do we change trains?

> ¿Ha cambiado Ud. de idea? Have you changed your mind?

> Cambiemos de tema. Let's change the subject.

> Cambiar la velocidad. To shift gears.

CAMBIO m. barter, exchange; rate of exchange; change.

> No tengo cambio. I haven't any change.

> ¿A cuánto está el cambio? What's the rate of exchange?

> En cambio. On the other hand. In return.

> Cambio de velocidad (de marchas). Gearshift.

camilla f. small bed; stretcher.

CAMINAR to walk; to march; to move along.

CAMINO m. road, way, highway.

> ¿Dónde va a este camino? Where does this road lead to?

> ¿Es éste el camino a Lima? Is this the road to Lima?

> ¿Voy bien por este camino? Am I on the right road? Am I going the right way?

> Indíqueme el camino. Show me the way.

camión m. truck; bus (Mex.).

CAMISA f. shirt, chemise.

> En mangas de camisa. In one's shirt sleeves.

camisería f. haberdashery; haberdashery store; shirt factory.

camiseta f. undershirt.

camisón m. nightshirt, nightgown.

camote m. sweet potato.

campamento m. camp, encampment.

campana f. bell.

> ¿Tocó Ud. la campanilla? Did you ring the bell?

> Parece ser una persona de muchas campanillas. He seems to be a very important person.

campeón m. champion.

campeonato m. championship.

campesino m. peasant.

campo m. field, country; space.

cana f. gray hair.

canal m. channel, canal.

canario m. canary.

canasta f. basket, hamper.

canasto m. large basket.

cancelar to cancel; to annul.

cáncer m. cancer.

CANCIÓN f. song.

cancha f. sports grounds, playing field.

candado m. padlock.

candelero m. candlestick.

candidato m. candidate.

candidatura f. candidacy.

candidez f. candor, simplicity.

cándido adj. candid, simple.

canela f. cinnamon.

cangrejo m. crab, crawfish.

canjear to exchange.

canoa f. canoe.

CANSADO adj. tired; tedious; annoying.

cansancio m. fatigue.

cansar to tire; to annoy, to bore.

cansarse *to get tired, to get annoyed, to become bored.*

cantante *m. and f. singer.*

CANTAR *to sing; to reveal a secret.*

cantidad *f. quantity; amount; sum (of money).*

cantina *f. barroom, saloon; canteen.*

canto *m. singing; song; border; edge; front edge of a book; back of a knife; pebble, stone.*

caña *f. cane, reed; leg, upper part of a boot.*
    Caña de pescar. *Fishing rod.*
    Caña de azúcar. *Sugar cane.*

cañada *f. ravine.*

cañaveral *m. reed field, sugar cane plantation.*

cañería *f. conduit, piping; water pipe; main (gas).*

caño *m. pipe, tube, spout.*

cañón *m. cannon, gun; gorge, canyon; tube; funnel (of a chimney).*

caoba *f. mahogany.*

capa *f. cape, cloak; layer; coat, coating.*

capacidad *f. capacity.*

capataz *m. foreman, overseer.*

CAPAZ *adj. capable, able; liable, apt; spacious, having plenty of room.*
    Es capaz de cualquier cosa. *He's capable of anything.*

capital *adj. principal, main; m. principal (money invested); capital (stock); f. capital (metropolis).*

capitán *m. captain; commander; ringleader.*

capítulo *m. chapter.*

CARA *f. face; front, façade.*
    Su cara no me es desconocida. *Your face is familiar.*
    Tiene Ud. muy buena cara. *You look very well.*
    Hacer cara a. *To face. To cope with. To meet.*
    Echar en cara. *To reproach. ("To throw in someone's face.")*
    De cara. *Facing.*
    Sacar la cara por uno. *To take someone's part. To defend someone.*
    ¿Cara o cruz? *Heads or tails?*

¡caray! *Good gracious! Goodness! Gosh!*

carbón *m. coal; charcoal; carbon.*
    Papel carbón. *Carbon paper.*

carcajada *f. hearty laughter.*
    Reírse a carcajadas. *To laugh uproariously. To split one's sides laughing.*
    Soltar una carcajada. *To burst out laughing.*
    Se ríe a carcajadas. *He has a hearty laugh.*

cárcel *f. prison, jail.*

CARECER *to lack, to be in want.*
    Carecemos del dinero suficiente para eso. *We lack (don't have) enough money for that.*
    Lo que dijo carece de lógica. *His words aren't logical. ("What he said lacks logic.")*

carestía *f. lack, scarcity; famine; high price.*

carga *f. freight; load; cargo; burden.*

cargado *adj. loaded; strong (tea).*

    Estaba cargado de razón. *He was absolutely right.*
    No quiero el té cargado. *I don't want my tea strong.*

cargamento *m. cargo; load.*

cargar *to load; to charge; to carry a load.*
    Cargar en cuenta. *To charge to an account.*

caricia *f. caress.*

caridad *f. charity.*

cariño *m. fondness, love, affection; pl. regards.*
    Tomar cariño a. *To become attached to.*
    Poner cariño a alguna cosa. *To take a liking to something.*
    Dar cariños. *To give one's regards.*

cariñoso *adj. affectionate, loving.*

caritativo *adj. charitable.*

carnaval *m. carnival.*

CARNE *f. flesh; meat; pulp (of fruit).*
    Carne asada. *Roast meat.*
    Carne de vaca. *Beef.*
    Ser carne y uña. *To be like two peas in a pod. To be hand in glove with each other. To be bosom friends.*

carnero *m. mutton.*

carnet *m. booklet; membership book, membership card.*

carnet de conducir *driver's license.*

carnicería *f. butcher shop, meat market; slaughter.*

carnicero *m. butcher.*

CARO *adj. dear; expensive.*
    Es muy caro. *It's too expensive (dear).*
    Un amigo caro. *A dear friend.*
    Lo pagará Ud. caro. *You'll pay dearly for it.*
    ¡Qué caro se vende Ud.! *How seldom you come to see us!*
    Cara mitad. *Better half.*

carpintero *m. carpenter.*

carrera *f. career; race.*

carreta *f. heavy cart, wagon.*

carrete *m. spool, reel, bobbin, coil; kind of hat (Mex.).*

carretel *m. spool, bobbin, reel.*

carretera *f. road, highway, drive.*
    ¿Dónde va esta carretera? *Where does this highway lead?*

carretilla *f. wheelbarrow.*

carrillo *m. cheek.*
    Echar carrillos. *To grow fat in the cheeks.*
    Comer a dos carrillos. 1. *To draw benefits from two sides.* 2. *To eat like a horse.*

carro *m. cart; car, motorcar (Amer.).*

carruaje *m. any kind of vehicle or carriage.*

CARTA *f. letter; map, chart; charter; playing card.*
    ¿Cómo tengo que dirigir la carta? *How shall (do) I address the letter?*
    Eche Ud. la carta en el buzón. *Put the letter in the mailbox.*
    ¿A qué hora reparten las cartas? *When is the*

mail delivered?

Carta certificada. *Registered letter.*

Carta urgente. *Special delivery letter.*

Carta de crédito. *Letter of credit.*

Carta de naturaleza. *Naturalization papers.*

Tomar cartas. *To take part. To take sides.*

Vamos a jugar a las cartas. *Let's play cards.*

cartel m. *placard, poster, cartel.*

cartera f. *portfolio; pocketbook, wallet.*

Le han robado la cartera. *They've stolen his wallet.*

carterista m. *pickpocket.*

cartero m. *mailman, letter carrier.*

cartilla f. *primer (book).*

cartón m. *cardboard.*

CASA f. *house, home; firm, concern.*

Vive en esa casa que hace esquina. *He lives in the corner house.*

Mándemelo a casa. *Send it to my house.*

Vamos a mudarnos de casa pronto. *We're going to move soon.*

¿Cuándo viene Ud. por mi casa? *When are you coming to my place?*

Estaré en casa todo el día. *I'll be (at) home all day.*

Está en la casa de Juan. *He's at John's house.*

Aquí tiene Ud. su casa. *Come again. ("This is your home.")*

"Su casa." *"Your house." (A polite form of giving one's address, implying my house is yours or at your disposal.)*

Esta casa goza de buena fama. *This firm has a good reputation.*

Casa de huéspedes. *Boarding house.*

Casa de apartamentos. *Apartment house.*

casado adj. *married.*

casamiento m. *marriage, wedding.*

casar *to marry; to match.*

casarse *to get married.*

cascanueces m. *nutcracker.*

cáscara f. *peel, husk, shell, bark.*

caserío m. *row of houses, hamlet.*

casero adj. *pertaining to the home, domestic.*

No hay nada como la comida casera. *There's nothing like home cooking.*

Remedios caseros. *Home remedies.*

CASI *almost, nearly.*

Casi he terminado. *I'm almost finished.*

La comida está casi lista. *Dinner is about ready.*

Casi nunca leo los periódicos. *I hardly ever read the newspapers.*

casilla f. *small house; post-office box (Amer.).*

casino m. *casino.*

CASO m. *case, event, accident.*

¿Qué caso tan singular! *What a strange case!*

Bien, vamos al caso. *Well, let's get to the point.*

Hacer caso. *To pay attention to. To mind.*

No le haga caso. *Pay no attention to him. Don't mind him.*

castañuela f. *castanet.*

castellano adj. *Castilian;* m. *Spanish language.*

castigar *to punish.*

castigo m. *punishment, penalty.*

castizo adj. *pure Spanish without foreign influence.*

casual adj. *accidental, casual.*

casualidad f. *chance, coincidence, accident.*

Me lo encontré de pura casualidad. *I met him by chance.*

¿Qué casualidad! *What a coincidence!*

catálogo m. *catalog.*

catarata f. *waterfall, cascade; cataract (of the eye).*

catarro m. *a cold.*

Tengo un catarro terrible. *I have a bad cold.*

cátedral f. *cathedral.*

catedrático m. *professor of a university.*

categoría f. *category, class.*

catolicismo m. *Catholicism.*

católico adj. *Catholic.*

CATORCE *fourteen; fourteenth.*

catre m. *cot.*

caudillo m. *leader, chieftain.*

CAUSA f. *cause, motive; lawsuit.*

No vino a causa de la lluvia. *He didn't come on account (because) of the rain.*

Sin causa. *Without cause. Without a reason.*

causar *to cause.*

Causa horror. *It's horrible!*

Causar daño. *To do harm. To cause damage. To injure.*

cautela f. *caution, prudence.*

cauto adj. *cautious, prudent.*

cavar *to dig up, to excavate.*

caverna f. *cave, cavern.*

cavidad f. *cavity.*

cavilar *to ponder.*

caza f. *hunting; game.*

cazador m. *hunter.*

cazar *to hunt, to chase.*

cazuela f. *casserole.*

cebada f. *barley.*

cebo m. *bait; priming.*

cebolla f. *onion.*

ceder *to grant; to give in, yield.*

cedro m. *cedar.*

cédula f. *warrant, certificate.*

Cédula de vecindad (cédula personal). *Identification papers.*

ceguera f. *blindness.*

ceja f. *eyebrow.*

celda f. *cell.*

CELEBRAR *to celebrate; to be glad; to praise; to hold, take place.*

Lo celebro mucho. *I'm very happy to hear it.*

Celebro que le haya ido bien. *I'm glad he's done well (that things have gone well with him*).

¿Cuándo se celebra la reunión? *When will the meeting take place?*

célebre *adj. famous, renowned.*

celeste *adj. light blue.*

celos *m. pl. jealousy.*

celoso *adj. jealous.*

célula *f. cell.*

cementerio *m. cemetery.*

cemento *m. cement.*

CENA *f. supper, dinner.*

cenar *to have supper, to dine.*

cenicero *m. ash tray.*

ceniza *f. ashes.*

censura *f. censorship; reproach.*

censurar *to censure; to reproach; to criticize.*

CENTAVO *m. cent.*

centena *f. a hundred, about a hundred.*

centenar *m. a hundred, about a hundred.*

A centenares. *By the hundreds.*

centenario *m. centenary.*

centeno *m. rye.*

centésimo *adj. hundredth.*

centígrado *adj. centigrade.*

centímetro *m. centimeter.*

céntimo *m. centime; a hundredth part of a peseta* (Spain).

CENTRAL *adj. central; f. main office.*

América Central. *Central America.*

¿Dónde está la central telefónica? *Where is the telephone exchange?*

CENTRO *m. center, middle; core; club, social circle.*

ceñirse *to limit oneself to.*

ceño *m. frown.*

cepillar *to brush; to plane, to polish.*

cepillo *m. brush; carpenter's plane.*

Cepillo de dientes. *Toothbrush.*

cera *f. beeswax, wax; wax candle.*

CERCA *near, about, close by; f. fence.*

¿Hay alguna farmacia cerca de aquí? *Is there a drugstore near here?*

Está muy cerca. *It's quite near.*

Esto me toca de cerca. *This concerns me very much.*

Por aquí cerca. *Near here. Somewhere around here.*

cercanías *f. vicinity, neighborhood.*

cercano *adj. nearby.*

cercar *to fence, inclose, surround; to besiege.*

cerciorarse *to ascertain, to make sure.*

cerco *m. fence; siege.*

cerdo *m. hog, pig.*

cereal *m. cereal.*

cerebro *m. brain.*

ceremonia *f. ceremony; formality.*

cereza *f. cherry.*

cerezo *m. cherry tree.*

cerilla *f. match (wax match).*

cero *m. zero; nought.*

Tenemos diez grados bajo cero. *It's ten degrees below zero.*

Ser un cero a la izquierda. *To be a nobody.*

cerrado *adj. closed, shut; stupid.*

Cerrado por reformas. *Closed for repairs.*

Las tiendas estarán cerradas mañana. *The stores will be closed tomorrow.*

Se trató el asunto a puerta cerrada. *The matter was discussed privately.*

cerradura *f. lock.*

CERRAR *to close, lock, shut; to turn off.*

Cierre la puerta. *Close (shut) the door.*

Cerrar con llave. *To lock. ("To close with a key.")*

Haga el favor de cerrar el grifo. *Please turn the water off.*

cerro *m. hill.*

cerrojo *m. bolt, latch.*

certeza *f. certainty, conviction.*

certidumbre *f. certainty.*

certificado *m. certificate.*

certificar *to certify; to register (a letter, etc.).*

Quisiera certificar esta carta. *I'd like to register this letter.*

cervecería *f. brewery, beer saloon.*

cerveza *f. beer, ale.*

cesante *adj. unemployed; dismissed, fired.*

CESAR *to cease, stop; to leave (a job).*

Quédese aquí hasta que cese la lluvia. *Stay here until the rain stops.*

Ha cesado en su cargo. *He left his job.*

césped *m. grass, lawn.*

cesta *f. basket, hamper.*

cesto *m. hand basket.*

cicatriz *f. scar.*

ciclista *m. and f. bicyclist.*

ciclón *m. cyclone.*

ciego *adj. blind; m. a blind person.*

cielo *m. sky; heaven.*

CIEN *(contraction of ciento; used before nouns), one hundred.*

¿Le bastará a usted con cien pesos? *Will one hundred pesos be enough for you?*

ciencia *f. science.*

científico *adj. scientific.*

CIENTO *adj. and n. one hundred; one hundredth.*

CIERTO *adj. certain.*

Es cierto. *It's certain. It's true.*

Eso no es cierto. *That's not certain. That's not true.*

Lo dimos por cierto. *We assumed that it was true.*

Hasta cierto punto eso es verdad. *That's true to a certain extent.*

Esto me lo dijo cierta persona. *A certain person told me that.*

¡Sí, por cierto! Yes, indeed!

ciervo m. deer.

cifra f. number; cipher; code.

cigarrera f. woman who makes or sells cigars; cigarette case.

Le regalaron una cigarrera. They gave him a cigarette case as a present.

CIGARRILLO m. cigarette.

cigarro m. cigar; cigarette (Mex.).

cigüeña f. stork.

cilindro m. cylinder.

cima f. summit, top.

Dar cima. To carry through successfully.

Dió cima a su projecto. He concluded his project successfully.

cimiento m. foundation, base.

CINCO adj. and n. five; fifth.

CINCUENTA adj. and n. fifty; fiftieth.

cincuentavo m. fiftieth (part).

CINE m. movies, motion picture, cinema.

cinema m. movies, cinema.

cinematógrafo m. movie, motion picture.

cinta f. ribbon; tape; film.

Cinta magnetofónica. Tape (for a tape recorder).

cintura f. waist.

cinturón m. belt.

ciprés m. cypress.

circo m. circus.

circulación f. circulation; traffic.

circular adj. circular.

circular to circulate.

círculo m. circle; circuit; club.

circunferencia f. circumference.

circunstancia f. circumstance.

Lo exigen las circunstancias. The circumstances demand it. The situation requires it.

ciruela f. plum, prune.

cirujano m. surgeon.

cisne m. swan.

CITA f. appointment, date; summons; quotation.

Deseo hacer una cita con Ud. I'd like to make an appointment with you.

Nunca llega a tiempo a sus citas. He's never on time for his appointments.

Tengo una cita esta noche con mi novia. I've a date tonight with my girl.

citar to cite; to make an appointment; to summon.

Me ha citado con él para el lunes. I've made an appointment with him for next Monday.

Citó una porción de casos semejantes. He cited a number of similar cases.

CIUDAD f. city.

Ciudad natal. Home town. City in which one is born.

ciudadanía f. citizenship.

ciudadano m. citizen.

civil adj. civil; courteous, polite.

civilización f. civilization.

civilizar to civilize.

clara f. white of an egg.

claridad f. clearness; light; distinctness, plainness.

Escriba Ud. la dirección con claridad. Write the address clearly.

Hablar con claridad. To speak clearly (plainly).

clarín m. bugle; bugler.

clarinete m. clarinet; clarinetist.

CLARO adj. clear; intelligible; obvious, evident; plain, frank; transparent; pure (water, etc.); light (color); bright (room, etc.); m. skylight; space (in writing); gap.

Escriba claro. Write clearly.

Poner en claro. To make (something) clear. To clarify. To clear (something) up. To set right.

Claro que lo haré. Certainly I'll do it. Of course I'll do it.

¡Claro que sí! Certainly! Of course!

¡Claro que no! Of course not!

Decir las cosas claras. To speak plainly.

Pasé la noche en claro. I couldn't sleep a wink all night.

CLASE f. class; kind; sort; classroom; lesson.

Clase de español. Spanish class.

Tomó clases de español pero no adelantó mucho. He took Spanish lessons but he didn't get very far (make much progress).

Es el primero de la clase. He's at the head of his class.

El niño no asistió hoy a clase. The child didn't attend school today.

¿Qué clase de fruta es esa? What kind of fruit is that?

La clase obrera. The working class.

clásico m. classic, typical.

Este es un caso clásico. This is a typical case.

clavar to nail, fasten; to drive in, to pierce; to cheat.

Clavar la vista en. To stare at.

CLAVE f. key; cipher, code.

clavel m. carnation.

clavo m. nail; clove.

Por fin ha dado Ud. en el clavo. At last you've hit the nail on the head.

clero m. clergy.

cliente m. and f. client; customer.

clientela f. clientele, customers.

clima m. climate.

clínica f. clinic; dispensary.

cloaca f. sewer.

cloroformo m. chloroform.

club m. club.

cobarde adj. timid, cowardly; m. coward.

cobija f. bed cover, blanket.

cobrador m. conductor (bus, streetcar, etc.); collector.

COBRAR to collect, receive (money); to charge (price).

Quisiera cobrar este cheque. *I'd like to have this check cashed.*

Cobre Ud. de este dólar. *Take it out of this dollar.*

Cobramos a primero de mes. *We're paid on the first of the month.*

¿Cuánto cobra Ud. por la hechura de un abrigo? *How much do you charge for making a coat?*

Cobrar ánimo. *To take courage.*

cobre *m. copper.*

cocer *to cook, boil, bake.*

cocido *m. dish made of boiled meat and vegetables.*

cocina *f. kitchen; cuisine.*

cocinar *to cook.*

cocinero *m. chef, cook.*

coco *m. coconut tree; coconut.*

COCHE *m. couch, carriage; car.*

Vaya Ud. por un coche. *Call a cab (taxi).*

Coche comedor. *Dining car. Diner.*

Coche cama. *Sleeping car. Sleeper.*

Coche de fumar. *Smoking car.*

Coche salón. *Parlor car.*

codazo *m. a shove with the elbow.*

Me dió un codazo. *He gave me a shove (with his elbow).*

codiciar *to covet, to desire eagerly.*

codicioso *adj. covetous, greedy; diligent.*

codo *m. elbow.*

Hablar hasta por los codos. *To be a chatterbox.*

codorniz *f. quail.*

COGER *to catch, to take hold of; to gather; to take, to seize; to have room or capacity for. (It's a bad word in Argentina or Uruguay. In those countries use "tomar.")*

Coja Ud. bien la pluma. *Hold your pen properly.*

Coja Ud. un lápiz y escriba. *Take a pencil and write.*

He cogido un resfriado. *I've caught a cold.*

Esa pregunta me ha cogido de sorpresa. *That question took me by surprise.*

Esta alfombra no cogerá toda la sala. *This carpet won't cover the whole room.*

Los niños desbarataron todo lo que cogen. *Children destroy everything they get hold of (lay their hands on).*

Ha cogido mi sombrero en vez del suyo. *He took my hat instead of his own.*

Le cojo la palabra. *I'll take you up on that.*

cogote *m. neck.*

cohecho *m. bribery.*

cohete *m. rocket.*

coincidencia *f. coincidence.*

Nos encontramos por una simple coincidencia. *We met by pure chance (coincidence).*

coincidir *to coincide.*

cojear *to limp.*

Sé de que pie cojea. *I know his weakness.*

cojera *f. lameness.*

cojo *adj. lame.*

cola *f. tail; rear of a train; glue; line (of people).*

Hacer cola. *To stand in line.*

colaboración *f. collaboration.*

colaborar *to collaborate.*

colar *to strain.*

colcha *f. bedspread.*

colchón *m. mattress.*

colección *f. collection.*

coleccionar *to collect.*

colecta *f. collection, collect.*

colectar *to collect; to solicit.*

colegio *m. school; association (means "college" only in the sense of a body of persons having common interests or corporate functions; for example, the electoral college or college of cardinals).*

No ha debido aprender gran cosa en el colegio. *I don't think he learned much at school.*

Colegio de abogados. *Lawyers association. The bar.*

Colegio de médicos. *Medical association.*

El colegio de cardinales. *The College of Cardinals.*

Colegio electoral. *Electoral college.*

cólera *f. anger, fit of temper, rage; m. cholera.*

Se le pasó la cólera fácilmente. *He got over his fit of temper easily.*

COLGAR *to hang, to suspend.*

Colgaron al criminal. *The criminal was hanged. ("They hanged the criminal.")*

Cuelgue su abrigo en la percha. *Hang your coat on the clothes-rack.*

¡No cuelgue Ud.! *Don't hang up!*

Cuelgue el receptor. *Hang up the receiver.*

cólico *m. colic.*

coliflor *f. cauliflower.*

colilla *f. cigar or cigarette stub.*

colina *f. small hill.*

colmena *f. beehive.*

colmillo *m. eyetooth, canine tooth, premolar.*

colmo *m. heap; climax, limit.*

¡Es el colmo! *That's the limit! That's the last straw!*

colocación *f. employment, situation; arrangement.*

Anda buscando una colocación. *He's looking for a job.*

Ha obtenido una buena colocación. *He has a good job. He got a good job.*

colocar *to place, to give employment to; to dispose of, to sell; to invest.*

Colóquelo en su lugar. *Put it back in its place.*

Se ha colocado en una casa de comercio. *He got a job in a business firm.*

colonia *f. colony; residential section in the outskirts of a town.*

colonial *adj. colonial.*

COLOR *m. color; paint; tendency, policy; aspect; pretext.*

    Es un color muy de moda. *It's a very stylish color.*

    Este color va bien con el verde. *This color goes well with green.*

    Color firme (solido). *Fast Color. Color that doesn't fade.*

    Color vivo. *Bright color.*

    Color claro. *Light color.*

    Color muerto. *Dull (dead) color.*

    De color. *Colored.*

    ¿Qué color tiene ese periódico? *What's that newspaper's policy? How does that newspaper stand politically?*

colorado *adj. red.*

    Ponerse colorado. *To blush.*

colorete *m. rouge.*

colorido *m. colorful.*

columna *f. column, pillar.*

columpiar *to swing.*

columpio *m. swing.*

collar *m. necklace, collar.*

coma *f. comma.*

comadre *f. term applied both to the godmother and to the mother of a child; a gossip.*

comadrear *to gossip.*

comadrona *f. midwife.*

comandante *m. commander, commandant.*

comarca *f. territory, district.*

combate *m. combat.*

    Poner fuera de combate. *To knock out.*

combatiente *noun and adj. combatant, fighter.*

    No combatiente. *Noncombatant.*

combatir *to combat, fight.*

combinación *f. combination; a slip (for women).*

combinar *to combine.*

combustible *m. combustible, fuel.*

comedia *f. comedy, play; farce.*

    La comedia agradó mucho al auditorio. *The audience liked the play very much.*

    Es una comedia. *It's a farce.*

comediante *m. comedian.*

comedor *m. dining room.*

    Coche comedor. *Diner. Dining car.*

comensal *m. and f. guest (at the table); boarder.*

comentar *to comment.*

comentario *m. comment, commentary.*

    Comentarios del día. *News commentary.*

    Eso se entiende sin comentarios. *That's a matter of course. That's very clear (obvious, self-evident).* ("*It's clear without any comments; it needs no comments.*")

COMENZAR *to begin, to commence.*

    ¿A qué hora comienza la función? *(At) What time does the play begin?*

COMER *to eat, to dine.*

¿Qué tiene Ud. de comer? *What do you have to eat?*

¿Qué quiere Ud. comer? *What do you want (would you like) to eat?*

¿Come Ud. con gana? *Are you enjoying your food? How do you like the food?*

Tengo ganas de comer. *I'm hungry.*

No tengo ganas de comer ahora. *I don't feel like eating just now.*

Dar de comer. *To feed.*

Ser de buen comer. *To have a hearty appetite.*

Se ha comido Ud. una línea. *You've omitted a line.*

Se comen el uno al otro. *They fight like cats and dogs.*

Ud. se come las palabras. *You don't enunciate clearly. You swallow half of your words.*

comerciar *to deal, to trade.*

comercio *m. commerce, trade.*

comestible *adj. edible; m. pl. food, groceries.*

cometer *to commit; to make (a mistake).*

    Todos cometemos errores. *We all make mistakes. Anyone can make a mistake.*

cometido *m. mission, trust, task; duty.*

    Yo he cumplido con mi cometido. *I've done my duty.*

    Desempeñó su cometido muy bien. *He carried out his mission faithfully. He fulfilled his obligation (commitment) faithfully.*

comezón *f. itching, itch.*

cómico *adj. comic, comical.*

COMIDA *f. food; meal; dinner.*

    La comida es muy sabrosa. *The food's very tasty.*

    No debe Ud. tomar nada entre comidas. *You mustn't eat anything between meals.*

    No hay nada como la comida casera. *There's nothing like home cooking.*

    ¿Está la comida? *Is dinner ready?*

    La comida está servida. *Dinner's served. Dinner's on the table.*

comienzo *m. beginning, start.*

comillas *f. quotation marks.*

comisaría *f. police station.*

comisario *m. commissioner.*

comisión *f. commission.*

comité *m. committee.*

COMO *how; as, like.*

    ¿Cómo lo pasa Ud.? *How do you do? How are you getting along?*

    ¿A cómo estamos? *What's the date?*

    ¿Cómo se llama Ud.? *What's your name?*

    ¿A cómo se venden estas medias? *How much are these stockings?*

    ¿Cómo no? *Why not?*

    ¡Cómo no! *Yes, of course.*

    Como Ud. quiera. *As you wish (like).*

    Habla español tan bien como ella. *He speaks*

Spanish as well as she.

El pasaje en autobús cuesta tanto como en tranvía. *It costs as much to ride on a bus as it does on a streetcar.*

Hace como que trabaja para que no la regañen. *She pretends to work so they won't scold her.*

Como si tal cosa. *As if nothing had happened.*

Según y como. *It all depends.*

cómoda *f. chest of drawers, a dresser.*

comodidad *f. comfort; convenience.*

Para su comodidad. *For your convenience.*

Esta casa tiene muchas comodidades. *This house has many (modern) conveniences.*

Comodidades de la vida moderna. *Modern conveniences.*

cómodo *adj. comfortable; convenient, handy.*

Estoy muy cómodo aquí. *I'm very comfortable here.*

Esta silla es un poco más cómoda. *This chair's a bit more comfortable.*

compadecer *to pity, to sympathize with.*

Le compadezco. *I pity him. I sympathize with him.*

compadre *m. term applied both to the godfather and to the father of a child; friend, pal, buddy (coll.).*

compañero *m. companion, comrade, pal; fellow member.*

En poco tiempo pasó a sus compañeros de estudios. *In a short time he was doing better than his fellow students.*

Es mi compañero de cuarto. *He's my roommate.*

compañía *f. company; partnership, society.*

Suárez y Cía. *Suárez and Co.*

comparación *f. comparison.*

En comparación con. *In comparison with.*

COMPARAR *to compare.*

compartir *to share.*

compás *m. compasses, dividers; compass; time (in music).*

compasión *f. pity, sympathy.*

compatible *adj. compatible, consistent with.*

compatriota *m. and f. countryman, countrywoman.*

compensación *f. compensation, reward.*

compensar *to compensate, to reward.*

competencia *f. competition; competence.*

competente *adj. competent, fit.*

competir *to compete, to contend.*

complacer *to please, to accommodate.*

Uno no puede complacer a todo el mundo. *One can't please everybody.*

Lo siento, pero no puedo complacerle. *I'm sorry but I can't accommodate you.*

complacerse *to be pleased.*

Se complace mucho en lo que hace. *He's very pleased (satisfied) with what he's doing.*

complaciente *adj. accommodating, agreeable, pleasing.*

complemento *m. complement, object (grammar).*

COMPLETAR *to complete.*

Completar un trabajo. *To complete a job (task).*

COMPLETO *adj. full; complete, finished.*

El autobús va completo. *The bus is full.*

Hay un lleno completo esta noche. *There's a full house tonight.*

Por completo. *Completely.*

complicado *adj. complicated.*

complicar *to complicate.*

cómplice *m. and f. accomplice.*

complot *m. conspiracy, plot, intrigue.*

componer *to repair, to mend; to manage; to compose.*

Quiero que me compongan los zapatos. *I'd like to have my shoes repaired.*

Quiero que componga Ud. esta radio. *I'd like you to fix this radio.*

Ya sabré componérmelas. *I'll know how to manage. I'll manage all right (one way or another).*

comportamiento *m. behavior.*

comportar *to suffer, to tolerate.*

comportarse *to behave.*

composición *composition.*

compositor *m. composer; typesetter.*

compostura *f. repair; neatness; modesty; composure.*

compota *f. preserves, stewed fruit.*

COMPRA *f. purchase, shopping.*

Ir de compras. *To go shopping.*

Tengo que hacer unas compras. *I want to make a few purchases. I want to buy a few things.*

comprador *m. buyer, purchaser; customer.*

COMPRAR *to buy, to shop.*

Comprar a crédito. *To buy on credit.*

Comprar al fiado. *To buy on credit.*

Comprar al contado. *To buy for cash.*

Comprar de ocasión. *To buy secondhand.*

COMPRENDER *to understand; to comprise, to include.*

¿Me comprende Ud. bien? *Do you understand me ("all right")?*

Le entiendo perfectamente. *I understand you perfectly.*

¡Se comprende! *That's understood. That's clear. That's a matter of course.*

comprendido *adj. understood; including.*

comprensible *comprehensible.*

comprensión *f. comprehension, understanding.*

comprensivo *adj. comprehensive.*

comprimir *to compress; to repress, to restrain.*

comprimirse *to restrain oneself, to control oneself.*

comprobante *m. proof, voucher.*

comprobar *to prove, to verify.*

comprometerse *to commit oneself; to become engaged.*

compromiso *m. compromise; jeopardy; engagement;*

pledge, commitment.

compuesto adj. and n. compound.

compulsorio adj. compulsory.

computar to compute.

COMÚN adj. common.

> Sentido común. Common sense.
>
> En común. In common. Jointly.
>
> Por lo común. Generally.
>
> De común acuerdo. By mutual consent.

comunicación f. communication.

> Telefonista, nos ha cortado la comunicación. Operator, we've been cut off.
>
> Por favor, póngame en comunicación con el número . . . Kindly connect me with number . . .

comunicar to announce; to communicate; to inform.

comunidad f. community.

CON with, by.

> Se viene con nosotros. She's coming with us.
>
> Con mucho gusto. With ("great") pleasure. Gladly.
>
> No sea duro con él. Don't be hard on him.
>
> Con tal. Provided that.
>
> Con que. And so. So. Then. Well then.
>
> ¡Con que esas tenemos! So that's the story!
>
> Con todo. Notwithstanding. Nevertheless. However. Even so.
>
> Tratar con. To do business with. To deal with.
>
> Dar con. To find. To meet. To come across.
>
> Con tal que. On (the) condition that. Provided that.

concebir to conceive.

conceder to grant.

concentración f. concentration.

concentrar to concentrate.

concepto m. concept, idea.

concernir to concern.

> Eso no le concierne a Ud. That doesn't concern you.

concesión f. concession.

conciencia f. conscience, consciousness.

concierto m. concert; agreement.

conciliación f. conciliation.

conciliar to conciliate, to reconcile.

conciso adj. concise.

concluir to conclude; to finish; to close (a deal).

conclusión f. conclusion.

concluso adj. ended, concluded, closed.

concordancia f. concordance; harmony, agreement.

concordarse to agree.

concretar to make concrete, reduce to its simplest form.

concretarse to limit or confine oneself (to a subject).

> Concrétese a la pregunta. Stick to the point. Answer the question.

concreto adj. concrete.

En concreto. In short.

concurrencia f. audience, attendance; coincidence; competition.

concurrir to concur; to attend.

concurso m. competition, contest.

concha f. shell.

conde m. count (title).

condecoración f. decoration, medal.

condena f. sentence, penalty.

condenar to condemn, to convict; to disapprove.

> Se le condenó a muerte. He was condemned to death.
>
> Condeno su proceder. I disapprove of his behavior.

condición f. condition, state; term.

> A condición que. On (the) condition that. Provided that.
>
> Convengo en sus condiciones. I agree to your terms.
>
> ¿Está todo en buenas condiciones? Is everything in good order?

condicional adj. conditional.

condimentar to season (food).

condimento m. seasoning, condiment.

condiscípulo m. fellow student, schoolmate.

condonar to forgive, to pardon.

cóndor m. condor.

CONDUCIR to drive; to conduct; to carry; to lead.

> ¿Sabe Ud. conducir? Do you know how to drive?
>
> Este camino nos conducirá al lago. This road will take us to the lake.

conducirse to conduct oneself, to behave.

conducta f. conduct, behavior.

conductor m. conductor, driver.

conejo m. rabbit.

confeccionar to make, to prepare.

conferencia f. conference, lecture; call (long distance).

> Asistimos a la conferencia del lunes. We attended Monday's lecture.
>
> Conferencia a larga distancia. Long distance call.
>
> Conferencia interurbana. Long distance call (Spain).

conferenciante m. and f. lecturer.

conferir to confer, to bestow.

confesar to admit, to confess.

> ¿Confiesa Ud. su falta? Do you admit your guilt?

confesión f. confession, acknowledgment.

confianza f. confidence; faith; familiarity.

> Digno de confianza. Reliable. Trustworthy.
>
> En confianza. In confidence.
>
> Tener confianza en. To trust.

confiar to confide; to trust in, to entrust.

confidencia f. confidence.

confidencial adj. confidential.

confidente adj. confident.

confirmación f. *confirmation.*

confirmar *to confirm. to ratify.*

confite m. *candy.*

conflicto m. *conflict, strife; predicament.*

conformar *to conform; to fit, to agree; to comply with.*

  Conformarse con. *To agree with. To be satisfied with.*

CONFORME *alike; according to; O.K., correct.*

  Conforme a. *According to.*

  Estar conforme. *To be in agreement.*

conformidad f. *conformity, resemblance.*

  De conformidad con. *In accordance with.*

confort m. *comfort.*

confortable adj. *comfortable.*

confortante adj. *comforting.*

confortar *to comfort, to cheer.*

confundir *to confuse; to mistake.*

confundirse *to become confused; to be perplexed.*

confusión f. *confusion, perplexity.*

confuso adj. *confused.*

congelar *to freeze.*

congeniar *to be congenial.*

congestión f. *congestion.*

congratulación f. *congratulation.*

congratular *to congratulate.*

congregación f. *congregation.*

congregar *to congregate, to assemble.*

conjetura f. *conjecture, guess.*

conjeturar *to conjecture, to guess.*

conjugación f. *conjugation.*

conjugar *to conjugate.*

conjunción f. *conjunction.*

conjunto adj. *joint, united; m. the whole.*

  En conjunto. *On the whole. In all. Altogether.*

conmemoración f. *commemoration.*

conmemorar *to commemorate.*

conmigo *with myself, with me.*

  ¿Quiere Ud. hablar conmigo? *Do you want to speak with (to) me?*

  Venga Ud. conmigo. *Come (along) with me.*

conmoción f. *commotion, tumult, disturbance.*

conmutador m. *electric switch; telegraph key.*

CONOCER *to know, to understand, to be acquainted with.*

  ¿Conoce Ud. a María? *Do you know Mary?*

  No la conozco. *I don't know her.*

  ¿Se conocen Uds.? *Have you met? Do you know each other?*

  ¿No se conocen Uds.? *Don't you know each other?*

  No tengo el gusto de conocerle. *No, I haven't had the pleasure (of meeting him).*

  Sí, ya nos conocemos. *Yes, we've already met.*

  Dar a conocer. *To make known.*

conocido adj. *well-known; m. acquaintance.*

  Es un antiguo conocido nuestro. *He's an old acquaintance of ours.*

conocimiento m. *knowledge, understanding, acquaintance; bill of lading.*

  Poner en conocimiento. *To inform. To let know.*

  Llegar a conocimiento de. *To come to the knowledge of.*

  Tomar conocimiento de. *To take notice of.*

conque *and so, so then, well then.*

  Conque ¿te vas? *So you're leaving.*

conquista f. *conquest; winning somebody's affection, ingratiating oneself.*

conquistar *to conquer, to win over.*

consciente adj. *conscious.*

consecuencia f. *consequence.*

  No es de ninguna consecuencia. *It's of no consequence.*

  Como consecuencia. *In consequence. As a consequence.*

  En consecuencia. *Therefore. In consequence.*

CONSEGUIR *to obtain, to attain, to get.*

  Será difícil conseguirlo. *It'll be difficult to get it.*

  No pude conseguir ningún dinero. *I couldn't get (obtain) any money.*

consejero m. *member of a board (council); counselor, advisor.*

consejo m. *advice; council, advisory board.*

  Seguiré sus consejos. *I'll follow your advice.*

  Consejo de ministros. *Cabinet (government).*

  Consejo de guerra. *Court-martial.*

consentimiento m. *consent.*

consentir *to consent; to agree, to be willing to; to tolerate; to spoil (a child).*

  ¿Consentirá Ud. en ello? *Will you consent to it?*

  Nunca consentiré tal cosa. *I'll never tolerate such a thing.*

conserje m. and f. *janitor, concierge.*

conserva f. *preserve, canned food; convoy (of ships).*

conservación f. *conservation, upkeep, maintenance.*

conservador adj. and n. *preserver; conservative.*

CONSERVAR *to preserve, to keep, to conserve.*

  Lo conservé como recuerdo. *I kept it as a souvenir.*

considerable adj. *considerable, large.*

consideración f. *consideration, regard; importance.*

considerar *to consider, to take into account; to treat well.*

consigna f. *watchword; check room.*

  Dejaré esta maleta en la consigna. *I'll check this bag. I'll leave this suitcase in the check room.*

consigo *with oneself; with himself; with herself; with yourself, yourselves.*

  ¿Lo trajo consigo? *Did you bring it with you?*

  Lléveselo consigo. *Take it along with you.*

consiguiente adj. *consequent, consecutive; consis-*

tent, logical.

Por consiguiente. *Consequently.*

consistencia f. consistence, consistency; stability, solidity, firmness.

consistente adj. consistent, solid, firm.

consistir to consist, to be composed of.

consolación f. consolation.

consolar to console, to comfort, to cheer.

conspicuo adj. conspicuous.

constante adj. constant.

constitución constitution.

constituir to constitute.

construcción f. construction, building.

CONSTRUIR to construct, to build.

cónsul m. consul.

consulado m. consulate.

consulta f. consultation.

consultar to consult, to seek advice.

Vaya Ud. a consultar al médico. *Go and consult the doctor.*

¿Ha consultado Ud. a un médico? *Have you seen a doctor?*

Consultar algo con la almohada. *To sleep on something. ("To consult with one's pillow.")*

consultorio m. doctor's office; bureau of information.

consumidor m. consumer.

consumir to consume, to use.

consumo m. consumption; demand (goods).

Artículo de consumo. *Staple.*

contabilidad f. bookkeeping, accounting.

contado adj. rare, scarce; m. cash.

Por de contado. *Of course. As a matter of course.*

Vendemos sólo al contado. *We sell only for cash.*

Se lo pagaré al contado. *I'll pay cash for it.*

contador m. accountant, purser; meter (gas, electric, etc.).

contagiar to infect, to contaminate.

contagioso adj. contagious.

contaminar to contaminate.

CONTAR to count; to tell.

¿Contó Ud. su cambio? *Did you count your change?*

¿Tiene Ud. algo que contarme? *Have you anything to tell me?*

¿Qué cuenta Ud.? *What's new?*

¡Me lo cuenta a mí! *You're telling me!*

¿Puedo contar con Ud.? *Can I count (depend) on you?*

contemplación f. contemplation.

contemplar to contemplate, to consider, to have in view.

CONTENER to hold, to contain.

Esta botella contiene vino. *This bottle contains wine. There's wine in this bottle.*

contenerse to refrain, to restrain oneself.

No puede contenerse. *He can't restrain himself.*

contenido m. contents.

contentar to please, to satisfy.

contentarse to be pleased, to be contented.

No se contentará con palabras nada más. *He won't be satisfied with mere words.*

CONTENTO adj. glad, happy, pleased; m. contentment.

Parecía contenta. *She looked happy.*

Estamos contentos de su trabajo. *We're pleased with his work.*

contestación f. answer, reply.

CONTESTAR to answer, to reply; to attest; to dispute.

Le hice una pregunta y no supo contestarme. *I asked him a question and he didn't know the answer.*

Debe Ud. contestar su carta. *You ought to reply to his letter.*

No contestan. *They don't answer.*

contigo with you (familiar, singular).

contiguo adj. contiguous; close, near.

continente adj. moderate; m. continent.

continuación f. continuation.

CONTINUAR to continue.

continuo adj. continuous.

De continuo. *Continually.*

Sesión continua. *Continuous performance.*

CONTRA against, contrary to, counter to.

Lo hizo contra su voluntad. *She did it against her will.*

Apóyalo contra la pared. *Lean it against the wall.*

¿Sabe Ud. de algún remedio contra el mareo? *Do you know of a remedy for seasickness?*

contrabandista m. and f. smuggler.

contrabando m. contraband, smuggling.

contradecir to contradict.

contradicción f. contradiction.

contraer to contract.

Contraer matrimonio. *To get married.*

Contraer deudas. *To run into debt.*

contrahacer to counterfeit.

contrahecho adj. counterfeit; deformed.

contrariar to contradict; to annoy, to vex.

contrariedad f. mishap; disappointment; vexation.

¡Qué contrariedad! *What a disappointment!*

contrario adj. contrary, opposite; m. opponent.

A mí me pasa lo contrario. *With me it's the opposite.*

Dice lo contrario de lo que siente. *He says the opposite of what he thinks.*

Al contrario. *On the contrary.*

contraseña f. watchword; countersign, check.

contrastar to contrast.

contraste m. contrast; assayer.

contrata f. contract.

contratar *to engage, to hire; to bargain, to trade; to contract.*

contratiempo *m. mishap, setback, disappointment.*

contrato *m. contract.*

contribución *f. contribution; tax.*

contribuir *to contribute.*

contrincante *m. opponent, competitor.*

control *m. control.*

controlar *to control.*

contusión *f. bruise, contusion.*

convalecencia *f. convalescence.*

convaleciente *adj. and n. convalescent.*

convencer *to convince.*

conveniencia *f. convenience; fitness, advantage.*

conveniente *adj. convenient, suitable; advantageous.*

convenio *m. pact, agreement, covenant.*

CONVENIR *to agree; to suit, to be advisable.*

Eso me conviene. *That suits me.*

No me conviene. *It doesn't suit me. It won't do.*

Convengo con Ud. *I agree with you. I'm of your opinion.*

No convenimos en el precio. *We didn't agree on the price.*

Hágalo Ud. como más le convenga. *Do it in the way that's most convenient for you.*

Al tiempo y en el lugar convenidos. *At the time and place agreed on.*

convento *m. convent.*

conversación *f. conversation, chat, talk.*

Su conversación es agradable. *It's pleasant to talk with her. ("Her conversation is pleasant.")*

conversar *to converse, to chat.*

convertir *to convert, to change.*

convicción *f. conviction, belief, certainty.*

convicto *adj. guilty; convicted.*

convidado *adj. invited; m. guest.*

convidar *to invite, to treat.*

convoy *m. convoy.*

cónyuge *m. and f. husband or wife.*

coñac *m. cognac, brandy.*

cooperación *f. cooperation.*

cooperar *to cooperate.*

coordinar *to coordinate.*

copa *f. goblet, top of a tree; crown of a hat.*

copia *f. copy, transcript; abundance.*

Sacar una copia. *To make a copy.*

copiar *to copy.*

coqueta *f. flirt, coquette.*

coquetear *to flirt.*

coraje *m. courage; anger.*

CORAZÓN *m. heart; core.*

Poner el corazón en algo. *To set one's heart on something.*

corbata *f. necktie.*

corcho *m. cork.*

cordel *m. cord, rope.*

cordero *m. lamb.*

cordial *adj. cordial, effectionate.*

cordillera *f. mountain range.*

cordón *m. cord, string, lace.*

cordura *f. prudence, judgment, common sense.*

corona *f. crown; wreath; tonsure.*

corral *m. yard, court; corral.*

correa *f. leather strap, leash, thong.*

corredor *m. runner; broker.*

corregir *to correct.*

CORREO *m. post office; mail.*

¿Hay una oficina de correos cerca? *Is there a post office near by?*

¿A qué hora sale el correo? *(At) What time does the mail leave?*

¿Ha echado Ud. mi carta al correo? *Have you mailed my letter?*

A vuelta de correo. *By return mail.*

Por correo aéreo. *By air mail.*

Lista de correos. *General delivery.*

Apartado de correos. *Post-office box.*

CORRER *to run; to flow; to elapse; to blow (wind); to draw (curtains, etc.).*

Fuimos allí a todo correr. *We rushed there.*

Corre mucho aire. *There's a good breeze.*

Corra las cortinas. *Draw the curtains.*

¿Le corre a Ud. mucha prisa el trabajo? *Are you in a hurry for the work?*

No corre prisa. *There's no hurry.*

Esto corre de mi cuenta. *This is on me. This will be at my own expense.*

Corrió mucho riesgo. *He took quite a chance. He ran a great risk.*

correrse *to slide over, to move away; to make rash promises; to act or speak with undue haste; to overpay; to gutter (of a candle).*

Córrase un poco. *Move away a little.*

La vela se corre. *The candle's guttering.*

correspondencia *f. correspondence, mail.*

Estar en correspondencia con. *To correspond with.*

Mantener correspondencia con. *To correspond with.*

Llevar la correspondencia. *To be in charge of the correspondence. To take care of the mail.*

correspondiente *adj. corresponding.*

corresponsal *m. correspondent.*

corrida *f. run, race, course.*

Corrida de toros. *Bullfight.*

corriente *adj. current, present (month or year); ordinary, common; f. current; stream; draft (air).*

Cuenta corriente. *Current account.*

Salgo el quince del corriente. *I'm leaving on the fifteenth of this month.*

Hay una corriente de aire. *There's a draft.*

Quítese Ud. de la corriente. *Get out of the draft.*

Estar al corriente. *To be acquainted with. To be familiar with. To be abreast of.*

Poner al corriente. *To inform. To acquaint with.*

Tener al corriente. *To keep informed.*

Corriente alterna. *Alternating current (A. C.)*

Corriente continua. *Direct current (D. C.)*

Seguir la corriente. *To go with the tide. To follow the crowd.*

corroborar *to corroborate.*

corromper *to corrupt.*

corrupción *f. corruption.*

cortaplumas *m. penknife.*

cortar *to cut; to cut off; to shorten.*

Me he cortado. *I've cut myself.*

Este cuchillo no corta. *This knife doesn't cut well.*

Telefonista, nos ha cortado. *Operator, I've been cut off ("you've cut us off").*

Barbero, córteme el pelo. *("Barber,") Give me a haircut.*

Se ha cortado la leche. *The milk has turned sour.*

corte *cut; edge (of a knife, etc.); court; pl. congress (Spain).*

Corte de pelo. *Haircut.*

Las Cortes. *The Spanish congress.*

Llamar a Cortes. *To convoke the Cortes.*

Hacer la corte. *To court.*

cortejar *to court.*

cortés *adj. courteous, gentle, polite.*

El es muy cortés. *He's very polite.*

cortesía *f. courtesy, politeness.*

corteza *f. bark; peel; crust.*

Corteza del árbol. *Bark of a tree.*

cortina *f. curtain, screen.*

CORTO *adj. short; shy; stupid; backward.*

Las mangas son muy cortas. *The sleeves are very short.*

Es muy corto de genio. *He's very shy.*

A la corta o larga. *Sooner or later.*

Cuento corto. *Short story.*

Es corto de vista. *He's near-sighted.*

cortocircuito *m. short circuit.*

COSA *f. thing; matter.*

No hay tal cosa. *There's no such thing.*

¡Qué cosa más preciosa! *What a beautiful thing!*

Ninguna cosa. *Nothing.*

¿Desea Ud. alguna otra cosa? *Would you like anything else?*

Es poco más o menos la misma cosa. *It's more or less the same thing.*

Venga Ud. aquí, tengo que decirle una cosa. *Come here, I want to tell you something.*

Como si tal cosa. *As if nothing had happened.*

No es cosa de risa. *It's no laughing matter.*

Hace cosa de dos meses. *It was about two months ago.*

Cosa rara. *A strange thing.*

Eso es cosa suya. *That's his business.*

cosecha *f. harvest, crop; harvest time.*

cosechar *to reap, to gather in the crop.*

coser *to sew.*

Máquina de coser. *Sewing machine.*

cosmético *m. cosmetic.*

cosquillas *f. pl. tickling.*

cosquillear *to tickle.*

cosquilloso *adj. ticklish, easily offended.*

costa *f. coast, shore; cost, expense.*

A toda costa. *At all costs. By all means.*

A lo largo de la costa. *Coastwise. Along the coast.*

costado *m. flank; side.*

COSTAR *to cost.*

¿Cuánto cuestan estos zapatos? *How much do these shoes cost?*

¿Cuánto me costará más o menos? *About how much will it cost?*

Me cuesta trabajo creerlo. *It's hard for me to believe it.*

Cueste lo que cueste. *Whatever it costs. At all costs.*

Costar un ojo de la cara. *To cost a fortune.*

costear *to pay the expenses; to sail along the coast.*

costilla *f. rib; wife; stave.*

COSTO *m. cost, expense, price.*

Precio de costo. *Cost price.*

costoso *adj. dear, expensive.*

costumbre *f. custom; habit.*

De costumbre. *Usually.*

Como de costumbre. *As usual.*

Tener costumbre de. *To be used to. To be in the habit of.*

costura *f. sewing; needlework; seam.*

Alta costura. *High fashion.*

costurera *f. seamstress.*

cotejar *to confront, to check.*

cotejo *m. comparison, collation.*

cotidiano *adj. daily, everyday.*

cotización *f. quotation (of prices).*

cotizar *to quote (prices).*

coyuntura *f. articulation, joint; opportunity.*

coz *f. kick.*

cráneo *m. skull, cranium.*

crear *to create; to establish, to set up.*

CRECER *to grow; to increase.*

crecimiento *m. increase, growth, increment.*

credencial *f. credential.*

crédito *m. credit; credence; reputation, standing.*

Comprar a crédito. *To buy on credit.*

Vender a crédito. *To sell on credit.*

Dar crédito. *To give credit.*

Carta de crédito. *Letter of credit.*

creencia *f. credence, belief.*

CREER *to believe; to think.*

Creo que es una buena idea. *I think it's a good idea.*

Creo que sí. *I believe so. I think so.*

Creo que no. *I don't think so.*

Ya lo creo. *I should think (say) so! Of course! Naturally!*

Ver y creer. *Seeing is believing.*

crema *f. cream.*

. Crema de noche. *Night cream.*

Crema dentrífica. *Toothpaste.*

criada *f. maid, servant.*

criado *m. a manservant; valet.*

criar *to create, to produce; to nurse; to rear, to bring up.*

criatura *f. creature; baby, child.*

cribar *to sift.*

cribo *m. sieve.*

crimen *m. crime; guilt.*

criminal *m. and f. criminal.*

criollo *adj. and n. Creole (one born in Spanish America of European parents).*

crisantemo *m. chrysanthemum.*

crisis *f. crisis.*

cristal *m. crystal; glass.*

cristianismo *m. Christianity.*

cristiano *adj. and n. Christian.*

criterio *m. criterion, judgment, opinion.*

Lo dejo a su criterio. *I leave it up to you.*

crítica *f. criticism, review.*

criticar *to criticize.*

crítico *m. critic.*

crónica *f. chronicle.*

cronista *m. reporter.*

croqueta *f. croquette.*

cruce *m. crossing; crossroads.*

crucero *m. crossing; cruiser.*

crudo *adj. raw, crude.*

cruel *adj. cruel, hard.*

crueldad *f. cruelty.*

cruz *f. cross.*

cruzar *to cross; to cruise.*

cuaderno *m. notebook; memorandum book.*

cuadra *f. stable; block (of houses).*

cuadrado *adj. square.*

cuadrilla *f. gang, crew.*

cuadro *m. painting, picture; frame; scene (in a play).*

CUAL *which; what; like; as; el cual (m.); la cual (f.); los cuales (m. pl.); las cuales (f. pl.) who, which.*

¿Cuál de ellos prefiere Ud.? *Which one do you prefer (like best)?*

¿Cuáles son los últimos modelos? *What are the latest styles?*

Por lo cual. *For that reason.*

Cada cual. *Each one.*

Tal para cual. *Tit for tat. Two of a kind.*

cualquier *any (used immediately before a noun).*

See also **cualquiera.**

A cualquier hora. *At any time.*

En cualquier momento. *At any moment.*

Es capaz de cualquier cosa. *He's capable of anything.*

cualquiera *any; anyone; anybody. (**Cualquiera** and **cualquier** do not change for gender.)*

Cualquiera de los hombres. *Any of the men.*

Cualquiera puede hacer eso. *Anybody can do that.*

Tome Ud. cualquiera que le guste. *Take anyone (whichever one) you like.*

Un cualquiera. *A nobody.*

cuan *how, as (used only before adjectives or adverbs).*

¡Cuán lejos! *How far!*

¡Cuán hermoso! *How pretty!*

CUANDO *(written **cuándo** when interrogative), when.*

¿Cuándo se marcha Ud.? *When are you leaving?*

Cuando Ud. guste. *Whenever you say. Whenever you wish.*

¿Hasta cuándo? *Until when?*

¿De cuándo acá? *Since when? How come? How is that?*

De cuando en cuando. *From time to time.*

De vez en cuando. *Once in a while.*

Cuando más (mucho). *At best. At most.*

Cuando menos. *At least.*

CUANTO *as much as, as many as.*

Compre cuantas naranjas encuentre. *Buy as many oranges as you can find.*

Avíseme en cuanto esté libre. *Let me know as soon as it's free.*

Cuanto más le doy, tanto más me pide. *The more I give him, the more he asks for.*

Cuanto más gaste tanto menos tendrá. *The more you spend, the less you'll have.*

Cuanto antes mejor. *The sooner the better.*

Se quedó con tanto cuanto quiso. *He kept for himself as much as he wanted.*

Cuanto antes. *As soon as possible.*

Por cuanto. *Whereas. Inasmuch as.*

En cuanto a. *In regard to.*

Cuanto Ud. quiera. *All (as much as) you wish.*

CUÁNTO *how much; how long; how far; how, pl. how many.*

¿Cuánto? *How much?*

¿Cuántos? *How many?*

¿A cuántos estamos? *What's the date?*

¿Cuánto es? *How much is it?*

¿Cuánto vale? *How much is it worth?*

¿Cuánto hay de aquí a Zaragoza? *How far is it from here to Zaragoza?*

¿Cuánto tiempo se tarda en aeroplano? *How long does it take by airplane?*

¡Cuánto me alegro! *I'm very glad. ("How glad*

I am!")

¡Cuánto ha cambiado Ud.! *You have changed a lot! How (much) you've changed!*

CUARENTA *adj. and n.* forty; fortieth.

cuartel *m.* quarter; barracks; district of a city.
Cuartel general. *Headquarters.*

CUARTO *adj.* fourth, quarter; *m.* room.
Le daré la cuarta parte. *I'll give you a fourth of it.*
A las once menos cuarto. *At a quarter to eleven.*
A las cinco y cuarto. *At a quarter past five.*
¿Tiene Ud. un cuarto para dos personas? *Do you have a double room?*
Es mi compañero de cuarto. *He's my room-mate.*

CUATRO *adj. and n.* four; fourth.
Son las cuatro. *It's four o'clock.*
Soltar cuatro frescas. *To give (someone) a piece of one's mind.*

cuatrocientos *adj. and n.* four hundred.

Cuba *f.* Cuba.

cubano *adj. and n.* Cuban.

cubeta *f.* small barrel; pail, bucket; mercury cup (of a barometer).

cubierta *f.* cover; deck of a ship.

cubierto *m.* cover; place at a table; table d'hôte; shelter.

cubo *m.* bucket; tub; hub of a wheel.

cubrecama *f.* bedspread.

CUBRIR *to cover; to roof.*

cucaracha *f.* cockroach.

CUCHARA *f.* spoon.

cucharada *f.* spoonful.

cucharadita *f.* teaspoonful.

cucharetear *to stir with a spoon; to meddle in other people's affairs.*

cucharilla *f.* teaspoon.

cucharita *f.* teaspoon.

cucharón *m.* ladle; large spoon.

cuchichear *to whisper.*

cuchicheo *m.* whispering.

cuchilla *f.* large knife.

cuchillo *m.* knife.

cuello *m.* neck; collar.

CUENTA *f.* count; account; statement; bill; bead.
Tráigame Ud. la cuenta. *Let me have the bill.*
¿Cuál es el saldo de mi cuenta? *What's the balance of my account?*
Apúntelo en mi cuenta. *Charge it to my account.*
Caer en la cuenta. *To notice.*
Ya caigo en la cuenta. *Now I see the point.*
Abonar en cuenta. *To credit with.*
Cuenta corriente. *Current account.*
Cuenta pendiente. *Unpaid balance. Balance due.*
Dar cuenta de. *To report on.*

Darse cuenta. *To realize.*
Tener en cuenta. *To bear in mind. To take into account (consideration).*
Tomar por su cuenta. *To take upon oneself. To assume responsibility for.*

cuentagotas *m.* medicine dropper.

cuento *m.* story, tale; gossip.
Cuento de hadas. *Fairy tale.*
Cuento corto. *Short story.*
Traer a cuento. *To bring up. To turn the conversation to a certain point.*
Venir a cuento. *To be to the point. To be pertinent.*
Esto no viene a cuento. *That's beside the point. That's not the case.*
Dejarse de cuentos. *To stop beating around the bush.*

cuerda *f.* cord, rope; spring (of a watch).
Quiero un mozo de cuerda. *I want a porter.*
¿Le ha dado Ud. cuerda a su reloj? *Have you wound (up) your watch?*
Lo hizo por debajo de cuerda. *He did it in an underhand way.*

cuerdo *adj.* in one's senses; wise, prudent.

cuerno *m.* horn.

cuero *m.* leather; hide; skin.

CUERPO *m.* body; element; corps.

cuervo *m.* crow, raven.

cuesta *f.* slope, grade; hill; collection for charity.
Ir cuesta abajo. *To go downhill.*
Ir cuesta arriba. *To go uphill.*
Cuesta arriba. *With great trouble and difficulty. Painfully.*
A cuestas. *On one's back.*

CUESTIÓN *m.* question; dispute, quarrel; problem.

cuestionable *adj.* questionable, problematical.

cuestionar *to question.*

cueva *f.* cave; cellar.

CUIDADO *m.* care, attention; anxiety, worry.
¡Cuidado! *Be careful!*
Tener cuidado. *To be careful.*
¡Tenga cuidado! *Be careful!*
Me tiene sin cuidado. *I don't care.*
¡No tenga Ud. cuidado! *Don't worry!*
Estar con cuidado. *To be worried.*

cuidadoso *adj.* careful.

cuidar *to care, to take care, to mind, to look after.*
¡Cuídese Ud.! *Take good care of yourself.*
Cuidar de. *To take care of.*

culebra *f.* snake.

culpa *f.* fault, guilt; sin.
¿Quién tiene la culpa? *Whose fault is it?*
Yo no tengo la culpa. *It isn't my fault.*
Es culpa mía. *It's my fault.*
Echar la culpa a. *To blame.*
Tener la culpa de. *To be to blame. To be at fault.*

culpable *adj.* guilty.

culpar *to accuse, to blame.*

cultivar *to cultivate; to till; to improve.*

En Canadá se cultiva mucho el trigo. *They grow a lot of wheat in Canada.*

Este terreno me parece que está cultivado. *This ground appears to be cultivated.*

cultivo *m. farming, cultivation; tillage.*

culto *adj. well-educated; polished; m. worship; cult, religion.*

Es un hombre culto. *He's a well-read (cultured) man.*

cultura *f. culture; urbanity.*

cultural *adj. cultural.*

cumpleaños *m. birthday.*

cumplido *adj. courteous, polite; full, abundant; m. compliment, attention, courtesy.*

No gaste Ud. cumplidos. *Don't stand (so much) on ceremony.*

cumplimiento *m. compliment; accomplishment; compliance, fulfillment, carrying out.*

No se ande Ud. en cumplimientos conmigo. *You don't have to stand on ceremony with me.*

Ofrecer algo por cumplimiento. *To offer something out of courtesy.*

CUMPLIR *to carry out, to fulfill, to keep one's word; to expire.*

Siempre cumple con su deber. *He always does his duty. He always fulfills his obligations.*

El plazo se ha cumplido. *The time has expired.*

Al cumplir los veinte y un años será mayor de edad. *He'll be of age when he's twenty-one.*

Cumplir años. *To have a birthday.*

cuna *f. cradle; family, lineage.*

cuña *f. wedge.*

cuñada *f. sister-in-law.*

cuñado *m. brother-in-law.*

cuota *f. share; quota.*

cura *m. parson; priest; f. cure; curing; preserving.*

Los casó el cura. *The priest married them.*

Este mal tiene cura. *This sickness is curable.*

curable *adj. curable.*

curación *f. healing, cure.*

curar *to cure; to heal.*

curiosear *to pry into other people's affairs, to be a busybody.*

curiosidad *f. curiosity; neatness, cleanliness.*

curioso *adj. curious.*

curso *m. course, direction; succession; current.*

curva *f. curve.*

cúspide *f. summit, top.*

custodia *f. custody, guard; escort.*

custodiar *to guard, to take into custody.*

cutis *m. complexion; skin.*

cuya *(f. of* **cuyo***) whose, of which, of whom (pl.* **cuyas***).*

La señora a cuya hija le he presentado, es amiga de su padre. *The lady whose daughter I introduced you to is a friend of your father's.*

cuyo *whose, of which, of whom (pl.* **cuyos***).*

Era un pequeño pueblo, cuyo nombre no recuerdo. *It was a small town, the name of which I don't remember.*

CH

chabacano *adj. coarse, unpolished; m. kind of apricot (Mex.).*

chacal *m. jackal.*

chacota *f. noisy merriment; fun.*

Hacer chacota de. *To make fun of. To ridicule.*

chacra *f. farm (Arg.).*

chal *m. shawl.*

chaleco *m. vest.*

chalet *m. chalet; cottage.*

chalupa *f. sloop; small canoe.*

chambón *adj. awkward, clumsy.*

chambonada *f. blunder.*

champaña *m. champagne.*

champú *m. shampoo.*

chancear *to joke, to fool.*

chanclos *m. pl. galoshes, rubbers.*

chancho *adj. dirty, unclean; m. hog, pig.*

chantaje *m. blackmailing.*

chantajista *m. and f. blackmailer.*

chanza *f. jest, joke.*

chaqueta *f. jacket, coat.*

charco *m. pond, puddle.*

charla *f. chat, chatter.*

charlar *to chat, to chatter.*

charlatán *m. quack, charlatan; babbler, one who is always talking.*

chasco *m. disappointment; joke.*

chasis *m. chassis.*

chato *adj. flat; flat-nosed.*

chelín *m. shilling.*

cheque *m. check (money).*

chicle *m. chicle; chewing gum.*

chica *f. little girl; girl.*

Es una chica encantadora. *She's a charming girl.*

chico *adj. small, little; m. boy; pl. youngsters.*

Es un chico muy obediente. *He's a very obedient boy.*

chicharrón *m. crisp fried bacon or pork fat.*

chichón *m. lump on the head.*

chiflado *adj. silly, crazy.*

chillar *to scream, to screech; to squeak, to creak.*

chillido *m. scream.*

chillón *adj. loud, gaudy (color); m. bawler, screamer.*

chimenea *f. chimney; fireplace.*

chinche *f. thumbtack; bedbug; boring person.*

chinela *f. slipper.*

chiquero *m. pigsty, pigpen.*

chiquillada *f. childishness, childish action.*

chiquillo m. *little boy; f. little girl.*
chiquito adj. *small, tiny; m. little boy, f. little girl.*
chiripa f. *fluke; lucky chance; bargain.*
   De chiripa. *By mere chance. By a fluke.*
chirriar *to hiss; to squeak.*
chisme m. *gossip.*
chismear *to gossip, to tattle.*
chismorreo m. *gossip.*
chismoso adj. *talebearing, gossiping; m. talebearer, tattletale, one who gossips.*
chispa f. *spark.*
   Echar chispas. *To get raving mad.*
   Ser chispa. *To be full of life. To sparkle.*
chistar *to mutter, to mumble.*
   Ni siquiera chistó. *He didn't say a word. He didn't open his mouth.*
chiste m. *joke.*
chistoso adj. *witty, humorous.*
¡Chito! ¡Chitón! *Hush! Silence!*
chivo m. *kid, goat.*
chocar *to collide; to strike; to disgust; to shock.*
choclo m. *cob. green ear of corn.*
chocolate m. *chocolate.*
chófer m. *chauffeur.*
choque m. *collision; clash; shock.*
chorizo m. *sausage.*
chorro m. *gush, spurt, jet of water.*
choza f. *hut, hovel.*
chubasco m. *squall.*
chuchería f. *trinket, gewgaw, trifle.*
chuleta f. *cutlet; chop.*
   Chuleta de cordero. *Lamb chop.*
   Chuleta de puerco. *Pork chop.*
   Chuleta de ternera. *Veal chop.*
chupar *to suck, to absorb; to sponge on.*
churro m. *a kind of doughnut, fritter (Spain).*
chusco adj. *droll, amusing, funny.*

D

dactilógrafo m. *typist.*
dádiva f. *gift, present.*
dadivoso adj. *liberal, generous.*
dados m. pl. *dice.*
dama f. *lady, dame; king (in checkers).*
   Primera dama. *Leading lady.*
   Jugar a las damas. *To play checkers.*
daga f. *dagger.*
dalia f. *dahlia.*
danzón m. *a Cuban dance.*
dañado adj. *spoiled, damaged.*
dañar *to damage, to hurt; to spoil.*
dañino adj. *harmful.*
daño m. *damage, loss; hurt, harm.*
   ¿Te has hecho daño? *Did you get hurt?*
   ¿Le ha hecho daño la comida? *Did the food disagree with you?*
   Causar daño. *To do harm or damage.*

DAR *to give; to deal (cards); to show (a picture); to strike (hours); to hit; to take (a walk).*
   Dénos algo de comer. *Give us something to eat.*
   Déme un poco de pan. *Give me some bread.*
   ¿En cuánto me lo da Ud.? *How much will you sell ("give") it to me for?*
   Le doy dos pesetas por el libro. *I'll give you two pesetas for the book.*
   ¿A quién le toca dar? *Whose turn is it to deal?*
   Ud. da las cartas. *You deal (cards).*
   La radio dió la noticia. *The news came over the radio.*
   ¿Dónde dan esa película? *Where are they showing that picture (film)?*
   Este reloj da las horas y las medias horas. *This clock strikes the hours and the half-hours.*
   Acaban de dar las tres. *It's just struck three.*
   Dar un paseo. *To take a walk.*
   Vamos a dar un paseo. *Let's take a walk.*
   Dar memorias. Dar recuerdos. *To give one's regards.*
   Le doy la razón. *I admit you are right.*
   Dar palmadas. *To clap one's hands.*
   Dar a entender. *To insinuate. ("To give to understand.")*
   Dar el golpe. *To make a hit. To create a sensation.*
   Dar a conocer. *To make known.*
   Dar en el clavo. *To hit the nail on the head.*
   Dar razón de. *To inform about.*
   Dar que decir. *To give cause for criticism.*
   Dar de comer. *To feed.*
   Dar prestado. *To lend.*
   Dar los buenos días. *To say good morning. To greet. To pass the time of day.*
   Dar fiado. Dar a crédito. *To give credit.*
   Dar con. *To meet. To come across.*
   Dar a la calle. *To face the street.*
   Dar a luz. *To give birth.*
   Dar parte. *To report.*
   Dar la mano. *To shake hands.*
   Dar marcha atrás. *To put in reverse (a car).*
   Dar en el blanco. *To hit the mark. To hit the bull's-eye.*
   Darse prisa. *To hurry.*
   Darse cuenta. *To realize.*
dátil m. *date (fruit).*
dato m. *datum.*
DE *of; from; for; by; on; to; with.*
   La casa de mi amigo. *My friend's house.*
   ¿De quién es este libro? *Whose book is this?*
   No sé que ha sido de él. *I don't know what's become of him.*
   Estoy escaso de dinero. *I'm short of money.*
   El libro es de ella. *The book is hers.*
   ¿De dónde es usted? *Where are you from?*
   Soy de Madrid. *I'm from Madrid.*
   La chica del sombrero verde. *The girl with the green hat.*

Un reloj de oro. *A gold watch.*

Un vaso de vino. *A glass of wine.*

Una taza de café. *A cup of coffee.*

Tres pies de largo. *Three feet long.*

Máquina de coser. *Sewing machine.*

Hora de comer. *Time to eat. Dinnertime.*

De pie. *Standing.*

De puntillas. *On tiptoes.*

De prisa. *In a hurry.*

De buena gana. *Willingly.*

De todo un poco. *A little of everything.*

Un día de estos. *One of these days.*

De hoy en adelante. *From now on.*

De día. *In the daytime.*

De noche. *At night.*

De nada. *Don't mention it.*

DEBAJO under, underneath.

Debajo de los papeles estaba la carta. *The letter was under these papers.*

Lo hizo por debajo de cuerda. *He did it in an underhanded way.*

debate *m. debate.*

debatir *to debate, to discuss.*

deber *m. obligation, duty.*

DEBER *to owe; to be obliged; must; ought.*

¿Qué se debe hacer? *What can one do? What can be done? What ought (should) one do?*

Debemos irnos. *We must (have to) go.*

Ud. debiera comer más. *You should eat more.*

Debe Ud. aprovechar esta ocasión. *You should take advantage of this opportunity.*

El debe de haber recibido mi carta ya. *He must have received my letter already.*

¿Cuánto le debo a Ud.? *How much do I owe you?*

No me debe Ud. nada. *You don't owe me anything.*

Siempre cumple con su deber. *He always does his duty. He always fulfills his obligations.*

debido *adj. due, owing to, on account of; proper.*

Debido a la lluvia no pude venir ayer. *I couldn't come yesterday on account of the rain.*

Redacte Ud. la instancia en debida forma. *Draw up the petition in proper form.*

débil *adj. feeble, weak.*

debilidad *f. feebleness, weakness.*

debilitar *to weaken, to debilitate.*

débilmente *weakly.*

débito *m. debt; duty.*

debut *m. debut, first (public) appearance.*

década *f. decade.*

decadencia *f. decay, decadence, decline.*

decaer *to decay, to decline, to die down.*

decano *m. dean; senior.*

decapitar *to decapitate, to behead.*

decena *f. ten.*

decente *adj. decent; honest; neat.*

decepción *f. disappointment.*

decididamente *decidedly.*

decidido *adj. decided, firm, determined.*

Es una persona muy decidida. *He's a very determined person.*

DECIDER *to decide, to resolve, to determine.*

DECIDIRSE *to decide, to make up one's mind.*

No me he decidido todavía. *I haven't decided yet. I haven't made up my mind yet.*

decímetro *m. decimeter.*

décimo *adj. tenth.*

decimoctavo *adj. eighteenth.*

decimocuarto *adj. fourteenth.*

decimonono *adj. nineteenth.*

decimonoveno *adj. nineteenth.*

decimoquinto *adj. fifteenth.*

decimoséptimo *adj. seventeenth.*

decimosexto *adj. sixteenth.*

decimotercero *adj. thirteenth.*

decimotercio *adj. thirteenth.*

deciocheno *adj. eighteenth.*

decir *m. saying.*

Es sólo un decir. *It's just a saying.*

DECIR *to speak; to say, to tell.*

Dígame, por favor. *Please tell me.*

Dígame dónde está la estación. *Tell me where the station is.*

Dígaselo a él. *Tell it to him.*

Se lo diré. *I'll tell him.*

Dice Ud. bien. *You're right. That's correct. You've said the right thing.*

¡No me diga! *You don't say (so)! ("Don't tell me!")*

¡Diga! ¿Quién habla? *Hello! Who's speaking?*

Decir las cosas claras. *To speak plainly.*

Querer decir. *To mean.*

¿Qué quiere decir esta palabra? *What does this word mean?*

¿Qué me quiere Ud. decir? *What do you want to tell me? What do you mean?*

Por decirlo así. *As it were. So to speak.*

decisión *f. decision, determination.*

decisivo *adj. decisive.*

declaración *f. declaration.*

declarar *to declare; to state; to testify.*

¿Tiene Ud. algo que declarar? *Do you have anything to declare (customs)?*

Declararse en huelga. *To go on strike. To declare a strike.*

Juan se declaró a María. *John proposed to Mary.*

declinar *to decline; to decay.*

decoración *f. decoration; stage scenery.*

decorado *m. decoration; stage scenery; adj. decorated.*

decorar *to decorate.*

decoro *m. decency; decorum; honor.*

decrecer *to decrease.*

decreciente *adj. decreasing.*

decremento *m. decrease.*

decretar *to decree.*

decreto *m. decree.*

dedal m. thimble.

dedicar to dedicate; to devote.

La mañana la dedicamos a visitar los alrededores de la población. *We spent the morning visiting the suburbs of the town.*

Se dedica a los negocios. *He's a businessman.*

Se dedicó a la pintura. *He devoted himself to painting.*

dedicatoria f. dedication.

dedillo m. little finger.

Saber al dedillo. *To have at one's fingertips.*

Me sé la lección al dedillo. *I know the lesson by heart. ("I have it on my fingertips.")*

DEDO m. finger; toe.

Dedo meñique. *Little finger.*

Dedo índice. *Index finger.*

Dedo pulgar. *Thumb.*

Dedo del corazón. *Middle finger.*

Dedo anular. *Ring finger.*

Los zapatos me aprietan los dedos. *The shoes are tight around the toes.*

Está a dos dedos de la tumba. *He's on the brink of death.*

deducción f. deduction.

deducir to deduce; to gather, to understand.

Deduzco de su carta que no es muy feliz. *I gather from his letter that he's not very happy.*

defecto m. fault, defect.

Conozco sus defectos. *I know his faults.*

Tiene un defecto físico. *He has a physical defect.*

Poner defectos. *To find fault.*

defectuoso adj. defective.

defender to defend.

defensa f. defense.

defensiva f. defensive.

defensor m. supporter, defender; lawyer, counsel.

deferencia f. deference, respect, regard.

deficiencia f. deficiency.

deficiente adj. deficient.

déficit m. shortage, deficit.

definición f. definition, explanation.

definido adj. definite.

definir to define, to determine.

definitivamente definitely.

definitivo adj. definitive.

deformación f. deformation.

deformar to deform.

deforme adj. deformed; ugly.

deformidad f. deformity; ugliness.

defraudar to defraud, to swindle.

defunción f. death.

Acta de defunción. *Death certificate.*

degenerado adj. and n. degenerate.

degollar to slash the throat; to decapitate.

degradante adj. degrading.

degradar to degrade.

dejadez f. laziness; negligence.

dejado adj. lazy, negligent, sloppy.

dejamiento m. carelessness, indolence, self-neglect.

DEJAR to leave, to let; to quit, to give up.

Déjeme verlo. *Let me see it.*

Déjemelo en menos. *Can you let me have it cheaper? ("Give it to me for less.")*

No se nos dejó entrar. *They didn't let us come in.*

¿Puedo dejarle un recado? *May I leave a message for him?*.

Déjelo para mañana. *Leave it for tomorrow. Put it off until tomorrow.*

Déjeme en paz. *Let me alone. ("Leave me in peace.")*

Dejar de. *To stop.*

¿Por qué ha dejado Ud. de visitarnos? *Why have you stopped visiting us?*

Dejó su empleo por otro mejor. *He gave up his job for a better one.*

Dejó a su mujer y a sus hijos. *He abandoned his wife and children.*

Le dejaron plantado. *They left him in the lurch.*

No puedo dejar de creerlo. *I can't help believing it.*

Déjese enfriar y sírvase. *("Let") Cool and serve.*

dejarse to abandon oneself to; not to take care of oneself, to let oneself go.

dejo m. accent (in speech); taste, aftertaste; end; effect.

DEL (contraction of de + el) of the.

La casa del médico. *The doctor's house.*

Del principio al fin. *From (the) beginning to (the) end.*

No del todo. *Not quite.*

delantal m. apron.

DELANTE before; in front; in the presence of.

Nos aguarda delante del club. *He's waiting for us in front of the club.*

Firmó el testamento delante de testigos. *He signed his will before witnesses.*

No digas eso delante de ella. *Don't say that in front of her (in her presence).*

delantera f. front; start, lead.

delegación f. delegation.

delegado m. delegate, deputy, proxy.

deleitar to please, to delight.

deleite m. delight, pleasure; lust.

deletrear to spell.

deletreo m. spelling.

delgado adj. thin, slender.

deliberación f. deliberation.

deliberar to deliberate.

delicado adj. delicate; dainty, nice; exquisite, delicious; in poor ("delicate") health, having a weak constitution.

delicia f. delight, pleasure.

delicioso adj. delicious, delightful.

El postre está delicioso. *The dessert is delicious.*

Hemos pasado un rato delicioso. *We had a delightful time.*

delincuente *m. delinquent, offender.*

delinquir *to commit an offense against the law, to violate the law.*

delirar *to rave; to be delirious.*

Está delirando. *He's talking nonsense. He's raving.*

delirio *m. delirium; raving; wild excitement: nonsense.*

El delirio le duró toda la noche. *The delirium lasted all night.*

La quiere con delirio. *He's madly in love with her. He's head over heels in love with her.*

delito *m. misdemeanor, offense, crime.*

demacrarse *to become emaciated.*

demanda *f. claim, demand, request; inquiry.*

No atendieron su demanda. *They didn't pay any attention to his claim.*

Hay mucha demanda de este artículo. *There's a great demand for this article.*

demandante *m. and f. plaintiff.*

DEMANDAR *to demand, to claim; to take legal action, to enter a claim, to start a suit.*

demarcación *f. demarcation.*

DEMÁS *other; remaining, rest;* los (*m.*) **demás;** las (*f.*) **demás** *others; the others.*

Lo demás se lo contaré luego. *I'll tell you the rest later.*

Por lo demás me parece bien. *Aside (apart) from that (otherwise), it seems all right to me.*

Pensé que estaba por demás decírselo. *I didn't think it was necessary to mention it to you.*

Esperemos a los demás. *Let's wait for the others.*

DEMASIADO *excessive; too; too much.*

Es demasiado. *It's too much.*

Cuesta demasiado. *It costs too much.*

Es demasiado temprano aún. *It's too early yet.*

Este chaleco me aprieta demasiado. *This vest is too tight for me.*

demencia *f. insanity, madness.*

demente *adj. insane, crazy.*

democracia *f. democracy.*

demócrata *m. and f. democrat.*

democrático *adj. democratic.*

demoler *to demolish.*

demolición *f. demolition.*

demonio *m. demon, devil.*

Se puso hecho un demonio. *He became very angry.*

¿Para qué demonio lo querrá (coll.)? *What the devil does he need it for?*

¿Qué demonios hace Ud. aquí (coll.)? *What on earth are you doing here?*

demostración *f. demonstration.*

demostrar *to demonstrate, to prove, to show.*

Demuéstrelo Ud. *Prove it.*

Demostró que tenía razón. *He proved he was right.*

No demuestra el menor interés. *He doesn't show the slightest interest.*

demora *f. delay.*

Sin demora. *Without delay.*

demorar *to delay; to remain.*

Se demoraron en el camino. *They were delayed on the road.*

demovilizar *to demobilize.*

denegar *to refuse, to deny.*

denigrante *adj. defamatory, slanderous.*

denigrar *to blacken, to defame.*

denominación *f. denomination.*

denominar *to name.*

denotar *to denote, to indicate, to express.*

densidad *f. density.*

denso *adj. dense, thick.*

dentadura *f. set of teeth.*

dental *adj. dental.*

dentífrico *adj. and n. dentifrice.*

Pasta dentífrica. *Toothpaste.*

Polvo dentífrico. *Toothpowder.*

dentista *m. dentist.*

DENTRO *within, inside.*

Le espero dentro. *I'll wait for you inside.*

Hay más gente fuera que dentro. *There are more people outside than inside.*

El tren sale dentro de cinco minutos. *The train will leave in five minutes.*

Vuelva dentro de media hora. *Come back in half an hour.*

Dentro de poco. *Shortly.*

Hacia dentro. *Toward the inside.*

Por dentro. *On the inside.*

denuncia *f. complaint; denunciation.*

denunciar *to denounce; to give notice; to inform.*

departamento *m. department; apartment.*

dependencia *f. dependence, dependency; sales staff, personnel of an office, employees; branch office or store.*

DEPENDER *to depend, be dependent on.*

Mucho depende de lo que Ud. haga. *A great deal will depend on what you do.*

Depender de. *To depend on. To count on. To rely on.*

dependiente *m. clerk; subordinate; dependent.*

deplorable *adj. deplorable, pitiful.*

deplorar *to deplore, to be sorry, to regret.*

Deploro mucho lo ocurrido. *I'm sorry about what happened.*

deportar *to deport.*

deporte *m. sport.*

deportista *m. sportsman; f. sportswoman.*

deportivo *adj. having to do with sport(s).*

depositar *to deposit; to place; to put in a safe place; to entrust.*

Depositaron su dinero en el banco. *They deposited their money in the bank.*

Deposité en él toda mi confianza. *I placed all my trust in him.*

depositario m. *trustee; depositary.*

depósito m. *deposit; depot; warehouse; bond; reservoir; tank (of gasoline).*

Estos edificios son los depósitos de la fábrica. *These buildings are the warehouses of the factory.*

Lléneme el depósito. *Fill the tank up.*

En depósito. *As a deposit. In bond.*

depresión f. *depression.*

deprimir to *depress.*

DERECHA f. *right side; right hand.*

A la derecha. *To the right.*

Es su mano derecha. *He's his right-hand man ("He's his right hand.")*

Pertenece a un partido de derecha. *He belongs to a conservative party.*

No hace nada a derechas. *He doesn't do anything right.*

DERECHO m. *law, justice; claim, title; right; straight; direct.*

Es estudiante de derecho. *He's a law student.*

Obrar conforme a derecho. *To act according to law.*

Ud. no tiene derecho de quejarse. *You have no right to complain. You have no grounds for complaint.*

Siga derecho. *Keep straight ahead. Go straight ahead.*

Perdió el brazo derecho en la guerra. *He lost his right arm in the war.*

Fíjese que esté del derecho. *Make sure it's right side out.*

Ya es un hombre hecho y derecho. *He's now fully grown-up. He's now a man.*

Derechos de autor. *Copyright. Royalties.*

Derechos. *Rights. Fees. Duties.*

deriva f. *deviation; drift (of a ship or airplane).*

derogar to *annul; to repeal.*

derramamiento m. *spilling, shedding.*

derramar to *spill; to shed; to scatter; to spread.*

derrame m. *leakage; discharge (med.).*

derredor m. *circumference.*

Al derredor. (En derredor.) *About. Around.*

Mire en derredor suyo. *Look around you.*

derretir to *melt, to dissolve.*

derribar to *demolish; to knock down; to overthrow.*

Han derribado muchas casas viejas. *Many old houses have been torn down.*

De un golpe lo derribó al suelo. *He knocked him down with one punch (blow).*

derrocar to *overthrow.*

derrochador m. *spendthrift, squanderer.*

Es un derrochador. *He's a spendthrift. Money burns a hole in his pocket.*

derrochar to *squander; to waste away.*

derrota f. *ship's course; rout, defeat.*

derrotar to *rout, to defeat.*

derrotero m. *charts; course.*

derrumbamiento m. *collapse; landslide.*

derrumbar to *throw down, to demolish.*

desabotonar to *unbutton.*

desabrido adj. *insipid, tasteless.*

desabrigado adj. *uncovered; without shelter; without enough clothes on.*

desabrigar to *uncover; to leave without shelter.*

Desabrigarse. *To uncover. To take off one's coat or hat.*

desabrochar to *unbutton, to unclasp, to unfasten.*

desacierto m. *error, blunder.*

desacreditar to *discredit.*

desacuerdo m. *disagreement.*

desafiar to *challenge, to defy.*

desafío m. *challenge; competition.*

desafortunado adj. *unlucky, unfortunate.*

desagradable adj. *disagreeable, unpleasant.*

desagradar to *displease.*

desagradecido adj. *ungrateful.*

desagrado m. *displeasure, discontent.*

desagraviar to *vindicate; to give satisfaction.*

desagravio m. *vindication, justice.*

desaguar to *drain.*

desagüe m. *drainage.*

desahogarse to *find relief (from heat, fatigue, etc.); to free oneself from debt; to open one's heart.*

desahogo m. *ease, relief.*

desahuciar to *give up as hopeless.*

El médico ha desahuciado al enfermo. *The doctor has given up hope for the patient.*

desairar to *slight, to snub.*

No quiero desairarle. *I don't want to slight him.*

desaire m. *slight, snub.*

desalentar to *discourage.*

desaliento m. *discouragement; dismay.*

desalojar to *dispossess, to evict; to dislodge, to drive out.*

desalquilado adj. *vacant (for rent).*

desalquilar to *move out; to ask someone to vacate (a rented place).*

desamparado adj. *abandoned.*

desamueblado adj. *unfurnished.*

desamueblar to *remove the furniture, to take the furniture out.*

desangrar to *bleed.*

desanimado adj. *discouraged; dull.*

La fiesta estuvo muy desanimada. *The party was very dull.*

desanimar to *discourage.*

desánimo m. *discouragement.*

desaparecer to *disappear.*

desapercibido adj. *unprepared, not ready; unnoticed.*

desaprobar *to disapprove of.*

desaprovechar *to misuse, not to make good use of.*

    Desaprovechó la oportunidad. *He didn't make (good) use of the opportunity.*

desarmado *adj. unarmed.*

desarmar *to disarm; to dismount, to take apart.*

desarme *m. disarmament.*

desarraigar *to uproot, to extirpate.*

desarreglado *adj. immoderate; slovenly; disarranged, in disorder.*

desarreglar *to derange; to disarrange.*

desarreglo *m. disorder, derangement; irregularity.*

DESARROLLAR *to develop; to grow; to evolve; to unfold. (See* **revelar** *for "to develop" applied to film, etc.)*

desarrollo *m. development; evolution; growth.*

desaseado *adj. unclean, untidy.*

desaseo *m. slovenliness, untidiness, uncleanliness.*

desasosiego *m. uneasiness, restlessness.*

desastre *m. disaster, calamity.*

desatar *to untie, to loosen.*

desatender *to neglect; to disregard, to pay no attention, to take no notice of; to slight.*

desatento *adj. rude, not attentive.*

desatinar *to talk nonsense; to become confused.*

desatino *m. lack of tact; blunder; nonsense.*

desautorizar *to deprive of authority.*

desavenencia *f. disagreement, discord, misunderstanding.*

desayunarse *to breakfast.*

    ¿Se ha desayunado Ud. ya? *Have you had your breakfast yet?*

desayuno *m. breakfast.*

    Sírvame el desayuno. *Serve my breakfast.*

desbarrar *to act or talk foolishly; to slip out.*

desbarajuste *m. confusion, disorder.*

desbaratar *to thwart, to upset (a plan); to talk nonsense; to destroy; to disperse, to route (an army); to spoil, to ruin.*

desbocarse *to run away (a horse); to use vile language.*

descabellado *adj. crazy, wild, unrestrained.*

    ¡Qué ideas tan descabelladas tienes! *What crazy ideas you have!*

descalabro *m. calamity, great loss.*

descalificar *to disqualify.*

descalzarse *to take off one's shoes and stockings.*

descalzo *adj. barefoot(ed).*

DESCANSAR *to rest; to sleep.*

    ¿No quiere Ud. descansar un rato? *Don't you want to rest a little?*

    ¡Qué descanse Ud. bien! (¡Qué Ud. descanse!) *Good night, may you sleep well. I hope you sleep well.*

descanso *m. rest; quiet; landing (of a staircase); intermission (in Spain.)*

    Le santará muy bien un descanso. *A rest will do him good.*

descapotable *m. convertible (car).*

descarado *adj. brazen, impudent.*

descarga *f. discharge; unloading.*

descargar *to unload; to discharge; to acquit.*

descaro *m. boldness; impudence.*

descarrilamiento *m. derailment, running off the rails.*

descarrilar *to derail.*

descartar *to discard; to dismiss.*

    Hay que descartar esa posibilidad. *You must discard that possibility.*

    Me he descartado de un rey. *I discarded the king (at cards).*

descendencia *f. descent, origin.*

descender *to descend, to come down; to drop; to decrease.*

descendiente *adj. and n. descendant.*

descenso *m. descent; decline, fall.*

descifrar *to decipher; to decode.*

    No pude descifrarlo. *I couldn't figure it out. I couldn't make head or tail (out) of it.*

descolgar *to take down; to lift up, to pick up (the receiver).*

descolorido *adj. discolored, faded.*

descomedido *adj. immoderate; excessive; impolite; rude.*

    Es un muchacho muy descomedido. *He's very impolite.*

descomponer *to spoil, to break; to set at odds; to decompose; to disarrange.*

descomponerse *to rot; to be indisposed; to lose one's temper; to change for the worse (weather).*

    Parece que el tiempo se descompone. *It looks as though the weather will change (for the worse).*

descompuesto *adj. out of order, spoiled (food); impolite, brazen.*

desconcertante *adj. confusing, baffling, disconcerting.*

desconcertar *to disturb, to confuse, to baffle.*

desconectar *to disconnect.*

desconfianza *f. distrust.*

desconfiar *to distrust, to mistrust.*

    No tiene Ud. razón para desconfiar de él. *You have no reason to mistrust him.*

    El médico desconfiaba de poder salvarlo. *The doctor had little hope of saving him.*

desconocer *not to recognize; to disavow; to ignore.*

desconocido *adj. unknown; m. stranger.*

    Se la acercó un desconocido. *A stranger approached him.*

    La cara de Ud. no me es desconocida. *Your face is familiar.*

desconocimiento *m. ignorance; ingratitude.*

desconsiderado *adj. thoughtless, inconsiderate.*

desconsolador *adj. disheartening; sad.*

desconsuelo *m. affliction, grief.*

descontar to discount, to deduct; to take for granted.

descontento adj. not pleased, unhappy; m. discontent, dissatisfaction, disgust.

descorrer to draw (a curtain); to retrace one's steps.

descortés adj. discourteous, impolite.

descortesía f. lack of politeness, rudeness.

descoser to unstitch, to rip out the seams.

descote m. having a low neck (of a dress).

descrédito m. discredit.

DESCRIBIR to describe.

descripción f. description.

descubierto adj. discovered, uncovered; bareheaded; m. overdraft; deficit.

     Estar en descubierto. To have overdrawn a bank account.

descubrimiento m. discovery.

DESCUBRIR to discover, to find out; to disclose, to bring to light.

     Descubrimos que todo era mentira. We found out (discovered) that it was all a lie.

descubrirse to take off one's hat.

descuento m. discount.

descuidado adj. negligent, careless, slovenly.

descuidar to neglect, to overlook; to relieve from care.

     No descuide Ud. sus asuntos. Don't neglect your business.

     Descuide Ud. que no le pasará nada. Don't worry, nothing will happen to her!

descuido m. negligence, carelessness, omission, oversight.

DESDE since, after, from.

     Se siente enfermo desde ayer. He's been feeling sick since yesterday.

     ¿Se puede telefonear desde aquí? Can we phone from here?

     Estoy llamando desde hace rato. I have been ringing quite a while.

     Desde entonces. Since then. From then (that time) on.

     Desde luego. Of course.

     Desde que. Ever since.

     Desde niño. From childhood.

desdecirse to retract, to go back on one's word; to gainsay.

desdén m. disdain, scorn, contempt.

desdeñar to scorn, to disdain.

desdicha f. misfortune, calamity, unhappiness.

desdichado adj. wretched; unfortunate; unhappy; m. an unfortunate person, a poor fellow.

     Es un desdichado. He's a poor devil.

deseable adj. desirable.

DESEAR to wish, to desire.

     ¿Qué desea Ud.? What do you want (wish)? What would you like?

     ¿Desea Ud. alguna otra cosa? Do you wish anything else? Would you like anything else?

     Desearía hablar dos palabras con Ud. I'd like to have a few words with you. I'd like to speak with you a few minutes.

     Le deseo muchas felicidades. Lots of luck! ("I wish you much happiness.")

desechar to discard, to throw away, to scrap; to reject; to dismiss; to depreciate.

     Desecharon su propuesta. They rejected his proposal.

desecho m. remainder, residue; refuse; leftovers.

desembarazarse to rid oneself of difficulties or hindrances.

desembarcadero m. wharf, pier, landing place.

desembarcar to disembark, to go ashore.

desembarco m. landing, disembarkment; unloading.

desembarque m. landing, unloading.

desembolsar to pay out, to disburse.

desembolso m. expenditure, disbursement.

desembragar to release the clutch.

desempacar to unpack.

     Tengo que desempacar el equipaje. I have to unpack the baggage.

desempaquetar to unpack.

desempeñar to perform, to accomplish; to carry out; to redeem, to take out of pawn; to free from debt.

     Desempeñó muy bien su cometido. He carried out his mission very well. He fulfilled his obligation (commitment) faithfully.

desencantar to disappoint, to disillusion.

desencanto m. disappointment, disillusion.

desenfrenado adj. unbridled, wild.

desengañado adj. disappointed; disillusioned.

desengañar to disappoint, to become disillusioned; to disabuse, to rid of a false notion.

desengaño m. disappointment, disillusionment.

desengrasar to take out (remove) the grease; to scour.

desenlace m. outcome, result.

desenmascarar to unmask.

desenredar to disentangle.

desenredo m. disentanglement.

desenrollar to unwind, to unroll.

desentenderse to shirk; to ignore, to pay no attention.

desentendido adj. unaware; unmindful.

     No se haga Ud. el desentendido. Don't pretend you don't notice it. Don't pretend you don't know it.

desenterrar to disinter, to dig up.

desentonado adj. out of tune.

desentonar to be out of tune.

desenvoltura f. ease; self-possession; boldness; impudence.

desenvolver to unwrap, to unfold; to unravel; to develop.

DESEO m. wish, desire.

     No puede refrenar sus deseos. He has no self-control. He can't restrain his desires.

Tener deseo de. *To desire to.*

Tengo muchos deseos de conocerla. *I'm very eager to meet her.*

deseoso *adj. desirous.*

desequilibrado *adj. unbalanced.*

desequilibrio *m. lack of balance; state of being unbalanced (mind).*

desertar *to desert.*

desertor *m. deserter.*

desesperación *f. despair, desperation; fury.*

desesperado *adj. hopeless, desperate; raving mad.*

desesperarse *to despair, to lose hope; to exasperate.*

Eso me desespera. *That exasperates me.*

desfalcar *to embezzle.*

desfalco *m. embezzlement; diminution.*

desfallecer *to faint; to pine, to languish.*

desfallecimiento *m. fainting; languor.*

desfigurar *to disfigure; to misshape; to distort.*

desfiladero *m. defile, gorge.*

desfilar *to march in review; to parade.*

desfile *m. review, parade.*

desganarse *to lose interest; to lose one's appetite; to become disgusted.*

desgañitarse *to scream, to bawl.*

desgarrar *to tear, to rend.*

desgastar *to consume, to wear out; to waste.*

desgastarse *to lose strength; to wear out.*

desgaste *m. wear and tear; wastage.*

desgracia *f. misfortune; sorrow; accident. (Desgracia never means "disgrace." See* **vergüenza, deshonra.**)

¡Qué desgracia! *What a misfortune!*

Por desgracia. *Unfortunately.*

Por desgracia no lo supimos a tiempo. *Unfortunately we didn't know it in time.*

Acaba de ocurrir una desgracia en la calle. *There just was an accident outside ("in the street").*

Caer en desgracia. *To lose favor.*

desgraciadamente *unfortunately.*

desgraciado *adj. unhappy, unfortunate, unlucky; m. wretch, poor fellow.*

Es un desgraciado. *He's a poor devil. He's unlucky (unhappy, unfortunate).*

deshabitado *adj. deserted, uninhabited; vacant.*

deshabitar *to move out.*

deshacer *to undo; to unwrap; to take apart; to melt; to break up (a party); to liquidate (a business); to rout (an army).*

¿Quieres deshacer el paquete? *Would you please unwrap the package?*

Hemos deshecho el negocio. *We've liquidated the business.*

Deshacer el equipaje. *To unpack.*

deshacerse *to do one's best; to get rid of; to get out of order; to grow feeble; to be impatient; to grieve; to vanish.*

¿Se deshizo Ud. de su automóvil? *Did you sell*

(get rid of) your car?

Deshacerse en lágrimas. *To burst into tears.*

Deshacerse como el humo. *To vanish into thin air. ("To vanish like smoke.")*

deshecho *adj. wasted; in pieces; destroyed; undone; melted.*

deshelar *to melt, to thaw.*

desheredar *to disinherit.*

deshielo *m. thaw, thawing.*

deshilar *to ravel, to fray.*

deshilvanado *adj. incoherent; disconnected.*

deshojar *to strip off the leaves.*

deshonesto *adj. dishonest; immodest; indecent.*

deshonor *m. dishonor; disgrace.*

deshonra *f. dishonor; disgrace.*

El ser uno pobre no es deshonra. *Poverty is no disgrace.*

Tiene a deshonra el saludarme. *He thinks it beneath him to greet me.*

deshonrar *to dishonor; to disgrace.*

deshonroso *adj. dishonorable; disgraceful.*

deshora *f. inconvenient time.*

Viene siempre a deshora. *He always comes at the wrong time.*

desidia *f. idleness, indolence.*

desierto *adj. deserted; solitary; m. desert, wilderness.*

designar *to appoint; to designate.*

designio *m. intention, design, purpose.*

desigualdad *f. inequality; unevenness.*

El terreno era muy desigual. *The ground was very uneven.*

desilusion *f. disillusion.*

desilusionar *to disillusion.*

desinfectante *adj. disinfecting; m. disinfectant.*

desinfectar *to disinfect.*

desinflar *to deflate.*

desinterés *m. disinterestedness, unselfishness.*

desistir *to desist; to waive (one's right).*

Desistió de hacer el viaje. *He called off the trip. He didn't make the trip.*

desleal *adj. disloyal.*

deslealtad *f. disloyalty.*

desligar *to untie, to unbind; to free (from an obligation).*

deslindar *to demarcate, to mark off the limits.*

deslinde *m. demarcation.*

desliz *m. slip, lapse.*

deslizar *to slide; to slip; to lapse (in speech or conduct).*

Desliz de la lengua. *Slip of the tongue.*

deslumbramiento *m. glare, overpowering luster or brilliance; bewilderment.*

deslumbrar *to dazzle; to bewilder.*

desmayarse *to faint; to become dismayed.*

desmayo *m. swoon; faint; dismay.*

desmedido *adj. immoderate; out of proportion.*

desmejorarse *to grow worse, to decay.*

El enfermo está muy desmejorado hoy. *The patient is much worse today.*

desmemoriado *adj.* forgetful.

desmentir *to deny; to contradict.*

Lo desmintió rotundamente. *He denied it flatly.*

desmontar *to dismount; to clear (a wood); to take apart (a machine, etc.).*

desmoralizado *adj.* demoralized.

desmoralizar *to demoralize.*

desnatar *to skim milk.*

desnivel *m. unevenness (of ground).*

desnudarse *to undress, to take one's clothes off.*

desnudo *adj. naked, nude.*

desobedecer *to disobey.*

desobediencia *f. disobedience.*

desobediente *adj. disobedient.*

desocupación *f. unemployment; idleness.*

desocupado *adj. not busy; unemployed.*

Hablaré con Ud. cuando esté desocupado. *I'll speak with you when you're not busy.*

desocupar *to vacate; to empty.*

Tenemos que desocupar la casa antes del mes próximo. *We must vacate the house before next month.*

Voy a desocupar este armario para que Ud. lo use. *I'll empty this cabinet so that you can use it.*

desoír *to turn a deaf ear; to pretend not to hear; not to heed, to disregard.*

desorden *m. disorder; excess.*

desordenado *adj. disorderly; irregular; unruly.*

Lleva una vida desordenada. *He lives a very wild (irregular) life.*

desorganizar *to disorganize.*

desorientar *to lead astray, to confuse.*

despabilado *adj. wakeful, vigilant; lively.*

despabilar *to brighten up.*

despabilarse *to wake up; to snap out of.*

Despabílese. *Wake up. Snap out of it.*

Ud. verá como se despabila. *You'll see how he'll brighten up.*

despachar *to dispatch, to forward, to expedite, to send; to sell; to wait on; to attend to (the mail); to ship; to clear (at the customhouse).*

¿Quiere Ud. despacharme? *Will you wait on me?*

Despacharon un vagón de géneros. *They shipped out a wagonload of merchandise.*

No he despachado todavía la correspondencia de hoy. *I still haven't attended to ("sent out") today's correspondence (mail).*

despacho *m. dispatch; cabinet; office; shipment.*

Estaré en mi despacho entre las ocho y las nueve. *I'll be at my office between eight and nine.*

Acaban de recibir un despacho de la embajada. *They've just received a dispatch from the embassy.*

Esto lo despacho en un minuto. *I'll finish this in a minute.*

Despacho de localidades. *Box office.*

Despacho de billetes. *Ticket office.*

Despacho de equipajes. *Baggage room.*

DESPACIO *adj. slowly.*

Hable un poco más despacio. *Speak a little slower. Speak more slowly.*

Camine despacio. *Walk slowly.*

desparramar *to scatter, to squander.*

despecho *m. spite.*

despedazar *to tear or break into bits.*

despedir *to fire, to dismiss; to see off; to say good-by.*

despedirse *to take leave; to say good-by; to see off.*

despegar *to unglue, to detach; to take off.*

El sello se despegó. *The stamp came off.*

Acaba de despegar el avión. *The plane just took off.*

Se pasó la noche sin despegar los labios. *She didn't open her mouth ("lips") all night long.*

despegue *m. take-off (aviation).*

despeinar *to dishevel.*

despejado *adj. self-possessed; cloudless; smart, bright.*

No creo que llueva, el cielo está despejado. *I don't think it will rain. The sky is clear.*

¡Qué muchacho tan despejado! *What a smart boy!*

despejarse *to cheer up; to clear up (weather).*

Me parece que el tiempo se está despejando. *I think it's clearing up.*

despensa *f. pantry, provisions.*

desperdiciar *to waste; to squander.*

desperdicio *m. waste.*

desperezarse *to stretch oneself.*

desperfecto *m. slight damage; defect.*

despertador *m. alarm clock.*

Ponga el despertador a las siete. *Set the alarm for seven.*

DESPERTAR *to awaken; to wake up.*

¿Se acordará Ud. de despertarme? *Will you remember to wake me?*

despertarse *to wake up.*

Me desperté temprano. *I awoke early.*

despierto *adj. awake; vigilant; lively.*

despilfarrar *to squander, to waste.*

despilfarro *m. slovenliness; waste.*

despistar *to throw off the track; to confuse.*

desplazar *to displace.*

desplegar *to unfold, to unfurl; to hoist (the flag).*

desplomarse *to collapse; to fall flat on the ground.*

despoblado *adj. depopulated; m. deserted, uninhabited place.*

despojar *to despoil, to strip.*

Le han despojado hasta del último centavo.

They took everything he had down to the last penny.

Despójese Ud. de esas ideas. *Forget those ideas.*

desposar to marry.

déspota m. despot.

despreciable adj. despicable, contemptible.

despreciar to despise; to look down on.

desprecio m. contempt, scorn.

Lo trataron con desprecio. *They treated him with contempt.*

desprender to unfasten, to separate.

desprenderse to extricate oneself; to be inferred; to give away; to get rid of.

Se ha desprendido de toda su fortuna. *He gave away his whole fortune.*

desprendido adj. generous.

despreocupado adj. unconcerned; unconventional, free from prejudice.

despreocuparse to become unbiased; not to worry; to ignore, to forget, to pay no attention.

desproporcionado adj. disproportionate, out of proportion.

despropósito m. absurdity, nonsense.

desprovisto adj. unprovided.

DESPUÉS after, afterward, later.

¿Qué pasó después de eso? *What happened after that?*

Llegó media hora después. *He arrived half an hour later.*

Mas bien antes que después. *"Rather before than after."*

desquitarse to get even.

desquite m. revenge; making up for, getting even.

destacamento m. detachment (of troops).

destacar to detach (troops); to emphasize.

destajo m. piecework.

Trabajamos a destajo. *We do piecework.*

destapar to uncover; to open, to uncork.

desteñirse to fade (color).

desternillarse to split one's sides with laughter.

Desternillarse de risa. *To split with laughter.*

Me desternillé de risa. *I split my sides laughing.*

desterrado adj. exiled; m. exile.

desterrar to exile.

destinar to appoint; to allot; to assign; to station; to intend for; to address to.

La carta venía destinada a mí. *The letter was addressed to me.*

destinatario m. addressee.

destino m. destiny; destination; assignment; position.

Salió con destino a Buenos Aires. *He was bound for Buenos Aires.*

No sé que destino le van a dar a ese edificio. *I don't know what they'll use that building for.*

destornillador m. screwdriver.

destornillar to unscrew.

destreza f. skill.

destróyer m. destroyer (ship).

destrozar to destroy; to smash.

destrucción f. destruction.

destruir to destroy.

desvanecerse to vanish; to faint; to swell, to become puffed up (with pride).

desvelar to keep awake.

desvelo m. lack of sleep; anxiety.

desventaja f. disadvantage.

desventajoso adj. disadvantageous.

desventurado adj. unfortunate.

desvergonzado adj. impudent, unashamed, brazen.

desvergüenza f. impudence, brazenness.

desvestirse to undress.

desviación f. deviation; deflection.

desviar to divert; to deviate; to dissuade.

Desviar la mirada. *To turn one's head away.*

desvío m. deviation; detour.

desvivirse to long for; to be dying for.

desyerbar to weed.

detallar to detail; to retail.

detalle m. detail; retail.

Comprar al detalle. *To buy at retail.*

Vender al detalle. *To sell at retail.*

detallista m. retailer.

detective m. detective.

detención f. detention, arrest; delay.

detener to detain; to retain; to withhold; to stop.

DETENERSE to stay, stop over; to stop; to pause.

Nos tendremos que detener en Panamá dos días. *We'll have to stop in Panama for two days.*

Se detuvo un momento para pensarlo. *He paused a moment to think about it.*

detenidamente slowly, carefully.

detenido adj. under arrest.

detenimiento m. detention; care.

deteriorar to deteriorate.

deterioro m. damage, deterioration.

determinación f. determination; daring.

Tomar la determinación. *To resolve. To make the (a) decision.*

determinado adj. determined, resolute.

determinar to determine, to decide.

determinarse to resolve, to make up one's mind.

¿Se determinó a hacer el viaje? *Has he decided to take the trip?*

detestable adj. detestable.

detestar to detest, to abhor.

DETRÁS behind; behind one's back.

Detrás de la puerta. *Behind the door.*

Vienen detrás. *They're following behind.*

Por detrás hablaba mal de él. *He talked about him behind his back.*

deuda f. debt.

Pagó todas sus deudas. *He paid all his debts.*

Deuda pendiente. *An unpaid balance.*

Contraer deudas. *To incur debts.*

deudo *m. relative, kin, kindred.*

deudor *m. debtor.*

devastàción *f. devastation.*

devastar *to devastate, to ruin.*

devoción *f. devotion.*

devolución *f. restitution.*

devolver *to restore; to return.*

devorar *to devour, to consume.*

devoto *adj. devout, pious; devoted.*

DÍA *m. day.*

¡Buenos días! *Good morning!*

¿Qué día es hoy? *What's today?*

¿En qué día del mes estamos? *What day of the month is it?*

Dentro de ocho días. *In (within) a week ("eight days").*

Estaré en casa todo el día. *I'll be (at) home all day.*

La veo todos los días. *I see her every day.*

¿Cuál es el plato del día? *What's today's special? ("What's the plate of the day?")*

De día. *In the daytime.*

Un día sí y otro día no. *Every other day.*

Al día siguiente. Al otro día. *On the following day.*

Un día tras otro. *Day after day.*

De día en día. *From day to day.*

Día festivo. *Holiday.*

Día de trabajo. (Día laborable.) *Weekday. ("Working day.")*

Día entre semana. *Weekday.*

diabetes *f. diabetes.*

diablo *m. devil.*

¡Qué diablos! *What the devil!*

¿En dónde diablos te metiste? *Where on earth did you go? ("Where the devil did you hide yourself?")*

diagnóstico *m. diagnosis.*

diagrama *f. diagram.*

dialecto *m. dialect.*

diálogo *m. dialogue.*

diamante *m. diamond.*

Diamante en bruto. *Diamond in the rough.*

diámetro *m. diameter.*

diapositiva *f. slide.*

DIARIO *adj. and n. daily; diary; daily newspaper.*

He leído el diario sólo por encima. *I just glanced at (scanned) the paper.*

Nos vemos a diario. *We see each other every day.*

Los cuartos en este hotel no bajarán de diez pesos diarios. *The rooms in this hotel will cost at least ("won't cost less than") ten pesos a day.*

diarrea *f. diarrhea.*

dibujante *m. and f. draftsman, designer.*

dibujar *to draw, to design; to sketch.*

dibujo *m. drawing, design.*

diccionario *m. dictionary.*

DICIEMBRE *m. December.*

dictado *m. dictation.*

dictador *m. dictator.*

dictar *to dictate; to issue, to pronounce.*

Escriba Ud. Yo le dictaré. *Take this down. I'll dictate.*

El juez dictó sentencia. *The judge pronounced sentence.*

dicha *f. happiness; good luck.*

¡Qué dicha! *What luck!*

dicho *adj. said; m. saying.*

Niega que lo haya dicho. *He denies that he said it.*

Lo dicho, dicho. *I stick to what I've said. I'll (I'd) say it again.*

Dicho y hecho. *No sooner said than done. ("Said and done.")*

Es un dicho. *It's a saying.*

Tiene unos dichos muy graciosos. *She makes some very witty remarks.*

dichoso *adj. happy; fortunate.*

¡Dichosos los ojos que lo ven a Ud.! *What a pleasure (how nice) to see you! ("Happy are the eyes that see you.")*

DIECINUEVE *adj. and n. nineteen; nineteenth.*

diecinueveavo *adj. nineteenth.*

dieciochavo *adj. eighteenth.*

DIECIOCHO *adj. and n. eighteen; eighteenth.*

DIECISEIS *adj. and n. sixteen; sixteenth.*

dieciseisavo *adj. sixteenth.*

DIECISIETE *adj. and n. seventeen; seventeenth.*

diecisieteavo *adj. seventeenth.*

DIENTE *m. tooth.*

Tener buen diente. *To have a hearty appetite ("To have a good tooth.")*

Cepillo de dientes. *Toothbrush.*

Diente molar. *Molar.*

Diente de leche. *Milk tooth.*

Hablar entre dientes. *To mumble. To mutter. ("To speak between one's teeth.")*

DIESTRA *f. right hand.*

diestro *adj. and n. skillful, bullfighter.*

dieta *f. diet; doctor's fee.*

Estoy a dieta. *I'm on a diet.*

DIEZ *adj. and n. ten; tenth.*

difamación *f. defamation.*

difamar *to defame.*

DIFERENCIA *f. difference.*

Partir la diferencia. *To split the difference.*

DIFERENTE *adj. different.*

diferir *to defer, to put off; to differ.*

Telegrama diferido. *Night letter.*

DIFÍCIL *adj. difficult, hard.*

No es nada difícil. *It isn't difficult at all.*

Todo es difícil al principio. *Everything is hard in the beginning.*

Este escritor es difícil. *This author is difficult to understand.*

dificultad *f. difficulty.*

dificultar *to make difficult, to obstruct.*

dificultoso *adj. difficult; hard to please.*

difteria *f. diphtheria.*

difundir *to diffuse, to divulge; to broadcast.*

difunto *adj. deceased, dead; late; m. corpse.*

difusión *f. diffusion; broadcasting.*

digerir *to digest.*

digestión *f. digestion.*

dignarse *to deign, to condescend.*

dignidad *f. dignity.*

digno *adj. deserving, worthy; dignified.*

Digno de confianza. *Trustworthy.*

digresión *f. digression.*

dilación *f. delay.*

dilatar *to put off, to delay; to expand.*

dilección *f. love, affection.*

dilecto *adj. loved, beloved.*

dilema *m. dilemma.*

¡Vaya un dilema! *What a dilemma! What a difficult situation!*

diligencia *f. diligence; haste; business, errand.*

Estudia con diligencia sus lecciones. *He studies his lessons diligently.*

Hacer una diligencia. *To attend to some business. To do an errand.*

Hacer diligencias. *To try. To endeavor.*

Hay que resolverlo con toda diligencia. *You must solve it quickly.*

diligente *adj. diligent; prompt, swift.*

diluir *to dilute.*

diluviar *to rain heavily.*

Seguía diluviando cuando partimos. *It was still pouring when we left.*

dimensión *f. dimension.*

diminutivo *adj. diminutive.*

diminuto *adj. diminutive, minute.*

dimisión *f. resignation (from a position, society, etc.)*

dimitir *to resign, to retire.*

dinamita *f. dynamite.*

dínamo *f. dynamo.*

dineral *m. large amount of money.*

DINERO *m. money, currency.*

Ando mal de dinero. *I'm short of money.*

Dinero contante. *Ready money. Cash payment.*

Persona de dinero. *A well-to-do person.*

DIOS *m. God.*

¡Dios mío! *My God! Dear me!*

Dios mediante. *God willing. With the help of God.*

¡Por Dios! *For heaven's sake!*

¡Válgame Dios! *Goodness! My heavens! Good gracious!*

¡No, por Dios! *Good heavens, no!*

¡Vaya Ud. con Dios! *Good-by.*

¡Sabe Dios! *God knows!*

¡Qué Dios le oiga! *God grant it!*

diploma *m. diploma.*

diplomacia *f. diplomacy.*

diplomático *adj. diplomatic; m. diplomat.*

diptongo *m. diphthong.*

diputado *m. deputy; delegate; representative.*

DIRECCIÓN *f. address; direction, way; control, management, administration; manager's office.*

¿En qué dirección va Ud.? *Which way are you going?*

En esa dirección. *In that direction.*

Escriba la dirección. *Write (down) the address.*

Calle de dirección única. *One-way street.*

directamente *directly.*

directivo *adj. managing; f. governing board, board of directors.*

directo *adj. direct; straight; nonstop.*

¿Es éste un tren directo o tiene uno que cambiar? *Is that an express or must one change?*

director *adj. and n. directing; manager, director; chief editor; principal (of a school).*

Director de orquesta. *Orchestra conductor.*

directorio *m. directory; board of directors; executive committee.*

Presidente del directorio. *Chairman of the Board.*

dirigente *adj. leading, directing; m. leader.*

dirigible *m. dirigible, airship.*

DIRIGIR *to address; to direct; to conduct, to control; to guide; to drive.*

¿Cómo tengo que dirigir la carta? *How shall I address the letter?*

dirigirse *to apply to; to be bound for; to address.*

¿A quien tengo que dirigirme? *To whom shall I apply?*

Hágame el favor de dirigirme a. *Please direct me to.*

¿Se dirige Ud. a nosotros? *Are you speaking to us?*

El lugar hacia el cual se dirigen está aún muy lejos. *The place you're going to is still a good way off.*

discerniente *adj. discerning, discriminating.*

discernimiento *m. discernment.*

discernir *to discern; to distinguish.*

disciplina *f. discipline.*

disciplinar *to discipline.*

discípulo *m. disciple; pupil.*

disco *m. disk, record; telephone dial.*

discordante *adj. discordant.*

discordia *f. discord; disagreement; dissension.*

discreción *f. discretion; keenness; sagacity.*

A discreción. *At one's discretion. Left to one's discretion. Optional.*

discrepancia f. discrepancy.

discrepar to disagree; to differ from.

discreto adj. discreet.

disculpa f. excuse, apology.

disculpar to excuse.

discurrir to wander about; to think over; to flow (a liquid.)

Discurramos un poco más sobre esto. Let's consider that a little longer.

discurso m. speech.

Hacer un discurso. To make a speech. To deliver an address.

discusión f. discussion.

discutible adj. debatable.

DISCUTIR to discuss.

diseminar to disseminate; to scatter.

disensión f. dissension, strife.

disentería f. dysentery.

diseñar to draw, to design, to sketch.

diseño m. drawing; sketch, outline.

disfraz m. disguise; mask.

disfrazar to disguise.

DISFRUTAR to enjoy.

Disfrutaremos más si vamos en grupo. We'll have more fun if we all go together.

Disfruta de muy buena salud. He's enjoying good health.

disfrute m. enjoyment.

disgustar to displease, to disgust; to offend.

¿Le disgusta que fume? Do you mind my smoking? Do you mind if I smoke? Does my smoking bother you?

disgustarse to be displeased, to get angry; to quarrel.

¿No se disgustará Ud? Won't you be angry?

disgusto m. displeasure, disgust, annoyance; quarrel.

A disgusto. Against one's will. Not at ease.

Llevarse un disgusto. To be disappointed.

disidente adj. and n. dissident; dissenter.

disimulación f. dissimulation.

disimulado adj. dissembling.

A lo disimulado. Dissemblingly.

disimular to dissimulate; to overlook.

disimulo m. dissimulation; pretense; tolerance.

dislocación f. dislocation.

dislocarse to sprain; to dislocate.

disminución f. lessening, diminishing.

disminuir to diminish, to decrease.

disolver to melt; to dissolve; to break up (a crowd).

dispar adj. different, unlike.

disparar to shoot; to fire.

disparatado adj. nonsensical, absurd.

disparatar to ramble, to talk nonsense; to blunder.

disparate m. nonsense; blunder.

disparo m. discharge, shot.

DISPENSAR to excuse; to dispense; to exempt.

Dispénseme. Excuse me.

Dispense Ud. I beg your pardon.

Dispénseme, ¿qué hora es? Excuse me, what time is it?

Está dispensado. You're excused.

dispensario m. dispensary.

disperso adj. dispersed; scattered.

disponer to dispose; to arrange; to provide for; to prepare; to determine.

Disponga Ud. lo que quiera. Decide whatever you like (wish).

Me dispongo a salir mañana. I'm determined to leave tomorrow.

Dispongo de muy poco tiempo. I have very little time now ("at my disposal").

disponible adj. available.

disposición f. service; disposition; state of mind; regulation, order.

Estoy a su disposición. I'm at your service.

Tiene muy buena disposición. She has a very pleasant disposition.

Había que sujetarse a la nueva disposición. We had to submit to the new regulation.

dispuesto adj. disposed; ready, arranged; inclined; willing (to).

Bien dispuesto. Favorably disposed (inclined).

Mal dispuesto. Unfavorably disposed (inclined).

¿Tiene Ud. algo dispuesto para esta noche? Do you have anything arranged for tonight?

Estamos dispuestos a todo. We're prepared for anything.

La casa está bien dispuesta. The house is nicely arranged.

disputa f. dispute; contest; quarrel.

disputar to dispute; to quarrel.

DISTANCIA f. distance.

¿Qué distancia hay a Madrid? How far is it to Madrid?

Hemos recorrido toda la distancia a pie. We've walked the whole way.

Conferencia a larga distancia. Long distance call.

DISTANTE adj. distant, far off.

distar to be distant, to be far.

¿Dista mucho de aquí? Is it far from here?

Distaba mucho de ser cierto. It was far from certain.

distinción f. distinction; discrimination; difference.

Hay que hacer una distinción entre los dos sonidos. It's necessary to make a distinction between the two sounds.

Era un hombre de mucha distinción. He was a very distinguished man.

A distinción. In contradistinction.

distinguido adj. distinguished, eminent.

distinguir to distinguish; to discriminate; to tell (apart); to show regard for.

¿Cómo puede distinguirlos? How do (can) you tell them apart?

distinguirse to distinguish oneself, to excel.

distintivo adj. distinctive; m. badge, insignia.

DISTINTO adj. distinct; different.

distracción f. oversight; distraction; absence of mind; entertainment, recreation, pastime.

La lectura es su distracción favorita. Reading is his favorite diversion.

El cine es su distracción favorita. Going to the movies is his favorite entertainment (diversion).

Lo hizo por distracción. He did it absent-mindedly.

distraer to distract; to entertain.

Ese ruido me distrae. That noise distracts me.

distraerse to enjoy oneself, to have fun; to be absent-minded.

¿Se ha distraído en la fiesta? Did you have a good time at the party?

distraído adj. inattentive; absent-minded.

distribución f. distribution.

distribuidor adj. distributing; m. distributer.

distribuir to distribute; to divide; to allot, to allocate.

distrito m. district; region.

disturbar to disturb.

disturbio m. disturbance.

disuadir to dissuade.

disuasión f. dissuasion.

divagación f. wandering, digression.

divagar to wander.

diván m. couch.

divergencia f. divergence.

divergente adj. divergent.

diversidad f. diversity; variety.

diversión f. amusement, diversion, recreation.

diverso adj. diverse; various, several.

Le he visto en diversas ocasiones. I've seen him on several occasions.

divertido adj. entertaining, amusing; funny.

Este libro es muy divertido. This book is very entertaining.

Todo esto es muy divertido. All this is very amusing.

Es una muchacha divertidísima. She's lots of fun.

divertimiento m. diversion, amusement, sport, pastime.

divertir to distract; to divert; to amuse.

Nos contó unos chistes que nos divertieron mucho. He told us some jokes which amused us very much (a lot).

DIVERTIRSE to amuse oneself, to have a good time, to have fun.

¡Que se divierta! Have a good time! Enjoy yourself!

dividendo m. dividend.

DIVIDIR to divide.

divinamente splendidly; divinely, heavenly; very well.

Canta divinamente. She sings beautifully ("di-

vinely"). She has a beautiful voice.

Este sombrero le sienta divinamente. This hat is most becoming to you.

divinidad f. divinity.

divino adj. divine; excellent; heavenly.

divisa f. motto; badge; emblem.

divisar to perceive, to catch sight of.

división f. division; partition, compartment.

divorciarse to get a divorce, to be divorced.

divorcio m. divorce.

divulgar to divulge, to publish; to disclose.

dobladillo m. hem.

doblar to turn; to double; to fold; to bend.

Doble a la derecha. Turn to the right.

Doblar la esquina. To turn the corner.

Doble bien la carta antes de meterla en el sobre. Fold the letter well before putting (enclosing) it in the envelope.

doble adj. double, twofold; two-faced, deceitful.

No se fíe Ud. de él, es muy doble. Don't trust him, he's very deceitful.

Esto tiene doble sentido. This has a double meaning.

Al doble. Doubly.

doblement doubly; deceitfully.

doblez m. fold; crease; duplicity, double dealing.

DOCE adj. and n. twelve; twelfth.

DOCENA f. dozen.

Por docena. By the dozen.

dócil adj. docile; obedient; gentle.

doctor m. doctor.

doctrina f. doctrine.

documentación f. documentation, documents, papers.

documento m. document.

dólar m. dollar.

dolencia f. ailment; disease.

DOLER to ache, to cause pain, to hurt.

¿Dónde le duele? Where does it hurt you?

Me duele la cabeza. I've a headache.

El pie me duele muchísimo. My foot hurts a lot.

Me duelen los ojos. My eyes hurt.

Me duele una muela. My tooth aches.

Me duele la garganta. I have a sore throat.

dolerse (de) to be sorry (for); to regret; to pity; to complain (of).

DOLOR m. ache, pain; sorrow.

Tener dolor. To have a pain.

Tener dolor de cabeza. To have a headache.

Dolor de muelas. Toothache.

Dolor de garganta. A sore throat.

doloroso adj. sorrowful, afflicted; painful.

domar to tame; to subdue.

Sin domar. Untamed.

doméstico adj. domestic.

domicilio m. residence, domicile; home; address.

dominación f. domination.

dominante adj. dominant.

dominar to dominate; to master.

dominarse to control oneself.

DOMINGO m. Sunday.

dominio m. dominion; command, control.

    Tiene un buen dominio del español. He has an excellent command of Spanish.

    Tenía un gran dominio sobre sí mismo. He had great self-control. He had great control over himself.

don m. Don (title of respect used only before Christian names); natural gift.

    Dirija Ud. la carta a Don Antonio Sucre. Address the letter to Mr. Antonio Sucre.

    Tiene el don de hacer amigos. She has the gift of making friends.

    Don de gentes. Pleasant manners. Social graces. Savoir-faire.

donación f. gift, donation; grant.

donaire m. grace; elegance; witty saying.

donar to donate, to give as a gift, to make a gift to someone.

donativo m. gift, donation.

DONDE where.

    ¿Dónde vive? Where do you live?

    ¿Dónde está el teléfono? Where is the telephone?

    Iremos donde a Ud. le plazca. We'll go wherever you like.

    ¿De dónde? From where?

    ¿Hacia dónde? In what direction?

    ¿Por dónde? Which way?

dondequiera anywhere; wherever.

    Iré dondequiera que me mande. I'll go wherever you send me.

doña (f. of don) lady; madam.

dorado adj. gilt, gilded.

dormilón adj. fond of sleeping; m. sleepyhead.

DORMIR to sleep.

    ¿Ha dormido Ud. bien? Did you sleep well?

    No he podido dormir. I couldn't sleep.

DORMIRSE to fall asleep.

    Debo haberme dormido. I must have been asleep.

    Se ha quedado dormido. He's fallen asleep.

dormitar to doze, to be half asleep.

dormitorio m. dormitory; bedroom.

DOS adj. and n. two; second (day of the month).

    Dos a dos. Two by two.

    De dos en dos. Two abreast.

    En un dos por tres. In the twinkling of an eye.

    Para entre los dos. Between you and me.

    Son las dos. It's two o'clock.

    Las dos hermanas se parecen. Both sisters look alike.

    ¿Tiene Ud. un cuarto para dos personas? Do you have a double room?

    Está a dos pasos de aquí. It's only a few steps from here.

DOSCIENTOS m. pl. two hundred.

dosis f. dose.

dotación f. crew; equipment; allocation.

dotar to provide (with); to allocate; to give a dowry; to endow with.

dote m. and f. dowry; pl. gifts, talents.

drama m. drama.

dramático adj. dramatic.

dramatizar to dramatize.

drástico adj. drastic.

droga f. drug.

droguería f. drugstore.

ducha f. shower (bath).

DUDA f. doubt.

    Lo pongo en duda. I doubt it.

    No me cabe la menor duda. I haven't the slightest doubt.

    Sin duda. Without a doubt. Undoubtedly.

DUDAR to doubt.

    Lo dudo. I doubt it.

    Dudo que venga. I doubt if he'll come.

    Nadie lo duda. Nobody doubts it.

dudoso adj. doubtful; uncertain.

duelo m. duel; mourning; grief; affliction.

duende m. ghost.

dueña f. owner; landlady; mistress.

dueño m. owner; landlord; master.

    Hacerse dueño. To take possession.

    Dueño de sí mismo. Self-controlled. ("Master of oneself.")

DULCE adj. sweet; agreeable; m. candy.

dulcería f. candy store.

dulzura f. sweetness; gentleness.

dúo m. duo, duet.

duodécimo adj. twelfth.

duplicado m. duplicate; copy.

duplicar to duplicate, to repeat.

duque m. duke.

duquesa f. duchess.

durable adj. durable; lasting.

    ¿Es durable esta tela? Will this cloth wear well?

duración f. duration.

duradero adj. durable; lasting.

DURANTE during, for.

    Durante el día. During the day.

    Durante la noche. During the night.

    Durante algún tiempo. For some time.

DURAR to last; to continue; to wear well.

    ¿Cuánto dura la película? How long does the picture last?

    Este abrigo me ha durado mucho tiempo. This overcoat has lasted me a long time.

    El viaje en barco durará cinco días. The voyage will take five days.

    Todavía le dura el enfado. He's still angry.

durazno m. peach (Amer.).

dureza f. hardness; harshness.

    Dureza de oído. Hardness of hearing.

durmiente *adj. sleeping; m. sleeper.*

DURO *adj. hard; unbearable; obstinate; stingy; harsh; m. peso, dollar (Spain).*

No sea duro con él. *Don't be hard on him.*

Este pan es tan duro que es difícil cortarlo. *This bread is so hard that it's difficult to cut ("it").*

¿Me puede Ud. cambiar un billete de veinte duros? *(Spain) Can you change a twenty-dollar bill for me?*

A duras penas. *Scarcely. Hardly. With difficulty.*

E

e *and (used before words beginning with i or hi).*

Padre e hijo. *Father and son.*

ebanista *m. cabinetmaker.*

ebrio *adj. intoxicated, drunk.*

economía *f. economy, economics, saving.*

Economía política. *Political economy.*

económico *adj. economic; economical, not too expensive.*

economizar *to economize; to save.*

ECHAR *tó throw; to throw out; to fire; to sprout; to shoot; to lay down; to start to.*

Eche esto a la basura. *Throw this in the garbage.*

Lo echaron de su empleo por holgazán. *They fired him because he was too lazy.*

Eche un poco de agua caliente en la tetera. *Pour some hot water in the teapot.*

Eche Ud. la carta al buzón. *Put this letter in the mailbox.*

Echó la carta al correo. *He mailed the letter.*

Lo echaron a patadas. *They kicked him out.*

Eche la llave al salir. *Lock the door when you go out.*

¿Quiero Ud. echar una partida de damas? *Would you like to play a game of checkers?*

Echar de ver. *To notice. To perceive.*

Echar mano a. *To grab. To get hold of. To arrest.*

Echar a correr. *To start to run.*

Echar a perder. *To spoil.*

Echar la culpa a alguno. *To blame someone.*

Echar de menos. *To miss.*

Echar tierra a. *To forget.*

Echarla de. *To pretend. To claim to be.*

Echar el guante. *To arrest.*

Echar raíces. *To take root.*

Echar el ancla. *To drop anchor.*

ECHARSE *to lie down; to throw oneself, to plunge; to rush, to dash.*

Se echó en la cama. *He lay down on the bed.*

Se echó a reír. *He burst out laughing.*

EDAD *f. age; era, epoch, time.*

¿Qué edad tiene Ud? *How old are you? What's your age?*

Somos de la misma edad. *We're (of) the same age.*

Ser menor de edad. *To be a minor.*

Mayor de edad. *Of age.*

Es un hombre de edad. *He's well along in years.*

Edad media. *Middle Ages.*

edición *f. edition, issue; publication.*

edificar *to cónstruct, to build.*

Van a edificar una nueva escuela. *They are going to build a new school.*

edificio *m. building.*

Este edificio es bonito por fuera. *This building looks (is) nice from the outside.*

editor *adj. and n. publishing; m. publisher.*

Casa editora. *Publishing house.*

Fuí a ver a un editor. *I went to see a publisher.*

editorial *adj. editorial; f. publishing house.*

educación *f. education; bringing up, breeding.*

Es un hombre sin educación. *He's ill-bred. He has no breeding.*

educar *to educate; to bring up; to train.*

Es muy mal educado. *He has no breeding.*

Es una chica muy bien educada. *She's a very well-bred girl.*

educativo *adj. educational, instructive.*

efectivo *adj. effective, certain, real, actual; m. cash.*

Pagar en efectivo. *To pay in cash.*

Efectivo en caja. *Cash on hand.*

Valor efectivo. *Real value.*

Hacer efectivo. *To make effective. To put into effect. To cash (a check, etc.).*

Medidas efectivas. *Effective measures.*

EFECTO *m. effect, result, consequence; impression; pl. effects, assets, goods, belongings.*

Sus palabras causaron mal efecto. *His words made a bad impression.*

En efecto, no sabe nada. *In fact, he doesn't know anything.*

A tal efecto. *For this purpose.*

A cuyo efecto. *For the purpose of which. To which end.*

Por efecto de. *As a result of.*

Llevar a efecto. *To carry out. To put into practice (effect).*

Dejar sin efecto. *To cancel. To annul. To make (declare) void.*

Efectos personales. *Personal belongings.*

Efectos en cartera. *Securities in hand.*

Efectos públicos. *Public securities.*

eficaz *adj. effective, efficient.*

eficiente *adj. effective, efficient.*

eje *m. axle, axis.*

ejecución *f. execution, carrying out, performance.*

ejecutar *to execute, to carry out, to perform.*

ejecutivo *adj. executive.*

ejemplar *adj. exemplary, serving as an example; m. copy; sample.*

No pude conseguir otro ejemplar del libro. *I*

couldn't get another copy of the book.
EJEMPLO *m. example; pattern.*
   Por ejemplo. *For example.*
ejercer *to exercise, to perform, to practice.*
   Ejercer la medicina. *To practice medicine.*
ejercicio *m. exercise; drill.*
   Ejercicio de tiro. *Target practice.*
ejército *m. army.*
EL *(article m.) the.*
   El libro. *The book.*
   ¿No le gusta el frío? *Don't you like the cold?*
   ¿Cuál es el mejor hotel? *Which is the best hotel?*
   Hasta el lunes. *See you Monday.*
ÉL *(pronoun m.) he, him.*
   ¿Qué dijo él? *What did he say?*
   Dígaselo a él. *Tell it to him.*
elaboración *f. elaboration, working out.*
elaborado *adj. elaborate; manufactured.*
elaborar *to elaborate; to work out; to manufacture.*
elasticidad *f. elasticity.*
elástico *adj. and n. elastic.*
ele *f. name of the letter l.*
elección *f. election; choice.*
   Hoy se celebran las elecciones. *Elections will
     be held today.*
   Hizo una buena elección. *He made a good
     choice.*
electricidad *f. electricity.*
eléctrico *adj. electric.*
   Luz eléctrica. *Electric light.*
elefante *m. elephant.*
elegancia *f. elegance; refinement.*
   Viste con elegancia. *She dresses neatly.*
elegante *adj. elegant, refined, well dressed.*
elegir *to elect; to choose.*
elemental *adj. elementary; elemental.*
elemento *m. element; pl. elements, rudiments, first
     principles.*
elenco *m. catalogue, list, table, index.*
elevación *f. elevation.*
elevador *m. elevator; hoist.*
elevar *to elevate; to lift up.*
elevarse *to rise; to be elated, to be conceited.*
eliminación *f. elimination.*
eliminar *to eliminate.*
elocuencia *f. eloquence.*
elocuente *adj. eloquent.*
elogiar *to praise.*
elogio *m. praise, eulogy.*
elucidación *f. elucidation.*
eludir *to elude, to evade.*
   Deje de eludir la cuestión; vamos al grano.
     Stop evading the issue; let's get to the point.
ELLA(*f. of él*) *she, her.*
   ¿Cómo es ella? *What does she look like?*
   ¿Como se llama ella? *What's her name?*
ELLAS (*pl. of ella*) *they, them.*
   ¿Quiénes son ellas? *Who are they?*

   Ellas son mis hermanas. *They are my sisters.*
ELLO (*neuter of él and ella*) *it.*
   No doy en ello. *I don't get it.*
   Ello podrá ser verdad, pero no lo creo. *It may
     be true but I don't believe it.*
   Hablemos de ello. *Let's talk about that.*
   Para ello. *For the purpose.*
   Ello es que. *The fact is (that).*
ELLOS (*pl. of él*) *they, them.*
   Ellos se van, pero yo me quedo. *They're leav-
     ing but I'll stay.*
   Ninguno de ellos tiene dinero. *None of them
     has money.*
embajada *f. embassy.*
embajador *m. ambassador.*
embalaje *m. packing; putting in bales; packing-box.*
embalar *to pack in bales; to pack.*
embarcación *f. vessel, ship, boat; embarkation.*
embarcadero *m. wharf, place of embarkation.*
embarcar *to embark.*
embarcarse *to go on board a ship, to embark.*
embargo *m. embargo.*
   Sin embargo. *Nevertheless.*
embarque *m. embarkation, shipment, shipping.*
embestida *f. assault, attack.*
emborrachar *to intoxicate.*
emborracharse *to get drunk.*
emboscar *to ambush.*
emboscarse *to lie in ambush.*
embotellar *to bottle.*
embrollo *m. jumble, tangle; fix, jam.*
   No sé como salir de este embrollo. *I don't know
     how to get out of this fix (tight spot, jam).*
embrutecerse *to become stupid or coarse, to be-
     come brutalized.*
embustero *m. liar, fibber.*
embutido *m. inlaid work; sausage.*
emergencia *f. emergency.*
emigración *f. emigration.*
emigrante *m. emigrant.*
emigrar *to emigrate.*
eminente *adj. eminent.*
emisora *f. broadcasting station.*
emitir *to emit, to send forth; to issue (bonds, etc.);
     to utter, to express; to broadcast (news,
     etc.).*
emoción *f. emotion.*
emocionante *adj. touching.*
emocionar *to move, to arouse the emotions.*
emocionarse *to be moved.*
   Se emociona fácilmente. *He's easily moved. He's
     very emotional.*
empacar *to pack.*
empachar *to cause indigestion; to overeat, eat too
     much, to cram; to embarrass.*
empacho *m. indigestion; embarrassment.*
   Sin empacho. *Without ceremony. With ease.*
empalmar *to join; to splice.*

empanada *f. meat pie.*
empañar *to swaddle; to blur; to sully.*
empapar *to soak.*
empaparse *to be soaked, to be drenched.*
empapelar *to paper.*
empaquetar *to pack.*
emparedado *m. sandwich.*
emparentado *adj. related.*
emparentar *to become related.*
empastar *to paste; to bind (books); to fill (a tooth).*
empatar *to equal, to tie.*
 Los dos equipos empataron. *The game ended in a tie. ("The two teams tied.")*
empeñar *to pawn; to pledge; to engage.*
 Empeñé mi palabra. *I gave (pledged) my word.*
 Está empeñado hasta los ojos. *He's up to his neck in debt. He's head over heels in debt.*
empeñarse *to bind oneself; to get into debt.*
 Se empeñó en venir conmigo. *He (she) was determined to come with me. He (she) insisted on coming with me.*
empeño *m. pledge, obligation; determination; earnest desire; persistence.*
 Estudia con empeño. *He's studying diligently.*
 Tener empeño en. *To be bent on.*
EMPEZAR *to begin.*
empinar *to raise.*
 Empinar el codo. *To drink like a fish.*
empinarse *to stand on tiptoe; to stand on the hind legs; to rise high; to zoom (aviation).*
empleado *m. employee, clerk.*
EMPLEAR *to employ; to hire; to use; to spend.*
 ¿En qué empleó Ud. la tarde? *How did you spend the afternoon?*
 Empleamos dos días en hacerlo. *It took us two days to do it.*
 Estoy empleado en su casa. *I work in his firm.*
 Se acaba de emplear. *He just got a job.*
 Emplearon un centenar de obreros esta mañana. *They hired a hundred workers this morning.*
EMPLEO *m. employment, job, occupation; use.*
 Tiene un buen empleo. *He has a good job.*
 El empleo de esa palabra no es correcto. *That word is not used correctly.*
emprender *to undertake, to take up, to set off.*
empresa *f. undertaking; enterprise; company.*
empresario *m. impresario, contractor, manager.*
empréstito *m. loan.*
empujar *to push.*
 ¡No me empuje! *Don't push me!*
empuje *m. push; impulse.*
 Es un hombre de empuje. *He's an energetic man.*
empujón *m. push; shove.*
 A empujones. *By fits and starts.*
EN *in, into, on, at, by.*
 Lo tengo en la mano. *I have it in my hand.*

En buen estado. *In good condition.*
Entremos en esta tienda. *Let's go into this store.*
Métase en la cama. *Get into bed.*
He venido en avión. *I came by plane.*
¿En qué fecha? *On what date?*
En casa. *At home.*
En vano. *In vain.*
En general. *In general.*
En adelante. *From now on.*
En cambio. *On the other hand.*
En vez (lugar) de. *Instead of.*
En todas partes. *Everywhere.*
En medio de. *In the middle (midst) of.*
En seguida. *right away.*
enamorado *adj. in love.*
enamorarse *to fall in love.*
enano *m. dwarf; midget.*
encabezar *to write a heading; to register, to enroll; to head.*
encadenar *to chain, to link together.*
encajar *to fit in; to gear; to inlay; to sock, to hit; to palm, to pass off.*
encaje *m. lace.*
encaminar *to guide; to direct.*
encaminarse *to be on the way; to take the road to.*
encanecer *to turn gray, to grow old.*
encantador *adj. charming.*
 Es una chica encantadora. *She's charming. She's a charming girl.*
encantar *to enchant; to delight; to fascinate.*
 Me encantan las flores. *I love (am fond of) flowers.*
 Quedaré encantado. *I shall be delighted.*
encanto *m. charm; delight; fascination.*
 Es un encanto de criatura. *She's a charming girl.*
encapricharse *to become stubborn; to be infatuated; to indulge in whims.*
encarcelar *to imprison.*
encarecer *to raise the price; to entreat, to beg.*
 Le encarezco que lo haga con cuidado. *Please (I beg you to) do it carefully.*
 Ha encarecido el precio de la carne. *The price of meat has gone up.*
encargado *m. person in charge; agent.*
encargar *to ask, to have someone go on an errand; to entrust; to undertake; to instruct.*
 Le encargué que me lo comprara. *I asked her to buy it for me.*
encargarse *to take charge, to take care.*
 ¿Quién se encargará de los niños? *Who'll take care of the children?*
encargo *m. request; errand; order, charge.*
encarnado *adj. red; m. flesh color.*
 Se puso encarnada. *She blushed.*

encendedor *m. cigarette lighter.*
encender *to kindle; to light; to incite.*
 Haga el favor de encender la luz. *Please put*

on the light.

encerar *to wax.*

encerrar *to close in, to shut up, to confine; to contain.*

encerrarse *to lock oneself in; to live in seclusion.*

encía *f. gum (of the teeth).*

ENCIMA *above, over, at the top.*

> Encima de la mesa. *On the table.*
>
> Encima de los árboles. *Above the trees.*
>
> Por encima. *Superficially.*
>
> Por encima de todo. *Above all.*
>
> Estar muy por encima de. *To be far and away above.*
>
> ¿Cuánto dinero lleva Ud. encima? *How much money do you have with you?*

encina *f. evergreen oak.*

encolar *to glue.*

encomendar *to recommend; to commend; to entrust; to praise, to extol.*

encomendarse *to commit oneself, to place oneself into the hands of.*

encomienda *f. parcel; parcel post (Amer.).*

encono *m. irritation; soreness; animosity, rancor, bitter resentment.*

ENCONTRAR *to find; to meet.*

> ¿Encontraste lo que buscabas? *Did you find what you were looking for?*
>
> ¿Cómo encuentra Ud. el trabajo? *How do you find the work?*
>
> Debían encontrarnos aquí. *They were supposed to meet us here.*

ENCONTRARSE *to meet, to come across; to clash; to differ with; to be, to feel.*

> ¿Cómo se encuentra Ud.? *How do you feel? How are you?*
>
> Hoy me encuentro mejor. *I feel better today.*

encorvado *adj. bent; curved.*

encrespar *to curl; to frizzle.*

encresparse *to become rough (sea); to be involved (in an affair).*

encubrir *to hide, to conceal.*

ENCUENTRO *m. meeting; encounter.*

encharcar *to form puddles; to inundate.*

enchilada *f. a Mexican corn-flour pancake with chili.*

enchufar *to plug in; to fit one tube into another; to telescope.*

enchufe *m. plug, socket; coupling, joint (for pipes).*

enderezar *to straighten; to set right.*

endeudarse *to get into debt.*

endosar *to endorse.*

endurecer *to harden, to make hard.*

ene *f. name of the letter n.*

enemigo *adj. unfriendly, hostile; m. enemy, foe.*

> Es enemigo del tabaco. *He has an aversion to tobacco. He's against the use of tobacco.*

enemistad *f. enmity; hatred.*

energía *f. energy, power.*

enérgico *adj. energetic.*

ENERO *m. January.*

enfadar *to vex, to annoy, to make someone angry.*

enfadarse *to get angry, to become angry.*

enfado *m. vexation, anger.*

enfermar *to get ill; to fall sick.*

> Ud. va a acabar por enfermarse. *You'll end by getting sick.*

enfermizo *adj. infirm, not healthy, sickly.*

enfermo *adj. ill, sick; m. patient.*

> Me siento enfermo. *I feel ill. I don't feel well.*
>
> Está gravemente enfermo. *He's very ill.*
>
> ¿Cómo sigue el enfermo? *How is the patient getting along?*

enfocar *to focus.*

enfrentar *to face, to confront.*

ENFRENTE *in front of, opposite.*

> El automóvil está parado enfrente de aquel edificio. *The car's parked in front of that building.*
>
> Viven en la casa de enfrente. *They live in the house across the street.*

enfriamiento *m. cooling; refrigeration; cold.*

> Enfriamiento por aire. *Air cooling.*

enfriar *to cool.*

enfriarse *to cool off, to get cool.*

enfurecer *to infuriate, to enrage.*

enfurecerse *to become furious.*

enganchar *to hook; to get caught; to hitch; to couple; to recruit.*

engañar *to deceive, to fool.*

engañarse *to deceive oneself.*

> Ud. se engaña. *You're deceiving (fooling) yourself.*
>
> Se le engaña fácilmente. *He's easily fooled (taken in).*

engañoso *adj. deceitful; tricky.*

engendrar *to bring into existence; to produce, to create.*

engordar *to fatten; to grow fat.*

engranaje *m. gear.*

engrasar *to grease, to lubricate.*

engrase *m. lubrication.*

engreído *conceited, haughty.*

engreír *to spoil (a child, etc.).*

engreírse *to become conceited, to become haughty.*

engrudo *m. paste, glue.*

enhebrar *to thread a needle.*

enhorabuena *f. congratulation.*

> ¡La enhorabuena! *Congratulations!*

enjabonar *to soap; to wash with soap.*

enjaular *to cage; to imprison.*

enjuagar *to rinse.*

enjugar *to dry; to wipe off.*

enlace *m. connection; marriage; liaison, wedding, joining.*

> El enlace de trenes es excelente en esta estación. *The train connections are excellent*

at this station.

Un feliz enlace. *A happy marriage.*

enlazar *to join, to bind, to connect; to catch with a lasso.*

enmendar *to correct, to amend, to reform.*

enmudecer *to silence.*

enmudecerse *to become dumb; to be silent.*

enojado *adj. angry, cross.*

Estar enojado. *To be angry.*

enojar *to irritate, to make angry.*

enojarse *to get angry.*

enredar *to entangle; to make trouble; to upset.*

enredarse *to become entangled.*

enredo *m. entanglement.*

enriquecer *to enrich; to improve.*

enriquecerse *to get rich.*

ENROLLAR *to roll, to coil, to wind.*

enronquecer *to make hoarse.*

enronquecerse *to become hoarse.*

ensalada *f. salad.*

ensanchar *to widen, to enlarge.*

ENSAYAR *to try, to rehearse, to test.*

ensayarse *to train, to practice.*

ensayo *m. trial; rehearsal.*

enseñanza *f. teaching, instruction.*

ENSEÑAR *to teach; to point out, to show.*

¿Quiere Ud. enseñarme a hablar español?
Would you like to teach me to speak Spanish?

Enseñe Ud. el camino al señor. *Show this gentleman the way.*

No se lo enseñe a ella. *Don't show it to her.*

enseñarse *to accustom oneself.*

ensordecer *to deafen.*

ensordecerse *to become deaf.*

ensordecimiento *m. deafness.*

ensuciar *to dirty, to soil.*

ensuciarse *to get dirty; to lower oneself.*

entender *m. understanding; opinion.*

A mi entender. *In my opinion.*

ENTENDER *to understand.*

¿Entiende Ud. español? *Do you understand Spanish?*

No pude entender lo que decían. *I couldn't understand what they were saying.*

Entendido. *It's understood.*

Es un obrero muy entendido en su oficio. *He's very skilled in his trade.*

No darse por entendido. *To ignore. Not to take notice.*

Según tenemos entendido. *As far as we know.*

Entender de. *To be an expert in. To be familiar with.*

Entender en. *To be in charge of. To deal with. To attend to.*

Entendido. *Understood, right.*

entenderse *to understand one another; to come to an understanding, to agree, to arrange; to*

be understood; to be meant.

Entenderse con. *To have to do with. To deal with. To come to an understanding with. To arrange with.*

entendimiento *m. understanding.*

enteramente *entirely, completely, quite, fully.*

enterar *to inform, to acquaint.*

Estamos enterados de sus planes. *We know what his plans are.*

enterarse *to learn, to find out.*

Entérate de cuando sale el tren. *Find out when the train leaves.*

Acabo de enterarme de la noticia. *I've just heard the news.*

enternecer *to soften; to move, to touch.*

enternecerse *to pity; to be affected with emotion, to be moved.*

ENTERO *adj. entire, whole, complete.*

Por entero. *Entirely. Completely.*

Color entero. *Solid color.*

enterrar *to bury.*

entidad *f. entity.*

entierro *m. interment, burial, funeral.*

entonación *f. intonation; tone.*

entonar *to tune, to intone.*

ENTONCES *then, at that time.*

Era entonces un niño. *He was a child then.*

Por entonces. *At the time.*

Desde entonces. *Since then. From then on.*

entornar *to leave ajar.*

ENTRADA *f. entrance; entry; admission; ticket; entree.*

¿Cuánto cuesta la entrada? *How much is the admission?*

Debemos comprar las entradas ahora mismo. *We have to buy the tickets right away.*

¿Qué desea Ud. como entrada? *What would you like as an entree?*

"Se prohibe la entrada." *"No admittance."*

Entrada libre. *Admission free.*

entrante *adj. entering; coming; next (day, week, month, etc.); m. next month.*

ENTRAR *to enter, to go in; to fit in.*

¿Se puede entrar? *May I come in?*

Que no entre nadie. *Don't let anyone come in.*

El zapato no me entra, es muy pequeño. *I can't get my foot into this shoe; it's too small.*

ENTRE *between; in; among.*

Lo hicieron entre los dos. *They did it between the two of them.*

Mire entre los papeles. *Look among the papers.*

Parta Ud. 300 entre 3. *Divide 300 by 3.*

Reírse entre sí. *To laugh to oneself.*

Entre manos. *In hand.*

Entre tanto. *Meanwhile.*

Por entre. *Through.*

entreacto *m. intermission.*

entredós m. insertion (of lace, etc.).

entrega f. delivery; surrender.

entregar to deliver; to surrender.

¿A quién ha entregado Ud. la carta? Who(m) did you give the letter to?

No han entregado la mercancía todavía. They haven't delivered the goods yet.

entregarse to take to, to abandon oneself to; to give oneself up.

El criminal se entregó a la policía. The criminal gave himself up to the police.

Se ha entregado a la embriaguez. He's taken to drink.

entremeter to place between, to insert.

entremeterse to meddle, to intrude, to interfere.

entremetido m. meddler, busybody, intruder.

entrenador m. coach, trainer.

entrenamiento m. training.

entrenar to train, to coach.

entresuelo m. mezzanine.

ENTRETANTO meanwhile.

ENTRETENER to entertain, to amuse; to put off, to delay.

entretenido adj. pleasant, amusing.

entretenimiento m. amusement, entertainment.

entrevista f. interview, conference.

entristecer to grieve, to be unhappy.

entristecerse to be sad, to become sad.

entrometer. See entremeter.

enturbiar to make muddy; to muddle.

entusiasmar to fill with enthusiasm; to elate.

entusiasmarse to become enthusiastic.

entusiasmo m. enthusiasm.

entusiasta adj. enthusiastic; m. and f. enthusiast.

envasar to can; to barrel; to bottle.

envejecer to make old; to grow old.

envenenar to poison.

ENVIAR to send; to dispatch.

¿Puede Ud. enviar mi equipaje al hotel? Can you send my luggage to the hotel?

Se lo enviaré hoy mismo. I'll send it to him today ("this very day.").

Enviaron a buscar al médico. They sent someone for the doctor.

envidia f. envy.

envidiable adj. enviable.

envidiar to envy.

envidioso adj. envious, jealous.

envío m. sending, remittance, shipment.

enviudar to become a widow or a widower.

envoltorio m. bundle.

envolver to wrap up, to make into a package; to surround, to envelop; to disguise.

época f. epoch, age, era, period.

equipaje m. baggage; equipment; crew (of a ship).

Coche de equipaje. Baggage car.

Equipaje de mano. Hand luggage.

equipar to equip, to furnish.

equipo m. equipment; team (sports).

equis f. name of the letter x.

equivocación f. mistake.

EQUIVOCADO adj. mistaken, wrong.

Estoy equivocado. I'm mistaken. I'm wrong.

Ud. está muy equivocado. You're entirely mistaken.

equivocar to mistake.

EQUIVOCARSE to be wrong, to make a mistake.

Se equivoca Ud. You're wrong. You're making a mistake.

era f. era; threshing-floor; garden patch for vegetables.

ere f. name of the letter r.

erario m. public funds.

erección f. erecting, establishment.

erguir to erect, to raise.

erigir to erect, to build; to establish.

ERRAR to err, to go wrong, to make a mistake, to miss; to wander.

Todos somos susceptibles de errar. We are all liable to make mistakes. ("We are all subject to error.")

Errar el tiro. To miss the target.

errata f. erratum, error in writing or printing.

erre f. name of the letter rr.

ERROR m. error, fault, mistake.

erudición f. erudition, learning.

erudito adj. erudite, learned; m. scholar, erudite person.

ESA (f. of ese) that; pl. esas those.

Esa mujer. That woman.

Vamos por esa calle. Let's go down that street.

Esas mujeres. Those women.

No se ocupe Ud. de esas cosas. Don't pay any attention to such things. Don't bother about such things.

ÉSA (f. of ése) that, that one, that person, that thing; pl. ésas those.

Ésa es su mujer. That (woman) is his wife.

Deme ésa. Give me that one.

En ésa. In that place. In your town.

Ni por ésas. Not even so. Not even for that.

esbelto adj. slim, slender; elegant.

escabeche m. pickle; pickled fish.

escabroso adj. rugged, harsh.

escala f. stepladder; scale; port of call.

Hacer escala en. To stop. To call at a port.

escalera f. staircase; ladder.

escalofrío m. chill.

Tengo escalofríos. I have the chills.

escamoteo m. juggling; swindling.

escampar to stop raining; to clear up.

Si no escampa no iré. I won't go if it doesn't stop raining.

escapar to escape, to flee.

escaparate m. show window, glass case; cupboard; cabinet.

escape m. *escape.*

escarabajo m. *beetle.*

escarbar *to scratch (as fowls); to dig; to poke (fire); to probe.*

escarcha f. *frost.*

escarmentar *to learn by experience, to take warning; to make an example of.*

Ud. debe de escarmentar de eso. *That should be a lesson to you. You ought to profit from that.*

escaso adj. *scarce, scanty; short of.*

Estoy escaso de dinero. *I'm short of money.*

escena f. *stage; scene; view; episode.*

Poner en escena. *To stage (produce) a play.*

escenario m. *stage (theater).*

escenográfico adj. *scenic.*

escéptico adj. *skeptical; m. a skeptic.*

esclavitud f. *slavery.*

esclavo m. *slave.*

escoba f. *broom.*

ESCOGER *to choose, to pick out.*

escogido adj. *selected, choice.*

escolta f. *escort.*

escoltar *to escort.*

escombro m. *debris, rubbish.*

esconder *to hide, to conceal.*

esconderse *to hide, to remain hidden.*

escondido adj. *hidden.*

escopeta f. *shotgun.*

escribano m. *notary.*

ESCRIBIR *to write.*

Escriba claro. *Write clearly.*

¿Cómo se escribe esa palabra? *How is that word written (spelled)? How do you write that word?*

Escriba Ud. a estas señas. *Address it this way. Write this address.*

Escribir a máquina. *To typewrite.*

escrito adj. *written; m. writing; manuscript; communication.*

Por escrito. *In writing. In black and white.*

escritor m. *writer, author.*

escritorio m. *writing desk.*

escritura f. *writing; deed.*

Escritura social. *Deed of a partnership.*

escrutinio m. *scrutiny; election returns.*

escuadra f. *fleet; squad; square (instrument).*

ESCUCHAR *to listen; to heed.*

Escúcheme Ud. *Listen to me.*

No quiere escuchar razones. *He won't listen to reason.*

ESCUELA f. *school; schoolhouse.*

escupir *to spit.*

"Prohibido escupir." *"No spitting."*

escurrir *to drain; to wring; to slip; to glide.*

ese f. *name of the letter s.*

ESE (*demonstrative adjective m.*) *that; pl.* esos *those.*

Ese hombre. *That man.*

Esos hombres. *Those men.*

ÉSE (*demonstrative pronoun m.*) *that, that one, that person, that thing; pl.* ésos *those.*

Dígale a ése que no venga. *Tell that man not to come.*

Ésos no saben lo que dicen. *Those men don't know what they're talking about.*

Ése ya es otro cantar. *That's a different matter. That's something else (again).*

esencia f. *essence.*

esencial adj. *essential.*

esfera f. *sphere.*

esforzar *to strengthen; to force, to strain.*

esforzarse *to try hard, to endeavor, to strive, to make an effort.*

esfuerzo m. *effort; endeavor.*

Es inútil hacer mayores esfuerzos. *It's useless to continue trying ("to make further efforts").*

esgrima f. *fencing.*

eslabón m. *link (of a chain).*

esmalte m. *enamel.*

esmaltar *to enamel.*

esmeradamente *with the greatest care; nicely.*

esmerado adj. *done with care, carefully done.*

esmeralda f. *emerald.*

esmerar *to polish.*

esmerarse *to do one's best.*

Se esmera en todo. *She tries her hardest in everything (she does).*

esmeril m. *emery.*

ESO (*neuter of* ese *and* ése) *it; that, that thing.*

Eso es. *That's it.*

No es eso. *That's not it.*

Eso de. *That matter of.*

A eso de. *At about. Towards.*

Por eso. *Therefore. For that reason.*

¿Cómo es eso? *How's that?*

Éso no me gusta. *I don't like that.*

Éso no me importa. *That makes no difference to me. That doesn't matter to me.*

ESPACIO m. *space, room; distance.*

Un pequeño espacio de terreno. *A small piece of land.*

Anduvimos por espacio de dos horas. *We walked for two hours.*

espada f. *sword; spade (cards); m. bullfighter who uses a sword, matador.*

ESPALDA f. *back.*

¿Siente Ud. dolor en la espalda? *Does your back ache?*

A espaldas. *Behind one's back.*

Dar la espalda. *To turn one's back.*

espantar *to frighten; to chase out.*

espantarse *to be frightened.*

espanto m. *fright.*

espantosamente *frightfully.*

espantoso adj. *frightful.*

España f. Spain.
español adj. and n. Spanish; Spaniard; m. Spanish language.
   Yo soy español. I'm a Spaniard.
   Aquí se habla español. Spanish spoken here.
esparadrapo m. adhesive tape.
esparcir to scatter; to divulge, to make public.
especial adj. special, particular.
   En especial. Especially. Specially. In particular.
especialidad f. specialty.
especie f. species; motive; kind, sort.
espectáculo m. spectacle, show.
espectador m. spectator.
especulación f. speculation.
especular to speculate.
espejo m. looking glass, mirror.
   Mírese Ud. al espejo. Look at yourself in the mirror.
espera f. waiting; pause; adjournment.
   ¿Dónde está la sala de espera? Where's the waiting room?
esperanza f. hope.
ESPERAR to hope; to expect, to wait for.
   Así lo espero. I hope so.
   Espero que no. I hope not.
   Espéreme. Wait for me.
   Dígale que espere. Ask him to wait.
   ¿Espera Ud. visitas? Do you expect company?
   Espero volver a verle. I hope I'll see you again.
espeso adj. thick, dense.
espía m. and f. spy.
espiga f. ear (of corn, wheat, etc.); peg.
espina f. thorn; splinter; fishbone; spine.
espinaca f. spinach.
espíritu m. spirit, soul.
espiritual adj. spiritual.
espléndido adj. splendid, magnificent; brilliant.
esplendor m. splendor, magnificence.
ESPOSA f. wife.
esposas f. pl. handcuffs.
ESPOSO m. husband.
espuela f. spur; incentive.
espuma f. foam, froth.
esquela f. note, slip of paper.
esquí m. ski.
ESQUINA f. corner.
   La farmacia de la esquina. The drugstore on the corner.
   Doblar la esquina. To turn the corner.
   A la vuelta de la esquina. Around the corner.
ESTA (f. of este) this; pl. estas these.
   Esta mujer y aquel hombre son hermanos. This woman and that man are brother and sister.
   ¿De quién es esta casa? Whose house is this?
   Hágalo de esta manera. Do it this way. Do it in this manner.
   Esta mañana. This morning.
   Esta noche. Tonight.

   A estas horas. At the present time. By now.
ÉSTA (f. of éste) this, this one, the latter; pl. éstas these.
   En ésta no hay novedad. There's nothing new here.
   Ésta y aquélla. This one and that one.
establecer to establish.
establecerse to establish oneself, to set up in business.
   Un nuevo médico acaba de establecerse en esta calle. A new doctor has just opened his office ("established himself") on this street.
   Esto es lo que establece la ley. This is what the law provides.
establo m. stable.
ESTACIÓN f. station; railroad station; season of the year.
   ¿Dónde está la estación? Where is the station?
   El invierno es la estación más fría del año. Winter is the coldest season of the year.
estacionamiento m. parking.
estacionar to stop; to park.
ESTADO m. state; condition.
   ¿Cómo sigue el estado del enfermo? How is the patient's condition?
   En buen estado. In good condition.
   Estado de cuenta. Statement (of an account).
   Hombre de estado. Statesman.
   Ministerio de Estado. State Department.
   Estado Mayor. General Staff.
   Estado de guerra. State of war.
   Estados Unidos de América m. pl. United States of America.
estafa f. fraud, trick, swindle.
estampa f. picture; print; stamp.
estampilla f. postage stamp (Amer.).
estancia f. stay; ranch (in Latin America).
estanco adj. tight, water-tight; m. cigar store (Spain); monopoly.
estanque m. pond; reservoir.
estante m. shelf.
   Estante para libros. Bookcase.
estaño m. tin (metal).
ESTAR to be.
   ¿Cómo está Ud? How are you?
   Estoy bien, gracias. I'm well, thank you.
   Estoy cansado. I'm tired.
   Estamos listos. We're ready.
   ¿Qué está haciendo? What are you doing?
   Estoy afeitándome. I'm shaving.
   ¿Dónde está Juan? Where's John?
   Está en la oficina. He's at the office.
   He estado en Washington. I've been in Washington.
   ¿Dónde está el correo? Where's the post office?
   Está cerca. It's near.
   Está en la calle de Alcalá. It's on Alcala Street.
   Boston está en los Estados Unidos. Boston is in

the United States.

Hay que estar allí a las nueve. *We must be there at nine.*

Estaré de vuelta a las cinco. *I'll be back at five o'clock.*

¿A cuánto estamos? *What's the date?*

Hoy estamos a diez. *Today's the tenth.*

La ventana está abierta. *The window's open.*

Está muy nublado. *It's very cloudy.*

Estar de viaje. *To be on a journey.*

Estar de prisa. *To be in a hurry.*

Estar de pie. *To stand. To be on one's feet.*

estatua *f. statue.*

estatura *f. stature, height of a person.*

estatuto *m. statute, law, by-law.*

ESTE *m. east.*

Esa calle está al este de la ciudad. *This street is on the east side of the city.*

ESTE *(demonstrative adj. m.) this; pl. estos these.*

Este hombre. *This man.*

Estos libros. *These books.*

ÉSTE *(demonstrative pron. m.) this, this one; pl. éstos these.*

Éste es el mío y aquél es el tuyo. *This one is mine and that one is yours.*

Éstos y aquéllos. *These and those.*

Éstos no saben lo que dicen. *These men don't know what they're talking about.*

estenógrafa *f. stenographer.*

estibador *m. stevedore, longshoreman.*

estilar *to be customary, to be in the habit of.*

estilarse *to be in style.*

Ese modelo ya no se estila. *That model is not worn any more (is not in style any longer).*

ESTILO *m. style, manner; method, way.*

Por el estilo. *Of the kind. Like that. In that manner.*

Y así por el estilo. *And so forth.*

estilográfica *f. fountain pen.*

estima *f. esteem, respect; dead reckoning (navigation).*

estimación *f. estimation, valuation.*

estimar *to esteem; to estimate.*

Era muy estimado de cuantos le conocían. *He was held in esteem by all who knew him.*

Se estima que este trabajo costará mil dólares. *It's estimated that this work will cost a thousand dollars.*

estimular *to stimulate.*

estímulo *m. stimulus.*

estirar *to stretch; to pull.*

estirarse *to stretch, to put on airs.*

estirpe *f. race, stock, origin.*

ESTO *(neuter) this; this thing.*

¿Qué es esto? *What's this?*

¿Para qué sirve esto? *What's this for?*

Esto es mío. *This belongs to me.*

Todo esto es muy divertido. *All this is very amusing.*

Esto es todo cuanto tengo que decir. *This is all I have to say.*

Por esto. *For this. Hereby. Therefore. For this reason. On account of this.*

En esto. *At this time. At this juncture.*

Con esto. *Herewith.*

Esto es. *That is. Namely.*

estocada *f. stab, thrust.*

estofado *m. stew; stewed meat.*

estorbar *to hinder, to be in the way.*

¿Le estorba a Ud. esta maleta? *Is this suitcase in your way?*

estómago *m. stomach.*

estornudar *to sneeze.*

estornudo *m. sneeze.*

estrategia *f. strategy.*

estratégico *adj. strategic.*

estrechar *to tighten; to narrow; to squeeze.*

Estrechar la mano. *To shake hands.*

estrechez *f. tightness, narrowness.*

estrecho *adj. tight, narrow.*

estrella *f. star.*

estrellar *to dash, to hurl, to shatter; to fry (eggs).*

Por poco nos estrellamos. *We had a narrow escape.*

¿Quiere los huevos estrellados? *Do you want your eggs fried?*

estremecer *to shake, to tremble.*

estremecerse *to shudder, to tremble, to shake.*

estremecimiento *m. tremor; shudder; trembling; shaking; thrill.*

estrenar *to wear or put on something for the first time; to show for the first time.*

Estrené este traje ayer. *I wore this suit for the first time yesterday.*

estrenarse *to appear for the first time, to make one's debut.*

estreno *m. première, first public performance.*

estreñimiento *m. constipation.*

estribo *m. stirrup; running board.*

Perder los estribos. *To lose one's temper.*

estricto *adj. strict.*

estropear *to ruin, to damage, to spoil.*

estructura *f. structure.*

estruendo *m. loud noise, din, clatter; turmoil; ostentation.*

estrujar *to squeeze, to press.*

estuche *m. case, small box, kit; sheath.*

estudiante *m. and f. student.*

ESTUDIAR *to study.*

ESTUDIO *m. study; examination; consideration; survey; office; studio.*

Están haciendo un estudio de la situación. *They're making a survey of the situation.*

Estar en estudio. *To be under consideration (study).*

El estudio del profesor. *The professor's office*

(study).

El estudio del pintor. *The painter's studio.*

estudioso *adj. studious.*

estufa *f. stove; heater.*

Arrímese a la estufa. *Draw up (come closer) to the stove.*

estupendo *adj. stupendous, wonderful, terrific, great.*

estupidez *f. stupidity.*

estúpido *adj. stupid.*

etapa *f. daily ration, a day's march; stage, halt, stop.*

etcétera *f. et cetera.*

éter *m. ether.*

eternidad *f. eternity.*

eterno *adj. eternal, everlasting, endless.*

ética *f. ethics.*

ético *adj. ethical, moral.*

etiqueta *f. etiquette; label.*

Vestido de etiqueta. *Evening dress.*

¿Qué dice la etiqueta de la botella? *What does the label on the bottle say?*

evacuación *f. evacuation.*

evacuar *to evacuate; to quit; to vacate; to dispose of.*

evadir *to evade; to avoid.*

evaluación *f. evaluation.*

evaluar *to appraise, to value.*

evalúo *m. appraisal.*

evangelio *m. gospel.*

evaporar *to evaporate.*

evasión *f. evasion, escape.*

evasiva *f. pretext, excuse; subterfuge.*

evasivo *adj. evasive.*

evento *m. event.*

eventual *adj. eventual.*

evidencia *f. evidence.*

Poner en evidencia. *To make evident (clear, obvious). To make conspicuous. To display, reveal, show. To demonstrate.*

evidente *adj. evident.*

evitable *adj. avoidable.*

EVITAR *to avoid; to spare.*

Evitar un disgusto. *To avoid an unpleasant situation.*

evocar *to evoke.*

evolución *f. evolution.*

exactamente *exactly.*

exactitud *f. accuracy.*

EXACTO *adj. exact, just, accurate, correct.*

exageración *f. exaggeration.*

exagerar *to exaggerate.*

exaltación *f. exaltation.*

exaltar *to exalt, to praise.*

exaltarse *to become excited.*

examen *m. examination; test.*

EXAMINAR *to examine, to investigate, to look into, to study.*

exasperación *f. exasperation.*

exasperar *to exasperate.*

excedente *adj. excessive.*

exceder *to exceed.*

excederse *to overstep, to go too far.*

excelencia *f. excellence.*

EXCELENTE *adj. excellent.*

excelso *adj. lofty, exalted.*

excepción *f. exception.*

excepcional *adj. exceptional, unusual.*

excepto *except that, excepting.*

exceptuar *to except, to exempt.*

excesivo *adj. excessive, too much.*

exceso *m. excess, surplus.*

En exceso. *In excess.*

Exceso de equipaje. *Excess luggage.*

excitable *adj. excitable.*

excitación *f. excitement.*

excitante *adj. exciting.*

excitar *to excite, to stir up.*

exclamación *f. exclamation.*

exclamar *to exclaim.*

excluir *to exclude, to keep out; to rule out.*

exclusión *f. exclusion.*

exclusiva *f. exclusive (right); refusal, rejection.*

exclusivamente *exclusively.*

exclusive *exclusively.*

excursión *f. excursion, trip.*

excusa *f. excuse, apology.*

excusable *adj. excusable.*

excusado *adj. excused, exempted; m. toilet.*

excusar *to excuse; to apologize; to exempt.*

Excusamos decir. *It's needless to say.*

Excusarse de. *To apologize for.*

exención *f. exemption.*

exento *adj. exempt, free; duty free.*

Estar exento de. *To be exempt from. To be free from.*

exhalar *to exhale.*

exhibición *f. exhibition.*

exhibir *to exhibit.*

exhortar *to exhort, to admonish.*

exigencia *f. urgent need; demand for immediate action or attention, exigency.*

exigente *adj. demanding, hard to please.*

Es muy exigente. *He's a very hard person to please.*

No seas tan exigente. *Don't be so difficult (demanding, hard to please, particular).*

exigir *to demand; to require; to exact.*

Lo exigen las circunstancias. *The situation requires it.*

exiguo *adj. small, scanty, exiguous.*

eximir *to exempt, to excuse.*

existencia *f. existence; stock, supply.*

En existencia. *In stock.*

Agotarse las existencias. *To be out of stock.*

existente *adj. existing, existent.*

EXISTIR *to exist, to be.*
En mi opinión existen pruebas bastante claras de ello. *There are, it seems to me, pretty strong proofs of it.*

ÉXITO *m. end, outcome; success.*
Buen éxito. *Success.*
Le felicito por el éxito obtenido. *I congratulate you on your success.*

expedición *f. expedition; shipment.*
Gastos de expedición. *Shipping expenses.*

expedidor *m. dispatcher, sender.*

expediente *m. expedient; document, dossier; proceedings.*
Incoar expediente. *To start proceedings.*

EXPEDIR *to expedite; to dispatch, to send, to forward; to issue; to make out (a check, etc.).*

expeler *to expel.*

expendedor *m. dealer, retailer, seller.*

expensas *f. pl. expenses, charges, costs.*
A expensas de. *At the expense of.*

experiencia *f. experience; trial.*

experimentar *to experience; to experiment.*

experimento *m. experiment.*

experto *adj. experienced; able; m. expert.*

explicable *adj. explainable.*

explicación *f. explanation.*

EXPLICAR *to explain.*
Déjeme Ud. que se lo explique. *Let me explain it to you.*

explicarse *to explain oneself; to account for.*
No podemos explicárnoslo. *We can't make it out (account for it).*

explicativo *adj. explanatory.*

explícito *adj. explicit.*

exploración *f. exploration.*

explorador *m. explorer, scout.*

explorar *to explore.*

explosión *f. explosion, outburst.*
Hacer explosión. *To explode.*

explotar *to exploit; to operate; to profiteer.*

exponente *m. and f. exponent.*

exponer *to expound, to explain; to make clear; to expose.*

exponerse *to expose oneself; to run a risk.*

exportación *f. export.*

exportador *adj. exporting; m. exporter.*
Casa exportadora. *Export house (firm).*

exportar *to export.*

exposición *f. exposition, show, exhibition; explanation; peril, risk, exposure; statement.*

expositor *m. exhibitor; expounder, expositor.*

expresar *to express; to set forth, to state.*

expresarse *to express oneself.*

expresión *f. expression.*

expresivo *adj. expressive.*

expreso *adj. express; clear; m. express (train); special delivery.*

exprimidor *m. squeezer; wringer.*

exprimir *to squeeze.*
Exprimir un limón. *To squeeze a lemon.*

expuesto *adj. explained, stated; exposed (to); liable (to).*
Lo expuesto. *What has been stated.*
Todos estamos expuestos a equivocarnos. *Anyone is liable (apt) to make a mistake.*

expulsar *to expel, to eject, to throw out.*

expulsión *f. expulsion.*

exquisito *adj. exquisite, excellent, choice.*

extender *to extend, to stretch out; to make out (a check, a document).*

extensión *f. extension, extent.*
En toda su extensión. *To the full extent. In every sense.*

extensivo *adj. extensive, ample, far-reaching.*

extenso *adj. extensive, vast.*

extenuación *f. extenuation.*

extenuar *to extenuate.*

exterior *adj. exterior; foreign.*
Comercio exterior. *Foreign trade.*

externo *adj. external, on the outside.*

extinguir *to extinguish; to put out.*

extra *extra.*

extractar *to extract, to abridge, to summarize.*

extracto *m. extract, abridgment, summary.*

extraer *to extract, to pull out.*

EXTRANJERO *adj. foreign; m. foreigner, alien.*
Estar en el extranjero. *To be abroad.*
Ir al extranjero. *To go abroad.*

extrañar *to wonder at, to find strange.*
No es de extrañar que. *It's not surprising that.*

extrañarse *to be surprised.*
Me extraña su conducta. *I'm surprised at his behavior.*

extrañeza *f. wonder, surprise.*

extraño *strange, rare, odd, queer.*
Es un hombre extraño. *He's a queer fellow.*

extraoficial *adj. unofficial, off the record.*

extraordinario *adj. extraordinary.*
Tiene una memoria extraordinaria. *He has an extraordinary memory.*

extravagancia *f. folly; extravagance.*

extravagante *adj. queer, extravagant.*

extraviado *adj. astray; missing; mislaid.*

extraviar *to mislead; to mislay.*

extraviarse *to go astray; to get lost.*

extravío *m. straying; deviation, misplacement; misguidance.*

extremadamente *extremely, exceedingly.*

extremar *to go to extremes.*

extremarse *to exert oneself to the utmost.*

extremidad *f. extremity; very end.*

extremo *adj. and n. extreme, last, very end.*
En caso extremo. *As a last resort.*
Al extremo de que. *To such an extent that.*
De extremo a extremo. *From end to end.*
En extremo (Por extremo). *Extremely.*

F

fa m. *fa, F (fourth note in the musical scale).*
fabada f. *dish of pork and beans.*
fábrica f. *factory, mill, plant; fabrication; structure, building.*
  Precio de fábrica. *Factory price.*
  Marca de fábrica. *Trade mark.*
fabricación f. *manufacturing.*
fabricante m. *manufacturer.*
fabricar *to manufacture, to make; to build.*
fábula f. *fable, story, tale.*
fabuloso adj. *fabulous; incredible.*
FÁCIL adj. *easy.*
  Parece fácil pero es difícil. *It looks easy but it's difficult.*
  Es la cosa más fácil del mundo. *It's the easiest thing in the world.*
  Nada hay más fácil que eso. *Nothing could be easier than that.*
facilidad f. *ease, facility.*
  Con facilidad. *Easily. With ease.*
  Facilidad de pagos. *Easy terms. Easy payments.*
facilitar *to facilitate, to make easy; to supply, to provide.*
  Facilitar dinero. *To supply (provide) money.*
fácilmente *easily.*
  A mí no se me engaña tan fácilmente. *You can't fool me that easily.*
  No puedo expresarme fácilmente. *I can't express myself easily.*
factor m. *factor, element; agent; baggage master.*
factura f. *invoice, bill.*
  ¿A cuánto monta la factura? *What does the bill amount to?*
  La factura sube a mil pesetas. *The invoice amounts to one thousand pesetas.*
facturar *to bill, to invoice; to check (baggage).*
  Tendrá que facturar el baúl. *You'll have to check the trunk.*
facultad f. *faculty.*
facultar *to authorize, to empower.*
facultativo adj. *optional; m. physician.*
facha f. *appearance, look.*
fachada f. *façade; bearing (of a person).*
faena f. *work, task, labor.*
faja f. *band; girdle.*
fajar *to swaddle; to girdle.*
fajo m. *bundle; roll (bills).*
falda f. *skirt; the lap; slope (of a hill).*
falsear *to falsify; to forge, to distort, to adulterate.*
falsedad f. *falsehood, untruth.*
falsificación f. *falsification; forgery.*
falso adj. *false; incorrect; deceitful; counterfeit.*
  Esta noticia es falsa. *This news is false.*
  Me han dado una moneda falsa. *They've given me a counterfeit coin.*
FALTA f. *fault; defect; need; lack; absence, mistake.*

Tenemos que disculpar sus faltas. *We must excuse his faults.*
  Yo le corregiré las faltas. *I'll correct the mistakes.*
  Hacer falta. *To be needed. To be necessary.*
  ¿Qué le hace falta? *What do you need?*
  No hace falta. *It's not necessary. It's not needed.*
  Sin falta. *Without fail.*
  Tener falta de. *To be in need of.*
  Por falta de. *For lack of. Owing to the shortage of.*
  Falta de pago. *Non-payment.*
FALTAR *to be lacking; to be absent; to miss (classes); to fail; not to fulfill one's promise; to offend, to be rude.*
  Aquí faltan tres libros. *Three books are missing here.*
  Ud. faltó a su palabra. *You didn't keep your word.*
  Faltó a la oficina esta mañana. *He wasn't (present) at the office this morning.*
  Faltó a su padre. *He was rude to his father.*
  No faltes a clase. *Don't miss school.*
  Faltar a la verdad. *To lie.*
  No faltaba más. *That's the last straw.*
falto adj. *wanting, lacking, short of.*
  Estar falto de. *To be short of.*
  Falto de peso. *Underweight. Lacking the proper weight.*
falla f. *failure; fault.*
fallar *to deliver a verdict, pronounce a sentence; to fail.*
fallecer *to die.*
  Falleció repentinamente. *He died suddenly.*
fallo m. *sentence, verdict, judgment, finding, decision.*
  El juez dió el fallo. *The judge gave the verdict.*
fama f. *fame; reputation; rumor.*
FAMILIA f. *family; household.*
familiar adj. *familiar; m. close friend, relative.*
famoso adj. *famous; excellent.*
fanático adj. *fanatic.*
fanfarrón adj. *boasting; m. bully, boaster, braggart.*
fanfarronada f. *boast, bragging, bluff.*
fanfarronear *to boast, to brag.*
fango m. *mire, mud.*
fangoso adj. *muddy.*
fantasía f. *fantasy, fancy.*
fantasma m. *phantom; scarecrow; ghost.*
fantástico adj. *fantastic.*
fantoche m. *puppet; ridiculous fellow.*
fardo m. *bale of goods, parcel, bundle.*
faringe f. *pharynx.*
farmacéutico m. *pharmacist, druggist.*
farmacia f. *pharmacy, drugstore.*
faro m. *lighthouse; beacon; headlight.*
farol m. *lantern; street lamp; light.*
  Farol delantero. *Headlight.*

Farol trasero (de cola). *Taillight.*

farolero *adj. conceited, showing-off; m. a lamp-lighter.*

farsa *f. farce.*

farsante *adj. and n. impostor.*

fascinar *to fascinate, to charm; to allure.*

fase *f. phase; aspect.*

fastidiar *to annoy, to disgust.*

fastidio *m. disgust, annoyance; boredom.*

fastidioso *adj. squeamish; annoying, disgusting; tiresome.*

fatal *adj. fatal.*

fatiga *f. tiredness, fatigue, weariness, toil.*

fatigado *adj. tired, fatigued.*

fatigar *to tire; to annoy.*

fatigoso *adj. tiring; tiresome.*

fatuo *adj. fatuous, stupid, silly.*

fauna *f. fauna.*

fausto *adj. happy, fortunate; m. splendor.*

FAVOR *m. favor, good turn, service; good graces.*

Me hace Ud. un gran favor. *You're doing me a great favor (service).*

¡Es mucho favor que me hace! *You're flattering me!*

Por favor. *Please.*

Me hace Ud. el favor. *Please. If you please.*

Hágame Ud. el favor de. *Please ("Do me the favor of").*

Hágame el favor de ir con él. *Please go with him.*

Haga el favor de pasarme la sal. *Please pass me the salt.*

Haga el favor de indicarme el camino. *Please show me the way.*

Por favor, póngame en comunicación con el número . . . *Please connect me with number . . .*

Haga el favor de repetir lo que dijo. *Please repeat what you said.*

A favor de. *In favor of.*

favorable *adj. favorable.*

favorecer *to favor; to help.*

favorito *adj. favorite.*

faz *f. face, front.*

FE *f. faith; credit.*

Lo hizo de buena fe. *He did it in good faith.*

Lo dijo de mala fe. *He said it deceitfully.*

La fe católica. *The Catholic religion.*

La fe de bautismo. *Birth certificate.*

Dar fe. *To attest. To certify. To give credit.*

A fe mía. *Upon my word.*

FEBRERO *m. February.*

fecundo *adj. fruitful, productive, fecund, fertile, prolific.*

FECHA *f. date.*

¿Qué fecha es hoy? *What's the date today? What's today's date?*

¿En qué fecha estamos? *What day of the month is it?*

Hasta la fecha. *To date. Up to today.*

Para estas fechas. *By this time.*

A dos meses de la fecha. *Two months from today.*

fechar *to date (a letter).*

La carta está fechada el seis del corriente. *The letter is dated the sixth of this month.*

fechoría *f. misdeed, a wicked action.*

federación *f. federation.*

felicidad *f. happiness.*

¡Muchas felicidades! *Congratulations!*

felicitación *f. congratulation.*

felicitar *to congratulate, to felicitate.*

Le felicito a Ud. *Congratulations! ("I congratulate you.")*

FELIZ *adj. happy, fortunate.*

¡Feliz año nuevo! *Happy New Year!*

¡Feliz cumpleaños! *Happy birthday. Many happy returns of the day.*

¡Que las tenga Ud. muy felices! *Many happy returns of the day.*

Fué el día más feliz de mi vida. *It was the happiest day of my life.*

Vivían felices. *They lived happily.*

Feliz idea. *Clever (happy) idea.*

femenino *adj. feminine.*

fémur *m. femur, thigh bone.*

fenómeno *m. phenomenon.*

feo *adj. ugly, unpleasant.*

feria *f. fair, show.*

feriado *adj. relating to a holiday.*

Día feriado. *Holiday.*

fermentación *f. fermentation.*

fermentar *to ferment.*

fermento *m. ferment; leaven.*

feroz *adj. ferocious, fierce, cruel.*

férreo *adj. iron, ferrous.*

ferretería *f. hardware; hardware store.*

ferrocarril *m. railway, railroad.*

Por ferrocarril. *By railway.*

fértil *adj. fertile, fruitful.*

fervor *m. fervor, zeal.*

festejar *to celebrate.*

festividad *f. festivity; holiday.*

festivo *adj. festive, gay, merry.*

Día festivo. *Holiday.*

fiado *adj. on credit.*

Comprar al fiado. *To buy on credit.*

Dar fiado. *To give credit. To sell on credit.*

Se lo podemos dar fiado. *We can let you have it on credit.*

fiador *m. guarantor; stop, catch.*

fiambre *m. cold meat, cold cuts, cold lunch.*

fianza *f. guarantee, security, bail, bond.*

fiar *to trust, to confide; to sell on credit.*

Se lo puedo fiar. *I can sell it to you on credit.*

No me fío de él. *I don't trust him.*

Puede Ud. fiarse de su palabra. *You may rely*

(depend) on his word.

fibra *f. fiber.*

ficha *f. chip (used in games); card, token.*

fideo *m. vermicelli, noodle.*

fiebre *f. fever; rush, excitement.*

fiel *adj. faithful, loyal; true, right; m. pointer, needle (of a balance, scale).*

fiera *f. wild beast.*

fiero *adj. fierce, cruel.*

fierro *m. iron (Amer.).*

FIESTA *f. feast, party; holiday.*

¡Qué fiesta más agradable! *What a lovely party!*

Mañana es día de fiesta. *Tomorrow is a holiday.*

figura *f. figure, form, appearance, image.*

Tiene muy linda figura. *She has a nice figure.*

figurar *to figure; to appear.*

No figura en la lista de invitados. *His name was not on the guest list.*

figurarse *to imagine, to fancy.*

¡Figúrese! *Just imagine!*

figurín *m. costume; (fig) elegant person.*

fijar *to fix, set (a date); to post (a notice).*

"Prohibido fijar carteles." *"Post no bills."*

fijarse *to look at, to take notice, to pay attention to.*

Fíjese en la hora. *Look at the time. Look what time it is! Watch the time!*

¿Por qué no se fija Ud. mejor en lo que hace? *Why don't you pay more attention to what you're doing?*

fijo *adj. fixed, firm, fast; permanent.*

Precio fijo. *Fixed price.*

fila *f. row, line, rank.*

En fila. *In line. In a row.*

Una fila de sillas. *A row of chairs.*

filete *m. fillet, hem; tenderloin, filet mignon.*

filiación *f. relationship; file, record, description (of a person).*

filial *adj. filial; f. branch.*

film *m. film, picture, movie.*

filmadora *m. movie camera.*

filmar *to film, to make a moving picture.*

filosofía *f. philosophy.*

filósofo *m. philosopher.*

filtrar *to filter, to strain.*

filtrarse *to leak out, to leak through.*

filtro *m. filter.*

FIN *m. end; object, aim, purpose.*

A fin de mes. *At the end of the month.*

A fines de año. *In the latter part of the year. Towards the end of the year.*

Dar fin a. *To finish.*

Por fin. *Finally.*

Al fin. *At last.*

Sin fin. *Endless.*

Al fin y al cabo. *At last. In the end. At length. After all. In the long run.*

Con el fin de. *For the purpose of. With the ob-ject of.*

A fin de. *In order that.*

Con este fin. *To this end. With this end (purpose) in view.*

finado *m. deceased, late.*

FINAL *adj. final, last; m. end; pl. finals (in a contest).*

La letra final de una palabra. *The last letter of a word.*

Punto final. *Period. Full stop.*

Al final. *At the end. At the foot (of a page).*

Al final de la calle. *At the end of the street.*

El final de la línea. *The end of the line (street-car, bus, etc.).*

Final de trayecto. *Last stop.*

finalizar *to finish; to conclude, to expire.*

Al finalizar el contrato. *When the contract ex-pires.*

FINALMENTE *finally, at last.*

financiero *adj. financial; m. financier.*

finca *f. farm; real estate, property.*

fineza *f. fineness; delicacy; courtesy.*

fingir *to feign, to pretend.*

fino *adj. fine, delicate; cunning, keen; polite.*

Esta es una tela muy fina. *This is a very fine material.*

Es un niño muy fino. *He's a very polite boy.*

FIRMA *f. signature; firm; business concern.*

Trabaja con una firma norteamericana. *He works for a North American firm.*

El documento es nulo si no lleva la firma del cónsul. *The document isn't valid without the consul's signature.*

firmar *to sign.*

firme *adj. firm, fast, stable, secure, resolute.*

Mantenerse firme. *To stand one's ground.*

Color firme. *Fast color.*

fiscal *adj. fiscal; m. public prosecutor.*

física *f. physics.*

físico *adj. physical, m. physicist, face; physique.*

Tiene un defecto físico. *He has a physical de-fect.*

fisiología *f. physiology.*

fisonomía *f. features, physiognomy.*

flaco *adj. lean, thin, weak; m. weak point.*

flagrante *adj. flagrant.*

En flagrante. *In the very act. Red-handed.*

flamear *to flame; to flutter (flag).*

flan *m. custard.*

flaqueza *f. weakness, feebleness.*

flauta *f. flute.*

fleco *m. fringe, purl; bang (hair) (Mex.).*

flecha *f. arrow, dart.*

fletar *to charter (a ship, etc.).*

flete *m. freight, freightage.*

flexible *adj. flexible, pliable; docile.*

flirtear *to flirt.*

flojo *adj. lax, slack, lazy; loose; not tight; light.*

Es un hombre flojo. *He's a lazy man.*
La cuerda está floja. *The string's loose.*
Vino flojo. *Light wine.*
flor *f. flower.*
    ¿Cómo se llama esta flor? *What's the name of this flower?*
    Estar en flor. *To be in blossom.*
    Echar (decir) flores. *To flatter (a woman).*
florecer *to blossom; to bloom.*
florero *m. flower vase, flower stand.*
florista *m. and f. florist.*
flota *f. fleet.*
flote *m. floating.*
    A flote. *Afloat.*
    Sostenerse a flote. *To keep afloat.*
flúido *adj. fluid, fluent; m. fluid.*
foca *f. seal.*
foco *m. focus.*
fogón *m. fireplace; cooking stove.*
fogonazo *m. flash (of a gun).*
fogoso *adj. fiery, impetuous.*
folio *m. leaf of a book, folio.*
folklore *m. folklore.*
folletín *m. feuilleton, a novel in installments, serial story in a newspaper.*
folleto *m. pamphlet.*
fomenta *to foment, to encourage.*
fonda *f. inn, hotel, boarding house.*
fondear *to cast anchor.*
FONDO *m. bottom; background; fund.*
    Artículo de fondo. *Editorial.*
    En el fondo del pozo. *At the bottom of the well.*
    Los dibujos son de color pero el fondo es blanco. *The designs are in color (are colored) but the background is white.*
    Conocer a fondo. *To know well. To be thoroughly acquainted with.*
    En el fondo. *At heart. At bottom. Basically. As a matter of fact.*
    Irse a fondo. *To sink. To go to the bottom.*
    Fondos de reserva. *Reserve funds.*
fonética *f. phonetics.*
fonógrafo *m. phonograph.*
forastero *adj. foreign, strange; m. stranger, foreigner.*
forjar *to forge; to frame.*
FORMA *f. form, shape; mold; manner, way.*
    La forma de esta caja es interesante. *The shape of this box is interesting.*
    No hay forma de hacerlo. *There's no way of doing it.*
    ¿De qué forma se gana la vida? *How does he make a living?*
    En forma de. *In the shape of.*
    En forma. *In due form.*
    De forma que. *In order that. In such a manner that.*
formación *f. formation.*
formal *adj. formal, proper, serious.*

formalidad *f. formality.*
formar *to form; to shape.*
    La parada se formará a las doce. *The parade will form at twelve o'clock.*
    Formaron una sociedad. *They formed a society.*
formarse *to take form, to develop, to grow.*
    Formarse una idea. *To get an idea.*
formidable *adj. formidable.*
fórmula *f. formula; recipe.*
formular *to formulate.*
formulario *m. formulary; form, blank.*
    Llene este formulario. *Fill out this application blank.*
forrar *to line (clothes, etc.); to cover (books).*
    El abrigo está forrado por dentro. *The coat is lined inside.*
fortalecer *to fortify, to strengthen.*
fortaleza *f. fortress, stronghold; strength, fortitude.*
fortificación *f. fortification.*
fortificar *to fortify, to strengthen.*
fortitud *f. strength, fortitude.*
fortuito *adj. fortuitous, accidental.*
    Un caso fortuito. *An accident.*
fortuna *f. fortune.*
    Por fortuna. *Fortunately.*
forzar *to force, to compel, to oblige.*
forzosamente *necessarily, of necessity.*
forzoso *adj. compulsory, compelling.*
forzudo *adj. strong, robust.*
fosa *f. pit, hole; grave.*
fósforo *m. phosphorus; match (to light with).*
    ¿Tiene Ud. fósforos? *Do you have some matches?*
foto *f. (abbreviation of fotografía) photo, picture.*
    Las fotos salieron bien. *The pictures came out all right.*
fotografía *f. photography; photograph, photo, picture.*
fotografiar *to photograph.*
fotógrafo *m. photographer.*
frac *m. dress coat.*
fracasar *to fail, to come out badly.*
fracaso *m. failure.*
    La función fué un fracaso. *The play was a failure.*
fracción *f. fraction.*
fragancia *f. fragrance, pleasing odor.*
fragante *adj. fragrant.*
frágil *adj. fragile, brittle; weak, frail (morally).*
fragmento *m. fragment.*
fragua *f. forge.*
fraguar *to forge; to scheme, to plot.*
fraile *m. friar.*
frambuesa *f. raspberry.*
francamente *frankly, openly.*
francés *adj. French; m. Frenchman; French language, f. Frenchwoman.*
FRANCO *adj. frank, free, open, plain; m. French*

franc.

Puerto franco. *Free port.*

Franco de porte. *Freight prepaid.*

franela *f. flannel.*

franquear *to put a stamp on a letter, to prepay postage; to clear from obstacle; to free (a slave).*

¿Ha franqueado las cartas? *Did you put stamps on the letters?*

Franquear el paso. *To clear the way.*

franqueo *m. postage.*

franqueza *f. frankness, sincerity.*

Hable con franqueza. *Speak frankly.*

franquicia *f. franchise; exemption from duties (taxes).*

frasco *m. flask, bottle.*

frase *f. sentence.*

Esta frase no está bien escrita. *This sentence isn't well written.*

fraternidad *f. fraternity, brotherhood.*

frazada *f. blanket.*

frecuencia *f. frequency.*

Se veían con frecuencia. *They saw one another frequently.*

frecuentar *to frequent, to visit often.*

Este bar es muy frecuentado por mis amigos. *My friends go to this bar a lot.*

frecuente *adj. frequent.*

frecuentemente *often, frequently.*

fregar *to scrub; to wash dishes; to annoy.*

freír *to fry.*

frejol *m. kidney bean. See frijol.*

FRENAR *to put on the brakes, to slow up or stop by using a brake; to bridle; to curb.*

¡Frene! *Put on the brakes!*

frenético *adj. mad frantic.*

freno *m. brake; bridle, bit, curb.*

Quite el freno. *Release the brake.*

FRENTE *f. forehead; face; m. front; façade.*

En frente. *In front. Opposite. Across the way.*

Estar al frente de. *To be in charge of.*

Hacer frente a. *To face. To cope with.*

Frente a frente. *Face to face.*

fresa *f. strawberry.*

fresco *adj. cool; fresh; recent; bold; forward; m. fresco (painting); fresh air, breeze; a fresh person.*

El agua está fresca. *The water is cool.*

Ese es un fresco. *He's very fresh. He's a very impudent person.*

Tomar el fresco. *To go out for some fresh air.*

Aire fresco. *Fresh air.*

Un fresco agradable. *A nice breeze.*

frescura *f. freshness.*

fricasé *m. fricassee.*

fricción *f. friction, rubbing.*

frijol *m. kidney bean.*

FRÍO *adj. and n. cold.*

Tengo mucho frío. *I'm very cold.*

Hace frío. *It's cold (of the weather).*

Está frío. *It's cold (of an object).*

Sangre fría. *1. Cold blood. 2. Sang-froid. Presence of mind.*

Le mataron a sangre fría. *They killed him in cold blood.*

friolento *adj. allergic to cold.*

friolera *f. trifle.*

fritada *f. dish of fried fish or meat.*

frito *adj. fried.*

frontera *f. frontier, border.*

frontón *m. handball court; the wall of a handball court.*

frotar *to rub.*

fructífero *adj. fruitful.*

fructificar *to bear fruit; to yield profit.*

frugal *adj. frugal, thrifty.*

fruncir *to pleat; to knit (the brows).*

Fruncir las cejas. *To knit one's brows. To frown. To scowl.*

frustrar *to frustrate.*

fruta *f. fruit.*

frutería *f. fruit store.*

frutilla *f. strawberry (Chile, Arg., Peru).*

FUEGO *m. fire.*

No deje apagarse el fuego. *Don't let the fire go out.*

Prender fuego a. *To set fire to.*

Hacer fuego. *To fire (a gun).*

Armas de fuego. *Firearms.*

Fuegos artificiales. *Fireworks.*

FUENTE *f. spring, fountain, source; platter, large shallow dish.*

Lo sé de buena fuente. *I have it from a reliable ("good") source. I have it on good authority.*

FUERA *out, outside.*

Hay más gente fuera que dentro. *There are more people outside than inside.*

¡Fuera! *Get out!*

Estar fuera. *To be absent. To be out.*

Por fuera. *On the outside.*

Hacia fuera. *Outwards. Towards the outside.*

Fuera de eso. *Besides. Moreover. In addition (to that).*

Fuera de sí. *Frantic. Beside oneself.*

FUERTE *adj. strong; powerful; excessive; heavy (meal); loud (voice); deep (breath); hard; violent (quarrel); firm, fast; m. forte, strong point; fort, fortress.*

No hable tan fuerte. *Don't speak so loud.*

Este boxeador es más fuerte que el otro. *This boxer is stronger than the other one.*

Es una tela muy fuerte. *This material is very strong.*

Le pegó muy fuerte. *He hit him very hard.*

Respire Ud. fuerte. *Breathe deeply.*

Hubo un fuerte altercado. *There was a violent*

quarrel.

Comer fuerte. *To eat too much. To have a heavy meal.*

La música es su fuerte. *Music is his forte.*

FUERZA *f. force, strength, power.*

De por fuerza. *Forcibly. Necessarily. By force.*

Por fuerza. *By force.*

A fuerza de. *By dint of.*

A viva fuerza. *By main force.*

A la fuerza. *By sheer force.*

Por fuerza mayor. *Owing to circumstances beyond one's control. Act of God.*

Fuerza motriz. *Motive power.*

Fuerzas armadas. *Armed forces.*

fuga *f. escape; flight.*

Poner en fuga. *To put to flight. To rout.*

fugarse *to escape, to run away, to flee.*

fugaz *adj. short-lived, passing soon, not lasting, transient.*

fugitivo *adj. and n. fugitive.*

FULANO *m. So-and-so, What's-his-name.*

El señor fulano de tal. *Mr. So-and-So. Mr. What's-his-name.*

fumador *m. smoker.*

fumar *to smoke (cigarettes, etc.).*

Se prohibe fumar. *No smoking.*

función *f. function, performance, play.*

funcionar *to function; to work, to run (a machine).*

Esta máquina no funciona. *This machine doesn't work.*

Funcionar bien. *To be in good working condition.*

funcionario *m. official, officer, person who holds a public position.*

funda *f. pillowcase; sheath; case (of a pistol).*

Funda de almohada. *Pillowcase.*

fundación *f. foundation.*

fundador *m. founder.*

fundamental *adj. fundamental.*

fundamento *m. foundation, base, ground, cause.*

Sin fundamento. *Groundless.*

Carecer de fundamento. *To be without foundation, logic or reason.*

fundar *to found, to base.*

Han fundado una nueva sociedad. *They've founded a new society.*

fundarse *to base something on.*

¿En qué funda Ud. sus esperanzas? *On what do you base your hopes?*

fundición *f. foundry, casting, melting.*

fundir *to melt, fuse; to burn out (a bulb).*

fúnebre *adj. mournful, sad.*

funeral *adj. funeral, funereal; m. pl. funeral.*

furgón *m. baggage car; freight car.*

furia *f. fury, rage, fit of madness.*

furioso *adj. furious, mad, frantic.*

furor *m. fury.*

fusible *m. fuse (electricity).*

fusil *m. rifle.*

fusilar *to shoot.*

fútbol *m. football.*

FUTURO *adj. future; m. future; fiancé, husband.*

En un futuro próximo. *In the near future.*

En lo futuro. *In the future.*

Nos presentó a su futuro. *She introduced her fiancé to us.*

G

gabán *m. overcoat.*

gabardina *f. gabardine.*

gabinete *m. cabinet; study, studio, laboratory.*

Gabinete de lectura. *Reading room.*

gaceta *f. gazette, official government journal; newspaper.*

gacetilla *f. a newspaper column, newspaper squib.*

gachas *f. pl. porridge, mush, pap.*

Hacerse unas gachas. *To be very affectionate.*

A gachas. *On all fours.*

gafa *f. grapple hook; spectacles, eyeglasses.*

gaita *f. bagpipe.*

gaitero *m. piper.*

gajo *m. branch of a tree; each section or piece of an orange or lemon; part of a bunch of grapes.*

gala *f. gala occasion, gala affair; full dress.*

De gala. *Full dress.*

Hacer gala de. *To boast of.*

galán *m. leading man (theater); gallant, lover.*

Primer galán. *Leading man.*

galante *adj. gallant; generous.*

galantear *to court, to make love.*

galantería *f. gallantry, politeness and attention to women; elegance; generosity.*

galería *f. gallery.*

gales *m. Prince of Wales pattern.*

galgo *m. greyhound.*

galicismo *m. gallicism.*

galón *m. stripe (on uniform); gallon.*

galopar *to gallop.*

galope *m. gallop.*

galvanizar *to galvanize.*

gallardo *adj. gallant, brave, daring; handsome, spruce.*

galleta *f. cookie, biscuit; hardtack.*

gallina *f. hen; coward.*

Es un gallina. *He's a coward. He's yellow.*

gallinero *m. chicken coop; top gallery (in a theater).*

gallo *m. cock, rooster.*

gamo *m. buck, male of fallow deer.*

gamuza *f. suede, chamois.*

GANA *f. appetite, hunger; desire, inclination, will.*

No tengo ganas de comer ahora. *I'm not hungry now. I don't feel like eating now.*

De buena gana. *Willingly. With pleasure.*

De mala gana. *Unwillingly. Reluctantly.*

Trabajó de mala gana. *He worked unwillingly (against his will, reluctantly).*

Comer con gana. *To eat with an appetite.*

No me da la gana. *I don't want to. I don't feel like. I won't.*

Hace siempre lo que le da la gana. *She always does what she pleases.*

Tener ganas de. *To desire. To want to. To feel like. To have a mind to.*

Dan ganas de. *One feels inclined to. One feels like.*

ganadería f. *cattle raising, cattle ranch; livestock.*

ganadero m. *cattleman, cattle dealer; rancher.*

ganado m. *cattle, livestock.*

ganador m. *winner.*

ganancia f. *gain, profit.*

Ganancias y pérdidas. *Profit and loss.*

Sacar ganancia. *To make a profit.*

GANAR *to gain; to earn; to win; to reach.*

¿Cuánto quiere Ud. ganar? *What salary do you want?* ("How much do you want to earn?")

Le gané la apuesta. *I won the bet from him.*

Ganaron por dos tantos a cero. *They won two to nothing.*

No es capaz de ganarse la vida (ganarse el pan). *He's not capable of earning his living.*

El prófugo ganó la frontera en pocas horas. *The fugitive reached the border in a few hours.*

gancho m. *hook; hairpin; clip.*

gandul m. *tramp, loafer, vagabond.*

ganga f. *bargain; bargain sale.*

A precio de ganga. *At a bargain price.*

gangoso adj. *snuffling, speaking through the nose or with a nasal tone.*

ganso m. *gander, goose; a slow (clumsy) person; a simpleton.*

Hacer el ganso. *To try to be funny.*

Hablar por boca de ganso. *To be like a parrot. To repeat mechanically what other people say.*

ganzúa f. *picklock, skeleton key; thief, burglar.*

garaje m. *garage.*

¿Me puede decir dónde hay un garaje cerca? *Can you please tell me where there's a garage near here?*

garantía f. *guarantee; guaranty, bond.*

garantizar *to vouch, to guarantee.*

gardenia f. *gardenia.*

garganta f. *throat; neck; gorge; instep.*

Tengo dolor de garganta. *I have a sore throat.*

Me llegaba el agua a la garganta. *The water was up to my neck.*

gárgara f. *gargle; gargling.*

Hacer gárgaras. *To gargle.*

garra f. *claw, talon; clutch.*

garrafa f. *carafe, decanter.*

garrapata f. *tick (insect).*

garrocha f. *good; stock; pole (for jumping).*

Salto a la garrocha. *Pole vaulting.*

garrote m. *cudgel, club; garrote.*

garza m. *heron.*

Garza real. *Purple heron.*

gas m. *gas.*

Estufa de gas. *Gas stove.*

gasa f. *gauze.*

gasolina f. *gasoline.*

Me he quedado sin gasolina. *I've run out of gas.*

Estación de gasolina. (Puesto de gasolina.) *Gas station.*

gasolinera f. *gasoline pump or station (in Spain).*

GASTAR *to spend, to wear out; to waste; to wear, to use.*

Gastó más de cien pesos. *He spent more than a hundred pesos.*

Gastar bromas. *To make jokes. To joke.*

Nunca gasto sombrero en verano. *I never wear a hat in summer.*

Gasta muy buena salud. *He's always in good health.*

Gastar palabras en vano. *To waste words.*

GASTO m. *expense, cost; expenditure; consumption.*

Gastos menudos. *Petty cash.* ("Small expenses.")

Gastos generales. *General expenses, overhead.*

Gasto adicional. *Additional expense.*

gata f. *she-cat.*

A gatas. *On all fours.*

gatillo m. *trigger.*

gato m. *cat, tomcat; jack.*

El gato me ha arañado la mano. *The cat scratched my hand.*

Nos hace falta un gato para levantar el coche. *We need a jack to raise the car.*

gaucho m. *gaucho, cowboy (Arg.).*

gaveta f. *drawer (of a desk); locker.*

gavilán m. *sparrow-hawk.*

gavilla f. *sheaf (of wheat, etc.); a gang of thugs.*

gaviota f. *seagull.*

ge f. *name of the letter g.*

gelatina f. *gelatine, jelly.*

gema f. *gem; bud.*

gemelo m. *twin; pl. binoculars; cufflinks.*

gemido m. *groan, moan.*

gemir *to groan, to moan, to howl.*

generación f. *generation.*

GENERAL adj. *general, usual;* m. *general.*

Por lo general. *As a rule. Usually.*

En general. *In general. On the whole.*

Es general. *He's a general.*

generalmente *generally.*

GÉNERO m. *cloth, material, stuff; class, kind, sort; gender, sex; pl. goods.*

Género para vestidos. *Dress material.*

Género humano. *Mankind.*

generosidad f. *generosity.*

generoso adj. *generous, liberal.*

genial adj. *outstanding, brilliant, gifted; genial, pleasant.*

Tiene un carácter genial. *He's a pleasant person.*

Es una idea genial. *It's a brilliant idea.*

genio *m. genius; nature, disposition, temper.*

Es un verdadero genio. *He's a real genius.*

Tiene muy mal genio. *He has a bad temper.*

GENTE *f. people, crowd.*

Aquí hay mucha gente. *There are many people here.*

Don de gentes. *Pleasant manners. Social graces. Savoir-faire.*

gentil *adj. courteous; graceful; m. gentile, heathen.*

gentileza *f. politeness, courtesy, kindness.*

gentío *m. crowd.*

genuino *adj. genuine, real.*

geografía *f. geography.*

geometría *f. geometry.*

geranio *m. geranium.*

gerencia *f. management.*

gerente *m. manager.*

gerigonza *f. gibberish.*

germen *m. germ.*

germinar *to germinate, to sprout, to start growing or developing.*

gerundio *m. gerund, present participle.*

gesticular *to gesticulate, to make gestures.*

gestión *f. management; negotiation; attempt to obtain or accomplish.*

Encárguese Ud. de esa gestión. *You attend to that matter.*

Está haciendo gestiones para conseguir un puesto. *He's trying to get a job.*

¿Cuáles fueron los resultados de la gestión? *What were the results of the negotiations?*

gestionar *to manage; to negotiate; to try, to take the necessary steps to obtain or accomplish something; to attend to.*

Están gestionando la solución de la huelga. *They're trying to find a way to settle the strike.*

gesto *m. gesture; grimace; facial expression.*

gigante *adj. gigantic; m. giant.*

gimnasia *f. gymnastics, exercise.*

Hacer gimnasia. *To exercise.*

gimnasio *m. gymnasium.*

ginebra *f. gin (liquor); Geneva (Switzerland).*

GIRAR *to rotate, turn; to draw (a draft, etc.); to operate.*

La tierra gira alrededor del sol. *The earth rotates-around the sun.*

Esta casa gira bajo la razón social de. *This firm does business (operates) under the name of.*

Girar contra. *To draw on.*

girasol *m. sunflower.*

GIRO *m. turn; rotation; course (of events); draft, money order.*

Giro postal. *Money order.*

Giro bancario. *Bank draft.*

El giro de los acontecimientos. *The course of events.*

Tomar otro giro. *To take another turn (course).*

Tomar mal giro. *To take a turn for the worse.*

gitano *m. gypsy.*

glacial *adj. glacial, icy.*

Corre un viento glacial. *There's an icy wind.*

global *global, total.*

globo *m. globe; balloon.*

En globo. *In bulk. In a lump.*

gloria *f. glory; pleasure, delight.*

Esta comida sabe a gloria. *This food's delicious (wonderful).*

gloriarse *to be proud of, to boast, to take delight in.*

glorioso *adj. glorious.*

glosa *f. gloss, comment.*

glotón *adj. and n. gluttonous; glutton.*

goal *m. goal (at games).*

gobernación *f. administration, government. See gobierno.*

Ministerio de la gobernación. *Department of the Interior.*

gobernador *m. governor.*

gobernante *m. ruler.*

gobernar *to govern, to rule; to control, to steer; to regulate; to direct.*

Gobernar un barco. *To steer a ship.*

gobierno *m. government; control.*

Para su gobierno. *For your guidance.*

Hombre de gobierno. *Statesman.*

goce *m. enjoyment; possession.*

golf *m. golf.*

golfo *m. gulf; idler, tramp.*

golondrina *f. swallow (bird).*

golosina *f. dainty, delicacy, tidbit.*

goloso *adj. fond of sweets, having a sweet tooth.*

GOLPE *m. blow, stroke, hit; knock; shock.*

Eso fué un golpe muy fuerte. *That was a heavy blow.*

De golpe. *Suddenly. All at once.*

De golpe y porrazo. *Unexpectedly. All of a sudden.*

Golpe de estado. *Coup d'état.*

Golpe de gracia. *Coup de grâce. Finishing stroke.*

Golpe de fortuna. *Stroke of fortune.*

De un golpe. *With one blow.*

Golpe de mar. *Surf. Heavy sea.*

golpear *to strike, to hit, to beat; to knock; to pound.*

Deje de golpear la mesa. *Stop pounding the table.*

goma *f. gum, glue; rubber; eraser.*

Tacones de goma. *Rubber heels.*

Goma de mascar. *Chewing gum.*

gordo *adj. fat, stout; big; m. lard, suet; first prize in a lottery.*

Es un hombre muy gordo. *He's a fat man. He's very fat.*

Dedo gordo. *Thumb.*

gordura *f. stoutness, obesity.*

gorila m. gorilla.

gorra f. cap (for the head).

De gorra. Sponging. At someone else's expense.

gorrión n. sparrow.

gorro m. cap, hood.

gota f. drop (of liquid); gout.

Gota a gota. Drop by drop.

gotear to drip, to dribble; to leak.

gotera f. drip, leak; gutter.

GOZAR to enjoy; to have, to possess.

Goza de buena salud. He enjoys good health.

Goza de muy buena reputación. He has a very good reputation.

gozarse to rejoice; to find pleasure (in).

Se goza en . . . He finds pleasure in . . . He takes pleasure in . . .

gozo m. joy, pleasure.

No cabe en sí de gozo. He's very happy. ("He can't contain himself for joy.")

gozoso adj. cheerful, glad, merry.

grabado m. picture, illustration; engraving.

grabar to engrave; to impress upon the mind.

GRACIA f. grace; favor; pardon; wit, humor; name (of a person); pl. thanks.

Muchas gracias. Thank you very much.

Gracias a Dios. Thank God.

Un millón de gracias. Thanks a lot. ("A million thanks.")

Dar gracias. To thank.

¿Cuál es su gracia? What's your name?

Eso tiene gracia. That's funny.

Eso no me hace gracia. I don't think that's funny.

Caer en gracia. To take one's fancy.

Tener gracia. To be amusing (funny).

Hacer gracia. To amuse.

gracioso adj. graceful; witty, funny.

Un dicho gracioso. A witty remark.

grada f. step (of a staircase).

GRADO m. degree, rank; grade; will; pleasure.

Tenemos diez grados bajo cero. It's ten degrees below zero.

Acaba de recibir el grado de doctor. He has just received his doctor's degree.

Tenía un grado superior en el ejército. He held a high rank in the army.

Está en el cuarto grado. He's in the fourth grade.

De buen grado. Willingly. With pleasure.

Mal de su grado. Unwillingly. Much to one's regret.

En alto grado. In the highest degree.

gradual adj. gradual, by degrees.

graduar to graduate; to give military rank to; to adjust.

graduarse to graduate, to receive a degree.

gráfico adj. graphic; vivid; m. graph, diagram.

gramática f. grammar.

GRAN (contraction of **grande**) big, great.

Me hace Ud. un gran favor. You're doing me a great favor.

Es un hombre de gran talento. He's a man of great talent.

Es un gran embustero. He's a big liar.

granada f. pomegranate; grenade, shell.

GRANDE adj. great, large, huge; m. grandee, a Spanish nobleman.

Separe Ud. los grandes de los pequeños. Separate the large ones from the small.

Vive en una casa muy grande. She lives in a very large house.

Estos zapatos me quedan muy grandes. These shoes are too big for me.

Este jarrón es un poco más grande. This vase is a little larger.

En grande. On a large scale.

grandeza f. greatness.

grandioso adj. grand, magnificent.

granero m. granary, barn.

granizar to hail.

Graniza. (Está granizando.) It's hailing.

granizo m. hail.

granja f. grange, farm; country house.

granjear to gain, to win (somebody's affection or goodwill).

granjearse to gain the goodwill of another.

grano m. grain; cereal bean (of coffee); pimple.

Vamos al grano. Let's get to the point. Let's get down to brass tacks.

grasa f. grease, fat.

grasiento adj. greasy.

grasoso adj. greasy.

gratamente gratefully.

gratificación f. gratuity, tip, reward; allowance.

gratificar to reward, to gratify, to tip.

gratis adj. gratis, free.

La entrada será gratis. Admission will be free.

gratitud f. gratitude, thankfulness, gratefulness.

GRATO adj. pleasing, gratifying, pleasant.

Me es grato. I'm pleased to.

Me será grato hacerlo. I'll be glad to do it.

Su grata del 5 de mayo. Your letter ("favor") of May the 5th.

gratuito adj. gratis, free.

grave adj. grave; serious.

gravedad f. gravity, seriousness.

gremio m. trade union, guild.

grieta f. crevice, crack, fissure; chap (skin).

grifo m. faucet; griffin.

Haga Ud. el favor de cerrar el grifo. Please turn the water off.

grillo m. cricket (insect).

grillos pl. fetters, shackles.

gringo m. name given to Americans and Englishmen in Latin America.

gripe f. grippe, influenza.

gris adj. gray.

gritar *to shout, to scream.*

  No grites tanto. *Don't shout so. Don't scream like that.*

grito *m. cry, scream, shout.*

  Llamó a gritos. *He yelled (screamed). He called out loud.*

  Poner el grito en el cielo. *To complain bitterly. To make a big fuss. ("To cry to heaven.")*

  Estar en un grito. *To be in agony.*

grosella *f. currant (fruit).*

grosería *f. coarseness, rudeness.*

grosero *adj. coarse, rude, impolite.*

grúa *f. crane, derrick, hoist.*

gruesa *f. gross (144).*

GRUESO *adj. thick, coarse, bulky.*

  Una tajada gruesa. *A thick slice.*

  El tronco de ese árbol es muy grueso. *This tree has a very thick trunk.*

grulla *f. crane (bird).*

gruñido *m. grunt.*

gruñir *to grumble, to grunt.*

grupo *m. group.*

gruta *f. grotto, cavern.*

guano *m. guano, manure of sea birds, fertilizer.*

guante *m. glove.*

  Echar el guante. *To catch. To arrest.*

guapo *adj. good-looking, pretty, handsome; courageous, bold, brave (Amer.).*

  ¿Es guapa la hija? *Is the daughter pretty?*

  Es guapísima. *She's very pretty.*

guarda *f. and m. guard, watchman, keeper; custody, guardianship.*

guardapelo *m. locket.*

GUARDAR *to keep, to guard, to take care of.*

  Guarde su dinero en la caja fuerte. *Keep your money in the safe.*

  No le guardo ningún rencor. *I don't bear him any grudge.*

  Ha tenido que guardar cama. *He had to stay in bed. He was confined to bed.*

guardarse *to be on guard; to guard against; to abstain from.*

guardarropa *f. wardrobe; m. cloakroom, the cloakroom attendant.*

guardia *f. guard (a body of soldiers); watch (on a ship); m. guard (a person), policeman.*

  Cualquier guardia puede indicarle el camino. *Any policeman can direct you (show you the way).*

  Está de guardia. *He's on duty.*

guarecer *to shelter, to protect.*

guarnecer *to trim, to garnish; to garrison.*

guarnición *f. trimming, garniture; setting (in gold, silver, etc.); garrison; pl. harness.*

guasa *f. nonsense; dullness; joke, fun.*

guasón *adj. humorous, playful; m. teaser, joker.*

guayaba *f. guava (fruit).*

GUERRA *f. war; trouble.*

  Estar en guerra. *To be at war.*

  Hacer guerra. *To wage war.*

  Estos chicos dan mucha guerra. *These children are a lot of trouble.*

guerrero *adj. warlike; m. warrior.*

GUÍA *m. guide; cicerone; f. guidebook; directory.*

  ¿Dónde puedo encontrar un guía que me acompañe? *Where can I get a guide to accompany me?*

  Guía telefónica. *Telephone directory.*

  Servir de guía. *To serve as a guide.*

guiar *to guide, to direct; to drive.*

  ¿Sabe Ud. guiar? *Do you know how to drive?*

guijarro *m. pebble.*

guillotina *f. guillotine.*

guinda *f. kind of cherry.*

guiñar *to wink; to deviate (a ship).*

guión *m. hyphen; guidon (small flag).*

guisado *m. ragout, a stew of meat and vegetables.*

guisante *m. pea.*

guisar *to cook.*

guiso *m. stew.*

guitarra *f. guitar.*

gusano *m. worm.*

GUSTAR *to taste; to like.*

  ¿Le gusta a Ud. la fruta? *Do you like fruit?*

  A mí no me gusta el café. *I don't like coffee.*

  ¿Le gusta a Ud. eso? *Do you like that?*

  No me gusta. *I don't like it.*

  Nos gustó la comida. *We enjoyed the food.*

  Me gusta más el vino. *I like wine better.*

  Si Ud. gusta. *If you please. If you wish.*

  Como Ud. guste. *As you please.*

  Me gustaría mucho ir a España. *I'd like very much to go to Spain.*

GUSTO *m. taste; pleasure; liking.*

  Esto tiene un gusto extraño. *This has a strange (funny) taste.*

  Con (mucho) gusto. *With (much) pleasure.*

  Tengo mucho gusto en conocerle. *I'm glad to have met you. Glad to know you.*

  A mi gusto. *To my liking.*

  Se lo haré a su gusto. *I'll do it the way you want.*

  Estar (encontrarse, sentirse) a gusto. *To feel at home. To be comfortable.*

  Me siento a gusto aquí. *I feel at home here.*

  Dar gusto. *To please.*

  Tener gusto en. *To take pleasure in.*

gustoso *adj. tasty; glad, willing, with pleasure.*

  Aceptamos gustosos la invitación. *We accept your invitation with pleasure.*

gutapercha *f. gutta-percha.*

H

¡ha! *ah! alas!*

haba *f. broad bean.*

habano *m. Havana cigar.*

haber *m. credit (bookkeeping); assets.*

HABER *to have (as an auxiliary verb); to be, to exist.*

Hay. *There is. There are.*

Había. *There was. There were.*

Hubo. *There was. There were.*

Habrá. *There will be.*

Habría. *There would be.*

Haya. *There may be.*

Que haya. *Let there be.*

Hubiera (hubiese). *There might be.*

Si hubiera (hubiese). *If there were. If there should be.*

Ha habido. *There has (have) been.*

Había (hubo) habido. *There had been.*

Habría habido. *There should (would) have been.*

Hay que. *It's necessary.*

Habrá que. *It will be necessary.*

Hubo que. *It was necessary.*

Ha de ser. *It must be.*

He de hacer un largo viaje. *I have (I've got) to make a long trip.*

He aquí. *Here is.*

Poco ha. *A little while ago.*

¿Ha escrito la carta? *Has she written the letter?*

No la ha escrito todavía. *She hasn't written it yet.*

No he estado allí. *I haven't been there.*

Pudo haber sucedido. *It might have happened.*

Debían haber llegado anoche. *They were supposed to have come last night.*

Ayer hubo clase. *There was school yesterday.*

De haber sido Ud. no lo hubiera hecho. *If I had been you, I wouldn't have done it.*

Debe haber cartas para mí. *There must be some letters for me.*

¿Habrá alguien en la estación esperándome? *Will there be someone at the station to meet me?*

¿Qué distancia hay? *How far is it?*

Habrá unas cinco millas de aquí. *That must be about five miles from here.*

Hemos de ir el martes a su casa. *We must go (we have to go) to his (her) house on Tuesday.*

No habíamos comido desde hacía muchas horas. *We hadn't eaten for many hours.*

Así que hubo hablado se marchó. *He left as soon as he'd finished speaking.*

Me alegro de haberle visto. *I'm glad to have seen you.*

Dede haber hecho fortuna en América. *He must have made a fortune in America.*

Debe haber habido un edificio aquí en otros tiempos. *There must have been a building here formerly (in the past).*

Hace una semana que la vi. *I saw her a week ago.*

¿Qué se ha hecho? *What happened to her?*

¿Habráse visto cosa igual? *Did you ever see such a thing?*

Habérselas con. *To have to deal with. To cope with. To contend with.*

haberes *m. pl. possessions, property.*

habichuela *f. bean; kidney bean.*

Habichuelas verdes. *String beans.*

HABIL *adj. able; clever; skillful; capable.*

Es muy hábil. *He's very clever.*

Día hábil. *Working day.*

habilidad *f. ability, skill.*

habilitado *m. paymaster.*

habilitar *to qualify; to enable, to provide; to supply with.*

habitación *f. room; dwelling; place to live in.*

¿Cuántas habitaciones tiene el apartamento? *How many rooms does the apartment have?*

habitante *m. and f. inhabitant; tenant.*

habitar *to inhabit, to live in, to reside.*

¿Qué tal es el piso que habitan? *What kind of an apartment do you live in?*

hábito *m. habit, custom; cowl, habit (worn by members of a religious order).*

Tenía el hábito de levantarse temprano. *He was in the habit of getting up early.*

Colgó los hábitos. *He threw off the cowl.*

habituar *to accustom.*

habituarse *to become accustomed.*

habla *f. speech, talk.*

Perdió el habla. *He was speechless.*

Ponerse al habla con. *To get in touch with. To have a talk with.*

hablador *adj. talkative; m. gossip, chatterbox, talker.*

HABLAR *to speak, to talk.*

¿Habla Ud. español? *Do you speak Spanish?*

Yo no hablo español. *I don't speak Spanish.*

Aquí se habla español. *Spanish is spoken here.*

¡Hable! *Speak!*

¿Quién habla? *Who's speaking (telephone)?*

¡Diga! (¡Holá!) ¿Quién habla? *Hello! Who's this (telephone)?*

Hable más despacio. *Speak slower.*

Nunca habla mal de nadie. *He never says anything bad about anyone.*

Hablando en serio, eso no está bien. *Joking apart, that's wrong. Seriously, that's not right.*

Hablar con. *To speak with.*

Hablar por demás. *To talk too much. Not to talk to the point.*

Hablar por hablar. *To talk for the sake of talking.*

Hablar hasta por los codos. *To chatter. To talk constantly. To be a chatterbox.*

hacendado *m. rancher, landowner (Amer.).*

hacendoso *adj. diligent; industrious.*

Es una chica muy hacendosa. *She's a very industrious girl.*

HACER *to make; to do; to cause; to be (cold, warm, etc.).*

Hágame Ud. el favor de. *Please.*

Me hace Ud. el favor de. *Please.*

¡Haga el favor de pasarme la sal! *Please pass me the salt.*

¿Me permite que le haga una pregunta? *May I ask you a question?*

Hacen muy buenos pasteles aquí. *They make very good pies here.*

He mandado hacer un traje a la medida. *I'm having a suit made to order.*

Hicimos los planes de común acuerdo. *We made (laid) the plans by mutual agreement.*

Hágame un poco de sitio. *Make a little room for me.*

¿Tiene Ud. algo que hacer esta tarde? *Have you anything to do this afternoon?*

Tengo mucho que hacer hoy. *I've a lot to do today.*

¿Qué hago? *What shall I do?*

Haga Ud. lo que quiera. *Do as you please (like).*

¿Qué hace Ud.? *What are you doing?*

¿Qué hemos de hacer? *What are we to do?*

Hágalo Ud. de esta manera. *Do it this way.*

Hace lo que puede. *He does what he can. He does his best.*

Queda mucho por hacer. *Much still remains to be done.*

Me ha dado mucho que hacer. *He's given me a lot of trouble.*

Ya está hecho. *It's already done (finished).*

Dicho y hecho. *No sooner said than done.*

¿Le ha hecho daño la comida? *Did the food disagree with you?*

Ropa hecha. *Ready-made clothes.*

Yo le hacía en España. *I thought you were in Spain.*

Le hacíamos rico. *We thought he was rich.*

Haga Ud. por venir. *Try to come.*

Haga Ud. memoria. *Try to remember.*

Salió hace un rato. *He left a while ago.*

No hace mucho. *Not long ago.*

Hace cosa de dos meses. *It was about two months ago.*

Se va haciendo tarde. *It's getting late.*

Hace frío. *It's cold.*

Hace calor. *It's warm.*

Hace sol. *It's sunny.*

Hace viento. *It's windy.*

Hace mal tiempo. *The weather's bad. It's nasty out.*

Hacer falta. *To need. To be lacking.*

No hace falta. *It's not necessary.*

Hacer caso. *To pay attention.*

Hacer burla. *To make fun.*

Hacer alto. *To halt.*

Hacer un paréntesis. *To pause.*

Hacer de las suyas. *To be up to one's old tricks again.*

Hacer de cuenta. *To pretend.*

Hacer gimnasia. *To exercise.*

Hacer una convocatoria. *To call a meeting.*

Hacer cola. *To stand in line.*

Hacer frente a. *To face. To resist.*

Hacer ver. *To show.*

Hacer volver. *To send back.*

Hacer esperar. *To keep waiting.*

Hacer saber. *To make known. To inform.*

Hacer juego. *To match.*

Hacer por la vida. *To eat something.*

Hacer mal. *To do harm.*

Hacerlo bien (mal). *To do it well (badly).*

Hacer gasto. *To spend.*

Hacer fuego. *To fire. To shoot.*

Hacer cuentas. *To figure. To reckon.*

Hacer la corte. *To court. To woo.*

HACERSE *to become; to accustom oneself; to pretend; to be able to.*

¿Puede Ud. hacerse entender en inglés? *Can you make yourself understood in English?*

Juan está en camino de hacerse rico. *John's getting rich. ("John's on the way to becoming rich.")*

Se hacía más loco de lo que era. *He pretended to be crazier than he really was.*

La muñeca se hizo pedazos. *The doll broke into pieces.*

Me hice un lío. *I was all mixed up.*

Hacerse rogar. *To like to be coaxed.*

Hacerse cargo de. *To take charge of. To take into consideration.*

Hacerse atrás. *To fall back.*

Hacerse una sopa. *To become drenched. To get soaked to the skin.*

Hacerse a. *To become accustomed (used) to.*

Hacerse a la vela. *To set sail.*

Hacerse de. *To obtain. To get.*

Hacerse con alguna cosa. *To get hold of something. To obtain something.*

Hacerse el tonto. *To play the fool.*

¡Hazte allá! *Move on! Make way! Get out of the way!*

HACIA *toward, in the direction of.*

Péineme el pelo hacia atrás. *Comb my hair back.*

Iba hacia su casa. *He was going towards his house.*

El edificio está hacia el sur. *The building faces (the) south.*

Se dirigieron hacia la puerta. *They went towards the door.*

Hacia abajo. *Downwards.*

Hacia arriba. *Upwards.*

Hacia acá. *Over here. Towards this place.*

Hacia allá. *Over there. Towards that place.*

Hacia adelante. *Forward. Onward. Toward the front.*

hacienda *f. property, lands, ranch, plantation, large estate (Amer.); fortune, wealth; treasury; finance.*

Ministerio de Hacienda. *The Treasury.*

hacha *f. ax, hatchet.*

hache *f. name of the letter h.*

hada *f. fairy.*

Cuentos de hadas. *Fairy tales.*

hado *m. destiny, fate.*

halagar *to please, to flatter.*

halago *m. flattery, excessive praise.*

halagüeño *adj. pleasing, nice; flattering, attractive.*

halar *to pull (Amer.).*

Hale la cuerda. *Pull the rope.*

HALLAR *to find, to meet with.*

Hallé muchas faltas en esta carta. *I found many mistakes in this letter.*

No lo hallo en ninguna parte. *I can't find it anywhere.*

Lo hallará en el escritorio. *You'll find it on the desk.*

hallarse *to find oneself, to be.*

Se halla muy bien. *He's very well. He's fine.*

Me hallo sin dinero. *I find myself without any money.*

hallazgo *m. finding; thing found.*

hamaca *f. hammock.*

HAMBRE *m. hunger.*

Tengo hambre. *I'm hungry.*

No tengo hambre. *I'm not hungry.*

Me estoy muriendo de hambre. *I'm starving.*

hambriento *adj. hungry; starved; greedy.*

hangar *m. hangar.*

haragán *adj. and n. lazy; indolent; loafer.*

harapo *m. tatter; rag.*

harina *f. flour.*

hartarse *to stuff oneself, to gorge.*

Tomó helado hasta hartarse. *He stuffed himself with ice cream.*

harto *adj. satiated, full; fed up; enough.*

Estoy harto de todo esto. *I'm fed up with all this.*

HASTA *until; as far as; up to; also, even.*

Hasta luego. *So long. See you later.*

Hasta después. *I'll see you later.*

¡Hasta la vista! *Till we meet again! I'll be seeing you soon! See you soon!*

Hasta muy pronto. *I'll see you soon. See you later.*

Hasta mañana. *Until tomorrow. See you tomorrow.*

Hasta el lunes. *Until Monday.*

Fuimos andando hasta el parque. *We walked as far as the park.*

Hay ascensor hasta el quinto piso. *There is an elevator to the fifth floor.*

¿Hasta dónde va el camino? *How far does the road go?*

Estoy calado hasta los huesos. *I'm soaking wet. ("I'm soaked to the bones.")*

Hasta cierto punto. *To a certain extent.*

Hasta ahora. *Up to now. Up to this time.*

HAY *(see haber) there is, there are.*

¿Hay vino? *Is there any wine?*

No hay vino. *There is no wine.*

¿Hay cartas? *Are there any letters?*

¿Hay algo para mí? *Is there anything for me?*

¿Qué hay de bueno? *What's new?*

No hay novedad. *Nothing new. The same old thing. The same as usual.*

¿Qué hay? *What's the matter? What's up?*

¡No hay de qué! *Don't mention it! You're welcome!*

Hay un hombre esperándole. *There's a man waiting for you.*

Hay que ver lo que se puede hacer por ella. *We must see what can be done for her.*

haz *m. sheaf; fagot; f. face; right side (of a cloth); surface (of the earth).*

hazaña *f. prowess, feat, exploit.*

he *look here, take notice (used with aquí, ahí, allí, and me, te, la, le, lo, las and los).*

He aquí las razones. *These are the reasons (indicating what follows).*

He ahí las razones. *Those are the reasons (indicating what precedes).*

Héme aquí. *Here I am.*

¿Dónde está mi libro?—Hélo aquí. *Where's my book?—Here it is.*

hebilla *f. buckle.*

hebra *f. thread; fiber.*

Pasar la hebra por el ojo de la aguja. *To thread a needle.*

hectárea *f. hectare (10,000 square meters).*

hectólitro *m. hectoliter.*

hechicero *adj. fascinating, charming; m. wizard.*

Tiene un semblante hechicero. *She has a fascinating face.*

hechizar *to fascinate, to charm, to bewitch.*

HECHO *adj. made, done; m. fact; deed; action; event.*

Mal hecho. *That's wrong. Poorly made.*

Bien hecho. *Well done.*

Ropa hecha. *Ready-made clothes.*

El hecho es . . . *The fact is . . .*

Los hechos demostraron otra cosa. *The facts proved otherwise.*

Dicho y hecho. *Said and done.*

Hecho y derecho. *Perfect in every respect.*

De hecho. *In fact. Actually.*

De hecho y de derecho. *"By act and right."*

hechura *f. workmanship, making, cut, shape, form.*

heder *to stink.*

helada *f. frost.*

helado *adj. frozen; icy; astonished, amazed, astounded; m. ice cream.*

Traiga dos helados de chocolate. *Bring two orders of chocolate ice cream.*

La noticia me dejó helado. *The news astounded me.*

helar *to freeze; to astonish.*

hélice *f. propeller.*

hembra *f. female; woman; eye of a hook.*

hemisferio *m. hemisphere.*

hendedura *f. fissure, crevice.*

heno *m. hay.*

heredad *f. property, land, farm.*

heredar *to inherit.*

heredera *f. heiress.*

heredero *m. heir.*

hereditario *adj. hereditary.*

herencia *f. inheritance, heritage, legacy.*

herida *f. wound, injury.*

herido *adj. wounded, injured; m. wounded man.*

Fué herido en el brazo. *He was wounded in the arm.*

El herido sigue mejor. *The wounded man is improving.*

herir *to wound, to hurt.*

HERMANA *f. sister.*

hermanastro *m. stepbrother.*

HERMANO *m. brother.*

HERMOSO *adj. beautiful; lovely, fine.*

¡Qué paisaje tan hermoso! *What beautiful scenery! What a lovely landscape!*

¡Qué día más hermoso! *What a beautiful day!*

hermosura *f. beauty.*

héroe *m. hero.*

heroico *adj. heroic.*

hervir *to boil.*

Hierva el agua antes de beberla. *Boil the water before you drink it.*

Agua hirviendo. *Boiling water.*

herradura *f. horseshoe.*

herramienta *f. tool; set of tools.*

herrero *m. blacksmith.*

hidrofobia *f. hydrophobia; rabies.*

hidroplano *m. seaplane.*

hiedra *f. ivy.*

hiel *f. gall, bile.*

hielo *m. ice; frost; indifference.*

hiena *f. hyena.*

hierba *f. herb; weed; grass.*

hierbabuena *f. mint (plant).*

hierro *m. iron; poker.*

Remueva la lumbre con el hierro. *Stir the fire with the poker.*

hígado *m. liver.*

higiene *f. hygiene.*

higiénico *adj. hygienic, sanitary.*

higo *m. fig.*

higuera *f. fig tree.*

HIJA *f. daughter.*

hijastro *m. stepchild.*

HIJO *m. son; pl. children.*

¿Tiene Ud. hijos? *Do you have any children?*

Tal padre, tal hijo. *Like father, like son.*

hilar *to spin.*

hilero *f. row, file.*

HILO *m. thread; string; linen; wire.*

Pañuelo de hilo. *Linen handkerchief.*

No puedo seguir el hilo de la conversación. *I can't follow the conversation.*

Perder el hilo. *To lose the thread (of what one is saying, etc.).*

Sin hilos. *Wireless.*

Carrete (carretel) de hilo. *Spool of thread. Spool of cotton.*

hilván *m. tacking, basting.*

hilvanar *to tack, to baste; to do a thing hurriedly.*

himno *m. hymn.*

hincapié *m. unyielding.*

Hacer hincapié. *To insist on. To emphasize. To dwell on. To stand firm.*

hinchado *adj. swollen.*

hinchar *to swell, to inflate.*

hincharse *to swell; to become arrogant.*

hinchazón *m. swelling; vanity.*

hipnotismo *m. hypnotism.*

hipo *m. hiccough.*

hipocresía *f. hypocrisy.*

hipócrita *adj. and n. hypocritical, not sincere; hypocrite.*

hipódromo *m. racetrack; hippodrome.*

hipoteca *f. mortgage.*

hipotecar *to mortgage.*

hipótesis *f. hypothesis.*

hispano *adj. Hispanic, Spanish.*

hispanoamericano *adj. Spanish American.*

histérico *adj. hysterical.*

historia *f. history; story.*

Me vino con una larga historia. *He came to me with a long story.*

historiador *m. historian.*

histórico *adj. historic.*

historieta *f. short story; anecdote.*

hocico *m. snout; muzzle.*

Meter el hocico en todo. *To be nosy. To poke one's nose into everything.*

hogar *m. fireplace; home.*

hoguera *f. bonfire; blaze.*

HOJA *f. leaf; blade; sheet.*

En otoño caen las hojas. *The leaves fall in autumn.*

Doblemos la hoja. *Let's change the subject.*

Hoja en blanco. *Blank sheet.*

Hoja de servicio. *Service record.*
Hoja de afeitar. *Razor blade.*
Hoja de lata. *Tin plate.*

hojalata *f. tin plate.*

hojear *to turn the leaves or glance at a book; to look over hastily.*

holgar *to rest; to be idle; to go on strike.*
Huelga decir. *Needless to say.*

holgarse *to be pleased with, to take pleasure in, to amuse oneself.*

holgazán *adj. lazy, idle; m. a lazy person, idler.*

¡hola! *Hello!*

hombre *m. man.*
Es hombre de mundo. *He's a man of the world.*
Hombre de bien. *An honest man.*
Hombre de Estado. *Statesman.*

HOMBRO *m. shoulder.*
Se lastimó el hombro. *He hurt his shoulder.*
Arrimar el hombro. *To give a hand.*
Encogerse de hombros. *To shrug one's shoulders.*

homenaje *m. homage, honor, respect.*
Rendir homenaje. *To pay homage to.*

hondo *adj. profound; deep.*

honesto *adj. decent, honest.*

honor *m. honor.*
Dió su palabra de honor. *He gave his word of honor.*
Honores Militares. *Military honors.*

honra *f. honor, respect.*
Tener a honra. *To regard as an honor. To consider it an honor. To be proud of.*
A mucha honra. *I (we) consider it an honor. I (we) are honored. I'm (or we're) proud of it.*

honradez *f. honesty, integrity.*

honrado *adj. honest, honorable.*
Era un hombre honrado. *He was an honest man.*

honrar *to honor.*

honrarse *to deem something an honor, to be honored.*

HORA *f. hour; time.*
¿Qué hora es? *What time is it?*
¿Qué hora será? *I wonder what time it is.*
¿A qué hora empieza la función. (At) *What time does the show begin?*
¿A qué hora sale el correo? (At) *What time does the mail leave?*
Ya es hora de levantarse. *It's ("already") time to get up.*
Este reloj da las horas y las medias horas. *This clock strikes the hours and the half hours.*
Llegó media hora después. *He arrived half an hour later.*
A la hora. *On time.*
A la hora en punto. *On the dot.*
A la misma hora. *At the same time.*
A estas horas. *By this time. By now.*

horario *adj. hourly; m. hour-hand; timetable.*

horca *f. gallows; pitchfork.*

horizontal *adj. horizontal.*

horizonte *m. horizon.*

horma *f. form, model, mold; shoe last.*
Horma para zapatos. *Shoe last.*

hormiga *f. ant.*

hormigón *m. concrete (for building).*

hornada *f. batch (of bread).*

hornillo *m. portable stove; burner; blast hole.*

horno *m. oven; furnace.*

hortaliza *f. vegetables (for cooking), garden greens.*

horrible *adj. horrible.*

horror *m. horror.*

horroroso *adj. horrible, frightful, dreadful.*

hosco *adj. sullen, gloomy; dark-colored.*

hospedaje *m. lodging; board.*

hospedar *to lodge; to entertain (guests).*

hospicio *m. orphan asylum; poorhouse.*

hospital *m. hospital.*

hospitalizar *to hospitalize; to be taken to the hospital.*

hostelero *m. innkeeper, tavern keeper.*

hostia *f. host (in the Catholic Church).*

hostil *adj. hostile.*

hostilizar *to harass, to antagonize.*

HOTEL *m. hotel; villa; cottage.*
¿Dónde queda el hotel más próximo? *Where's the nearest hotel?*

HOY *today.*
¿Qué día es hoy? *What day is today? What's today?*
¿Cuál es el programa de hoy? *What's today's program?*
De hoy en adelante. *From now on. Henceforth.*
Hoy por hoy. Hoy día. *Nowadays.*

hoyo *m. hole, pit, excavation.*

hoz *f. sickle.*

hueco *m. hole, hollow, empty space.*

huelga *f. strike (of workers).*

huelguista *m. striker, a workman on strike.*

huella *f. track, footprint, trail.*
Huellas digitales. *Fingerprints.*

huérfano *m. orphan.*
Quedarse huérfano. *To be left an orphan.*

huerta *f. orchard; irrigated land.*

huerto *m. small orchard; vegetable garden.*

hueso *m. bone; stone (of fruit); drudgery.*
A otro perro con ese hueso. *Tell it to the marines. You expect me to believe that? ("Give that bone to another dog.")*

huésped *m. and f. guest; lodger; innkeeper, host.*
Casa de huéspedes. *Boarding house.*

HUEVO *m. egg.*
¿Cómo quiere Ud. los huevos? *How do you like your eggs?*
Huevos y tocino. *Bacon and eggs.*
Huevos fritos. *Fried eggs.*

Huevos pasados por agua. *Soft-boiled eggs.*

Huevos revueltos. *Scrambled eggs.*

huída f. *flight, escape.*

huir *to flee, to escape; to run away.*

hule m. *oilcloth; linoleum; India rubber.*

humanidad f. *mankind, humanity.*

humanitario adj. *humanitarian, philanthropic.*

HUMANO adj. *human; humane;* m. *man, human being.*

Eso fué un acto humano. *That was a humane act. That was a very humane thing to do.*

Un ser humano. *A human being.*

humear *to smoke (chimneys, etc.).*

humedad f. *humidity, dampness, moisture.*

humedecer *to moisten, to dampen.*

húmedo adj. *humid, moist, damp.*

humildad f. *humility, humbleness.*

humilde adj. *poor; humble; unaffected.*

humillación f. *humiliation; affront.*

humillante adj. *humiliating.*

humillar *to humiliate, to lower.*

humo m. *smoke; fume; pl. airs, conceit.*

HUMOR m. *humor; disposition; temper.*

Estar de buen humor. *To be in a good mood.*

Estar de mal humor. *To be in a bad mood. To have the blues.*

humorada f. *joke, witty remark, humorous saying.*

humorista m. and f. *humorist.*

hundimiento m. *sinking, scuttling; collapse, downfall.*

hundir *to sink; to submerge.*

hundirse *to sink; to cave in; to collapse.*

huraño *shy, not sociable.*

hurtadillas (a) *by stealth, on the sly.*

Me miró a hurtadillas. *He looked at me out of the corner of his eye.*

Lo hizo a hurtadillas. *He did it on the sly.*

hurtar *to steal, to rob.*

Hurtar el cuerpo. *To shy away.*

hurto m. *stealing; theft.*

¡hurra! *Hurrah!*

husmear *to smell, to scent; to pry into; to begin to smell (meat).*

I

ida f. *going; one-way trip, trip to a place.*

Billete de ida. *One-way ticket.*

Billete de ida y vuelta. *Round-trip ticket.*

IDEA f. *idea; mind.*

No tengo la menor idea. *I haven't the least idea.*

Creo que es una buena idea. *I think it's a good idea.*

No es mala idea. *That's not a bad idea.*

¿Ha cambiado Ud. de idea? *Have you changed your mind?*

ideal adj. and n. *ideal.*

idealizar *to idealize.*

idear *to think of, to conceive; to devise; to plan.*

Ideó un juego divertidísimo. *He thought up a very amusing game.*

Idear nuevos métodos. *To devise new methods.*

idem *the same, ditto.*

idéntico adj. *identical, the same.*

identidad f. *identity.*

¿Tiene Ud. sus documentos de identidad? *Do you have your identification papers?*

identificación f. *identification.*

identificar *to identify.*

idioma m. *language.*

idiota adj. *idiotic;* m. and f. *idiot.*

ídolo m. *idol.*

iglesia f. *church.*

ignominia f. *infamy; disgrace.*

ignorancia f. *ignorance.*

IGNORANTE adj. *ignorant; unaware;* m. *ignoramus, ignorant person.*

Estaba ignorante de lo que ocurría. *He was unaware of what was happening.*

Es un ignorante. *He's an ignorant man. He's an ignoramus.*

IGNORAR *to be ignorant of, not to know; to be unknown.*

Ignoro su nombre. *I don't know his name.*

Se ignora su paradero. *His whereabouts are unknown.*

IGUAL adj. *equal; similar, like; even.*

Mi corbata es igual que la suya. *My tie is like yours.*

Me es igual. *It's all the same to me. It makes no difference (to me).*

Al igual que los demás. *The same as the others.*

Igual a la muestra. *Like the sample.*

Por igual. *Equally. In a like manner.*

No tener igual. *To be matchless. To have no equal.*

igualar *to equalize; to compare, to liken; to make even.*

igualarse *to put oneself on the same level with someone else.*

igualdad f. *equality.*

En igualdad de condiciones. *On equal terms.*

ilegal adj. *illegal, unlawful.*

ilegible adj. *illegible.*

ilegítimo adj. *illegitimate, spurious.*

ileso adj. *unhurt, unscathed, not harmed.*

ilimitado adj. *unlimited.*

iluminación f. *illumination.*

iluminar *to illuminate.*

ilusión f. *illusion.*

ilustración f. *illustration.*

ilustrado adj. *illustrated;* m. *well-educated person.*

ilustrar to illustrate;- to explain.
ilustrarse to acquire knowledge.
ilustre adj. illustrious, celebrated.
imagen f. image, figure.
imaginación f. imagination.
IMAGINAR to imagine, to think, to suspect.
IMAGINARSE to imagine.
   ¡Imagínese Ud.! You can imagine!
   Me imagino lo que pensaría de mí. I can imagine what he thought of me.
imán m. magnet.
imbécil adj. and n. imbecile.
imbecilidad f. imbecility, stupidity.
imitación f. imitation.
imitar to imitate; to mimic.
impaciencia f. impatience.
impacientar to vex, to irritate, to make someone impatient.
impacientarse to become impatient.
impaciente adj. impatient, restless.
impar adj. odd, uneven.
   Números impares. Odd numbers.
imparcial adj. impartial, unbiased.
impedimento m. impediment, hindrance, obstacle; inability to act.
IMPEDIR to hinder, to prevent, to keep from.
   El ruido me impidió dormir. The noise kept me from sleeping. The noise kept me awake.
impenetrable adj. impenetrable; inscrutable, mysterious.
imperativo adj. and n. imperative.
imperdible m. safety pin.
imperfecto adj. imperfect, faulty; m. imperfect (tense).
imperio m. empire; dominion.
impermeabilizar to make waterproof.
impermeable adj. impermeable, waterproof; m. raincoat.
impersonal adj. impersonal.
impertinente adj. impertinent, out of place; importunate.
impetu m. impulse, impetus.
impetuoso adj. impulsive, impetuous.
impío adj. wicked; impious, ungodly.
implicar to implicate; to imply.
implícito adj. implicit.
implorar to implore; to beg.
imponer to impose; to acquaint with; to have personal knowledge of; to command (respect).
imponerse to assert oneself, to command respect.
importación f. import; importation.
IMPORTANCIA f. importance.
IMPORTANTE adj. important.
IMPORTAR to import; to matter; to cost, to amount to.
   Esta casa importa café del Brasil. This firm imports coffee from Brazil.
   Este libro importa un dólar. This book costs a dollar.
   ¿Cuánto importa la cuenta? What does the bill amount to?
   ¿Que importa? What difference does it make? No importa. Never mind. It doesn't matter.
   Importa mucho. It matters a lot. It's very important.
   No se meta en lo que no le importa. Mind your own business.
importe m. amount; value, cost.
importunar to importune, to annoy.
imposibilidad f. impossibility.
imposibilitar to make impossible.
IMPOSIBLE adj. impossible.
imposición f. imposition.
impostor m. impostor, deceiver.
impotencia f. inability, impotence.
impotente adj. powerless, helpless, impotent.
impracticable adj. impracticable, not practical.
imprenta f. printing; printing plant.
impresión f. impression; print, printing.
impresionante adj. impressive.
impresionar to impress; to move; to affect.
impreso adj. imprinted; stamped; m. printed matter.
impresor m. printer.
imprevisto adj. unforeseen, unexpected; sudden.
   Llegó de imprevisto. He arrived unexpectedly.
imprimir to print; to imprint.
improbable adj. unlikely, improbable.
impropio adj. improper, not correct, unfit; unbecoming.
improvisar to improvise, to extemporize; to make or do something offhand; to make for the occasion.
improviso adj. unexpected.
   De improviso. Unexpectedly.
imprudencia f. lack of prudence, imprudence.
imprudente adj. imprudent; indiscreet.
impuesto adj. imposed; informed; m. impost, tax, duty.
   Estar impuesto de. To be informed of (about).
impulsar to impel; to drive; to urge.
impulso m. impulse; spur; urge.
   Dar impulso a. To get something going (started).
impunidad f. impunity.
impureza f. impurity; contamination.
impuro adj. impure, not pure, adulterated.
imputar to impute, to blame, to attribute.
inaceptable adj. not acceptable.
inactivo adj. inactive, idle.
inadaptable adj. not adaptable.
inadecuado adj. inadequate, not adequate.
inadmisible adj. inadmissible, objectionable.
inadvertido adj. unnoticed.
inalámbrico adj. wireless.
inalterable adj. unalterable, changeless.
inauguración f. inauguration.

inaugurar to inaugurate; to begin.

incansable adj. untiring.

incapacidad f. incapacity, inability; incompetence, disability.

incapaz adj. incapable, inefficient, incompetent.
Es incapaz de hacerlo. He's incapable of doing it.

incautación f. seizure, taking over.

incautarse to take over, to seize.

incendiar to set on fire.

incendio m. fire.

incertidumbre f. uncertainty.

incesante adj. incessant, continual.
Un ruido incesante. A continual noise.

incidente adj. incidental; m. incident.

incierto adj. uncertain.

incisión f. incision.

inciso adj. incised, cut; m. partial meaning of a clause, parenthetic clause; comma.

incitar to incite, to stimulate.

inclemencia f. inclemency; severity.
La inclemencia del tiempo no nos permitió salir. The bad weather kept us at home.

inclinación f. inclination; leaning, tendency; bank (of an airplane).

inclinar to incline, to bend.

inclinarse to incline, to tend to, to lean towards.

INCLUIR to include; to enclose.
¿Está incluído el vino? Is wine included?
Incluya su nombre en la lista. Include his name on the list.
Incluí el recibo en la carta. I enclosed the receipt in the letter.

inclusive adj. inclusive, including.

incluso adj. enclosed; including.

incógnito adj. unknown; incognito.
Viajó de incógnito. He traveled incognito.

incoherente adj. incoherent; disconnected.

incombustible adj. incombustible.

incomodar to disturb, to inconvenience, to bother.
Si eso no le incomoda. If it doesn't inconvenience you.

incómodo adj. uncomfortable; inconvenient.

incomparable adj. matchless, without equal.

incompatible adj. incompatible.

incompetencia f. incompetency.

incompleto adj. incomplete, unfinished.

incomprensible adj. incomprehensible, impossible to understand.

incomunicado adj. incommunicado.

incomunicar to isolate, to hold someone incommunicado.

inconcebible adj. inconceivable, unthinkable, incredible.

incondicional adj. unconditional.

incongruencia f. incongruity, being out of place, being inconsistent.

inconsciencia f. unconsciousness.

inconsciente adj. unconscious.

inconstancia f. inconstancy, unsteadiness, fickleness.

inconveniente adj. inconvenient.
Tener inconveniente en. To object to.
No tener inconveniente en. Not to mind. Not to object to.

incorporar to incorporate; to join.

incorporarse to sit up or rise from a lying position.

incorrección f. incorrectness; inaccuracy.

incorrecto adj. incorrect, inaccurate, wrong, improper.

incorregible adj. incorrigible.

incredulidad f. incredulity, lack of belief.

incrédulo adj. incredulous.

increíble adj. incredible.

incremento m. increment, increase.
Tomar incremento. To increase.

increpar to reproach, to rebuke.

incubadora f. incubator.

inculcar to inculcate, to impress by repetition.

inculpar to inculpate, to involve, to blame.

inculto adj. uncultivated; uncultured, uneducated, boorish.

incumbencia f. duty, concern.
Eso no es de mi incumbencia. It doesn't concern me.

incumbir to concern, to pertain.
Esto te incumbe a ti. This concerns you.

incumplimiento m. nonfulfillment.

incurable adj. incurable; hopeless.

incurrir to incur, to run or get into; to make (a mistake).
Incurrir en deudas. To get into debt.
Ha incurrido en una falta terrible. He's made a terrible mistake.

indagar to inquire, to investigate.

indebidamente improperly, unduly, wrongly.

indebido adj. improper; wrong; undue; illegal.

indecente adj. indecent; unbecoming.

indecisión f. indecision, hesitation.

indeciso adj. undecided, hesitant.

indefenso adj. defenseless.

indefinido adj. indefinite.

indeleble adj. indelible.

indemnización f. indemnity, indemnification, compensation.

indemnizar to indemnify, to make good, to compensate.

independencia f. independence.

independiente adj. independent.

indeseable adj. undesirable.

indeterminado adj. indeterminate; doubtful; undecided.

indiano m. a Spaniard who returns to his birthplace after a long residence in Spanish America.

indicación f. indication, hint, sign; suggestion; pl. instructions.

Eso era una buena indicación. *That was a good sign.*

Lo hizo por indicación de su amigo. *He did it at his friend's suggestion.*

Una indicación de Ud. es bastante. *A hint from you is enough.*

Siguió las indicaciones del médico. *He followed the doctor's instructions.*

Para usarlo, siga las indicaciones siguientes. *To use it, follow these instructions.*

indicador *m. indicator, pointer, gauge.*

INDICAR *to indicate; to point out.*

Haga el favor de indicarme el camino. *Please show me the way.*

índice *m. index; hand (of a clock, etc.).*

Dedo índice. *Index finger.*

indicio *m. indication, mark, clue.*

indiferencia *f. indifference.*

indiferente *adj. indifferent.*

Me es indiferente. *It makes no difference to me.*

indígena *adj. native.*

indigencia *f. poverty, indigence.*

indigente *adj. poor, indigent.*

indigestión *f. indigestion.*

indigesto *adj. hard to digest.*

indignación *f. indignation, anger.*

indignar *to irritate, to annoy, to anger.*

indignidad *f. indignity.*

indigno *adj. unworthy, undeserving; unbecoming; disgraceful.*

índio *m. Indian; Hindu.*

indirecta *f. hint.*

indirecto *adj. indirect.*

indiscreción *f. indiscretion.*

indiscreto *adj. indiscreet, imprudent.*

indiscutible *adj. unquestionable, indisputable.*

indispensable *adj. indispensable, essential.*

indisponer *to indispose; to become ill; to cause enmity or quarrels.*

¿Está Ud. indispuesto? *Are you ill (indisposed)?*

indisposición *f. indisposition.*

individual *adj. individual.*

individualmente *individually.*

individuo *m. individual, person.*

índole *f. disposition, character; kind, class.*

inducir *to induce; to persuade.*

indudable *adj. indubitable, certain.*

indulgencia *f. indulgence.*

indulgente *adj. indulgent, lenient.*

indultar *to pardon (a prisoner, etc.).*

indulto *m. pardon.*

indumentaria *f. clothing, clothes, outfit.*

industria *f. industry; diligence.*

industrial *adj. industrial, manufacturing; m. industrialist.*

ineficacia *f. inefficiency.*

ineficaz *adj. inefficient.*

ineludible *adj. unavoidable.*

ineptitud *f. ineptitude, inability, unfitness.*

inepto *adj. inept, incompetent; unfit.*

inequívoco *adj. unmistakable.*

inerte *adj. inert; slothful, sluggish.*

inesperadamente *unexpectedly.*

inesperado *adj. unexpected, unforeseen.*

inevitable *adj. inevitable, unavoidable.*

inexactitud *f. inaccuracy.*

inexacto *adj. inexact, inaccurate.*

inexperto *adj. inexperienced; inexpert.*

inexplicable *adj. inexplicable, impossible to explain.*

infalible *adj. infallible.*

infamar *to disgrace, to dishonor, to defame.*

infame *adj. infamous, shameful.*

infamia *f. infamy, disgrace.*

infancia *f. childhood.*

infantería *f. infantry.*

infantil *adj. infantile; childish.*

Parálisis infantil. *Infantile paralysis.*

infatigable *adj. tireless, untiring.*

infección *f. infection.*

infectar *to infect, to spread disease.*

infectarse *to become infected.*

infeliz *adj. unhappy; unfortunate; m. a naive (good-hearted, gullible) person.*

INFERIOR *adj. inferior; lower; subordinate; m. an inferior, a subordinate.*

Es una tela de calidad inferior. *This material is of inferior quality.*

Trata muy bien a sus inferiores. *He treats his subordinates well.*

Labio inferior. *Lower lip.*

inferioridad *f. inferiority.*

inferir *to infer; to imply; to inflict (wounds, injuries, etc.).*

infiel *adj. unfaithful.*

Si no me es infiel la memoria. *If my memory doesn't fail me. If I remember correctly.*

infierno *m. hell, inferno.*

ínfimo *adj. lowest; least.*

No lo quiero vender a precio tan ínfimo. *I don't want to sell it at such a low price. I don't want to sell it for so little.*

infinidad *f. infinity; too many, a vast number.*

Hay infinidad de gente que no piensa así. *There are many (a lot of) people who don't think so.*

infinitamente *infinitely, immensely.*

infinitivo *m. infinitive (grammar).*

infinito *adj. infinite.*

inflamable *adj. inflammable.*

inflamación *f. inflammation.*

inflamar *to catch fire; to inflame.*

Tenga Ud. cuidado porque se inflama fácilmente. *Be careful, it's inflammable.*

Tiene los ojos inflamados. *His eyes are inflamed.*

inflar *to inflate.*

influencia *f. influence.*

influenza *f. influenza, grippe, flu.*

INFLUIR to *influence*.

La propaganda influye mucho en el público. *Advertising has a great influence on the public.* ("*Advertising influences the public very much.*")

Influya usted para que . . . *Use your influence to* . . .

INFORMACIÓN f. *information; inquiry; investigation.*

¿Dónde queda la ventanilla de información? *Where is the information window (in a railway station)?*

informal adj. *unreliable, not to be depended on; not serious; unbusinesslike.*

informalidad f. *informality; lack of reliability, not being dependable.*

informar to *report, to inform, to let know; to plead (law).*

informarse to *find out, to learn.*

Acabo de informarme del asunto. *I've just learned about the matter.*

informe adj. *shapeless; m. information; report; plea, allegation; pl. references.*

Dar un informe. *To give information. To make a report.*

informes m. *information.*

infortunado adj. *unlucky, unfortunate.*

infracción f. *infraction, violation, infringement.*

infranqueable adj. *insurmountable.*

infrecuente adj. *infrequent, unusual.*

infringir to *infringe, to violate.*

infructuoso adj. *unsuccessful, vain, fruitless.*

infundado adj. *unfounded, groundless, without cause or reason.*

infundir to *give (courage), to command (respect), to make (someone suspicious).*

Infundir ánimo. *To give courage.*

Infunde respeto. *It commands respect.*

Me infunde sospechas. *His actions make me suspect him.*

ingeniería f. *engineering.*

ingeniero m. *engineer.*

ingenio m. *ingenuity; talent; mill.*

Fué un escritor de mucho ingenio. *He was a very talented writer.*

Mi hermano trabaja en un ingenio de azúcar. *My brother works at a sugar mill.*

ingenioso adj. *ingenious, clever.*

ingenuidad f. *naïveté, simplicity.*

ingenuo adj. *naïve, simple.*

ingerir to *insert; to ingest, to take food.*

INGLÉS adj. and n. *English; Englishman; English language.*

Se habla inglés. *English spoken here.*

Habla muy mal el inglés. *He speaks English very badly.*

El señor es inglés. *The gentleman is an Englishman (is English).*

ingratitud f. *ingratitude, lack of gratitude.*

ingrato adj. *ungrateful.*

ingresar to *enter.*

ingreso m. *entry (bookkeeping); money received; pl. f. income, revenue, returns.*

Ingresó en el ejército como soldado. *He joined the army as a private.*

Hubo más gastos que ingresos. *There were more expenses than profits.*

íngrimo adj. *alone (Amer.).*

Estaba íngrimo. *He was all alone.*

inhábil adj. *incapable; unfit, unqualified.*

inhalar to *inhale.*

inhospitalario adj. *inhospitable.*

inhumación f. *burial.*

inhumano adj. *inhuman, cruel, hard-hearted.*

inicial adj. *initial; f. initial.*

iniciar to *initiate; to begin.*

iniciativa f. *initiative.*

Tomar la iniciativa. *To take the initiative.*

inicuo adj. *wicked.*

iniquidad f. *wickedness, iniquity.*

injerto m. *graft (of trees).*

injuria f. *insult, injury, offense.*

injustamente *unjustly.*

injusticia f. *injustice.*

injusto adj. *unjust, unfair.*

Eso es injusto. *That's not fair. That's unjust.*

inmediación f. *contiguity, nearness; vicinity.*

INMEDIATAMENTE *immediately.*

inmediato adj. *immediate; contiguous.*

inmejorable adj. *the very best, unsurpassable.*

inmensamente *immensely.*

inmenso adj. *immense, huge, vast.*

inmerecido adj. *undeserved.*

inmensurable adj. *boundless, immeasurable.*

inmiscuir to *mix.*

inmiscuirse to *meddle, to interfere.*

inmoderado adj. *immoderate, not moderate.*

inmoral adj. *immoral.*

inmortal adj. *immortal.*

inmóvil adj. *immovable, firmly fixed; deathlike.*

inmovilizar to *immobilize.*

inmueble m. *property; real estate.*

inmundicia f. *filth, dirt.*

inmundo adj. *filthy, dirty, unclean.*

inmutable adj. *unchangeable, immutable, neverchanging.*

innecesario adj. *unnecessary, not necessary.*

innegable adj. *undeniable, unquestionable.*

inocencia f. *innocence.*

inocente adj. *innocent.*

inodoro adj. *odorless; m. toilet.*

¿Dónde está el inodoro? *Where's the toilet?*

inofensivo adj. *inoffensive, harmless.*

inoportuno adj. *inopportune, untimely; said or done at the wrong time.*

No sea Ud. inoportuno. *Don't come at the*

wrong time (do things at the wrong time, say the wrong things).

inquebrantable adj. tenacious, unyielding.

inquietar to disturb, to cause anxiety.

inquietarse to become anxious or worried; to be uneasy or restless.

inquieto adj. restless, uneasy, worried.

Pasó toda la noche inquieto. He was restless all night.

inquietud f. uneasiness, anxiety, restlessness.

inquilino m. tenant.

inquirir to inquire.

insalubre adj. unhealthful.

insano adj. insane, mad.

inscribir to inscribe; to register, to record.

inscribirse to register (at a school, etc.).

inscripción f. inscription.

insecticida adj. insecticide.

Polvo insecticida. Insect powder. Insecticide.

insecto m. insect.

inseguro adj. uncertain.

insensatez f. foolishness, stupidity.

insensato adj. stupid, foolish.

insensible adj. not sensitive, unfeeling, heartless.

inseparable adj. inseparable.

insertar to insert; to introduce.

inservible adj. useless, good-for-nothing.

insidioso adj. insidious, sly.

insigne adj. famous, noted.

insignia f. badge; pl. insignia.

insignificante adj. insignificant.

insinuar to insinuate, to hint.

insipidez f. insipidity; lack of flavor (taste).

insípido adj. insipid, tasteless.

insistencia f. insistence, persistence.

insistir to insist.

insolación f. sunstroke.

insolencia f. insolence, rudeness.

insolente adj. insolent, rude.

insolvente adj. insolvent, not able to pay, broke.

insomnio m. insomnia, sleeplessness.

inspección f. inspection.

inspeccionar to inspect, to examine.

inspector m. inspector; superintendent.

inspiración f. inspiration.

inspirar to inspire; to inhale.

Le inspiró mucha simpatía. He found her very congenial.

instalación f. installation; fixtures.

Instalación eléctrica. Electrical fixtures.

instalar to install; to set up.

Todavía no han instalado la luz eléctrica. They haven't yet installed the electric lights.

instancia f. instance; request.

A instancia de. At the request of.

instantánea f. snapshot.

instantáneamente instantly, at once.

Contestó instantáneamente. He answered at

once (right away).

INSTANTE m. instant.

Aguárdame un instante. Wait for me a moment.

Me contestó al instante. He answered me right away.

instar to urge, to press.

instaurar to establish, to restore.

instintivamente instinctively.

instinto m. instinct.

institución f. institution, establishment.

instituir to institute, to establish.

instituto m. institute; high school.

institutriz f. governess.

instrucción f. instruction; education; pl. directions.

Instrucción pública. Public education.

¿Tiene Ud. las instrucciones para el manejo de esta máquina? Do you have the directions for the use of this machine?

instructivo adj. instructive.

instructor m. instructor, teacher.

instruir to instruct, to teach.

instrumento m. instrument.

¿Qué instrumento toca Ud.? What instrument do you play?

insubordinado adj. insubordinate.

insubordinarse to rebel; to mutiny.

insuficiencia f. insufficiency.

insuficiente adj. not enough, insufficient.

insufrible adj. unbearable.

insultar to insult.

insulto m. insult, offense.

insuperable adj. insuperable, insurmountable.

intacto adj. intact, untouched, whole.

intachable adj. irreproachable, faultless.

integral adj. integral; whole.

Pan integral. Whole-wheat bread.

integrar to integrate.

integridad f. integrity.

ÍNTEGRO adj. entire, whole, in full; upright, honest.

Es un hombre íntegro. He's an honest man. He's very upright.

La suma íntegra. The amount in full.

Se comió un pan íntegro. He ate a whole loaf of bread.

intelectual adj. and n. intellectual.

inteligencia f. intelligence; understanding.

En la inteligencia de que. With the understanding that.

INTELIGENTE adj. intelligent.

inteligible adj. intelligible.

intemperie f. rough or bad weather.

A la intemperie. Outdoors. In the open.

INTENCIÓN f. intention, mind, meaning.

¿Cuál es su intención? What does he intend to do?

Lo dijo con segunda intención. What he said had a double meaning.

Tener buena intención. *To mean well.*
Tener mala intención. *Not to mean well.*
Tener la intención de. *To intend to.*
intendencia f. *administration, management; quartermaster (corps).*
intendente m. *quartermaster (officer); superintendent.*
intensidad f. *intensity.*
intenso *adj. intense.*
intentar *to try, to attempt, to intend, to endeavor.*
Es inútil que intente. *It's useless to try.*
intento m. *intent, purpose.*
No lo hice de intento. *I didn't do it on purpose.*
intercalar *to intercalate, to put in between.*
intercambio m. *interchange; exchange.*
interceder *to intercede, to plead in another's behalf.*
interceptar *to intercept; to block.*
INTERÉS m. *interest.*
No demuestra el menor interés. *He doesn't show the slightest interest.*
Pone interés en hacerlo bien. *He tries hard to do it well.*
Devengar intereses. *To pay interest.*
interesado *adj. interested, concerned.*
INTERESANTE *adj. interesting.*
Es una novela poco interesante. *It's not a very interesting novel.*
INTERESAR *to interest, to concern.*
No me interesa. 1. *It doesn't interest me.* 2. *I don't care for him (her, it, etc.).*
INTERESARSE *to be concerned; to become interested.*
Se interesó mucho en el negocio. *He became very interested in the business.*
interino *adj. provisional, temporary, acting.*
INTERIOR *adj. interior, internal; m. interior; inside.*
Un cuarto interior. *An inside room.*
Lo dijo para su interior. *He said it to himself.*
El comercio interior. *Domestic trade.*
El Ministerio de lo Interior. *Department of the Interior.*
Ropa interior. *Underwear.*
Navegación interior. *Inland navigation.*
intermediar *to mediate.*
intermediario *adj. and n. intermediary.*
intermedio *adj. intermediate; m. interval, recess.*
internacional *adj. international.*
internar *to intern, to confine.*
interno *adj. internal; interior; m. boarding student; intern.*
Para uso interno. *For internal use.*
interponer *to interpose.*
interpretación f. *interpretation, meaning, acting.*
interpretar *to interpret; to understand.*
Interpretar bien. *To understand correctly.*
No interpretar bien. *To misunderstand.*
intérprete m. *and f. interpreter.*
intervalo m. *interval.*

intervenir *to intervene; to mediate.*
interrogación f. *interrogation, questioning; question, inquiry; question mark.*
Signo de interrogación. *Question mark.*
interrogar *to interrogate, to question.*
interrogatorio f. *cross examination.*
INTERRUMPIR *to interrupt.*
Dispense Ud. que le interrumpa. *Pardon me for interrupting you.*
interrupción f. *interruption; stop.*
Sin interrupción. *Without stopping.*
interruptor m. *switch (electricity).*
intestino *adj. intestinal; domestic, internal; m. pl. intestines.*
intimar *to intimate, to hint; to order; to become intimate.*
intimidad f. *intimacy, close friendship.*
intimidar *to intimidate, to frighten.*
íntimo *adj. intimate, close.*
Eran amigos íntimos. *They were very close friends.*
Tuvimos una conversación íntima. *We had an intimate conversation. We had a tête-à-tête.*
intolerable *adj. intolerable, unbearable.*
intolerancia f. *intolerance.*
intolerante *adj. intolerant.*
intoxicación f. *intoxication, poisoning.*
intranquilo *adj. restless.*
intransigencia f. *uncompromisingness, intransigence.*
intransigente *adj. uncompromising, unyielding, die-hard, intransigent.*
intransitable *adj. impassable.*
intratable *adj. hard to deal with; hidebound; not sociable.*
intrepidez f. *intrepidity, courage.*
intrépido *adj. intrepid, fearless.*
intriga f. *intrigue, plot.*
intrigante *adj. intriguing; m. intriguer.*
intrincado *adj. intricate, entangled, complicated.*
introducción f. *introduction. See presentación and recomendación.*
introducir *to introduce, to put in. See presentar.*
Introduje la carta en el buzón. *I put the letter in the mailbox.*
intromisión f. *interference.*
intruso *adj. intruding; m. and f. intruder.*
intuición f. *intuition.*
inundar *to inundate, to flood.*
INÚTIL *useless; fruitless; unnecessary.*
Es inútil que se lo pida. *There's no use (in) asking him.*
Es un hombre inútil. *He's good-for-nothing. He can't do anything.*
inutilidad f. *inutility, uselessness.*
inutilizar *to spoil, to ruin, to disable.*
INÚTILMENTE *uselessly, in vain.*
Hicimos el viaje inútilmente. *We made the*

    trip in vain.

invadir *to invade.*

invalidar *to invalidate, to nullify, to render void.*

inválido *adj. invalid, null; crippled; m. an invalid; a cripple.*

invariable *adj. unchangeable, invariable.*

invasión *f. invasion.*

invención *f. invention.*

inventar *to invent.*

inventario *m. inventory.*

invento *m. invention.*

inverisímil *adj. See inverosímil.*

invernar *to winter, to spend the winter.*

    Fueron a invernar a California. *They went to spend the winter in California.*

inverosímil *adj. improbable, unlikely; incredible.*

    Me pareció inverosímil el relato. *The story seemed improbable to me.*

invertir *to invert, to turn upside down; to spend, to take (time); to invest (money).*

investigación *f. investigation.*

investigar *to investigate.*

INVIERNO *m. winter.*

invisible *adj. invisible.*

invitación *f. invitation.*

INVITADO *adj. invited; m. guest.*

    Estamos invitados a una reunión mañana. *We are invited to go to a meeting tomorrow.*

    Hoy tendremos invitados. *We're having guests today.*

INVITAR *to invite.*

inyección *f. injection.*

inyectar *to inject.*

iodo *m. iodine. See yodo.*

IR *to go; to be; to concern, to have to do with.*

    ¡Vámonos! *Let's go!*

    ¡Voy! *I'm coming!*

    Me voy. *I'm going away. I'm leaving.*

    Voy a mi casa. *I'm going home.*

    Debemos irnos. *We must go.*

    ¡Váyase! *Go away!*

    ¡Qué se vaya! *Let him go!*

    No se vaya Ud. *Don't go away.*

    No puedo ir. *I can't go.*

    ¿Cómo le va? (¿Cómo vamos?) *How are you? How are you getting along?*

    ¿Cómo van los negocios? *How's business?*

    El paciente va mucho mejor. *The patient is much better.*

    Van a dar las doce. *It will soon be twelve.*

    Vamos a ver. *Let's see.*

    Vamos a dar un paseo. *Let's take a walk.*

    Vamos, Juan, dígamelo Ud. *Go on, John, tell it to me.*

    Vamos, déjame ya. *Come on, let me alone (don't bother me).*

    ¡Qué se le ha de hacer! *It can't be helped!*

    Vamos al grano. *Let's get to the point.*

    ¿Quién va? *Who's there?*

    ¡Vaya! *Go on! I don't believe it!*

    ¡Vaya una ocurrencia! *What an idea!*

    ¡Vaya Ud. con Dios! *Good-by! Good luck to you! ("Go with God.")*

    ¡Vaya Ud. a paseo! *Go to the dickens! Go to blazes!*

    ¡Vaya por Dios! *Good gracious!*

    Váyase con la música a otra parte. *Go away, don't bother me.*

    ¡Qué va! *Nonsense!*

    Ahora va de veras. *Now it's really serious.*

    ¡Ahí va eso! *Here it comes! Catch!*

    Ahí van dos dólares a que yo llego. *I bet you two dollars that I'll get there first.*

    La situación va de mal en peor. *The situation is getting worse and worse (is going from bad to worse).*

    Eso no me va ni me viene. *It (that) doesn't concern me in the least.*

    Eso no va conmigo. *That doesn't concern me.*

    Va de punta en blanco. *She's all dressed up.*

    El buque se fué a pique. *The ship sank.*

    Ir a pie. *To walk. To go on foot.*

    Ir a caballo. *To ride. To go on horseback.*

    Ir en coche. *To drive.*

    Ir de brazo. *To walk arm-in-arm.*

    Ir a medias. *To go half-and-half. To share equally.*

ira *f. anger, fury, rage.*

    Tuvo un repente de ira. *He had a fit of temper.*

iracundo *adj. irate, angry; enraged.*

    Estaba iracunda por lo que dije. *She was furious at what I said.*

ironía *f. irony.*

irónico *adj. ironical.*

irradiar *to irradiate.*

irreal *adj. unreal.*

irreflexivo *adj. thoughtless, rash.*

irregular *adj. irregular.*

irrespetuoso *adj. disrespectful, showing no respect.*

irresponsabilidad *f. irresponsibility, lack of responsibility.*

irresponsable *adj. irresponsible.*

irrigar *to irrigate.*

irritado *adj. irritated, angry.*

irritar *to irritate, to exasperate.*

    Ella le irrita. *She exasperates him.*

irrompible *adj. unbreakable.*

isla *f. isle, island.*

italiano *adj. and n. Italian.*

itinerario *adj. and n. itinerary; route; timetable, schedule.*

    ¿Qué itinerario seguirán? *Which route will you take?*

    Quisiera un itinerario de trenes. *I'd like a timetable.*

IZQUIERDO *adj. left; left-handed; f. left hand.*

A la izquierda. *To the left.*

Estaba sentado a mi izquierda. *He was sitting on my left.*

Es un cero a la izquierda. *He doesn't count. He's a nonentity.*

J

jabalí *m. wild boar.*

jabón *m. soap.*

jabonar *to soap.*

jabonera *f. soapdish.*

jaca *f. nag, pony.*

jacinto *m. hyacinth.*

jactancia *f. boasting.*

jactarse *to boast, to brag.*

Se jacta de haber viajado mucho por el mundo. *He boasts of having traveled all over the world.*

jalea *f. jelly.*

jalear *to encourage (a dancer); to sic (a dog).*

jaleo *m. clapping of hands to encourage a dancer; Andalusian dance; noisy party, revelry, racket.*

jalón *m. pole; surveying staff.*

JAMÁS *never.*

Jamás he visto una corrida de toros. *I've never seen a bull fight.*

Jamás lo hubiera hecho yo. *I'd never have done it.*

Nunca jamás. *Never. Never again.*

Para siempre jamás. *For ever and ever.*

Jamás de los jamases. *Never again.*

jamón *m. ham (smoked or cured).*

jaque *m. check (in chess); boaster.*

Jaque mate. *Checkmate.*

jaqueca *f. migraine, headache.*

Tengo jaqueca. *I have a very bad headache.*

jarabe *m. syrup.*

Jarabe para la tos. *Cough syrup.*

Jarabe tapatío. *A typical Mexican dance.*

jardín *m. garden.*

jardinero *m. gardener.*

jarra *f. jug, pitcher.*

En jarras. *With arms akimbo.*

jarro *m. pitcher, pot, jug; babbler.*

jarrón *m. vase, large jar.*

jaula *f. cage.*

jazmín *m. jasmine.*

jazz *m. jazz.*

jefatura *f. headquarters; leadership; office of a chief.*

Jefatura de Policía. *Police headquarters.*

JEFE *m. chief; head, principal; leader; boss, employer.*

Jefe de taller. *Foreman.*

El jefe del gobierno. *The head of the government.*

El jefe de la oficina. *The office manager.*

Jefe de estación. *Stationmaster.*

jerarquía *f. hierarchy.*

jerez *m. sherry wine.*

jeringa *f. syringe.*

Jesucristo *m. Jesus Christ.*

jesuíta *m. Jesuit; hypocrite.*

Jesús *m. Jesus.*

¡Jesús! *Good heavens! God bless you (said when someone sneezes)!*

jilguero *m. linnet (bird).*

jinete *m. horseman, rider.*

JIRA *f. outing, excursion, picnic; tour.*

Jira campestre. *Picnic.*

Jira de inspección. *Tour of inspection.*

jirafa *f. giraffe.*

jornada *f. journey, trip; day's travel; one day's work.*

Una jornada de cinco días. *A five days' journey (trip).*

Los obreros trabajan jornadas de ocho horas. *The laborers work eight hours a day.*

jornal *m. day's pay; wages.*

Trabaja a jornal. *He works by the day.*

Gana un buen jornal. *He earns good wages.*

jornalero *m. day laborer.*

joroba *f. hump.*

jorobado *m. hunchback.*

jorobar *to importune, to annoy.*

jota *f. name of the letter j; a typical Spanish dance.*

No saber ni jota. *To be very ignorant.*

JOVEN *adj. young; m. young man; f. young lady.*

Todavía es muy joven. *She's still very young.*

¿Quién es esa joven? *Who's that young lady?*

Es un joven muy simpático. *He's a very nice young man.*

jovial *adj. jovial, merry.*

joya *f. jewel, gem; precious, wonderful.*

Llevaba muy lindas joyas. *She wore very beautiful jewels.*

Esa muchacha es una joya. *She's a wonderful girl.*

joyas *f. jewelry.*

jubilar *to pension off, to retire from service.*

judía *f. bean; string bean; Jewess.*

Déme una libra de judías. *Give me a pound of beans.*

Estas judías verdes son excelentes. *These string beans are excellent.*

judío *adj. Jewish; m. Jew.*

JUEGO *m. play, game; gambling; set; play, movement.*

¿Qué juego prefiere? *Which game do you like best?*

Este sombrero no hace juego con mi vestido. *This hat doesn't match my dress.*

Ya te veo el juego. *I see what your intentions are. I see what you're driving (getting) at.*

Compró un juego de loza. *She bought a set of dishes.*

Juego de té. *Tea set.*
Juego de azar. *Game of chance.*
Juego de naipes (cartas). *Card game.*
Juego de prendas. *A game of forfeits.*
Hacer juego. *To match.*
Estar en juego. *To be at stake.*
Poner en juego. *To bring to bear upon. To put into play.*

JUEVES m. *Thursday.*

juez m. *judge.*
Juez de paz. *Justice of the peace.*

jugada f. *play; move (chess); turn (cards); mean trick.*
Jugada de bolsa. *Stock market speculation.*

jugador m. *gambler; player.*

JUGAR *to play; to gamble; to stake; to take part.*
Juega bien al tenis. *He plays tennis well.*
Ha jugado todo su dinero. *He's gambled all his money.*
Juega su última carta. *He's playing his last card. That's his last card.*

jugarreta f. *bad play; bad turn, nasty trick.*

jugo m. *juice.*

jugoso adj. *juicy.*

juguete m. *toy, plaything; laughing stock.*
Le regalaron un juguete. *They gave him a toy as a present.*
Está sirviendo de juguete. *He's being made a laughingstock.*

juicio m. *judgment; mind; opinion; wisdom, good judgment; lawsuit, trial.*
¿Ha perdido Ud. el juicio? *Have you lost your mind?*
Es un hombre de juicio. *He's a man of good judgment. He has good judgment.*
A mi juicio. *In my opinion.*
Someter a juicio. *To bring to trial.*
Pedir en juicio. *To sue (at law).*

juicioso adj. *prudent, sensible, wise, well-behaved.*

JULIO m. *July.*

JUNIO m. *June.*

junta f. *board, council, junta, committee; meeting; joint, coupling, union, junction.*
¿A qué hora fué la junta? *What time did the meeting take place?*
Junta directiva. *Board of directors. Executive committee.*
Junta de comercio. *Board of trade.*
Junta de acreedores. *Creditors' meeting.*
Junta de sanidad. *Board of health.*
Junta remachada. *Riveted joint.*

JUNTAR *to join, to unite; to assemble, to gather; to pile up (money); to leave ajar (door).*
Junte toda la ropa y póngala en la maleta. *Get all the clothes together and put them in the suitcase.*
Junte la puerta. *Leave the door ajar (open).*
Juntar dinero. *To pile up money.*

JUNTARSE *to get together, to meet; to join, to associate with, to keep company.*
Se junta con mala gente. *He keeps bad company.*
Se juntó mucha gente para oír al orador. *Quite a crowd gathered to hear the speaker.*
No me gusta con quien se junta. *I don't like the people you associate with.*

JUNTO near, *close to; together.*
Déjalo junto a la puerta. *Leave it near the door.*
Pasar por junto de. *To pass near. To pass by.*
Emprenderemos el negocio juntos. *We're going into this business together.*
Si Ud. quiere, vamos juntos. *If you wish, we'll go together.*

jura f. *oath of allegiance.*

jurado m. *jury, juryman, juror.*

jurar *to swear, to take oath.*
No se lo creo aunque me lo jure. *I won't believe you even if you swear that it's true.*

justicia f. *justice; fairness; law.*
Hacer justicia. *To do justice. To be just.*
Hacerse justicia por sí mismo. *To take the law into one's hands.*
La justicia. *The police.*

justificación f. *justification.*

justificar *to justify.*

JUSTO adj. *just; fair; exact, to the point; scarce; tight;* m. *a just and pious man.*
Eso no es justo. *That's not fair.*
Al año justo de. *Just a year after.*
El peso justo. *The exact weight.*
El sombrero me está muy justo. *My hat is very tight.*
Vivimos muy justos. *We live from hand to mouth.*

juvenil adj. *juvenile, youthful.*

juventud f. *youth, youthfulness.*

juzgado m. *tribunal, court (of justice).*

JUZGAR *to judge; to think.*
Lo ha juzgado Ud. mal. *You have judged it wrongly.*
¿Lo juzga Ud. conveniente? *Do you think it's advisable?*

K

ka f. *name of the letter k.*

kermese f. *charity festival; bazaar.*

kilo m. *kilo, kilogram (2.2046 pounds).*
Déme un kilo de azúcar. *Give me a kilogram of sugar.*

kilogramo m. *kilogram.*

kilometraje m. *mileage.*

kilométrico *kilometric; mileage (ticket).*

kilómetro m. *kilometer.*

kimono m. *kimona, dressing gown.*

kiosco m. *kiosk, newsstand.*

kodak m. *Kodak.*

L

LA (f. article) the; m. pl. **los**; f. pl. **las** the. See **los**.

La muchacha. The girl.

Las muchachas. The girls.

Las dos hermanas se parecen. Both sisters look alike.

Los padres. The parents.

LA (f. direct object pronoun) you, her, it; pl. **las** them, you. See **los** and **les**.

¿La vió Ud. en la fiesta? Did you see her at the party?

No la vi. I didn't see her.

Me alegro de verla. I'm glad to see you (a woman).

Dámela. Give it (f.) to me.

Traduzca estas palabras al español y léalas en voz alta. Translate these words into Spanish and read them aloud.

la m. la, A (sixth note of the musical scale).

labia f. sweet, winning talk.

Tiene mucha labia para vender. He has a good sales talk.

LABIO m. lip.

Lápiz de labios. Lipstick.

labor f. labor, task; needlework, embroidery.

laborable adj. workable; working.

Día laborable. Working day.

laborar to labor; to work; to till.

laboratorio m. laboratory.

laborioso adj. laborious; hardworking.

labrador m. farmer, peasant.

labranza f. farming; farm.

labrar to till, to cultivate (land); to carve (wood, etc.).

labriego m. peasant.

lacerar to lacerate; to mangle.

lacio adj. withered; languid; straight (hair).

lacónico adj. laconic, brief.

lacrar to communicate (a disease); to seal (with wax).

lacre m. sealing wax.

ladear to tilt, to incline; to skirt.

ladino adj. shrewd; crafty, cunning.

LADO m. side; party, faction.

Siéntese a mi lado. Sit next to me. Sit beside me.

Al otro lado de la calle. Across the street. On the other side of the street.

Vive en la casa de al lado. She lives next door. She lives in the next house.

Ese edificio queda al otro lado del parque. That building's on the other side of the park.

Nos quedamos a este lado del lago. We'll stay on this side of the lake.

Por un lado. On the one hand. On one side.

Por un lado me gusta, pero por el otro no. On the one hand I like it, on the other I don't.

¡Mire Ud. al otro lado! Look on the other side!

¿Quiere hacerse a un lado? Please move aside.

No cabe de lado. It won't fit sideways.

Trabajaron lado a lado. They worked side by side.

Mirar de lado. To look askance. To look out of the corner of one's eye. To look down on.

Dejemos esto a un lado. Let's put this aside.

Conozco muy bien su lado flaco. I know his weakness (weak side) very well.

ladrar to bark.

ladrido m. barking; criticism; calumny.

ladrillo m. brick, tile.

ladrón m. thief, robber.

lagartija f. small lizard.

lagarto m. lizard; alligator (Amer.).

lago m. lake.

lágrima f. tear; drop.

laguna f. pond; gap, blank.

lamentable adj. regrettable, deplorable.

Es lamentable. It's regrettable.

lamentar to regret, to deplore; to mourn.

Lo lamento mucho. I'm very sorry.

Lamento mucho lo ocurrido. I regret what happened. I'm sorry about what happened.

lamer to lick.

lámina f. plate, sheet of metal; engraving, print, picture.

lámpara f. lamp.

lana f. wool.

lance m. hazard; trouble, accident; quarrel.

De lance. Secondhand. At a bargain.

Libros de lance. Secondhand books. Used books.

lancha f. launch, boat.

langosta f. locust; lobster.

lánguido adj. languid, faint, weak.

lanzallamas m. flame thrower.

lanzamiento m. launching (of a ship); throwing, dispossessing.

lanzar to throw; to launch; to dispossess.

lapicero m. pencil holder.

lápida f. a flat stone with an inscription; gravestone.

LÁPIZ m. pencil; crayon.

Lápiz de labios. Lipstick.

lapso m. lapse (of time).

larga f. delay, adjournment.

A la larga. In the long run.

Dar largas a. To put off. To quibble. To delay.

largar to loosen; to let go; to heave (a ship).

Largarse. To leave. To go away.

¡Lárguese de aquí! Get out of here (not polite)!

LARGO adj. long; lengthy; m. length.

Tiene los brazos muy largos. He has very long arms.

Tiene cinco pies de largo. It's five feet long.

Conferencia a larga distancia. Long distance call.

No ponga Ud. esa cara tan larga. Don't pull such a long face.

Tres horas largas. *Three whole hours.*

¿Entró Ud. en casa de Juan?—No, pasé de largo. *Did you stop in at John's house?—No, I (just) passed by.*

A lo largo. 1. *In the distance.* 2. *Lengthwise.*

A lo largo de. *Along.*

A la corta o a la larga. *Sooner or later.*

A lo más largo. *At most.*

¡Largo de aquí! *Get out of here!*

Largo de mano. *Light-fingered.*

laringe f. *larynx.*

laringitis f. *laryngitis.*

larva f. *larva.*

las f. pl. See **la** the.

LÁSTIMA f. *pity; compassion.*

Es lástima. *It's a pity.*

¡Qué lástima! *What a pity! It's too bad! What a shame!*

Me da mucha lástima. *I feel very sorry for him.*

lastimar to *hurt; to injure.*

¿Se ha lastimado Ud.? *Have (did) you hurt yourself?*

Me lastimé una pierna al caer. *I hurt my leg when I fell (down).*

lastre m. *ballast.*

lata f. *tin; tin can; nuisance.*

lateral adj. *lateral.*

latido m. *beat; throbbing.*

latigazo m. *lash; crack (of a whip).*

látigo m. *whip.*

latín m. *Latin.*

latino adj. *Latin.*

latir to *palpitate, to beat.*

latoso adj. *tiresome; boring.*

lava f. *lava.*

lavable adj. *washable.*

lavabo m. *washstand; washroom.*

lavadero m. *laundry, washing-place.*

lavado m. *washing.*

Lavado y planchado. *Laundry.* ("*Washing and ironing.*")

lavandera f. *laundress, washwoman.*

lavandería f. *laundry.*

lavaplatos m. and f. *dishwasher.*

lavar to *wash; to launder.*

Láveme estos calcetines. *Wash these socks for me.*

¿Le lavo la cabeza? *Do you want a shampoo?* ("*Do you want to have your hair washed?*")

lavarse to *wash oneself.*

Lavarse las manos. *To wash one's hands.*

¿Quiere lavarse antes de comer? *Do you want to wash up before eating?*

lavativa f. *enema.*

laxante adj. and n. *laxative.*

lazo m. *bow; lasso, loop.*

Corbata de lazo. *Bow tie.*

LE *him, her, it; to him, to her, to it.* See **les**.

¿Qué le pasa? *What's the matter with him (her)?*

Le conozco. *I know him.*

Le di el libro (a ella). *I gave her the book.*

Le hablé hace un momento. *I spoke to him a little while ago.*

Le expliqué el caso a mi esposa. *I explained the matter to my wife.*

leal adj. *loyal.*

lealtad f. *loyalty.*

lección f. *lesson.*

lector adj. *reader.*

lectura f. *reading.*

LECHE f. *milk.*

lechería f. *dairy.*

lechero m. *milkman.*

lecho m. *bed; bed of a river; stratum.*

lechón m. *little pig, suckling pig.*

lechuga f. *lettuce.*

lechuza f. *owl.*

LEER to *read.*

Puedo leer español pero no lo puedo hablar. *I can read Spanish but I can't speak it.*

legajo m. *bundle of papers.*

legal adj. *legal, lawful; standard.*

Peso legal. *Standard weight.*

legalizar to *legalize.*

legar to *bequeath; to delegate.*

legendario adj. *legendary.*

legible adj. *legible.*

legión f. *legion.*

legislación f. *legislation.*

legislar to *legislate.*

legislatura f. *legislature.*

legitimar to *make legitimate, to legalize.*

legítimo adj. *legitimate; authentic.*

legua f. *league (measure of distance—about three miles).*

legumbre f. *vegetable.*

leído adj. *well-read, well-educated.*

Es un hombre muy leído. *He's a well-read man.*

lejano adj. *distant, remote, far.*

Un país lejano. *A distant country.*

LEJOS *far, far away, distant.*

¿Es muy lejos de aquí? *Is it very far from here?*

¿Queda lejos el hotel? *Is the hotel far from here?*

Está muy lejos de aquí. *It's very far from here. It's a long way from here. It's quite a distance from here.*

Algo lejos. *Rather far.*

Más lejos. *Further. Farther. More distant.*

A lo lejos. *In the distance.*

Desde (de) lejos. *From afar. From a distance.*

lema m. *motto.*

lencería f. *linen goods, linen shop; linen trade.*

LENGUA f. *tongue; language.*

Lengua española. *Spanish language.*

Lengua madre. *Mother tongue.*

Tirar de la lengua. *To draw one out.*

No morderse la lengua. *Not to be afraid to talk.*

Morderse la lengua. *To hold one's tongue. ("To bite one's tongue.")*

Irsele a uno la lengua. *To speak out of turn.*

Pegarse la lengua al paladar. *To be speechless with excitement or fear.*

lenguaje *m. language; style.*

LENTAMENTE *slowly.*

lente *m. lens; pl. eyeglasses.*

lenteja *f. lentil.*

lentitud *f. slowness.*

LENTO *adj. slow; sluggish.*

leña *f. firewood.*

A falta de carbón quemaremos leña. *If there's no coal, we'll burn wood.*

Echar leña al fuego. *To add fuel to the fire.*

leñador *m. woodcutter.*

leño *m. log, block.*

león *m. lion.*

leona *f. lioness; brave woman.*

leopardo *m. leopard.*

lepra *f. leprosy.*

LES *to them; to you (pl.); them, you (pl.). See le.*

Les escribiré. *I'll write to them.*

Les estimo mucho. *I have a high regard for them (you, pl.).*

Les querrás mucho. *You'll like them a lot.*

Les encantará (a Uds.). *You (pl.) will love it. You'll be charmed by it.*

lesión *f. lesion, injury, wound.*

lesionar *to hurt; to wound; to injure.*

LETRA *f. letter; handwriting; printing type; words of a song; draft, bill (of exchange).*

Tiene buena letra. *She has a good handwriting.*

A la letra. *To the letter. Literally. Verbatim.*

letrado *adj. learned, erudite; m. lawyer.*

letrero *m. inscription; sign; label.*

No me había fijado en el letrero. *I didn't notice the sign.*

letrina *f. latrine.*

levadura *f. leaven, yeast.*

levantamiento *m. raising, uprising, revolt.*

LEVANTAR *to raise, to lift, to pick up; to remove, to clear (the table); to draw (a map).*

¿Puede Ud. levantar ese peso? *Can you lift that weight?*

Levante la mesa. *Clear the table.*

Levanta ese papel del suelo. *Pick up that paper from the floor.*

Levantar cabeza. *To raise one's head again. To get on one's feet again.*

Empezó a levantar la voz. *He began to raise his voice.*

Levantar un plano. *To draw a map (of a place).*

Llegamos en el momento de levantar el telón. *We arrived just as the curtain was going up.*

Levantar la vista. *To lift one's eyes. To look up.*

LEVANTARSE *to rise, to get up.*

¿A qué hora se levanta Ud.? *What time do you get up?*

Me levanto temprano. *I get up early.*

Es hora de levantarse. *It's time to get up.*

leve *adj. light (weight); slight.*

levita *f. frock coat.*

léxico *m. lexicon.*

LEY *f. law, act; legal standard of quality, weight or measure.*

Proyecto de ley. *Bill (of Congress).*

La ley fué aprobada en el senado. *The law was passed in (by) the Senate.*

De ley. *Standard (gold, etc.).*

leyenda *f. legend; inscription (on coins, metals, etc.).*

lezna *f. awl.*

liar *to tie, to bind; to enroil.*

liberación *f. liberation.*

liberal *adj. and n. liberal.*

liberar *See libertar.*

libertad *f. liberty, freedom.*

libertador *adj. liberating; m. liberator.*

libertar *to liberate, to free.*

libertino *adj. and n. dissolute, licentious; libertine.*

libra *f. pound.*

Déme media libra de café. *Give me half a pound of coffee.*

Libra esterlina. *Pound sterling.*

libranza *f. draft; money order.*

LIBRE *adj. free.*

Avíseme en cuanto esté libre. *Let me know as soon as he's free.*

Libre a bordo. *Free on board (F.O.B.).*

Entrada libre. *Admission free.*

librería *f. bookstore; library; bookcase.*

librero *m. bookseller.*

libreta *f. memorandum book; loaf of bread weighing une pound (in Madrid).*

Libreta de apuntes. *Notebook.*

Libreta de depósitos. *Bankbook.*

LIBRO *m. book.*

Libro en rústica. *Paper-bound book.*

Libro de caja. *Cashbook.*

Libros de lance. *Secondhand books.*

Firme en el libro de registro. *Sign the register.*

licencia *f. license; leave, furlough; permit; certificate; degree.*

licenciado *m. license; lawyer.*

licenciar *to license; to allow; to discharge (a soldier).*

licitador *m. bidder.*

lícito *adj. licit, lawful, just, fair.*

licor *m. liquor.*

licorería *f. liquor store.*

líder *m. leader.*

lidiar *to combat, to fight; to contend.*

liebre *f. hare.*

Donde menos se piensa salta la liebre. *Things happen unexpectedly. ("The hare leaps from the bush where we least expect her.")*

lienzo m. linen cloth; canvas (painting).

liga f. garter; birdlime; league; alloy.

ligar to bind, to tie; to alloy.

ligereza f. lightness; fickleness; hastiness.

LIGERO adj. quick, swift, light (weight); hasty.

Hágalo ligero. Do it quickly.

Es muy ligero de cascos. He's very silly (feather-brained, light-headed).

lija f. sandpaper; dogfish.

lila f. lilac; lilac color.

lima f. lime (fruit); file (tool).

limar to file (with a tool); to polish.

limitación f. limitation, limit.

limitado adj. limited.

limitar to limit; to restrain.

Limitarse a decir. To say only. To confine oneself to.

límite m. limit, boundary, border.

Todo tiene sus límites. There's a limit to everything. One must draw the line somewhere.

limón m. lemon.

limonada f. lemonade.

limosna f. alms, charity.

Pedir limosna. To beg.

limpiabotas m. bootblack.

limpiador m. cleaner; cleanser.

limpiar to clean, to cleanse; to mop up.

Quiero que me limpie en seco este traje. I'd like this suit dry-cleaned.

Quiero que me limpien los zapatos. I want my shoes shined. I want a shoeshine.

limpiaúñas m. nail cleaner.

limpieza f. cleaning; cleanliness; honesty.

LIMPIO adj. clean; neat; pure.

Tiene su casa muy limpia. She keeps her house very clean.

Tráigame una toalla limpia. Bring me a clean towel.

Poner en limpio. To make a good (final, "clean") copy.

Sacar en limpio. To make out. To conclude. To infer.

Jugar limpio. To play fair. To deal fairly.

linaza f. linseed; flaxseed.

lince adj. keen, sharp-sighted; m. lynx.

linchar to lynch.

lindar to adjoin, to border.

linde m. limit, boundary; landmark.

lindero adj. adjoining, bordering; m. boundary.

LINDO adj. pretty; neat.

¡Qué muchacha tan linda! What a pretty girl!

Nos divertimos de lo lindo. We had a wonderful time. ("We enjoyed ourselves wonderfully.")

LÍNEA f. line.

Tire Ud. una línea recta. Draw a straight line.

La línea está ocupada. The line is busy.

Escribir cuatro líneas. To write a few lines. To drop someone a note.

Línea telefónica. Telephone line.

Línea férrea. Railway.

Línea aérea. Air line.

En toda la línea. All along the line.

lingote m. ingot.

lingüista m. and f. linguist.

linimento m. liniment.

lino m. flax; linen.

linóleo m. linoleum.

linotipia f. linotype.

linotipista m. linotype operator.

linterna f. lantern; flashlight.

lío m. bundle, parcel; row, fix, mess.

Me hice un lío. I was all mixed up.

En buen lío nos hemos metido. We got ourselves in quite a fix.

Armar un lío. To start a row.

liquidación f. liquidation.

liquidar to liquidate.

LÍQUIDO adj. liquid; clear, net; m. liquid, fluid.

Producto líquido. Net proceeds.

lírico adj. lyric, lyrical.

lirio m. lily.

lisiado adj. maimed, crippled.

liso adj. smooth, even; plain.

Tela lisa. Plain cloth.

lisonja f. flattery.

lisonjear to flatter; to please.

lisonjero adj. flattering, pleasing; n. flatterer.

El habla de Ud. de una manera muy lisonjera. He speaks well of you. ("He speaks of you in a very flattering manner.")

LISTA f. list; roll, muster; menu; strip of cloth; stripe.

Tráigame la lista de vinos. Bring me the wine list.

Aquí está la lista de platos. Here is the menu.

Pasar lista. To call the roll.

Tela a listas. Striped cloth.

Lista de correos. General delivery.

listado adj. striped.

listín m. telephone book.

LISTO adj. ready; quick; bright, clever, smart, cunning.

¿Está Ud. listo? Are you ready?

Todo está listo. Everything's ready.

No crea, es más listo de lo que parece. Don't get the wrong idea; he's smarter than he looks.

litera f. litter.

literario adj. literary.

literato m. learned man: writer.

literatura f. literature.

litigio m. litigation, lawsuit.

litografía f. lithography.

litoral adj. littoral; m. coast; seacoast.

litro m. liter.

liviano adj. light (weight); fickle; lewd.

Es liviano; Ud. puede alzarlo facilmente. *It's light; you can lift it easily.*

lívido *adj. livid; pale.*

Se puso lívido. *He became pale.*

LO *(neuter article) the.*

Lo más hermoso. *The prettiest.*

Lo mejor. *The best.*

Lo peor. *The worst.*

Lo dicho. *What's said.*

Lo mío y lo tuyo. *Mine and yours. What's mine and what's yours.*

Lo demás importa poco. *The rest doesn't matter a great deal. The rest is not very important.*

Eso es lo que quiero. *That's what I want.*

A lo lejos. *At a distance. In the distance.*

A lo sumo. *At the most.*

LO *(m. and neuter direct object pronoun) it, him, you.*

¿Quién lo quiere? *Who wants it?*

¿Me lo das? *Will you give it to me?*

Démelo. *Give it to me.*

No me lo diga Ud. *Don't tell it to me.*

Dígaselo a ella. *Tell it to her.*

¿Están Uds. listos? —Lo estamos. *Are you ready? —We are.*

No lo conozco. *I don't know him.*

Se lo llevaron a casa. *They took (carried) him home.*

No lo puedo remediar. *I can't help it.*

¿Por qué no se lo pides? *Why don't you ask him for it?*

No lo suelte Ud. *Hold it. Don't let it go.*

lobo *m. wolf.*

lóbulo *m. lobule, lobe.*

lóbrego *adj. murky, dark; sad.*

local *adj. local; m. place; quarters.*

Costumbre local. *Local custom.*

Este local es muy pequeño. *This place (hall, etc.) is very small.*

localidad *f. locality, place; seat (theater).*

localizar *to localize, to locate.*

loción *f. lotion, wash.*

loco *adj. mad, insane, crazy; m. madman.*

Volverse loco. *To lose one's mind. To become insane.*

Estar loco. *To be crazy.*

Está loco por ella. *He's head over heels in love with her. He's crazy about her.*

Hablar a tontas y a locas. *To tell idle stories (tales).*

locomoción *f. locomotion.*

locuaz *adj. loquacious, talkative.*

locura *f. insanity, madness, folly.*

Eso es una locura. *That's a crazy thing to do. That's absurd.*

lodo *m. mud, mire.*

lógica *f. logic.*

Carece de lógica y de sentido común. *It lacks logic and common sense.*

lógico *adj. logical, reasonable.*

LOGRAR *to obtain, to get; to attain; to manage, to succeed.*

Por fin logró lo que quería. *He finally got what he wanted.*

Debe haber algún medio de lograrlo. *There must be some way of getting it (of obtaining it).*

Lograron hacerlo. *They managed to do it.*

Hemos logrado que nos paguen. *We have succeeded in getting them to pay us.*

Nada lograba influenciarle. *Nothing could influence him.*

logro *m. gain; attainment; achievement.*

loma *f. hillock, little hill.*

lombriz *f. earthworm.*

lomo *m. loin; back (of a book); ridge (agriculture).*

Llevar a lomo. *To carry on one's back.*

lona *f. canvas.*

longaniza *f. a kind of sausage.*

longitud *f. longitude.*

lonja *f. slice, rasher; exchange market.*

loro *m. parrot.*

LOS *(pl. of el) the. See la, lo.*

Los hombres. *The men.*

Los dos. *Both. The two of them.*

Los míos. *My people. My family. My folks.*

Lávese las manos. *Wash your hands.*

Límpiate los dientes. *Brush your teeth.*

LOS *(pl. direct object pronoun) they, them; you (pl.). See le and les.*

¿Cómo los quiere Ud.? *How do you want them?*

Los aguardábamos (a Uds.). *We were waiting for you (pl.).*

Se los daré mañana. *I'll give them to you (them) tomorrow.*

Ya no los queremos. *We don't want them any longer.*

¿Ve Ud. a los soldados? —Los veo. *Do you see the soldiers? —I see them.*

lote *m. lot; portion, share.*

loza *f. chinaware; crockery.*

lozanía *f. vigor; exuberance, liveliness.*

lozano *adj. healthy; sprightly, lively.*

lubricación *f. lubrication.*

lubricante *adj. lubricating; m. lubricant.*

lubricar *to lubricate.*

lucidez *f. lucidity, clearness.*

lúcido *adj. lucid, brilliant.*

luciérnaga *f. glowworm, firefly.*

lucir *to shine; to show off.*

lucirse *to outshine; to show off.*

lucrativo *adj. lucrative, profitable.*

lucro *m. gain, profit.*

lucha *f. fight, struggle, strife.*

La lucha por la vida. *The struggle for existence.*

luchador *wrestler, fighter.*

luchar *to fight, to wrestle, to struggle.*

LUEGO *immediately, soon, afterwards, then, later.*

¡Hasta luego! *See you later. So long.*

¿Qué haremos luego? *What will we do after-wards?*

Cenaremos y luego iremos al teatro. *We'll have dinner and then we'll go to the theater.*

Quiero que lo hagas muy luego. *I want you to do it right away.*

Lo haré luego. *I'll do it later.*

Desde luego. *Of course.*

Avíseme luego que lo reciba. *As soon as you receive it, let me know.*

LUGAR *m. place; time; occasion; motive, cause.*

Nos encontraremos en el lugar de costumbre. *We'll meet at the usual place.*

Ponga las cosas en su lugar. *Put the things in their place. Put everything in its place.*

Yo en su lugar, no iría. *If I were you (in your place) I wouldn't go.*

¿A qué hora tendrá lugar la boda? *What time will the wedding take place?*

En lugar de. *Instead of.*

Dar lugar a. *To give cause for. To give occa-sion for. To lead up to.*

lugarteniente *m. deputy, substitute, lieutenant.*

lujo *m. luxury.*

Edición de lujo. *De luxe edition.*

lujoso *adj. luxurious.*

lujuria *f. lust; excess.*

LUMBRE *f. fire, light.*

Déme lumbre. *Give me a light.*

Sentémonos junto a la lumbre. *Let's sit near the fire.*

luminoso *adj. shining, luminous.*

LUNA *f. moon; glass plate for mirrors.*

Hay luna esta noche. *The moon is out tonight.*

Luna de miel. *Honeymoon.*

lunático *adj. lunatic, mad, eccentric.*

LUNES *m. Monday.*

lustrar *to polish, to shine.*

lustre *m. luster, gloss; splendor.*

luto *m. mourning; grief, sorrow.*

De luto. *In mourning.*

LUZ *f. light, daylight.*

Encienda la luz. *Put the light on.*

Apaque la luz. *Turn the light off. Put the light out.*

Se apagaron las luces. *The lights went out.*

Luz eléctrica. *Electric light.*

Dar a luz. 1. *To give birth.* 2. *To publish.*

Salir a luz. *To be published. To appear (a book).*

A todas luces. *In every respect.*

LL

llaga *f. ulcer, wound.*

llama *f. flame; llama (animal).*

llamada *f. call; marginal note.*

Llamada telefónica. *Phone call.*

llamamiento *m. calling; call; appeal.*

LLAMAR *to call; to appeal; to name; to send for; to knock (at the door).*

¿Ha llamado Ud.? *Did you call?*

Llamar por teléfono. *To phone.*

Llámeme por teléfono. *Give me a ring. Phone me. ("Call me on the telephone.")*

Llame Ud. un taxi, por favor. *Please call a taxi.*

Llaman a la puerta. *Somebody's knocking at the door. Someone's at the door.*

Llama a la criada y pide café y tostadas. *Ring for the maid and order coffee and toast.*

Mandar a llamar. *To send for.*

Mande a llamar al doctor. *Send for the doctor.*

Llamar la atención. *To call attention to.*

Llamar a gritos. *To call out loud. To yell for someone.*

LLAMARSE *to be called or named.*

¿Cómo se llama Ud.? *What's your name?*

Me llamo . . . *My name is . . .*

¿Cómo se llama esta calle? *What's the name of this street?*

llamarada *f. blaze; flushing (of the face).*

llamativo *adj. conspicuous, striking, attractive, showy.*

llanamente *simply, plainly, clearly; sincerely, frankly.* Hable llanamente. *Speak plainly (simply). Speak frankly.*

llaneza *f. simplicity, plainness.*

llano *adj. even, smooth, flat; frank; m. plain, flat-land.*

Un campo llano. *A smooth terrain.*

llanta *f. rim; tire.*

llanto *m. weeping, crying.*

llanura *f. plain, flatlands.*

LLAVE *f. key; wrench; faucet, spigot.*

¿Dónde está la llave de mi cuarto? *Where's the key to my room?*

Cerrar con llave. *To lock.*

Cierre la puerta con llave cuando salga. *Lock the door when you leave.*

Llave inglesa. *Monkey wrench.*

llavero *m. key-ring.*

llegada *f. arrival, coming.*

Avíseme de su llegada. *Let me know when you'll (he'll) arrive.*

LLEGAR *to arrive; to come; to reach, to succeed; to amount.*

¿A qué hora llega el tren? *(At) What time does the train arrive?*

El tren llega con dos horas de retraso. *The train is two hours late.*

Llegué ayer. *I came home yesterday. I got back (here) yesterday.*

¿Llegó Ud. a tiempo? *Were you in time?*

¿Cuándo llegamos a la frontera? *When will we reach the border?*

Llegó a hacerlo. *He managed to do it.*

Llega Ud. de improviso. *You've come rather unexpectedly.*

Tenía prisa por llegar a la hora. *He was in a hurry to get there on time.*

Ha llegado a mis oídos que . . . *I've heard that . . .*

Llegar a ser. *To become.*

Llegar a las manos. *To come to blows.*

LLENAR *to fill, to stuff; to occupy; to satisfy; to fulfill.*

Llene la botella de vino. *Fill the bottle with wine.*

La noticia la llenó de alegría. *The news made her very happy. The news filled her with joy.*

Al verla se llenó de gozo. *He was glad to see her. ("He was very happy when he saw her.")*

No me llena su explicación. *His explanation doesn't satisfy me.*

Llenar completamente. *To fill up (completely).*

LLENO *adj. full; complete; m. fullness, abundance; full house (theater).*

Estoy lleno. *I'm full. I've had enough.*

El vaso está lleno. *The glass is full.*

Hay un lleno completo esta noche. *There's a full house tonight.*

llevadero *adj. bearable, tolerable.*

LLEVAR *to carry, to take; to take away; to set (a price); to wear (clothes); to be (older, late, etc.).*

Lléveme allí. *Take me there.*

Taxi, lléveme a la estación. *Taxi, take me to the station.*

Lleve estas cartas al correo. *Take these letters to the post office.*

Lleve Ud. este paquete a mi casa. *Take this package to my house.*

¿Llevamos paraguas? *Shall we take umbrellas?*

No llevo bastante dinero. *I don't have enough money on me. ("I'm not carrying enough money on me.")*

Ayúdeme a llevar este hombre en la camilla. *Help me carry this man on the stretcher.*

¿Cuánto le llevó el tendero por esto? *How much did the storekeeper charge you for this?*

Me lo llevo si me lo deja en tres dólares. *I'll take it if you'll let me have it for three dollars.*

Llevamos un tanto por ciento de interés. *We charge so much (per cent) interest.*

Hace una semana que llevo este traje. *I've worn this suit for a week.*

Llevar al revés. *To wear on the wrong side. To wear wrong side out.*

¿Cuánto tiempo lleva Ud. esperándome? *How long have you been waiting for me?*

El tren lleva una hora de retraso. *The train is an hour late.*

Le llevo cinco años. *I'm five years older than he.*

Llevar a cuestas. *To carry on one's shoulders.*

Llevar a cabo. *To carry out. To bring about. To put through.*

Llevar consigo. *To carry along with one. To carry with it. To imply.*

Llevar la delantera. *To lead. To be ahead.*

Llevar los libros. *To keep books (bookkeeping).*

Llevar la correspondencia. *To take care of the correspondence.*

Llevar lo mejor. *To get the best. To get the best part of.*

llevarse *to take or carry away; to get along.*

Llévese Ud. estos libros. *Take these books away.*

Se llevó la palma. *He carried the day. He carried off the laurels.*

Llevarse bien. *To get along well (together).*

Llevarse mal. *To be on bad terms.*

Llevarse un chasco. *To suffer a bitter disappointment.*

llorar *to weep, to cry; to lament.*

lloro *m. weeping, crying.*

LLOVER *to rain, to shower.*

Está lloviendo. *It's raining.*

Parece que va a llover. *It looks as if it's going to rain.*

Llueve a cántaros. *It's pouring. It's raining cats and dogs.*

Eso ya es llover sobre mojado. *That's adding insult to injury.*

llovizna *f. drizzle.*

lloviznar *to drizzle.*

LLUVIA *f. rain, shower.*

M

macana *f. (Arg.) blunder, nonsense, joke.*

Déjate de macanas. *Stop talking nonsense. Stop doing foolish things.*

macanear *(Arg.) to do silly things, to talk nonsense.*

macanudo *adj. (Amer.) fine, excellent, grand, dandy, first-rate.*

macarrones *m. pl. macaroni.*

maceta *f. flowerpot; mallet.*

macizo *adj. solid; massive; firm.*

machacar *to pound; to crush; to harp; to dwell (on a subject).*

machete *m. machete.*

macho *adj. male; masculine; vigorous; m. male animal; he-mule.*

machucar *to pound, to bruise.*

madama *f. madam.*

madeja *f. hank, skein; lock of hair.*

MADERA *f. wood; lumber; timber.*

Esto es de madera. *This is made of wood.*

maderero *m. dealer in lumber.*

madero *m. beam; timber; piece of lumber.*

madrastra f. stepmother.

madre f. mother; bed (of a river).

madreselva f. honeysuckle.

madriguera f. burrow; den.

madrina f. godmother; bridesmaid; sponsor, patroness.

madrugada f. dawn; early morning.

    De madrugada. At dawn.

    En la madrugada. In the early morning.

    Telegrama de madrugada. Night letter.

madrugador adj. early riser.

    ¡Ud. es muy madrugador! You're an early bird!

madrugar to get up early; to get ahead of.

    Caray, tú, sí que has madrugado. My, but you're up early!

    A quien madruga Dios le ayuda. The early bird catches the worm.

madurar to ripen; to mature.

madurez f. maturity; ripeness.

maduro adj. ripe; mature.

    La fruta todavía no está madura. The fruit isn't ripe yet.

maestro adj. masterly, master; m. teacher; skilled craftsman; master.

    Una obra maestra. A masterpiece.

    Es un maestro. He's a teacher.

    Maestro de obras. Builder.

magia f. magic.

mágico adj. magic; marvelous.

magisterio m. teaching profession; teachers (as a class).

magistrado m. magistrate.

magnánimo adj. magnanimous.

magnesia f. magnesia.

magnético adj. magnetic.

magnífico adj. magnificent, fine, splendid, wonderful.

    Habrá que felicitarle por su magnífica labor. We ought to (must) congratulate him on his wonderful achievement.

    Tenemos un magnífico surtido de corbatas. We have a fine selection of ties.

magnitud f. magnitude; importance, greatness.

magno adj. great.

    Alejandro Magno. Alexander the Great.

    Es una obra magna. It's an excellent piece of work.

magnolia f. magnolia.

mago m. magician, wizard.

maguey m. maguey (fruit), American aloe.

mahometano adj. and n. Mohammedan.

maicena f. corn flour.

maíz m. maize, Indian corn.

maizal m. corn field.

majadero adj. and n. silly; bore, pest.

majestad f. majesty.

majestuoso adj. majestic, imposing.

MAL adj. (shortening of **malo** used before masc.

nouns) bad; adv. badly, poorly; m. evil; harm; disease; illness.

    Hace mal tiempo. The weather's bad.

    Está de muy mal humor. He's in a very bad mood.

    Ud. no tiene mal aspecto. You don't look ill.

    No está mal pensado. It's (that's) not a bad idea.

    No está mal. Not bad. It's not bad.

    Este libro está mal escrito. This book is badly written.

    Ando mal de dinero. I'm short of money.

    El enfermo va mal. The patient is getting worse.

    De mal en peor. Worse and worse. From bad to worse.

    Hacer mal. To do harm. To do wrong. To act wrongly.

    Eso no puede hacerle mal. That can't hurt him.

    Este abrigo me está mal. This coat doesn't fit me.

    Mal hecho. Badly done.

    Mal que le pese. In spite of him.

    Mal de su grado. Unwillingly.

    El bien y el mal. Right and wrong. Good and evil.

    Tomemos del mal el menos. Let's choose the lesser of the two evils.

    Mal de garganta. Sore throat.

    Este mal tiene cura. This sickness (disease) is curable.

malagradecido adj. ungrateful.

malaria f. malaria; paludism.

malbaratar to undersell; to squander.

malcriado adj. ill-bred; naughty.

maldad f. wickedness.

maldecir to damn, to curse.

maldición f. curse.

maldito adj. wicked; damned; cursed.

malecón m. sea wall, jetty.

maleficio m. witchcraft, enchantment.

malestar m. indisposition, discomfort.

    Sentir un malestar. To be indisposed.

maleta f. valise, suitcase.

    Lleve estas maletas, por favor. Please carry these suitcases.

maleza f. underbrush, thicket.

malgastar to squander, to waste.

malhablado adj. foul-mouthed.

malhechor m. malefactor, criminal.

malhumorado adj. ill-humored, peevish.

malicia f. malice; suspicion.

malicioso adj. malicious, suspicious.

maligno adj. malignant.

malintencionado adj. evil-minded, ill-disposed.

MALO adj. bad; wicked; ill; difficult; poorly.

    No es mala idea. That's not a bad idea.

    ¿Qué hay de malo en eso? What harm is there in that? What's wrong with it?

    ¿Te sientes malo? Do you feel ill?

Está muy malo. *He's very sick.*

Es un escritor bastante malo. *He's a very poor writer.*

¿Tiene Ud. los ojos malos? *Are your eyes sore?*

Ese niño es muy malo. *This child is very bad.*

Estos huevos están malos. *These eggs are bad.*

Lo dijo de mala fe. *He said it deceitfully.*

Lo malo es que no tengo tiempo. *The trouble is that I've no time.*

Llevaba muy mala vida. *He led a very dissolute life.*

Tiene mala cabeza. *He's reckless.*

Trabajó de mala gana. *He worked unwillingly.*

Hoy ando de malas. *I have no luck today.*

Tener malas pulgas. *To be hot-tempered. To be hot-headed (hot-blooded).*

Por malas o por buenas. *Willingly or unwillingly. Willy-nilly.*

malsano *adj. unhealthy, unhealthful.*

Es un clima muy malsano. *It's a very unhealthful climate.*

maltratar *to treat roughly, to mistreat, to abuse; to harm.*

maltrato *m. ill-treatment.*

malvado *adj. wicked.*

mamá *f. mamma.*

mamar *to suck; to cram.*

mamarracho *m. daub; ridiculous thing.*

mamey *m. mamee (tree and its fruit).*

mamífero *adj. mammalian; m. pl. mammals.*

manantial *m. spring, source.*

manar *to flow; to ooze.*

manco *adj. one-handed; one-armed; crippled.*

mancomún (de) *adj. jointly, in common; by mutual consent.*

mancomunar *to associate; to subject; to joint liability.*

mancha *f. stain, spot; blemish.*

manchado *adj. stained, spotted.*

manchar *to stain, to spot, to soil.*

mandadero *m. messenger; errand boy.*

mandado *m. errand.*

¿Puede Ud. hacerme un mandado? *Will (can) you do (run) an errand for me?*

mandamiento *m. mandate; commandment.*

MANDAR *to send; to will, bequeath; to order; to command; to govern.*

Mándamelo a casa. *Send it to my house.*

Mande el paquete a estas señas. *Send the package to this address.*

Quiero mandar un telegrama (cable). *I want to send a telegram (cable).*

¿Me ha mandado Ud. llamar? *Did you send for me? Have you sent for me?*

Le mandé venir inmediatamente. *I had him come immediately.*

Mande por una ambulancia. *Send for an ambulance.*

¿Qué ha mandado Ud. a pedir para comer?

What have you ordered for dinner?

He mandado hacer un traje a la medida. *I'm having a suit made to order.*

Lo he hecho porque Ud. me lo ha mandado. *I did it because you told me to.*

Si no manda Ud. otra cosa, me retiro. *If you don't need anything else, I'll leave now. If you'll excuse me, I'll leave now.*

Mandar decir. *To send word.*

mandarina *f. mandarin, tangerine.*

mandatario *m. attorney; agent; proxy.*

mandato *m. mandate, order.*

mandíbula *f. jaw, jawbone.*

mando *m. command, authority, control.*

mandolina *f. mandolin.*

mandón *adj. domineering, bossy.*

manecilla *f. small hand; hand of a clock or watch.*

manejar *to handle; to drive; to manage.*

¿Sabe Ud. manejar? *Do you know how to drive?*

manejo *m. management; handling.*

MANERA *f. manner, way, method.*

Hágalo Ud. de esta manera. *Do it this way.*

Hágalo de cualquier manera. *Do it any way you can. Do it any old way.*

No hay manera de traducirlo. *There's no way to translate it.*

No tiene buenas maneras. *He has no manners.*

Lo dijo de mala manera. *He said it in a rude way.*

¿Qué manera es ésa de contestar? *Is that the way to answer?*

¿De manera que no viene Ud.? *So you're not coming?*

Le alabó en gran manera. *He praised him very highly.*

En cierta manera. *To a certain extent.*

De ninguna manera. *By no means.*

De todas maneras iremos. *We'll go in any case.*

De manera que. *So then. So as to. In such a manner as to.*

Escríbalo de manera que se pueda leer. *Write it so that it can be read (that one can read it).*

manga *f. sleeve; hose (for water); waterspout.*

Tener manga ancha. *To be broad-minded.*

En mangas de camisa. *In shirt sleeves.*

mangante *m. sponger.*

mango *m. handle, haft; mango (tree and its fruit).*

mangonear *to sponge; to loaf; to meddle, to pry.*

mangoneo *m. meddling; pettifogging; sponging.*

manía *f. mania, frenzy, whim.*

maniático *adj. and n. maniac.*

manicomio *m. insane asylum.*

manicura *f. manicure.*

manifestación *f. manifestation, demonstration.*

manifestar *to manifest; to state; to reveal.*

manifiesto *adj. manifest; clear, obvious.*

maniobra *f. maneuver; handiwork.*

manipulación *f. handling, manipulation.*

manipular *to handle, to manipulate; to manage.*

maniquí *m. mannikin.*

manivela *f. crank.*

Manivela de arranque. *Crank for starting.*

manjar *m. dish, food; victuals.*

MANO *f. hand; forefoot; coat (of paint, etc.); first hand (cards).*

Lo tengo en la mano. *I have it in my hand.*

Dénse la mano. *Shake hands.*

Le dió la mano al verle. *He shook hands with him when he saw him.*

Mano izquierda. *Left hand.*

Mano derecha. *Right hand.*

El es mi mano derecha. *He's my right-hand man.* ("He's my right hand.")

Pidió la mano de mi hermana. *He asked for my sister's hand (in marriage).*

Dejo el asunto en sus manos. *I leave the matter in your hands. I leave it up to you.*

¡Manos a la obra! *Get it started! Get to work! Let's start (it)!*

Suelte Ud. las manos. *Let go!*

Vinieron a las manos. *They came to blows.*

Se lavó las manos como Pilatos. *He washed his hands of the affair.* ("He washed his hands like Pontius Pilate.")

Bajo mano. (Debajo de mano.) *Underhandedly. In an underhand manner.*

De buena mano. *On good authority. From a reliable source.*

A manos llenas. *Liberally. Abundantly.*

Mano a mano. *Even. On equal terms.*

A mano. 1. *At hand. Near-by.* 2. *By hand.*

Hecho a mano. *Made by hand. Hand-made.*

De primera mano. *First-hand.*

manojo *m. handful, bunch.*

manosear *to handle; to feel; to rumple.*

mansión *f. mansion; residence.*

manso *adj. tame; gentle.*

manta *f. blanket.*

manteca *f. lard; fat; butter.*

mantecado *m. vanilla ice cream; buttercake.*

mantel *m. tablecloth.*

mantener *to feed, to support, to maintain; to keep up; to uphold (an opinion).*

Tiene que mantener dos familias. *He has to support two families.*

Mantener correspondencia. *To keep up a correspondence.*

Mantener una opinión. *To hold to (maintain) an opinion.*

mantenerse *to support oneself, to earn one's living; to stick to; to hold one's own; to remain; to stay.*

En este termos el agua se mantiene fresca. *The water stays cold in this thermos bottle.*

El barco se mantuvo a flote depués de torpedeado. *The ship remained afloat after be-*

ing torpedoed.

Me mantengo en lo dicho. *I maintain (stick to) what I've said.*

Se mantuvieron firmes hasta el fin. *They held their ground till the very end.*

mantenimiento *m. maintenance, support.*

MANTEQUILLA *f. butter.*

mantequillera *f. butter dish.*

manto *m. mantle, cloak.*

mantón *m. large shawl.*

manual *adj. manual; m. handbook; manual.*

manufacturar *to manufacture.*

manuscrito *adj. written by hand; m. manuscript.*

manutención *f. support, maintenance.*

manzana *f. apple; block of houses.*

manzanilla *f. camomile (plant); manzanilla (a strong white wine).*

manzano *m. apple tree.*

maña *f. dexterity, skill, cunning; knack, trick, habit.*

mañana *f. morning, forenoon; tomorrow.*

Esta mañana. *This morning.*

Hasta mañana. *See you tomorrow. Until tomorrow.*

Mañana por la mañana. *Tomorrow morning.*

Pasado mañana. *The day after tomorrow.*

mañoso *adj. handy, skillful; cunning.*

mapa *m. map, chart.*

mapamundi *m. map of the world.*

máquina *f. machine; engine.*

Máquina de escribir. *Typewriter.*

A máquina. *By machine.*

maquinaria *f. machinery.*

maquinilla *f. small machine.*

Maquinilla de afeitar. *Safety razor.*

maquinista *m. machinist; engineer, engine driver.*

MAR *m. and f. sea.*

Iremos por mar. *We'll go by sea.*

Viaje por mar. *Sea voyage.*

En el mar. *At sea.*

maraca *f. maraca (musical instrument).*

maraña *f. entanglement, perplexity, puzzle.*

maravilla *f. marvel, wonder.*

A maravilla. *Marvelously.*

maravillarse *to marvel, to admire.*

maravilloso *adj. marvelous, wonderful.*

Pasamos un tiempo maravilloso. *We had a wonderful time.*

marca *f. mark; brand; make.*

Es una marca renombrada. *It's a well-known brand.*

marcar *to mark; to brand; to register.*

El termómetro marca treinta grados a la sombra. *The thermometer registers thirty degrees in the shade. It's thirty degrees in the shade.*

Marcar un número. *To dial (a number).*

marco *m. frame.*

marcha *f. march.*

marchante m. customer; client.

MARCHAR to go; to go off; to leave; to march.

¿Se marcha Ud. ya? Are you leaving already?

Tengo que marcharme en seguida. I have to go immediately.

Se marcha al extranjero. He's going abroad.

Las cosas marchan viento en popa. All's well. Everything's going nicely.

Al negocio marcha a pedir de boca. Business is progressing splendidly.

El sargento marchaba delante de la compañía. The sergeant was marching in front of the company.

marchitar to wither, to fade.

marchito adj. faded, withered.

marea f. tide.

mareado adj. seasick.

marearse to get seasick.

mareo m. seasickness.

marfil m. ivory.

margarina f. margarine.

margen m. and f. margin, border; bank (of a river).

marido m. husband.

Marido y mujer. Husband and wife.

marina f. navy.

marinero adj. seaworthy; m. sailor.

marino m. seaman.

mariposa f. butterfly; rushlight.

marítimo adj. maritime.

marmita f. kettle.

mármol m. marble.

marqués m. marquis.

marquesa f. marchioness.

MARTES m. Tuesday.

martillar to hammer.

martillazo m. a hammer blow.

martillo m. hammer.

mártir m. martyr.

MARZO m. March.

marrano m. hog, pig; dirty person.

MAS conj. but, yet, however.

Parecen distintos mas no lo son. They seem different but they're not.

MÁS adv. more; most; over; besides; plus.

Más o menos. More or less.

¿Cuánto me costará, más o menos? About how much will it cost?

¿Desean algo más? Will you have anything more?

¿Quiere Ud. más ensalada? Would you like some more salad?

¿Nada más? Is that all? Nothing else?

No se me ocurre nada más. I can't think of anything else.

No hay más. There are (there is) no more.

No tengo más. I haven't got any more.

¿A quién quiere Ud. más? Who(m) do you like (love) the best (more)?

La madre es más bonita que la hija. The mother's prettier than the daughter.

Cinco más dos son siete. Five plus two are seven.

Es la cosa más fácil del mundo. It's the easiest thing in the world.

Más adelante se lo explicaré. Later on, I'll explain it to you.

Más acá del río. On this side of the river.

La casa está más allá. The house is further on.

Son más de las diez. It's after ten o'clock.

Corre más que yo. He runs faster than I do.

¡Qué papel más malo! What bad (poor, awful) paper!

¡Más vale así! So much the better!

Eso es lo más acertado. That's the best thing to do.

No faltaba más que eso. That's all we needed. That's the limit.

Acérquese un poco más al micrófono. Come little closer to the microphone.

Las más de las veces. Most of the time.

Lo más pronto. As soon as possible.

A lo más. At most.

Más tarde o más temprano. Sooner or later.

A más tardar. At the latest.

Más de. More than. Over.

De más. Too much. Too many.

Sin más ni más. Without much ado.

Más bien. Rather.

masa f. dough; mass; crowd.

En masa. In bulk.

masaje m. massage.

Dar un masaje. To massage. To give a massage.

masajista m. and f. masseur, masseuse.

mascar to chew.

máscara f. mask; disguise.

mascota f. mascot.

masculino adj. masculine.

Género masculino. Masculine gender.

masón m. Freemason.

masonería f. Freemasonry.

masticar to chew, to masticate.

Mastique bien la comida. Chew your food well.

mástil m. mast, post.

mata f. plant, shrub.

matadero m. slaughterhouse.

matanza f. slaughter, massacre.

matar to kill, to murder.

No matarás. Thou shalt not kill!

Matar el tiempo. To kill time.

Me ha matado con su pelmacería. He's so dull he bores me to death.

mate adj. dull (finish); m. checkmate; maté, Paraguay tea; dull color.

matemáticas m. mathematics.

matemático m. mathematician.

materia f. matter; material; subject.

Materia prima. *Raw material.*
material *adj. material; m. material; equipment.*
   Ese material no sirve. *This material is no-good.*
   Material rodante. *Rolling stock.*
materializar *to materialize; to realize.*
maternal *adj. maternal.*
maternidad *f. maternity.*
materno *adj. maternal, motherly.*
matiz *m. shade of color.*
matón *m. bully.*
matorral *m. thicket, bushes.*
matrícula *f. register; list; matriculation.*
matricular *to matriculate, to register.*
   ¿En qué escuela te has matriculado? *At what school did you register?*
matrimonio *m. marriage, matrimony; married couple.*
mausoleo *m. mausoleum.*
máxima *f. maxim, rule; proverb.*
máximo *adj. maximum, highest, largest, chief, principal.*
   Máxima altura. *Highest point. Peak.*
   El precio máximo es de diez dólares. *The maximum price is ten dollars.*
MAYO *m. May.*
mayonesa *f. mayonnaise.*
MAYOR *adj. greater, greatest; larger, largest; elder, eldest; m. major.*
   Fué Mayor en el ejército. *He was a major in the army.*
   ¿Cuál es la ciudad mayor del mundo? *What is the largest city in the world?*
   ¿Es su hermana mayor o menor que Ud.? *Is your sister older or younger than you?*
   Ser mayor de edad. *To be of age.*
   Este asunto es del mayor ínterés. *This matter is of the greatest interest.*
   La mayor parte de la gente lo cree. *Most (of the) people believe it.*
   Pasé la mayor parte de la noche en vela. *I stayed awake most of the night.*
   Viven en la calle Mayor. *They live on Main Street.*
   Sólo vendemos al por mayor. *We sell wholesale only.*
mayordomo *m. majordomo, steward, butler; administrator.*
mayoría *f. majority; plurality.*
   Así piensan la mayoría de los hombres. *Most men think that way.*
   Fué electo por una gran mayoría. *He was elected by a large majority.*
mayúscula *f. capital letter.*
mazapán *m. marzipan.*
mazorca *f. cob of corn.*
   Déme unas mazorcas de maíz. *Give me some corn on the cob.*
ME *pron. me; to me; myself.*
   Me lo dió. *He gave it to me.*

Dámelo. *Give it to me.*
   Vino a verme. *He came to see me.*
   Me es indiferente. *It makes no difference to me.*
   Me ha convencido Ud. *You've convinced me.*
   Me duele la cabeza. *I have a headache.*
   Me he cortado. *I've cut myself.*
   Me dije para mis adentros. *I said to myself.*
mecánica *f. mechanics; kitchen police (military).*
mecánico *adj. mechanical; m. mechanic.*
mecanismo *m. mechanism.*
mecanógrafa *f. typist.*
   Se necesita una mecanógrafa. *Typist wanted.*
mecanógrafo *m. typist.*
mecedora *f. rocking chair.*
mecha *f. wick; fuse; lock of hair.*
mechar *to lard.*
mechón *m. lock of hair.*
medalla *f. medal.*
media *f. stocking; mean (mathematics).*
   ¿Quiere Ud. medias de seda o de nilón? *Do you want silk or nylon stockings?*
   Media diferencial. *Arithmetical mean.*
mediación *f. mediation, intervention.*
mediador *mediator, go-between.*
mediados *about the middle.*
   A mediados de marzo. *About the middle of March.*
mediano *adj. medium, middling, not so good, mediocre.*
medianoche *f. midnight.*
   A medianoche. *At midnight.*
mediante *by means of, by virtue of.*
   Lo obtuve mediante su ayuda. *I got it through his help.*
   Dios mediante. *God willing.*
mediar *to mediate, to intercede.*
medicina *f. medicine; remedy.*
médico *adj. medical; m. physician, doctor.*
MEDIDA *f. measure; measurement.*
   Medida patrón. *Standard measure.*
   Se tomaron las medidas necesarias en contra de la epidemia. *They took the necessary measures against the epidemic.*
   Esta chaqueta me queda como a la medida. *This jacket fits me perfectly.*
   A la medida. *Made to order (suit, dress, etc.).*
   A medida de su deseo. *According to your wish.*
   A medida que reciba la mercadería, envíemela. *Send me the goods as you receive them.*
   Escriba estos números a medida que se los vaya diciendo. *Write these numbers down as I give them to you.*
MEDIO *adj. and adv. half; half-way; midway; means; average; m. middle, center; way, method; pl. means.*
   Déme media libra de café. *Give me half a pound of coffee.*
   A las dos y media. *At half past two.*
   Una hora y media. *An hour and a half.*

La clase media. *The middle class.*

En un término medio. *On an average.*

Los telegramas diferidos se pagan a media tasa. *You pay only half rate for a night letter.*

Estoy medio muerto de cansancio. *I'm exhausted. I'm half dead.*

Hicimos el trabajo a medias. *We did the work between (the two of) us.*

La criada viene día por medio a hacer la limpieza. *The maid comes every other day to do the cleaning.*

Lo puso de vuelta y media. *He gave him a dressing down.*

¡Quítese de en medio! *Get out of the way!*

No había medio de saberlo. *There was no way of finding out.*

Vive según sus medios. *He lives according to his means.*

Media vuelta. *About face. Right about-face.*

En medio. *In the middle.*

Medio en broma, medio en serio. *Half in fun, half in earnest.*

Medio muerto de hambre. *Half-starved.*

A medio vestir. *To be half dressed.*

Medio asado. *Medium (of roasted meat). ("Half roasted.")*

mediocre *adj.* mediocre.

mediocridad *f.* mediocrity.

mediodía *m.* midday, noon; south.

Al mediodía. *At noon.*

medir *to measure.*

meditación *f.* meditation.

meditar *to meditate.*

médula *f.* medulla, marrow; pitch.

mejilla *f.* cheek.

Mejillas rosadas. *Rosy cheeks.*

MEJOR *adj. and adv.* better, rather.

Me siento mejor. *I feel better.*

Es el mejor hombre del mundo. *He's the best man alive. ("He's the best man in the world.")*

Esta es la mejor señal de mejoría. *That's the best sign of improvement.*

Escribe el español mejor que yo. *He writes Spanish better than I do.*

Tal vez eso sea mejor. *Perhaps that would be better.*

Hice lo mejor que pude. *I did the best I could.*

Tanto mejor. *All the better. So much the better.*

Tanto mejor si no viene. *So much the better if he doesn't come.*

Cuanto antes mejor. *The sooner the better.*

A lo mejor mañana no llueve. *Perhaps it won't rain tomorrow.*

Mejor que escribir ponga Ud. un telegrama. *It would be better to send a telegram than to write.*

Mejor que mejor si Ud. puede venir. *So much the better (all the better) if you can come.*

mejora *f.* improvement.

Eso es una gran mejora. *That's a great improvement.*

mejorar *to improve; to outbid.*

Sigue mejorando. *He's improving.*

El tiempo ha mejorado. *The weather has improved.*

mejoría *f.* improvement; recovery.

melaza *f.* molasses.

melocotón *m.* peach.

melodía *f.* melody.

melón *m.* melon.

mella *f.* notch; dent; gap; impression.

Hacer mella. *To make an impression. To impress.*

mellizo *adj.* twin.

membrete *m.* letterhead; memorandum, note.

membrillo *m.* quince (tree and its fruit).

memorable *adj.* memorable.

MEMORIA *f.* memory; memoir, report; *pl.* regards, compliments.

Tiene una memoria extraordinaria. *He has an extraordinary memory.*

Si la memoria no me es infiel. *If my memory doesn't fail me. If I remember correctly.*

Déle Ud. memorias mías. *Give her my regards.*

Apréndaselo de memoria. *Learn it by heart.*

Haga Ud. memoria. *Try to remember.*

Hágame Ud. memoria de ello mañana. *Remind me of it tomorrow.*

menaje *m.* household goods, furnishings, furniture.

Menaje de casa. *Household goods. Furniture.*

mencionar *to mention.*

mendigar *to beg, to ask charity.*

mendigo *m.* beggar.

mendrugo *m.* a piece of bread.

menear *to move, to stir; to wag.*

menester *m.* need; occupation.

Es menester que lo hagamos. *We must do it. It's necessary that we do it.*

menesteroso *adj.* needy.

mengua *f.* decrease; decline; poverty; disgrace.

menguar *to decay; to diminish, to wane.*

MENOR *adj.* less; smaller; younger; *m.* minor, a person under age.

No me cabe la menor duda. *I haven't the slightest doubt.*

No le hicieron el menor caso. *They didn't pay the slightest attention to him.*

El es menor que ella. *He's younger than she is.*

Es menor de edad. *She's a minor (underage).*

MENOS *adj. and adv.* less; least; minus; except.

Es poco más o menos la misma cosa. *It's more or less the same thing.*

Tengo cinco pesetas de menos. *I'm five pesetas short.*

Eso es lo de menos. *That's the least of it.*

Todos fueron menos yo. *Everyone went but me.*

A las once menos cuarto. *At a quarter to eleven.*

Echar de menos a. *To miss someone or something.*

¿Echa Ud. de menos algo? *Is anything missing? Do you miss anything?*

No puedo menos que hacerlo. *I can't help doing it.*

No pude menos de reirme de él. *I couldn't help laughing at him.*

Menos mal que no le vió. *It's a good thing that he didn't see you.*

Tiene a menos hablarles. *He considered it beneath him to speak to them.*

¡Si yo tuviera veinte años menos! *If only I were twenty years younger!*

Tiene poco más o menos treinta años. *He's about thirty.*

No iré a menos que Ud. me acompañe. *I won't go unless you go with me (accompany me).*

Su familia ha ido muy a menos. *His family has become poor.*

Es lo menos que puede Ud. hacer. *It's the least you can do.*

menoscabo *m. damage, loss; detriment.*

Con menoscabo de. *To the detriment of.*

menospreciar *to underrate; to despise, to slight.*

menosprecio *m. underrating; scorn, contempt.*

mensaje *m. message.*

Quisiera enviarle un mensaje. *I'd like to send him a message.*

mensajero *m. messenger.*

mensual *adj. monthly.*

mensualidad *f. monthly salary; monthly allowance.*

menta *f. mint, peppermint.*

mental *adj. mental.*

mentalidad *f. mentality.*

mentar *to mention.*

Lo mentó en el discurso. *He mentioned it in his speech.*

MENTE *f. mind, understanding.*

Téngalo siempre en mente. *Always bear it in mind.*

mentecato *adj. silly, stupid; m. fool.*

mentir *to lie, to tell lies.*

mentira *f. lie, falsehood.*

mentiroso *adj. lying, false, deceitful; m. liar.*

menudeo *m. detail; retail trade.*

menudillos *m. pl. giblet (of fowl).*

MENUDO *adj. small; minute; m. change (money); entrails (of animals).*

¿Tiene Ud. menudo? *Do you have any change?*

Déjese Ud. ver más a menudo. *Come around more often.*

Sucede a menudo. *It happens very often.*

Gente menuda. *Children.*

meñique *m. little finger.*

El dedo meñique. *The little finger.*

mercader *m. merchant, dealer.*

mercadería *f. commodity, merchandise, goods.*

mercado *m. market; marketplace.*

La sirvienta fué de compras al mercado. *The maid went to the market to do the shopping.*

mercancía *f. merchandise, goods.*

mercante *adj. merchant, mercantile.*

Barco mercante. *Merchant ship.*

Marina mercante. *Merchant Marine.*

merced *f. gift, favor; mercy.*

Hacer merced. *To do someone a favor.*

Tener merced. *To show mercy. To be merciful.*

Merced a. *Thanks to.*

A la merced de. *At the mercy of.*

Estar a merced de. *To be at someone's mercy.*

mercenario *adj. mercenary.*

mercería *f. haberdashery; sort of five-and-ten.*

merecer *to deserve, to merit.*

Se lo merece. *He deserves it.*

merecido *m. deserved punishment.*

merendar *to lunch, to eat a light meal.*

merengue *m. meringue (pastry).*

meridiano *adj. and n. meridian.*

merienda *f. lunch, light meal.*

mérito *m. merit, worth; value.*

merma *f. decrease; waste; drop, loss.*

mermar *to decrease, to dwindle, to diminish.*

mermelada *f. marmalade.*

mero *adj. mere, only, pure, simple.*

Es una mera broma. *It's only a joke.*

Por mera casualidad. *By a mere coincidence.*

MES *m. month; monthly wages.*

¿Qué día del mes tenemos? (¿En qué día del mes estamos?) *What day of the month is it?*

Hace cosa de dos meses. *It was about two months ago.*

El mes que viene. *Next month.*

El mes pasado. *Last month.*

A últimos de mes. *Toward the end of the month.*

A principios del mes que viene. *In the early part of next month.*

MESA *f. table; chair, chairman and other officers of an assembly.*

¿Quién va a servir a la mesa? *Who's going to wait on the table?*

Levante la mesa. *Clear the table.*

Ponga la mesa. *Set the table.*

Los invitados se sentaron a la mesa. *The guests sat around the table. The guests sat down to eat.*

meseta *f. plateau; landing (of staircase).*

mestizo *adj. and n. half-breed; mestizo.*

mesura *f. moderation; politeness.*

meta *f. object, end, goal.*

Alcanzó la meta. *He reached his goal.*

metal *m. metal.*

metálico *adj. metallic.*

METER *to put in; to smuggle; to insert.*

Meter la mano en el bolsillo. *To put one's hand in one's pocket.*

Meta Ud. el dinero en el bolsillo. *Put the money in your pocket.*

No atino a meter la llave en la cerradura. *I can't get the key in the lock.*

Haga el favor de meter un poco las costuras de la chaqueta. *Please take in the seams of the jacket a little.*

Meter bulla. *To make a lot of noise.*

Meter la pata. *To put one's foot in it.*

METERSE *to meddle, to interfere; to become; to choose a profession or trade; to pick (a quar-rel); to give oneself to; to get oneself in.*

No quiero meterme en líos. *I don't want to get myself involved in difficulties.*

En buen lío nos hemos metido. *We got our-selves in quite a fix.*

No se meta en lo que no le importa. *Mind your own business. Don't meddle in other peo-ple's affairs.*

Mete las narices en todo. *He's a busybody.*

No se meta Ud. de por medio. *Don't interfere in this.*

Meterse en vidas ajenas. *To meddle in other people's affairs.*

Se metió a cura. *He became a priest.*

Jamás se me metió en la cabeza idea semejante. *Such an idea never entered my head.*

¿Por qué se mete Ud. conmigo? *Why do you pick on me?*

Meterse en la cama. *To get into bed.*

¿En dónde diablos se ha estado metido Ud.? *Where on earth have you been?*

Este frío se le mete a uno hasta los huesos. *This cold's very penetrating. This cold goes right through you ("goes to the bones").*

metódico *adj. methodical.*

método *m. method.*

metralla *f. grape-shot, shrapnel.*

metro *m. meter (39.37 inches), subway (in Spain.)*

metrópoli *f. metropolis.*

mezcla *f. mixture, blending; mortar (for holding bricks or stones together).*

Sin mezcla. *Unmixed. Pure.*

mezclar *to mix, to blend, to mingle.*

No mezcle estas cosas. *Don't mix these things.*

mezquino *adj. stingy; mean; petty.*

MI *(possessive adj.) my; pl. mis.*

Mi libro. *My book.*

Mis libros. *My books.*

Siéntese a mi lado. *Sit next to me. ("Sit at my side.")*

MÍ *(pron. used after a preposition) me.*

Para mí. *For me.*

Me llaman a mí. *They're calling me.*

¡Me lo cuenta a mí! *You're telling me!*

MÍA *(f. of mío) mine; pl. mías.*

Esta corbata es mía. *This tie is mine. This is my tie.*

Es una amiga mía. *She's a friend of mine.*

Son amigas mías. *They're friends of mine.*

¡Querida mía! *My darling!*

Muy señora mía (in a letter). *Dear Madam.*

'miaja *f. crumb, small piece.*

microbio *m. microbe.*

microscópico *adj. microscopic.*

microscopio *m. microscope.*

miedo *m. fear, dread.*

Tener miedo. *To be afraid.*

No tengas miedo. *Don't be afraid.*

miedoso *adj. fearful, easily frightened.*

miel *f. honey.*

Luna de miel. *Honeymoon.*

miembro *m. member, limb.*

MIENTRAS *in the meantime, while.*

Entró mientras leía. *He came in while I was reading.*

Mientras tanto. *Meantime. In the meantime. In the meanwhile.*

¿Qué hizo mientras tanto? *What did he do in the meantime?*

MIÉRCOLES *m. Wednesday.*

Miércoles de ceniza. *Ash Wednesday.*

miga *f. crumb, fragment, bit.*

Hacer buenas migas. *To be in perfect harmony.*

MIL *m. thousand.*

Su carta está fechada el veintitres de mayo de mil novecientos cuarenta y seis. *Your letter is dated May the twenty-third, nineteen hun-dred and forty-six.*

De mil amores. *With great pleasure.*

Lo hizo a las mil maravillas. *He did it won-derfully.*

Mil gracias. *Many thanks. ("A thousand thanks.")*

milagro *m. miracle, wonder.*

milagroso *adj. miraculous, marvelous.*

milésimo *adj. and n. thousandth.*

miligramo *m. milligram.*

milímetro *m. millimeter.*

militante *adj. militant.*

militar *adj. military; m. military man, soldier.*

milla *f. mile.*

¿Cuántas millas hay de aquí a Madrid? *How many miles is it from here to Madrid?*

Madrid dista veinte millas de aquí. *Madrid está a veinte millas de aquí. Madrid is twenty miles from here.*

millar *m. thousand; pl. a great number.*

millón *m. million.*

millonario *adj. and n. millionaire.*

mimado *adj. spoiled.*

Es un niño mimado. *He's a spoiled child.*

mimar *to spoil (a child).*

mina *f. mine.*

mineral *adj. and n. mineral.*

minería *f. mining, working of a mine.*

miniatura f. miniature.

mínimo adj. minimum; least, smallest.
> La cosa más mínima. The smallest thing.
> Una suma mínima. A very small sum.
> Este es el precio mínimo. This is the lowest price.

ministerio m. cabinet, ministry; secretary's office.

ministro m. Secretary (Cabinet); minister.

minorista m. retailer (Arg.).

minuta f. minutes (record); memorandum.

minutero m. minute hand.

minuto m. minute (of an hour).
> ¡Espere un minuto! Wait a minute!
> Estará listo dentro de unos minutos. It will be ready in a few minutes.

MÍO mine; pl. míos.
> Este pañuelo no es mío. This handkerchief is not mine.
> Son amigos míos. They're friends of mine.
> Esto es mío. This is mine. This belongs to me.
> Lo que es mío es suyo. What's mine is yours.
> El gusto es mío, señor. The pleasure is mine, sir.
> Hijo mío. My son.
> Muy señor mío (in a letter). Dear Sir.

miope adj. and n. nearsighted.
> ¿Es Ud. miope? Are you nearsighted?

mirada f. glance, look.
> Mirada triste. A sad look.
> Mirada fija. A fixed look.

mirado adj. looked at.
> Es una persona bien mirada. He's very respected (well-considered).

MIRAR to look, to behold; to observe; to watch; to consider.
> ¡Mire Ud! Look!
> ¡Mírelo, ahí está! Look at it, there it is!
> Déjeme mirarle bien. Let me take a good look at you.
> Mire Ud. donde pisa. Watch where you're going. Watch your step.
> Mire Ud. bien lo que hace. Consider carefully ("well") what you're doing.
> ¿No tienen a nadie que mire por ellos? Don't they have anyone to look after them?
> Dos de las habitaciones miran a la calle. Two of the rooms face the street.
> Miraba lo que estábamos haciendo. He watched what we were doing.
> Mirar de reojo. To look askance. To look out of the corner of one's eye.
> Bien mirado. 1. Carefully considered. 2. Well-considered. Respected.

mirarse to look at oneself; to look at each other.
> Mírese Ud. al espejo. Look at yourself in the mirror.

misa f. mass.

miserable adj. miserable, wretched; miserly, avaricious.

> Vive una vida miserable. He leads a miserable life.

miseria f. misery, destitution; stinginess; trifle.

misericordia f. mercy.

misión f. mission, errand.

misionero m. missionary.

MISMA (f. of mismo) same; similar; equal; self.
> Ella misma lo dice. She says it herself.
> No es ya la misma persona. He's no longer the same person. He's changed a great deal.
> Somos de la misma edad. We're (of) the same age.

MISMO adj. same; similar; equal; self.
> El mismo día. The same day.
> Es el mismo hombre que ví ayer. He's the same man I saw yesterday.
> No es ya lo mismo. It's no longer the same (thing).
> Yo mismo lo ví. I myself saw it.
> Yo mismo lo haré. I'll do it myself.
> Soy del mismo parecer. I'm of the same opinion.
> No piensa sino en sí mismo. He only thinks of himself.
> Ahora mismo. Right now.
> Allí mismo. In that very place.
> Te espero aquí mismo. I'll wait for you right here.
> Ayer mismo. Only yesterday.
> Mañana mismo. Tomorrow for sure. Tomorrow without fail.
> Mañana mismo voy. I'll come tomorrow without fail.
> Te estás engañando a tí mismo. You're fooling yourself.
> Me da lo mismo. It's all the same to me. It makes no difference to me.
> Siempre me pasa lo mismo. The same thing always happens to me.
> Lo mismo que si. Just as if.
> Pienso precisamente lo mismo. I think exactly the same thing (the same way).

misterio m. mystery.

misterioso adj. mysterious.

MITAD f. half; middle, center.
> Déme la mitad. Give me half.
> Mi cara mitad. My better half.
> Fuí la mitad del camino a pie y la otra mitad a caballo. I went one half of the way on foot and the other half on horseback.

mitigar to mitigate; to quench.

mitin m. meeting.

mito m. myth.

mitología f. mythology.

mixto adj. mixed, mingled.
> Ese es un tren mixto. That's both a passenger and a freight train. That train carries both passengers and freight.
> Una escuela mixta. A mixed school (for both boys and girls). Co-educational school.

mobiliario m. furniture.

mocedad f. youth.

moción f. motion.

Ambas mociones fueron rechazadas. Both motions were rejected.

mochila f. knapsack.

moda f. fashion, style.

¿Están aún de moda los sombreros de paja? Are straw hats still worn? Are straw hats still in style?

Es un color muy de moda. It's a fashionable color. You see that color worn a lot now.

Estar de moda. To be in style.

Ya no está de moda. To be out of style.

La última moda. The latest style.

modales m. pl. manners, breeding.

Este niño tiene muy buenos modales. This child has very good manners.

Sus modales le hacen odioso. His manners make people dislike (hate) him.

modalidad f. modality; form.

modelo m. model, pattern; style.

¿Cuáles son los últimos modelos? What are the latest styles?

Ese modelo ya no se estila. That model isn't worn any more (any longer).

moderación f. moderation.

moderado adj. moderate; mild.

moderar to moderate, to restrain; to slow up.

Modere la velocidad. Slow up. Slow down.

modernista m. and f. modernist.

MODERNO adj. modern.

Métodos modernos. Modern methods.

Adelantos modernos. Modern improvements.

modestia f. modesty.

modesto adj. modest.

módico adj. moderate; m. reasonable price.

Es un precio módico. It's a reasonable price.

modificar to modify, to alter.

modismo m. idiom.

modista f. modiste, dressmaker; milliner.

MODO m. mode; method, manner; mood.

Es el mejor modo de hacerlo. It's the best way to do it.

De este modo. In this way.

No me parece bien su modo de hablar. I don't approve of (like) his manner of speaking.

De modo que. So that.

Hable de modo que se le pueda oír. Speak so that they can hear you (you can be heard).

Hágalo de cualquier modo. Do it any way.

De todos modos. Anyway.

De todos modos iré a su casa. I'll go to his house anyway (anyhow).

De ningún modo. By no means. In no way. Not at all.

mofa f. mockery; scoff, sneer.

mofarse to mock, to scoff, to jeer.

mojar to wet; to moisten; to dampen.

Las calles están mojadas. The streets are wet.

Eso ya es llover sobre mojado. That's adding insult to injury.

molde m. mold; pattern, model.

En letras de molde. In print.

moldura f. molding.

moler to grind; to mill; to bore; to pound.

molestar to disturb, to trouble, to bother, to annoy; to tease.

No se moleste Ud. Don't trouble yourself. Don't bother.

Siento mucho molestarle. I'm sorry to bother you.

¿Le molesta a Ud. el humo? Does the smoke bother you?

No se moleste Ud., lo haré yo mismo. Don't bother, I'll do it myself.

Deje Ud. de molestarme. Stop bothering me.

molestia f. trouble, bother, annoyance.

No es ninguna molestia. Why, it's no bother. It's no trouble at all.

Siento darle a Ud. tanta molestia. I'm sorry to trouble you so much.

Este asunto me ha ocasionado muchas molestias. This business has given me a great deal of trouble.

Tomarse la molestia de. To take the trouble to.

molesto adj. bothersome; uncomfortable; annoying, boring.

Visitas tan largas son molestas. Such long visits become annoying.

¡Qué molesto es! How annoying he is!

No tenía porque sentirse molesto. He had no reason to be annoyed.

molino m. mill.

momentáneo adj. momentary.

MOMENTO m. moment.

No tengo ni un momento libre. I don't have a free moment.

Un momento, que suena el teléfono. Just a moment, the phone is ringing.

Le ví abajo hace un momento. I saw him downstairs a moment ago.

Le espero de un momento a otro. I expect him any minute now.

Estamos en un momento crítico. We are at the critical point now.

Por el momento. For the moment. For the present.

En cualquier momento. At any moment.

Al momento. In a moment. Immediately.

monarca m. monarch.

monarquía f. monarchy.

mondadientes m. toothpick.

mondadura f. peeling.

mondar to clean; to husk, to remove the bark; to peel.

moneda f. coin; money.

monja *f. nun.*

monje *m. monk.*

mono *adj. pretty, cute, nice; m. monkey, ape.*

¡Qué mono! ¿Verdad? *Isn't it cute! It's cute, isn't it?*

Tiene dos hijas muy monas. *He has two very pretty daughters.*

He conseguido un apartamento monísimo. *I found the coziest apartment.*

monólogo *m. monologue, soliloquy.*

monopolio *m. monopoly.*

monopolizar *to monopolize.*

monotonía *f. monotony.*

monótono *adj. monotonous.*

monstruo *m. monster.*

monstruosidad *f. monstrosity.*

monstruoso *adj. monstrous; huge.*

monta *f. amount, total sum.*

De poca monta. *Of little importance.*

montacargas *m. hoist.*

montaña *f. mountain.*

montar *to mount; to ride; to amount to; to set (a diamond); to put together, to fit together, to assemble.*

¿Monta Ud. a caballo? *Can you ride (a horse)?*

¿Monta Ud. en bicicleta? *Can you ride a bicycle?*

¿A cuánto monta la cuenta? *How much does the bill come to?*

Monte esta máquina. *Assemble this machine. Put this machine together.*

monte *m. mountain; wood, forest; monte (card game).*

montón *m. heap, mass.*

montura *f. mount, saddle horse; saddle and trappings.*

monumental *adj. monumental.*

monumento *m. monument.*

mora *f. delay; mulberry; blackberry.*

morada *f. dwelling, abode.*

morado *adj. purple.*

morador *m. resident, inhabitant.*

moral *adj. moral; f. ethics; morale; m. mulberry tree; blackberry bush.*

morar *to inhabit, to reside.*

mordedura *f. bite.*

morder *to bite.*

mordisco *m. bite; biting; a piece bitten off.*

morena *f. brunette.*

moreno *adj. brown; dark, swarthy.*

morera *f. white mulberry tree.*

moribundo *adj. dying.*

MORIR *to die.*

Murió de pena. *She died of a broken heart.*

Morirse de hambre. *To starve.*

Morirse de frío. *To freeze to death.*

morral *m. nosebag; knapsack.*

mortadela *f. bologna sausage.*

mortaja *f. shroud, winding sheet.*

mortal *adj. mortal, fatal.*

mortalidad *f. mortality; death rate.*

mortero *m. mortar.*

mortificación *f. mortification, humiliation.*

mortificar *to humiliate, to vex.*

mosca *f. fly; dough, money (coll.).*

moscatel *m. muscatel (grape or wine).*

mosquito *m. mosquito.*

mostaza *f. mustard; mustard seed.*

mosto *m. must, grape juice; new wine.*

mostrador *m. counter.*

MOSTRAR *to show; to exhibit; to prove.*

¿Me lo puede mostrar? *Can you show it to me?*

¿Puede mostrarnos como hacerlo? *Can you show us how to do it?*

motivo *m. motive, reason; motif.*

No tiene motivo para quejarse. *You have no reason to complain. You have no grounds for complaint.*

No hay motivo para preocuparse tanto. *There's no need to be so worried.*

Sus afirmaciones dieron motivo a una seria disputa. *His statements led to a serious quarrel.*

motocicleta *f. motorcycle.*

motociclista *m. and f. motorcyclist.*

motor *m. motor; engine.*

El motor no funciona. *The motor doesn't work.*

MOVER *to move; to stir up; to shake.*

No mueva la mesa. *Don't shake the table.*

No dejó piedra que no moviese. *He left no stone unturned. He searched high and low.*

Apenas podía hablar ni moverse. *He could scarcely talk or move.*

móvil *adj. movable; mobile; m. motive.*

movilización *f. mobilization.*

movilizar *to mobilize.*

movimiento *m. movement, motion; traffic.*

moza *f. girl; maid, servant.*

mozo *adj. young; m. young man; waiter; porter.*

¡Vaya con el mozo! *What a man!*

Mozo, tráigame una cerveza. *Waiter, bring me a (glass of) beer.*

El mozo le subirá la maleta al tren. *The porter will put your suitcase on the train.*

Quiero un mozo de cuerda. *I want a porter.*

MUCHA *adj. (f. of mucho) much, very much, a great deal, a lot; very; pl. many, a great many, too many.*

Mucha agua. *A lot of water.*

Había mucha gente. *There was a big crowd.*

Muchas veces. *Many times.*

Muchas cosas. *Many things.*

Esto y muchas otras cosas más. *This and many other things.*

Muchísimas gracias. *Thank you very much.*

MUCHACHA *m. girl; servant, maid.*

¡Qué muchacha tan encantadora! *What a lovely girl! What a charming girl!*

MUCHACHO *m. boy; lad.*

Es un muchacho muy inteligente. *He's a very intelligent boy.*

muchedumbre *f. multitude; crowd.*

MUCHO *adj. much, very much, a great deal of, a lot; very; long (time); pl. many, a great many, too many; very.*

Mucho dinero. *A lot of money.*

Escribe mucho. *He writes a great deal.*

Mucho más grande. *Much larger.*

Muchos libros. *Many books. A lot of books.*

Tiene muchos amigos. *He has a lot of friends.*

Esto es mucho mejor. *This is much better.*

Mucho menos lejos. *Much nearer.*

Tengo mucho que hacer hoy. *I've a lot to do today.*

Con mucho gusto. *Gladly. With (much) pleasure.*

Lo celebro mucho. *I'm very happy to hear it.*

Hace mucho tiempo. *It's been a long time. A long time ago.*

Hace mucho frío. *It's very cold.*

Se lo agradezco muchísimo. *Thank you very much.*

Tengo muchísimo trabajo. *I have a great deal of work to do.*

Lo cuidaré mucho. *I'll take good care of it.*

muda *f. change of clothes, change of linen; molting.*

mudanza *f. change; moving out.*

MUDAR *to change; to alter; to remove; to molt.*

He mudado de parecer. *I've changed my mind.*

MUDARSE *to change (clothes); to move (household).*

Tengo que mudarme de ropa. *I have to change my clothes.*

Mi amigo se ha mudado de casa. *My friend has moved.*

Vamos a mudarnos de casa pronto. *We're going to move soon.*

mudo *adj. dumb, mute, silent.*

MUEBLE *m. piece of furniture.*

Con muebles. *Furnished.*

Una habitación sin muebles. *An unfurnished room.*

mueca *f. grimace, wry face.*

muela *f. millstone; molar tooth.*

muelle *adj. tender, soft; easy (life); m. pier, quay, dock, wharf; spring (metal).*

MUERTE *f. death.*

Se le condenó a muerte. *He was condemned to death.*

Muerte repentina. *Sudden death.*

muerto *adj. dead; languid; m. corpse.*

Muerto de hambre. *Starved.*

Muerto de cansancio. *Dead tired.*

Medio muerto. *Half dead.*

Estar muerto por alguna persona. *To be madly in love with someone.*

muestra *f. sample; specimen.*

muestrario *m. collection of samples.*

MUJER *f. woman; wife.*

¡Qué mujer más hermosa! *What a beautiful woman!*

Su mujer es joven. *His wife is young.*

mula *f. she-mule.*

muleta *f. crutch; stick on which the matador displays his red cape.*

mulo *m. mule.*

multa *f. fine, penalty.*

multar *to mulct; to fine.*

múltiple *adj. multiple.*

multiplicar *to multiply.*

multitud *f. multitude; crowd.*

MUNDO *m. world; multitude; great quantity.*

Quiere ver el mundo. *He (she) wants to see the world.*

Tengo que comprar un mundo de cosas. *I have to buy a lot of things.*

Todo el mundo quiere ir. *Everyone wants to go.*

Critica a todo el mundo. *He criticizes everybody.*

Este hombre se ríe de todo el mundo. *He ("this man") laughs at (ridicules) everybody.*

Tener mundo. *To be a man of the world.*

munición *f. ammunition.*

municipal *adj. municipal.*

municipalidad *f. municipality; town hall.*

municipio *m. municipality.*

muñeca *f. wrist; doll; figure (in dressmaking).*

muñeco *m. puppet; doll; pl. comics, funnies.*

Nunca se cansa de leer los muñecos. *She never gets tired of reading the comics (funnies).*

muralla *f. wall; rampart.*

murmuro *m. murmur, whisper.*

murmurar *to murmur, to whisper.*

muro *m. wall; rampart.*

músculo *m. muscle.*

museo *m. museum.*

¿Qué días está abierto el museo? *What days is the museum open?*

música *f. music.*

Tiene talento para la música. *She has a gift for music.*

Váyase con la música a otra parte. *Go away, don't bother me.*

musical *adj. musical.*

músico *m. musician.*

muslo *m. thigh.*

mutilar *to mutilate.*

mutuo *adj. mutual.*

Se detestan mutuamente. *They detest each other.*

MUY *very; greatly.*

Muy bien, gracias. *Very well, thank you.*

No muy bien. *Not so well. Not very well.*

Muy mal. *Very bad.*

Ese vestido le cae muy bien. *That dress fits her*

very well.

Vino muy de mañana. *He came very early in the morning.*

Estoy muy molesto. *I'm very much annoyed.*

Es muy española. *She's very Spanish. She's a typical Spanish woman (girl).*

Está muy lejos de aquí. *It's a long way from here. It's very far from here.*

N

nabo m. *turnip.*

NACER *to be born; to sprout; to rise (sun); to originate.*

Nació en Madrid. *He was born in Madrid.*

nacimiento m. *birth; origin; source.*

Partida de nacimiento. *Birth certificate.*

nación f. *nation.*

nacional adj. *national.*

nacionalidad f. *nationality.*

NADA *nothing; by no means.*

No quiero nada. *I don't want anything.*

Nada de particular. *Nothing special. Nothing in particular.*

Nada más que una taza de café negro. *Just a cup of black coffee.*

De nada. *Don't mention it.*

No es nada. *It's nothing at all.*

No importa nada. *It doesn't matter at all.*

No vale nada. *It's worthless.*

¿Nada más? *Is that all?*

Nada de eso. *None of that. Nothing of the sort.*

No sé nada de eso. *I know nothing about it. I don't know a thing about it.*

Por nada. *For nothing. Under no circumstances.*

¿No se puede hacer nada? *Can't something be done?*

¿Qué tiene Ud.?—No tengo nada. *What's the matter (with you)?—Nothing's the matter.*

No quiero nada con él. *I don't want to have any dealings with him. I don't want to have anything to do with him.*

No me acuerdo de nada. *I don't remember it at all. I don't remember anything.*

Déme un poquito, nada más. *Give me just a little.*

Antes que nada. *First of all. Before anything else.*

nadador m. *swimmer.*

nadar *to swim, to float.*

Sabe nadar muy bien. *She swims very well.*

Se me nadan los pies en los zapatos. *These shoes are much too big for me. ("My feet are swimming in these shoes.")*

NADIE *nobody, anybody, no one, anyone, none.*

Nadie lo duda. *Nobody doubts it.*

Eso no lo cree nadie. *Nobody believes it.*

Nunca habla mal de nadie. *He never says anything bad about anyone.*

No teme a nadie. *He's not afraid of anyone.*

Importa a Ud. más que a nadie. *It concerns you more than anyone else.*

No le gusta rozarse con nadie. *She doesn't like to have anything to do with anybody.*

nado (a) *swimming.*

Pasar el río a nado. *To swim across a (the) river.*

naipe m. *playing card.*

naranja f. *orange.*

naranjada f. *orangeade.*

naranjo m. *orange tree.*

narcótico adj. and n. *narcotic.*

NARIZ f. *nose; nostril.*

Nariz parfilada. *A straight nose.*

Nariz aguileña. *An aquiline nose.*

Nariz chata. *A flat nose.*

Mete las narices en todo. *He's a busybody.*

Le dieron con la puerta en las narices. *They slammed the door in his face ("nose").*

Tener de (por) las narices. *To have someone under control. To lead someone by the nose.*

narración f. *account, narration; story.*

narrar *to narrate; to relate.*

nata f. *cream; best part.*

Es de la flor y nata. *He's crème de la crème. He's in the highest society.*

natación f. *swimming.*

natal adj. *natal, native.*

natalidad f. *birth rate.*

nativo adj. *native.*

natural adj. and n. *natural; native.*

Eso es muy natural. *That's quite natural.*

Dibujar del natural. *To draw from life.*

Son naturales de esta isla. *They're natives of this island.*

naturaleza f. *nature.*

NATURALMENTE *of course, naturally.*

Naturalmente que lo haré. *Of course I'll do it.*

¿Estará Ud. allí?—Naturalmente. *Will you be there?—Naturally.*

naturismo m. *vegetarianism; nudism.*

naturista m. and f. *nature-lover; vegetarian; nudist.*

naufragar *to be shipwrecked; to fail.*

naufragio m. *shipwreck; failure.*

náusea f. *nausea, nauseousness.*

náutica f. *navigation.*

naval adj. *naval.*

nave f. *ship, vessel.*

navegable adj. *navigable.*

navegación f. *navigation; shipping.*

navegante m. *navigator.*

navegar *to navigate; to sail.*

navidad f. *Nativity; Christmas.*

Por navidad. *For Christmas.*

¡Felices Navidades! ¡Felices Pascuas! *Merry Christmas!*

naviero adj. shipping; m. shipowner.

navío m. warship, ship.

neblina f. mist, light fog.

necesariamente necessarily.

NECESARIO adj. necessary.

Es necesario hacer esto inmediatamente. It's necessary to do this right away.

¿Cree Ud. que tendrá los medios necesarios? Do you think you'll have the necessary means?

Carecemos de lo más necesario. We lack even the essentials.

NECESIDAD f. necessity; need, want.

No hay necesidad de certificar la carta. It's not necessary to register the letter.

Tengo necesidad de ir al banco. I have (need) to go to the bank.

Tienen muchas necesidades. They need many things.

Verse en la necesidad de. To be in need of. To be compelled to.

necesitado adj. very poor; needy; m. person in need.

Está necesitado. He's in want. He's down and out.

NECESITAR to need; to be in need; to want.

¿Necesita Ud. algo más? Do you need anything else (in addition)?

Necesito un nuevo par de zapatos. I need a new pair of shoes.

Necesita tomar un taxi para ir al aeropuerto. He has to take a taxi to get to the airport.

Le prestaré el dinero que necesita. I'll lend you the money you need.

Se necesita una mecanógrafa. Typist wanted.

necio adj. ignorant, stupid; fool.

necrología f. necrology, obituary.

nefasto adj. ill-fated; unlucky.

Día nefasto. Unlucky day.

NEGAR to deny; to refuse; to disown.

No lo niegue Ud. Don't deny it.

No lo niego. I don't deny it.

Lo negó de plano. He denied it flatly.

Ella se negó a aceptarlo. She refused to accept it.

Le niega hasta el saludo. He even refused to greet her.

negativa f. refusal.

negativo adj. negative.

Una respuesta negativa. A negative answer. An answer in the negative.

negligencia f. negligence, neglect.

negligente adj. negligent, careless.

negociado m. bureau, department.

Preséntese Ud. al negociado de inmigración. Report to the Immigration Department.

negociante m. merchant, trader, businessman.

Es un negociante muy hábil. He's a clever

(good) businessman.

negociar to negociate.

NEGOCIO m. business; affair; transaction.

¿A qué negocio se dedica Ud.? What business are you in?

¿Qué tal van sus negocios? How's business?

Se dedica a los negocios. He's a businessman.

Hacer negocios. To do (conduct) business.

Retirarse de los negocios. To retire from business.

NEGRO adj. black; gloomy; m. Negro.

Vestirse de negro. To dress in black.

nervio m. nerve.

Tengo los nervios de punta. My nerves are on edge.

nervioso adj. nervous.

neto adj. neat, pure; net.

Peso neto. Net weight.

neumático m. tire.

Se me ha pinchado un neumático. I have a flat (tire). One of my tires blew out.

neurastenia f. neurasthenia.

neurótico adj. neurotic.

neutral adj. neutral.

nevar to snow.

Está nevando. It's snowing.

nevera f. icebox.

NI neither, either, nor.

Ni come ni bebe. He doesn't eat or drink.

No iré ni con Ud. ni con ellos. I won't go either with you or with them.

Ni mi hermano ni yo le podíamos ayudar. Neither my brother nor I could (were able to) help him.

Ni siquiera eso. Not even that.

Ni aún viene a verme. She doesn't even come to see me.

Ni por asomo creí volver a verlo. I never dreamed I would see him again.

nicho m. niche.

nicotina f. nicotine.

nido m. nest.

niebla f. fog, haze.

Hay niebla. It's foggy.

nieta f. granddaughter.

nieto m. grandson.

nieve f. snow.

nilón m. nylon.

NINGÚN adj. (shortening of ninguno used only before a masculine noun) no, none, any.

Ningún hombre. No man.

De ningún modo. By no means. In no way.

A ningún precio. Not at any price.

NINGUNA adj. (f. of ninguno) no, none, any, no one, nobody.

Ninguna de las chicas. None of the girls.

No he visto a ninguna de las chicas. I haven't seen any of the girls.

Al presente no tenemos ninguna noticia. At

present we have no news (haven't any news).

No quiero ir a ninguna parte esta noche. *I don't want to go anywhere tonight.*

De ninguna manera. *By no means. In no way.*

NINGUNO *adj. no, none, not one, any; indefinite pronoun none, no one, nobody.*

No tengo ninguno. *I haven't any.*

Ninguno ha venido. *Nobody has come.*

Ninguno de nosotros. *None of us.*

NIÑA *f. girl; pupil (of the eye).*

niñez *f. childhood, infancy.*

NIÑO *m. child; pl. children.*

níquel *m. nickel (metal).*

NO *no, not.*

No fumo. *I don't smoke.*

No, gracias. *No, thank you.*

Le tuve que decir que no. *I had to say no to him.*

Ciertamente que no. *Certainly not.*

¡Por supuesto que no! *No, indeed!*

Todavía no. *Not yet.*

No sé. *I don't know.*

No la conozco. *I don't know her.*

¿Cómo dice? No oigo nada. *What are you saying? I can't hear anything.*

¿No quiere Ud. sentarse? *Won't you take a seat (sit down)?*

No hay nadie aquí. *There's no one here.*

No tengo más. *I haven't got any more. I don't have any more.*

No está mal. *It's not bad.*

No corre prisa. *There's no hurry.*

Ya no. *No longer.*

No del todo. *Not quite. Not altogether.*

No tengo mucho tiempo. *I haven't much time.*

No hay de que. *Don't mention it.*

¡No importa! *It doesn't matter!*

¡No me diga! *You don't say (so)! Don't tell me!*

noble *adj. noble; m. nobleman.*

nobleza *f. nobleness, nobility.*

noción *f. notion, idea.*

No tenía noción de que fuera posible. *I had no idea that it would be possible.*

nocivo *adj. harmful.*

nocturno *adj. nocturnal, night, in the night.*

Trabajo nocturno. *Night work.*

NOCHE *f. night.*

¡Buenas noches! *Good night!*

Esta noche. *Tonight.*

Mañana por la noche. *Tomorrow night.*

¿Sale Ud. todas las noches? *Do you go out every night?*

Se hace de noche. *It's getting dark.*

Ya es de noche. *It's dark.*

Hace una noche deliciosa. *It's a delightful evening.*

Por la noche. *At night.*

Durante la noche. *During the night.*

A medianoche. *At midnight.*

A altas horas de la noche. *Late at night.*

Que pase Ud. buena noche. *I hope you have a good night's sleep (rest).*

Pasar la noche. *To spend the night.*

nochebuena *f. Christmas Eve.*

Esta noche es nochebuena. *Tonight's Christmas Eve.*

nombramiento *m. nomination; appointment.*

nombrar *to appoint, to nominate; to name.*

Fué nombrado gobernador de la isla. *He was appointed Governor of the island.*

Al niño le nombraron José. *They named the child Joseph.*

NOMBRE *m. name; noun.*

¿Su nombre y profesión, por favor? *Your name and occupation?*

Ponga el nombre y las señas del remitente en el reverso del sobre. *Put the sender's name and address on the back of the envelope.*

La conozco de nombre. *I know her by name.*

No conozco a nadie con ese nombre. *I don't know anyone by that name.*

Salúdele en mi nombre. *Remember me to him.*

Va a poner a su hijo el nombre de Antonio. *He's going to name his son Anthony.*

nómina *f. payroll.*

norma *f. rule, standard, model.*

normal *adj. normal, f. normal school.*

normalidad *f. normality.*

NORTE *m. north.*

norteamericano *adj. and n. North America; American (restricted to persons or things from the United States).*

NOS *we; us; to us.*

Nos hace falta dinero. *We need money.*

Nos reuníamos todos los lunes a cierta hora. *We used to meet at a certain hour every Monday.*

Dénoslo. *Give it to us.*

No nos dejaron entrar. *They didn't let us in.*

El mismo nos lo dijo. *He told us so himself.*

NOSOTRAS *(f. of nosotros) we; us; ourselves.*

(Nosotras) Somos sus hermanas. *We're his sisters.*

Nosotras las mujeres. *We women.*

NOSOTROS *we; us; ourselves.*

(Nosotros) Somos vecinos. *We're neighbors.*

Lo haremos nosotros mismos. *We'll do it ourselves.*

Quiere venir con nosotros. *She wants to come with us.*

Nosotros los norteamericanos. *We Americans.*

nostalgia *f. nostalgia, homesickness.*

NOTA *f. note.*

Tomar nota. *To take note.*

Cuaderno de notas. *Notebook.*

Nota marginal. *Marginal note.*

Nota musical. *Musical note.*

The notes of the scale in Spanish are: *do C,*

re D, mi E, fa F, sol G, la A, si B.

Do agudo. *Upper C.*

Do grave. *Lower C.*

Do sostenido. *C sharp.*

Re bemol. *D flat.*

Redonda. *Semibreve.*

Blanca. *Minim.*

Negra. *Crotchet.*

Corchea. *Quaver.*

Semicorchea. *Semiquaver.*

Fusa. *Demisemiquaver.*

Semifusa. *Semidemisemiquaver.*

notable *adj. notable; worthy of notice.*

Es un hecho notable. *It's an outstanding fact.*

Es un hombre notable. *He's an outstanding man.*

notar *to note; to notice.*

¿Notó Ud. algo raro? *Did you notice anything strange?*

notario *m. notary.*

NOTICIA *f. piece of news; information; notice; pl. news.*

La radio dió la noticia. *The news came over the radio.*

Las noticias del día. *The news of the day.*

Hay buenas noticias. *There's good news. Good news!*

No he tenido noticias de mi familia. *I haven't heard from my family.*

notificación *f. notification.*

notificar *to notify; to inform.*

notorio *adj. well-known, evident.*

novato *adj. novice, beginner.*

novecientos *adj. and n. nine hundred.*

NOVEDAD *f. novelty; latest news or fashion.*

¿Qué hay de novedad? *What's new?*

Sin novedad. *As usual. Nothing new.*

Llegamos a Toluca sin novedad. *We arrived in Toluca safely.*

Ultima novedad. *Latest style.*

novela *f. novel.*

novelista *m. and f. novelist.*

noventa *adj. and n. ninety.*

novia *f. sweetheart, girl friend; fiancée; bride.*

noviazgo *m. engagement, betrothal.*

novicio *adj. novice; apprentice.*

novio *m. sweetheart, boy friend; fiancé; bridegroom.*

Los novios. *The newlyweds.*

nube *f. cloud; film (on the eyeball).*

Hay muchas nubes. *There are many clouds. It's cloudy.*

nublado *adj. cloudy.*

Está nublado. *It's cloudy.*

nuca *f. nape, back of the neck.*

nudo *m. knot.*

nuera *f. daughter-in-law.*

NUESTRA *(f. of nuestro) our, ours; pl. nuestras.*

Nuestra hermana. *Our sister.*

Nuestras hermanas. *Our sisters.*

Ella es vecina nuestra. *She's a neighbor of ours.*

La nuestra. *Ours.*

NUESTRO *our; ours; pl. nuestros.*

Nuestro amigo. *Our friend.*

Nuestros derechos. *Our rights.*

Nuestro deber. *Our duty.*

Es un antiguo conocido nuestro. *He's an old acquaintance of ours.*

Es en nuestro beneficio. *It's to our advantage (benefit).*

El nuestro. *Ours.*

Lo nuestro. *Ours. What's ours.*

Los nuestros. *Our folks (people).*

NUEVE *adj. and n. nine.*

NUEVO *adj. new.*

¿Es nuevo ese sombrero? *Is that hat new? Is that a new hat?*

¿Qué hay de nuevo? *What's new?*

¿Sabe Ud. algo de nuevo? *Have you heard anything new? ("Do you know anything new?")*

¿Tiene Ud. alguna obra nueva? *Have you any recent books?*

Hágalo Ud. de nuevo. *Do it again.*

¡Feliz año nuevo! *Happy New Year!*

nuez *f. walnut; nut; Adam's apple.*

nulidad *f. nullity; nonentity; incompetent person.*

nulo *adj. null, void; not binding.*

numerar *to number.*

número *m. number; figure; issue (of a magazine), act.*

¿Qué número es el de su casa? *What's your house number? What's your address?*

¿Cuál es su número de teléfono? *What is your telephone number?*

Escriba el número. *Write the number.*

Por favor, póngame en comunicación con el número . . . *Kindly connect me with number . . .*

En números redondos. *In round numbers (figures).*

No me gustó ese número. *I didn't like that act.*

NUNCA *never, ever.*

¡Nunca! *Never!*

Nunca tomo café. *I never take coffee.*

Nunca lo consentiré. *I'll never consent (agree to it).*

Casi nunca leo los periódicos. *I hardly ever read the newspapers.*

Más vale tarde que nunca. *Better late than never.*

nupcial *adj. nuptial.*

nupcias *f. pl. nuptials, wedding.*

nutrición *f. nutrition, nourishment.*

nutrir *to nourish, to feed.*

nutritivo *adj. nutritious, nourishing.*

Ñ

ñame *m. yam (plant).*

ñato *adj. flat-nosed.*

O

O *or, either.*

Más o menos. *More or less.*

Más tarde o más temprano. *Sooner or later.*

Le he visto o en Roma o en París. *I saw him either in Rome or in Paris.*

obcecado *adj. stubborn, obdurate.*

obedecer *to obey.*

Quiero que me obedezcan. *I expect to be obeyed.*

Eso obedece a otras razones. *This is due to other reasons.*

obediencia *f. obedience.*

obediente *adj. obedient.*

obeso *adj. obese, extremely fat.*

obispo *m. bishop; ray (fish).*

objetar *to object, to oppose.*

objetivo *m. objective, aim.*

OBJETO *m. object, thing, article; purpose, aim.*

No tengo objetos de valor que declarar. *I have nothing ("no articles of value") to declare.*

Por fin logró su objeto. *Finally he reached his goal.*

Al objeto de. *For the purpose of.*

Ser objeto de. *To be the cause of. To be the object of.*

Ser objeto de burla. *To be the laughingstock.*

Llenar su objeto. *To suit one's purpose.*

Objetos de escritorio. *Office equipment.*

oblicuo *adj. oblique.*

obligación *f. obligation; duty; pl. liabilities.*

obligar *to oblige; to compel; to obligate.*

Me veré obligado a dar parte a la policía. *I'll have (be compelled) to report it to the police.*

Me dió un resfriado terrible que me obligó a guardar cama por una quincena. *I caught a bad cold which kept me in bed for two weeks.*

obligatorio *adj. obligatory, compulsory.*

OBRA *f. work; labor; book; play (theater); building; repairs (in a house); means; deed, action.*

¿Dan ya esa obra? *Are they giving that play yet?*

Es una obra de tres tomos. *The work is in three volumes.*

Toda obra importante requiere trabajo. *All important work requires labor.*

Obra maestra. *Masterpiece.*

Obras públicas. *Public works.*

Poner en obra. *To put into practice. To set into operation.*

Obra de arte. *Work of art.*

obrar *to work; to act; to do things.*

No me gusta su modo de obrar. *I don't like the way he does things.*

Obrar conforme a derecho. *To act in accordance with the law.*

obrero *m. worker, workman.*

obscurecer *to darken; to grow dark.*

obscurecerse *to get dark.*

Está obscureciendo. *It's getting dark.*

obscuridad *f. obscurity; darkness.*

obscuro *adj. obscure; dark.*

Una noche obscura. *A dark night.*

obsequiar *to entertain, to treat; to make a present, to give a gift.*

Le obsequiamos con motivo de su cumpleaños. *We entertained him on his birthday.*

Me han obsequiado un libro. *They gave me a book (as a gift).*

obsequio *m. entertainment; gift, present.*

Le agradezco mucho su obsequio. *Thank you very much for your present.*

En obsequio de. *For the sake of.*

observación *f. observation; remark.*

observar *to observe, to notice; to keep, to follow (the law, etc.); to make a remark; to look.*

observatorio *m. observatory.*

obsesión *f. obsession.*

obstáculo *m. obstacle.*

obstante *(preceded by no) notwithstanding, in spite of.*

No obstante. *Notwithstanding. Regardless.*

obstinación *f. obstinacy, stubbornness.*

obstinado *adj. obstinate.*

obstinarse *to be obstinate; to persist.*

obstruir *to obstruct, to block.*

Obstruir el tráfico. *To block traffic.*

obtención *f. attainment; accomplishment.*

OBTENER *to obtain, to get; to attain.*

Ha obtenido una buena colocación. *He got a good job.*

obturador *m. shutter (of a camera); plug, stopper.*

obtuso *adj. obtuse, blunt.*

obús *m. howitzer, shell (of a gun).*

obvio *adj. obvious, evident.*

OCASIÓN *f. occasion; opportunity.*

He perdido una buena ocasión. *I lost (missed) a good opportunity.*

Iré a Bolivia en la primera ocasión. *I'll go to Bolivia at the first opportunity.*

Celebro la ocasión de conocerla. *I'm very happy to know you.*

Dar ocasión a. *To give rise to.*

Aprovechar la ocasión. *To take advantage of the occasion (opportunity).*

De ocasión. *Secondhand.*

Con (en) ocasión de. *On the occasion of.*

ocasionar *to cause; to bring about.*

occidental *adj. western, occidental.*

occidente *m. occident, west.*

océano *m. ocean.*

Océano Atlántico. *Atlantic Ocean.*

Océano Pacífico. *Pacific Ocean.*

ocio m. idleness, leisure; pastime.

ociosidad f. idleness, leisure.

ocioso adj. idle, useless.

octavo adj. eighth.

OCTUBRE m. October.

oculista m. and f. oculist.

ocultar to conceal; to hide.

　No se pueden ocultar las penas. It's impossible to conceal one's troubles (sorrows, grief).

　No se le ocultará a Ud. que . . . You must be aware that . . .

oculto adj. concealed, hidden.

ocupación f. occupation, business, trade.

　¿Cuál es su nombre y ocupación? What is your name and occupation?

OCUPADO adj. occupied; busy; engaged.

　Ultimamente he estado muy ocupado. I've been very busy lately.

　La línea está ocupada. The line is busy.

　Ese taxi está ocupado. That cab is taken.

OCUPAR to occupy; to take possession of; to give work to; to hold a position.

　¿Está este asiento ocupado? Is this seat taken (occupied)?

　Ocupa un puesto muy importante. He holds a very important position.

　Han ocupado más obreros en la fábrica. They have employed (taken on) more workers at the factory.

　Nuestras tropas han ocupado la ciudad. Our troops have occupied the city.

　El edificio ocupa toda una manzana. The building occupies an entire block.

OCUPARSE to pay attention to; to be concerned about; to attend to; to be encouraged in; to have as one's business.

　No se ocupe Ud. de esas cosas. Don't bother about such things. Don't pay attention to such things.

　Se ocupaba poco de aquellos rumores. He paid little attention to those rumors.

　Ocuparse de. To look into. To take care of.

　El asunto que nos ocupa. The matter in question.

　¿En qué se ocupa Ud.? What's your occupation?

ocurrencia f. occurrence, incident; wisecrack, joke.

　Fué una ocurrencia desgraciada. It was an unfortunate incident.

　¡Qué ocurrencia! 1. What an idea! 2. What a joke!

　Siempre dice muchas ocurrencias. He's always telling jokes.

OCURRIR to occur, to happen.

　¿Qué ocurre? What's the matter? What's happening? What's up?

　No ha ocurrido nada de nuevo. Nothing new has happened.

　¿Cuando ocurrió eso? When did that happen?

　El accidente ocurrió aquí mismo. The acci-

dent happened right here (in this very place).

ocurrirse to occur to one, to strike one (an idea).

　Se me ocurre una idea. An idea occurred to me. I have an idea.

　No se me ocurrió ponerles un telegrama. I didn't think of sending them a telegram. It didn't occur to me to send them a telegram.

OCHENTA adj. and n. eighty.

OCHO adj. and n. eight.

　Dentro de ocho días. A week from today.

odiar to hate.

odio m. hatred.

odioso adj. hateful.

OESTE m. west.

ofender to offend.

ofenderse to take offense, to be offended.

　Se ofende por nada. He (she) gets offended over (takes offense at) the least little thing (over trifles).

ofensa f. offense.

ofensiva f. offensive.

　Tomar la ofensiva. To take the offensive.

oferta f. offer; offering, gift.

　Es su última oferta. That's his last (final) offer.

　Oferta y demanda. Supply and demand.

oficial adj. official; m. officer, official; trained worker.

oficialmente officially.

oficina f. office; workshop.

　¿Cuál es la dirección de su oficina? What's your office address?

oficinista m. and f. office worker.

oficio m. occupation, work, trade, business; written communication.

　¿Qué oficio tiene? What's your profession? What do you do for a living?

OFRECER to offer; to present.

　Ofrézcales un poco. Offer them some.

　Nos ofreció su ayuda. He offered us his help. He offered to help us.

　¿Qué se le ofrece? What would you like? What can I do for you?

　Me ofreció dos dólares por el libro. He offered me two dollars for the book.

ofrecimiento m. offer.

oh! Oh!

OÍDO m. hearing; ear.

　Tengo dolor de oído. I have an earache.

　Tiene oído para la música. He has a good ear for music.

　Le dijo algo al oído y se marchó. He whispered something in his ear and left.

　Ha llegado a mis oídos que . . . I've heard that . . .

OÍR to hear; to listen.

　¡Oye! (¡Oiga! ¡Oígame!) Say! Say there! Listen! Look here!

　¿Cómo dice? No oigo nada. What are you saying? I can't hear a thing.

　No oí el despertador. I didn't hear the alarm

clock.

¿Ha oído Ud. la última noticia? *Have you heard the latest news?*

¡Qué Dios le oiga! *Let's hope so! ("God grant it!")*

ojal m. buttonhole.

¡Ojalá! God grant (it)! Would that . . .

¡Ojalá que venga! *I wish she would come.*

¡Ojalá fuera así! *I wish it were so! Would that it were so!*

OJO m. eye; attention, care; keyhole.

Tengo los ojos cansados de tanto leer. *My eyes are tired from reading so much.*

No pude pegar los ojos en toda la noche. *I couldn't sleep a wink ("close my eyes") all night.*

Hay que tener mucho ojo. *One should be very careful.*

Le costó un ojo de la cara. *It cost him a mint of money. It cost him a small fortune.*

ola f. wave (of water).

OLER to smell.

Huelo algo. *I smell something.*

Me huele a quemado. *I smell something burning.*

Esto no me huele bien. *There's something fishy about it.*

Oler a soga. *To deserve to be hanged.*

Huele a chamusquina. *It looks like a fight.*

olfatear to smell.

olfato m. sense of smell.

oliva f. olive.

Aceite de oliva. *Olive oil.*

olivo m. olive tree.

olor m. scent, odor.

oloroso adj. fragrant.

OLVIDAR to forget.

Olvidé los guantes. *I forgot my gloves.*

Se me olvidó el paraguas. *I forgot my umbrella.*

Siempre se me olvida su nombre. *I always forget his name.*

¡Ah, se me olvidaba! *Oh, I almost forgot!*

Olvidemos lo pasado. *Let bygones be bygones.*

olvido m. forgetfulness; oversight.

Nos ha echado al olvido. *He's forgotten us.*

Fué un olvido. *It was an oversight.*

olla f. pot.

ombligo m. navel; center, middle.

omisión f. omission.

omitir to omit, to leave out.

Ud. ha omitido varias frases. *You've omitted several sentences.*

ómnibus m. bus.

¿Dónde para el ómnibus? *Where does the bus stop?*

¿Dónde queda la parada del ómnibus? *Where is the bus stop?*

ONCE adj. and n. eleven.

onda f. wave; ripple.

Onda corta. *Short wave.*

Onda larga. *Long wave.*

onza f. ounce.

opaco adj. opaque; dull; not transparent.

opción f. option, choice.

ópera f. opera.

operación f. operation.

operar to operate; to act, to take effect; to operate on.

La medicina empieza a operar. *The medicine is beginning to take effect.*

Hay que operar al enfermo. *It's necessary to operate on the patient.*

operario m. worker; operator.

opinar to give an opinion.

Opino que debes hacerlo. *I think you should do it ("It's my opinion that . . .")*

¿Qué opina Ud. de esto? *What do you think of that? What's your opinion about that?*

opinión f. opinion.

Esta es la opinión de todos. *Everyone is of that opinion.*

He cambiado de opinión. *I've changed my mind.*

oponer to oppose, to go against.

No opuso la menor dificultad. *He didn't raise any difficulties.*

oponerse to be against, to object to.

Me opongo a eso. *I'm against that.*

oportunamente opportunely, in good time.

oportunidad f. opportunity, good chance.

oportuno adj. opportune.

oposición f. opposition; competition for a position.

opositor m. opponent; competitor.

opresión f. oppression.

opresivo adj. oppressive.

opresor m. oppressor.

oprimir to press, to squeeze; to oppress.

optar to choose, to pick up.

Optar por. *To choose.*

óptico adj. optic, optical; m. optician.

optimismo m. optimism.

optimista m. and f. optimist.

opuesto adj. opposed, opposite, contrary.

ora whether; either; now, then.

Ora esto, ora estotro. *Now this (one), now that (one).*

oración f. prayer; sentence (grammar).

orador m. orator, speaker.

oral adj. oral.

orar to pray.

ORDEN m. order, arrangement; f. order, command; brotherhood, society, order.

A sus órdenes. *At your service.*

Por orden de. *By order of.*

Llamar al orden. *Call to order.*

En orden. *In order.*

Dar orden. *To instruct.*

Hasta nueva orden. *Until further instructions.*
Until further orders. Until further notice.
La orden del día. *The order of the day.*
El orden del día. *Agenda.*
Mantener el orden público. *To preserve the*
("public") peace.

ordenanza *f. order; statute, ordinance; m. orderly.*
ordenar *to arrange; to order; to command; to ordain.*
ordeñar *to milk.*
ordinariamente *ordinarily.*
ORDINARIO *adj. ordinary; vulgar, unrefined; m.*
carrier, mailman; delivery boy; daily house-
hold expense.
Es una mujer ordinaria. *She's vulgar.*
De ordinario. *Usually. Ordinarily.*
oreja *f. ear (external); flange, lug.*
Enseñar la oreja. *To let the cat out of the bag.*
orfandad *f. orphanage.*
orgánico *adj. organic.*
organillo *m. barrel organ.*
organismo *m. organism.*
organización *f. organization.*
organizar *to organize; to form; to arrange.*
órgano *m. organ; means, agency.*
orgullo *m. pride; haughtiness.*
orgulloso *adj. proud; haughty.*
oriental *adj. oriental, eastern; m. oriental.*
orientar *to orient.*
orientarse *to find one's bearings, to find one's way*
around.
Es difícil orientarse en una ciudad desconocida.
It's difficult to find one's way around in a
strange city.
ORIENTE *m. orient, east.*
origen *m. origin, source.*
original *adj. and n. original.*
originalidad *f. originality.*
originar *to cause, to originate.*
Los gastos originados. *The cost.*
orilla *f. border, edge; shore; bank (of a river).*
ornamento *m. ornament, decoration.*
ornar *to adorn.*
ORO *m. gold; pl. diamonds (at cards).*
Perdí mi reloj de oro. *I lost my gold watch.*
orquesta *f. orchestra, band.*
ortografía *f. orthography, spelling.*
oruga *f. caterpillar; rocket (planet).*
os *(dative and accusative of vos and vosotros) you,*
to you.
oscuro *m. dark.*
oso *m. bear.*
ostentar *to display; to show off, to boast.*
OTOÑO *m. autumn, fall.*
otorgar *to consent, to agree to; to grant.*
Quien calla otorga. *Silence gives consent.*
("Whoever keeps silent, consents.")
OTRA *(f. of otro) other, another; pl. otras.*
Déme otra manzana. *Give me another apple.*
Mi otra hija. *My other daughter.*

Sus otras fincas. *His other estates.*
¿Desea alguna otra cosa? *Would you like any-*
thing else?
Y otras muchas cosas. *And many other things.*
Parece otra. *She looks quite different. She looks*
changed.
Otra vez. *Again. Once more.*
Otras veces. *Other times.*
OTRO *adj. other, another; pl. otros.*
¡Otro vaso de cerveza! *Another glass of beer!*

Busco otro. *I'm looking for another (one).*
Busco el otro. *I'm looking for the other (one).*
Queremos otros. *We want some others.*
Queremos los otros. *We want the others.*
Otro tanto. *As much more.*
Otros tantos. *As many more.*
¿Quiénes son los otros invitados? *Who are the*
other guests?
Debe haber otros dos. *There must be two more.*
Al otro lado de la calle. *Across the street.*
Algún otro. *Someone else.*
Otro día. *Another day.*
El otro día. *The other day.*
De otro modo. *Otherwise.*
Si no manda Ud. otra cosa, me retiro. *If you*
don't need anything else, I'll leave (go) now.
ovación *f. ovation.*
oval *adj. oval.*
oveja *f. sheep.*
oyente *m. and f. hearer; listener; pl. audience,*
listeners.

P

pabellón *m. pavilion; flag, colors.*
pacer *to pasture; to graze.*
paciencia *f. patience.*
Tenga paciencia. *Be patient. Have patience.*
Estoy perdiendo la paciencia. *I'm losing my*
patience.
paciente *adj. patient; m. patient.*
pacífico *adj. peaceful; mild.*
pactar *to reach an agreement, to sign a pact, to*
agree upon.
pacto *m. pact, agreement.*
padecer *to suffer; to be liable to.*
¿Qué es lo que Ud. padece? *What seems to be*
the matter with you?
Ha padecido mucho. *He's suffered a lot.*
Padezco mucho de dolores de cabeza. *I suffer*
from headaches a lot.
padecimiento *m. suffering.*
padrastro *m. stepfather.*
PADRE *m. father; pl. parents.*
De tal padre, tal hijo. *Like father, like son.*
padrino *m. godfather; best man (at a wedding);*
second (in a duel); sponsor.
paella *f. a popular Valencian dish.*
paga *f. payment; pay, wages, fee.*

pagadero adj. payable.

pagador m. payer; paymaster; paying teller.

pagaduría f. paymaster's office.

pagano m. pagan, heathen.

PAGAR to pay, to pay for; to return (a visit, a favor).

    ¿Nos pagarán hoy? Will they pay us today?

    Pagar al contado. To pay cash.

    Pagar en la misma moneda. To pay back in the same coin.

    Pagar una visita. To return a visit.

    Me las pagará. I'll make him pay for it.

    Pagar el pato. To be blamed for something. To take the blame for something.

    Pagarse de. To be pleased with. To be fond of. To be conceited.

    Está muy pagado de sí. He has a high opinion of himself.

pagaré m. promissory note, I.O.U.

PÁGINA f. page (of a book, etc.).

    La página siguiente. The following page.

pago m. payment; reward.

    En pago de. In payment of.

    Suspender los pagos. To stop payment.

país m. country (nation).

paisaje m. landscape, view.

paisano adj. coming from the same country; m. fellow countryman; civilian.

    Somos paisanos. We are fellow countrymen.

    Iba vestido de paisano. He was dressed in civilian clothes.

paja f. straw.

pájaro m. bird.

PALABRA f. word; promise.

    ¿Qué quiere decir esta palabra? What does this word mean?

    No entiendo palabra. I don't understand a word.

    Desearía hablar dos palabras con Ud. I should like to have a few words with you.

    Me quitó la palabra de la boca. He took the words right out of my mouth.

    No falte a su palabra. Don't break your promise.

    Pido la palabra. May I have the floor?

    Esas son palabras mayores. That's no joking matter.

    Dió su palabra de honor. He gave his word of honor.

    Le cojo la palabra. I'll take you up on that.

    Libertad de palabra. Freedom of speech.

    De palabra. By word of mouth.

    Dirigir la palabra. To address.

    Palabra de matrimonio. Promise of marriage.

    El que lleva la palabra. The spokesman.

    Empeñar la palabra. To give one's word.

palacio m. palace.

paladar m. palate; taste.

palanca f. lever; crowbar.

palangana f. washbowl; basin.

palco m. grandstand; box (in a theater).

palidecer to turn pale.

pálido adj. pale.

palillo m. toothpick; pl. chopsticks; castanets; drumsticks.

paliza f. spanking; beating.

palma f. palm tree; palm leaf; palm (of the hand).

    Llevarse la palma. To carry the day. To carry off the laurels.

palmada f. pat, clap; clapping.

    Dar palmadas. To clap one's hands.

palmo m. span, measure of length.

    Palmo a palmo. Inch by inch.

palo m. stick; cudgel; timber; blow; suit (of cards).

    Palo de escoba. Broomstick.

    De tal palo tal astilla. A chip off the old block. Like father, like son.

paloma f. pigeon; dove.

    Paloma mensajera. Homing pigeon. Carrier pigeon.

palomar m. pigeon house, dovecot.

palpable adj. palpable, evident.

palpar to feel, to touch.

palpitar to beat, to throb, to palpitate.

paludismo m. paludism; malaria.

pampa f. pampas, vast treeless plain.

PAN m. bread; loaf.

    Pan con mantequilla. Bread and butter.

    ¿Tienen Uds. bastante pan? Have you (pl.) enough bread?

    Se comió un pan entero. He ate a whole loaf.

panadería f. bakery.

panadero m. baker.

panal m. honeycomb; hornet's nest.

pandereta f. tambourine.

pandilla f. gang.

panecillo m. roll (bread).

panera f. breadbasket; granary.

pánico adj. panic; m. panic.

panorama m. landscape, view.

panorámico adj. panoramic.

pantalón m. trousers.

pantalla f. lamp shade; screen.

pantano m: marsh, swamp.

pantera f. panther.

pantomima f. pantomime.

pantorrilla f. calf (of the leg).

panza f. paunch, belly.

pañal m. swaddling cloth; diaper.

paño m. woolen material, cloth, fabric; (by extension) ar.y woven material.

    ¿Le queda a Ud. bastante paño para hacer otro traje? Have you enough material left to make another suit?

    Paños menores. Underwear.

pañuelo m. handkerchief.

papa f. potato; m. Pope.

papá m. papa, daddy.

papagayo m. parrot.

papel m. paper; role; part (in a play).

    ¿Quiere darme un pliego de papel? Will you please give me a sheet of paper?

    Escríbalo en este papel. Write it on this paper.

    Hay papel de escribir en el cajón. There's some writing paper in the drawer.

    Hizo el papel de tonto. He played the fool.

    Hacer un papel. To play a part. To play a role.

    Papel moneda. Paper money (currency).

    Papel secante. Blotting paper. Blotter.

    Papel para calcar. Tracing paper.

    Papel de estraza. Wrapping paper.

    Papel de seda. Tissue paper.

    Papel de fumar. Cigarette paper.

papelera f. writing desk; (paper) folder.

papelería f. stationery store.

PAQUETE m. package; parcel.

    Mande el paquete a estas señas. Send the package to this address.

PAR adj. equal; par (value); even (number); m. pair, couple; team; peer.

    Es una mujer sin par. There's nobody like her.

    La peseta estaba a la par. The peseta was at par value.

    La puerta estaba abierta de par en par. The door was wide open.

    Un par de zapatos. A pair of shoes.

    Llegará dentro de un par de días. He'll arrive in a couple of days.

    ¿Toma Ud. pares o nones? Do you take odds or evens?

PARA for, to, until, about, in order to, toward.

    ¿Para qué? What for? For what purpose?

    ¿Para quién es esto? For whom is this?

    Esta carta es para Ud. This letter is for you.

    ¿Para quién es este libro? Who's this book for?

    ¿Para qué sirve esto? What's this for? What's this good for?

    Tengo una cita para las cuatro. I have an appointment for four o'clock.

    Déjelo para mañana. Leave it until tomorrow.

    Tiene talento para la música. She has a gift for music.

    Me abrigo para no tener frío. I dress warmly so as not to be cold.

    Bueno para comer. Good to eat.

    Dije para mí. I said to myself.

    Está para llover. It's going to rain.

    Estoy para salir. I'm about to leave.

    El tren está para partir. The train is about to leave.

    Quisiera algo para leer. I'd like something to read.

    Trabajar para comer. To work for a living.

    Estudia para médico. He's studying to be a doctor.

    Para siempre. Forever.

    Para entre los dos. Between ourselves.

parabién m. congratulation.

parábola f. parable; parabola.

parabrisa m. windshield.

paracaídas m. parachute.

paracaidista m. parachutist.

parada f. stop; pause; halt; parade; wager.

    ¿Dónde está la parada más cerca del tranvía? Where is the nearest streetcar stop?

    Cinco minutos de parada. Five minutes' stop.

    La parada se formará a las doce. The parade will form at twelve o'clock.

paradero m. whereabouts; terminus; end.

parado adj. stopped, at a standstill; closed (a factory); unemployed; standing up (Amer.).

paradoja f. paradox.

PARAGUAS m. umbrella.

    ¿Llevamos paraguas? Shall we take (our) umbrellas?

paraíso m. paradise.

paraje m. place, spot.

paralelo adj. and n. parallel.

parálisis f. paralysis.

paralítico adj. paralytic.

paralizar to paralyze; to bring to a standstill; to impede, to hinder.

PARAR to stop, to halt, to stay; to bet; to stand (Amer.).

    ¿Por qué para el tren? Why is the train stopping?

    ¿Paramos aquí? Do we stop here?

    Pare Ud. en frente de la estación. Stop in front of the station.

    Mi reloj se paró. My watch stopped.

    No para de llover desde ayer. It hasn't stopped raining since yesterday.

    Con estas cartas yo voy a parar cincuenta pesos. With these cards I'm going to bet fifty pesos.

    ¿En qué hotel pararán sus amigos? At what hotel will your friends stay?

    Paró la oreja para oír lo que decíamos. He pricked up his ears to hear what we were saying.

    No paró bien aquel negocio. That business didn't end very well.

    ¿Dónde irá a parar todo esto? How's all this going to end?

pararse to stop; to stand up (Amer.).

    Se pararon (Amer.) al verla llegar. They stood up when they saw her coming.

    Párese (Amer.) en esta esquina que ahorita pasará el autobús. Stand on this corner; the bus will pass by in a little while.

pararrayos m. lightning rod.

parásito m. parasite.

parcela f. parcel; piece of land.

parcial adj. partial.

parcialidad f. partiality, bias.

parcialmente partially, partly.

pardo adj. brown; dark.

PARECER to appear, to show up, to turn up; to seem, to look, to be like, to resemble; m. opinion; appearance.

¿Qué le parece? What do you think of it? How do you like it? How does it seem to you?

Léalo Ud. despacio y dígame lo que le parece. Read it carefully and let me know what you think of it.

¿Le parece que vayamos al cine? What do you say to our going to the movies?

Me parece barato a ese precio. I think it's cheap at that price.

Está enfermo, pero no lo parece. He's sick but he doesn't look it.

Al parecer vendrá la semana próxima. Apparently he's coming next week.

Parece que va a llover. It looks as if it's going to rain.

Déme Ud. su parecer. Give me your opinion (about it).

¿Cuál es su parecer respecto a eso? What's your opinion about that?

También soy yo del mismo parecer. I'm also of the same opinion.

No me gusta su parecer. I don't like his appearance.

parecerse to look alike, to resemble.

Este niño se parece a su padre. This child looks like his father.

Las dos hermanas se parecen. Both sisters look alike.

Se parecen como dos gotas de agua. They are as alike as two peas in a pod.

PARECIDO adj. like, similar, resembling; (good or bad) looking; m. likeness.

Yo tengo un traje muy parecido al suyo. I have a suit very much like yours.

Los dos trabajos son muy parecidos. The two jobs are very similar.

Su hijo es muy bien parecido. Your son is very good-looking.

PARED f. wall.

Apóyalo contra la pared. Lean it against the wall.

Entre la espada y la pared. Between the devil and the deep blue sea. ("Between the wall and the sword.")

pareja f. pair; couple; team (of horses); dancing partner.

paréntesis m. parenthesis.

PARIENTE m. relative, relation.

¿Tiene Ud. parientes en esta ciudad? Do you have any relatives in this town?

Fuí a visitar a unos parientes. I went to visit some relatives.

parir to give birth.

parlamento m. parliament; parley.

paro m. unemployment; stoppage of work.

Paro forzoso. Lockout.

párpado m. eyelid.

parque m. park.

parra f. grapevine.

párrafo m. paragraph.

Echar un párrafo. To have a chat.

parrilla f. gridiron, broiler.

parroquia f. parish; clientele, customers.

parroquiano m. parishioner; customer.

Somos sus parroquianos. We're his (your) customers.

PARTE f. part; portion; share; side; role; party; m. report, communication, dispatch.

¿Qué parte del pollo le gusta más? What part of the chicken do you like best?

¿En qué parte de la ciudad vive Ud.? In what part of the city do you live?

Hagamos el trabajo por partes iguales. Let's divide the work equally. ("Let's do the work in equal parts.")

Cada uno pagó su parte. Each one paid his share.

Traigo esto de parte del señor Sucre. This is from Mr. Sucre.

Salude a Juan de mi parte. Give John my regards.

Recibimos felicitaciones de ambas partes. We received congratulations from both sides.

He leído la mayor parte del libro, pero no todo. I've read most of the book, but not all.

No tengo arte ni parte en el asunto. I've nothing to do with the matter.

¿Le ha visto en alguna parte? Have you seen him anywhere?

No lo hallo en ninguna parte. I can't find it anywhere.

No iremos a ninguna parte. We won't go anywhere.

¿Ha leído Ud. el parte de guerra? Have you read the communiqué?

En todas partes. Everywhere.

En parte. In part.

En gran parte. Largely.

De algún tiempo a esta parte. For some time past.

De cinco días a esta parte. Within the(se) last few days.

Haré todo de mi parte. I'll do all in my power.

Parte de la oración. Part of speech.

Dar parte. To inform. To notify.

Le he dado parte de mi llegada. I've sent him word of my arrival.

Por mi parte. As far as I'm concerned. For my part.

Por una parte. On one hand.

Por otra parte. On the other hand. Besides.

La parte interesada. The party concerned. The

interested party.

¿De parte de quién? *Who's calling?*

participación *f. participation, share.*

participar *to participate, to take part, to share; to inform, to notify.*

No se crea que yo participo de sus ideas. *Don't think that I share his views.*

Le participo mi decisión. *I'm informing you of my decision.*

¿Participaron Uds. en el juego? *Did you take part in the game?*

particular *adj. particular, unusual, peculiar; m. private citizen; individual.*

Eso no tiene nada de particular. *There's nothing unusual about it.*

¿Qué tiene de particular? *What's there strange about it? What's so strange about it?*

¿Hay algo de nuevo?—Nada de particular. *Anything new?—Nothing in particular.*

En particular. *In particular.*

particularidad *f. particularity, peculiarity.*

particularmente *particularly, especially.*

partida *f. departure; entry, item (in an account); lot; one game; certificate (birth, etc.).*

Punto de partida. *Point of departure. Starting point.*

Partida de nacimiento. *Birth certificate.*

Echemos una partida de ajedrez. *Let's play a game of chess.*

Partida doble. *Double entry.*

partidario *adj. and n. partisan, follower, supporter.*

Soy partidario de los paseos al aire libre. *I like to take walks in the fresh air.*

Es partidario de la política del buen vecino. *He's in favor of the Good-Neighbor Policy.*

partido *adj. divided, split; broken; m. party; advantage; game.*

Ese vaso está partido. *That glass is broken.*

La tabla esta partida. *The board is split.*

¿Qué partido tomaremos? *What course shall we take?*

No sabía que partido tomar. *I didn't know what to do.*

Pertenecen al mismo partido. *They belong to the same party.*

¿Quiere Ud. ver el partido de fútbol? *Would you like to see the football game?*

¿Cuál fué el .esultado del partido? *What was the final score of the game?*

PARTIR *to divide, to split; to leave; to cut; to break.*

El tren está para partir. *The train is about to leave.*

Partiremos el primero del mes. *We'll leave on the first of the month.*

Seguía diluviando cuando partimos. *It was still pouring when we left.*

Necesito un cuchillo para partir este pan. *I need*

a knife to cut this bread.

La tabla se ha partido en dos. *The board broke in two.*

Partió la manzana en dos. *He divided (split) the apple in two.*

Parta Ud. 300 entre 3. *Divide 3 into 300.*

Partieron el terreno en varios lotes. *They divided the land into several lots.*

Al partirse el hielo cayeron al agua. *When the ice broke, they fell into the water.*

Partir la diferencia. *To split the difference.*

parto *m. childbirth.*

parvo *adj. small, little.*

párvulo *m. child.*

Escuela de párvulos. *Kindergarten.*

pasa *f. raisin.*

PASADO *m. past; past tense.*

Pasados dos días. *After two days.*

Lo pasado. *The past.*

El martes pasado, tres de marzo. *Last Tuesday, March the third.*

Pasado mañana. *The day after tomorrow.*

pasaje *m. passage; fare; strait.*

¿Cuánto cuesta el pasaje? *What's the fare?*

pasajero *adj. passing, transitory; m. passenger.*

pasaporte *m. passport.*

PASAR *to pass, to go by, to go across; to come over, to come in, to call (visit); to spend (the time); to get along; to be taken for; to put on, to pretend; to overlook; to surpass; to happen.*

Pásame la sal, por favor. *Pass the salt, please.*

Pase Ud. y siéntese. *Come in and sit down.*

Pase Ud. por aquí. *Come this way.*

Pase por aquí otro día. *Drop in again some time.*

¿Puede Ud. pasar por mi oficina mañana? *Can you call at my office tomorrow?*

Pasamos el río a nado. *We swam across the river.*

Ya pasó el tren. *The train has already passed.*

Pasó el rápido a las nueve. *The express went by at nine.*

Pasaron por aquí hace poco. *They went by this place a moment ago.*

Pasamos por la calle de Arenal. *We passed through Arenal Street.*

Pasa por norteamericano, pero no lo es. *He passes for an American but he isn't really.*

Los años se pasan rapidamente. *The years pass quickly.*

¿Cómo se llama este pueblo que acabamos de pasar? *What's the name of the village we just passed?*

Se pasó todo el día leyendo. *She spent the whole day reading.*

Se pasa la vida refunfuñando. *He's always grumbling about something.*

¿Qué pasa? *What's the matter?*

¿Cómo lo pasa Ud.? *How are you getting along? How are things with you?*

Ud. lo pase bien. *Good-by! Have a good time.*

¿Qué le pasa a Ud.? *What's the matter with you?*

Que pase Ud. buena noche. *I hope you have a good night's sleep (rest). Sleep well.*

Lo pasa uno bien allí. *Life is pleasant there.*

Yo no sé lo que le pasa. *I don't know what's the matter with him.*

Ud. no sabe lo que ha pasado. *You don't know what has happened.*

Sólo Dios sabe qué pasará. *(Only) God knows what will happen.*

Esta lluvia pasará pronto. *The (this) rain will stop soon.*

Ya se le pasará. *He'll get over it.*

Ya pasó aquello. *That's gone (past) and forgotten.*

Eso ha pasado de moda. *That's gone out of style.*

Se pasa de buena. *She's too good.*

El papel se pasa. *The paper blots.*

Se me pasó por alto. *I overlooked it. I didn't (take) notice.*

Voy a pasar lista a la clase. *I'm going to call the class roll.*

Estamos pasando el rato. *We're killing time. We're having fun.*

pasatiempo *m. pastime, amusement.*

Pascua *f. Christmas; Easter; Passover.*

¡Felices Pascuas! *Merry Christmas!*

Está como unas pascuas. *He's as merry as a cricket.*

pase *m. pass, permit; thrust.*

paseante *m. stroller.*

PASEAR *to walk; to ride; to take a walk.*

Vamos a pasear. *Let's go for a walk.*

Saca los niños a pasear. *Take the children out for a walk.*

pasearse *to go for a walk.*

PASEO *m. walk, stroll; ride; drive; avenue or road bordered by trees.*

Demos un paseo. *Let's take a walk.*

Vamos a dar un paseo en coche. *Let's go for a drive.*

Hay muchos árboles en el paseo de Recoletos. *There are a lot of trees on Recoletos Avenue.*

pasillo *m. corridor; aisle; hall; basting stitch.*

Iré al pasillo para llamar por teléfono. *I'll go out into the hall to phone.*

pasión *f. passion.*

pasivo *adj. passive; m. liabilities.*

PASO *m. step; pass; passage; place; gait.*

Está a dos pasos de aquí. *It's only a few steps from here.*

Los pasos que sentí no parecían de mujer. *The steps I heard didn't sound like a woman's.*

Tuvimos que abrirnos paso por entre la multi-

tud. *We had to make our way through the crowd.*

Este caballo tiene un paso excelente. *This horse has a fine gait.*

Apretemos el paso para llegar a tiempo. *Let's hurry so that we'll get there on time.*

De paso. *By the way. Incidentally.*

Salir de paso. *To get out of a difficulty.*

Dar los pasos necesarios. *To take the necessary steps.*

Paso a paso. *Step by step.*

Llevar el paso. *To keep in step.*

Marcar el paso. *To mark time.*

"Prohibido el paso." *"Keep out." "No trespassing."*

pasta *f. paste; dough; binding (of a book).*

Pasta dentífrica. *Toothpaste.*

pastel *m. pie, cake.*

pastelería *f. pastry shop; pastry.*

pastelero *m. pastry cook; a temporizer.*

pastilla *f. drop, lozenge; cake (of soap).*

Pastillas de menta. *Mint drops.*

Pastillas para la tos. *Cough drops.*

pastor *m. shepherd; pastor.*

pata *f. foot and leg of an animal; leg (of a table, chair, etc.); duck.*

Ha roto la pata de la mesa. *He broke the leg of the table.*

A pata *(coll.). On foot.*

Patas arriba. *Upside down.*

Meter la pata. *To make a blunder. To put one's foot in it.*

patalear *to stamp (the foot).*

patata *f. potato.*

patente *adj. patent, obvious; f. patent; grant, privilege.*

Hacer patente. *To make clear.*

patín *m. skate.*

Patín de ruedas. *Roller skates.*

patinar *to skate; to skid.*

patio *m. patio; yard; pit (theater).*

pato *m. drake, duck.*

Pagar el pato. *To be made the scapegoat.*

patraña *f. falsehood, fib.*

patria *f. native country, fatherland.*

patriota *m. patriot.*

patriótico *adj. patriotic.*

patriotismo *m. patriotism.*

patrocinar *to patronize.*

patrón *m. master, skipper (of a ship); employer, boss; pattern; standard (gold).*

patrono *m. employer; patron saint.*

patrulla *f. patrol.*

paulatinamente *slowly, by degrees.*

paulatino *adj. slow, gradual.*

pausa *f. pause.*

pauta *f. paper ruler; guide lines; example, model.*

pava *f. turkey hen.*

Pelar la pava. *To flirt.*

PAVIMENTO *m. pavement.*

pavo *m. turkey.*

Pavo real. *Peacock.*

pavor *m. fear, terror.*

payaso *m. clown.*

PAZ *f. peace.*

¿Por qué no hacen las paces? *Why don't they bury the hatchet? Why don't they make up?*

En paz. *Even. Quits. On even terms.*

Déjeme en paz. *Let me alone. ("Leave me in peace.")*

pe *f. name of the letter p.*

De pe a pa. *Entirely. Thoroughly. From top to bottom. From beginning to end.*

peatón *m. pedestrian.*

pecado *m. sin, trespass.*

pecar *to sin.*

peculiar *adj. peculiar.*

peculiaridad *f. peculiarity.*

PECHO *m. chest; breast; bosom.*

Me duele el pecho. *My chest hurts me.*

Es un hombre de pelo en pecho. *He's a daring (bold, brave, aggressive) fellow.*

No lo tome Ud. a pecho. *Don't take it to heart.*

Dar el pecho. *To suckle.*

pechuga *f. breast (of a fowl).*

pedagogo *m. pedagogue, teacher.*

pedal *m. pedal, treadle.*

PEDAZO *m. bit, piece, morsel.*

Sírvame otro pedazo de carne. *May I have another piece of meat? ("Serve me another piece of meat.")*

Hágame el favor de un pedazo de papel. *May I have a piece of paper?*

Hacer pedazos. *To break into pieces.*

¡Pedazo de alcornoque! *Blockhead!*

pedestal *m. pedestal; support.*

pedido *m. order (for goods); request.*

No podemos servir el pedido. *We can't fill the order.*

Hacer un pedido. *To order (goods). To place an order.*

A pedido de. *At the request of.*

PEDIR *to ask for; to beg; to demand; to wish; to order (goods).*

Me ha pedido que le haga un favor. *He asked me to do him a favor.*

¿Ya pidió Ud. el desayuno? *Have you ordered breakfast?*

Tengo que pedirle permiso. *I have to ask his permission.*

Pido la palabra. *May I have the floor?*

Coma lo que le pida el cuerpo. *Eat whatever you like.*

El negocio marcha a pedir de boca. *Business is going splendidly. Business is excellent.*

Pidió socorro a voces. *She cried out for help.*

El público entusiasmado pidió la repetición. *The enthusiastic audience called for an encore.*

Pedir informes. *To ask for information. To inquire.*

pegajoso *adj. sticky, viscous; contagious.*

pegar *to paste, to glue; to sew on; to hit, to beat; to stop.*

Pegue las etiquetas. *Paste the labels on.*

Pegar a una persona. *To hit (beat up) a person.*

Pésegueme un botón a esta camisa. *Sew a button on this shirt.*

Pegar fuego a. *To set fire to.*

No pude pegar los ojos en toda la noche. *I couldn't sleep a wink all night.*

peinado *m. hairdressing; hair style, coiffure, hairdo.*

¿Qué peinado prefiere? *What hair style do you prefer?*

peinar *to comb.*

Péineme el pelo hacia atrás. *Comb my hair back.*

peinarse *to do or to comb one's hair.*

Ella se peina muy bien. *She does her hair very nicely.*

Sólo me falta peinarme. *I just (only) have to comb my hair.*

PEINE *m. comb.*

peineta *f. dress comb.*

pelado *adj. plucked, bare, bald; penniless, broke (Amer.).*

pelar *to peel; to cut somebody's hair; to pluck, to rob, to cheat.*

Péleme esa manzana. *Peel that apple for me.*

Es duro de pelar. *He's (it's) a hard nut to crack.*

peldaño *m. step (of staircase).*

pelea *f. fight, struggle.*

pelear *to fight.*

peletería *f. furrier's, fur shop.*

película *f. film.*

La película resultó muy aburrida. *The picture was dull.*

¿Qué película dan esta noche? *What's showing tonight? ("What film are they giving tonight?")*

peligro *m. peril, danger.*

No hay peligro. *There's no danger.*

peligroso *adj. dangerous.*

PELO *m. hair.*

Quiero que me corten el pelo. *I want a haircut.*

¡No me tome Ud. el pelo! *Don't make fun of me! Don't kid me! Don't tease me!*

Para más pelos y señales. *In more detail.*

pelota *f. ball.*

peluca *f. wig.*

peluquería *f. barber shop.*

Peluquería de señoras. *Beauty parlor.*

peluquero *m. barber; wigmaker.*

pellejo *m. skin; peel; rawhide.*

pellizcar *to pinch.*

pena *f. penalty, punishment; grief, sorrow, hardship, toil.*

  Murió de pena. *She died of a broken heart.*

  Ha sufrido muchas penas. *He has been through many hardships.*

  Lo hizo a duras penas. *He did it with great difficulty.*

  No vale la pena hacerlo. *It's not worth while doing.*

  So pena de. *Under penalty of.*

  Pena capital. *Capital punishment. Death penalty.*

penal *adj. penal; m. prison.*

penalidad *f. hardship; penalty.*

penar *to suffer; to be in agony.*

pender *to hang; to be pending.*

pendiente *adj. pendent; pending; m. earrings. f. slope.*

  Cuestión pendiente. *An open question. A question still pending.*

  Eso queda pendiente. *That's still pending.*

  Deuda pendiente. *Balance due.*

  Lleva unos pendientes muy bonitos. *She's wearing very pretty earrings.*

  Bajar una pendiente. *To descend (go down) a hill.*

penetrante *adj. penetrating, piercing.*

penetrar *to penetrate; to fathom, to comprehend.*

península *f. peninsula.*

penitente *adj. and n. penitent.*

penoso *adj. painful; difficult, arduous; distressing.*

pensado *adj. deliberate; thought out.*

  Está muy bien pensado. *It's (very) well thought out.*

  Tengo pensado comprarlo. *I intend to buy (buying) it.*

pensador *m. thinker; thinking.*

pensamiento *m. thought; idea; pansy.*

PENSAR *to think; to consider, to intend.*

  Piense antes de hablar. *Think before you speak.*

  Lo hice sin pensar. *I did it without thinking.*

  ¿En qué piensa Ud.? *What are you thinking about?*

  Esto me da en que pensar. *This gives me something to think about. This gives me food for thought.*

  Pienso igual que Ud. *I think the way you do. I think the same as you. I agree with you.*

  Pensaban estar aquí para el lunes. *They planned to be here about Monday.*

  ¿Cuándo piensa Ud. marcharse? *When do you intend to leave?*

  ¿En qué hotel piensa Ud. parar? *At what hotel do you expect to stop.*

pensativo *adj. pensive, thoughtful.*

pensión *f. pension; board; boarding house.*

pensionista *m. and f. pensioner; boarder.*

penúltimo *adj. penultimate, last but one.*

peña *f. rock, large stone; circle (of friends).*

peñón *m. large rock; cliff; rocky mountain.*

  El peñón de Gibraltar. *The rock of Gibraltar.*

peón *m. peon; pawn (in chess); pedestrian; (spinning) top.*

PEOR *adj. and adv. worse; worst.*

  Sigue peor. *He's getting worse.*

  Eso es lo peor. *That's the worst of it.*

  Tanto peor. *All the worse. So much the worse.*

  Llevar la peor parte. *To get the worst of it.*

  El mes pasado fué el peor de todos. *Last month was the worst of all.*

  La situación va (sigue) de mal en peor. *The situation is going from bad to worse.*

pepinillos *m. pl. pickles.*

pepino *m. cucumber.*

pequeñez *f. a trifle; pettiness.*

  Discutieron sobre una pequeñez. *They argued over a trifle.*

PEQUEÑO *adj. little, small, tiny; young; m. child.*

  Su hijo es muy pequeño. *His child is very young.*

  Tiene los dientes blancos y pequeños. *She has small white teeth.*

  ¿Cómo están los pequeños? *How are the children?*

PERA *f. pear.*

  Partir peras con alguno. *To treat a person familiarly. To be on familiar terms with someone.*

peral *m. pear tree.*

percal *m. percale.*

percance *m. misfortune, mishap, accident.*

percepción *f. perception.*

perceptible *adj. perceptible, perceivable.*

percibir *to perceive, to get.*

  No percibo bien lo que dice. *I don't quite get what he's saying.*

  Percibe un sueldo de cien pesos. *He has (receives) a salary of a hundred dollars a month.*

percha *f. perch, pole, staff.*

PERDER *to lose.*

  He perdido mi cartera. *I've lost my wallet.*

  No tengo tiempo que perder. *I haven't any time to lose.*

  Estuvo a punto de perder la vida. *He nearly lost his life.*

  Han echado a perder el jardín. *They've spoiled the garden.*

  Está echado a perder. *He's spoiled.*

  No lo pierdas de vista. *Don't lose sight of him.*

  He perdido una buena ocasión. *I missed a good opportunity.*

  Lo hice a ratos perdidos. *I did it in my spare moments (time).*

  Está borracho perdido. *He's dead drunk.*

  ¿Este color no pierde? *Is this a fast color? ("Does this color fade?")*

Ha perdido la razón. *He's lost his reason (mind).*

Perdió la vista. *He lost his eyesight.*

Perder la vergüenza. *To lose all sense of shame.*

Perder el respeto. *To lose respect for.*

Perder el habla. *To become speechless. ("To lose one's tongue.")*

perderse *to get lost; to spoil, to get spoiled; to go astray.*

La comida se va a perder si no se come hoy. *The food will spoil if it's not eaten today.*

Perderse en el bosque. *To get lost in the woods.*

perdición *f. perdition; ruin.*

pérdida *f. loss; damage; leakage.*

Reparar una pérdida. *To recover a loss.*

perdidamente *desperately.*

Está perdidamente enamorado. *He's head over heels in love.*

perdiz *f. partridge.*

perdón *m. pardon.*

¡Perdón! *Pardon me!*

PERDONAR *to excuse, to pardon, to forgive.*

Perdóneme Ud. *Excuse me.*

Le suplico a Ud. que me perdone. *Please excuse me.*

Perdone mi tardanza. *Pardon my lateness.*

Esta vez se lo perdono. *This time I forgive you.*

No perdonar una fiesta. *Not to miss a party.*

No perdonar ni un detalle. *To leave nothing untold. To tell every detail.*

perecer *to perish, to die.*

Perecer ahogado. *To drown.*

peregrino *adj. migratory; odd, strange.*

perejil *m. parsley.*

pereza *f. laziness, idleness.*

perezoso *adj. lazy, indolent.*

perfección *f. perfection, improvement, perfecting.*

perfeccionar *to make perfect, to improve.*

perfeccionarse *to improve oneself, to increase one's knowledge.*

PERFECTO *adj. perfect.*

Es un trabajo perfecto. *It's a perfect piece of work.*

perfidia *f. perfidy, treachery, foul play.*

perfil *m. profile; outline.*

perfume *m. perfume; scent, fragrance*

perfumería *f. perfume store.*

pericia *f. skill; knowledge.*

perilla *f. knob, doorknob.*

Déle vuelta a la perilla. *Turn the knob.*

Eso me viene de perilla. *That just fits the purpose.*

periódico *adj. periodic(al); m. newspaper, magazine, periodical.*

periodismo *m. journalism.*

periodista *m. and f. journalist, newspaperman, newspaperwoman.*

período *m. period, time.*

perito *adj. experienced, skillful; m. expert; appraiser.*

perjudicar *to damage, to injure, to hurt.*

perjudicial *adj. prejudicial, harmful.*

perjuicio *m. prejudice; damage, harm.*

perjuro *adj. perjured; m. perjurer.*

perla *f. pearl.*

permanecer *to remain, to stay.*

¿Cuánto tiempo permanecerá Ud. fuera de la ciudad? *How long will you be (remain) out of town?*

permanencia *f. permanence; stay.*

PERMANENTE *adj. and n. permanent.*

Un lugar permanente. *A permanent place.*

Ondulado permanente. *Permanent wave.*

permeable *adj. permeable.*

PERMISO *m. permission; permit, authorization, consent.*

Tener permiso de. *To have permission to.*

Con su permiso. *If I may. With your permission ("by your leave")*

No lo haga Ud. sin mi permiso. *Don't do it without my permission.*

Permiso de llevar armas de fuego. *A permit to carry firearms.*

Permiso para guiar. *A driving license.*

permitir *to permit, to let, to allow.*

¿Me permite Ud. que fume? *May I smoke? Do you mind if I smoke?*

¿Me permite que le haga una pregunta. *May I ask you a question?*

No permitiré tal cosa. *I won't allow such a thing.*

Permítame Ud. que le presente a mi amigo. *Allow me to introduce you to my friend.*

permuta *f. permutation; exchange; barter.*

permutar *to permute; to barter, to exchange.*

pernicioso *adj. pernicious, injurious, harmful.*

PERO *but, yet, except; m. defect, fault.*

Ud. no querrá ir, pero yo sí. *You may not want to go, but I do.*

Quisiera ir, pero no puedo. *I'd like to go, but I can't.*

Pero no es así. *But it's not so. But that's not the case.*

Pero él dice otra cosa. *But he tells a different story.*

¡Pero qué calor hace! *How hot it is! It's certainly hot!*

Es hermoso sin pero. *It's very beautiful. ("It's beautiful with no buts about it.")*

No hay pero que valga. *No buts.*

Poner peros. *To find fault.*

perpendicular *adj. and n. perpendicular.*

perpetuar *to perpetuate.*

perpetuidad *f. perpetuity.*

perpetuo *adj. perpetual, everlasting.*

perplejo *adj. perplexed, bewildered, puzzled.*

Me siento perplejo. *I'm perplexed (puzzled).*

perra *f. bitch; drunkenness; copper coin (Spain).*

Perra gorda. *Ten centime copper coin (Spain).*

Perra chica. *Five centime copper coin (Spain).*

PERRO *m. dog.*

persecución *f. persecution.*

perseguir *to persecute; to pursue; to harass.*

perseverancia *f. perseverance.*

perseverar *to persevere, to persist.*

persiana *f. window blind; pl. Venetian blind.*

persistencia *f. persistence, obstinacy.*

persistente *adj. persistent, firm.*

persistir *to persist.*

PERSONA *f. person.*

Es muy buena persona. *He's a very nice person.*

Esto me lo dijo cierta persona. *A certain person told me that.*

En este salón caben más de cien personas. *This hall can accommodate over a hundred people.*

personaje *m. personage; character (in a play).*

personal *adj. personal; m. personnel, staff.*

Estos artículos son de mi uso personal. *These articles are for my personal use.*

personalidad *f. personality.*

perspectiva *f. perspective.*

perspicacia *f. perspicacity.*

perspicaz *adj. perspicacious, acute, sagacious, quick-sighted.*

persuadir *to persuade; to convince.*

persuasión *f. persuasion.*

pertenecer *to belong.*

Esto pertenece a . . . *This belongs to . . .*

Esa pluma me pertenece. *That pen belongs to me.*

Pertenece al Cuerpo de Sanidad. *He belongs to (is in) the Medical Corps.*

pertinente *adj. pertinent.*

perturbar *to perturb, agitate.*

perversidad *f. perversity, wickedness.*

perversión *f. perversion.*

perverso *adj. perverse.*

pervertir *to pervert.*

pesadilla *f. nightmare.*

pesado *adj. heavy; tedious; tiresome; m. bore.*

El hierro es pesado. *Iron is heavy.*

Es un pesado. *He's a bore.*

pésame *m. condolence; message of condolence.*

PESAR *to weigh, to be of weight; to cause regret; m. grief, sorrow; regret.*

¿Cuánto pesa Ud.? *How much do you weigh?*

¿Pesa demasiado la carta? *Does the letter weigh too much?*

Antes de entrar en el avión hay que pesarse. *Before boarding the plane you have to be weighed.*

Vale lo que pesa. *It's worth its weight in gold.*

Me pesa mucho haberle ofendido. *I'm sorry I offended him.*

Aunque me pese no puedo menos que hacerlo.

Although I regret it, I can't help doing it.

Lo haremos a pesar de todo. *We'll do it in spite of everything.*

pesca *f. fishing; fishery.*

PESCADO *m. fish (after it is caught; see* **pez***).*

pescar *to fish; to catch.*

pesebre *m. crib, manger.*

peseta *f. peseta (Spanish silver coin).*

pesimismo *m. pessimism.*

pesimista *adj. pessimistic; m. and f. pessimist.*

pésimo *adj. very bad.*

peso *m. weight; weighing; scales; importance; burden; peso (standard monetary unit in some Spanish American countries).*

Las ramas se doblan bajo el peso de la fruta. *The branches are bending under the weight of the fruit.*

Le presté cinco pesos. *I lent him five pesos.*

Ponga Ud. esto en el peso. *Put that on the scales.*

Me han quitado un peso de encima. *That took a load off my mind.*

Sobre nosotros cayó todo el peso de la lucha. *We bore the brunt of the struggle.*

Eso cae de su peso. *That goes without saying.*

Peso neto. *Net weight.*

Peso bruto. *Gross weight.*

De peso. *Of weight. Of importance.*

pestaña *f. eyelash; fringe, edging.*

peste *f. plague; pestilence.*

pestillo *m. door latch.*

petición *f. petition; claim; demand; plea.*

petróleo *m. petroleum; mineral oil.*

pez *m. fish (in the water; see* **pescado***); f. pitch, tar.*

pezuña *f. hoof.*

piadoso *adj. pious; merciful.*

pianista *m. and f. pianist.*

piano *m. piano.*

picadillo *m. hash; minced meat.*

picadura *f. prick; puncture; bite (of an insect or snake); cut tobacco.*

picante *adj. hot, highly seasoned; cutting, sarcastic, pungent (wit).*

picaporte *m. latch.*

picar *to bite, to sting; to prick; to itch; to chop; to nibble; to spur; to be hot (pepper, etc.).*

Me ha picado una abeja. *I was stung by a bee.*

Me pica la espalda. *My back itches.*

Picar la carne. *To chop (up) meat.*

Esta pimienta pica mucho. *This pepper is very hot (strong).*

El sol pica. *The sun is scorching.*

Picar el caballo. *To spur a horse.*

Picar alto. *To aim too high.*

picarse *to begin to rot (fruit); to decay; to be piqued; to be moth-eaten; to become choppy (sea).*

El vino empieza a picarse. *The wine is turning sour (fermenting).*

Tengo un diente picado. *I have a cavity in one of my teeth.*

picardia f. *knavery; deceit; malice.*

pícaro adj. *roguish; mischievous; m. and f. rogue, rascal, scoundrel.*

Tiene trazas de ser un pícaro. *He looks like a rascal.*

pico adj. *odd, left over; m. beak, bill; pick; spout; peak.*

Subieron al pico más alto de la sierra. *They climbed to the highest peak of the mountain ridge.*

Tiene mucho pico. *She's a chatterbox.*

Son las once y pico. *It's a little after eleven.*

Veinte dólares y pico. *Twenty dollars and some odd cents.*

picor m. *itching.*

PIE m. *foot, leg; footing, basis.*

Me duele mucho el pie. *My foot hurts a lot.*

Esta mesa tiene seis pies de largo. *This table is six feet long.*

A pie. *On foot.*

Nos fuimos a pie al hotel. *We walked to the hotel.*

Al pie del cerro. *At the foot of the hill.*

A los pies de Ud., señora. *At your service, madam. ("At your feet, madam.")*

De (en) pie. *Standing (up).*

Al pie de la letra. *Literally. To the letter.*

Ponerse en pie. *To stand up.*

Quedar en pie. *To hold good. To be (still) pending.*

No tiene pies ni cabeza. *It doesn't make any sense.*

Tiene buenos pies. *She's a good walker.*

Ha nacido de pie. *He was born with a silver spoon in his mouth.*

piedad f. *mercy; pity.*

piedra f. *stone; gravel; hail.*

Piedras preciosas. *Precious stones.*

Este pan es duro como una piedra. *The bread's hard as a rock.*

No dejar piedra por mover. *To leave no stone unturned. To move heaven and earth.*

PIEL f. *skin; hide; fur.*

Tiene la piel como seda. *She has very soft skin. Her skin is soft as silk.*

Abrigo de pieles. *Fur coat.*

Quiero este libro encuadernado en piel de Rusia. *I want this volume bound in Russian leather.*

PIERNA f. *leg.*

Dormir a pierna tendida. *To sleep soundly.*

PIEZA f. *piece; part; room; a play.*

Esta pieza tiene dos ventanas. *This room has two windows.*

Géneros de pieza. *Piece goods. Yard goods.*

Piezas de repuesto. *Spare parts.*

pijamas m. pl. *pajamas.*

pila f. *stone trough or basin; fountain; holy-water basin; font; sink (kitchen, etc.); pile, heap; battery.*

Pila de cocina. *Kitchen sink.*

Una pila de leña. *A pile of wood.*

Pila seca. *Dry cell (battery).*

Nombre de pila. *Christian name. ("Baptismal name.")*

pilar m. *pillar, column, post.*

píldora f. *pill.*

piloto m. *pilot; first mate.*

pillo m. *rogue, rascal.*

pimentón m. *ground red pepper; paprika.*

pimienta f. *pepper.*

pimiento m. *pepper, pimento.*

pincel m. *artist's brush.*

pinchar *to prick, to puncture.*

Se pinchó el dedo. *He pricked his finger.*

Se me ha pinchado un neumático. *I have a flat tire. One of my tires blew out.*

pinchazo m. *puncture; flat tire; prick.*

pino m. *pine.*

pintado adj. *painted; spotted; just right, exact.*

Ese traje le queda como pintado. *That dress fits her just right.*

Pintado de rojo. *Painted red.*

No puedo verle ni pintado. *I can't stand the sight of him.*

pintar *to paint; to describe; to begin to ripen.*

¿Qué pinta Ud.? *What are you painting?*

Pinte de azul la pared. *Paint the wall blue.*

Empiezan a pintar las uvas. *The grapes are becoming (getting) ripe.*

pintor m. *painter.*

pintura f. *painting.*

La pintura no está seca. *The paint is still wet ("isn't dry").*

Pintura al óleo. *Oil painting.*

Esa es una pintura histórica. *That's an historical painting.*

piña f. *pineapple.*

piojo m. *louse.*

pipa f. *tobacco pipe; cask, barrel (wine).*

pique (a) *sink (used with the verb echar and ir).*

El buque se fué a pique. *The ship sank.*

Echar a pique. *To sink. To send to the bottom.*

pirámide f. *pyramid.*

pirata m. *pirate.*

piropear *to flatter (a girl or a woman).*

pisada f. *footstep; footprint.*

pisar *to tread, to step on; to press; to cover.*

Mire Ud. donde pisa. *Watch your step. Watch where you're going.*

Pise el acelerador. *Step on the gas ("accelerator").*

piscina *f. swimming pool.*

PISO *m. floor; pavement; story, apartment.*

¿Se alquila este piso? *Is this apartment for rent?*

¿Cuántos roperos tiene este piso? *How many closets are there in this apartment?*

Ella vive en el segundo piso. *She lives on the second floor.*

Suban Uds. un piso más. *Walk up another flight.*

pisotear *to tread, to trample; to step on someone's foot.*

pisotón *m. tread; stepping on someone's foot.*

Me dió un pisotón. *He stepped on my foot.*

pista *f. trail, track, footprint; trace, clue; race-track.*

Seguir la pista. *To follow the trail.*

Le estamos siguiendo la pista. *We're on his trail (track).*

pisto *m. a dish made of fried peppers, tomatoes and eggs.*

Darse pisto. *To show off.*

pistola *f. pistol.*

pitillera *f. cigarette case.*

pitillo *m. cigarette.*

No tengo ni pitillos ni cerillas. *I have neither cigarettes nor matches.*

pito *m. whistle.*

Eso no vale un pito. *It isn't worth a hang. It isn't worth a tinker's dam.*

pivote *m. pivot.*

pizarra *f. slate; blackboard.*

pizca *f. mite, bit; pinch.*

Tiene su pizca de gracia. *It has its funny side.*

placa *f. plate; plaque, tablet; badge.*

Una placa fotográfica. *A photographic plate.*

Una placa metálica. *A metal plate.*

PLACER *to please; m. pleasure, enjoyment.*

Iremos donde a Ud. le plazca. *We'll go wherever you like.*

Es un placer conversar con ella. *It's a pleasure to talk to (with) her.*

Tener placer en. *To take pleasure in.*

Tendré mucho placer en hacerlo. *I'll be very pleased (happy) to do it.*

Me será un gran placer conocerle. *I'd be very happy ("it would be a great pleasure for me") to meet him (you).*

plaga *f. plague; epidemic.*

plan *m. plan; scheme; drawing.*

plana *f. page; plain (land).*

Lo leí en primera plana. *I read it on the first page of the newspaper.*

La plana mayor del regimiento. *The regimental staff.*

plancha *f. plate (metal); iron (for clothes); blunder; gangplank.*

La plancha está muy caliente. *The iron is very hot.*

Plancha de acero. *Steel plate.*

Hizo una plancha. *He made a blunder. He put his foot in it.*

planchado *m. ironing; linen to be ironed.*

Lavado y planchado. *Washed and ironed laundry.*

planchar *to iron, to press (clothes).*

Quiero que me planchen el traje. *I'd like to have my suit pressed.*

Ella misma lava y plancha la ropa. *She washes and irons the clothes herself.*

planeta *m. planet.*

planicie *f. plain (land).*

plano *adj. level, flat; m. plane, map; plan.*

Lo negó de plano. *He denied it flatly.*

Quisiera un plano de la ciudad. *I'd like a map of the city.*

Levantar un plano. *To draw a map (of a place).*

planta *f. plant; sole (of the foot).*

La planta ha echado raíces. *The plant has taken root.*

He alquilado un cuarto en la planta baja. *I've rented a room on the ground floor.*

plantación *f. plantation; planting.*

plantar *to plant; to drive in (the ground); to hit, to punch; to throw out.*

Van a plantar unos árboles en el jardín. *They're going to plant some trees in the garden.*

Lo dejaron plantado. *They left him in the lurch.*

Se plantó en Guadalajara en dos horas. *It took him two hours to get to Guadalajara.*

Plantar una bofetada. *To slap in the face.*

Lo plantaron en la calle. *They threw him out. They put him out on the street.*

plantilla *f. insole; payroll; pattern.*

plástico *adj. plastic.*

PLATA *f. silver; silver coin.*

¿Tiene Ud. dinero en plata? *Have you any silver (money)?*

Plata fina. *Sterling silver.*

plátano *m. banana.*

platillo *m. saucer; cymbal; pan of a balance.*

platino *m. platinum.*

PLATO *m. dish, plate, course.*

Este plato está a pedir de boca. *This dish is delicious.*

¿Cuál es el plato del día? *What's today's special? ("What's the plate of the day?")*

Hay que secar los platos. *We have to dry the dishes.*

¿Puedo repetir de este plato? *May I have a second helping?*

Pagar los platos rotos. *To be made the scape-goat. To be blamed for everything.*

Plato hondo (sopero). *Soup plate.*

Plato llano (de mesa). *Dinner plate.*

Ser plato de segunda mesa. *To play second*

fiddle.

playa *f. shore, beach.*

PLAZA *f. plaza, square; market; fortified place.*

Vamos a dar una vuelta por la plaza. *Let's take a stroll around the square.*

Hoy no habían naranjas en la plaza. *There weren't any oranges in the market today.*

Plaza de toros. *Bull-ring.*

Plaza fuerte. *Stronghold. Fortress.*

plazo *m. term, time; credit.*

¿En cuántos plazos debo pagar este automóvil? *How many payments do I have to make on this car?*

A plazos. *On credit. On the installment plan.*

Comprar a plazos. *To be on the installment plan.*

Pagar a plazos. *To pay in installments.*

El plazo se ha cumplido. *The time has expired.*

plegable *adj. folding; pliable.*

plegar *to fold; to plait.*

pleito *m. litigation; lawsuit; dispute, quarrel.*

Tuvo un pleito con él. *He had a quarrel with him.*

plenamente *fully, completely.*

plenitud *f. plenitude, fullness.*

PLENO *adj. full, complete.*

Plenos poderes. *Full powers.*

Sesión plena. *Joint session.*

En pleno. *In full. As a whole.*

pliego *m. sheet of paper; letter or document sealed in an envelope.*

¿Quiere darme un pliego de papel? *Will you please give me a sheet of paper?*

Pliego de valores declarados. *Sealed envelope containing money.*

pliegue *m. plait; crease; fold.*

plomo *m. lead; a bore, a dull person.*

El plomo se funde fácilmente. *Lead melts easily.*

Ande con pies de plomo. *Proceed cautiously.*

pluma *f. pen; feather.*

plural *adj. and n. plural.*

población *f. population; town.*

poblado *m. town, village, inhabited place.*

poblar *to populate, to inhabit, to colonize; to bud, to put forth leaves.*

POBRE *adj. poor; m. a poor person; a beggar.*

Es un hombre muy pobre. *He's a very poor man.*

El pobre no da pie en bola. *The poor fellow can't do anything right.*

El pobre ha venido muy a menos. *The poor fellow has come down in the world.*

¡Pobrecito! *Poor little thing!*

¡Qué de pobres hay en esta ciudad! *What a lot of beggars there are in this city!*

pobreza *f. poverty.*

POCO *adj. and adv. little; small; scanty; m. a little, a small part; pl. a few.*

¿Le sirvo un poco de vino? *May I serve (offer) you some wine?*

Déme un poco de leche. *Give me a little milk.*

Acérquese un poco más al micrófono. *Come a little closer to the microphone.*

Me gusta un poco. *I like it a little. I rather like it.*

Sabe un poco de todo. *He knows a little about everything.*

Hágame un poco de sitio. *Make a little room for me.*

Es hombre de poco talento. *He doesn't have much ability.*

Me queda muy poco dinero. *I have very little money left.*

Llegará dentro de poco. *He'll arrive soon.*

Poco importa. *It's not very important. It doesn't matter.*

Por poco se muere. *He almost died.*

Lo demás importa poco. *The rest doesn't matter very much.*

Lo tiene en poco. *He attaches very little value to it.*

Era poco tolerante. *He wasn't very tolerant.*

Poco a poco. *Little by little.*

Hace poco. *A little while ago.*

Pocas veces. *A few times.*

A pocos pasos de aquí. *A few steps from here. Very near.*

podar *to prune (trees).*

PODER *to be able; can; may; m. power, authority; capacity.*

¿En qué puedo servirle? *What can I do for you?*

¿Puedo ir? *May I go?*

¿Podrá Ud. venir? *Will you be able to come?*

¿Puedo entrar? *May I come in?*

¡No puede ser! *That can't be! That's impossible!*

¿Puede dejarme la regla? *Can you let me have a ruler?*

¿Qué puedo ofrecerle a Ud.? *What can I offer you?*

¿Puedo contar con Ud.? *Can I count (depend) on you?*

Hice lo mejor que pude. *I did the best I could.*

A ese tipo no lo puedo ni ver. *I can't bear the sight of that fellow.*

No puedo con él. *I can't stand him.*

Puede que vaya a Australia el próximo año. *I may go to Australia next year.*

Querer es poder. *Where there's a will there's a way.*

Ha dado poder general a su padre. *He has given his father power of attorney.*

El dictador se arrogó el poder. *The dictator usurped power.*

Estudia a más no poder. *He studies as much as he possibly can.*

poderoso adj. mighty, powerful; wealthy.

podrir. (See pudrir.)

poema m. poem.

poesía f. poetry.

poeta m. poet.

polémica f. polemics; controversy (literary or political).

polémico adj. polemical.

policía f. police; public order; m. policeman.

　Un policía acudió en nuestra ayuda. A policeman came to our aid.

　La policía registró su casa. The police searched his house.

polígamo adj. polygamist.

polilla f. moth.

política f. politics; policy.

　Tener influencia política. To have good political connections.

político adj. politic, political; in-law; m. politician.

póliza f. policy (insurance, etc.).

　Póliza de seguro. Insurance policy.

polo m. pole; polo (game).

polvera f. woman's compact; powder box.

POLVO m. dust; powder.

　Hay mucho polvo. It's very dusty.

　Polvo dentífrico. Toothpowder.

　Una caja de polvos para la cara. A box of face powder.

pólvora f. gunpowder.

polla f. pullet, chicken; pool (cards); young lady (coll.).

POLLO m. chicken; nestling; young man (coll.).

　Pollo frito. Fried chicken.

　Pollo asado. Roast chicken.

　Arroz con pollo. Chicken and rice.

pomada f. pomade, salve.

pómulo m. cheek bone.

ponche m. punch (drink).

poncho m. poncho (a kind of cloak worn in South America).

ponderación f. weighing, consideration, prudence; exaggeration; description.

　Tiene mucha ponderación. He's very prudent.

ponderar to ponder, to weigh; to praise highly.

　Lo ponderan mucho. It's highly recommended.

PONER to put; to set (a table); to suppose; to lay (eggs); to send (a telegram); to write.

　Ponga el libro en su lugar. Put the book in its place. Put the book back.

　Mandó poner otra cama en su cuarto. He had another bed put in his room.

　Hay que poner punto final a esto. We must put a stop to this.

　Ponga la mesa. Set the table.

　Le pondré unas líneas. I'll drop him a few lines.

　Póngalo por escrito. Put it in writing.

　El médico me ha puesto a régimen. The doctor has put me on a diet.

¿Dónde habré puesto mi sombrero? Where can I have put my hat?

　Acaba de poner una tienda. He's just opened a store.

　Hay que poner en claro este lío. We must clear up this mess. We must get to the bottom of this.

　Poner huevos. To lay eggs.

　Aquí se necesita alguien que ponga orden. We need someone here who'll keep order.

　Pone en tela de juicio todo lo que le dicen. He questions everything they tell him.

　Yo pondré de mi parte todo lo que pueda. As far as I'm concerned, I'll do my best.

　Poner un telegrama. To send a telegram.

　Poner precio. To set a price.

　Poner al corriente. To inform.

　Poner al sol. To put in the sun. To expose to the sun.

PONERSE to set (the sun); to put on (clothes); to become; to make one become; to reach, to come to; to start to.

　El sol se pone más temprano en invierno. The sun sets earlier in winter.

　Se puso el sombrero y salió. He put on his hat and left.

¿Qué me pondré? What shall I wear (put on)?

　Se puso encarnada. She blushed.

　Al oír aquello se puso pálida. When she heard that, she turned pale.

　Se ha puesto muy gordo. He's become (gotten) very fat.

　Se puso a reír. She began to laugh.

　Se puso en la frontera en unas cuantas horas. He reached the border in a couple of hours.

　Se pone mal con todos. He gets in bad with everybody.

　Ponerse a trabajar. To start working.

　Ponerse en marcha. To start. To put out (a train).

　Ponerse de acuerdo. To agree. To come to an agreement.

　Ponerse nervioso. To become (get) nervous.

　Ponerse en pie. To stand up.

　Ponerse al día. To be up-to-date.

poniente m. west; west wind.

popular adj. popular.

　Es una canción popular. It's a popular song.

popularidad f. popularity.

POR for; by; through; about.

　Por correo aéreo. By air mail.

　Ganó por pocos puntos. He won by a few points.

　"Don Quijote" fué escrito por Cervantes. "Don Quixote" was written by Cervantes.

　La casa está por alquilar. The house is for rent.

¿Quiere Ud. ir por el correo? Will you go for (go get) the mail?

　Queda una cosa por hacer. Something still remains to be done.

No votaré ni por el uno ni por el otro. *I won't vote for either one.*

El pasaporte es válido por un año. *The passport is valid just for a year.*

Nos pagan por quincena. *They pay us every two weeks.*

Entrar por la puerta. *To enter through the door.*

Pasar por la casa. *To pass by the house.*

Lo hace por miedo. *He does it out of fear.*

Por grande que sea. *However large it may be.*

Haga Ud. por venir. *Try to come. Do your best to come.*

Ella se interesa mucho por él. *She's very much interested in him.*

Por el buen parecer. *For the sake of appearances.*

Por poco me caigo. *I almost (nearly) fell down.*

Viven por aquí cerca. *They live near here.*

Eso está por ver. *That remains to be seen.*

Quedan diez páginas por copiar. *Ten pages remain to be copied.*

Por la calle no pasaba un alma. *Not a soul was passing in the street.*

Por adelantado. *In advance.*

Por docena. *By the dozen.*

Por mes. *By the month.*

Por mucho tiempo. *For a long time.*

Por la mañana. *In the morning.*

Por la tarde. *In the afternoon.*

Por la noche. *At night.*

Por ahora. *For the present.*

Por dentro. *On the inside.*

Por fuera. *On the outside.*

Por entonces. *At that time.*

Por consiguiente. *Consequently.*

Por fin. *Finally.*

Por dicha. *Fortunately.*

De por sí. *By himself.*

¿Por qué? *Why?*

Por todas partes. *Everywhere.*

¡Por Dios! *For heaven's sake!*

Por más que. *No matter how. However much.*

Por lo visto. *Apparently.*

Por lo demás. *Furthermore. Aside from this. As to the rest.*

Por esto. *For this reason.*

Por cuanto. *For that reason. Since. Considering that. Whereas.*

Por tanto. *So. For that reason.*

Por otra parte. *On the other hand.*

Por ejemplo. *For example.*

Por supuesto. *Of course.*

porcelana f. *porcelain; chinaware.*

La vajilla es de porcelana. *The dinner set is of porcelain.*

porción f. *portion, part; a great many.*

Ya se lo había dicho una porción de veces. *I'd already told him so several times.*

pordiosero m. *beggar.*

porfía f. *insistence; obstinacy.*

porfiado adj. *stubborn, obstinate.*

porfiar *to persist.*

pormenor m. *detail; pl. particulars.*

Eso es simplemente un pormenor. *It's just a detail.*

Para más pormenores averigüe en . . . *For further details inquire at . . .*

PORQUE *because, on account of, for, as.*

No vino porque estaba ocupado. *He didn't come because he was busy.*

Corrían porque tenían prisa. *They ran because they were in a hurry.*

porqué m. *cause, reason.*

No acierto a explicarme el porqué de su actitud. *I can't understand the reason for his behavior.*

¿POR QUÉ? *why?*

¿Por qué no vino Ud. ayer? *Why didn't you come yesterday?*

¿Por qué se apura Ud.? *What are you worrying about?*

No sé por qué. *I don't know why.*

porquería f. *filth; nastiness; worthless thing.*

porrazo m. *blow (with a stick).*

portaaviones m. *aircraft carrier.*

portada f. *cover (of a book, etc.)*

portador m. *bearer; holder, carrier.*

portaequipajes m. *luggage-rack.*

portal m. *vestibule; hall, entrance, doorway; portico.*

portamonedas m. *pocketbook, purse.*

portarse *to behave, to act.*

¿Cómo se porta? *How does he behave?*

Se portó muy mal conmigo. *He didn't behave very well towards me.*

portátil adj. *portable.*

portazo m. *banging (of a door).*

porte m. *carriage, postage, freight (cost); department.*

¿Ha pagado Ud. el porte? *Did you pay the postage?*

Franco de porte. *Free delivery.*

portento m. *wonder, portent, prodigy.*

portería f. *superintendent's office (of a building), doorkeeper's lodge.*

portero m. *doorman, janitor.*

portezuela f. *carriage door; small door.*

Cierre la portezuela del coche. *Close the car door.*

porvenir m. *future, time to come.*

En lo porvenir. *In the future.*

pos (en) *after; in pursuit (of).*

Ir en pos de. *To go after.*

posada f. *inn, lodging house, boarding house.*

posadero m. *innkeeper.*

posar *to pose (for an artist); to lodge; to perch (birds).*

POSEER *to possess, to have; to master, to know (a subject).*

Posee una casa en el campo. *He has a house in the country.*

Posee bien el español. *He knows Spanish well. He has a good command of Spanish.*

posesión *f. possession.*

posesionar *to give possession.*

posesionarse *to take possession.*

posibilidad *f. possibility.*

POSIBLE *adj. possible; m. pl. means, wealth.*

No me será posible hacerlo. *It won't be possible for me to do it.*

Haré por Ud. cuanto me sea posible. *I'll do as much as I can for you.*

Todo cabe en lo posible. *Everything's possible.*

posición *f. position; status, situation.*

Goza de una posición holgada. *He's well-to-do.*

Una posición estratégica. *A strategic position.*

positivamente *positively.*

Estoy positivamente seguro. *I'm positively certain.*

positivo *adj. positive, sure, certain.*

postal *adj. postal.*

Giro postal. *Money order.*

Paquete postal. *Parcel post.*

postergar *to defer, to put off, to delay.*

posteridad *f. posterity.*

posterior *adj. rear, back; later, subsequent.*

La parte posterior de la cabeza. *The back of the head.*

Esta ley ha quedado anulada por otra posterior. *This law was superseded by a later one.*

posteriormente *subsequently.*

postguerra *f. postwar period.*

postizo *adj. artificial, false.*

Dientes postizos. *False teeth.*

postor *m. bidder.*

Al mejor postor. *To the highest bidder.*

postración *f. depression, exhaustion, state of being depressed.*

postrado *adj. depressed, exhausted.*

postre *adj. last in order; m. dessert.*

Llegamos a los postres. *We came when they were having dessert.*

A la postre. *In the long run. At last.*

postrer *(a shortening of postrero used before a noun) last.*

Un postrer deseo. *A last wish.*

postrero *adj. last.*

póstumo *adj. posthumous.*

postura *f. posture, position; bid; wager.*

potable *adj. drinkable.*

¿Hay agua potable aquí? *Is there any drinking water here?*

potaje *m. pottage, thick soup.*

potencia *f. power; strength, force; faculty.*

Las grandes potencias. *The Great Powers.*

potentado *m. potentate, monarch; rich man.*

potente *adj. potent, powerful, mighty.*

potro *m. colt.*

pozo *m. well; pit.*

práctica *f. practice, exercise.*

practicante *adj. practicing; m. practitioner; hospital intern; graduate nurse.*

práctico *adj. practical; skillful; m. (harbor) pilot.*

Es un hombre muy práctico. *He's very practical.*

pradera *f. meadow, prairie.*

prado *m. lawn, meadow, pasture ground.*

preámbulo *m. preamble, introduction.*

Es un preámbulo interesante. *It's an interesting preface.*

Déjese Ud. de preámbulos, y diga lo que quiere. *Stop beating around the bush (stop evading the issue) and tell me what you want.*

precario *adj. precarious.*

precaución *f. precaution, prudence.*

precaver *to prevent.*

precaverse *to take precautions; to be on one's guard.*

precedencia *f. precedence.*

precedente *adj. preceding; m. precedent.*

preceder *to precede.*

precepto *m. precept, order.*

preciar *to value, to appraise.*

preciarse *to take pride in, to boast.*

Se precia de saber español. *He boasts (is very proud) about his knowledge of Spanish.*

PRECIO *m. price; value.*

¿Qué precio tiene? *What's the price?*

Es precio fijo. *It's a fixed price.*

Precio de fábrica. *Cost price.*

Precio corriente. *Regular price.*

Ultimo precio. *Lowest price.*

A ningún precio. *Not at any price.*

A precio de ganga. *At a bargain price.*

preciosidad *f. preciousness; precious or beautiful object; a beauty.*

Es una preciosidad de criatura. *She's a beautiful child. ("She's a beauty of a child.")*

precioso *adj. precious; beautiful, delightful.*

Piedras preciosas. *Precious stones.*

Es un sitio precioso para pasar el verano. *It's a delightful spot to spend the summer.*

Hay una luna preciosa esta noche. *There's a beautiful moon tonight.*

precipicio *m. precipice; ruin, destruction.*

precipitación *f. rash haste.*

precipitadamente *hastily, in a rush.*

precipitar *to precipitate; to hasten, to rush; to hurl.*

precipitarse *to rush headlong into; to rush, to hurry.*

precisamente *precisely.*

precisar *to fix, to set; to compel.*

Hay que precisar la hora de la cita. *We have to set the time for the appointment.*

Me ví precisado a hacerlo. *I was compelled to do it.*

precisión *f. precision, accuracy; necessity; compul-*

sion.

Instrumento de precisión. *Precision instrument.*

Tengo precisión de hacer eso. *I'm obliged to do that.*

Habla con precisión. *He's very precise in his speech. He speaks to the point.*

PRECISO *adj. necessary; precise; clear.*

Es preciso que Ud. reuna el dinero hoy mismo. *You must get the money today.*

Es preciso practicar un idioma para dominarlo. *It's necessary to practice a language in order to master it.*

Será preciso obrar con prudencia. *It will be necessary to act prudently.*

precoz *adj. precocious.*

predecir *to predict, to foretell.*

predicar *to preach.*

predicción *f. prediction.*

Saliéron mal mis predicciones. *My predictions didn't come true.*

predilección *f. predilection, preference.*

Tener predilección por. *To have a fondness for. To have a predilection for.*

predilecto *adj. favorite.*

Es mi primo predilecto. *He's my favorite cousin.*

predispuesto *adj. predisposed.*

predominar *to prevail, to predominate.*

prefacio *m. preface.*

prefecto *m. prefect, chief administrative official of a county or province.*

prefectura *f. office, jurisdiction, territory and official residence of a prefect; prefecture.*

preferencia *f. preference, choice.*

La tratan con preferencia. *She's given preferential treatment. She's treated with favoritism.*

preferente *adj. preferable, preferring.*

preferible *adj. preferable.*

Es preferible ir personalmente. *It's preferable to go in person.*

PREFERIR *to prefer, to like best.*

¿Prefiere vino o cerveza? *Do you prefer wine or beer?*

Prefiero el vino a la cerveza. *I prefer wine to beer?*

¿Cuál de estos colores prefiere Ud.? *Which one of these colors do you like best?*

prefijo *m. prefix.*

pregonar *to proclaim in public, to make known.*

PREGUNTA *f. question.*

¿Me permite que le haga una pregunta? *May I ask you a question?*

Estar a la cuarta pregunta. *To be penniless. To be broke.*

PREGUNTAR *to ask, to inquire.*

¿Por qué me lo preguntas? *Why do you ask me?*

¿Le preguntó a Ud. algo? *Did he ask you anything?*

¿Quién pregunta por mí? *Who's asking for me?*

Alguien pregunta por Ud. *Someone's asking for*

you.

preguntarse *to wonder.*

preguntón *m. inquisitive person.*

prehistórico *adj. prehistoric.*

prejuicio *m. prejudice, bias.*

preliminar *adj. and n. preliminary.*

preludio *m. prelude, introduction.*

Ser el preludio de. *To lead to.*

prematuro *adj. premature.*

premeditación *f. premeditation.*

premeditar *to premeditate, to think out.*

premiar *to reward, to remunerate.*

premio *m. prize; reward.*

premura *f. haste, hurry, urgency.*

prenda *f. pledge, security, pawn; piece of jewelry; garment; forfeit; a very dear person; token; pl. qualities, talents.*

Prendas de vestir. *Articles of clothing.*

Juego de prendas. *Forfeits. The game of forfeits.*

Es un hombre de buenas prendas. *He's a man of fine qualities.*

prendar *to pledge, to give or take something as security; to ingratiate oneself.*

prendarse *to take a fancy to, to be taken with (the beauty of something, etc.), to become fond of, to fall in love.*

prendedor *m. clasp; breastpin, brooch.*

PRENDER *to clasp, to grasp; to catch; to arrest; to take root (a plant); to burn.*

Prender con alfileres. *To fasten with pins.*

¿Quién prendió al ladrón? *Who arrested (caught) the thief?*

La leña no prende. *The wood won't burn.*

La planta ha prendido. *The plant has taken root.*

PRENSA *f. press (newspaper).*

preñada *adj. pregnant.*

preocupación *f. preoccupation, concern, worry.*

preocupar *to preoccupy; to prejudice; to cause concern.*

Está algo preocupado. *He has something on his mind.*

preocuparse *to be worried, to care about, to be concerned.*

No se preocupe tanto. *Don't worry so much.*

Se preocupa por la suerte de su hija. *He's concerned (worried) about his daughter.*

preparación *f. preparation.*

preparado *adj. prepared; m. (medicinal) preparation.*

PREPARAR *to prepare, to get ready.*

Nos preparamos a partir. *We're getting ready to start.*

Prepare Ud. su billete. *Get your ticket ready.*

Tenme preparada la comida. *Have dinner ready for me.*

prepararse *to prepare oneself, to be prepared.*

Prepárese. *Get ready.*

Prepararse para un viaje. *To get ready (prepare)*

for a trip.
preparativo *m. preparation.*
    Estamos haciendo los preparativos para el viaje. *We're making preparations for the trip.*
preparatorio *adj. preparatory.*
preponderancia *f. preponderance.*
preponderar *to prevail.*
preposición *f. preposition.*
presa *f. capture; prey; dam.*
presagiar *to predict, to give warning.*
presagio *m. omen, prediction.*
prescindir *to do without, to dispense with, to do away with.*
prescribir *to prescribe.*
prescripción *f. prescription.*
presencia *f. presence.*
    Se exige su presencia. *His presence is required. It's necessary that he be present.*
    Lo dije en su presencia. *I said it in his presence.*
    Hacer acto de presencia. *To put in an appearance.*
    Presencia de ánimo. *Presence of mind.*
presenciar *to be present, to witness, to see.*
    Acabamos de presenciar . . . *We've just witnessed . . .*
PRESENTAR *to present; to introduce; to show.*
    No la conozco, preséntemela. *I don't know her. Will you introduce me? (Introduce her to me.)*
    Le presento a mi prometido. *I'd like you to meet my fiancé.*
    Presente este talón al reclamar su equipaje. *Present this check when you claim your baggage.*
    Presentaron una queja a la dirección. *They complained to the management.*
presentarse *to put in an appearance, to show up.*
    Se presentó inesperadamente. *He showed up unexpectedly.*
PRESENTE *adj. present; m. gift; present.*
    ¡Presente! *Present (in a roll call)!*
    Al presente no tenemos ninguna noticia. *At present we have no news.*
    Tengo presente lo que me dijo. *I'm bearing in mind what he told me.*
    Tendré siempre presente su bondad. *I shall always remember your kindness.*
    "La presente es para saludarle y decirle . . ." *(in a letter). "This is to greet you and to say . . ."*
    Lo dije en voz alta a fin de que lo oyesen todos los presentes. *I said it out loud, so that everyone present could hear it.*
    Un presente de valor. *An expensive (valuable) gift.*
presentimiento *m. presentiment.*
presentir *to have a presentiment.*
preservación *f. preservation.*

preservar *to preserve; to maintain; to keep.*
presidencia *f. presidency; (presidential) chair; chairmanship.*
    Ocupar la presidencia. *To preside. ("To occupy the chair.")*
presidente *m. president; chairman.*
presidiario *m. convict.*
presidio *m. penitentiary, prison.*
presidir *to preside; to direct, to lead.*
presión *f. pressure.*
preso *adj. and n. imprisoned, prisoner.*
prestado *adj. lent, loaned.*
    Vino a pedirme prestado un libro. *He came to borrow a book from me.*
    Dar prestado. *To lend.*
    Tomar (pedir) prestado. *To borrow.*
prestamista *m. and f. money lender; pawnbroker.*
préstamo *m. loan.*
PRESTAR *to lend, to aid; to pay (attention).*
    Me prestó un libro muy interesante. *He lent me a very interesting book.*
    Le presté cinco pesos. *I lent him five dollars.*
    ¿Quiere Ud. prestarnos su ayuda? *Will you give (lend) us a hand?*
    Prestar atención. *To pay attention.*
    Se ruega prestar atención. *May I have your attention? ("Your attention is requested.")*
    Me ha prestado Ud. un gran servicio. *You've done (rendered) me a great service.*
prestarse *to offer to; to be apt to, to lend itself to.*
    Se prestó a ayudarnos. *He offered to help us.*
    Eso se prestará a malas interpretaciones. *That is apt to be misinterpreted.*
presteza *f. quickness, speed, haste.*
    Con presteza. *Quickly..*
prestigio *m. prestige; good name.*
prestigioso *adj. famous.*
PRESTO *adj. quick, prompt; ready; adv. quickly; soon.*
    Estamos prestos para salir. *We're ready to go out.*
    Vístete presto. *Get dressed quickly.*
    De presto. *Promptly. Swiftly.*
presumido *adj. and n. vain, conceited; conceited person.*
    Es muy presumida. *She's very conceited.*
presumir *to presume; to assume; to be conceited.*
    Presume ser listo. *He thinks he's smart.*
    Era de presumir que . . . *It was to be expected that . . . It was to be presumed . . .*
presunción *f. presumption; presumptuousness, conceit.*
presunto *adj. presumed; apparent.*
    Presunto heredero. *Heir apparent.*
presuntuoso *adj. presumptuous, vain.*
presuponer *to presuppose, to take for granted in advance, to assume beforehand.*
presupuestar *to estimate, to make an estimate, to make a budget.*

presupuesto *m.* budget; *estimate.*

pretencioso *adj. presumptuous, conceited.*

pretender *to pretend; to apply for; to try, to endeavor.*

Pretender un empleo. *To apply for a job.*

Pretende su mano. *He's asking for her hand in marriage.*

Pretendió convencerme. *He tried to convince me.*

pretendiente *adj. and n. pretender; suitor; candidate.*

pretensión *f. pretension; contention.*

pretexto *m. pretext.*

prevalecer *to prevail.*

prevención *f. prevention; foresight; prejudice.*

prevenir *to prepare; to prevent; to foresee; to forewarn, to warn.*

Estámos prevenidos. *We're prepared (on guard).*

Le prevengo a Ud. que no lo haga. *I warn you not to do it.*

prever *to foresee, to see ahead, to anticipate, to provide for.*

Prevemos el éxito. *We anticipate success.*

Es de prever. *It's to be expected.*

previamente *previously.*

prévio *adj. previous; prior to.*

Una cuestión previa. *Previous question (parliamentary procedure).*

Previo pago de. *Upon payment of.*

previsto *adj. foreseen.*

En las condiciones previstas en el acuerdo . . . *Under (In) the conditions which have been provided for in the agreement . . .*

prima *f. first string (in musical instruments); premium; female cousin.*

Prima de seguro. *Insurance premium.*

María es mi prima. *Mary is my cousin.*

primario *adj. primary.*

Escuela primaria. *Elementary school. Primary school.*

PRIMAVERA *f. spring (the season).*

PRIMER *(a shortening of primero used before a noun) first.*

Primer galán. *Leading man.*

En primer lugar. *In the first place.*

El primer año. *The first year.*

Este es mi primer vuelo en avión. *This is my first flight.*

primeramente *first, firstly, in the first place.*

PRIMERO *adj. and n. first; former.*

Tráiganos primero un poco de sopa. *Bring us some soup first.*

Es el primero de la clase. *He ranks highest in his class.*

Veamos primero la hora que es. *Let's first see what time it is.*

Sírvase Ud. darme dos billetes de primera para Madrid. *Two pullman ("first class") tickets to Madrid, please.*

Es un nadador de primera. *He's an excellent swimmer.*

Primera velocidad. *First gear.*

Primera dama. *Leading lady.*

La primera casa. *The first house.*

La primera vez. *The first time.*

Primera enseñanza. *Primary education.*

De primera clase. *First class.*

De primera. *Of superior quality. Highest grade.*

Al primero del mes que viene. *On the first of next month.*

A primeros del mes que viene. *In the early part of next month.*

Primeros auxilios. *First aid.*

De buenas a primeras. *All of a sudden.*

primitivo *adj. primitive.*

primo *m. cousin; a fool (coll.).*

Primo hermano. *First cousin.*

primor *m. beauty, exquisiteness; dexterity, skill.*

Ese bordado es un primor. *That embroidery is very lovely.*

princesa *f. princess.*

PRINCIPAL *adj. principal, main, chief, most important; m. capital; head (of a concern); first floor.*

Este es uno de los argumentos principales de su tesis. *This is one of the main arguments of his thesis.*

Vivimos en el princpal. *We live on the first floor.*

príncipe *m. prince; ruler.*

principiante *adj. and n. beginner, apprentice.*

principiar *to begin, to commence.*

Van a principiar la construcción. *They're beginning to build.*

PRINCIPIO *m. beginning; origin; principle.*

Al principio me parecía fácil. *It seemed easy to me at first.*

Le pagarán a principios del mes que viene. *They'll pay you the early part of next month.*

Al principios de la semana entrante. *Early next week.*

Al principio. *At the beginning. At first.*

Dar principio. *To begin.*

¿En qué principio basa Ud. su teoría? *On what principle do you base your theory?*

En principio no me parece mal la idea. *That idea doesn't seem bad in principle.*

prioridad *f. priority.*

PRISA *f. haste, hurry; urgency.*

Tengo mucha prisa. *I'm in a great hurry.*

No corre prisa. *There's no hurry.*

Siempre anda de prisa. *He's always in a hurry.*

¡Démonos prisa, que es tarde! *Let's hurry, it's late.*

¿Por qué tanta prisa? *Why such a hurry?*

Déle Ud. prisa. *Make him (get him to) hurry up.*

prisión *f. imprisonment; prison.*

prisionero *m. prisoner.*

privación f. *privation, want.*

privado adj. *private, intimate; personal.*

   Vida privada. *Private life.*

   En privado. *Confidentially.*

   Carta privada. *Personal letter.*

privar to *deprive; to forbid.*

   Privarse de. *To do without.*

   No se priva de nada. *He doesn't deprive himself of anything.*

   Privado del conocimiento. *Unconscious.*

privilegiado adj. *privileged.*

privilegio m. *privilege.*

pro m. and f. *profit, advantage; pro.*

   En pro de. *In favor of.*

   El pro y el contra. *The pros and the cons.*

proa f. *prow, bow (of a ship).*

probabilidad f. *probability, likelihood.*

PROBABLE adj. *probable, likely.*

   Es poco probable. *It's not likely.*

   Es más que probable. *It's more than probable.*

PROBABLEMENTE *probably, likely.*

probado adj. *proved, tried.*

   Eso está probado. *That's been proved.*

PROBAR to *try; to taste; to prove; to try on.*

   Pruebe Ud. este vino, a ver si le gusta. *Taste this wine and see if you like it.*

   Me probaré estos zapatos. *I'll try these shoes on.*

   Pruebe otra vez. *Try again. Try once more.*

PROBLEMA m. *problem.*

procaz adj. *insolent, impudent, bold.*

procedencia f. *origin; place of sailing.*

procedente adj. *coming or proceeding from; according to law, rules or practices.*

PROCEDER to *proceed; to act, to behave;* m. *behavior, conduct.*

   Procedió correctamente. *He acted properly.*

   Procede con mucho tiento. *He uses a great deal of tact.*

   Lo que procede hacer. *The correct and proper thing (to do).*

   Proceder a. *To proceed with.*

   Proceder de. *To come from.*

   Proceder contra. *To proceed against. To take action against.*

   No me gusta su proceder. *I don't like his behavior.*

procedimiento m. *procedure; method.*

procesado adj. *indicted;* m. and f. *defendant.*

procesar to *sue; to indict.*

procesión f. *procession, parade.*

proceso m. *legal proceedings, (legal) process, lawsuit.*

proclamación f. *proclamation.*

proclamar to *proclaim; to promulgate.*

   La República Española fué proclamada el 14 de abril de 1931. *The Spanish Republic was proclaimed on April 14th, 1931.*

   Se ha proclamado la ley marcial. *Martial law*

has been proclaimed.

procrear to *procreate.*

PROCURAR to *endeavor, to try.*

   Procuraré estar a tiempo. *I'll try to be on time.*

   Procuró levantarse pero no pudo. *He tried to get up but he couldn't.*

   Procure no faltar. *Don't fail to come (do it, etc.). Try your best to come (do it, etc.).*

prodigar to *squander, to lavish.*

prodigio m. *wonder, marvel.*

prodigioso adj. *prodigious, marvelous.*

pródigo adj. *prodigal, wasteful, lavish.*

producción f. *production; output.*

PRODUCIR to *produce; to yield, to bear; to bring as evidence (law).*

   Producen 200 aeroplanos al día. *They turn out (produce) 200 planes per day.*

   Todo aquello le producía risa. *That made him laugh.*

producirse to *be produced.*

productivo adj. *productive.*

producto m. *product; amount.*

   Productos alimenticios. *Foodstuffs. Food products. Food.*

profanación f. *profanation.*

profanar to *profane.*

profano adj. *profane; secular; irreverent.*

profecía f. *prophecy.*

proferir to *utter, to say.*

profesar to *profess; to declare openly.*

profesión f. *profession.*

   ¿Su nombre y profesión, por favor? *Your name and profession?*

profesional adj. *professional.*

profesor m. *professor, teacher.*

profeta m. *prophet.*

profético adj. *prophetic.*

prófugo adj. *fugitive;* m. *draft dodger, slacker.*

profundamente *deeply; soundly (sleep).*

   Lo siento profundamente. *I regret it deeply.*

   Anoche, dormí profundamente. *I slept soundly last night.*

profundidad f. *profundity, depth.*

   ¿Qué profundidad tiene este lago? *What's the depth of this lake?*

   200 pies de profundidad. *200 feet deep.*

profundizar to *deepen; to delve into, to fathom.*

PROFUNDO adj. *profound, deep, intense.*

   Dolor profundo. *Intense pain.*

   Es un pozo muy profundo. *It's a very deep well.*

   Nos perdimos en lo más profundo del bosque. *We were lost in the depths of the woods.*

programa m. *program, plan; curriculum.*

   ¿Cuál es el programa de hoy? *What is today's program?*

   ¿Hasta qué punto del programa han estudiado? *How far did they get in the curriculum?*

progresar to *progress, to make progress.*

progreso m. progress.

Hacer progresos. To progress. To make progress.

prohibición f. prohibition.

prohibido adj. forbidden.

"Prohibido fumar." "No smoking."

"Prohibido por la ley." "Prohibited by law."

"Prohibido pasar." "No thoroughfare." "Do not pass beyond here." "No trespassing."

"Prohibido el tráfico." "Closed to traffic."

"Prohibida la entrada." "No admittance."

PROHIBIR to prohibit, to forbid.

Le prohibo hacer eso. I forbid you to do that.

Está prohibido llevar perros en los autobuses. *Dogs are not allowed on the busses.*

"Se prohibe la entrada." "No admittance."

"Se prohibe fumar." "No smoking."

prójimo m. fellow man, neighbor.

proletariado m. proletariat, working class.

proletario adj. proletarian; of the working class.

La clase proletaria. The working class.

prolijo adj. prolix, too long, using too many words.

prólogo m. prologue, preface, introduction.

prolongación f. prolongation, lengthening.

prolongar to prolong, to extend.

promedio m. average, mean.

promesa f. promise, assurance.

PROMETER to promise.

¿Por qué no me ha escrito Ud. como me prometió? Why haven't you written to me as you promised?

Nunca cumple lo que promete. He never does what he promises.

Este negocio no promete mucho. This business is not very promising.

prometido adj. promised; m. fiancé; f. fiancée.

Cumplir lo prometido. To keep a promise.

Mi prometido. My fiancé.

prominencia f. prominence; protuberance.

prominente adj. prominent; conspicuous.

Ocupa un puesto prominente en el gobierno. He occupies a prominent position in the government.

promover to promote; to advance.

promulgar to promulgate, to publish.

pronombre m. pronoun.

pronosticar to forecast.

pronóstico m. forecast, prediction; prognosis.

Pronóstico del tiempo. Weather forecast.

prontitud f. promptness, swiftness.

PRONTO adj. prompt, quick; ready; adv. promptly, quickly; soon; m. impulse, fit (of temper).

Hasta muy pronto. So long. I'll see you soon.

¡Venga pronto! Come quickly! Come right away!

Mientras más pronto mejor. The sooner the better.

Hizo muy pronto el trabajo. He did the work very quickly.

Me dijo que estaría de vuelta pronto. She told me she would be back soon.

Su respuesta fué muy pronta. He replied (very) promptly. ("His reply was very prompt.")

Estoy pronto para empezar. I'm ready to begin.

Está arrepentido de aquel pronto que tuvo. He still regrets that sudden impulse.

De pronto. Suddenly. All of a sudden.

De pronto ocurrió algo. All of a sudden something happened.

Por de pronto. For the time being.

pronunciación f. pronunciation.

pronunciar to pronounce; to utter; to deliver (a speech).

Ud. pronuncia muy bien el español. You pronounce Spanish very well.

Pronunciará un discurso sobre historia contemporánea. He's going to give a lecture on Modern History.

Pronunciar sentencia. To pronounce sentence.

propagación f. propagation, dissemination.

propaganda f. propaganda.

propagandista m. and f. propagandist.

propagar to propagate; to spread (news, knowledge, etc.)

propasarse to take undue liberties; to exceed one's authority.

propender to tend, to incline to.

propensión f. propensity, inclination.

propenso adj. inclined to, disposed to.

Está propenso a hacerlo. He's inclined to do it.

propiamente properly.

propicio adj. propitious, favorable.

Una ocasión propicia. A favorable opportunity.

propiedad f. ownership; property.

Esas casas son de su propiedad. Those houses belong to him (are his property).

El jabón tiene la propiedad de quitar la mugre. Soap has the property of removing dirt.

Acabo de comprar esa propiedad. I've just bought that property.

propietario m. proprietor, owner, landlord.

propina f. tip, gratuity.

PROPIO adj. own, self; proper, fit, suitable.

Sus propias palabras. His own words.

Le deseo lo propio. I wish you the same. The same to you.

Eso es un juego propio de niños. It's a game suitable for children.

Eso sería lo propio. That would fit the case.

Estimación propia. Self-respect.

Amor propio. Self-conceit.

proponer to propose; to suggest; to move.

Me propongo ir a verle. I intend to go to see him.

Propongo que vayamos todos a casa. I suggest we all go home.

Señor presidente, propongo que se levante la sesión. Mr. Chairman, I move that the meeting be adjourned.

Le será difícil llevar a cabo lo que se propone. *It will be hard to carry out what you have in mind (intend).*

proporción f. *proportion.*

proporcional adj. *proportional.*

proporcionar *to provide, to furnish, to supply; to proportion, to fit.*

proposición f. *proposition; proposal, motion.*

PROPÓSITO m. *purpose, intention.*

Lo hizo de propósito. *He did it on purpose.*

A propósito. *By the way.*

Fuera de propósito. *Not to the point. Irrelevant. Foreign to the subject.*

A propósito de. *With regards to. Regarding.*

propuesta f. *proposal, offer; nomination.*

Aceptaron nuestra propuesta. *They accepted our proposal.*

prórroga f. *extension of time, renewal.*

Dar prórroga. *To extend the time of payment. To grant an extension.*

prorrogar *to extend (time), to prolong.*

prosa f. *prose.*

prosaico adj. *prosaic.*

proseguir *to pursue, to carry on, to go on, to continue, to proceed.*

prosista m. *prose writer.*

prospecto m. *prospectus, catalogue.*

prosperar *to prosper, to thrive, to be successful, to get rich.*

próspero adj. *prosperous.*

protagonista m. and f. *protagonist.*

protección f. *protection, support.*

protector m. *protector.*

proteger *to protect; to support.*

protesta f. *protest.*

protestante adj. and n. *protesting; Protestant.*

protestar *to protest.*

PROVECHO m. *profit; benefit, advantage.*

Ser de provecho. *To be useful.*

Sacar provecho. *To derive profit from. To turn to advantage.*

En su provecho. *In your favor. To your advantage.*

¡Buen provecho (said at meals)! *I hope you enjoy your food. Hearty appetite!*

provechoso adj. *profitable, beneficial.*

proveer *to provide; to furnish, to supply; to dispose.*

Proveer de fondos. *To provide with funds.*

Proveerse de. *To supply oneself with.*

provenir *to be due to; to derive from, to come from.*

Eso puede provenir de un resfrío. *That can come from (be caused by) a cold.*

proverbio m. *proverb.*

providencia f. *providence; pl. dispositions, measures.*

Tomar providencias. *To take measures.*

provincia f. *province.*

provisión f. *provision; stock, supply.*

Provisiones alimenticias. *Foodstuffs. Food.*

provisional adj. *provisional, temporary.*

provisionalmente adv. *provisionally, temporarily.*

provisto adj. *provided for, supplied.*

La tienda está muy bien provista de mercaderías. *The store is well stocked with merchandise.*

provocación f. *provocation.*

provocador m. *trouble maker.*

provocar *to provoke, to vex, to make angry.*

PRÓXIMO adj. *near, next, neighboring.*

La próxima estación. *The next station.*

La semana próxima. *Next week.*

¿Cuál es la calle próxima? *What's the street after this?*

proyecto m. *project; plan, scheme; design.*

prudencia f. *prudence; moderation.*

prudente adj. *prudent, cautious.*

PRUEBA f. *proof; test; fitting (of garments).*

Existen pruebas bastante claras de ello. *There are pretty strong proofs of it.*

Me han sacado dos pruebas. *I had two proofs made.*

Sala de pruebas. *Fitting room.*

A prueba de fuego. *Fireproof.*

psicología f. *psychology.*

psicológico adj. *psychological.*

psicólogo m. *psychologist.*

psiquiatra m. *psychiatrist.*

psiquiatría m. *psychiatry.*

púa f. *sharp point, prong.*

Alambre de púas. *Barbed wire.*

publicación f. *publication.*

publicar *to publish; to announce.*

Acaba de publicarse este libro. *This book has just been published.*

Va a publicar un artículo en el periódico de mañana. *He's going to publish an article in tomorrow's paper.*

Publíquese y ejecútese. *Let it be made public and put into effect. ("Let it be published and enforced.")*

publicidad f. *publicity.*

PÚBLICO adj. *public, not private; m. public, crowd, audience.*

Sacarán la casa a pública subasta. *They'll sell the house at public auction.*

En público. *Publicly. In public.*

"Aviso al público." *"Notice to the public."*

El público silbó la comedia. *The audience booed the comedy.*

puchero m. *earthen pot; dish of stewed vegetables and meats.*

pudiente adj. *powerful; wealthy, rich.*

pudín m. *pudding.*

pudor m. *modesty, shyness.*

pudrir *to rot.*

Las manzanas se están pudriendo. *The apples are spoiling (rotting).*

PUEBLO *m. village, town; population; people.*

¿Qué pueblo es éste? *What town is this?*

Pueblo natal. *Native town.*

El pueblo español. *The Spanish people.*

puente *m. bridge.*

puerco *adj. nasty, filthy, dirty; m. hog.*

PUERTA *f. door; doorway; gate.*

Abra la puerta. *Open the door.*

Cierre la puerta. *Shut the door.*

Cierre la puerta con llave cuando salga. *Lock the door when you leave.*

La puerta trasera da al jardín. *The back door opens out into the garden.*

puerto *m. port, harbor; haven; pass through the mountains.*

Puerto franco. *Free port.*

Puerto de destino. *Port of destination.*

PUES *as, since; so; well; then; why; now; indeed.*

Pues hágalo Ud. *Then do it.*

Pues vamos. *Then let's go.*

¿Pues qué quiere? *What do you want?*

¡Pues sí! *Yes, indeed!*

¡Pues hombre! *Why, man!*

¡Pues mira, chico! *Now look here, pal!*

Pues vámonos ya. *Let's run along.*

¡Pues no faltaba más! *Well, that's the last straw!*

Pues, como no fumo, no compro tabaco. *Since I don't smoke, I don't buy tobacco.*

Pues bien. *Well, then.*

¿Y pues? *What of it? So what?*

¿Pues qué? *Why not?*

¿Pues y qué? *So what?*

Pues no. *Not at all.*

¡Pues bien, iré! *All right then, I'll go!*

Pues no puede ser. *But it can't be. But it's impossible.*

puesta *f. set, setting; laying (eggs).*

La puesta del sol. *The sunset.*

PUESTO *adj. put, placed; on; set (table); m. place; stand; post; position, employment.*

La mesa está puesta. *The table is set.*

Esto está mal puesto. *This is in the wrong place.*

Llevaba puesto su traje nuevo. *He had his new suit on.*

Puesto que. *Since. Inasmuch as.*

Le compré en un puesto del mercado. *I bought it at a stand in the market.*

¿Dónde habrá un puesto de gasolina? *Where do you suppose there's a filling station?*

Tiene un buen puesto. *He has a good position.*

Puesto militar. *Military post.*

Puesto a bordo. *Free on board.*

Puesto en Neuva York. *Delivered free in New York.*

púgil, pugilista *m. prizefighter.*

pugna *f. struggle.*

pulcro *adj. neat, tidy.*

pulga *f. flea.*

Tiene malas pulgas. *He's bad-tempered.*

pulgada *f. inch.*

pulgar *m. thumb.*

pulir *to polish.*

pulmón *m. lung.*

pulmonía *f. pneumonia.*

pulpa *f. pulp.*

pulsera *f. bracelet.*

pulso *m. pulse; steadiness of the hand; tact.*

Déjeme tomarle el pulso. *Let me feel your pulse.*

Obra con gran pulso. *He acts with great circumspection.*

punta *f. point; tip; edge; cape, headland.*

La punta del lápiz. *Pencil point.*

Sáquele punta al lápiz. *Sharpen the pencil.*

Tengo los nervios de punta. *My nerves are on edge.*

Va de punta en blanco. *She's all dressed up.*

puntada *f. stitch.*

puntapie *m. kick.*

puntería *f. aim, aiming, marksmanship.*

puntiagudo *adj. sharp-pointed.*

puntilla *adj. narrow lace edging.*

De puntillas. *On tiptoe.*

PUNTO *m. point; dot; period; place; stitch; loop (in knitting); net (cloth material); hole (in a stocking).*

Punto de partida. *Starting point. Point of departure.*

¿Donde está el punto en esta máquina de escribir? *Where's the period on this typewriter?*

Punto y coma. *Semicolon.*

Dos puntos. *Colon.*

Ganó por pocos puntos. *He won by a few points.*

Nos veremos en el mismo punto. *We'll meet at the same place.*

Punto por punto. *Point by point.*

Ha dado Ud. en el punto. *You've put your finger on it.*

Llevaba un traje de puntos blancos. *She wore a dress with white polka dots.*

Un vestido de punto. *A knitted dress.*

Hay que poner punto final a esto. *We must put a stop to this.*

Estábamos a punto de salir cuando llegaron. *We were just about to leave (on the point of leaving) when they arrived.*

A la hora en punto. *On the dot.*

Estaré a la una en punto. *I'll be there at one o'clock sharp.*

Hasta cierto punto es verdad. *To a certain extent it's true.*

Desde cierto punto de vista Ud. tiene razón.

You're right from a certain standpoint.

Estuvo a punto de perder la vida. *He nearly lost his life.*

Su cólera subía de punto. *He became angrier by the minute.*

No sé a punto fijo. *I don't know for certain.*

La comida está en su punto. *The food is just right.*

Punto cardinal. *Cardinal point.*

En punto a. *In regard to.*

Punto menos que imposible. *Almost impossible.*

puntuación *f. punctuation.*

Signos de puntuación *Punctuation marks.*

puntual *adj. punctual, prompt, on time; exact.*

Sea Ud. puntual. *Be on time. Be punctual.*

puntualizar *to give a detailed account of; to emphasize.*

puntualmente *punctually, on time.*

punzada *f. puncture, prick; acute pain.*

punzante *sharp.*

punzar *to prick, to puncture, to stick.*

puñado *m. handful; a few.*

Un puñado de soldados defendieron la posición. *A few soldiers defended the position.*

puñal *m. dagger.*

puñetazo *m. a punch*

puño *m. fist; cuff; hilt (of a sword); haft (of a tool); handle (of an umbrella); head (of a cane).*

Firmado de mi puño y letra. *Signed by me.*

pupila *f. pupil (of the eye).*

pupilo *m. ward (under someone's guardianship); boarder; a day student.*

pupitre *m. writing desk.*

puré *m. puree, thick soup.*

Puré de guisantes. *Pea soup.*

Puré de patatas (papas). *Mashed potatoes.*

pureza *f. purity.*

purga *f. purge, physic.*

purgante *m. laxative; purgative.*

purgatorio *m. purgatory.*

Está pasando las penas del purgatorio. *He's suffering many hardships. ("He's going through purgatory.")*

purificar *to purify.*

PURO *adj. pure; clean; plain; m. cigar.*

Aire puro. *Pure air.*

Le digo a Ud. la pura verdad. *I'm telling you the plain truth.*

Me lo encontré de pura casualidad. *I met him by ("pure") chance.*

Pruebe estos puros. *Try these cigars.*

pútrido *adj. putrid, rotten.*

Q

QUE *(rel. pron.) that, which, who, whom; conj. that, than, whether.*

El que. *He who, the one which.*

La que. *She who, the one which.*

Los que (m. pl.). *They who, those who, the ones who.*

Las que (f. pl.). *They who, those who, the ones who.*

Lo que. *That which, which, that, what.*

Yo fuí la que lo dijo. *It's I who said it. I was the one who said it.*

El que está hablando. *The one who's speaking. The one speaking.*

Yo no sé lo que le pasa. *I don't know what's the matter with him.*

Eso es lo que yo digo. *That's what I say.*

Alguno que otro. *Someone or another.*

Dice que lo hará. *He said he'd (he'll) do it.*

Vale mucho más de lo que se figuran. *It's worth much more than they imagine.*

Que le guste o no. *Whether he likes it or not.*

Que no entre nadie. *Don't let anyone come in.*

Q.E.S.M. (Que estrecha su mano). *Yours truly. ("Who shakes your hand.")*

QUÉ *(interrogative pron.) what; how.*

¿Por qué? *Why?*

¿Por qué se apura Ud.? *What are you worrying about?*

¿Qué es esto? *What's this?*

¿Qué hora es? *What time is it?*

¿Qué busca Ud.? *What are you looking for?*

¿Qué pasa? *What's going on?*

¿Qué van a tomar Uds.? *What are you going to have?*

¿Qué hora será? *I wonder what time it is?*

¿Pues y qué? *So what?*

No sé qué hacer. *I don't know what to do.*

¿De qué está hablando? *What's he talking about?*

¿En qué quedamos? *How do we stand?*

¡Qué va! *Nonsense!*

¡Qué barbaridad! *How awful!*

¿Qué sé yo? *How do I know?*

¡Qué gracia! *How amusing!*

¡Ay qué risa! *How funny! What a joke!*

¡Qué hombre! *What a man!*

No hay de qué. *Don't mention it. You're welcome.*

quebrada *f. ravine, gorge.*

quebradizo *adj. brittle, fragile.*

quebrado *adj. broken; bankrupt; ruptured; m. fraction (math.).*

quebradura *f. fissure; fracture; rupture, hernia.*

quebrantado *adj. tottering, broken down; failing (health).*

Salud quebrantada. *Failing health.*

quebrantamiento *m. breaking, breach (of law, promise, etc.)*

quebrantar *to break, to crash; to trespass; to violate (the law).*

quebranto *m. weakness; failure; great loss, severe damage; grief.*

QUEBRAR *to break; to rupture (hernia); to become*

bankrupt.

Al caer se quebró un brazo (*Amer.*). *He broke his arm when he fell.*

El negocio quebró. *The business failed.*

QUEDAR *to remain; to stop; to be; to fit; to be left; to agree.*

¿Cuántos dólares le quedan? *How many dollars do you have left?*

¿Queda lejos el hotel? *Is the hotel far from here?*

Este traje le queda como mandado a hacer. *This suit fits you as if it were made to order.*

Me quedan un poco estrechos. *They're a little tight for me.*

Todo quedó muy mal. *Everything came off (turned out) badly.*

Quedó más pobre que una rata. *He became poorer than a church mouse.*

No le queda a Ud. mucho tiempo. *You haven't much time left.*

Quedaron en hacer el trabajo. *They agreed to do the work.*

Quédese sentado. *Remain seated. Keep your seats.*

Nuestro amigo se quedó en Europa. *Our friend stayed in Europe.*

Me quedaré aquí un ratio. *I'll stay here (for) awhile.*

Me quedaré hasta el viernes. *I'll stay until Friday.*

¿En qué quedamos? *How do we stand? What's the final agreement?*

Esto queda entre los dos. *This is just between the two of us.*

Quedarse con. *To keep. To take.*

Se quedó con el libro. *He kept the book. He didn't return the book.*

Me quedo con esta camisa. *I'll take (buy) this shirt.*

Quedarse sin dinero. *To be left penniless.*

quehacer *m. occupation, work.*

Quehaceres domésticos. *Housework.*

queja *f. complaint; resentment; groan.*

quejarse *to complain.*

Ella se queja de Ud. *She complains (is complaining) about you.*

Se queja de dolor de cabeza. *She complains of a headache.*

Eso le dará motivo para quejarse. *That will give him grounds for complaint.*

quejoso *adj. complaining; plaintive.*

quemado *adj. burnt.*

Huele a quemado. *I smell something burning. ("It smells burnt.")*

quemadura *f. burn; scald.*

QUEMAR *to burn; to scald; to parch; to be very hot.*

Cuidado con quemarse. *Be careful, don't burn yourself.*

Por poco me quemo la lengua. *I nearly (almost) burned my tongue.*

Este teatro se ha quemado dos veces. *This theater has burned down twice.*

El sol quema hoy. *The sun's scorching today.*

¡Que te quemas! *You're warm! (i.e. You've almost found or guessed it.)*

querella *f. complaint; quarrel.*

querellarse *to complain.*

querencia *f. affection, fondness.*

QUERER *to wish, to want, to desire; to like; to love.*

¿Qué quiere Ud.? *What do you want? What would you like?*

¿Quiere Ud. ver el piso? *Do you want (would you like) to see the apartment?*

¿Quiere Ud. callarse? *Will you keep quiet?*

¿Lo quiere? *Do you want it?*

Yo no lo quiero. *I don't want it.*

Si Ud. quiere. *If you like.*

Haz lo que quieras. *Do as you please.*

Pide lo que quieras. *Order whatever you want.*

Iremos donde quieras. *We'll go wherever you wish.*

Como quieras. *As you like.*

¿A quién quieres más? *Who (m) do you love most? Who (m) do you love the best?*

La quiere mucho. *He loves her very much.*

Quisiera un helado. *I'd like some ice cream.*

Yo quisiera un vaso de vino tinto. *I would like a glass of red wine.*

Quiero comprar un reloj. *I want to buy a watch.*

Hubiera querido ver aquella película. *I should like to have seen that film. ("I should have liked to see . . .")*

No quiero nada más. *I don't care for anything more.*

¿Qué quiere decir esta palabra? *What does this word mean?*

Sin querer. *Without wanting (wishing) to.*

Querer es poder. *Where there's a will there's a way.*

Como Ud. quiera. *As you wish (like).*

Si Ud. quiere. *If you like.*

querido *adj. beloved, dear; m. lover; f. mistress.*

Querido amigo. *Dear friend.*

queso *m. cheese.*

¡quiá! *Come now! Not at all! No, indeed!*

quicio *m. hinge.*

Estar fuera de quicio. *To be out of one's mind. To be unbalanced. ("To be unhinged.")*

Sacar de quicio. *To drive one crazy. To exasperate. ("To unhinge.")*

QUIEN *who, which; pl. quienes.*

¿Quién es Ud.? *Who are you?*

¿Quiénes son los otros invitados? *Who are the*

other guests?
¿Quién habla? *Who's speaking?*
¿Quién lo quiere? *Who wants it?*
¿De quién es este sombrero? *Whose hat is this?*
¿Para quién es? *For whom is it?*
¿Quién va? *Who's there?*
¿A quién busca Ud.? *Who(m) are you looking for?*
Quien así piensa se equivoca. *Whoever thinks so is wrong.*
¡Quién sabe! *Who knows! Heaven knows!*
¿A quién de ellos conoce Ud.? *Which one of them do you know?*

quienquiera *whoever.*
QUIETO *adj. quiet, still.*
¡Estése quieto! *Be quiet!*
quietud *f. quietness, quiet, tranquillity.*
quilla *f. keel.*
química *f. chemistry.*
químico *adj. chemical, m. chemist.*
quimono *m. kimona.*
QUINCE *adj. and n. fifteen; fifteenth.*
Hace quince días estaba aquí. *He was here two weeks ago.*
quincena *f. fortnight, period of two weeks, fifteen days; semi-monthly pay.*
Nos pagan por quincena. *They pay us every two weeks.*
quincenal *biweekly, fortnightly.*
quinientos *adj. and n. five hundred.*
quinina *f. quinine.*
quinta *f. country house; levy, draft.*
quintal *m. quintal, hundredweight.*
quinto *adj. and n. fifth; m. drafted soldier.*
quintuplicar *to quintuplicate.*
quíntuplo *adj. quintuple, fivefold.*
quiosco *m. kiosk, stand.*
Quiosco de periódicos. *Newspaper stand.*
quirúrgico *adj. surgical.*
quisquilloso *adj. touchy, too sensitive, difficult.*
QUITAR *to remove; to take away; to rob.*
Quite esa silla de aquí. *Take this chair away.*
Quita los pies de la silla. *Take your feet off the chair.*
Me han quitado el reloj. *They have stolen my watch.*
Esta crema quita las pecas. *This cream removes freckles.*
Quite el freno. *Release the brake.*
quitarse *to get rid of; to take off.*
Al entrar en la iglesia se quitó el sombrero. *He took his hat off when he entered the church.*
Ya se me quitó el resfriado. *I've gotten rid of my cold.*
Quitarse a uno de encima. *To get rid of someone.*
QUIZÁ, QUIZÁS *perhaps, maybe.*

Quizá sea verdad lo que dice. *Perhaps what he says is true.*
Quizá lo haga. *I might do it. Maybe I'll do it.*

R

rábano *m. radish.*
rabia *f. rabies, hydrophobia; rage, anger.*
Me da rabia. *It makes me angry (mad).*
rabiar *to be furious, to rage, to be angry.*
Rabiar por. *To be extremely eager (anxious) for something.*
rabioso *adj. furious, mad.*
Perro rabioso. *Mad dog.*
rabo *m. tail.*
racimo *m. bunch (grapes), cluster.*
ración *f. ration.*
racional *adj. rational, reasonable.*
racionar *to ration.*
radiador *m. radiator.*
radiar *to radiate; to broadcast.*
radical *adj. and n. radical.*
RADIO *m. radius; radium; f. radio.*
radiodifusión *f. broadcasting.*
radioemisora *f. broadcasting station.*
radioescucha *m. and f. radio listener.*
radiografía *f. radiography, X-ray photography.*
radiograma *m. radiogram.*
radioyente *m. and f. radio listener.*
radiotelefonía *f. radiotelephony.*
radiotelegrafía *f. radiotelegraphy.*
raid *m. raid.*
raíz *f. root; foundation.*
El árbol fué arrancado de raíz. *The tree was uprooted.*
Echar raíces. *To take root.*
rajar *to split, to cleave.*
rejarse *to crack; to back out.*
rallador *m. grater.*
rallar *to grate.*
Queso rallado. *Grated cheese.*
rama *f. branch; chase (printing).*
Tabaco en rama. *Leaf tobacco.*
Algodón en rama. *Cotton wool. Raw cotton.*
Andarse por las ramas. *To beat around the bush.*
ramal *m. strand (of a rope); halter; branch, line (railway); ramification.*
ramificación *f. ramification.*
ramillete *m. bouquet.*
ramo *m. branch, line; bunch; bouquet.*
Esa clase de mercancía no es de nuestro ramo. *That type of merchandise is not in our line.*
Le obsequió un ramo de flores. *He gave her a bouquet of flowers.*
rampa *f. ramp, slope.*
rana *f. frog.*
rancio *adj. rancid, stale.*
ranchero *m. mess attendant; rancher.*

rancho *m. mess; hut; hamlet; ranch.*

Sirvieron el rancho a las doce. *Mess was served at twelve.*

Tiene un rancho muy grande. *He has a big ranch.*

rango *m. rank; position.*

ranura *f. slot, groove.*

RAPIDAMENTE *rapidly.*

rapidez *f. rapidity, swiftness.*

RAPIDO *adj. rapid; fast; swift; quick; m. express train.*

Fué una opercaión rápida. *It was a swift move.*

¿Es este tren rápido? *Is this an express train?*

Será mejor que tomemos el rápido. *It would be better if we took the express.*

rapiña *f. robbery, plundering.*

raptar *to abduct, to kidnap.*

rapto *m. kidnapping, abduction.*

raqueta *f. racket (tennis).*

raramente *seldom.*

Raramente vamos a su casa. *We rarely go to his house.*

rareza *f. rarity; queer habit, queer way.*

Ese chico tiene muchas rarezas. *That boy has many queer habits.*

RARO *adj. rare; unusual; odd, queer, strange.*

Es muy raro que haya mosquitos en esta época del año. *It's strange there should be mosquitos at this time of the year.*

Es un hombre muy raro. *He's a very queer person.*

Era raro el día que no recibía cartas. *Hardly a day would go by without her getting a letter.*

Se equivoca raras veces. *He seldom makes a mistake.*

rascacielos *m. skyscraper.*

rascar *to scratch.*

rasgadura *f. tent, tear.*

rasgar *to tear, to rend, to rip.*

rasgo *m. dash, stroke (in writing); feature, characteristic; deed, feat.*

Rasgo de pluma. *A stroke of the pen.*

Rasgo característico. *Outstanding feature.*

Un rasgo heroico. *A heroic action.*

A grandes rasgos. *In bold strokes. Broadly. In outline.*

rasguño *m. scratch.*

raso *adj. clear; flat; plain; m. satin.*

Cielo raso. *Ceiling.*

Un soldado raso. *Private. Buck private.*

Pasamos la noche al raso. *We spent the night in the open air.*

raspador *m. scraper; eraser.*

raspar *to scrape; to rasp; to erase.*

rastrillo *m. rake; hackle.*

rastro *m. track; trail; trace, sign; harrow, rake; slaughterhouse (Amer.); a junkyard (Madrid).*

Ni encontrar rastro de. *Not to find any trace of.*

rata *f. rat.*

ratero *m. petty thief; pickpocket.*

ratificación *f. ratification.*

ratificar *to ratify, to sanction.*

RATO *m. little while, short time.*

¿No quiere Ud. descansar un rato? *Won't you take a little rest? Don't you want to rest awhile?*

Salió hace un rato. *He left for a little while ago.*

Lo haré a ratos perdidos. *I'll do it in my spare time.*

ratón *m. mouse.*

ratonera *f. mousetrap.*

raya *f. dash; stripe, line; part (hair).*

Prefiero esa camisa de rayas. *I'd rather have that striped shirt.*

Tener (poner) a raya. *To hold at bay (at a distance). To keep within limits.*

rayado *adj. striped.*

Tela rayada. *Striped material (cloth).*

rayar *to draw lines; to rule (paper); to dawn.*

Al rayar el alba. *At daybreak.*

rayo *m. ray, beam; spoke (of wheel); thunderbolt; flash of lightning.*

Rayo de sol. *Sunbeam.*

Rayos X. *X-rays.*

raza *f. race (of people, animals, etc.).*

RAZON *f. reason; cause; rate; right.*

Tener razón. *To be right.*

No tener razón. *To be wrong.*

Tiene Ud. razón. *You're right.*

No tiene razón. *He's wrong.*

No tener razón de ser. *To be without foundation. To have no raison d'être.*

Atender a razones. *To listen to reason.*

Por razones. *For reasons.*

A razón de. *At the rate of.*

Ponerse en razón. *To be reasonable.*

Dar razón de. *To give an account of. To account for. To give information about.*

Dar la razón. *To agree with.*

En razón a. *Concerning. As regards. In regard to.*

Perder la razón. *To lose one's reason.*

Razón social. *Firm. Name of a concern. Firm name.*

Aquí no hay quien dé razón. *There's no one here to give any information.*

¡Con razón! *I can see it now!*

razonable *adj. reasonable, fair.*

razonamiento *m. reasoning.*

razonar *to reason; to argue.*

re *m. D, re (musical note).*

reacción *f. reaction.*

reaccionar *to react.*

Reaccionó violentamente al oír esas palabras.

He reacted violently when he heard that ("those words").

reaccionario adj. reactionary.

reacio adj. obstinate, stubborn.

REAL adj. real, actual; royal; m. a silver coin.

realidad f. reality; truth.

En realidad. In reality. Really. Actually.

realismo m. realism.

realizar to realize, to sell out; to accomplish, to fulfill; to materialize.

realmente in reality, really, actually.

reanudar to renew; to resume.

Reanudar un negocio. To resume a business.

reaparecer to reappear.

rebaja f. reduction; deduction; abatement, diminution.

¿Puede Ud. hacerme una rebaja en el precio? Can you let me have it cheaper?

rebajar to reduce; to lower; to diminish.

Han rebajado un poco los precios. They've reduced the prices a little.

rebajarse to lower oneself.

rebanada f. a slice of bread.

rebanar to slice.

rebaño m. flock, herd of cattle.

rebatir to repel; to refute.

rebelarse to rebel, to revolt.

rebelde adj. hard to manage, rebellious; stubborn; m. rebel.

rebelión f. rebellion.

rebosar to muffle up; to dip into batter; to overflow.

rebotar to bounce, to rebound.

rebuscar to search; to glean.

recado m. message; gift; compliment; daily marketing; errand.

Lo mandaron a un recado. They sent him on an errand.

¿Tiene Ud. algún recado para mí? Have you a message for me?

recaer to fall back; to relapse; to devolve.

Recayó a los pocos días de haberse levantado. He had a relapse a few days after he got up (got out of bed).

recaída f. relapse.

recalcar to emphasize, to stress.

recalentar to heat again; to overheat.

recámara f. dressing room; breech (of a gun).

recapacitar to think over, to recollect, to recall.

recargado adj. overloaded; strong; heavy. ·

recargar to overcharge; to overload; to make an additional charge; to increase (a sentence).

recargo m. overload; extra charge; overcharge; additional tax; new charge or accusation; increase (of sentence).

recatado adj. circumspect, prudent, cautious.

recatarse to act carefully, to be cautious.

recaudación f. collection (of rent, taxes, etc.); collector's office.

recaudar to collect (rent or taxes).

recelar to suspect, to distrust.

recelo m. misgiving, suspicion, mistrust.

receloso adj. suspicious, apprehensive.

recepción f. reception.

receptor m. receiver.

Descuelgue el receptor. Pick up the receiver.

Cuelgue el receptor. Hang up the receiver.

receta f. prescription; recipe.

¿Puede Ud. prepararme esta receta? Can you fill this prescription for me?

Receta de cocina. Recipe.

recetar to prescribe a medicine.

RECIBIR to receive; to accept.

Recibí hoy una carta de mi hermano. I received a letter from my brother today.

recibirse to graduate (as a doctor, lawyer, etc.).

recibo m. receipt.

Acusar recibo. To acknowledge receipt.

recién (used immediately before past participles) recently; lately.

Recién casado. Newly wed.

El recién llegado. The newcomer.

RECIENTE adj. recent, new, fresh; modern.

Un acontecimiento reciente. A recent event.

RECIENTEMENTE recently.

Falleció recientemente. He died recently.

recinto m. precinct; inclosure; place.

recio adj. strong, vigorous; loud (voice); coarse, thick; severe (weather).

Hombre de recia constitución. A man of strong constitution.

Hablar recio. To talk in a loud voice.

De recio. Strongly. Violently.

recipiente adj. receiving; m. container.

reciprocar to reciprocate.

recíproco adj. reciprocal, mutual.

A la recíproca. Reciprocally.

Deben Uds. ayudarse recíprocamente. You should help each other.

reclamación f. reclamation; complaint.

reclamante m. and f. claimant.

reclamar to reclaim, to claim.

reclamo m. advertisement; decoy bird; claim.

recluir to shut up, to confine.

recluso adj. imprisoned; m. recluse; convict.

recluta f. recruiting; m. recruit.

reclutar to recruit.

recobrar to recover; to regain.

Recobrar la salud. To regain one's health.

RECOGER to pick up; to call for someone; to gather; to collect; to shelter.

Recoja Ud. eso que se le ha caído. Pick up what you dropped.

Puedes venir a recogerme a las seis. You can come to pick me up at six o'clock.

recogerse to retire, to go home, to take a rest.

Se recoge temprano. He goes to bed early.

recolección f. gathering; compilation; harvest; sum-

mary.
recolectar to gather, to harvest.
recomendable adj. recommendable.
recomendación f. recommendation; praise.
    Carta de recomendación. Letter of introduction. Letter of recommendation.
RECOMENDAR to recommend; to commend; to advise.
    La persona a quien me recomendó Ud. me ha prometido un empleo. The person you recommended me to has promised me a job.
    Le recomiendo a Ud. que lo haga de prisa. I advise you to do it quickly.
recompensa f. reward, compensation.
    En recompensa. In return.
recompensar to recompense, to reward, to make up for.
reconciliación f. reconciliation, bringing together again.
reconciliar to reconcile, to make friends again.
RECONOCER to recognize; to admit; to inspect, to reconnoiter; to consider; to appreciate.
    ¿Reconoce Ud. esta letra? Do you recognize this handwriting?
    Fué necesario reconocer todo el equipaje. All the baggage had to be inspected.
    Le estoy muy reconocido por sus atenciones. I'm grateful to you for your attention.
reconocimiento m. recognition, acknowledgment; appreciation, gratitude; reconnoitering, reconnaissance.
reconstituyente m. tonic (medicine).
reconstrucción f. reconstruction.
reconstruir to reconstruct, to rebuild.
recopilar to compile, to collect.
record m. record (sports, etc.).
    Batir el record. To break the record.
recordar to remind.
    No puedo recordar su apellido. I don't recall his name.
    Se lo recordaré. I'll remind you of it.
recordatorio m. reminder.
recorrer to travel over; to go over; to look over.
    Ayer recorrimos diez millas. Yesterday we covered ten miles.
    Esta mañana recorrimos casi todas las tiendas. This morning we went to nearly all the stores.
recorrido m. distance traveled; run, way, line.
    ¿Es éste el final del recorrido? Is this the end of the line (streetcar, bus, etc.)?
recortar to cut, to trim, to clip; to shorten.
recorte m. clipping; outline; pl. cuttings, trimmings.
    Le envié un recorte del periódico. I sent him a newspaper clipping.
recostar to lean against.
recostarse to lean back, to recline.
recreación f. recreation, diversion, amusement.
recrear to entertain, to amuse, to delight.

recrearse to have a little distraction, to have a good time.
recreo m. recreation, diversion, amusement.
rectángulo m. rectangle.
rectificar to rectify; to correct.
rectitud f. rectitude, straight-forwardness, honesty.
RECTO adj. straight; just, upright; erect.
    Trace una linea recta. Draw a straight line.
    Era un hombre recto. He was a very upright man.
rector m. rector, the head of a college or university.
recuento m. checking, recount, inventory.
recuerdo m. recollection; memory; souvenir.
    Este pañuelo es un recuerdo. This handkerchief is a souvenir.
    Déle recuerdos de mi parte. Remember me to him. Give him my regards.
recuperar to recuperate, to recover.
recurrir to recur, to appeal; to resort to, to turn to.
    Tuvimos que recurrir a su ayuda. We had to turn to him for help.
recurso m. recourse; appeal; resource; pl. means.
    Sin recursos. Without means.
rechazar to repulse, to reject, to refuse.
red f. net; network; trap, snare.
    Los pescadores tendieron la red. The fishermen spread out the net.
    Cayó en las redes que le tendieron. He fell into the trap they set for him.
    Red ferroviaria. Railroad system.
redacción f. wording; editing.
redactar to edit; to word, to write.
    Redactar una carta. To word a letter.
    El manuscrito estaba bien redactado. The manuscript was well written.
redactor m. editor.
rededor m. surroundings.
    Al rededor. Around. Roundabout.
    Al rededor de. Around. About. More or less. Nearly.
redención f. redemption; recovery.
redimir to redeem, to recover, to buy back.
rédito m. interest; revenue, yield of invested capital.
redoblar to double, to redouble; to clinch (a nail); to roll (a drum); to toll (bells).
redonda f. neighborhood; semibreve (music).
    Tres millas a la redonda. Three miles around.
    A la redonda. Roundabout.
REDONDO adj. round.
    La mesa es redonda. The table is round.
    En números redondos. In round numbers.
    Boleto de viaje redondo (Mex.). Round-trip ticket.
reducción f. reduction, decrease.
REDUCIR to reduce; to cut down; to make smaller; to subdue.

De hoy en adelante reduciré mis gastos. *From now on I'll cut down on my expenses.*

Todo se redujo a nada. *It didn't amount to anything.*

Reducir la marcha. *To slow down.*

Reducir a polvo. *To pulverize.*

redundancia *f. redundance.*

redundante *adj. redundant.*

redundar *to redound, to turn to, to result.*

Redundará todo en nuestro beneficio. *Everything will turn out to be to our advantage.*

reelección *f. re-election.*

reelegir *to re-elect.*

reembolsar *to get one's money back, to get a refund.*

reembolso *m. refund.*

reemplazar *to replace; to restore.*

reemplazo *m. replacement; substitution.*

reexpedir *to forward.*

Tenga la bondad de reexpedir mi correspondencia a esta dirección. *Please forward my mail to this address.*

referencia *f. reference; account, report.*

¿Quién puede dar referencia de Ud.? *Who(m) can you give as reference?*

El asunto de referencia. *The matter in question.*

referente *adj. referring, relating.*

REFERIR *to refer; to relate; to report.*

referirse *to refer to.*

¿A qué se refiere Ud.? *What are you referring to?*

refinado *adj. refined; polished.*

refinería *f. refinery.*

reflector *adj. reflecting; m. searchlight.*

reflejar *to reflect.*

Eso refleja su carácter. *That reflects his character.*

reflejo *m. reflex; glare.*

Es un fiel reflejo de la verdad. *It's an exact account. This is the (plain) truth. ("It's an exact reflection of the truth.")*

reflexión *f. reflection; thinking something over carefully.*

reflexionar *to think over, to think carefully, to meditate; to reflect.*

Reflexiónelo bien. *Think it over carefully.*

Tengo que reflexionar sobre eso. *I have to think about that. I have to think that over.*

reflexivo *adj. reflexive.*

reforma *f. reform; reformation; alteration.*

Cerrado por reformas. *Closed for alterations (repairs).*

reformar *to reform; to correct; to alter.*

Hay que reformar esta americana. *This coat has to be altered.*

reformatorio *adj. reforming; m. reformatory.*

reforzar *to reinforce; to strengthen.*

refrán *m. proverb, saying.*

refrenar *to curb, to restrain, to refrain.*

refrendar *to legalize; to countersign, to authenticate.*

refrescar *to refresh; to cool; to brush up.*

refresco *m. refreshment; cold drink.*

refriega *f. fray, skirmish, strife.*

refrigerador *adj. refrigerating; m. refrigerator.*

refrigerar *to refrigerate, to cool.*

refuerzo *m. reinforcement.*

refugiado *adj. and n. refugee.*

refugiar *to shelter.*

refugiarse *to take shelter (refuge).*

refugio *m. refuge, shelter, haven.*

refunfuñar *to growl, to grumble.*

No refunfuñe tanto. *Don't grumble so much.*

regadera *f. sprinkler; watering pot.*

regalado *adj. free, given away for nothing; cheap; easy.*

Hace una vida muy regalada. *He leads an easy life.*

regalar *to make a gift; to entertain; to treat; to caress.*

Le regalaré este libro. *I'll make him a present of this book. I'll give him this book as a gift.*

Es muy amigo de regalarse. *He's very fond of good living.*

REGALO *m. gift, present; comfort, good living.*

Ese regalo es para Ud. *This present is for you.*

Recibió un bonito regalo. *He received a nice gift.*

Vivía con mucho regalo. *He lived in luxury.*

regañar *to scold; to quarrel; to growl.*

La regañaron por llegar tarde. *They scolded her for being late.*

Ese hombre se pasa la vida regañando. *That man is always quarreling.*

regaño *m. reprimand, scolding.*

regañón *adj. and n. growling; growler; a scolding person.*

regar *to water, to irrigate.*

regata *f. boat race, regatta.*

regatear *to bargain, to haggle; to stint; to dodge, to evade.*

regateo *m. haggling.*

regeneración *f. regeneration.*

regenerar *to regenerate.*

regente *m. regent; foreman (printing press); registered pharmacist.*

régimen *m. regime; diet.*

El médico me ha puesto a régimen. *The doctor has put me on a diet.*

El país cambió de régimen. *The country changed its government. The country has a new regime.*

regimiento *m. regiment.*

regio *adj. royal, regal; splendid, magnificent.*

región *f. region.*

regional *adj. regional, local.*

REGIR *to rule, to govern; to go by; to prevail; to be in force (law, etc.).*

Regía los destinos del pueblo. *He governed ("ruled the destinies of") the people.*

¿Por qué método se rige Ud.? *What method (system) do you use? What rules do you go by?*

Aún rige ese decreto. *That decree is still in effect.*

Los precios que rigen. *The prevailing prices.*

registrar *to inspect, to examine; to search; to register, to put on record.*

Es preciso registrarse en el Consulado. *You have to register at the Consulate.*

En este libro se registran las compras y ventas. *Purchases and sales are entered in this book.*

La policía registró su casa. *The police searched his house.*

¿Dónde registrarán el equipaje? *Where will they examine the baggage?*

registro *m. inspection; search; record, register.*

Firme en el libro de registro. *Sign the register.*

REGLA *f. ruler; rule; principle.*

¿Puede dejarme la regla? *Can you let me have the ruler?*

¿Tiene Ud. el pasaporte en regla? *Is your passport in order?*

Todo está en regla. *Everything is in order.*

Estas son las reglas del juego. *These are the rules of the game.*

Por regla general. *As a general rule.*

reglamentario *adj. according to regulations; usual, customary.*

reglamento *m. rules and regulations, by-laws.*

regocijar *to make glad (happy).*

regocijarse *to rejoice, to be glad.*

Se regocijó mucho por la noticia. *The news made him very glad. He was very happy at the news.*

regocijo *m. rejoicing, pleasure.*

REGRESAR *to return, to go or come back.*

Regresará por Navidad. *He'll come back for Christmas.*

Regresaré a España en junio. *I'll go back to Spain in June.*

regreso *m. return, coming back.*

En nuestro viaje de regreso. *On our voyage back. On our return voyage.*

A mi regreso. *On my return.*

REGULAR *to regulate; to adjust; adj. regular, ordinary; fair, moderate; medium in size, quality, grade, etc.*

Regular el tráfico. *To regulate traffic.*

Estoy regular. *I'm so, so. Can't complain!*

Disfrutaba de un salario regular. *He received a moderate salary.*

De tamaño regular. *Of medium size.*

Por lo regular le veía todos los días. *Ordinarily I used to see him every day.*

regularmente *regularly.*

rehabilitación *f. rehabilitation.*

rehabilitar *to rehabilitate; to restore.*

rehacer *to make over; to refit.*

rehacerse *to recover, to regain strength; to rally (military).*

rehuir *to withdraw; to shun, to avoid; to refuse.*

Siempre rehuye verme. *He always avoids me.*

rehusar *to refuse; to reject.*

Rehusó la invitación. *He refused the invitation.*

reimprimir *to reprint.*

reina *f. queen.*

reinado *m. reign.*

reinar *to reign; to predominate, to prevail, to exist.*

La reina Victoria reinó durante sesenta años. *Queen Victoria reigned sixty years.*

Reina un malestar general. *There's a general unrest.*

reincidir *to relapse, to fall back into a former state or way of acting, to backslide.*

reino *m. kingdom, reign.*

reintegrar *to restore; to refund.*

Hay que reintegrar la suma. *We have to make good (replace) the sum.*

Le reintegrarán el importe. *They'll refund your money.*

reintegrarse *to recuperate; to return.*

Reintegrarse al trabajo. *To return to work.*

reintegro *m. restitution; refund.*

REÍR *to laugh.*

Se echó a reír. *He burst out laughing.*

Reír a carcajadas. *To laugh uproariously. To laugh out loud.*

reírse *to scoff, to make fun, to laugh.*

¿Por qué se ríe de él? *Why are you laughing at him?*

Se ríe por nada. *The least little thing makes him laugh. ("He laughs over nothing.")*

Reírse entre sí. *To laugh up one's sleeve.*

reiterar *to reiterate.*

reja *f. plowshare; grate; railing, iron fence; iron bars.*

rejuvenecer *to rejuvenate.*

RELACIÓN *f. relation, connection; report, account; pl. connections; relations.*

No hay relación entre estas dos cosas. *There's no relation (connection) between these two things.*

Hizo una relación del suceso. *He gave an account of what happened.*

Tiene muy buenas relaciones. *He has very good connections.*

Relaciones diplomáticas. *Diplomatic relations.*

relacionado *adj. acquainted, related, well-connected.*

Está muy bien relacionado. *He has very good connections.*

relacionar *to relate; to connect; to be acquainted.*

Estamos relacionados con la firma. *We do business (have dealings) with the firm.*

relacionarse *to associate oneself with, to get ac-*

quainted, to make connections.
Se relaciona mucho con artistas y escritores.
He associates a lot with artists and writers.
Cuanto se relaciona con. *Everything which relates to.*
Entiende todo cuanto se relaciona con la
mecánica. *He understands everything that has to do with mechanics.*

relámpago m. *lightning.*

relampaguear *to lighten (lightning).*
Relampaguea (Está relampagueando). *It's lightning.*

relatar *to relate, tell.*

relativo adj. *relative.*
Relativo a. *With regard to. With reference to.*

relato m. *account, statement; story.*
Hizo un relato de lo que ocurrió. *He gave an account of what had happened.*

releer *to read over again.*

relieve m. *relief.*

religión f. *religion.*

religioso adj. *religious.*

RELOJ m. *clock, watch.*
Reloj de bolsillo. *Pocket watch.*
Reloj de pulsera. *Wristwatch.*
Reloj de pared. *Clock.*

relojero m. *watchmaker.*

relucir *to shine, to sparkle, to glitter; to excel, to be brilliant.*
Sacó a relucir aquella vieja cuestión. *He brought up that old question (problem) again.*

relumbrar *to shine, to sparkle, to glisten.*

rellenar *to refill; to stuff; to pad.*

relleno adj. *stuffed; filled;* m. *stuffing.*
Pimientos rellenos. *Stuffed peppers.*

remar *to row, to paddle.*

rematar *to complete, to put the finishing touches on; to sell at auction.*

remate m. *end, conclusion; auction.*
De remate. *Utterly, Irremediably.*
Por remate. *Finally.*

remedar *to imitate; to mimic.*

remediar *to remedy; to make good; to help; to avoid.*
No lo puedo remediar. *I can't help it. I can't do anything about it.*
Eso se puede remediar. *That can be remedied.*
Lo que no se puede remediar, se ha de aguantar. *What cannot be cured must be endured.*

REMEDIO m. *remedy; medicine; redress; resource, resort.*
¿Sabe Ud. de algún remedio contra el mareo? *Do you know of any medicine for seasickness?*
Esto no tiene remedio. *There's no remedy for this. This can't be helped. This is hopeless.*
No tuvo más remedio que aceptarlo. *He had no alternative but to accept it. There was*

nothing he could do—he had to accept it.
¡No hay más remedio! *There's nothing else to do. Nothing (else) can be done!*
Sin remedio. *Inevitable. Nothing can be done about it.*
Es un caso sin remedio. *It's a hopeless case.*

remendar *to mend, to patch; to darn.*

remesa f. *remittance; shipment.*

remiendo m. *patch; repair.*

remitente adj. *remittent;* m. and f. *sender, shipper, dispatcher.*

REMITIR *to remit; to send, to forward, to ship.*
Me hace el favor de remitir mis cartas a estas señas. *Please forward my mail ("letters") to this address.*
Le remitimos los géneros. *We sent you the goods.*

remo m. *oar.*

remojar *to soak, to steep, to dip.*

remojo m. *soaking, steeping.*
Ponga las judías en remojo. *Let the beans soak.*

remolcador m. *tugboat; lighter.*

remolcar *to tow; to haul.*

remolino m. *whirlpool; whirlwind; cowlick.*

remolque m. *towing; towline.*
Llevar a remolque. *To tow.*

remontar *to remount; to repair saddles.*

remontarse *to soar, to fly upward, to fly at a great height; to date back.*
Remontarse a. *To date back to.*

remorder *to feel remorse.*
Le remuerde la conciencia. *His conscience is bothering him. He has a guilty conscience.*

remordimiento m. *remorse.*

remover *to remove; to stir; to dismiss.*

remuneración f. *remuneration; reward.*

remunerar *to remunerate, to reward.*

renacer *to be reborn; to grow again.*

rencilla f. *quarrel; grudge.*

rencor m. *rancor, grudge.*
No le guardo ningún rencor. *I don't bear him any grudge.*

rencoroso adj. *resentful, spiteful.*

rendición f. *rendering; surrendering.*

rendido adj. *tired, worn-out, exhausted, overcome.*
Estoy rendido, no puedo andar más. *I'm exhausted. I can't walk any further.*

rendija f. *slit, crevice, crack.*

rendir *to subdue; to surrender; to produce, to yield; to tire out.*
Este negocio rinde poco. *This business is not very profitable.*

rendirse *to give up, to surrender; to be tired.*
Está por rendirse. *He's about to give up.*
Rendirse incondicionalmente. *To surrender unconditionally.*

renegado m. *renegade.*

renglón m. *line (written or printed).*

Le pondré unos renglones. *I'll drop him a few lines.*

Fijese en el tercer renglón. *Look at the third line.*

Leer entre renglones. *To read between the lines.*

A renglón seguido. *Then. Immediately afterwards.*

renombre m. *renown, fame; surname, family name.*

renovación f. *renovation; renewal.*

renovar *to renovate; to renew; to reform, to transform.*

renta f. *rent, income; profit; rental; revenue, annuity.*

Vive de sus rentas. *He lives on his income.*

renuncia f. *resignation; renunciation, giving up; waiving.*

Presentó su renuncia. *He turned in his resignation.*

renunciar *to renounce, to resign; to waive; to drop (a claim); to refuse.*

Renunciaré a mi empleo. *I'll resign my position.*

Renunciar un derecho. *To give up a right.*

Renunció el ofrecimiento. *He refused (declined) that offer.*

reñir *to quarrel, to fight; to scold.*

Ha reñido con sus suegros. *She quarreled with her in-laws.*

No le riñas al niño. *Don't scold the child.*

reo m. *criminal; defendant.*

reojo m. *(look) askance.*

Mirar de reojo. *To look askance. To look out of the corner of one's eye.*

reorganización f. *reorganization.*

reorganizar *to reorganize.*

reparable adj. *reparable, remediable.*

reparación f. *reparation, repair; amends; satisfaction.*

REPARAR *to repair; to notice; to make up for.*

Hay que reparar la radio. *Our radio needs to be fixed.*

¿Dónde me podrán reparar esto? *Where can I get this repaired (fixed)?*

¿Reparó Ud. en su acento cubano? *Did you notice his Cuban accent?*

reparo m. *remark, hint; consideration; objection; parry (fencing).*

Poner reparo. *To object. To raise an objection.*

Sin ningún reparo. *Without any consideration.*

repartición f. *distribution; partition.*

Repartición de premios. *Distribution of prizes.*

repartidor m. *distributor, delivery-man.*

repartir *to distribute; to divide; to deliver (the mail).*

Se repartieron las ganancias. *They divided the profits between (among) themselves.*

Reparten el correo a eso de las ocho. *The mail is delivered at about eight o'clock.*

reparto m. *distribution; delivery; cast (in a play).*

¿A qué hora se hace el reparto? *At what time is the mail delivered?*

repasar *to check, to look over; to go over; to mend (clothes).*

Repase Ud. esa cuenta detenidamente. *Check that account carefully.*

Repasar la lección. *To go over one's lessons.*

Está repasando la ropa. *She's mending the clothes.*

repaso m. *review (of a lesson); revision.*

repatriar *to repatriate.*

REPENTE m. *sudden movement.*

Tuvo un repente de ira. *She had a fit of temper.*

De repente. *Suddenly. All of a sudden.*

De repente se apagaron todas las luces. *All of a sudden the lights went out.*

repentino adj. *sudden.*

Murió de muerte repentina. *He died suddenly. His death was sudden.*

repercusión f. *repercussion; reaction.*

repercutir *to have a repercussion; to echo, to reverberate.*

Eso repercutirá en la situación. *That will have an effect on the situation.*

repetición f. *repetition, encore.*

El informe estaba lleno de repeticiones. *The report was full of repetitions.*

El público entusiasmando pidió la repetición. *The enthusiastic audience called for an encore.*

REPETIR *to repeat; to have a second helping.*

Haga el favor de repetir lo que dijo. *Please repeat what you said.*

¿Puedo repetir de este plato? *May I have a second helping?*

repisa f. *bracket; shelf.*

REPLETO adj. *full, replete.*

El autobús está repleto. *The bus is full.*

Tiene la cartera repleta de billetes. *His wallet is full of bills.*

La tienda está repleta de mercadería. *The store is well stocked ("is full of merchandise").*

réplica f. *reply, answer.*

Su réplica fué acertadísima. *His reply was very much to the point.*

replicar *to reply; to retort, to talk back.*

¡No me repliques! *Don't answer back! Don't talk back to me!*

reponer *to replace; to restore.*

Repuso los fondos. *He replaced the funds.*

reponerse *to recover; to retrieve.*

No podrá reponerse. *She can't possibly recover.*

Ya me he repuesto de mis pérdidas. *I have already retrieved my losses.*

reporter, reportero m. *reporter.*

reposar *to rest; to lie down.*
  Está reposando. *She's resting.*
  Reposar la comida. *To rest after eating. To take a nap after lunch (dinner).*
reposarse *to settle (liquids).*
  Deja que se repose el café. *Let the coffee settle.*
reposo *m. rest.*
  Después de un reposo se sentirá mejor. *You'll feel better after a short rest.*
repostería *f. confectioner's, pastry shop; pantry.*
reprender *to reprimand, to reprehend.*
represión *f. reproof, reproach, reprimand.*
representación *f. representation; play, performance.*
  ¿A qué hora empieza la representación? *When does the performance (play) begin?*
  Ostentó la representación de su país en Rusia. *He went to Russia as his country's representative.*
representante *adj. representing; m. and f. representative, agent.*
representar *to represent; to stage, to play on the stage.*
  ¿Qué casa representa Ud.? *Which firm do you represent?*
  No representa su edad. *She doesn't look her age.*
reprimir *to repress, to check, to hold in check.*
  No me pude reprimir por más tiempo. *I couldn't contain myself any longer.*
reprobación *f. reprobation.*
reprobar *to reprove, to condemn, to find fault with.*
reprochar *to reproach; to upbraid.*
reproducción *f. reproduction.*
reproducir *to reproduce.*
reproducirse *to recur.*
reptil *m. reptile.*
república *f. republic.*
republicano *adj. and n. republican.*
repudiar *to repudiate; to disown.*
repuesto *adj. recovered; m. provisions, supply set apart; sideboard; pl. spare parts.*
  De repuesto. *Spare. Extra.*
  Envíeme Ud. algunas piezas de repuesto. *Send me some spare parts.*
  Repuestos. *Spare parts.*
repugnante *adj. repugnant, distasteful.*
repugnar *to be distasteful, to be repugnant; to detest; to act with reluctance.*
  Me repugna. *I detest it. It's repugnant to me.*
repulsión *f. repulsion; aversion.*
repulsivo *adj. repulsive, repelling.*
reputación *f. reputation, name.*
  Gozar de buena reputación. *To have a good name.*
requerimiento *m. request; summons.*
requerir *to summon; to notify; to require.*
  Eso requiere mucha atención. *That requires a lot of attention.*
requisito *m. requisite, requirement.*
  Llenar los requisitos. *To meet the requirements.*
res *f. steer, cow, bull (Amer.).*
  Carne de res. *Beef.*
resaltar *to rebound; to stand out; to be conspicuous.*
  Hacer resaltar. *To emphasize. To call attention to.*
  Resaltar a la vista. *To be self-evident. To be very obvious. To stare one in the face.*
resbaladizo *adj. slippery.*
resbalar *to slip, to slide.*
resbalarse *to slip.*
  Cuidado con resbalarse. *Watch out you don't slip.*
resbalón *m. slip, slipping.*
resbaloso *adj. slippery.*
  La acera está resbalosa. *The sidewalk is slippery.*
rescatar *to ransom; to redeem.*
rescate *m. ransom.*
resentirse *to begin to give way, to fail; to feel the effects of; to resent, to be offended, to feel hurt, to show displeasure; to hurt.*
  Está resentida. *She's resentful. She feels hurt.*
  Resentirse por nada. *To become offended over trifles. To take offense at unimportant things.*
  Se resiente del trabajo pesado que hace. *He's beginning to feel the effects of the hard work he's doing.*
  Tengo el cuerpo resentido. *My body aches all over.*
reseña *f. sketch; brief account.*
reseñar *to outline, to give a brief account.*
reserva *f. reserve; reservation; caution; secret.*
  Se lo digo a Ud. en reserva. *I'm telling you this in confidence.*
  Con la mayor reserva. *In strict(est) confidence.*
  Está en la reserva. *He is in the reserve (Army or Navy).*
  Reserva mental. *Mental reservation.*
  Sin reserva. *Without reservation. Unreservedly. Openly.*
  De reserva. *Extra. In reserve.*
  Tengo una reserva en el banco. *I have some money put away in the bank.*
reservadamente *secretly, confidentially.*
reservado *adj. reserved; cautious; confidential.*
  Es muy reservado. *He's very reserved.*
reservar *to reserve; to save; to keep; to conceal.*
  Queremos que nos reserve un asiento de Pullman. *We want a Pullman reservation.*
  Le reservó su habitación hasta su regreso. *He reserved the room for him until his return.*
  El Club se reserva el derecho de admisión. *The Club reserves the right of admission.*
  Reserve algún dinero para el viaje. *Save some money for the trip.*

Se reservaron una parte de las ganancias. *They kept a share of the profits.*

reservarse *to preserve oneself; to bide one's time; to be cautious.*

resfriado m. *a cold.*

He cogido un resfriado. *I've caught a cold.*

resfriar *to cool; to cool off.*

resfriarse *to catch a cold.*

Se resfrió anoche. *He caught a cold last night.*

El niño va a resfriarse. *The boy is going to catch a cold.*

resfrío m. *a cold.*

Tengo un fuerte resfrío. *I have a bad cold.*

resguardar *to reserve, to keep safe, to protect.*

resguardarse *to take care of oneself; to be on one's guard; to take shelter.*

resguardo m. *voucher; security; safekeeping; guard; customs official.*

Poner a resguardo de. *To keep safe. To preserve from.*

residencia f. *residence.*

residente *adj. residing; resident;* m. *resident, inhabitant.*

residir *to reside, to live.*

¿En dónde reside su familia actualmente? *Where does your family live at present?*

residuo m. *residue, remainder.*

resignación f. *resignation, patience, state of being resigned.*

resignarse *to be resigned, to resign oneself to.*

resistencia f. *resistance.*

resistente *adj. resistant, strong.*

resistir *to resist, to hold out, to withstand, to endure.*

Resistir la tentación. *To resist temptation.*

Resistir un ataque. *To resist (withstand) an attack.*

Ha resistido la prueba. *It stood the test.*

Esto ya no se puede resistir. *This can't be tolerated any longer.*

resistirse *to offer resistance; to refuse.*

Se resistió a hacerlo. *He refused to do it.*

resolución f. *resolution, determination, decision; solution.*

Tenemos que tomar una resolución. *We must come to some decision.*

resoluto *adj. resolute.*

resolver *to resolve, to determine, to decide; to solve; to dissolve; to settle.*

Estoy resuelto a hacerlo yo mismo. *I'm determined to do it myself.*

Este problema es difícil de resolver. *This problem is hard to solve.*

Puede ser que haya resuelto hacerlo. *It may be that he has decided to do it.*

Es necesario resolver este asunto con toda urgencia. *It's necessary to settle this affair immediately.*

resolverse *to resolve, to make up one's mind, to reach a decision.*

No se resuelve a tomar una decisión. *He couldn't bring himself to the point of making a decision. He couldn't make up his mind.*

resonancia f. *resonance.*

resonante *adj. resonant, resounding.*

resonar *to resound.*

resorte m. *spring (metal); pl. means, resources.*

respaldo m. *back (of a seat); back, reverse (of a sheet of paper); endorsement.*

Al respaldo. *On the back of.*

respectivamente *respectively.*

respectivo *adj. respective.*

RESPECTO m. *relation, respect, reference.*

Con respecto a. *With regards to.*

Al respecto. *Relative to.*

A este respecto. *In regard to this.*

Por todos respectos. *By all means.*

respetable *adj. respectable, honorable.*

respetar *to respect, to honor.*

RESPETO m. *respect, regard, consideration.*

Mis respetos a su señor padre. *My best regards to your father.*

Perder el respeto. *To lose respect for.*

Faltar al respeto. *To be disrespectful.*

Por respeto a. *Out of consideration for.*

Pieza de respeto. *Spare part.*

respetuoso *adj. respectful, polite.*

respiración f. *respiration; breathing.*

Le faltó la respiración. *He was out of breath.*

respirar *to breathe.*

Respire Ud. fuerte. *Breathe deeply.*

Déjeme Ud. respirar. *Give me a chance to get my breath.*

Con aquel dinero pudo respirar un mes más. *With that money he could get by for another month.*

respiro m. *respite, time of relief.*

resplandor m. *splendor; glare.*

RESPONDER *to answer; to respond; to talk back; to correspond; to be responsible.*

Ni siquiera me respondió. *He didn't even answer me.*

Ese niño siempre responde a sus padres. *That child always talks back to his parents.*

¿Y qué responde Ud. a esto? *And what do you say to that?*

Ha respondido muy bien al tratamiento. *He responded to the treatment very well.*

Respondo de las consecuencias. *I'll answer for the consequences.*

¿Hay alguien que responda por él? *Is there anyone who will stand up for him?*

respondón *adj. saucy, fresh;* m. *a person who is always answering back.*

responsabilidad f. *responsibility.*

responsable *adj. responsible, liable.*

RESPUESTA f. answer, reply; retort; response.

¿Cuál es su respuesta? What is your answer?

Respuesta favorable. Favorable answer.

Respuesta pagada. Reply prepaid.

resquebrajar to crack, to split.

resta f. subtraction; remainder.

restablecer to re-establish; to restore.

restablecerse to recover.

Restablecerse de una enfermedad. To recover from an illness.

restante adj. remaining; m. remainder.

Hay muchas cosas restantes. There are many things left over (remaining).

restar to subtract; to deduct; to remain; to be left.

Resta dos de cinco. Subtract two from five.

Me restan cinco pesos. I have five pesos left.

No nos resta más que marcharnos. There's nothing left for us to do but leave.

Restan muchas cosas por hacer. Many things remain to be done.

restauración f. restoration.

RESTAURANT, RESTAURANTE m. restaurant.

restaurar to restore; to recover.

restitución f. restitution.

restituir to restore.

Le restituyeron sus propiedades. His property was restored to him.

RESTO m. rest, remainder, residue; pl. remains, left-overs.

Esa cocinera sabe aprovechar los restos. This cook knows how to make good use of left-overs.

Echar el resto. To stake one's all. To bet everything one has.

Le juego mi resto. I bet everything I have.

restricción f. restriction, curtailment.

restringir to restrain; to curtail; to restrict, to limit.

resucitar to resurrect; to revive; to come or bring back.

Resucitar una moda. To revive a style.

resuelto adj. resolute, daring; determined; prompt; settled, resolved.

Es un hombre muy resuelto. He's a very determined person.

Es cosa resuelta. It's a (a) settled (matter).

resulta f. result, effect, consequence.

De resultas. As a consequence. Consequently.

RESULTADO m. result; score.

¿Cuál será el resultado? What will be the result?

¿Cuál fué el resultado del partido? What was the final score of the game?

RESULTAR to result, to turn out to be.

No resultó muy bien la combinación. The combination didn't turn out to be a good one.

Si tomamos un cuarto juntos nos resultará más barato. If we take a room together, it will be cheaper for us.

Nos resultó muy caro. It was very expensive for us.

¿Qué traje le ha resultado mejor? Which suit wore better?

La película resultó muy aburrida. The picture was boring.

Resultó herido. He was wounded.

Esto no me resulta. This doesn't suit me.

resumen m. summary, summing up, recapitulation.

resumido adj. abridged.

En resumidas cuentas. In short. To make a long story short.

resumir to abridge, to cut short; to summarize, to sum up.

Resumir un discurso. To cut a speech short.

resurgimiento m. revival.

resurgir to reappear.

retaguardia f. rear guard.

retar to challenge; to reprimand.

retardar to retard; to delay.

¿Qué le ha retardado a Ud.? What made you so late?

retardo m. delay.

Eso fué la causa del retardo. That caused the delay. That was the cause of the delay.

Temo que el retardo sea fatal. I'm afraid that the delay may be fatal.

retazo m. remnant, piece (material, cloth).

retener to retain; to withhold; to hold, to keep; to remember.

Le retuvieron el sueldo aquel mes. They withheld his salary that month.

Retuvieron aquella posición una semana. They held that position for a week.

No puede retener las fechas en la cabeza. He can't remember dates. ("He can't keep dates in his head.")

retina f. retina.

retirada f. retreat, withdrawal.

El enemigo se bate en retirada. The enemy is retreating.

retirar to withdraw; to retire; to take away; to back up (printing).

Quiero retirar cien dólares. I'd like to withdraw a hundred dollars.

Retire un poco la silla para que se pueda pasar. Pull the chair aside a little so there will be room to pass.

Retire esta silla. Take this chair away.

retirarse to go away; to retire; to retreat.

Se ha retirado de los negocios. He has retired from business.

Nuestras fuerzas se retiraron. Our forces withdrew.

Se retiró a su cuarto. He went to his room.

Retírese del fuego. Get away from the fire.

Puede Ud. retirarse. You may go now.

retocar to retouch, to improve.

retoñar *to sprout, to reappear.*

retoño *m. shoot, sprout.*

retoque *m. retouching; finishing touch.*

retorcer *to twist; to contort; to distort; to retort.*

retornar *to return, to shuttle; to give back; to repay; to reciprocate.*

retorno *m. return; repayment; exchange.*

retozar *to frisk, to jump and run about playfully, to frolic.*

retractar *to retract, to withdraw.*

retractarse *to retract, to go back on one's word.*

retraer *to dissuade; to draw back.*

retraerse *to keep aloof; to shy away; to retire, to withdraw from; to live a retired life.*

retraído *aloof, solitary, not communicative, secretive.*

     Se muestra retraído. *He holds himself aloof. He holds back. He's withdrawn.*

     Es un hombre retraído. *He's not communicative.*

retraimiento *m. shyness; reserve; retreat, seclusion.*

retrasar *to retard, to delay, to be slow; to put off; to set back.*

     Hemos retrasado el viaje. *We have put off the trip.*

     Mi reloj retrasa. *My watch is slow.*

     El tren viene retrasado. *The train's late.*

retrasarse *to be late; to fall behind (in payment); to be backward.*

     Siento haberme retrasado tanto. *I'm sorry to be so late.*

     Nos hemos retrasado en los pagos. *We've fallen behind in our payments.*

retraso *m. delay.*

     Habrá un corto retraso. *There will be a short delay.*

     Con retraso. *Late.*

     El tren ha tenido retraso. *The train's late.*

retratar *to portray; to draw a portrait; to photograph, to take a picture.*

retrato *m. portrait; photograph, picture; image.*

     Es un retrato muy bien hecho. *It's a very good picture.*

     Este retrato no se parece en nada a ella. *This portrait doesn't resemble her at all.*

     Es el vivo retrato de su padre. *He's the living image of his father.*

retrete *m. toilet, washroom.*

retribución *f. retribution; reward.*

retribuir *to pay back; to remunerate.*

retroactivo *adj. retroactive.*

retroceder *to back up, to move backward; to draw back, to fall back; to recoil; to grow worse.*

     El auto retrocedió hasta quedar enfrente de la puerta. *The car backed up until it was in front of the door.*

     Retrocedió unos pasos para reunirse con nosotros. *He came back a few steps to join us.*

     No podía retroceder en su decisión. *He couldn't reverse his decision.*

retroceso *m. recoil, drawing back.*

retrógrado *adj. retrogressive.*

retrospectivo *adj. retrospective.*

reuma *m. rheumatism.*

reumatismo *m. rheumatism.*

reunión *f. reunion; meeting, assembly.*

     Habrá una reunión a las cinco. *There will be a meeting at five o'clock.*

reunir *to gather; to collect, to get (money), to bring together.*

     Es preciso que Ud. reuna el dinero hoy mismo. *You must get the money today.*

     Reunieron mucho dinero en la función de beneficencia. *They collected a lot of money at the benefit.*

     Reunió a sus amigos en una fiesta. *He brought all his friends together at a party.*

     Se han reunido todos contra él. *They've all united against him.*

reunirse *to get together; to meet; to unite; to join.*

     ¿A qué hora podríamos reunirnos? *At what time could we get together?*

     Se reunen en su casa todos los sábados. *They meet at his home every Saturday.*

revelación *f. revelation.*

revelar *to reveal, to show, to disclose; to develop (photography).*

     Revelar un secreto. *To reveal a secret.*

     El autor revela gran talento en este libro. *The author shows great talent in this book.*

     ¿Reveló Ud. ya las fotografías? *Have you developed the pictures yet?*

revendedor *m. retailer.*

revender *to retail; to resell.*

reventar *to burst, to blow up; to blow out; to break; to sprout, to blossom; to tire, to exhaust, to vex.*

     Reventar de risa. *To burst into laughter.*

     Reventó el neumático. *The tire blew out.*

     Estoy reventado de tanto caminar. *I'm exhausted from walking so much.*

     Aquel gasto me reventó. *The expense ("that expenditure") just about finished me (left me broke).*

     Ese tipo me revienta. *I can't stand that fellow.*

reventarse *to burst.*

     Se reventó un neumático en el camino. *We had a blowout on the road.*

reventón *m. bursting; blowout; explosion; steep slope; hard work.*

     Tuvo que darse un reventón para terminar el trabajo. *He almost worked himself to death to finish the work.*

reverencia *f. reverence.*

reverso *m. reverse.*

REVÉS *m. reverse; wrong side; backhand slap;*

misfortune.

Este es el revés. *This is the wrong side.*

La chaqueta está del revés. *The jacket is wrong side out.*

Llevas puestas las medias al revés. *You're wearing your stockings the wrong side out.*

No es así, precisamente es al revés. *It's not like that, it's just the opposite.*

So lo dije al revés. *I told him just the opposite.*

Todo le salía al revés. *Everything he did went wrong.*

revisar *to look over, to go over; to check; to overhaul; to examine, to audit (accounts).*

Revisar las cuentas. *To audit accounts.*

Hágame el favor de revisar el motor. *Please check the engine.*

revisión *f. checking; verification; overhauling.*

Revisión de cuentas. *Audit.*

revisor *m. overseer; conductor.*

revista *f. review, parade; magazine.*

El general pasó revista a los soldados. *The general reviewed the soldiers.*

Tomaré un ejemplar de esta revista. *I'll take a copy of this magazine.*

revivir *to revive.*

revocación *f. revocation, repeal.*

revocar *to revoke, to repeal, to cancel; to plaster, to cover with plaster.*

revolcar *to knock down, to tread on; to confuse; to floor (an opponent).*

revolcarse *to wallow, to welter.*

revoltoso *adj. rebellious, hard to manage; boisterous; naughty, full of pranks.*

revolución *f. revolution.*

revolucionario *adj. revolutionary; m. revolutionist.*

revolver *to revolve; to turn upside down; to stir up.*

El niño lo revolvía todo en la casa. *The child turned the house upside down.*

Revuélvalo Ud. con una cuchara. *Stir it with a spoon.*

revólver *m. revolver.*

revoque *m. plaster.*

revuelo *m. commotion, sensation.*

revuelta *f. revolt.*

revuelto *adj. turned upside down; scrambled; boisterous, restless.*

Huevos revueltos. *Scrambled eggs.*

rey *m. king.*

reyerta *f. quarrel, brawl.*

rezagado *adj. straggling; m. straggler, someone left behind.*

rezagar *to leave behind; to defer.*

rezagarse *to remain behind; to lag.*

rezar *to pray.*

Rezaba todos los días sus oraciones. *He said his prayers every day.*

Eso no reza conmigo. *That's none of my business. That's no affair of mine. That has nothing to do with me.*

ría *f. mouth of a river, estuary.*

riachuelo *m. brook, stream, rivulet.*

ribera *f. shore, bank.*

ribete *m. border, trimming; pretense; binding (on seams).*

ricacho, ricachón *m. very rich.*

ricino *m. castor-oil plant.*

Aceite de ricino. *Castor oil.*

RICO *adj. rich, wealthy; delicious.*

Si yo fuera rico no trabajaría tanto. *I wouldn't work so much if I were rich.*

¡Qué sabor más rico el de esta carne! *What a delicious flavor this meat has!*

ridiculizar *to ridicule.*

RIDÍCULO *adj. ridiculous; odd, queer; m. ridicule.*

Es una moda ridícula. *It's a ridiculous fashion.*

Poner en ridículo. *To ridicule.*

Ponerse en ridículo. *To make oneself ridiculous.*

riego *m. irrigation, watering.*

riel *m. rail, track.*

rienda *f. rein; restraint.*

Sujete Ud. bien las riendas. *Hold on to the reins.*

Corrió a rienda suelta. *He ran fast.*

Dar rienda suelta. *To give free rein. To give vent to.*

riesgo *m. risk, danger, hazard.*

Corrió mucho riesgo. *He took a big risk.*

Sin riesgo. *Without risk. Safely.*

rifa *f. raffle; quarrel.*

rifar *to raffle; to quarrel.*

rifle *m. rifle.*

rigidez *f. rigidity, sternness.*

rígido *adj. rigid; severe, hard, stern.*

rigor *m. rigor.*

riguroso *adj. rigorous, severe, strict.*

rima *f. rhyme.*

rincón *m. corner (of a room, etc.); nook; hidden spot, secluded place.*

Ponga Ud. la silla en el rincón. *Put the chair in the corner.*

rinconera *f. corner piece.*

rinoceronte *m. rhinoceros.*

riña *f. quarrel, fray, fight.*

riñon *m. kidney.*

río *m. river.*

El Río Grande. *Rio Grande ("The big river").*

riqueza *f. riches; wealth; fertility.*

RISA *f. laugh, laughter.*

Todo aquello le producía risa. *That ("all that") made him laugh.*

No es cosa de risa. *It's no laughing matter.*

Desternillarse de risa. *To split one's sides laughing.*

¡Ay que risa! *My, how funny! That's very funny!*

risco m. steep rock; cliff.

risible adj. laughable.

risueño adj. smiling; pleasing.
Es un niño muy risueño. *The child is very good-natured ("always smiling").*

ritmo m. rhythm.

rito m. rite, ceremony.

rival m. rival.

rivalidad f. rivalry.

rivalizar to vie, compete.

rizo m. curl, frizzle; loop (aviation).

robar to rob, to steal; to draw (a card).
Me han robado. *I've been robbed.*
Me han robado la cartera. *My wallet's been stolen.*
Ahora le toca a Ud. robar. *Now it's your turn to draw (in cards).*

roble m. oak.

robo m. robbery, theft; cards drawn (in certain card games).

robusto adj. robust, strong.
Es de constitución robusta. *He has a strong constitution.*

roca f. rock.

roce m. friction; continual dealing with acquaintances.
Tiene mucho roce con ellos. *He associates a lot with them.*

rociar to spray, to sprinkle.

rocío m. dew.

rodada f. rut, track of a wheel.

rodar to roll; to roam around; to shoot (a film).
Rodó la escalera. *He went rolling down the stairs.*
Ahora rueda el dinero más que nunca. *The money's coming in now hand over fist. ("The money rolls in more than ever now.")*
Desde muy joven empezó a rodar por el mundo. *He began to roam around the world when he was very young.*
Se empezó a rodar la película. *They started shooting the picture.*

rodear to surround, to encircle; to go around.

rodeo m. turn; roundabout way; roundup, rodeo.
Ese camino da un rodeo muy grande. *That road makes a wide turn.*
Hubo un rodeo la semana pasada. *There was a rodeo last week.*
Déjese de rodeos y conteste claramente. *Stop beating around the bush and give me a straight answer.*

RODILLA f. knee.
De rodillas. *On one's knee.*
Ponerse de rodillas. *To kneel.*

rodillo m. roller; rolling-pin; inking roller (printing).

roer to gnaw, to nibble; to pick (a bone); to annoy.

rogar to pray, to beg, to entreat, to request.
Le ruego que . . . *I beg you to . . . Please . . .*

ROJO adj. red.
La cruz roja. *The Red Cross.*

rol m. roll, list, muster roll, crew list; role.

rollizo adj. plump; m. log.

rollo m. roll.

Roma f. Rome.

romadizo m. catarrh, cold in the head; hay fever.

romance m. romance; ballad.

romanticismo m. romanticism.

romántico adj. romantic.

romería f. pilgrimage; excursion, tour.

romero m. rosemary; pilgrim.

rompecabezas m. riddle; puzzle.

rompenueces m. nutcracker.

rompeolas m. breakwater; mole.

ROMPER to break; to smash; to tear; to rip; to fracture; to start, to begin.
¿Ha roto Ud. la botella? *Have you broken (did you break) the bottle?*
Se cayó del caballo y se rompió una pierna. *He fell from his horse and broke a leg.*
Rompió el documento. *He tore up the document.*
Se me ha roto la media. *I've ripped my stocking.*
Romper relaciones. *To break relations.*
Romper con alguno. *To break with someone.*
Al romper el día. *At daybreak.*

ron m. rum.

roncar to snore; to roar; to brag.

ronco adj. hoarse.

roncha f. swelling caused by a bite or by a blow; wheal, welt.

ronda f. night patrol; making the rounds; a round (of drinks, etc.).

rondar to patrol.

ronquido m. snore; roaring.

roña f. scab; filth, dirt; bark of pine trees.

ROPA f. wearing apparel, clothing; clothes.
Tengo que mudarme de ropa. *I have to change my clothes.*
Quiero que me laven la ropa. *I want my clothes washed.*
Ropa hecha. *Ready-made clothes.*
Ropa interior. *Underwear.*
Ropa sucia. *Dirty clothes. Laundry (to be washed).*
Ropa limpia. *Laundry (washed). Clean clothes (laundry).*

ropero m. wardrobe; closet; dealer in clothes.

rosa f. rose.

rosado adj. pink, rosy.

rosal m. rosebush.

rosario m. rosary.

rosca f. ring (bread or cake); thread (of a screw).
Déme Ud. una rosca de esas. *Give me one of those rings (bread or cake).*
La rosca de un tornillo. *The thread of a screw.*

rosquilla f. jelly-roll; doughnut.

rostro m. face, countenance.

roto adj. torn; broken; ragged; m. tramp (Chile).

rotular to label.

rótulo m. label; poster, placard.

rotura f. breaking, rupture; crack.

rozar to grub, to clear (the ground); to nibble (grass); to graze.

El avión rozó ligeramente el suelo. *The plane grazed the ground.*

rozarse to fret, to rub against; to bump one's foot against another; to associate, to rub elbows, to be on familiar terms.

Se roza mucho con ellos. *He associates a lot with them.*

rubí m. ruby.

rubio adj. blond; f. blonde.

rubor m. blush; bashfulness.

ruborizarse to blush.

rudeza f. coarseness, roughness.

rudimento m. rudiment.

rudo adj. rude, rough; severe.

rueda f. wheel; sunfish.

ruedo m. hem; round mat; bull-ring.

ruego m. request, petition.

Dirigió un ruego a la Cámara. *He submitted a petition to the legislature.*

A ruego de. *At the request of.*

rugido m. roar; rumbling.

rugir to roar; to bellow.

RUIDO m. noise.

El ruido me impidió dormir. *The noise kept me awake. ("The noise kept me from sleeping.")*

Meter (hacer) ruido. *To make noise. To create a sensation. To attract attention.*

ruin adj. mean, vile, low.

ruina f. ruin; downfall; bankruptcy; pl. ruins.

ruinoso adj. ruinous; in ruins.

ruiseñor m. nightingale.

ruleta f. roulette.

rumba f. rumba (Cuban dance).

rumbo m. course; road, route; pomp, showy display.

Tomaremos otro rumbo. *We'll take another course (road).*

Con rumbo a. *Bound for.*

Era un hombre de rumbo. *He was a spendthrift.*

rumiar to ruminate; to ponder.

rumor m. rumor.

ruptura f. rupture; breaking off.

rural adj. rural, rustic.

ruso adj. and m. Russian.

rústico adj. rustic.

Un libro en rústica. *A paper-bound book.*

ruta f. route, course.

rutina f. routine, habit; rut.

rutinario adj. according to routine; mechanical.

S

SÁBADO m. Saturday.

sábana f. bedsheet.

sabana f. savanna; grassy plain (Cuba).

sabandija f. small reptile or insect.

sabañón m. chilblain.

saber m. learning, knowledge.

SABER to know; to know how; to be able to; to taste; to hear, to find out. (To know a person or a place = conocer.)

¿Sabe Ud. dónde vive? *Do you know where he lives?*

¿Sabe Ud. a qué hora abren las tiendas? *Do you know at what time the stores open?*

¿A ver qué sabe Ud.? *Let's see what (how much) you know.*

Sabe tanto como su profesor. *He knows as much as his teacher (professor).*

¿Sabe Ud. lo que pasó? *Do you know what happened?*

¿Sabe Ud. patinar? *Do you know how to skate?*

¿Sabe Ud. escribir? *Can you write?*

¿Sabe Ud. nadar? *Can you swim?*

Sabe nadar muy bien. *She swims very well.*

¿Sabe Ud. bailar la conga? *Can you dance the conga?*

¿Sabe Ud. algo de nuevo? *Have you heard anything new?*

Celebro saberlo. *I'm glad (delighted) to hear it.*

¿Le sabe mal? *Isn't it all right with you? Don't you like it?*

¿Sabe la noticia? *Have you heard the news?*

¿Cómo ha sabido Ud. eso? *How did you find that out (learn that)?*

¿Qué sé yo? *How do I know? How should I know?*

¡Ya lo sé! *I know it!*

Yo no sé. *I don't know.*

¡Quién sabe! *Who knows!*

¿Quién lo sabe? *Who knows it?*

No se sabe. *Nobody knows. It's not known.*

No se sabe nunca. *One never knows.*

¡Sabe Dios! *God knows!*

Esto sabe mal. *This tastes bad.*

Esta comida sabe a gloria. *This food's delicious. ("This food tastes wonderful.")*

Le remitimos los géneros siguientes, a saber: *We are sending you the following goods:*

Hacer saber. *To make known.*

Como es sabido. *As is known.*

Que yo sepa. *To my knowledge. As far as I know.*

No que yo sepa. *Not that I'm aware of.*

Saber de sobra. *To know well enough.*

¿Sabe Ud. una cosa? *Do you know what? (Do) You know something?*

sabiduría f. learning, knowledge, wisdom.

sabio adj. wise, learned; m. scholar.

sable m. saber; cutlass.

sabor m. savor, taste, flavor.

saborear to flavor; to savor, to relish.

saborearse to relish, to enjoy (eating or drinking); to be delighted.

sabotaje m. sabotage.

sabroso adj. delicious, tasty.

La comida es muy sabrosa. The food is very tasty.

sacacorchos m. corkscrew.

sacamanchas m. cleaning fluid; stain remover.

SACAR to take out, to put out, to bring out, to get out; to draw; to remove, to pull out; to infer; to publish; to win (a prize); to take (a picture); to buy, to get.

Sacar una copia. To make a copy.

¿Cuánto saca por día? How much does he make a day?

Saque Ud. la cuenta. Figure out the bill.

Esta mañana saqué un poco de dinero del banco. I drew some money from the bank this morning.

Saqué un premio en el sorteo. I won a prize at the lottery.

¿Dónde puedo sacar mis billetes? Where can I buy my tickets?

Sacaré tres butacas. I'll buy three orchestra seats.

Saque las manos de los bolsillos. Take your hands out of your pockets.

¿De dónde ha sacado Ud. esa idea? Where did you get that idea?

¿De dónde sacará tanto dinero? Where does he get so much money?

Nos sacó de apuro. He got us out of trouble (out of a difficulty).

Saca los niños a pasear. Take the children out for a walk.

Sacó una moneda de su monedero. She took a coin out of her purse.

Ese hombre saca partido de todo. That man turns everything to profit.

Sacarán la casa a subasta pública. They're going to sell the house at public auction.

Sacar una foto. To take a picture.

Sacar una muela. To pull out a tooth.

Sacar a luz. To print. To publish. To make public.

Sacar en limpio. To infer.

No sacar nada en limpio. Not to be able to make anything out of. Not to be able to make head or tail out of.

saco m. sack, bag; coat (Amer.).

¿Qué hay en este saco? What's in this bag?

El viajero llevaba un saco a cuestas. The traveler carried a bag on his shoulders.

Quítese el saco. Take your coat off.

Caer en saco roto. To come to nothing.

sacramento m. sacrament.

sacrificar to sacrifice.

sacrificio m. sacrifice.

sacrilegio m. sacrilege.

sacristía f. sacristy, vestry.

sacudida f. shock, shake; beating.

Le dió una buena sacudida. He gave him a good beating.

sacudir to shake; to jerk; to beat; to dust; to shake off.

sacudirse to get rid of, to object.

saeta f. arrow; shaft.

sagacidad f. sagacity, shrewdness.

sagaz adj. sagacious, shrewd.

sagrado adj. sacred.

sainete m. farce, burlesque act.

SAL f. salt; wit, humor; charm.

Haga el favor de pasarme la sal. Please pass me the salt.

Tiene mucha sal esta niña. This girl is very witty.

SALA f. living room, parlor; large room; room.

Vamos a la sala a escuchar un poco de música. Let's go to the living room (parlor) and listen to some music.

¿Dónde está la sala de espera? Where is the waiting room?

Sala de pruebas. Fitting room.

Sala de fiestas. Nightclub (in Spain).

salado adj. salty; witty.

Esta carne está muy salada. This meat is very salty.

Es muy salada. She's very witty.

salario m. salary, wages.

salchicha f. sausage.

salchichón m. large sausage.

SALDO m. balance, remainder; sale, bargain.

La tienda anuncia un saldo. The store is advertising a sale.

Queda todavía a mi favor un pequeño saldo. A small sum still remains to my credit.

salero m. salt shaker, saltcellar; gracefulness, charm.

Tenga la bondad de alcanzarme el salero. Please pass me the salt shaker.

Es hermosa y además tiene mucho salero. She's pretty and she's also very charming.

SALIDA f. departure; exit; outlet; sale; sortie, sally; witty remark; loophole, subterfuge.

Salida y llegada de trenes. Departure and arrival of trains.

¿Dónde está la salida? Where is the exit?

Le veré a la salida. I'll see you on my way out.

Tener salida. To sell well.

Dar salida. To dispose of. To sell.

Salida del sol. Sunrise.

Callejón sin salida. Dead-end street.

SALIR to go out; to leave; to depart; to appear;

to come out; to get out; to come off; to turn
out; to rise (the sun); to cost; to take after.

¿A qué hora sale el tren? *What time does the
train leave?*

El tren está por salir. *The train is about to
leave.*

¿Piensa Ud. salir esta noche? *Are you going out
tonight?*

Voy a salir a tomar un poco el aire. *I'm going
out for some air.*

Salió hace un rato. *He left a while ago,*

He salido sin dinero. *I left the house without
any money.*

Me sale a peseta la yarda. *It costs me a peseta
a yard.*

Ella sale a su madre. *She takes after her mother.*

Mi madre salió de compras hoy. *My mother
went shopping today.*

Eche la llave al salir. *Lock the door ("with the
key") when you go out.*

¡Salga de aquí! *Get out!*

Muy en breve saldrá el libro. *The book will be
out (appear) very soon.*

El preiódico sale todos los días. *The paper
comes out (appears) every day.*

Estas manchas no salen. *These spots don't come
off.*

Se le sale mucho el pañuelo del bolsillo. *His
handkerchief sticks way out of his pocket.*

Salió bien en los exámenes. *He passed his examination with good marks.*

¿Quién salió ganando? *Who was the winner?*

Los negocios han salido mal. *Business has
turned out badly.*

Todo le salía al revés. *Everything he did went
wrong.*

Al salir el sol. *At sunrise.*

El sol sale para todos. *The sun shines on the
just and on the unjust.*

El anillo se me ha salido del dedo. *The ring
slipped off my finger.*

salirse *to leak; to overflow.*

Esta jarra se sale. *This jar is leaking.*

¡Cuidado que se sale la leche! *Look out, the
milk is going to overflow!*

Salirse con la suya. *To get one's way. To accomplish one's end.*

saliva *f. saliva.*

salmón *m. salmon.*

salón *m. hall; salon; parlor.*

¿Hay algún salón de belleza por aquí? *Is there
a beauty parlor near here?*

En este salón caben más de cien personas. *This
hall can accommodate over a hundred people.*

Salón de baile. *Dance hall.*

salpicar *to splash, to spatter.*

salsa *f. sauce, gravy, dressing.*

salsera *f. gravy dish.*

SALTAR *to jump, to leap, to hop; to skip, to omit;
to bounce; to fly off.*

¿Puede Ud. saltar por encima de esa tapia? *Can
you jump over that fence?*

Al pasar lista saltó mi nombre. *When he called
the roll he skipped my name.*

Esta pelota no salta. *This ball doesn't bounce.*

Saltó una astilla del leño. *A chip flew off the
log.*

Saltó en su defensa. *He sprang to his (her) defense.*

Hacer saltar. *To blow up.*

Saltar a la vista. *To be obvious. To stare one
in the face.*

salteador *m. highwayman.*

SALTO *m. jump, leap; sudden promotion; waterfall, cascade.*

Salto de agua. *Waterfall.*

A saltos. *By fits and starts.*

Dar saltos. *To jump.*

De un salto. *At one jump.*

Salto mortal. *A somersault.*

SALUD *f. health.*

Disfruta de muy buena salud. *He's enjoying
good health.*

Bueno para la salud. *Good for the health.
Healthful.*

Estar bien de salud. *To be in good health.*

Estar mal de salud. *To be in poor health.*

Bebamos a la salud de nuestro anfitrión. *Let's
drink to our host ("to the health of our
host").*

¡Salud! *Hello! Good luck! To your health!*

¡Salud y pesetas! *Here's to health and wealth!
("Health and money!")*

saludable *adj. healthful, good for the health; sal-
utary, beneficial.*

saludar *to salute, to greet.*

Le saludó muy afectuosamente. *He greeted him
(her) affectionately.*

Y a mí, ¿no me saluda Ud.? *(Well,) Aren't you
going to say hello to me?*

Cuando le vea, salúdele mi nombre. *Remember me to him when you see him.*

Salude a Juan de mi parte. *Give John my regards.*

saludo *m. salute, greeting.*

Saludos a. *Greetings to.*

salva *f. salvo, volley.*

Una salva de aplausos. *Thunderous applause.*

salvación *f. salvation.*

salvado *m. bran.*

salvaje *adj. savage; wild.*

salvamento *m. salvage, rescue.*

salvar *to salvage; to save; to clear (an obstacle);
to avoid (a danger); to jump over (a ditch,
etc.), to cover (a distance).*

El médico ha perdido la esperanza de salvarle.
*The doctor has given up hope for him. The
doctor has given up hope of saving him.*

Salvando pequeños detalles. *Apart from minor
details.*

salvarse *to escape from danger; to be saved.*

Se salvó por un pelo. *He had a narrow escape.
He escaped with his skin.*

salvavidas m. *lifesaver; life preserver; lifeboat, life-
belt, life buoy.*

salvedad f. *reserve, exception, qualification.*

SALVO adj. *saved, safe; excepted; save, exempt-
ing; but, unless.*

Todos vinieron salvo él. *Everyone came except
him.*

Salvo los casos imprevistos. *Except for unforeseen cases.*

Salvo que. *Unless.*

Poner a salvo. *To safeguard. To keep safe.*

En salvo. *Safe. With safety.*

Sano y salvo. *Safe and sound.*

Ponerse a salvo. *To escape.*

Quedar a salvo. *To be safeguarded.*

A su salvo. *To one's satisfaction.*

salvoconducto m. *pass, safe-conduct.*

sanar *to cure, to heal; to recover.*

La herida sanó pronto. *The wound healed
quickly. The wound soon healed.*

sanatorio m. *sanatorium, sanitarium.*

sanción f. *sanction.*

sancionar *to sanction; to ratify, to confirm.*

sandalia f. *sandal.*

sandía f. *watermelon.*

saneamiento m. *sanitation; surety, bail.*

sanear *to drain, to improve (lands); to take sanitary
measures, to make sanitary; to make good,
to indemnify; to give bail.*

sangrar *to bleed; to drain.*

SANGRE f. *blood.*

A sangre fría. *In cold blood.*

A sangre y fuego. *Without mercy. With fire and
sword.*

sangriento adj. *bloody; sanguinary; cruel.*

sanidad f. *health; health department.*

Sanidad pública. *Public health.*

Cuerpo de Sanidad. *Medical Corps.*

sanitario adj. *sanitary; hygienic.*

SANO adj. *sound, healthy; sane; safe.*

Está más sano de lo que parece. *He's healthier
than he looks.*

Regresó sano y salvo. *He returned safe and
sound.*

santiamén m. *instant, twinkling of an eye, jiffy.*

Lo haré en un santiamén. *I'll do it in a jiffy
(before you can say Jack Robinson).*

santiguarse *to cross oneself, to make the sign of the
cross (on oneself).*

santo adj. *very good, saintly; saint, holy, sacred.*

Esa chica es una santa. *She's a very good girl.*
("That girl is a saint.")

Semana Santa. *Holy Week (Easter).*

Se ha quedado para vestir santos. *She's going
to be (is) an old maid.*

saña f. *rage, fury, anger, passion.*

sapo m. *toad.*

saquear *to sack, to loot, to pillage.*

sarampión m. *measles.*

sarcasmo m. *sarcasm.*

sardina f. *sardine.*

sargento m. *sergeant.*

sarmiento m. *vine shoot.*

sarpullido m. *rash, skin eruption.*

sartén f. *frying pan.*

sastre m. *tailor.*

Lleve este traje al sastre. *Take this suit to the
tailor.*

sastrería f. *tailor shop, tailoring.*

Satán, Satanás m. *Satan.*

sátira f. *satire, sarcasm, irony.*

satírico adj. *satirical.*

SATISFACCIÓN f. *satisfaction; pleasure; apology.*

Tuve la satisfacción de conocerla. *I had the
pleasure of meeting her.*

Eso fué una gran satisfacción para mí. *That
was a great satisfaction for me.*

El dió un suspiro de satisfacción. *He gave a
sigh of relief.*

A satisfacción. *To one's satisfaction. Satisfactorily.*

Dar satisfacciones. *To apologize.*

SATISFACER *to satisfy; to please; to pay (debt);
to gratify.*

No me satisface su trabajo. *His work doesn't
satisfy me.*

Eso no me satisface. I'm not satisfied with
that. *That isn't satisfactory to me.*

Satisfacer una deuda. *To pay a debt.*

satisfactorio adj. *satisfactory.*

SATISFECHO adj. *satisfied, content.*

Deseamos que todos estén satisfechos. *We want
everyone to be satisfied.*

Hágalo Ud. de modo que él quede satisfecho.
Do it in a way that will please him.

No deseo comer más, estoy satisfecho. *I don't
want to eat any more, I've had enough.*

sauce m. *willow.*

sazón f. *maturity; seasoning, taste, flavor; opportunity.*

A la sazón estaba yo en Inglaterra. *At that time
I was in England.*

En sazón. *In season. Ripe. Seasonably.*

sazonado adj. *seasoned; ripe; expressive.*

Un plato bien sazonado. *A well-seasoned dish.*

sazonar *to season; to mature, to ripen.*

SE *(third person object and reflexive pronoun) to
him, to her, to it, to you, etc.; self, one-*

self, himself, herself, itself, etc. (Se is often used as a reciprocal pronoun and also to introduce the passive form.)

Se lo diré. *I'll tell it to him.*

Se dice. *It's said.*

¡Figúrese Ud.! *Just imagine!*

Se me figura. *I can imagine.*

Déselo. *Give it to him.*

Lávese. *Wash yourself.*

Se engañan. *They're fooling themselves.*

Se conocen. *They know each other (one another).*

Se aman. *They love each other.*

¿Cómo se llama Ud.? *What's your name?*

Se sabe. *It's known.*

No se sabe. *No one knows.*

Se habla español. *Spanish spoken here.*

Se alquila. *For rent.*

Se prohíbe fumar. *No smoking allowed.*

SÉ (imperative of ser and first person indicative of saber) be; I know.

Sé bueno. *Be good.*

No lo sé. *I don't know.*

seca f. drought, dry season.

Lo dijo a secas. *He told it in a matter-of-fact way ("dryly").*

secante m. blotter, blotting paper; f. secant.

¿Dónde está el secante? *Where's the blotter?*

SECAR to dry, to desiccate; to wipe.

Hay que secar los platos, *We have to dry the dishes.*

Séquese bien. *Dry yourself well (thoroughly).*

Puso a secar la ropa cerca del fuego. *He put the clothes near the fire to dry.*

sección f. section; division; department; cutting.

¿En qué sección trabaja Ud.? *In what section (division) do you work?*

SECO adj. dry; withered; lean; curt; rude.

Tengo la garganta seca. *My throat is dry.*

Quiero que me limpie en seco este traje. *I'd like this suit dry-cleaned.*

Era un hombre muy seco. *He was a very curt ("dry") person.*

Consérvese seco. *Keep dry.*

"Consérvese en un lugar seco." *"Keep in a dry place."*

Clima seco. *Dry climate.*

Vino seco. *Dry wine.*

Lavar en seco. *To dryclean.*

secretamente secretly.

secretaria f. woman secretary.

secretaría f. secretaryship; secretary's office.

secretario m. secretary.

secreto adj. secret; private; m. secret; secrecy; mystery.

Lo he guardado en secreto. *I've kept it a secret.*

Temo que Ud. no guarde el secreto. *I'm afraid you won't keep the secret.*

Era un secreto a voces. *It was an open secret.*

secuestro m. kidnapping.

secundar to second, to back up, to aid.

Lo secunda en todo y por todo. *He supports him in everything ("and for everything").*

secundario adj. secondary, subsidiary.

SED f. thirst; desire, craving.

Tengo sed. *I'm thirsty.*

seda f. silk.

Tiene la piel como seda. *Her skin is soft as silk.*

Papel de seda. *Tissue paper.*

Ir como seda. *To go smoothly (without a hitch). To work like magic (like a charm). To be smooth sailing.*

sedería f. silks, silk goods; silk shop.

sedición f. sedition, mutiny.

sediento adj. thirsty.

sedimento m. sediment.

seducir to seduce; to tempt, to fascinate; to bribe.

segadora f. reaper, harvester (machine).

segar to reap; to mow.

segregar to segregate, to separate.

SEGUIDA f. succession, continuation.

En seguida. *Right away. Immediately.*

¡Venga en seguida! *Come right away!*

De seguida. *Successively. In succession.*

seguidamente successively; immediately after, right after that, then.

seguidilla f. seguidilla (a lively Spanish dance); the song and music that go with it.

seguido adj. continued; straight (ahead).

Vaya todo seguido y luego tome la bocacalle a la mano derecha. *Go straight ahead and then take the side street to your right.*

SEGUIR to follow; to pursue; to continue, to go on, to keep on.

Sígame. *Follow me.*

Le sigo a Ud. *I'll follow you.*

Seguiré sus consejos. *I'll follow your advice.*

¡Siga adelante! 1. *Go straight ahead!* 2. *Go ahead! Continue!*

Siga derecho. *Keep straight ahead.*

¿Qué sigue después? *What comes afterwards?*

Como sigue: *As follows:*

Siga tal como empezó. *Go on just as you started.*

Siguió hablando. *He went on talking. He kept (on) talking.*

La situación sigue de mal en peor. *The situation is going from bad to worse.*

El herido sigue mejor. *The wounded man is improving.*

Seguía diluviando. *It was still pouring.*

Sigo sin comprender. *I still don't understand.*

SEGÚN according to; in the same way as, just as; it depends.

Según el informe que me dió. *According to the*

report he gave me.

Esto está hecho según los planos. *This was done according to plans.*

Claro que esto es según se mire. *Of course, this depends on how you look at it.*

Según vayan llegando hágalos Ud. entrar. *Have them enter in their order of arrival.*

Según y conforme. *That depends.*

¿Irá Ud.?—Según y cómo. *Will you go?—That all depends.*

SEGUNDO *adj. and n.* second; mate (of a ship).

Espéreme un segundo, ahora vuelvo. *Wait a second, I'll be right back.*

Ella vive en el segundo piso. *She lives on the second floor.*

¿Qué tomo desea Ud., el primero o el segundo? *Which volume do you want, the first or second?*

Segunda velocidad. *Second gear.*

En segundo lugar. *In the second place. Secondly. On second thought.*

Un billete de segunda. *A coach ticket. ("A second-class ticket.")*

De segunda mano. *Secondhand.*

seguramente certainly, surely.

Seguramente que sí. *Yes, certainly.*

seguridad *f.* security; certainty; safety.

Puede Ud. tener la seguridad de que lo haré. *You may be sure that I'll do it.*

Con toda seguridad. *With absolute certainty.*

Para mayor seguridad. *For safety's sake. For greater safety.*

SEGURO *adj.* secure, sure, safe, certain; *m.* insurance; safety; stop, safety catch.

¿No está Ud. seguro? *Aren't you sure?*

Tener por seguro. *To be sure. To consider certain.*

Ir sobre seguro. *To be on safe ground.*

A buen seguro. *Certainly.*

Compañía de seguros. *Insurance company.*

Póliza de seguro. *Insurance policy.*

Prima de seguro. *Insurance premium.*

Seguro de vida. *Life insurance.*

Seguro contra incendios. *Fire insurance.*

Tomar un seguro. *To take out insurance. To take out an insurance policy.*

SEIS *adj. and n.* six; sixth.

seiscientos *adj. and n.* six hundred; six hundredth.

selección *f.* selection, choice, digest.

selecto *adj.* select; distinguished.

Había un público muy selecto. *There was a very distinguished audience.*

selva *f.* forest, woods.

sellar to seal; to stamp.

¿Es necesario sellar esta carta con lacre? *Is it necessary to use sealing wax on this letter?*

Selle Ud esas localidades. *Stamp those tickets.*

SELLO *m.* seal; stamp; postage stamp.

El sello se despegó. *The stamp came off.*

Sello de urgencia. Sello de entrega inmediata. *Special delivery stamp.*

semáforo *m.* semaphore.

SEMANA *f.* week; week's pay.

Voy al cine cada semana. *I go to the movies every week.*

Lo veremos la semana que viene. *We'll see him next week.*

Al parecer vendrá la semana próxima. *Apparently he's coming next week. It seems he's coming next week.*

La semana pasada. *Last week.*

En una semana más o menos. *In a week or so.*

Semana inglesa. *Five-day week.*

Semana Santa. *Holy Week (Easter).*

Un día entre semana. *A weekday.*

A la semana. *Per week.*

Hace una semana. *A week ago.*

semanal *adj.* weekly.

Una revista semanal. *A weekly magazine.*

semanalmente weekly, by the week, every week.

Esta revista sale semanalmente. *This magazine appears every week.*

semanario *adj.* weekly; *m.* weekly publication.

semblante *m.* countenance, look; aspect.

Hoy tiene Ud. muy buen semblante. *You look very well today.*

sembrar to sow; to scatter, to spread.

semejante *adj.* similar; such; *m.* fellow man.

¿Tiene Ud. algo semejante? *Do you have something (anything) similar?*

Los dos relatos son muy semejantes. *The two stories are very similar.*

No creo en semejante cosa. *I don't believe such a thing.*

Piense que son sus semejantes. *Remember that they are your fellow men.*

semejanza *f.* similarity, resemblance, likeness.

semejar to resemble, to be like.

semestral *adj.* semi-annually.

semestre *m.* space of six months, half-year, semester; half-year's income or pension.

semi (prefix) semi, half, partially.

Semicircular. *Semi-circular.*

Semibreve. *Semi-breve.*

semilla *f.* seed.

seminario *m.* seminary.

seminarista *m.* seminarist.

sempiterno *adj.* everlasting.

senado *m.* senate.

senador *m.* senator.

sencillez *f.* simplicity, lack of affectation, plainness; candor.

Atraía por la sencillez de su carácter. *She attracted people by her lack of affectation.*

Vestía con mucha sencillez. *She dressed very*

simply.

SENCILLO adj. *simple; plain; single.*

Era un problema muy sencillo. *It was a very simple problem.*

Aquel trabajo era muy sencillo. *That work (job) was very simple.*

Un vestido sencillo. *A plain dress.*

Le apuesto doble contra sencillo. *I'll bet you two to one.*

senda f. *path, footpath.*

sendero m. *path, footpath.*

senil adj. *senile.*

seno m. *breast, bosom; lap; sinus; womb.*

sensación f. *sensation.*

sensacional adj. *sensational.*

sensatez f. *good sense, discretion.*

sensato adj. *sensible, discreet.*

sensibilidad f. *sensibility; sensitivity.*

SENSIBLE adj. *sensitive; regrettable; f. sensible, seventh note (music).*

Los ojos son sensibles a la luz. *The eyes are sensitive to light.*

Es una chica muy sensible. *She's a very sensitive girl.*

Un corazón sensible. *A tender heart.*

Una pérdida sensible. *A regrettable loss.*

sensual adj. *sensual, voluptuous.*

sensualidad f. *sensuality, lust.*

sentado adj. *seated; judicious; sensible.*

Estaba sentado a mi izquierda. *He was sitting on my left.*

Dar por sentado. *To take for granted.*

Puede esperar sentado. *You'll have to wait for it till doomsday.*

SENTAR to fit, *to be becoming; to agree with one (food, etc.); to seat.*

Este sombrero le sienta divinamente. *This hat is very becoming to you.*

¿No le ha sentado bien el desayuno? *Didn't your breakfast agree with you?*

Le sentará muy bien un descanso. *A rest will do him good.*

Sentar plaza. *To enlist (as a soldier).*

Sentarle a alguien. *To fit (referring to clothing).*

SENTARSE to sit down, *to take a seat.*

Sentémonos aquí. *Let's sit down here.*

¿Dónde me siento? *Where shall I sit?*

Siéntese Ud. en esta butaca. *Sit down in this armchair.*

Los invitados se sentaron a la mesa. *The guests sat at the table.*

sentencia f. *sentence, verdict; maxim.*

sentenciar to sentence.

sentencioso adj. *sententious.*

SENTIDO adj. *felt; experienced; offended; disgusted; touchy; m. sense; meaning; understanding; direction.*

Es muy sentida. *She's very touchy.*

Está sentida con ellos. *She's disgusted with them.*

Su muerte fué muy sentida. *His death affected everyone deeply.*

En el sentido de. *In the sense of.*

Sin sentido. *Senseless. Meaningless.*

Carece de lógica y de sentido común. *It lacks logic and common sense.*

No lo tome Ud. en ese sentido. *Don't take it that way. I didn't mean it that way.*

Caminaba en sentido contrario. *He was walking in the opposite direction.*

Pondré mis cinco sentidos al hacerlo. *I'll put everything I've got into it.*

Perder el sentido. *To become unconscious.*

sentimental adj. *sentimental, showing a great deal of feeling.*

Es muy sentimental. *She's very sentimental.*

sentimentalismo m. *sentimentalism.*

sentimiento m. *sentiment, feeling; grief; resentment.*

Era persona de malos sentimientos. *He was a malicious person.*

Le acompaño a Ud. en el sentimiento. *I'm very sorry to hear about your loss.*

SENTIR to feel; *to be sorry; to grieve; to hear; to sense; to be (happy, cold, warm, etc.); m. feeling; opinion.*

Lo siento muchísimo. *I'm very sorry.*

Siento no poder ir. *I'm sorry I can't go.*

Siento haberme retrasado tanto. *I'm sorry to be so late.*

Sentí en el alma la pérdida de tan fiel amigo. *I felt very deeply the loss of such a faithful friend.*

Ahora siento frío. *I'm cold now.*

Siento mucha alegría. *I'm very happy (glad).*

Pasaron las horas sin sentir. *The hours passed without our knowing it. Time passed without our noticing it.*

Siento que viene alguien. *I hear someone coming.*

Díganos cuál es su sentir. *Tell us how you feel (about it).*

Es de sentir. *It's to be regretted. It's regrettable.*

Dar que sentir. *To hurt one's feelings.*

SENTIRSE to resent; *to feel (well, sick, sad, etc.); to ache; to crack (a wall, etc.).*

¿Se siente Ud. mejor? *Do you feel better?*

Me siento mal. *I don't feel well.*

¿Siente Ud. dolor en la espalda? *Do you have a backache?*

Se siente del pecho. *His chest aches.*

No tenía porque sentirse molesto. *He has no reason to feel annoyed.*

SEÑA f. *signal; sign, mark, password; pl. address.*

¿Cuáles son sus señas? *What's your address?*

Escriba Ud. a estas señas. *Write to this address.*

No dejaron ni señas del pastel. *They ate up every bit of the cake.* ("*They didn't leave a sign of the cake.*")

Hacer señas. *To motion. To signal.*

SEÑAL *f. sign, mark; signal; trace; scar; deposit (paid as a pledge); token.*

Esta es la mejor señal de mejoría. *That's the best sign of improvement.*

Ponga una señal en esa página. *Put a mark on that page. Mark that page.*

La señal de alarma. *The alarm signal.*

Se daba a entender por señales. *He made himself understood by signs.*

¿Quiere Ud. que deje algún dinero en señal? *Do you want me to leave you some money as a deposit?*

Tiene una señal en la cara. *He has a scar on his face.*

Para más pelos y señales. *In more detail.*

En señal de. *As a token of. In proof of.*

Código de señales. *Signal code.*

señalado *adj. distinguished, noted; marked; appointed (time).*

Al (en el) tiempo señalado. *At the appointed time.*

señalar *to mark; to signal; to point out; to set (the date).*

Hay que señalar el día de la reunión. *The date of the meeting must be set.*

Señale Ud. los errores que encuentre. *Point out the errors you find.*

Señalar con el dedo. *To point one's finger at. To point.*

SEÑOR *m. mister, sir; gentleman; master; lord.*

Señor Navarro. *Mr. Navarro (used when addressing the person directly).*

Buenos días, señor Navarro. *Good morning, Mr. Navarro.*

El señor Navarro no podrá venir. *Mr. Navarro will not come (used when speaking of the person).*

Gracias, señor. *Thank you, sir.*

El gusto es mío, señor. *The pleasure is mine, sir.*

El señor es inglés. *The gentleman is an Englishman (is English).*

Hay un señor esperándole. *There's a gentleman waiting for him.*

Los señores de Sucre. *Mr. and Mrs. Sucre.*

SEÑORA *f. Mrs., madam, lady; wife.*

Señora de García. *Mrs. García (direct address).*

La señora de García. *Mrs. García (when speaking of the person).*

¿Puedo hablar con la señora de Navarro? *May I speak to Mrs. Navarro?*

La señora no está en casa. *The lady of the house is not at home.*

Sí, señora. *Yes, madam.*

Mucho gusto en conocer a Ud., señora. *I'm very happy (pleased) to know you, madam.*

A los pies de Ud., señora. *Your humble servant, madam.* ("*At your feet, madam.*")

Déle una silla a esta señora. *Give this lady a chair.*

¿Cómo está su señora? *How is your wife?*

SEÑORITA *f. miss; young lady.*

Mucho gusto en conocerla, señorita Navarro. *I'm very glad to meet you, Miss Navarro.*

Que pase la señorita Navarro. *Have Miss Navarro come in. Ask Miss Navarro to come in.*

Esta señorita es norteamericana. *This young lady is an American.*

separación *f. separation.*

separar *to separate.*

Separe Ud. los grandes de los pequeños. *Separate the large ones from the small.*

Una cortina separa las dos habitaciones. *A curtain divides the two rooms.*

Separe Ud. un poco la mesa de la pared. *Move the table from the wall a bit.*

separarse *to part company; to get out of the way; to retire (from business, etc.).*

Decidieron separarse legalmente. *They decided to separate legally.*

SEPTIEMBRE *m. September.*

séptimo *adj. seventh.*

septuagenario *adj. and n. septuagenarian.*

sepulcro *m. grave, tomb, sepulcher.*

sepultar *to bury, to inter; to hide.*

sepultura *f. burial; grave; tomb.*

sequedad *f. dryness.*

sequía *f. drought, lack of rain.*

ser *m. being, creature.*

Ser viviente. *Living being. Living creature.*

Seres humanos. *Human beings.*

SER *to be.*

¿Quién es? *Who is it?*

Soy yo. *It's me (I).*

¿Quién será? *Who can it be?*

¿Es Ud. el Sr. Smith? *Are you Mr. Smith?*

¿De dónde es Ud.? *Where are you from?*

Soy de Boston. *I'm from Boston.*

Somos norteamericanos. *We're Americans.*

Somos viejos amigos. *We are old friends.*

¿Qué será de él? *What will become of him?*

¿En qué puedo serle útil? *What can I do for you? Can I help you?*

¿De quién es este lápiz? *Whose pencil is this?*

Es mío. *It's mine.*

Es de Juan. *It belongs to John.*

¿De quién será esta casa? *Whose house can (could) this be?*

Es la casa de Juan. *It's John's house.*

¿De qué es esta maleta? *What is this suitcase made of?*

Es una maleta de cuero. *It's a leather suitcase.
It's made of leather.*

¿Cómo es? *How is it?*

Es algo sordo. *He's rather hard of hearing.*

¿Es guapa la hija? *Is the daughter pretty?*

Es guapísima. *She's very pretty.*

¿Qué es Ud.? *What are you?*

Yo soy escritor. *I'm a writer.*

¿Qué es su hermano? *What is your brother?
What does your brother do?*

Es médico. *He is a doctor.*

¿Qué es eso? *What is that?*

¿Cuánto es? *How much is it?*

¿Qué tal ha sido el viaje? *How was the trip?*

¿Qué hora es? *What time is it?*

Es la una. *It's one o'clock.*

Son las dos. *It's two o'clock.*

¿Qué hora será? *I wonder what time it is.*

Ya son las doce pasadas. *It's after twelve. It's
past twelve already.*

Son más de las diez. *It's after ten o'clock.*

Es temprano todavía. *It's still early.*

¿Cuándo será la boda? *When will the wedding take place?*

¿Qué fecha es hoy? *What's the date today?*

¿Qué día es hoy? *What day is today?*

Hoy es lunes. *Today is Monday.*

Mañana será otro día. *Tomorrow is another
day.*

Es fácil. *It's easy.*

Es difícil. *It's difficult.*

¿Es verdad? *Is it true?*

No es verdad. *It's not true.*

No creo que sea cierto. *I don't believe it's
(that's) true.*

¿Será posible? *Would that be possible?*

Puede ser. *That may be. Maybe. Perhaps.*

Eso no puede ser. *That can't be.*

¿Quién quiere ser mano? *Who wants to deal
first (cards)?*

Después llegaron a ser buenos amigos. *Afterwards they became good friends.*

Eso no era con Ud. *It wasn't meant for you.*

Haré por Ud. cuanto me sea posible. *I'll do as
much as I can for you.*

¿Qué ha sido de su amigo? *What became of
your friend?*

Sea Ud. puntual. *Be on time.*

No seas tonto. *Don't be foolish.*

No sea Ud. inoportuno. *Don't come at the
wrong time (do things at the wrong time,
¡say the wrong things).*

¡Sé bueno, hijo mío! *Be good, my child!*

Ha llegado a ser gerente. *He became manager.*

Sea quien fuera. *Whoever he might be.*

Son tal para cual. *They're two of a kind.*

serenamente coolly, calmly.

serenar to clear up; to calm down; to pacify.

Está serenando. *It's clearing up.*

¡Serénese Ud.! *Calm yourself! Calm down!*

serenata f. serenade.

serenidad f. serenity, coolness.

sereno adj. serene, calm; clear (sky); m. dew;
night watchman.

Era un hombre sereno. *He was a calm man.
He was very calm.*

El cielo está muy sereno. *The sky is very clear.*

Hay mucho sereno en las flores. *There's a lot
of dew on the flowers.*

Esta calle no tiene sereno. *This street has no
night watchman.*

serie f. series.

Pertenece a la serie A. *It belongs to series A.*

seriedad f. seriousness, reliability; earnestness.

SERIO adj. serious; earnest; businesslike.

Es un hombre serio. *He's businesslike.*

La situación se pone seria. *The situation is
becoming serious.*

Lo dijo en serio. *He said it in earnest.*

Hablando en serio, eso no está bien. *Joking
apart, that's wrong.*

Tomar en serio. *To take seriously.*

sermón m. sermon; lecture, reproof.

serpiente f. serpent.

serrano m. mountaineer.

serrar to saw.

servicial adj. serviceable; obliging, accommodating.

SERVICIO m. service, favor, good turn; set,
service.

Servicio de mesa. *Table service.*

Me ha prestado Ud. un gran servicio. *You've
done me a great favor. ("You've rendered
me a great service.")*

Ud. podría hacerme un gran servicio. *You
could do me a great favor.*

Se quejó del servicio en el hotel. *He com-
plained about the service in the hotel.*

El servicio de trenes es muy malo aquí. *The
train service is very bad here.*

Es muy difícil conseguir servicio doméstico.
It's very difficult to get any domestic help.

Tenemos que tomar en cuenta sus buenos
servicios. *We must take into consideration
the work he did.*

De servicio. *On duty.*

Estar a servicio de. *To be working for.*

servidor m. servant, waiter.

¡Servidor de Ud.! *At your service. ("Your
servant.")*

"Quedo de Ud. atento y seguro servidor."
"Sincerely yours."

Tiene muy buenos servidores. *She has excellent servants.*

servidumbre f. servants, help; servitude.

servil adj. servile, low, mean.

servilleta f. napkin.

SERVIR to serve; to do a favor; to do for, to be useful, to answer the purpose; to be for; to wait on (the table).

Para servir a Ud. At your service.

¿En qué puedo servirle? What can I do for you? Can I help you?

¿Le sirvo a Ud. un poco de vino? Shall I give (serve) you a little wine?

Permítame servirle otra taza de café. Let me give you another cup of coffee.

La comida está servida. Dinner is served.

El camarero sirvió a la mesa. The waiter waited on the table.

¿Para qué sirve esta máquina? What's this machine for?

Sirvió cuatro años en las fuerzas aéreas. He was in the Air Corps for four years.

No lo tire, que puede servir para algo. Don't throw it away! It may be good for something.

No sirve. It's no good.

No sirve para nada. It's no good. It's good for nothing. It's worthless.

El puede servir de intérprete. He can act as interpreter.

De nada le servirá escribirles. Writing to them won't do you any good.

servirse to deign, to please; to help oneself (food); to make use of.

Sírvase venir conmigo. Please come with me.

Tenga la bondad de servirse. Please help yourself.

Me sirvo del diccionario para traducir. I use the dictionary for translating.

SESENTA adj. and n. sixty.

sesentón m. sexagenarian.

sesgo adj. sloped, oblique; m. slope; slant; bias.

Tomar mal sesgo. To take a bad turn. To take a turn for the worse. To look bad.

sesión f. session, meeting.

En sesión. In session.

SESO m. brain; brains.

Devanarse los sesos. To rack one's brains.

Perder el seso. To lose one's head.

No tiene sesos. He has no brains (coll.).

seta f. mushroom.

setecientos adj. seven hundred; seven hundredth.

SETENTA adj. and n. seventy.

setentón m. septuagenarian.

seudónimo adj. relating to a pseudonym; m. pseudonym; pen name.

severidad f. severity, strictness.

severo adj. severe, strict.

sexo m. sex.

sexteto m. sextet, sextette.

sexto adj. sixth.

SI conj. if; whether; m. si, B (the seventh note of the musical scale).

Si Ud. quiere. If you like.

Si Ud. gusta. If you please.

Si tuviese dinero, lo compraría. I'd buy it if I had money.

Si le parece nos citamos para las cuatro. Let's meet at four o'clock if that's convenient for you.

Si bien. Although.

Si por acaso. If by any chance. In case.

¡Si lo acabo de ver! But I just saw it!

Si no. If not. Otherwise.

SÍ adv. yes; indeed; refl. pron. himself, herself, itself, oneself, themselves; m. consent, assent.

Sí señor. Yes, sir.

Pues sí. Yes, indeed.

¿Sí o no? Yes or no?

Le dije que sí. I told him yes.

Eso sí que no. I should say not.

Creo que sí. I think so.

Espero que sí. I hope so.

Habla demasiado de sí misma. She talks too much about herself.

Lo quiere para sí. He wants it for himself.

Todavía no ha vuelto en sí. He hasn't recovered consciousness yet.

Estaban fuera de sí. They were beside themselves (with anger, etc.).

Reírse entre sí. To laugh up one's sleeve.

¿A que sí? I'll bet I do.

De sí. Spontaneously. Of itself (himself, etc.).

Lo dijo de sí. He said it spontaneously (of his own accord).

Dar el sí. To say yes. To give one's consent. To accept a marriage proposal.

sidra f. cider.

siega f. harvest.

siembra f. sowing; seedtime; sown ground.

SIEMPRE always; ever.

Siempre llega tarde. He's always late.

Es lo de siempre. It's the same old story.

Siempre que pueda le escribiré. I'll write you provided I'm able.

Para siempre. For good. Forever.

Para siempre jamás. Forever (and ever).

siempreviva f. everlasting, immortelle (plant).

sien f. temple.

sierra f. saw; sierra, mountain range.

No corta bien la sierra. The saw doesn't cut well.

La Sierra Madre está en Mexico. Sierra Madre is in Mexico.

siesta f. siesta, nap.

¿Va Ud. a dormir la siesta? Are you going to take your nap?

SIETE adj. and n. seven.

sigilo m. seal, secrecy; discretion; caution.

Obra con sigilo. *He acts cautiously.*

sigiloso *adj. secretivo; reserved.*

SIGLO *m. century, age; a long time.*

Vivió en el siglo décimo. *He lived in the tenth century.*

Hace un siglo que no le veo. *I haven't seen him for ages.*

El Siglo de Oro. *The Golden Age.*

significación *f. signification; significance, meaning.*

significado *m. significance; meaning.*

¿Cuál es el significado de esta palabra en inglés? *What does that word mean in English?*

SIGNIFICAR *to mean, to signify.*

¿Qué significa eso? *What's the meaning of that? What does that mean?*

No sé qué significa esa palabra. *I don't know what that word means. I don't know the meaning of that word.*

significativo *adj. significant.*

signo *m. sign, mark.*

El signo de la cruz. *The sign of the cross.*

SIGUIENTE *adj. following, next.*

Al día siguiente. *On the following day. On the next day.*

La página siguiente. *The next page.*

La aduana está en la siguiente cuadra. *The customhouse is on the next block.*

Lo siguiente: *The following:*

sílaba *f. syllable.*

silbar *to whistle; to hiss, to boo.*

El público silbó la comedia. *The audience booed the comedy. (Whistling indicates disapproval in Spanish-speaking countries.)*

silbido *m. whistling, whistle; hiss.*

silencio *m. silence; quiet.*

¡Silencio! *Silence!*

Todo estaba en silencio. *Everything was quiet.*

Su silencio me inquieta. *I'm worried because I haven't had any word from her.*

Eso lo pasó Ud. en silencio. *You avoided mentioning that.*

Sufrir en silencio. *To suffer in silence.*

silencioso *adj. silent, noiseless.*

Quiero una máquina de escribir silenciosa. *I want a noiseless typewriter.*

silueta *f. silhouette.*

silvestre *adj. wild, rustic, uncultivated.*

Flores silvestres. *Wild flowers.*

SILLA *f. chair; saddle.*

Ponga la silla aquí. *Put the chair here.*

Ponga al caballo la silla. *Put the saddle on the horse. Saddle the horse.*

sillón *m. armchair.*

simbólico *adj. symbolic.*

simbolizar *to symbolize.*

símbolo *m. symbol.*

simetría *f. symmetry.*

simétrico *adj. symmetrical.*

SIMILAR *adj. similar, resembling. (See parecido.)*

Es un producto similar. *This is a similar product.*

similitud *f. resemblance, similarity, similitude.*

simpatía *f. sympathy, liking.*

Le inspiró mucho simpatía. *He found him (her) very congenial.*

simpático *adj. nice, pleasant, congenial, nice.*

Es muy simpático. *He's very nice. He's very congenial.*

simpatizar *to sympathize; to like.*

SIMPLE *adj. simple; plain; silly, foolish; m. fool; simple (pharm.).*

Por la simple razón. *For the simple reason.*

A simple vista. *At first sight.*

El procedimiento es muy simple. *The system is very simple.*

Es una mujer muy simple. *She's a very simple woman.*

A un simple cualquiera le engaña. *Anyone can cheat a fool.*

simplemente *simply, merely.*

Eso es simplemente un detalle. *That's simply a detail.*

simpleza *f. naivete, foolishness.*

simplicidad *f. simplicity.*

simplificar *to simplify.*

simulación *f. simulation; fake.*

simulacro *m. sham, feign.*

simulado *adj. simulated, sham.*

simular *to simulate, to feign, to sham.*

simultáneo *adj. simultaneous.*

SIN *without, besides.*

Iremos sin él. *We'll go without him.*

No puedo leer sin mis anteojos. *I can't read without my glasses.*

Lo hice sin pensar. *I did it without thinking.*

Lo hice sin querer. *I did it without meaning to. I didn't mean to do it.*

Estaba sin dinero. *He was penniless.*

Es un hombre sin educación. *He's ill-bred.*

Es una mujer sin par. *She's in a class by herself. There's no one like her.*

Me he quedado sin gasolina. *I've run out of gas.*

Sin falta. *Without fail.*

Sin duda. *Without a doubt. Undoubtedly.*

Sin novedad. *Nothing new. The same as usual.*

Sin embargo. *Nevertheless. Notwithstanding.*

Un sin fin de cosas. *A million and one things.*

sinceridad *f. sincerity.*

sincero *adj. sincere.*

Es un amigo sincero. *He's a true friend.*

síncope *f. faint, fainting spell.*

sincronizar *to synchronize.*

sindical *adj. pertaining to a trade union.*

sindicato *m. trade union; syndicate.*

sinfonía *f. symphony.*

sinfónico *adj.* symphonic.

SINGULAR *adj.* singular; unusual; exceptional; strange, odd.

"Niño" es singular, y "niños" es plural. *"Boy" is singular, "boys" plural.*

¡Qué caso tan singular! *What a strange case!*

Es un hombre singular. *He's an exceptional man.*

Es un caso singularísimo. *It's a very singular (unusual) case.*

singularidad *f.* singularity; peculiarity.

siniestro *adj.* sinister; unfortunate; *m.* shipwreck, damage.

Lado siniestro. *Left side.*

Tiene un aspecto siniestro. *It looks sinister. It has a sinister look.*

¿Dónde ocurrió el siniestro? *Where did the shipwreck occur?*

sinnúmero *m.* a great many, too many, numberless, no end.

SINO (used after a negative) but; except; only; instead; *m.* fate, luck.

No es rojo sino rosado. *It's not red, but pink.*

No iré hoy, sino mañana. *I'll go tomorrow instead of today.*

Nadie puede hacerlo sino tú. *No one but you can do it.*

No piensa sino en sí mismo. *He only thinks of himself.*

Es su triste sino. *It's his hard luck.*

sinónimo *adj.* synonymous; *m.* synonym.

sintaxis *f.* syntax.

síntesis *f.* synthesis.

sintético *adj.* synthetic.

síntoma *f.* symptom.

sintonizar to tune in (radio).

sinvergüenza *m.* and *f.* shameless person.

SIQUIERA at least; even; although.

Siquiera un poquito. *Even a little bit.*

Ni siquiera eso. *Not even that.*

Una vez siquiera. *Once at least.*

Déme siquiera agua fría. *At least give me some cold water.*

Ni me dió las gracias siquiera. *He didn't even thank me.*

sirena *f.* siren; whistle; foghorn; mermaid.

sirviente *m.* servant.

sisa *f.* petty theft.

sisar to steal small quantities of something; to take in (sewing).

sistema *m.* system.

Sistema métrico. *Metric system.*

sistemático *adj.* systematic.

sitiar to besiege.

SITIO *m.* place; space, room; *m.* siege.

Ponlo otra vez en su sitio. *Put it back in the same place.*

No hay bastante sitio para todos. *There isn't enough room for everybody.*

Ocupe Ud. su sitio. *Take your seat.*

Me ofreció un sitio en su coche. *He offered me a lift ("seat") in his car.*

Está en algún sitio en la casa. *It's somewhere around the house.*

¿En qué sitio le duele? *Where does it hurt you?*

Hacer sitio. *To make room.*

Poner sitio. *To besiege.*

SITUACIÓN *f.* situation; position; circumstances; site, location.

Está en mala situación. *He's in a bad situation.*

situado *adj.* situated, located; *m.* allowance, annuity.

situar to place, to locate; to situate; to allot funds.

situarse to place oneself, to settle in a place.

so under, below.

So (capa) pretexto de. *Under the pretext of.*

So pena de. *Under penalty of.*

sobar to knead; to soften; to pummel; to pet; to beat, to whip.

soberanía *f.* sovereignty.

soberano *adj.* and *n.* sovereign.

soberbia *f.* pride, haughtiness.

soberbio *adj.* proud, haughty; ill-tempered; superb; magnificent.

Un edificio soberbio. *A magnificent building.*

Es muy soberbio. *He's very proud.*

sobornar to suborn, to bribe.

soborno *m.* bribe.

SOBRA *f.* too much, too many, more than is needed; leftover.

Tengo tiempo de sobra. *I've plenty of time.*

Tengo de sobra con lo que Ud. me dió. *I've more than enough with what you gave me.*

Estar de sobra. *To be superfluous.*

Tiene Ud. razón de sobra. *You're quite right.*

Hay de sobra. *There's more than enough.*

Aproveche las sobras. *Use up the leftovers.*

sobradamente abundantly.

Saber sobradamente. *To know only too well.*

sobrante *adj.* remaining; *m.* remainder, surplus; leftover.

SOBRAR to be more than enough; to have more than is needed; to remain; to be left.

Sobró mucha comida. *A great deal of food was left over.*

Nos sobran poquísimas provisiones. *We've got very few supplies (provisions) left.*

Más vale que sobre que no falte. *It's better to have too much than (to have) too little.*

Me parece que aquí sobro. *It seems to me that I'm intruding ("that I'm one too many") here.*

Sobran cinco. *There are five too many.*

SOBRE on; over; above; about; *m.* envelope.

Ponga el vaso sobre la mesa. *Put the glass on the table.*

Desgracia sobre desgracia. *Misfortune on misfortune. Trouble after trouble. Just one thing after another.*

¿Qué opina Ud. sobre esto? *What do you think about this?*

Tengo noticias ciertas sobre su paradero. *I've got reliable information concerning (about) his whereabouts.*

Ha escrito un libro sobre los Estados Unidos. *He has written a book about the United States.*

¿Sobre qué están discutiendo? *What are they discussing?*

Discurramos un poco más sobre esto. *Let's consider that a little longer.*

Tenía un gran dominio sobre sí. *He had great self-control.*

Sobre las tres. *At about three o'clock.*

Tengo sobre cincuenta dólares. *I have about fifty dollars.*

Estar sobre aviso. *To be on guard.*

Sobre todo. *Above all.*

Sobre que. *Besides.*

Déme un sobre. *Give me an envelope.*

sobrealimentación *f. overfeeding.*
sobrealimentar *to overfeed.*
sobrecama *f. bedspread.*
sobrecarga *f. overload; overcharge.*
sobrecargar *to overload; to overcharge.*
sobrecargo *m. purser; supercargo (on a ship).*
sobrecoger *to surprise, to take by surprise.*
sobreentenderse *to be understood, to go without saying.*

Eso se sobreentiende. *That's understood. That goes without saying.*

sobrellevar *to shoulder, to ease (another's burden); to bear; to endure.*

El es el que sobrelleva toda la carga. *He's the one who shoulders the whole burden.*

Sobrelleva sus penas con paciencia. *He endures his difficulties (troubles) patiently.*

sobremanera *excessively, exceedingly.*
sobremesa *f. table cover; dessert; after dinner; after-dinner talk (around the table).*

Después de comer, fuma su cigarro de sobremesa. *After eating he smokes his after-dinner cigar.*

Estuvimos cerca de una hora de sobremesa. *After dinner we sat around the table and talked for about an hour.*

sobrenatural *adj. and m. supernatural.*
sobrepaga *m. extra pay.*
sobrepasar *to exceed, to surpass.*
sobreponer *to place over; to overlay; to overlap.*
sobreponerse *to master, to overcome; to prevail on another; to show (prove) oneself superior to.*

sobresaliente *adj. outstanding; excelling.*
sobresalir *to stand out, to excel.*
sobresaltar *to frighten, to startle; to assail, to fall upon.*
sobresaltarse *to be frightened, to be startled.*

Se sobresalta por la menor cosa. *The least (little) thing frightens her. She gets frightened at the least (little) thing.*

sobresalto *m. start, shock.*
sobresueldo *m. extra pay; bonus.*
sobrevenir *to happen, to take place; to supervene.*

Sobrevino algo inesperado. *Something unexpected happened.*

sobriedad *f. sobriety, temperance, moderation.*
sobrina *f. niece.*
sobrino *m. nephew.*
sobrio *adj. sober, temperate.*
sociable *adj. sociable.*
social *adj. social.*

Tenía muy buen trato social. *He was very agreeable socially.*

Movimiento social. *Social movement.*

¿Quién representa a esta razón social? *Who's the representative of this firm?*

socialismo *m. socialism.*
socialista *adj. socialistic; m. socialist.*
socializar *to socialize.*
sociedad *f. society; social life; company, corporation; partnership.*

Le gustaba frecuentar la buena sociedad. *He liked to move in society.*

Formaron una sociedad. *They formed a partnership.*

Sociedad anónima. *Corporation.*

socio *m. partner, associate; fellow member.*

Le presento a mi socio, Sr. Smith. *Meet my partner, Mr. Smith.*

¿Es Ud. socio de ese club? *Are you a member of that club?*

sociología *f. sociology.*
sociólogo *m. sociologist.*
socorrer *to aid, to help, to assist; to rescue.*

Hay que socorrerlo. *We have to help him.*

socorro *m. succor, aid, help.*
soda *f. soda.*
soez *adj. indecent, obscene; outspoken, rude, coarse.*
sofá *m. sofa.*
sofocante *adj. suffocating.*
sofocar *to suffocate, to stifle, to choke; to vex; to make a person blush; to put out (fire).*

El calor le ha sofocado. *He was suffocated by the heat.*

No se sofoque Ud. *Don't get excited. Don't overexert yourself.*

Sofocar el fuego. *To put out a fire.*

Sofocar una rebelión. *To crush (subdue) a rebellion.*

sofocón *m. chagrin.*

soga f. rope; halter, cord.

SOL m. sun, sunshine; C, sol (the fifth note of the musical scale).

Hace sol. The sun's shining. The sun's out.

Vamos a tomar el sol. Let's go for a walk in the sun.

Antes de bañarse estuvieron tomando el sol mucho rato. They took a long sunbath before bathing.

Salida del sol. Sunrise.

Puesta del sol. Sunset.

De sol a sol. From sunrise to sunset.

SOLAMENTE solely, only.

Aprendí solamente un poco de español. I learned only a little Spanish.

Déme Ud. solamente la mitad. Give me just half.

solapa f. lapel.

solar m. lot, plot (land); real estate; mansion.

solas (a) all alone, by oneself.

A mis solas. By myself. All alone.

A sus solas. By himself (herself). All alone.

SOLDADO m. soldier, private.

Soldado raso. Buck private.

soldar to solder; to weld.

Todavía no han soldado la cañería. They haven't soldered the pipe yet.

soledad f. solitude, loneliness.

solemne adj. solemn; serious, grave.

solemnidad f. solemnity.

Pobre de solemnidad. Very poor.

SOLER to be unusual, to be accustomed to, to be in the habit of.

Suele comer despacio. He usually eats slowly.

Suele venir los domingos. He usually comes on Sundays.

Como suele acontecer. As often happens. As is apt to be the case.

solfear to sing the scale (music).

SOLICITAR to solicit; to ask; to apply for.

Solicita un empleo. She's applying for a position.

Hay que solicitar un permiso para visitar ese edificio. You'll have to ask for a pass to visit that building.

Solicitó su mano. He proposed to her.

solicitud f. application; request.

Llene Ud. el pliego de la solicitud. Fill out the application.

solidaridad f. solidarity.

solidario adj. jointly responsible.

solidez f. solidity, firmness, soundness.

SÓLIDO adj. solid, sound, strong, firm; m. solid.

Tiene una base muy sólida. It has a very solid base.

Cuerpo sólido. Solid substance.

Tiene una educación sólida. He has a sound education.

solitario adj. solitary, lonely; m. solitary; hermit; solitaire (game).

SOLO adj. alone; single; m. solo (music).

¿Está Ud. solo? Are you alone?

Ni una sola palabra. Not a single word.

Quiero estar solo. I want to be alone.

Vive solo. He lives alone.

Estoy muy solo. I'm very lonely.

¿Ha venido Ud. solo? Have you come alone?

No lo puedo hacer yo solo. I can't do this all alone (by myself).

SÓLO adv. only, solely.

Sólo tengo dos pesos. I have only two dollars.

Sólo para adultos. Adults only.

Hace sólo un rato que almorcé. I had breakfast only a little while ago.

Sólo Dios sabe lo que pasará. (Only) God knows what will happen.

SOLTAR to untie; to loosen; to set free; to let out; to let go.

Soltaron al preso. They set the prisoner free.

¡No lo suelte Ud! Hold it! Don't let go!

Soltaron las amarras. They loosened the cables.

De repente soltó una carcajada. Suddenly he burst into laughter (burst out laughing).

Tengo unas ganas de soltarle cuatro frescas a ése. I would like to give that fellow a piece of my mind.

soltarse to get loose; to become wild; to lose restraint, to become more dexterous; to start.

Se soltó a correr. He started to run.

Soltarse el pelo. To let one's hair down.

soltero adj. single, unmarried; m. bachelor.

¿Es Ud. casado o soltero? Are you single or married?

Todavía soy soltero. I'm still a bachelor.

solterón m. old bachelor.

solterona f. old maid.

soltura f. ease; ability; agility; release; looseness.

Bailaba con mucha soltura. She dances with great ease (gracefully).

Hablar con soltura. To speak freely.

soluble adj. soluble; solvable.

SOLUCIÓN f. solution, answer, way out; denouement, outcome (of a plot in a play, story, etc.).

Esto no tiene solución. This doesn't have a solution. There's no solution to this.

¿Dónde encontraré la solución? Where can I find the answer?

Esa es la mejor solución. That's the best way out. That's the best solution.

solvencia f. solvency.

solvente adj. solvent.

sollozar to sob.

sollozo m. sob.

SOMBRA f. shade; shadow; darkness.

El termómetro marca treinta grados a la

sombra. *The thermometer registers thirty
degrees in the shade.*

Se sentó a descansar a la sombra de un árbol.
He sat down to rest in the shade of the tree.

Le pusieron a la sombra. *They imprisoned
him.*

sombrerera *f.* milliner; hatbox.

sombrerería *f.* hat shop; millinery.

sombrerero *m.* hatter.

SOMBRERO *m.* hat.

Se puso el sombrero y salió. *He put on his
hat and left.*

Quítese Ud. el sombrero al entrar. *Take off
your hat on entering (when you enter).*

sombrilla *f.* parasol.

sombrío *adj.* shady; gloomy.

Tenía un semblante muy sombrío. *He had a
very gloomy face.*

someter *to subject; to subdue; to put (to a test);
to submit.*

Fué difícil someter a los rebeldes. *It was
difficult to subdue the rebels.*

Someta Ud. esto a nuevo estudio. *Give it
further study.*

somnámbulo *m.* sleepwalker, somnambulist.
(Also written **sonámbulo**.)

SON *m.* sound, tune; guise; a Cuban musical
rhythm.

¿A son de qué? *Why? For what reason?*

En son de. *In the guise of. As.*

En son de broma. *As a joke.*

Sin son ni ton. *Without rhyme or reason.*

Bailar uno al son que le tocan. *To adapt
oneself to the circumstances.*

sonaja *f.* jingles; tambourine.

sonámbulo *m.* sleepwalker.

SONAR *to sound; to ring; to be mentioned, to
sound familiar.*

Esa nota no me suena bien. *That note doesn't
sound right.*

Suena el timbre. *The bell's ringing.*

Ese nombre no me suena. *That name doesn't
sound familiar to me.*

Suena mucho su nombre para candidato. *His
name is often mentioned as a candidate.*

Sonó un disparo. *There was the sound of a shot.*

sonarse *to blow one's nose.*

sonata *f.* sonata.

sondar (See **sondear**).

sondear *to sound, to fathom; to find out, to learn
about.*

Estuvieron sondeando la bahía. *They were
sounding the bay.*

Sondee Ud. sus intenciones. *Find out his
intentions. Sound him out.*

soneto *m.* sonnet.

sonido *m.* sound.

sonoridad *f.* sonority.

sonoro *adj.* sonorous; sounding.

Tiene una voz muy sonora. *He has a sonorous
voice.*

Una película sonora (hablada). *A talking picture. A sound film.*

sonreír *to smile.*

Todos sonrieron satisfechos. *Everyone smiled
with satisfaction.*

sonrisa *f.* smile.

Una amable sonrisa. *A pleasant smile.*

sonrojar *to make one blush.*

sonrojarse *to blush.*

Se sonroja por nada. *Anything makes her
blush. She blushes at the least little thing.*

sonsacar *to wheedle.*

soñador *m.* dreamer.

SOÑAR *to dream.*

No debería Ud. soñar con tales cosas. *You
shouldn't even dream of such things.*

Vive soñando. *His head's in the clouds. ("He
lives in a daydream.")*

soñoliento *adj.* sleepy, drowsy.

SOPA *f.* soup.

¿Le sirvo un poco de sopa? *Shall I serve you
some soup?*

Estoy hecho una sopa. *I'm soaked to the skin.*

sopapo *m.* a blow under the chin, uppercut; slap.

sopera *f.* soup tureen.

sopetón *m.* blow; toasted bread dipped in oil.

Se presentó de sopetón. *Suddenly he appeared.
He appeared all of a sudden.*

soplar *to blow; to inflate; to steal, to rob.*

Soplaba un viento suave. *A very gentle wind
was blowing.*

Le soplaron el reloj. *They stole his watch.*

soplo *m.* blowing; puff (of wind); hint; denunciation.

soplón *m.* stoolpigeon.

sopor *m.* stupor; drowsiness.

soportar *to stand, to endure, to bear.*

Ha soportado muchas penas. *He endured
many hardships.*

No puedo soportarlo por más tiempo. *I can't
stand it any longer.*

soprano *m.* soprano.

sorber *to sip; to suck; to absorb; to swallow.*

sorbete *m.* sherbet.

sorbo *m.* sip, draught, gulp.

Tómeselo a sorbos. *Sip it.*

sordera *f.* deafness.

SORDO *adj.* deaf; not able to hear; not willing to
hear; muffled; silent; *m.* a deaf person.

Sordo como una tapia. *As deaf as a post.*

Ser sordo a. *To be deaf to.*

sordomudo *adj. and n.* deaf and dumb; deaf-mute.

SORPRENDER *to surprise; to take by surprise.*

No se sorprenda Ud. por eso. *Don't be surprised at that.*

Su llegada nos sorprendió a todos. *His arrival surprised everybody.*

SORPRESA *f.* surprise.

Es una verdadera sorpresa. *This is a real surprise.*

De sorpresa. *By surprise.*

Me ha cogido de sorpresa. *It has taken (it took) me by surprise.*

sortear to draw lots; to raffle; to avoid, to evade, to dodge.

sorteo *m.* lottery, raffle.

sortija *f.* ring; lock of hair.

sosa *f.* soda.

Sosa cáustica. *Caustic soda.*

sosegado *adj.* calm, quiet.

sosegar to appease, to calm; to rest.

sosegarse to calm down; to be quiet.

Cuando Ud. se sosiegue, hablaremos. *We'll talk it over when you calm down.*

sosiego *m.* peace, calmness, quiet.

No tenía un minuto de sosiego. *He hadn't had a moment's peace.*

soslayo *m.* slant, askance.

Mirar de soslayo. *To look askance. To look out of the corner of one's eye.*

soso *adj.* insipid, tasteless; uninteresting; simple, homely.

La comida está sosa. *The food is tasteless.*

Es una chica sosa. *She's an uninteresting girl.*

sospecha *f.* suspicion.

Eso da motivos de sospecha. *That gives ground for suspicion.*

sospechar to suspect, to have a suspicion.

Sospecho de él. *I'm suspicious of him. I suspect him.*

sospechoso *adj.* suspicious; suspecting.

Es un individuo sospechoso. *He's a suspicious character.*

sostén *m.* support, prop.

SOSTENER to support, to sustain; to maintain; to hold; to carry (a conversation).

Sostenía a su familia. *He supported his family.*

Ahora podemos sostener una conversación en español. *We can now carry on a conversation in Spanish.*

Lo digo y lo sostengo. *I'll stand by what I'm saying. ("I'm saying it and I maintain it.")*

sostenerse to support oneself, to keep up, to hold out.

Estaba tan borracho que no podía sostenerse. *He was so drunk, he couldn't stand up.*

sostenido *adj.* sustained; *m.* sharp (music).

sostenimiento *m.* support, maintenance; upkeep.

sota *f.* jack, knave (playing cards).

sotana *f.* cassock.

sótano *m.* cellar.

soya *f.* soy bean. (Also **soja**.)

SU *pron.* his, her, its, their; your; *pl.* sus.

Su libro. *His book.*

Sus libros. *His books.*

Su hermana. *His sister.*

Sus hermanas. *His sisters.*

Su novio. *Her fiancé.*

¿Dónde están sus hijos?—Están con sus abuelos. *Where are your children?—They're with their grandparents.*

Este procedimiento tiene sus ventajas y desventajas. *This procedure has its advantages and disadvantages.*

SUAVE *adj.* soft, smooth, mild, gentle, mellow.

Esta tela es muy suave. *This cloth is very soft.*

Es un vino suave. *This wine is very mellow.*

Tabaco suave. *Mild tobacco.*

suavemente smoothly, softly, mildly; gently, sweetly.

suavidad *f.* softness; suavity.

suavizar to soften; to make smooth.

subalterno *adj.* and *n.* subaltern, subordinate.

subarrendar to sublet.

subasta *f.* auction.

subconsciente *adj.* and *n.* subconscious.

subdirector *m.* assistant director.

súbdito *m.* subject (of a king, etc.).

subdivisión *f.* subdivision.

subido *adj.* bright, loud, deep (color); high (price).

Es de un color muy subido. *It's a loud color.*

Es algo subido el precio. *The price is a little high.*

SUBIR to go up, to walk up; to ascend, to rise; to climb; to mount; to come up; to take up; to bring up; to get on; to raise.

Suba Ud. a mi cuarto. *Go up to my room.*

Subamos. 1. *Let's go up.* 2. *Let's get on (train, bus, etc.)*

Suban Uds. un piso más. *Walk up another flight.*

Oigo subir a alguien. *I hear someone coming upstairs.*

Me tienes que ayudar a subir el baúl. *You must help me bring the trunk up.*

El mozo le subirá la maleta al tren. *The porter will put your suitcase on the train.*

Subió a lo alto del árbol. *He climbed to the top of the tree.*

El globo subió hasta diez mil pies. *The balloon rose to ten thousand feet.*

Le subió la temperatura. *His temperature rose.*

Los precios suben cada vez más. *Prices are constantly going up (rising).*

Tendrá Ud. que subir un poco la voz, es muy sordo. *You'll have to raise your voice a little; he's very deaf.*

Ha subido muy de prisa ese muchacho. *That boy has made rapid progress.*

¿A cuánto sube la cuenta? *How much is the bill?*

Subir a caballo. *To mount a horse.*

Subir de punto. *To increase. To grow.*

Se le subieron los tragos a la cabeza. *The drinks went to his head.*

SÚBITAMENTE *suddenly.*

SÚBITO *adj. sudden.*

De súbito. *Suddenly. All of a sudden.*

subjefe *m. second in command; chief assistant.*

subjetividad *f. subjectivity.*

subjetivo *adj. subjective.*

subjuntivo *m. subjunctive.*

sublevación *f. insurrection, uprising.*

sublevar *to stir up, to excite to rebellion.*

sublevarse *to revolt.*

sublime *adj. sublime.*

submarino *adj. and n. submarine.*

subordinado *adj. subordinate.*

subordinar *to subordinate.*

subrayar *to underline, to emphasize.*

subsanar *to rectify, to make right, to repair, to make up; to excuse.*

Subsanar un error. *To rectify an error.*

subscribir *to subscribe.*

subscribirse *to subscribe to.*

¿Quiere Ud. subscribirse a esta revista? *Would you like to subscribe to this magazine?*

subscripción *f. subscription.*

subscriptor *m. subscriber.*

subsecretario *m. under secretary; assistant secretary.*

subsecuente *adj. subsequent.*

subsidio *m. subsidy, aid.*

subsistencia *f. subsistence.*

Han subido mucho las subsistencias. *The cost of living has risen (gone up) a great deal.*

Subsistencias alimenticias. *Foodstuffs. Food.*

subsistente *adj. subsistent; subsisting.*

subsistir *to subsist; to exist; to last.*

substancia *f. substance; essence.*

En substancia. 1. *In substance.* 2. *In short. In brief.*

substancial *adj. substantial.*

substanciar *to substantiate.*

substancioso *adj. juicy; nourishing; substantial.*

substantivo *adj. substantive; m. substantive, noun.*

substitución *f. substitution.*

substituir *to substitute.*

substituto *m. substitute.*

substracción *f. subtraction.*

substraer *to subtract.*

subterráneo *adj. subterranean, underground; m. subway (Arg.).*

subtítulo *m. subtitle.*

suburbio *m. suburb.*

subvención *f. subsidy.*

subvencionar *to subsidize.*

subyugar *to subdue, to subjugate.*

SUCEDER *to happen; to succeed; to inherit.*

¿Qué sucedió después? *What happened then (next)?*

¿Qué le ha sucedido? *What happened to you?*

Suceda lo que suceda. yo estaré aquí. *No matter what happens, I'll be here.*

Se cree que su hijo le sucederá. *It's thought that his son will succeed him.*

sucesión *f. succession; estate, inheritance; off-spring.*

sucesivamente *successively.*

sucesivo *adj. successive.*

En lo sucesivo. *In the future. Hereafter.*

suceso *m. event; incident.*

Sucesos de actualidad. *Current events. News of the day.*

sucesor *m. successor.*

suciedad *f. dirt, filth.*

sucio *adj. dirty, filthy, nasty.*

Una jugada sucia. *A dirty trick.*

Palabras sucias. *Nasty (dirty) words.*

sucumbir *to die; to succumb; to give way, to yield.*

sucursal *adj. subsidiary; m. branch, annex.*

sud *m. south. (See sur.)*

sudar *to sweat, to perspire; to toil.*

sudeste *m. southeast.*

sudoeste *m. southwest.*

sudor *m. sweat, perspiration, toil, hard work.*

suegra *f. mother-in-law.*

suegro *m. father-in-law.*

suela *f. sole (of shoe); sole leather.*

sueldo *f. salary.*

SUELO *m. soil; ground; floor.*

Levanta ese papel del suelo. *Pick up that paper from the floor.*

Dígale a la criada que barra el suelo. *Tell the servant to sweep the floor.*

El suelo está resbaladizo (resbaloso). *The pavement is slippery.*

Este suelo produce mucho. *This land is very fertile.*

Venirse al suelo. *To fall to the ground.*

Estar por los suelos. *To be very cheap (price).*

Suelo natal. *Native land.*

SUELTO *adj. loose; swift; free; fluent (style), single, odd (copy); m. change (money); newspaper item, short editorial.*

Sus cordones están sueltos. *Your shoelaces are untied (loose).*

Tenemos unos números sueltos de esa revista. *I have some odd copies of that magazine.*

Ese muchacho anda suelto. *That boy's running wild.*

Suelto de lengua. *Outspoken.*

Corrió a rienda suelta. *He ran fast.*

¿Tiene Ud. suelto? *Have you any change?*

No tengo suelto. *I haven't any change.*

SUEÑO *m. sleep; dream.*

¿Tiene Ud. sueño? *Are you sleepy?*

Tengo mucho sueño. *I'm very sleepy.*

Sueño con mucha frecuencia. *I dream very often.*

Todo me parece un sueño. *Everything seems like a dream.*

suero m. *serum.*

SUERTE f. *chance, lot, fortune, luck; manner, way, kind.*

¡Buena suerte! *Good luck!*

Mala suerte. *Bad luck.*

Envidio tu suerte. *I envy your luck.*

Tiene mucha suerte. *He's very lucky.*

Echemos suertes. *Let's draw lots.*

¿A quién le tocó la suerte? *Who won the lottery?*

De la misma suerte. *The same way.*

De suerte que. *So that. So. Thus.*

suficiencia f. *sufficiency, capacity.*

SUFICIENTE adj. *enough; sufficient.*

Eso no es suficiente. *That's not enough.*

Por más que trabaja, nunca gana lo suficiente. *He never earns enough no matter how hard he works.*

sufijo adj. *suffixed;* m. *suffix.*

sufragar *to pay, to defray; to aid.*

Sufragará todos los gastos del viaje. *He'll pay all the expenses of the trip.*

sufragio m. *suffrage, vote; aid.*

sufrido adj. *patient, enduring; practical (color).*

Es una mujer sufrida. *She's a very patient woman.*

El traje tiene un color sufrido. *The dress is of a practical color.*

sufrimiento m. *suffering.*

sufrir *to suffer, to stand.*

¿De qué dolencia sufre Ud.? *What (illness) are you suffering from? What do you have?*

No puedo sufrirlo por más tiempo. *I can't stand it any more.*

sugerencia f. *suggestion*

SUGERIR *to suggest, to hint.*

¿Qué me sugiere Ud.? *What do you suggest ("to me")?*

SUGESTION f. *suggestion, hint.*

Esa fué una buena sugestión. *That was a good suggestion.*

sugestionar *to suggest through hypnotism; to influence.*

sugestivo adj. *suggestive.*

suicida m. and f. *suicide (person).*

suicidarse *to commit suicide.*

suicidio m. *(the act of) suicide.*

sujetapapeles m. *paper clip, paper holder.*

SUJETAR *to fasten; to hold; to subdue, to subject.*

Sujete Ud. bien las riendas. *Hold on to the reins.*

No está bien sujeto el cinturón. *The belt isn't fastened well.*

Sujete al perro con una cadena. *Put a leash ("chain") on the dog.*

sujetarse *to submit to, to keep to, to abide by.*

Había que sujetarse a la nueva disposición. *We had to submit to the new regulations.*

SUJETO adj. *subject, liable, likely;* m. *subject; (coll.) fellow, guy.*

Estar sujeto a. *To be subject to.*

¿Quién es ese sujeto? *Who's that fellow (coll.)?*

Es un buen sujeto. *He's a nice guy (coll.).*

sulfuro m. *sulphide.*

SUMA f. *sum, amount; addition.*

¿Cuánto es la suma total? *What's the total amount?*

Ha menester cincuenta dólares para completar la suma. *Fifty dollars is needed to complete the sum.*

Una suma crecida. *A large sum of money.*

Es hombre de suma cortesía. *He's very (extremely) polite.*

En suma. *In short.*

sumamente *extremely, exceedingly.*

Es Ud. sumamente amable. *You're extremely kind.*

sumar *to add; to sum up.*

Suma muy bien. *He adds accurately.*

Sumarse a. *To join.*

Se sumó al movimiento. *He joined the movement.*

sumario adj. *summary;* m. *summary; indictment, table of contents.*

sumergir *to submerge.*

sumidero m. *sewer, drain, sink.*

suministrar *to supply, to furnish.*

suministro m. *supply.*

sumisión f. *submission, resignation, obedience.*

sumiso adj. *submissive, obedient, docile.*

SUMO adj. *high, great, supreme.*

Con sumo gusto. *With great pleasure.*

En sumo grado. *In the highest degree.*

A lo sumo. *At the most.*

suntuosidad f. *sumptuousness.*

suntuoso adj. *sumptuous, magnificent.*

supeditar *to subject.*

Estar supeditado a. *To be subject to.*

superabundante adj. *superabundant, very abundant.*

superar *to exceed, to excel, to surpass; to overcome.*

superchería f. *deceit, fraud.*

superficial adj. *superficial.*

superficialidad f. *superficiality.*

superficie f. *surface; area.*

superfluo adj. *superfluous.*

superintendente m. *superintendent; supervisor; quartermaster.*

SUPERIOR adj. *superior; higher, better; above;* m. *superior.*

Es superior a todo elogio. *It's above all praise.*

Labio superior. *Upper lip.*

Es un hombre superior. *He's a great man.*

Este es un vino superior. *This is an excellent wine.*

superioridad *f. superiority; higher authority.*

superlativo *adj. superlative.*

supernumerario *adj. supernumerary.*

superproducción *f. overproduction.*

superstición *f. superstition.*

supersticioso *adj. superstitious.*

superviviente *adj. and n. survivor; surviving.*

suplantar *to supplant, to displace.*

suplementario *adj. supplementary.*

suplemento *m. supplementing; supplement, extra (in Spain.)*

suplente *adj. and n. substituting, replacing; alternate, substitute.*

súplica *f. request, entreaty, petition.*

No cedió a sus súplicas. *He didn't give in to her pleas.*

suplicación *f. supplication; request; petition.*

suplicar *to beg, to implore, to beseech, to entreat; to petition.*

Suplico a Ud. que le perdone. *I beg of you (entreat you) to forgive him.*

Le suplicó que le ayudara. *She implored him to help her.*

suplicio *m. ordeal, torment, torture; execution (death penalty).*

Pasó por el suplicio de . . . *He went through the ordeal of . . .*

suplir *to supply; to make up; to substitute.*

SUPONER *to imagine, to suppose, to surmise; to amount to; to expect.*

Ud. podrá suponer lo que ocurrió. *You can imagine what happened.*

¿Cuánto supone todo esto? *What does all this amount to? How important is all this?*

Es de suponer que . . . *It's to be expected that . . .*

suposición *f. supposition, conjecture, assumption; falsehood.*

supremacía *f. supremacy.*

supremo *adj. supreme; highest.*

supresión *f. suppression.*

SUPRIMIR *to suppress; to abolish; to eliminate; to omit, to leave out; to do away with.*

Suprima Ud. los huevos. *Eliminate eggs from your diet.*

Suprimieron los impuestos sobre las diversiones. *The amusement taxes were abolished.*

SUPUESTO *adj. supposed, assumed; m. supposition, assumption.*

Usaba un nombre supuesto. *He used an alias.*

Ud. parte de un supuesto equivocado. *You're starting with a false assumption (from a wrong premise).*

Por supuesto, tendrá Ud. que tener el pasaporte en regla. *Of course, you have to have your passport in order.*

En el supuesto de que. *On the assumption that.*

SUR *m. south. (See sud.)*

surco *m. furrow; wrinkle.*

surgir *to spurt; to arise; to appear.*

Han surgido algunas dificultades. *Some (several) difficulties have arisen.*

surtido *adj. assorted; m. assortment, stock, supply.*

Quiero una caja de galletas surtidas. *I want a box of assorted cookies.*

Hemos recibido un surtido de medias de varios tamaños. *We've received an assortment of stockings of various sizes.*

Un surtido selecto. *A select stock. A selection (of articles, etc.).*

surtidor *m. jet, spout; caterer.*

Surtidor de gasolina. *Filling station (gasoline).*

surtir *to supply, to furnish.*

¿Se ha surtido de todo lo necesario? *Have you supplied yourself with everything necessary?*

SUS *(pl. of su). (See su.)*

susceptibilidad *f. susceptibility.*

susceptible *adj. susceptible, sensitive to.*

suscitar *to stir up, to excite.*

susodicho *adj. above-mentioned; aforesaid.*

SUSPENDER *to suspend; to lay off; to postpone; to put off; to discontinue; to stop (payment); to adjourn.*

La lámpara estaba suspendida del techo. *The lamp was suspended from the ceiling.*

Se ha suspendido la publicación de la revista. *The publication of the magazine was suspended.*

Lo han suspendido de su cargo. *He was laid off from his job.*

Suspendieron el partido por la lluvia. *The game was postponed on account of rain.*

Suspender los pagos. *To stop payment.*

suspensión *f. suspension, cessation, stop.*

suspensivo *adj. suspensive.*

Puntos suspensivos. *Suspension points.*

suspenso *adj. suspended; hung; m. suspense; abeyance.*

El libro lo tiene a uno en suspenso. *The book keeps one in suspense.*

En suspenso. *In suspense. Pending.*

Dejar en suspenso. *To hold over (for future action or consideration). To hold in abeyance.*

suspicacia *f. suspicion; distrust.*

suspicaz *adj. suspicious, distrustful.*

suspirar *to sigh.*

Suspirar por. *To crave. To long for.*

suspiro *m. sigh, breath.*

sustancia *f. (See substancia.)*

sustantivo m. (See **substantivo**.)

sustentar to support, to feed, to sustain, to assert.

sustento m. maintenance, support.

sustituto m. (See **substituto**.)

sustituir (See **substituir**.)

sustituto adj. (See **substituto**.)

susto m. fright.

Dar un susto. To scare.

Recuperarse de un susto. To recover from a shock.

sustraer (See **substraer**.)

sutil adj. subtle.

sutileza f. subtleness.

SUYA (f. of suyo) yours; his; hers; theirs; your own; his own; her own; their own; f. view, way. (See suyo.)

Mi corbata es igual que la suya. My tie is like yours.

Una amiga suya. A friend of hers.

Esta pluma es suya. This pen is yours.

Ha tomado mi pluma y me ha dado la suya. He took my pen and gave me his own.

Ver la suya. To see one's chance.

Salirse con la suya. To have one's way.

Es una de las suyas. It's one of his tricks (pranks).

SUYAS (pl. of suya). (See suya.)

Son vecinas suyas. They're neighbors of yours.

Estas chicas son amigas suyas. These girls are friends of hers. These girls are her friends.

SUYO yours; his; hers; theirs; one's; your own; his own; her own; their own; its own; sometimes used with the article el, la, lo, los, las. (El suyo, la suya, lo suyo, los suyos and las suyas are equivalent to el de Ud., el de él, el de ella, el de ellos, el de ellas, los de Ud., los de él, los de ella, los de ellos, las de Ud., las de él, las de ellas, las de ellos.)

¿Es Ud. primo suyo? Are you his cousin?

¿Es suyo este lápiz? Is this pencil yours?

Me gustaría tener un anillo como el suyo. I'd like to have a ring like yours.

Un conocido suyo. An acquaintance of theirs.

De suyo. Of one's own accord. Spontaneously. In itself. Of itself.

SUYOS (pl. of suyo). (See suyo.)

Estos libros son los suyos. These are your books.

Unos amigos suyos. Some friends of yours.

¿Cómo está Ud. y los suyos? How are you and your family ("yours")?

T

tabaco m. tobacco.

Tabaco suave (flojo). Mild tobacco.

Tabaco en rama. Leaf tobacco.

tabaquera f. snuffbox; tobacco pouch.

tabaquería f. cigar store.

tabaquero m. tobacconist.

taberna f. tavern, inn, bar.

tabernero m. tavern keeper.

tabique m. partition wall, partition.

tabla f. table (of information); board, plank (of wood); pl. stage.

Con esta tabla haré un banco. I'll make a bench with this board.

Tabla de multiplicar. Multiplication table.

tablado m. platform; stage; scaffold.

tablero m. panel, board.

Tablero de damas. Checkerboard.

Tablero de ajedrez. Chessboard.

tableta f. tablet.

tablilla f. slab, small board; bulletin board.

tuburete m. stool; tabouret.

tacañería f. stinginess.

tacaño adj. stingy, miserly.

tácito adj. tacit.

taciturno adj. taciturn.

taco m. plug, stopper; pad, wad; billiard cue.

tacón m. heel; heelpiece of a shoe.

Tacones de goma. Rubber heels.

taconear to tap with the heels.

taconeo m. the act of tapping with the heels.

táctica f. tactics.

tacto m. touch; tact; skill; feel.

Es un hombre de mucho tacto. He's a very tactful man.

Es suave al tacto. It feels soft. ("It's soft to the touch.")

tacha f. fault, blemish.

Poner tacha (a). To find fault. To make objections.

Sin tacha. Without fault (blemish).

tachar to find fault with; to erase, to cross out; to censure.

tachuela f. tack, small nail.

tafetán m. taffeta.

tahona f. bakery, baker shop.

tahur m. gambler; cardsharp.

tajada f. slice, cut.

tajo m. cut, incision.

TAL adj. such, so, as.

¿Qué tal? How are you? How are things? What do you say?

¿Qué tal ha sido el viaje? How was the trip?

¿Qué tal está su familia? How is your family?

¿Qué tal se porta? How is she behaving?

No permitiré tal cosa. I won't allow such a thing.

En mi vida nihe visto ni oído tal cosa. I haven't seen or heard of such a thing in my life.

Encontramos el país tal como nos lo habíamos imaginado. We found the country just as we had imagined it to be.

Tal era el frío que tuvimos que encender la lumbre. *It was so cold that we had to light a fire.*

Como si tal cosa. *As if nothing had happened.*

Lo dejaron todo tal como estaba. *They left everything just as it was.*

Me lo dijo un tal Smith. *A certain Smith told me so.*

Tal vez. *Maybe.*

Con tal que. *Provided that.*

No hay tal. *No such thing.*

Tal para cual. *Two of a kind.*

tala *f. felling of trees; havoc.*

talabartería *f. saddlery, saddler's shop.*

talabartero *m. saddler.*

taladrar *to drill, to bore.*

taladro *m. auger, bit, drill; drill hole, bore.*

talar *to fell trees; to destroy.*

talco *m. talcum, talc; tinsel.*

talego *m. bag, sack; a clumsy person.*

talento *m. talent; cleverness.*

Es un escritor de gran talento. *He's a very talented writer.*

talón *m. heel; check, stub, receipt.*

Presente este talón al reclamar su equipaje. *Present this check when you claim your baggage.*

talonario *m. stub; stub book, checkbook.*

talla *f. stature, size; wood carving; sculpture, engraving.*

Es un hombre de talla media. *He's of medium height.*

tallador *m. engraver.*

tallar *to carve; to engrave.*

tallarín *m. noodle.*

talle *m. waist; size; shape; figure.*

Tiene un talle muy pequeño. *She has a very small waist.*

taller *m. workshop, factory; laboratory.*

Taller de sastre. *Tailor shop.*

Taller de reparaciones. *Repair shop.*

tallo *m. stem; stalk; sprout.*

tamal *m. tamale.*

¿Le gustan los tamales? *Do you like tamales?*

TAMAÑO *adj. of such and such a size; such, so great, so large, so small, etc.; m. size, dimensions.*

Nunca había visto tamaño descaro. *I'd never seen such impudence.*

¿De qué tamaño es? *What size is it?*

¿Tiene Ud. tornillos de este tamaño? *Have you screws of this size?*

Hemos recibido un surtido de medias de varios tamaños. *We've received an assortment of stockings of various sizes.*

De gran tamaño. *Very large.*

De poco tamaño. *Small.*

TAMBIÉN *also, too; as well; likewise.*

Yo también. *I also.*

¿Va Ud. también? *Are you going too?*

También Ud. puede venir. *You may also come. You can come too.*

tambor *m. drum; drummer.*

tamiz *m. fine sieve, sifter.*

tamizar *to sift.*

TAMPOCO *neither (used after a negative).*

A decir verdad, no quiero verle.—Ni yo tampoco. *To tell the truth I don't want to see him.—Neither do I.*

Su mujer tampoco dijo nada. *His wife didn't say anything either.*

TAN *(shortening of tanto) so, as, so much, as well, as much.*

¿Qué le ha hecho volver tan pronto? *What made you return so soon?*

Siendo tan tarde no iré. *Since it's so late, I won't go.*

Tan pronto como sea posible. *As soon as possible.*

Tan largo tiempo. *Such a long time.*

No tan de prisa. *Not so fast.*

Ya es tan alto como su padre. *He's now as tall as his father.*

Habla español tan bien como ella. *He speaks Spanish as well as she.*

Tan bien. *So well. As well.*

Tan mal. *So bad. As bad.*

Además de ser tan encantadora, es inteligente. *She's intelligent as well as charming.*

No le creí tan niño. *I didn't think he was so childish. ("I didn't think him such a child.")*

¿Tan aficionado es su hermano al esquí? *Is your brother that enthusiastic about skiing?*

tanda *f. rotation, turn; (work) shift; batch; team.*

tangible *adj. tangible.*

tango *m. tango.*

tanque *m. tank.*

tantear *to measure; to try, to sound somebody out; to keep the score in a game; to estimate.*

tanteo *m. estimate; sounding (somebody out); score (games).*

TANTO *adj. so much, as much; adv. so, in such a manner; such a long (time); m. point (in games), pl. score.*

Tanto gusto, señora. *I'm very glad (pleased) to know you, Madam.*

¡Lo siento tanto! *I'm so sorry!*

No beba Ud. tanto. *Don't drink so much.*

¡Tanto bueno por aquí! *Look who's here! I'm glad to see you.*

¿Por qué tanta prisa? *Why the hurry? ("Why such a hurry?")*

Tanta gente. *So many people.*

Ciento y tantas libras. *A hundred and some*

pounds.

Tener tantos años de edad. *To be so many years old.*

A tantos de mayo. *On such and such a date in May.*

¿Tanto le costó? *Did it cost you as much as that?*

A tanto la yarda. *At so much a yard.*

Algún tanto. *A little. Somewhat.*

Otro tanto. *Just as much. As much more.*

Otros tantos. *Just as many.*

Ni tanto, ni tan poco. *Neither too much nor too little.*

Tanto por tanto. *For the same price.*

Tantos a tantos. *Equal numbers.*

Tanto uno como otro. *The one as well as the other. Both of them.*

Cuanto más le doy, tanto más me pide. *The more I give him, the more he asks for (wants).*

Tanto más cuanto (que). *All the more (because).*

Tanto como. (Tanto cuanto.) *As much as.*

En tanto. (Entre tanto.) *In the meanwhile.*

Hay tanta gente aquí. *There are so many people here.*

Por lo tanto. *Therefore. For the reasons mentioned.*

Estar al tanto de. *To be informed of. To be aware of.*

Tanto mejor. *So much the better.*

Tanto peor. *So much the worse.*

tapa f. *cover, lid, cap.*

tapadera f. *cover, lid.*

tapar *to cover; to conceal, to hide.*

tapia f. *mud wall; fence.*

¿Puede Ud. saltar por encima de esta tapia? *Can you jump over that fence?*

Es sordo como una tapia. *He's deaf as a post.*

tapicería f. *tapestry; upholstery.*

tapioca f. *tapioca.*

tapiz m. *tapestry.*

tapizar *to hang with tapestry; to upholster.*

tapón m. *cork; plug.*

taponar *to plug.*

taquígrafo m. *stenographer.*

taquilla f. *letter file; ticket or key rack; ticket office or window.*

¿Dónde está la taquilla? *Where's the ticket office?*

taquimecanógrafo m. *stenographer-typist.*

tardanza f. *slowness, delay.*

Perdone mi tardanza. *Pardon my lateness.*

TARDAR *to delay; to be late; to be slow.*

No tarde Ud. *Don't be long. Don't take too long. Don't be late.*

No tardaré en volver. *I'll be back before long.*

No creo que tarde mucho. *I don't think he'll be long.*

Tardó una hora en ir allí. *It took him an hour to go (get) there.*

¿Cuánto tiempo se tarda en aeroplano? *How long does it take by airplane?*

Tarda mucho en decidirse. *He's slow in making up his mind. It takes him a long time to decide.*

A más tardar. *At the latest.*

TARDE f. *afternoon; adv. late.*

¡Buenas tardes! *Good afternoon!*

¡Qué hermosa tarde! *What a lovely afternoon!*

¿De modo que pasaron Uds. allí la tarde? *So you spent the afternoon there?*

Esta tarde a las cuatro. *This afternoon at four o'clock.*

En la tarde. *In the afternoon.*

Mañana por la tarde. *Tomorrow afternoon.*

Ya es tarde. *It's late.*

Más vale tarde que nunca. *Better late than never.*

No quiero llegar tarde. *I don't want to be late.*

Puede ser que venga más tarde. *Maybe he'll come later.*

Más tarde o más temprano. *Sooner or later.*

Hacerse tarde. *To grow late.*

tardío adj. *tardy, slow; late.*

tardo adj. *slow; sluggish, dull.*

tarea f. *job, task, work.*

La tarea está concluida. *The job is finished.*

tarifa f. *tariff; fare, rate.*

tarima f. *movable platform; stand.*

tarjeta f. *card.*

Aquí tiene Ud. mi tarjeta. *Here's my card.*

Tarjeta de visita. *Visiting card. Calling card.*

Tarjeta postal. *Postcard.*

tarro m. *jar; can, pot.*

tartamudear *to stammer, to stutter.*

tartamudo adj. *stammering; stuttering; m. stammerer, stutterer.*

tarugo m. *wooden peg.*

tasa f. *assessment; appraisement; measure; standard; rate; valuation.*

tasajo m. *hung beef.*

tasar *to appraise, to assess; to value.*

tatarabuela f. *great-great-grandmother.*

tatarabuelo m. *great-great-grandfather.*

tataranieta f. *great-great-granddaughter.*

tataranieto m. *great-great-grandson.*

tatuaje m. *tattoo; tattooing.*

tatuar *to tattoo.*

tauromaquia f. *bullfighting.*

TAXI m. *taxi, taxicab.*

¿Iremos a pie o en taxi? *Shall we walk or take a taxi?*

taxímetro m. *meter (of a cab).*

TAZA f. *cup; bowl.*

Haga el favor de darme otra taza de café. *Please give me another cup of coffee.*

tazón m. *large bowl.*

TE pron. *(objective and dative cases of* tú) *you, to you.*

    ¿Te duele la cabeza? *Do you have a headache?*

    ¿Qué te parece? *What do you think of it?*

    Te lo dió a tí. *He gave it to you.*

    Si me escribes te contestaré. *I'll answer you if you write to me.*

te f. *name of the letter* t.

té m. *tea.*

    Ya está el té. *Tea is ready.*

teatral adj. *theatrical.*

TEATRO m. *theater; playhouse.*

tecla f. *key (of a piano, typewriter, etc.).*

teclado m. *keyboard (of a piano, typewriter, etc.).*

técnica f. *technique.*

técnico adj. *technical;* m. *technician, expert.*

techo m. *roof; ceiling.*

tedio m. *boredom, tediousness.*

tedioso adj. *tiresome, tedious.*

teja f. *tile.*

    Á toca teja. *Cash payment.*

tejado m. *roof, tiled roof.*

tejer *to weave, to knit.*

tejido m. *texture, fabric, web; tissue.*

tela f. *cloth, material; web, fabric.*

    Esta tela tiene un metro de ancho. *This material (cloth) is one meter wide.*

    ¿Se encoge esta tela? *Does this material shrink?*

    Ese es el revés de la tela. *That's the wrong side of the material.*

telaraña f. *cobweb.*

TELEFONEAR *to phone.*

    Telefonéeme. *Phone me. Give me a ring.*

    ¿Se puede telefonear desde aquí? *Can we phone from here?*

    Telefoneo de parte del Sr. López. *I'm calling for ("in behalf of") Mr. Lopez.*

telefonema m. *telephone message, call.*

telefónico adj. *relating to a telephone.*

    ¿Dónde está la central telefónica? *Where's the telephone exchange?*

    Guía telefónica. *Telephone directory (book).*

    Cabina telefónica. *Telephone booth.*

telefonista m. and f. *telephone operator.*

TELÉFONO m. *telephone.*

    ¿Dónde está el teléfono? *Where's the telephone?*

    Llámeme por teléfono. *Phone me. Give me a ring.*

    Le llaman por teléfono. *There's a telephone call for you. You're wanted on the phone.*

    ¿Qué número tiene su teléfono? *What's your phone number?*

    Un momento, que suena el teléfono. *Just a minute, the phone is ringing.*

telegrafiar *to telegraph, to wire.*

    Tendremos que telegrafiarle. *We'll have to wire him.*

telegráficamente *by telegraph.*

telegrafista m. and f. *telegraph operator.*

telégrafo m. *telegraph.*

    ¿Dónde está la oficina de telégrafos? *Where's the telegraph office?*

telegrama m. *telegram.*

    Quiero mandar un telegrama. *I want to send a telegram.*

    Le pondré un telegrama en cuanto llegue. *I'll send you a telegram as soon as I arrive. I'll send you a wire as soon as I get there.*

    Telegrama de madrugada. *Night letter.*

telescopio m. *telescope.*

televisión f. *television.*

telón m. *curtain (theater).*

tema m. *theme; subject.*

    Cambiemos de tema. *Let's change the subject. Let's talk about something else.*

temblar *to tremble, to shake, to shiver.*

temblor m. *trembling, tremor; earthquake.*

TEMER *to fear, to dread, to be afraid.*

    No tiene Ud. nada que temer. *You have nothing to fear. There's nothing to be afraid of.*

    Temo que esté enfermo. *I'm afraid he's sick.*

    No tema, que no le hará daño. *Don't be afraid, it won't hurt you.*

    Temo que sea demasiado tarde. *I'm afraid that it's too late.*

temerario adj. *reckless, rash.*

temeridad f. *temerity, rashness, recklessness; folly.*

temeroso adj. *timid; afraid, fearful.*

temible adj. *dreadful, terrible.*

temor m. *fear, dread.*

temperamento m. *temperament, temper, nature.*

temperatura f. *temperature.*

tempestad f. *tempest, storm.*

templado adj. *moderate, temperate, tempered; lukewarm.*

templo m. *temple; church.*

temporada f. *season; period.*

    Este espectáculo es el mejor de la temporada. *This is the best show of the season.*

temporal adj. *temporary;* m. *storm.*

TEMPRANO *early.*

    Salimos por la mañana temprano. *We left early in the morning.*

    Me gusta acostarme temprano. *I like to go to bed early.*

    Es demasiado temprano aún. *It's too early yet.*

    Se sabrá más tarde o más temprano. *It'll become known sooner or later.*

tenacidad f. *tenacity.*

tenaz adj. *tenacious; stubborn.*

tenazas f. pl. *pincers, tongs, pliers; forceps.*

tendencia f. *tendency, leaning; trend.*

tender *to hang (clothes); to stretch out, to spread*

out, to tend.

Tengo que tender la ropa para que se seque. *I have to hang the clothes out to dry.*

Los pescadores tendieron la red. *The fisherman spread out the net.*

Cayó en las redes que le tendieron. *He fell into the trap they set for him.*

tendero *m. storekeeper.*

tendón *m. tendon.*

tenebroso *adj. dark; gloomy.*

TENEDOR *m. fork; holder.*

    Déme un tenedor. *Let me have a fork.*

    Tenedor de libros. *Bookkeeper.*

    Tenedor de póliza. *Policyholder.*

teneduría *f. keeping (of books).*

    Teneduría de libros. *Bookkeeping.*

TENER *to have, to possess; to keep; to hold; to contain; to take; to be (hungry, thirsty, cold, warm, etc.).*

    ¿Qué tiene Ud. en ese paquete? *What do you have in that package?*

    Tendrá que facturar el baúl. *You'll have to check the trunk.*

    Tengo que irme ahora. *I have to go now.*

    No tengo mucho tiempo. *I haven't much time.*

    Tengo mucho que hacer hoy. *I've a lot to do today.*

    No tengo suelto. *I haven't any change.*

    No tengo más. *I haven't (got) any more. I don't have any more.*

    ¿Qué tiene Ud. que ver con eso? *What do you have to do with it?*

    Aquí tenemos que cambiar de tren. *We have to change trains here.*

    Tiene su casa muy limpia. *She keeps her house very clean.*

    ¿Qué edad tiene Ud.? *How old are you?*

    Tengo treinta años. *I'm thirty years old.*

    Aquí tiene Ud. un libro interesante. *Here's an interesting book.*

    ¿Qué día del mes tenemos? *What day of the month is it?*

    ¿Qué número tiene su teléfono? *What's your phone number?*

    ¿Qué tiene Ud.? *What's the matter with you?*

    No tengo nada. *There's nothing the matter with me.*

    No tenga Ud. miedo. *Don't be afraid.*

    Tengo hambre. *I'm hungry.*

    No tengo ganas de comer ahora. *I don't feel like eating now.*

    Tengo sed. *I'm thirsty.*

    Tengo mucho frío. *I'm very cold.*

    Tengo dolor de cabeza. *I have a headache.*

    Tengo dolor de garganta. *I have a sore throat.*

    Tengo escalofríos. *I have the chills.*

    Tengo un fuerte resfriado. *I have a bad cold.*

    ¿Tiene Ud. sueño? *Are you sleepy?*

    Tenga paciencia. *Be patient. Have patience.*

    ¡Tenga cuidado! *Be careful! Watch out!*

    Tiene buena cara. *It looks very nice. It looks good.*

    Tener razón. *To be right.*

    ¿Quién tiene razón? *Who's right?*

    No tener razón. *To be wrong.*

    Tiene los brazos muy largos. *He has very long arms.*

    Tiene mucha suerte. *He's very lucky.*

    Tener prisa. *To be in a hurry.*

    Tener lugar. *To take place.*

    Tener malas pulgas. *To be hot-tempered. To be hot-headed (hot-blooded).*

    Tener buen diente. *To have a hearty appetite.*

    Lo tendré en cuenta. *I'll bear it in mind.*

    No tengo en mucho a Juan. *I don't think much of John.*

    Lo tiene en poco. *He attaches little value to it.*

    No puedo tenerme de sueño. *I can't keep awake.*

    Tuve un buen día. *I spent a pleasant day.*

    ¿Con qué ésas tenemos? *So that's the story!*

    Tiene mucho pico. *He's a chatterbox.*

    No tengo arte ni parte en el asunto. *I've nothing to do with the matter.*

tenis *m. tennis.*

tenor *m. tenor; text; purport.*

tensión *f. tension; voltage.*

tentación *f. temptation.*

tentar *to touch, to feel; to grope; to tempt; to try, to attempt.*

tentativa *f. attempt, try.*

tenue *adj. tenuous, thin, delicate.*

teñir *to dye, to tinge.*

teoría *f. theory.*

teórico *adj. theoretical.*

terapéutica *f. therapeutics.*

TERCER *(shortening of tercero) third.*

    Vive en el tercer piso. *He lives on the third floor.*

    El tercer día. *The third day.*

TERCERO *adj. third; m. third person; mediator, intermediary.*

    La tercera parte. *The third part. A third.*

    La tercera lección. *The third lesson.*

    El sirvió de tercero en la negociación. *He was an intermediary in the negotiations.*

    Ya está en tercera (velocidad). *It's in third (gear).*

tercio *adj. third; m. a third; the Foreign Legion (Spain).*

terciopelo *m. velvet.*

terco *adj. stubborn, headstrong.*

tergiversar *to distort, to misrepresent.*

terminación *f. termination; ending.*

terminal *adj. terminal, final; m. terminal.*

TERMINAR *to end, to terminate; to finish.*

    Casi he terminado. *I've almost finished. I'm*

almost finished.

La reunión terminó cerca de las diez. *The meeting ended about ten o'clock.*

término *m. term; manner; end; word; boundary.*

¿En qué términos? *On what terms?*

En estos términos. *On these terms. In these words.*

Poner término a. *To put an end to.*

En un término medio. *On an average.*

Me ha hablado en términos lisonjeros de su obra. *She spoke to me in a very flattering way ("in high terms") about your work.*

terminología *f. terminology.*

termómetro *m. thermometer.*

termos *m. thermos bottle.*

ternera *f. veal; heifer.*

Chuletas de ternera. *Veal cutlets.*

ternero *m. calf.*

ternura *f. tenderness, fondness.*

terraplén *m. embankment; mound; banquette.*

terrateniente *m. landowner.*

terraza *f. terrace.*

terremoto *m. earthquake.*

terreno *m. land, soil, field, piece of ground.*

Partieron el terreno en varios lotes. *They divided the land into several lots.*

Sobre el terreno. *On the spot.*

terrestre *adj. ground, terrestrial.*

Fuerzas terrestres. *Ground forces.*

TERRIBLE *adj. terrible, dreadful.*

territorio *m. territory.*

terrón *m. clod; lump.*

Un terrón de azúcar. *A lump of sugar.*

terror *m. terror.*

terruño *m. piece of land, native country.*

tertulia *f. evening party, social gathering, friendly conversation.*

tesis *f. thesis.*

tesorería *f. treasury, treasurer's office.*

tesorero *m. treasurer.*

tesoro *m. treasure; treasury.*

testamento *m. testament, will.*

testar *to make a will; to bequeath.*

testarudo *adj. headstrong, stubborn, obstinate.*

No seas tan testarudo y haz lo que te piden. *Don't be so stubborn and do as you are told.*

testigo *m. and f. witness.*

testimonio *m. testimony; attestation; affidavit; evidence; deposition.*

tetera *f. teapot.*

textil *adj. and n. textile.*

texto *m. text.*

Libro de texto. *Textbook.*

textual *adj. textual.*

textualmente *textually, according to the text, word for word.*

tez *f. complexion, skin.*

Tiene una tez muy suave. *She has a very delicate complexion. Her skin is very*

smooth.

TI *you (prepositional form of tú).*

Para ti. *For you.*

A ti te hablan. *They're talking to you.*

Te estás engañando a ti mismo. *You're fooling yourself.*

tía *f. aunt.*

tibia *f. tibia, shinbone.*

tibio *adj. lukewarm; indifferent.*

Agua tibia. *Lukewarm water.*

tiburón *m. shark.*

TIEMPO *m. time; tense; weather; tempo.*

¿Qué tiempo hace? *How's the weather? What's the weather like?*

Hace muy buen tiempo. Hace un tiempo muy bueno. *The weather's fine. The weather's very nice.*

Hace mal tiempo. *The weather's bad.*

El tiempo se pone bueno. *The weather's getting very nice.*

Parece que el tiempo se descompone. *It looks as though the weather will change (for the worse).*

El tiempo está muy variable. *The weather's very changeable.*

El tiempo se está despejando. *The weather's clearing up.*

Durante algún tiempo. *For some time.*

Por mucho tiempo. *For a long time.*

Hace mucho tiempo. *It's been a long time.*

¿Cuánto tiempo se tarda en aeroplano? *How long does it take by airplane?*

¿Cuánto tiempo hace que vive Ud. aquí? *How long have you been living here?*

¡Si hay tiempo de sobra! *There's plenty of time. There's time to spare.*

Tengo tiempo de sobra. *I have plenty of time.*

No tengo tiempo. *I have no time.*

No hay tiempo que perder. *There's no time to waste.*

Es tiempo de que Ud. hable. *It's time for you to speak.*

Aprovechar el tiempo. *To make good use of one's time.*

Darse buen tiempo. *To amuse oneself.*

Andar con el tiempo. *To keep up with the times.*

Obedecer al tiempo. *To act as circumstances require. To go with the times.*

Matar el tiempo. *To kill time.*

A tiempo. *In time.*

Fuera de tiempo. *Out of season.*

A un tiempo. *At the same time.*

Con tiempo. *Timely.*

Con el tiempo. *In time. In the course of time.*

El tiempo es oro. *Time is money.*

TIENDA *f. store, shop; awning; tent.*

¿A qué hora abren las tiendas? *What time do*

the stores open?

¿Hasta qué hora está la tienda abierta? *Until what time does the store stay open? How late does the store stay open?*

Esta tienda anuncia un saldo. *This store is advertising a sale.*

Poner (abrir) tienda. *To open up a store.*

Acamparon en tiendas (de campaña). *They camped in tents.*

tientas (a) *in the dark.*

Andar a tientas. *To feel one's way in the dark. To grope in the dark.*

Encienda la luz, no busque a tientas. *Turn the light on. Don't look for it in the dark.*

tierno *adj. tender; soft; affectionate; young.*

TIERRA *f. earth; soil; land; ground; native country.*

Su fortuna consiste en tierras y valores. *His fortune consists of land and securities.*

Iremos por tierra. *We'll go by land (overland).*

Iremos a tierra en cuanto atraque el barco. *We'll go ashore as soon as the ship docks.*

Ver tierras. *To see the world. To travel.*

Echar tierra. *To forget.*

Echar a tierra. *To bring down.*

Tomar tierra. *To anchor. To land.*

En tierra. *On land. Ashore.*

Tierra adentro. *Inland.*

Echar por tierra. *To overthrow. To ruin. To destroy.*

¡Tierra a la vista! *Land in sight!*

tieso *adj. stiff, hard; firm, strong; solemn; stubborn.*

Tenérselas tiesas. *To hold to one's opinion. To be stubborn (opinionated).*

tiesto *m. flowerpot.*

tifus *m. typhus.*

tigre *m. tiger.*

tijeras *f. pl. scissors; shears.*

tila *f. linden tree; flower of the linden; infusion of linden flowers.*

tildar *to cross out; to put a tilde over; to brand, to criticize.*

tilde *f. tilde, a mark (˜) used over n; trifle, bit.*

timador *m. swindler.*

timar *to swindle, to cheat.*

TIMBRE *m. stamp, seal; bell, buzzer, tone.*

Hay que ponerle un timbre a este certificado. *You have to put an official stamp on this certificate.*

Tocar el timbre. *To ring the bell.*

Abrí la puerta luego que sonó el timbre. *I opened the door as soon as the bell rang.*

timidez *f. timidity, shyness.*

tímido *adj. timid, shy.*

tímpano *m. kettledrum; tympanum, eardrum; tympan.*

tina *f. large earthen jar; tub; bathtub; vat.*

tinaja *f. large earthen jar for water.*

tino *m. skill, knack; judgment, tact; a good hit.*

Sacar de tino. *To exasperate. To confound.*

tinta *f. ink; dye.*

La tinta es demasiado espesa, no corre bien. *The ink is too thick; it doesn't flow well.*

Lo sé de buena tinta. *I have that on good authority. I learned that from a reliable source.*

tinte *m. dye; tint, hue; cleaner's.*

Lleve esto al tinte. *Take this to the cleaner's.*

tintero *m. inkstand, inkwell.*

tintorería *f. cleaner's.*

tintorero *m. dyer.*

tintura *f. dyeing; m. tincture; tint; dye.*

Tintura para el pelo. *Hair-dye.*

TÍO *m. uncle; (coll.) fellow.*

Mis tíos. *My uncle and aunt.*

¿Quién es ese tío? *Who's that fellow?*

típico *adj. typical, characteristic.*

tiple *m. and f. treble, soprano.*

tipo *m. type; rate; standard; class; (coll.) fellow.*

¿Cuál es el tipo de cambio hoy? *What is the rate of exchange today?*

Ese tipo me revienta. *I can't stand that fellow.*

Ese es un tipo muy malo. *He's a bad character.*

tipografía *f. printing; printing shop; typography.*

tipógrafo *m. printer, typographer, typesetter.*

tira *f. strip; stripe.*

tirabuzón *m. corkscrew; curl of hair.*

tirada *f. edition, issue; printing; cast, throw; distance; stretch.*

De una tirada. *At a stretch.*

tirador *m. marksman, sharpshooter.*

tiranía *f. tyranny.*

tirano *m. tyrant.*

tirante *adj. strained, taut, tight; m. brace, trace; pl. suspenders.*

TIRAR *to throw, to toss, to cast; to shoot; to pull; to squander; to draw; to print.*

No lo tire. *Don't throw it away.*

Tíremelo. *Toss it over to me. Throw it to me.*

El niño la tiraba de la falda. *The child tugged at her skirt.*

Tire una línea recta. *Draw a straight line.*

Ha tirado su fortuna. *He's squandered his fortune.*

Han tirado una nueva edición. *They've printed a new edition.*

Veamos cual de nosotros puede tirar mejor. *Let's see which one of us is the better shot.*

Tirar a los dados. *To shoot dice.*

Tirar al blanco. *To shoot at a target.*

Tira de la cuerda. *Pull the cord.*

¡Voy tirando! *I manage to get along.*

Se tiró por la ventana. *He threw himself out the window.*

Vimos como se tiraban los paracaidistas. *We saw the parachutists jump.*

tiritar *to shiver.*

tiro *m. shot; report (of a gun); throw, fling; range; reach, mark made by a throw; team (of draft animals); draft of a chimney.*

Tiro al blanco. *Target practice.*

Errar el tiro. *To miss the mark.*

Matar a tiros a. *To shoot to death.*

¿Cuántos tiros ha disparado Ud.? *How many shots did you fire?*

tirón *m. tug, pull.*

De un tirón. *All at once. At one stroke.*

Dormí toda la noche de un tirón. *I slept all night through.*

tiroteo *m. shooting.*

tísico *adj. and n. consumptive; person who has tuberculosis.*

tisis *f. tuberculosis, consumption.*

titere *m. puppet.*

titiritar *to shiver.*

titubear *to hesitate, to doubt.*

El testigo contestaba sin titubear. *The witness answered without hesitation.*

titular *to title; to entitle; adj. and n. titular; head, holder; headline.*

título *m. title, diploma, degree; heading, headline; inscription; pl. shares, securities.*

Recibió el título de abogado. *He became a lawyer.*

A título de. *On the pretense of. Under the pretext of.*

Títulos al portador. *Shares payable to the bearer.*

Títulos ferroviarios. *Railway stock.*

tiza *f. chalk.*

tiznar *to smut, to smudge.*

toalla *f. towel.*

tobillo *m. ankle.*

tocado *adj. touched; tainted; m. headdress, coiffure.*

tocador *m. vanity, dressing table; boudoir, dressing room.*

tocante *adj. touching, respecting, concerning.*

Tocante a. *Concerning. As regards.*

En lo tacante a. *In regard to. Regarding.*

TOCAR *to touch; to play (an instrument); to ring; to toll; to concern, to interest; to be one's turn; to fall to one's share; to call (at a port).*

¡Toque Ud. qué suave es esta tela! *Feel how soft this cloth is.*

¡No tocar! *Don't touch! Hands off!*

Toque el timbre. *Ring the bell.*

¿Qué instrumento toca Ud.? *What instrument do you play?*

La orquesta está tocando un tango. *The band is playing a tango.*

¿A quién le toca ahora? *Whose turn is it now?*

Ahora me toca a mí. *It's my turn now.*

Le toca jugar. *It's your turn to play.*

¿A quién le tocó la suerte? *Who won the lottery?*

Nos tocarán partes iguales. *We'll get equal shares.*

Por lo que toca a mí. *As far as I'm concerned. As regards myself.*

El barco no tocará en Cádiz. *The ship won't call (stop) at Cadiz.*

Tocar a la puerta. *To knock at the door.*

A toca teja. *Cash payment.*

tocayo *m. namesake.*

Es mi tocayo. *He's my namesake. He has the same name I have.*

tocino *m. bacon; salt pork.*

Huevos y tocino. *Bacon and eggs.*

TODAVÍA *yet; still.*

Todavía es temprano. *It's still early.*

Todavía no han dado las diez. *It's not ten o'clock yet.*

¿Terminó la carta?—Todavía no. *Have you finished the letter?—Not yet.*

¿Todavía anda Ud. por aquí? *Are you still around?*

TODO *adj. all, each, every; m. the whole, everything, everyone.*

Todo o nada. *All or nothing.*

Eso es todo. *That's all.*

Estoy todo rendido. *I'm all tired out.*

No estoy del todo satisfecho. *I'm not quite (altogether) satisfied.*

Ha perdido toda su fortuna. *He's lost his whole fortune.*

Todo lo cual no es verdad. *All of which isn't true.*

¡Ya estamos todos! *We're all here!*

Nos han convidado a todos. *They've invited all of us.*

Esta es la opinión de todos. *This is everyone's opinion.*

Todos son uno. *They're all the same.*

Me es todo uno. *It's all the same to me. It makes no difference to me.*

Todos los días. *Every day.*

La veo todos los días. *I see her every day.*

Todo el día. *All day long.*

He esperado todo el día. *I've been waiting all day.*

¿Sale Ud. todas las noches? *Do you go out every night?*

Según parece lloverá toda la tarde. *It looks as if it will rain all afternoon.*

Todo el año. *All year round.*

Espero quedarme todo el otoño. *I hope to stay through the autumn.*

Toda la familia. *The whole family.*

Todo el que. *Whoever. All that. All who.*

Todo el mundo. *Everybody.*

Todo el mundo lo sabe. *Everybody knows it.*

Sabe un poco de todo. *He knows a little about everything.*

Todo cuanto Ud. dice me interesa. *Everything ("all that") you say interests me.*

Le daré todo lo que necesita. *I'll give him everything he needs.*

Todo tiene sus límites. *There's a limit to everything.*

¿Está todo en buenas condiciones? *Is everything in good order?*

Estamos dispuestos a todo. *We're prepared for anything.*

Ella siempre está en todo. *She doesn't miss a thing.*

Todo está arreglado. *Everything has been arranged.*

Fuimos allí a todo correr. *We rushed there.*

Ante todo. *First of all.*

Después de todo. *After all.*

De todos modos. *At any rate. Anyway.*

A toda costa. *By all means. At any price. At all cost. At all hazards.*

Una vez por todas. *Once (and) for all.*

Del todo. *Wholly. Completely. Entirely.*

No del todo. *Not completely. Not quite.*

A toda velocidad. *At full speed.*

Así y todo. *In spite of all.*

Con todo, prefiero no ir. *Still, I prefer not to go. I still would rather not go.*

Jugar el todo por el todo. *To stake or risk all.*

Todo cabe en él. *He's capable of anything.*

Perdido por uno, perdido por todo. *In for a penny, in for a pound.*

toldo *m. awning.*

tolerable *adj. tolerable.*

tolerancia *f. tolerance.*

tolerante *adj. tolerant.*

tolerar *to tolerate.*

No podemos tolerar tal atropello. *We can't tolerate such an outrage.*

No toleraba nunca ninguna intervención de nadie. *He never tolerated any interference from anyone.*

toma *f. seizure, capture; dose (of medicine); tap (of a water main or electric wire); intake (water, gas, etc.).*

TOMAR *to take; to get; to seize; to have (drink or food).*

¿Qué quiere tomar? *What will you have to drink?*

Tomaremos café en lugar de té. *We'll take coffee instead of tea.*

¿Qué toma Ud.? *What will you have (to drink)?*

Tomo vino de vez en cuando. *I drink wine occasionally. I have some (take a little) wine every once in a while.*

Tomemos un bocadillo. *Let's have a bite.*

¿Qué toma Ud. para desayunarse? *What do you eat for breakfast?*

¿Qué tomamos para postre? *What shall we have for dessert?*

Tome la medicina un día sí y otro no. *Take the medicine every other day.*

Tomemos un taxi. *Let's take a taxi.*

Le aconsejo que tome el tren de las ocho. *I advise you to take the eight o'clock train.*

Tome él que más le guste. *Take the one you like best.*

Tomaré un ejemplar de esta revista. *I'll take a copy of this magazine.*

Tomar asiento. *To take a seat. To sit down.*

¿Quiere Ud. tomar asiento? *Would you like to sit down? Won't you sit down?*

Tome dos de ocho. *Take (subtract) two from eight.*

Tomar nota de. *To take note of.*

Lo toman por tonto. *They take him for a fool.*

No lo tome Ud. en ese sentido. *Don't take it that way.*

Tomar a bien. *To take (it) in the right way. To take (it) well.*

Tomar a mal. *To take (it) in the wrong way.*

Tomar a broma. *To take as a joke.*

Esto debe tomarse en consideración. *This should be taken into consideration.*

Tómelo con calma. *Take it easy.*

No lo tome Ud. a pecho. *Don't take it to heart.*

El médico le tomó el pulso. *The doctor took (felt) his pulse.*

Se tomaron las medidas necesarias en contra de la epidemia. *They took the necessary measures against the epidemic.*

No tomaron más tiempo que el necesario para comer. *They only took the time necessary to eat.*

Tomaron la ciudad de noche. *They took (captured) the city during the night.*

Tomar el pelo. *To make fun of. To tease.*

No me tome el pelo. *Don't make fun of me. Don't kid me.*

Voy a salir a tomar un poco el aire. *I'm going out for some air.*

Vamos a tomar el fresco. *Let's go out and get some fresh air.*

Está tomando alas (coll.). *He's putting on airs. He's getting high-hat. He's getting too big for his breeches. ("He's putting on wings.")*

Tomó razón de todo lo que dijo. *He made a record of all that was said.*

Tomar cariño. *To become attached to. To become fond of. To take a liking to.*

Tomar las once. *To have a light lunch or some appetizers about noon.*

Tomar la responsabilidad. *To assume (the) responsibility.*

Tomar una resolución. *To make a decision. To decide. To resolve.*

La ha tomado conmigo. *He picked a quarrel with me.*

Ya le estoy tomando el gusto a este juego. *I'm beginning to enjoy this game.*

tomate *m. tomato.*

tomo *m. volume (book).*

Es una obra en tres tomos. *The work's in three volumes.*

ton *m. tone.*

Sin ton ni son. *Without rhyme or reason.*

tonel *m. barrel, cask.*

tonelada *f. ton.*

tónico *adj. and n. tonic.*

tono *m. tone; tune; key tone; accent; manner; conceit; shade (color).*

Darse tono. *To show off.*

Gente de buen tono. *Fashionable people.*

tontear *to act foolishly; to talk nonsense.*

tontería *f. foolishness, nonsense.*

No digas tonterías. *Don't talk nonsense. Don't say foolish things.*

TONTO *adj. silly, stupid; m. fool.*

No sea Ud. tonto. *Don't be foolish.*

Es un tonto de cuatro suelas. *He's a downright fool.*

Hablar a tontas y a locas. *To tell idle stories (tales).*

topacio *m. topaz.*

topar *to collide; to run into; to butt.*

tope *m. top, butt; stop (device); buffer (railway); collision, bump.*

topografía *f. topography.*

topógrafo *m. topographer.*

toque *m. touch; ringing, peal; call (bugle).*

tórax *m. thorax.*

torbellino *m. whirlwind; rush, hurly-burly, hurry-scurry.*

torcedura *f. twisting; sprain.*

torcer *to twist; to turn; to sprain; to distort.*

Se me ha torcido el pie. *I've sprained my ankle.*

Tuerza a la derecha. *Turn right.*

torcido *adj. twisted; crooked.*

toreo *m. bullfighting.*

torear *to be a bullfighter; to banter.*

torero *m. bullfighter.*

tormenta *f. storm, tempest.*

tormentoso *adj. stormy.*

tornar *to return; to repeat, to do again; to change.*

tornasol *m. sunflower; litmus.*

torneo *m. tournament.*

tornillo *m. screw.*

La rosca de un tornillo. *The thread of a screw.*

torniquete *m. turnstile; tourniquet.*

torno *m. lathe; winch, windlass; spindle.*

toro *m. bull.*

Vamos a los toros. *Let's go to the bullfight.*

toronja *f. grapefruit.*

torpe *adj. dull, clumsy, slow; awkward.*

torpedero *m. torpedo boat.*

torpedo *m. torpedo.*

torpeza *f. dullness, slowness; awkwardness.*

torre *f. tower; turret; belfry; castle (in chess).*

torrente *m. torrent.*

tórrido *adj. torrid.*

torta *f. cake, tart; font (printing).*

tortilla *f. omelet; a kind of pancake (Mex.).*

Tráigame Ud. una tortilla de cebolla. *Bring me an onion omelet.*

tórtola *f. turtledove.*

tortuga *f. turtle; tortoise.*

tortura *f. torture.*

torturar *to torture.*

tos *f. cough.*

Pastillas para la tos. *Cough drops.*

tosco *adj. rough, coarse, clumsy.*

toser *to cough.*

tostada *f. toast.*

Tráigame una taza de café, tostadas y mantequilla. *Bring me a cup of coffee and some toast and butter.*

tostado *adj. toasted; tanned.*

Pan tostado. *Toast (bread).*

tostar *to toast; to roast; to tan (by exposure to sun).*

TOTAL *adj. and n. total, whole, in all.*

¿Cuál es el importe total? *What's the total amount?*

¿Cuántos hay ahí en total? *How many are there in all?*

Total, ¿qué se adelanta con eso? *In short, where will it get you (what's the good of it)?*

totalitario *adj. totalitarian.*

tóxico *adj. toxic, poisonous; m. poison.*

traba *f. obstacle, hindrance; trammel, hobble, fetter.*

trabajador *adj. hard-working, industrious; m. worker, laborer.*

TRABAJAR *to work; to labor.*

¿En qué trabaja Ud.? *What work do you do?*

Se gana la vida trabajando. *He works for a living.*

TRABAJO *m. work, labor; workmanship; toil, trouble, hardship.*

Se garantiza el trabajo. *The work is guaranteed.*

Este trabajo está hecho a medias. *This work is only halfway done.*

Todo esto es trabajo perdido. *All this work is wasted. This is all wasted effort.*

¡Qué trabajo más bien hecho! *What an excellent piece of work!*

Sin trabajo. *Unemployed. Out of work.*

Costar trabajo. *To be difficult. To require a lot of work (effort).*

Cuesta trabajo creerlo. *It's hard to believe it.*

Día de trabajo. *Working day.*

Tomarse el trabajo de. *To take the trouble to.*

Trabajo nocturno. *Night work.*

Trabajos forzados. *Hard labor. ("Forced labor.")*

trabar *to join, to unite, to bind; to shackle.*

Trabar conversación. *To open a conversation.*

Trabar amistad. *To make friends.*

Trabar conocimiento. *To make someone's acquaintance. To strike up an acquaintance.*

tractor *m. tractor.*

tradición *f. tradition.*

tradicional *adj. traditional.*

traducción *f. translation.*

TRADUCIR *to translate.*

Traduzca esta carta al inglés. *Translate this letter into English.*

No hay manera de traducirlo. *There's no way to translate it.*

traductor *m. translator.*

TRAER *to bring, to carry; to wear.*

¡Mozo! Tráigame una cerveza. *Waiter, bring me a glass of beer.*

¿Me han traído el traje? *Have they brought my suit?*

¿Lo trajo consigo? *Did you bring it with you?*

¿Qué le trae a Ud. acá? *What brings you here?*

¿Qué trae el diario? *What's new in the paper today?*

Todos los días trae un vestido nuevo. *Every day she wears a new dress.*

Traer a cuento. *To bring into the conversation.*

traficante *adj. trading; m. trader.*

traficar *to traffic, to trade, to do business.*

tráfico *m. traffic; trading; trade.*

tragaluz *f. skylight.*

tragar *to swallow; to devour, to glut.*

tragedia *f. tragedy.*

trágico *adj. tragic.*

trago *m. drink, draught.*

Vamos a echarnos un trago. *Let's have a drink.*

Beber a tragos. *To gulp (down).*

tragón *adj. gluttonous; m. glutton.*

traición *f. treason; treachery.*

Hizo traición a su patria. *He betrayed his country.*

traicionar *to betray, to act treacherously.*

traidor *adj. treacherous; m. traitor.*

traje *m. suit; dress; gown.*

Traje de sastre. *Tailored suit.*

Traje hecho. *Ready-made suit.*

Traje de etiqueta. *Evening dress. Formal dress.*

Traje de calle. *Business suit.*

trajinar *to carry, to convey; to travel about.*

trama *f. weft (in weaving), web; plot; conspiracy.*

tramar *to weave; to plot, to scheme.*

Se trama algo. *Something's brewing. Some-thing's in the air.*

tramitar *to conduct, to transact.*

trámite *m. procedure; transaction; pl. formalities.*

trampa *f. trap; fraud; bad debt.*

Trampa para ratones. *Mousetrap.*

tramposo *adj. and n. deceitful; trickster, cheater, deceiver.*

tranca *f. crossbar.*

trance *m. danger; critical moment.*

A todo trance. *By all means. At all costs. To the bitter end.*

tranco *m. a long stride; threshold.*

tranquilidad *f. tranquillity, peace, quietness.*

tranquilizar *to calm, to reassure.*

tranquilo *adj. tranquil, quiet, calm.*

Este es un lugar muy tranquilo. *This is a very quiet place.*

transacción *f. compromise; transaction.*

transatlántico *adj. transatlantic; m. (transatlantic) liner.*

transbordar *to transship; to transfer, to change (trains, busses, etc.).*

transbordo *m. transshipment; transfer.*

transcurso *m. course, lapse (of time).*

transcurrir *to pass, to elapse (time).*

transeúnte *m. and f. passer-by.*

transferencia *f. transference; transfer.*

Déme una tranferencia. *Give me a transfer.*

transformación *f. transformation.*

transformador *adj. transforming; m. transformer.*

transformar *to transform.*

transfusión *f. transfusion.*

transigir *to compromise; to give in.*

transitar *to pass by, to walk along; to travel.*

tránsito *m. passage, transit, transition.*

De tránsito. *In transit.*

transitorio *adj. transitory.*

transmisor *adj. transmitting; m. transmitter.*

transmitir *to transmit, to send, to convey.*

transparencia *f. slide.*

transparente *adj. transparent; m. window shade.*

transpiración *f. perspiration.*

transportar *to transport, to convey; to transpose (music).*

transporte *m. transport; transportation.*

Transporte pagado. *Carriage paid.*

tranvía *m. tramway, street car.*

¿Qué tranvía debo tomar? *Which streetcar should I take?*

¿Dónde está la parada más cerca del tranvía? *Where is the nearest streetcar stop?*

trapecio *m. trapeze.*

trapero *m. junkman, ragman.*

trapo *m. rag; pl. old clothes; rags.*

Poner como un trapo. *To reprimand severely. To give someone a dressing down.*

Trapo de limpiar. *Cleaning rag.*

TRAS *after, behind, besides.*

Uno tras el otro. *One after the other.*

Pónlo tras ese biombo. *Put it behind that screen.*

Buscamos en una tienda tras otra. *We tried store after store.*

trascendencia f. *transcendency, importance.*

trascendental adj. *transcendental; very important, far-reaching.*

trascender *to smell; to spread, to pervade; to leak out, to become known.*

trasero adj. *back, rear.*

La puerta trasera da al jardín. *The back door opens out into the garden.*

Asiento trasero. *Back seat.*

trasladar *to move; to transport; to transfer; to postpone; to transcribe, to translate.*

Se trasladaron de casa. *They moved to another house.*

Acaban de trasladarlo a otra sucursal. *He's just been transferred to another branch.*

traslado m. *transfer; notification (law); transcript, copy.*

trasmitir (See transmitir.)

trasnochador adj. and n. *night owl; one who stays up late, one who keeps late hours.*

trasnochar *to keep late hours, to stay up late, to sit up all night.*

traspasar *to cross; to transfer, to trespass.*

Traspasar de un lado a otro. *To cross from one side to the other.*

Traspasar un negocio. *To transfer a business.*

traspaso m. *transfer; assignment; trespass.*

Acta de traspaso. *Deed of assignment.*

traspié m. *slip; trip.*

trasplantar *to transplant.*

trasquilar *to clip, to shear.*

traste m. *fret (on a guitar, etc.).*

Dar al traste con. *To ruin. To spoil. To destroy.*

trastienda f. *back room (in a store).*

trasto m. *an old piece of furniture; trash.*

Trastos de cocina. *Kitchen utensils.*

trastornar *to upset; to turn upside down; to disturb, to disarrange.*

trastorno m. *upsetting; disturbance.*

trata f. *slave trade.*

tratable adj. *sociable, easy to deal with; amenable.*

tratado m. *treaty; treatise.*

tratamiento m. *treatment; form of address.*

Ha respondido muy bien al tratamiento. *He responded to the treatment very well.*

tratante m. *dealer, trader, merchant.*

TRATAR *to treat; to deal; to try; to discuss.*

¿De qué se trata? *What's it all about? What's it a question of?*

Se trata de un asunto importante. *The matter in question is important.*

De eso se trata. *That's the point. That's what it's about.*

De nada de eso se trató. *That wasn't discussed.*

¿De qué trata este artículo de fondo? *What does this editorial deal with? What's this editorial about?*

Este libro trata de la vida de Washington. *This book deals with (is about) the life of Washington.*

Prefiero tratar con personas serias. *I prefer to deal with reliable (serious) people.*

Todos los que la tratan la quieren. *She's liked by everyone who meets her.*

Tratan mal a sus empleados. *They don't treat their employees well.*

La trataron como a una hermana. *They treated her like a sister.*

Trató de hacerlo pero no pudo. *He tried to do it but couldn't.*

Trate de ser más puntual en lo futuro. *Try to be more punctual in the future.*

Trataron de un asunto importantísimo. *They discussed a very important matter.*

Le trataron de tonto. *They called him a fool.*

Eso es lo que trataba de decir. *That's what I was trying to say.*

Tratarse con. *To be on friendly terms with. To deal personally with (someone).*

No se tratan desde hace mucho tiempo. *They haven't been on friendly terms for a long time.*

Tratándose de Ud. *In your case.*

Por tratarse de Ud. *In so far as concerns you. In what concerns you.*

trato m. *treatment; form of address; agreement, deal.*

He tenido poco trato con ellos. *I haven't had much to do with them.*

Cerrar el trato. *To close a (the) deal.*

Entrar en tratos. *To start a deal. To enter into (start) negotiations.*

Hagamos un trato. *Let's make a deal.*

Tener buen trato. *To be pleasant. To be nice.*

Tener mal trato. *To be rude. To be impolite.*

TRAVÉS m. *bias; misfortune; crossbeam; traverse.*

A través de. *Through. Across.*

Mirar de través. *To look sideways. To look out of the corner of one's eyes.*

travesaño m. *crosspiece, crossbeam.*

travesía f. *ocean crossing, sea voyage; crossing.*

Es una larga travesía. *It's a long voyage.*

travesura f. *mischief, prank, trick.*

traviesa f. *tie (railway).*

travieso adj. *mischievous, naughty.*

trayecto m. *distance; stretch; route.*

Final del trayecto. *Last stop.*

trayectoria f. *trajectory.*

traza f. *sketch, outline; appearance.*

Llevar trazas de. *To look like.*

Según todas las trazas. *According to all appear-*

ances.

trazar *to draw, to plan, to outline.*

Trace una línea recta. *Draw a straight line.*

Los ingenieros trazaron los planos para un nuevo muelle. *The engineers drew up plans for a new dock.*

trébol *m. trefoil, clover.*

trece *adj. and n. thirteen; thirteenth.*

Estarse (mantenerse) en sus treces. *To stick to one's opinion.*

trecho *m. distance, stretch.*

A trechos. *At intervals.*

tregua *f. truce; respite.*

TREINTA *adj. and n. thirty.*

tremendo *adj. tremendous, dreadful, awful.*

TREN *m. train; equipment; retinue; ostentation.*

¿A qué hora sale el próximo tren? *(At) What time does the next train leave?*

El tren va a salir. *The train's about to leave.*

¿Dónde va este tren? *Where does this train go?*

¿Para este tren en todas las estaciones? *Does this train stop at all stations?*

trenza *f. braid, tress.*

trenzar *to braid.*

trepar *to climb; to creep (a plant).*

tres *adj. three, third.*

trescientos *adj. and n. three hundred; three hundredth.*

treta *f. trick, wile.*

triángulo *m. triangle.*

tribu *f. tribe.*

tribuna *f. tribune; platform.*

tribunal *m. court (of justice).*

tributar *to pay taxes; to pay tribute, to render homage.*

tributo *m. tribute, tax.*

trigo *m. wheat.*

trigonometría *f. trigonometry.*

trigueña *f. brunette, swarthy.*

trigueño *m. swarthy, having the color of wheat.*

trilla *f. threshing.*

trilladora *f. thresher, threshing machine.*

trillar *to thresh.*

trimestral *adj. quarterly.*

trimestre *m. quarter (of a year).*

trinchar *to carve (meat).*

trinchera *f. trench.*

trineo *m. sleigh, sled, sledge.*

trío *m. trio.*

tripa *f. tripe; intestines; belly (coll.).*

triple *adj. triple, treble.*

triplicar *to triple, to treble.*

tripulación *f. crew.*

tripulante *m. and f. crew member.*

tripular *to man (a ship); to equip.*

triquiñuela *f. trickery; dodge.*

TRISTE *adj. sad; gloomy.*

Esto es muy triste. *That's very sad.*

Parecía triste y cansado. *He looked tired and depressed.*

Al oír la noticia se puso muy triste. *She became very sad when she heard the news.*

tristeza *f. sadness, grief, gloom.*

Se muere de tristeza. *She's heartbroken. She's broken-hearted.*

triturar *to grind, to pound.*

triunfal *adj. triumphal.*

triunfante *adj. triumphant.*

triunfar *to triumph, to succeed.*

Triunfó porque era muy determinado. *He succeeded because he was very determined.*

triunfo *m. triumph; trump card.*

trivial *adj. trivial.*

Es algo trivial. *It's a trifling matter. It's a trifle.*

trocar *to change; to barter.*

trofeo *m. trophy; prize.*

trompa *f. trumpet; trunk (of an elephant).*

trompada *f. punch, blow with the fist.*

trompeta *f. trumpet; m. trumpeter.*

trompo *m. top, spinning-top.*

tronar *to thunder.*

Por lo que pudiera tronar. *As a precaution. In case of an emergency. In case something happens.*

tronco *m. trunk (of wood); log; stem.*

trono *m. throne.*

tropa *f. troop.*

tropezar *to stumble, to trip; to come across, to meet accidentally, to run into; to meet with difficulties.*

Por poco me caigo al tropezar con esa piedra. *I almost tripped over that stone. ("I almost fell when I tripped over that stone.")*

¿Ha tropezado Ud. por casualidad con mi libro? *Have you by any chance come across my book?*

Acabo de tropezar con Juan en la calle. *I just ran across John in the street.*

Trepezaron con muchas dificultades al principio. *In the beginning they encountered many difficulties.*

tropezón *m. stumbling; tripping.*

Dar un tropezón. *To stumble.*

A tropezones. *By fits and starts. Painfully. Stumbling along.*

tropical *adj. tropical.*

trópico *m. tropic.*

tropiezo *m. stumble, trip; slip, fault; difficulty.*

Sin tropiezo. *Without any difficulty. Without a hitch ("slip").*

trotar *to trot.*

trote *m. trot.*

trozo *m. bit, piece, morsel; passage of a literary work.*

truco *m. trick; pocketing a poolball.*

trucha *f. trout.*

trueno m. thunder.
    Truena. (Está tronando.) It's thundering.
trueque m. barter, exchange.
    A trueque de. In exchange for.
TÚ you (familiar form).
    Hablarse de tú. To address each other in the familiar form.
    Tú eres un buen muchacho. You're a good boy.
    Tú debías saberlo. You ought to know it.
TU (possessive singular of tú) your; pl. tus.
    Tu libro. Your book.
    Tus libros. Your books.
tuberculosis f. tuberculosis.
tuberculoso adj. and n. tubercular.
tubería f. pipe line; tubing.
tubo m. tube; pipe.
tuerca f. nut (of a screw).
tuétano m. marrow.
    Helarse hasta los tuétanos. To be frozen to the marrow.
tufo m. vapor, exhalation; unpleasant odor; snobbishness.
tul m. tulle, thin fine silk net.
tulipán m. tulip.
tullido adj. and n. crippled, partially paralyzed.
tumba f. tomb, grave.
tumbar to knock down; to tumble.
tumor m. tumor.
tumulto m. tumult, commotion; mob.
tunante adj. leading a wild life; m. rascal, rogue.
    El muy tunante se ha burlado de nosotros. The rascal has fooled us.
túnel m. tunnel.
tupido adj. dense, thick, close-woven.
turba f. mob, rabble, crowd.
turbación f. perturbation; embarrassment.
turbante m. turban.
turbar to disturb, to upset; to embarrass.
turbina f. turbine.
turbio adj. turbid, muddy; troubled.
turbulencia f. turbulence, disturbance.
turbulento adj. turbid; turbulent.
turismo m. touring.
    Barco de turismo. Boat for tourists.
    Coche de turismo. Touring car.
    Agencia de turismo. Travel agency.
    Guía de turismo. Travel guide.
turista m. and f. tourist.
turístico adj. touristic.
turnar to alternate; to take turns.
turno m. turn.
    Espere su turno. Wait for your turn.
    Es mi turno. It's my turn now.
turquesa f. turquoise.

turrón m. nougat, almond and honey paste.
tute m. a kind of card game (Spain).
tutear to address each other in the familiar form.
    To use "tú."

tutela f. guardianship, tutelage.
tutor m. tutor, guardian.
TUYA (f. of tuyo) yours, of yours; pl. tuyas.
    Una hermana tuya. One of your sisters.
    Unas amigas tuyas. Some (girl) friends of yours.
    Esa camisa es tuya. This shirt is yours.
    Prefiero la tuya a la mía. I prefer yours to mine.
    Las tuyas. Yours (pl.).
TUYO yours, of yours (familiar form); pl. tuyos.
    Eso es tuyo. That's yours.
    Un amigo tuyo. A friend of yours.
    Unos amigos tuyos. Some friends of yours.
    Este libro es tuyo. This book is yours.
    Prefiere el tuyo al mío. I prefer yours to mine.
    Los tuyos. Yours (pl.).
    Lo mío y lo tuyo. Mine and yours.
    Lo mío es tuyo. What's mine is yours.

U

u (used instead of o when the following word begins with an "o", f. name of the letter u.
    Siete u ocho. Seven or eight.
    Uno u otro. One or the other. Either one.
ufano adj. proud, haughty; satisfied, contented, happy.
    Vive muy ufano en Nueva York. He lives very happily in New York.
Ud. (abbreviation of usted) you (polite form).
úlcera f. ulcer.
ulterior adj. ulterior.
ÚLTIMAMENTE lately.
    Ha estado malo últimamente. He's been sick lately.
    Se ha avejentado últimamente. He's aged lately.
ultimátum m. ultimatum.
ÚLTIMO adj. last, latest; late, latter; final; lowest (price).
    Fué el último en llegar. He was the last one to arrive.
    A última hora. At the last moment.
    A últimos de mes. Toward the end of the month. In the latter part of the month.
    ¿Es ésta la última edición? Is this the latest (last) edition?
    El último precio. The lowest price.
    Última moda. Latest style.
    Está en las últimas. He's at the end of his rope.
    Por último. Finally. At last.
ultrajar to outrage; to offend; to abuse, to insult, to humiliate.
ultraje m. outrage, great offense, insult.
ultramarino adj. overseas.
ultramarinos m. pl. grocery; fancy groceries usually from overseas.

ultravioleta *adj. ultraviolet.*

umbral *m. threshold, doorway.*

UN *(ind. article) a, an; adj. (shortening of uno) one.*

   Un hombre. *A man.*

   Tráigame un vaso de cerveza. *Bring me a glass of beer.*

   Un pedazo de pan. *A piece of bread.*

   Un poco. *A little.*

   Sabe un poco de todo. *He knows a little about everything.*

   Hace un tiempo magnífico. *The weather is fine (lovely, wonderful).*

   Compraré solamente un libro. *I'll buy only one book.*

UNA *(f. of un) a, an, one; (f. of uno) one; some-one; pl. a few, some.*

   Una mujer. *A woman.*

   Unas señoras preguntan por Ud. *Some ladies are asking for you.*

   Quiero decirle unas palabras. *I'd like to say a few words to you.*

   Es una bailarina. *She's a dancer.*

   Es una chica encantadora. *She's a charming girl.*

   Tengo una sola maleta. *I have only one suitcase.*

   Salimos a la una. *We'll leave at one.*

   Una vez. *Once.*

   Unas veces. *Sometimes.*

   Lo intentó una y otra vez. *He tried it time and time again.*

unánime *adj. unanimous.*

unanimidad *f. unanimity.*

   Por unanimidad. *Unanimously.*

undécimo *adj. and n. eleventh.*

ungüento *m. unguent, ointment, liniment.*

   Este ungüento le quitará el dolor. *This oint-ment will ease the pain.*

únicamente *only, simply, merely.*

ÚNICO *adj. only, only one, singular, unique, alone.*

   Era su hijo único. *It was her only son.*

   Es algo único en su género. *It's something unique.*

unidad *f. unity; conformity; unit.*

unido *adj. united, joined.*

unificar *to unify.*

uniforme *adj. uniform, always the same; m. uni-form.*

   Uniforme militar. *Military uniform.*

uniformidad *f. uniformity.*

UNIÓN *f. union; unity; coupling; joint.*

   La unión hace la fuerza. *In union there is strength.*

   La Unión de los Obreros del Transporte. *The Transport Workers Union.*

   En unión de. *Together with. In company with.*

unir *to unite, to join together, to put together.*

   Hay que unir esos dos alambres. *Those two wires have to be joined.*

   Una Ud. esas dos mesas. *Put those two tables together.*

unirse *to become united; to merge.*

   Se han unido las dos firmas. *The two firms have merged.*

universal *adj. universal.*

universidad *f. university.*

universitario *adj. collegiate; pertaining to a uni-versity.*

universo *m. universe.*

UNO *adj. and n. one; ind. pron. one, someone; pl. some, a few.*

   El número uno. *The number one.*

   Déme uno nada más. *Give me just one.*

   Uno más. *One more.*

   Unos señores quieren verle. *Some gentlemen would like to see you.*

   Tenía unos cigarros y los he regalado. *I had a few cigars and gave them away.*

   Unos cuantos. *Some. A few.*

   ¿Qué puede uno hacer? *What can one do?*

   Uno pregunta por Ud. *Someone is asking for you.*

   Uno no es infalible. *One is not infallible.*

   Nos parecemos el uno al otro. *We resemble one another.*

   Se aman uno a otro. *They love each other.*

   No se pueden ver unos a otros. *They can't stand each other.*

   Uno y otro. *Both.*

   Uno y otro son peruanos. *They are both Peruvian.*

   Cada uno. *Each one.*

   Uno u otro. *Either of the two. Either one.*

   Ni uno ni otro. *Neither one.*

   Uno a uno. *One by one.*

   Uno por uno. *One at a time.*

   Uno tras otro. *One after the other.*

   Todo es uno. *It's all the same.*

untar *to grease; to rub; to bribe; to anoint.*

   Untelo de aceite. *Rub some oil on it.*

unto *m. grease, fat (of animals).*

untura *f. rubbing with salve, unguent, etc.; unguent, salve, ointment.*

uña *f. nail (of finger or toe); claw; hoof.*

   Cortarse las uñas. *To cut one's nails.*

   Carne y uña. *To be very close friends.*

uñero *m. ingrown nail.*

urbanidad *f. urbanity, good manners, politeness.*

urbano *adj. urban, living in a city; urbane, refined, polite.*

urbe *f. large city.*

urdir *to warp; to scheme, to plot.*

urgencia *f. urgency, pressure.*

   La urgencia de los negocios. *The pressure of*

business.

Con urgencia. *Urgently.*

De urgencia. *Urgent. Pressing.*

urgente *adj. urgent.*

Es urgente que sepan la noticia. *It's urgent for them to know the news.*

urgir *to urge, to be pressing.*

Nos urgen mucho estos géneros. *We're greatly in need of these goods. We have urgent need of these goods.*

usado *adj. used, secondhand; worn-out.*

Ropa usada. *Secondhand clothing. Used clothes.*

usanza *f. usage, custom.*

USAR *to use; to be accustomed to; to wear.*

¿Me permite Ud. usar su teléfono? *May I use your phone? ("Will you allow me to use your telephone?")*

Uso anteojos porque no veo bien. *I wear (use) eyeglasses because I can't see well.*

Usar de su derecho. *To exercise one's right.*

USO *m. use; usage, customary; wearing, wear.*

Estos artículos son de mi uso personal. *These articles are for my personal use.*

Para uso interno. *For internal use.*

En buen uso. *In good condition.*

Se viste al uso del día. *She keeps up with the style. She dresses according to the latest style.*

USTED *you (polite form). Usually abbreviated to* Ud. *(or* Vd.).

Ud. y yo. *You and I.*

¿Cómo está Ud.? *How are you?*

¿Y Ud.? *And you? And how are you?*

¿Es Ud. francés? *Are you French?*

¿Qué toma Ud.? *What will you have (to drink)?*

Después de Ud. *After you.*

¡Cuídese Ud.! *Take good care of yourself!*

USTEDES *(pl. of* usted) *you. Usually abbreviated to* Uds. *(or* Vds.).

Todos Uds. son muy amables. *You are all very kind.*

Uds. llegaron antes que nosotros. *You (pl.) arrived before we did.*

USUAL *adj. usual, customary.*

Lo usual. *What's customary (usual). That which is customary.*

Eso es muy usual. *That's very common (usual).*

Son cosas usuales. *They're common (everyday) things.*

usura *f. usury.*

usurero *m. usurer; money-lender.*

usurpación *f. usurpation.*

usurpar *to usurp.*

utensilio *m. utensil.*

Utensilios de cocina. *Kitchen utensils.*

ÚTIL *adj. useful, profitable; m. pl. implements,*

tools, equipment.

¿En qué puedo serle útil? *What can I do for you? Can I help you in any way?*

Lo encontrará muy útil. *You'll find it very useful.*

Útiles para la escuela. *School supplies.*

Útiles de carpintería. *Carpenter's tools.*

utilidad *f. utility, usefulness; profit.*

Esto les será de mucha utilidad. *You'll find this very useful.*

utilizar *to utilize.*

uvas *f. pl. grapes.*

V

VACA *f. cow; beef.*

Carne de vaca. *Beef.*

vacación *f. vacation; pl. holidays.*

vacante *adj. vacant; f. vacancy.*

vaciar *to empty; to pour out; to cast, to mold; to make hollow.*

vaciarse *to give vent to one's feelings; to talk too much.*

vacilación *f. vacillation, hesitation.*

vacilante *adj. vacillating, wavering, uncertain, hesitating.*

vacilar *to vacillate, to waver, to hesitate.*

No vaciló en hacerlo. *He didn't hesitate to do it.*

vacío *adj. empty; vacant; m. void; vacuum.*

vacuna *f. vaccination; vaccine.*

vacunar *to vaccinate.*

vadear *to ford; to surmount.*

vado *m. ford (of a river).*

vagabundo *adj. vagabond, tramp.*

vagancia *f. vagrancy.*

vagar *to rove, to roam, to wander about; to be idle.*

vago *adj. vague; vagrant; m. tramp, vagabond.*

vagón *m. coach, car; wagon, freight car.*

vahído *m. dizziness, vertigo.*

vaho *m. exhalation, vapor, steam.*

vaivén *m. sway; fluctuation.*

vajilla *f. table service, dinner set.*

vale *m. promissory note, voucher; I.O.U. (This word is often written after a postscript to a letter to show that the addition is valid.)*

Firmó el vale. *He signed the I.O.U.*

valentía *f. valor, courage, bravery; boast.*

VALER *to be worth, to amount to; to be valid, to hold good.*

¿Cuánto vale? *How much is it worth?*

¿Cuánto puede valer ese automóvil? *I wonder how much that car would cost?*

Vale lo que pesa. *He's (it's) worth his (its) weight in gold.*

Vale más que su hermano. *He's better than his brother.*

Haga valer su autoridad. *Use your authority. Make your authority felt.*

Hacer valer. *To assert (one's rights). To make good (a claim).*

Más vale. *It's better.*

Más valiera. *It would be better.*

Más vale así. *It's just as well. It's better this way.*

Más vale tarde que nunca. *Better late than never.*

Vale la pena. *It's worth while.*

No vale la pena. *It's not worth while.*

valerse *to avail oneself of, to make use of.*

Se valió de mi influencia. *He made use of my influence.*

valeroso *adj. courageous, brave, valiant.*

validar *to make valid.*

validez *f. validity.*

válido *adj. valid, binding.*

El pasaporte es válido por un año. *The passport is valid for a year.*

valiente *adj. brave, courageous, valiant.*

valija *f. valise, grip; sack; mail bag.*

valioso *adj. valuable; of great influence.*

VALOR *m. value; price; courage, valor; pl. securities, bonds, shares.*

No tuvo valor de decirlo. *He hadn't the courage to say it.*

No tengo objetos de valor que declarar. *I have nothing (of value) to declare (in the custom-house).*

Aumentar el valor. *To increase the value.*

De poco valor. *Of little value.*

Sin valor. *Of no value. Worthless.*

Valor nominal. *Face value.*

Valor real. *Actual value.*

Estimar en su justo valor. *To attach the proper value to something.*

valorar *to value, to appraise.*

vals *m. waltz.*

valuación *f. valuation, appraisal, appraisement.*

valuar (en) *to rate, to price, to appraise, to value.*

válvula *f. valve.*

Válvula de seguridad. *Safety valve.*

Válvula de escape. *Exhaust valve.*

valla *f. fence, stockade; obstacle.*

vallado *m. enclosure; stockade.*

valle *m. valley.*

¡vamos! *Well! Come now! Go on! Let's go! (See ir.)*

vanagloria *f. vainglory, boasting, vanity, extreme self-pride.*

vanagloriarse *to boast.*

vanamente *vainly, in vain.*

vanguardia *f. vanguard.*

vanidad *f. vanity.*

Lo hace por vanidad. *He does it out of vanity.*

vanidoso *adj. vain, conceited.*

VANO *adj. vain; of no use.*

Esperé en vano toda la tarde. *I waited all afternoon in vain.*

Tratamos en vano de hacerlo. *We tried in vain to do it.*

Toda tentativa fué en vano. *Every attempt was in vain.*

vapor *m. vapor, steam; steamboat, steamer.*

Compañía de vapores. *Steamship company.*

A todo vapor. *At full steam.*

vaquero *m. herdsman; cowherd; cowboy.*

vara *f. measure of about 33 inches; yardstick; rod, pole, stick; wand; twig; baton, symbol of office or authority; shaft.*

No se meta Ud. en camisa de once varas. *Don't be so inquisitive.*

varar *to run aground; to be stranded; to launch (a ship).*

variable *adj. variable, changeable.*

variación *f. variation, change.*

Sin variación. *Unchanged.*

Las variaciones del tiempo. *Changes in the weather.*

variado *adj. varied; of different kinds.*

variante *adj. varying; deviating; f. textual variation; variant reading.*

variar *to vary, to change.*

No varía. *It doesn't change.*

variedad *f. variety.*

VARIO *adj. changeable; various; pl. several, some, a few.*

Un carácter muy vario. *A very changeable character.*

Hemos recibido un surtido de medias de varios tamaños. *We've received an assortment of stockings of various sizes.*

Varios hombres descargaban el camión. *Several men were unloading the truck.*

He comprado varios libros. *I bought a few books.*

Llevo ya escritas varias cartas. *I have already written several letters.*

El cajón del armario tiene varias divisiones. *The bureau drawer has several sections.*

varón *m. man, male.*

varonil *adj. manly, manful.*

vaselina *f. vaseline.*

vasija *f. vessel (pitcher, jar, container, etc.).*

VASO *m. glass (for drinking); vessel (anatomy).*

Déme otro vaso de cerveza. *Give me another glass of beer.*

vástago *m. stem; shoot; offspring.*

vasto *adj. vast, immense.*

vaticinar *to forecast, to predict, to foretell.*

vaticinio *m. forecast, prediction.*

¡vaya! *Go on! Come on! Indeed! Certainly! Go! (See ir.)*

¡Vaya historia! *Some story! What a story!*

ve *f. name of the letter v.*

vecindad *f. vicinity, neighborhood.*

vecindario *m. neighborhood; people of a neighbor-*

hood.

VECINO *adj. neighboring, next; m. neighbor; resident.*

El vecino de al lado. *Next-door neighbor.*

veda *f. prohibition, interdiction by law; season when hunting is forbidden.*

vegetación *f. vegetation.*

vegetal *m. vegetal, vegetable.*

vegetariano *adj. and n. vegetarian.*

vehemencia *f. vehemence.*

vehemente *adj. vehement, violent.*

VEINTE *adj. and n. twenty; twentieth.*

vehículo *m. vehicle.*

veintena *f. a score, twenty.*

vejación *f. annoyance, vexation.*

vejar *to vex, to annoy.*

vejez *f. old age.*

vejiga *f. bladder; blister.*

vela *f. candle; vigil; watch, wake; sail; sailboat; night work.*

Apaque las velas por favor. *Please blow out the candles.*

Pasé la noche en vela. *I didn't sleep all night.*

Darse (hacerse) a la vela. *To set sail.*

velada *f. evening entertainment, soiree, party.*

velador *m. watchman; lamp table, lamp stand.*

velar *to watch; to keep vigil; to work at night; to veil.*

Velar a un paciente. *To keep vigil over a patient.*

Velar por. *To watch over. To take care of.*

Velar un cuadro. *To veil a picture.*

velero *adj. fast sailer (ship); m. sailboat.*

velo *m. veil.*

VELOCIDAD *f. velocity, speed; gear.*

Pasaron a toda velocidad. *They tore past at full speed.*

Modere la velocidad. *Slow up.*

Cambio de velocidad. *Gearshift.*

Primera velocidad. *First gear.*

Segunda velocidad. *Second gear.*

Ya está en tercera velocidad. *It's in third gear.*

Tren de pequeña velocidad. *Freight train. Slow train.*

Tren de gran velocidad. *Express train.*

En pequeña velocidad. *By freight train.*

En gran velocidad. *By express.*

veloz *adj. swift, fast.*

vello *m. fuzz, down, nap; gossamer.*

vellón *m. fleece; lock of wool; an ancient copper coin.*

velludo *adj. downy, hairy, shaggy.*

vena *f. vein.*

venado *m. deer, venison.*

vencedor *adj. and n. victorious; winner, victor.*

vencer *to conquer, to vanquish.*

vencerse *to control oneself.*

vencido *adj. defeated; due (to be paid).*

¡Me doy por vencido! *I give up!*

Letra vencida. *Overdue draft.*

vencimiento *m. maturity, falling due, expiration (of term); victory.*

Al vencimiento. *When due.*

Mañana es el vencimiento de la letra. *The draft becomes due tomorrow.*

venda *f. bandage.*

vendaje *m. bandage, dressing (of wounds).*

vendar *to bandage, to dress a wound; to blindfold.*

vendaval *m. gale, strong wind.*

vendedor *m. seller, trader, dealer, salesman (-woman), vendor.*

VENDER *to sell.*

¿A cómo se venden estos libros? *What's the price of these books?*

Quiero vender mi automóvil. *I want to sell my car.*

Vender a crédito. *To sell on credit.*

Vender al contado. *To sell for cash.*

Vender a ojo. *To sell in bulk.*

Vender al por mayor. *To sell wholesale.*

Vender al por menor. *To sell retail.*

¡Qué caro se vende Ud.! *You're a sight for sore eyes! You're quite a stranger!*

vendible *adj. saleable; easily sold.*

vendimia *f. vintage.*

veneno *m. venom, poison.*

venenoso *adj. poisonous.*

venerable *adj. venerable.*

veneración *f. veneration.*

venerar *to venerate.*

vengador *m. avenger.*

venganza *f. vengeance.*

vengar *to avenge, to take revenge.*

vengativo *adj. vindictive, revengeful.*

VENIR *to come; to fit, to suit.*

¡Ven acá! *Come here!*

¡Venga pronto! *Come quickly!*

¿A qué hora vendrá Ud.? *(At) What time will you come?*

¿De manera que no viene Ud.? *So you're not coming?*

¡Venga en seguida! *Come at once!*

Los veo venir. *I see them coming.*

El mes que viene. *Next month.*

Estos zapatos me vienen anchos. *These shoes are too wide for me.*

Le viene como un guante. *It fits you like a glove.*

¡Venga el dólar! *Come on, give me the dollar.*

¿A qué viene eso? *What does that have to do with the case? What's that got to do with it?*

Venirse al suelo. *To fall to the ground.*

Eso te viene de no hacer caso. *That comes from not paying attention.*

Me vino el deseo de hacerlo. *I felt like doing it.*

Venga lo que venga. *Come what may.*

El tren viene retrasado. *The train's late.*

El pobre ha venido muy a menos. *The poor fellow ι as come down in the world.*

Lo que Ud. dice no viene al caso. *What you're saying is beside the point.*

Esto no viene cuento. *That's beside the point.*

Venir a pelo. *To fit the case. To come to the point.*

Eso ni me va ni me viene. *That doesn't concern me.*

VENTA *f. sale, selling; roadside inn.*

Estos días han disminuído las ventas. *Sales have decreased (fallen off) recently (these days).*

Poner a la venta. *To put on sale.*

Está a la venta. *It's for sale.*

Ventas al por mayor. *Wholesale.*

Ventas al por menor. *Retail.*

ventaja *f. advantage; profit; odds (games); handicap (sports).*

Este procedimiento tiene sus ventajas y desventajas. *This procedure has its advantages and disadvantages.*

Llevar ventaja. *To have an (the) advantage over.*

Llevar la ventaja. *To get the upper hand.*

ventajoso *adj. advantageous, profitable.*

VENTANA *f. window; window shutter; nostril.*

Las ventanas dan a la calle. *The windows face the street.*

Asómese Ud. a la ventana. *Lean out of the window.*

Las ventanas de la nariz. *Nostrils.*

Tirar por la ventana. *To squander. To waste.*

ventanal *m. large window.*

ventanilla *f. small window.*

ventilación *f. ventilation.*

Este cuarto necesita ventilación. *The (this) room needs to be aired.*

ventilador *m. ventilator; electric fan.*

ventilar *to ventilate, to air; to winnow; to discuss.*

Favor de ventilar el cuarto. *Please air the room.*

Abra las ventanas para que se ventile la habitación. *Open the windows to air out the room.*

Ventilar una cuestión. *To discuss a question.*

ventisca *f. blizzard.*

ventosa *f. cupping; cupping glass; vent.*

ventura *f. happiness; fortune, chance, venture.*

venturoso *adj. lucky, fortunate.*

VER *to see; to see; to look into; to visit; to meet; m. sense of sight; seeing; look; opinion.*

Déjeme verlo. *Let me see it.*

¿Se le puede ver? *May I see him?*

Me alegro mucho de verla aquí. *I'm very glad to see you here.*

Hasta más ver. *So long. See you later. Good-by.*

A más ver. *So long. See you later. Good-by.*

¿Dónde nos vemos antes de la comida? *Where shall we meet before dinner?*

Nos veremos esta noche. *We'll meet tonight.*

¿Qué cuadros desea Ud. ver? *Which paintings do you wish to see?*

Me marché sin ver a nadie. *I went away without seeing anybody (anyone).*

Vamos a ver. *Let's see.*

¿A ver si le gusta esto? *See whether you like it.*

Vea Ud. esta carta. *Look at this letter.*

Veamos el menú. *Let's have a look at the menu.*

A ver, otro chiste. *Come on, tell another joke.*

Ya veremos más adelante. *We'll see about that later.*

¡Allá veremos! (¡Ya veremos!) *We'll see. Time will tell.*

Ya se ve. *It's evident. It's obvious. It's plain.*

A lo que se ve. *Apparently. As it seems.*

¡Para que veas! *There you are! I told you so.*

Ver y creer. *Seeing is believing.*

No lo puedo ver ni pintado. *I can't bear the sight of him.*

Eso queda por ver. *That remains to be seen.*

Aquello era de ver. *It was worth while seeing.*

No tener nada que ver con. *To have nothing to do with.*

A mi ver. *In my opinion. As it seems to me.*

Hacer ver. *To show.*

Hacer ver que . . . *To make it clear that . . .*

VERANO *m. summer.*

VERAS *f. pl. truth, reality; earnestness.*

¿Pero de veras es Ud.? *Is it really you?*

¿De veras? *Really? No fooling? Do you really mean it?*

¡De veras! *You don't say so! You don't mean it! Really! Indeed!*

De veras. *In earnest. Absolutely so. Really.*

veraz *adj. veracious, truthful.*

verbal *adj. verbal, oral.*

verbalmente *verbally, orally.*

verbigracia *for example, for instance, e.g.*

verbo *m. verb.*

VERDAD *f. truth.*

Todo lo cual no es verdad. *All of which isn't true. There's not a shred of truth in it.*

Diga Ud. la verdad. *Tell the truth.*

Quiero averiguar si es verdad. *I want to find out if it's true.*

Falta Ud. a la verdad. *You're lying. You're not telling the truth.*

Hace frío, ¿no es verdad? *It's cold, isn't it?*

¿Verdad? *Is that so? Is it? Isn't it? Doesn't it?*

Ya no me necesita Ud., ¿verdad? *You don't need me any more, do you?*

¿De verdad? *Really?*

De verdad. *In earnest.*

La pura verdad. *The plain truth.*

En verdad. *Truly.*

A la verdad. *Truly. In fact.*

A decir verdad. *As a matter of fact. To tell the truth.*

Bien es verdad que . . . *It's true that . . .*

Decir cuatro verdades. *To give someone a piece of one's mind.*

verdaderamente *truly, really; in fact, indeed.*

Es verdaderamente bonito. *It's really very pretty.*

verdadero *adj. true, real, veritable; sincere.*

Es una verdadera sorpresa. *This is a real surprise.*

Es un amigo verdadero. *He's a true friend.*

verde *adj. green; immature, unripe; m. green color.*

El verde le cae muy bien. *Green is very becoming to you.*

Legumbres verdes. *Greens. Green vegetables.*

Uvas verdes. *Sour grapes.*

Estas judías verdes son excelentes. *These string beans are excellent.*

Fruta verde. *Green (unripe) fruit.*

Darse un verde. *To take time out for relaxation. To take it easy for a little while.*

verdugo *m. hangman; very cruel person; young shoot of a tree.*

verdulero *m. vegetable man.*

verdura *f. verdure; vegetables, greens.*

vereda *f. path, footpath, trail; sidewalk (Amer.).*

veredicto *m. verdict.*

vergonzoso *adj. bashful, shy; shameful, disgraceful.*

Este niño es muy vergonzoso. *This child is very bashful.*

vergüenza *f. shame; disgrace.*

¿No le da vergüenza? *Aren't you ashamed of yourself?*

¡Qué vergüenza! *What a shame!*

Perder la vergüenza. *To lose all sense of shame.*

Tener vergüenza. *To be ashamed.*

Sin vergüenza. *Shameless.*

verídico *adj. truthful, veracious.*

verificación *f. verification.*

verificar *to check up, to verify; to take place.*

Verifique la cuenta. *Check the account.*

La reunión se verificará mañana. *The meeting will take place tomorrow.*

verisímil *adj. likely, probable, credible.*

verja *f. grate, grating; iron gate; iron railing.*

vermut *m. vermouth.*

versar *to go about; to deal with; to be about.*

versátil *adj. versatile.*

versatilidad *f. versatility.*

VERSE *to see each other; to be seen; to find oneself; to be (in).*

Nos vemos con frecuencia. *We see each other quite often.*

Se veía pobre y sin amigos. *He found himself poor and friendless.*

Verse obligado a. *To find it necessary to. To be compelled to.*

Verse con alguien. *To see someone. To have a talk with someone.*

Verse en apuro. *To be in trouble.*

Verse negro. *To be in a fix.*

Véase la página . . . *See page . . .*

versión *f. version.*

Cada uno de ellos dió una versión distinta del suceso. *Each one of them gave a different version of the incident.*

Esta es la mejor versión del Quijote en inglés. *This is the best version of "Don Quixote" in English.*

verso *m. verse; pl. verses, poetry; poem.*

vértebra *f. vertebra.*

vertebrado *adj. vertebrate.*

vertedero *m. sewer, drain.*

verter *to pour; to spill; to empty; to translate.*

vertical *adj. vertical.*

vértice *m. vertex, apex, top.*

vertiente *f. flowing; stream; watershed; slope.*

vértigo *m. dizziness; giddiness, vertigo.*

vestíbulo *m. hall, lobby.*

Hay un teléfono en el vestíbulo. *There's a phone in the lobby.*

VESTIDO *adj. dressed; m. dress; garment; clothing.*

Siempre va bien vestida. *She's always well dressed.*

¿Cómo estaba vestida? *What was she wearing? How was she dressed?*

Iba vestido de paisano. *He was dressed in civilian clothes.*

¿Cuánto tardaría Ud. en teñirme este vestido? *How long would it take to dye this dress for me?*

Vestido de etiqueta. *Evening dress.*

Vestido de verano. *Summer dress.*

Vestido de casa. *House dress.*

vestigio *m. vestige.*

VESTIR *to dress; to put on; to cover.*

Tengo que vestir a los niños. *I have to dress the children.*

Eso viste mucho. *That's very stylish.*

Se ha quedado para vestir santos. *She's an old maid.*

VESTIRSE *to dress oneself, to get dressed; to wear.*

Date prisa y vístete que se nos hace tarde. *Hurry up and get dressed—we're late.*

Iba vestida de punta en blanco. *She was all dressed up.*

Se viste muy bien. *She dresses well. She dresses in good taste.*

Se viste de uniforme. *He wears a uniform.*

Se viste siempre de negro. *She's always dressed in black.*

Estoy a medio vestir. *I'm (only) half dressed.*

vestuario m. *clothes, wardrobe, wearing apparel; dressing room (in a theater).*

veterano m. *veteran.*

veterinario m. *veterinarian.*

veto m. *veto.*

VEZ f. *time; turn.*

Una vez. *Once.*

Dos veces. *Twice.*

Tres veces. *Three times.*

Otra vez. *Again.*

Repetidas veces. *Again and again.*

De una vez. *At once.*

De una vez para siempre. *Once (and) for all.*

Rara vez. *Seldom.*

Muchas veces. *Often.*

Tal vez. *Perhaps.*

Cada vez. *Each time. Every time.*

Cada vez más. *More and more.*

Todas las veces que. *Whenever. As often as. Every time that.*

De vez en cuando. *Now and then.*

Alguna (una) que otra vez. *Sometimes. Once in a while.*

Una vez que otra. *Sometimes. Once in a while.*

A la vez que. *While.*

Esta vez. *This time.*

VÍA f. *road, way;   vía; track, line (railroad).*

Por vía de. *By way of.*

Vía ancha. *Broad gauge (railroad).*

Vía angosta. *Narrow gauge (railroad).*

Doble vía. *Double track.*

Vía férrea. *Railroad. Railway.*

Vía aérea. *Airway.*

Por la vía marítima. *By sea. By boat.*

Vía terrestre. *Land route.*

En vía de fabricación. *In process of manufacture.*

En vías de. *Under way.*

Vía pública. *Public road. Thoroughfare. Street.*

viable adj. *viable, capable of maintaining life; feasible.*

VIAJAR *to travel.*

¿Ha viajado Ud. alguna vez por avión? *Have you ever traveled by plane?*

Ha viajado mucho por Europa. *He's traveled a lot in Europe.*

VIAJE m. *trip, voyage, journey, travel.*

¡Buen viaje! *Bon voyage! Pleasant journey!*

¡Feliz viaje! *A pleasant journey!*

Tuvimos una tormenta durante el viaje de ida. *We ran into a storm on our way over.*

En viaje para. *En route for.*

Estar de viaje. *To be on a trip. To be away traveling.*

Viaje redondo. *A round trip.*

Viaje de novios. *Honeymoon.*

Viaje de recreo. *Pleasure trip.*

Viaje de ida. *A one-way trip. Trip to a place.*

Viaje de vuelta (regreso). *A return trip. A trip back.*

Viaje de ida y vuelta. *A round trip.*

VIAJERO m. *traveler; passenger.*

¡Señores viajeros, al tren! *(Passengers.) All aboard!*

vianda f. *food, viands; pl. vegetables for a Cuban dish called* ajiaco.

víbora f. *viper.*

vibración f. *vibration.*

vibrar *to vibrate, to throb.*

vicealmirante m. *vice-admiral.*

vicecónsul m. *vice-consul.*

vicepresidente m. *vice-president.*

viciar *to vitiate, to mar; to spoil; to corrupt; to tamper with, to forge; to make void.*

El aire aquí está viciado. *The air here is impure.*

Este manuscrito está viciado. *The manuscript has been tampered with.*

Las raspaduras vician el documento. *The erasures make the document void.*

viciarse *to give oneself up to vice; to acquire vices.*

vicio m. *vice; habit; bad habit; defect; exuberance; growth of plants.*

Ese niño llora de vicio. *That child is always crying.*

Este árbol lleva mucho vicio. *This tree is rich in foliage.*

Dinero para los vicios. *Pocket money.*

Quejarse de vicio. *To complain without cause. To be in the habit of complaining.*

Tener el vicio de. *To be in the habit of.*

Vivir en el vicio. *To lead a dissolute life.*

vicioso adj. *vicious; having bad habits, given to vice.*

Es muy vicioso. *He has many bad habits.*

Círculo vicioso. *Vicious circle.*

vicisitud f. *vicissitude.*

víctima f. *victim.*

victoria f. *victory.*

victorioso adj. *victorious.*

VIDA f. *life; living.*

En mi vida he visto ni oído tal cosa. *I've never seen or heard of such a thing in my life.*

Me gano la vida escribiendo. *I write for a living. I make my living by writing.*

Mi vida. *My dearest. My darling.*

Vida mía. *My dearest. My darling.*

Buscar la vida. *To try to make a living.*

Ganarse la vida. *To earn (make) a living.*

Darse buena vida. *To live comfortably.*

Dar mala vida. *To mistreat. To abuse.*

Vida alegre (airada). *A merry life.*

Pasar la vida. *To live frugally. To eke out an*

existence.

El coste de la vida. *The cost of living.*

Entre la vida y la muerte. *Between life and death.*

En su vida. *Never.*

¡Por mi vida! *My word!*

Escapar con vida. *To have a narrow escape.*

vidriera f. *showcase; show window.*

vidrio m. *glass.*

Vidrio de aumento. *Magnifying glass.*

Vidrio tallado. *Cut glass.*

Pagar los vidrios rotos. *To be made the scapegoat.*

viejecito m. *a little old man.*

VIEJO adj. *old; worn-out; ancient;* m. *an old man.*

Somos viejos amigos. *We're old friends.*

Le creí más viejo. *I thought you were older.*

Su madre es muy vieja. *His mother is very old.*

Ese viejo tiene muy mal genio. *That old man has a bad (vile) temper.*

VIENTO m. *wind; scent (hunting); airs.*

Hace mucho viento. *It's very windy.*

Corre un viento glacial. *There's an icy wind.*

Sus negocios van de viento en popa. *His business is very successful.*

vientre m. *belly, stomach.*

VIERNES m. *Friday.*

viga f. *beam, rafter, girder.*

vigésimo adj. and n. *twentieth.*

vigilancia f. *vigilance.*

vigilante adj. *vigilant; watchful;* m. *watchman.*

vigilar to *watch over, to look after.*

vigilia f. *vigil; fast; eve; burning the midnight oil.*

Pasamos la noche de vigilia. *We sat up all night.*

Esta novela es el producto de sus vigilias. *He spent his nights working on this novel.*

Comer de vigilia. *To abstain from meat.*

vigor m. *vigor, strength.*

vigoroso adj. *vigorous, strong.*

vil adj. *mean, low, vile, despicable.*

vileza f. *meanness, infamous deed.*

villa f. *village; villa.*

vinagre m. *vinegar.*

vinicultura f. *viniculture, wine growing.*

vinicultor m. *wine grower.*

VINO m. *wine.*

¿Le sirvo a Ud. un poco de vino? *Shall I pour (serve) you a little wine?*

Jerez es famoso por sus vinos. *Jerez is famous for its wines.*

Vino tinto. *Red wine.*

Vino blanco. *White wine.*

Vino espumoso. *Sparkling wine.*

Vino de Jerez. *Sherry.*

Vino de Oporto. *Port wine.*

viña f. *vineyard.*

viñedo m. *vineyard.*

violación f. *violation, breach.*

violar to *violate, to infringe, to offend.*

violencia f. *violence.*

violento adj. *violent.*

violeta f. *violet (plant).*

violín m. *violin.*

violinista m. and f. *violinist.*

violoncelo m. *violoncello.*

virar to *tack, to veer, to change direction, to turn.*

Vire a la derecha (izquierda). *Turn right (left).*

virgen f. *virgin.*

viril adj. *virile, manly.*

virilidad f. *virility.*

virtud f. *virtue, a good quality.*

En virtud de. *By virtue of.*

Por virtud de. *Because of. On account of.*

En tal virtud. *In view of which. On account of which.*

virtuoso adj. and n. *virtuoso.*

viruela f. *smallpox.*

Viruelas locas. *Chicken pox.*

virulencia f. *virulence.*

virulento adj. *virulent; malignant.*

visar to *visa, to visé; to O.K.*

Deseo hacer visar mi pasaporte para México. *I want to get a visa for Mexico.*

Tengo mi pasaporte visado. *My passport's stamped.*

viscosidad f. *viscosity.*

viscoso adj. *viscous, clammy.*

visibilidad f. *visibility.*

visible adj. *visible.*

visión f. *vision, sight; revelation.*

VISITA f. *visit, call.*

Está esperando la visita en la sala. *The guest is waiting in the living room.*

Tenemos visitas. *We have company.*

Hacer una visita. *To pay a call.*

Visita de cumplido. *A formal call.*

Visita de inspección. *Inspection tour.*

Pagar una visita. *To return a call.*

VISITAR to *visit; to call on.*

¿Por qué ha dejado Ud. de visitarnos? *Why have you stopped visiting us? Why have you stopped coming to see us?*

Los visito de vez en cuando. *I call on them now and then. I go to see them once in a while.*

visitarse to *call on one another, to be on visiting terms.*

víspera f. *eve.*

Estar en vísperas de. *To be on the eve of.*

VISTA f. *sight; view; glance; looks; trial (law);* m. *a customhouse officer, a customs official.*

¡Hasta la vista! *I'll be seeing you! See you soon!*

Solamente le conozco de vista. *I know him only by sight.*

No lo pierdas de vista. *Don't lose sight of him.*

Bajar la vista. *To look down.*

Alzar la vista. *To look up.*

A la vista. *On sight.*

A primera vista. *At first sight.*

Corto de vista. *Nearsighted.*

Cansar la vista. *To strain one's eyes.*

En vista de. *In view of. Considering.*

Hacer la vista gorda. *To connive.*

Echar una vista a. *To glance at.*

Vista de pájaro. *A bird's-eye view.*

Hay una hermosa vista desde aquí. *There's a nice view from here.*

¡Qué vista! *What a view!*

vistazo *m. glance.*

Echar un vistazo. *To glance.*

visto *adj. seen; obvious, clear.*

Está visto. *It's obvious. It's evident.*

Nunca visto. *Unheard of.*

Por lo visto. *Evidently. Apparently.*

Visto Bueno. *(V°.B°.) O.K. All right. Approved.*

Visto que. *Considering that.*

Bien visto. *Respected. Highly regarded. Proper. Well considered. On second thought.*

Mal visto. *Not respected. Looked down on.*

vistoso *adj. beautiful, showy; dressy.*

visual *adj. visual.*

vital *adj. vital.*

vitalicio *adj. for life; during life.*

Renta vitalicia. *Life pension.*

vitalidad *f. vitality.*

vitamina *f. vitamin.*

vitorear *to acclaim, to cheer.*

vituperio *m. vituperation, bitter abuse; infamy, shame.*

viuda *f. widow; mourning bride (plant).*

viudez *f. widowhood.*

viudo *f. widower.*

¡viva! *Long live! Hail! Hurrah!*

¡Viva España! *Long live Spain!*

Es un viva la virgen. *He's a simpleton.*

vivamente *vividly, deeply, very much.*

vivaracho *adj. lively, sprightly, frisky.*

vivaz *adj. lively; vivid, ingenious, bright, witty.*

vivero *m. warren; hatchery; nursery (plants).*

viveza *f. liveliness; vividness; perspicacity, keenness; sparkling (eyes).*

VIVIR *to live; to last; m. life, living.*

Vive solo. *He lives alone.*

¿Dónde vive? *Where do you live?*,

¿Cuánto tiempo hace que vive Ud. aquí? *How long have you been living here?*

Se viene a vivir con nosotros. *He's coming to live with us.*

Ella vive en el segundo piso. *She lives on the second floor.*

Se vive bien aquí. *One can live well (nicely, comfortably) here.*

Vive de su pluma. *He makes his living as a writer.*

Tiene para vivir. *He has enough to live on.*

Vive soñando. *His head's in the clouds. ("He lives in a daydream.")*

Vivir para ver. *Live and learn.*

VIVO *adj. living, alive; lively; smart.*

Está vivo. *He's alive.*

Copia al vivo. *Facsimile.*

Es un hombre muy vivo. *He's a very smart man.*

Color vivo. *Bright color.*

A lo (al) vivo. *To the life. Like the model. Very like the original.*

De viva voz. *By word of mouth.*

Tocar en lo vivo. *To cut to the quick.*

Los vivos y los muertos. *The quick and the dead.*

vizconde *m. viscount.*

vizcondesa *f. viscountess.*

vocablo *m. word, term.*

vocabulario *m. vocabulary.*

vocación *f. vocation.*

vocal *adj. vocal, oral; f. vowel, m. voter (in an assembly); member of a board of directors.*

vocear *to cry out.*

vocero *m. spokesman; advocate.*

vociferar *to vociferate, to shout, to cry out loudly.*

volandas (en) *in the air; in a jiffy.*

Lo llevaron en volandas. *They carried him on their shoulders.*

volante *adj. flying; m. steering wheel; balance wheel (watch).*

VOLAR *to fly; to blow up, to blast; to spread, to disseminate (news, a rumor).*

Volamos desde Madrid a Barcelona. *We flew from Madrid a Barcelona.*

Las horas vuelan. *The hours flew by.*

La noticia voló de boca en boca. *The news spread from mouth to mouth.*

Echar a volar la imaginación. *To let one's imagination run away with one.*

Sacar (echar) a volar. *To spread. To publish.*

Volaron el puente. *They blew up the bridge.*

volátil *adj. volatile, changeable.*

volcán *m. volcano.*

volcar *to overturn; to turn upside down; to turn over; to tilt.*

voltear *to turn over (position); to tumble, to roll over (an acrobat).*

voltereta *f. somersault.*

volubilidad *f. volubility.*

voluble *adj. voluble; fickle, changeable.*

volumen *m. volume; size; bulk. (For "volume" in the sense of "volume two of a set," see tomo.)*

voluminoso *adj. voluminous, bulky.*

VOLUNTAD *f. will, desire; disposition, consent; intention.*

Lo puede hacer pero le falta voluntad. *He can do it but he's unwilling to.*

Lo hice contra mi voluntad. *I did it against my own will.*

Mala voluntad. *Bad disposition.*

De buena voluntad. *With pleasure. Willingly.*

De mala voluntad. *Unwillingly.*

A voluntad. *At will.*

Ultima voluntad. *Last will and testament.*

voluntariamente *voluntarily, of one's own free will.*

voluntario *adj. voluntary, willing; m. volunteer.*

voluptuoso *adj. voluptuous, sensual.*

VOLVER *to come back, to return; to turn; to turn back; to put back.*

Vuelva mañana. *Come back tomorrow.*

No ha vuelto todavía. *He hasn't returned yet.*

Volverá pronto. *He'll come back soon.*

Se ha marchado para no volver. *He's gone for good.*

Vuelva la página. *Turn the page.*

El camino vuelve hacia la izquierda. *The road turns to the left.*

Vuelve el libro a su sitio. *Put the book back in its place.*

Volvió a salir. *He went out again.*

No vuelvas a hacer eso. *Don't do that again.*

No la volvió a ver más. *He didn't see her again.*

Vuelva a hacerlo. *Do it again.*

Volver la cabeza. *To turn one's head.*

Volver a trabajar. *To resume work.*

Volver atrás. *To come or go back.*

Volver en sí. *To recover one's senses.*

Volver a uno loco. *To drive someone crazy.*

VOLVERSE *to turn, to become.*

Este papel se ha vuelto amarillo. *This paper has turned yellow.*

Se ha vuelto loco. *He's become insane.*

Volverse atrás. *To retract.*

Volverse la tortilla. *To turn the tables.*

vomitar *to vomit, to throw out.*

vomitivo *adj. and n. emetic.*

vómito *m. vomiting.*

voracidad *f. voracity, greediness.*

vorágine *f. vortex, whirlpool.*

voraz *adj. voracious, greedy.*

vos *(pers. pron.) you (singular and familiar; used in Arg., Costa Rica and Uruguay).*

Vos y yo. *You and I.*

Es como vos. *He's like you.*

Vos tenés que venir mañana. *(Arg.) You have to come tomorrow.*

VOSOTRAS *(f. pl. of tú) you (familiar).*

Vosotras sois sus hermanas. *You're his sisters.*

Esto es para vosotras. *This is for you (pl. f.).*

VOSOTROS *(m. pl. of tú) you (familiar).*

Vosotros sois mis amigos. *You (pl.) are my friends.*

Vosotros tenéis la culpa. *You're (pl.) to blame.*

Vosotros os engañáis. *You're (pl.) fooling yourselves.*

Os aguardábamos a vosotros. *We were waiting for you (pl.).*

votación *f. voting.*

Votación secreta. *Ballot. Secret vote.*

Poner a votación. *To put to a vote.*

votante *m. and f. voter, elector.*

votar *to vote; to vow.*

No votaré ni por el uno ni por el otro. *I won't vote for either one.*

voto *m. vote; ballot; vow; wish.*

Fué elegido por una gran mayoría de votos. *He was elected by a large majority (of votes).*

Hacemos votos por que obtenga lo que desea. *We hope you'll get your wish.*

Hacemos votos por su felicidad. *We wish you a lot of happiness.*

Hago votos por su prosperidad. *I wish you success.*

VOZ *f. voice; outcry; word; rumor.*

Tiene muy buena voz. *He has a very good voice.*

El es quien lleva la voz cantante. *He's the spokesman.*

Pidió socorro a voces. *She cried out for help.*

Alzar la voz. *To raise one's voice.*

Anudarse la voz. *To be unable to speak (because of excitement, emotion, etc.).*

Tener voz y voto. *To have a voice in a (the) matter.*

Voz de mando. *Word of command.*

La voz pasiva. *The passive voice (grammar).*

A media voz. *In an undertone. In a whisper.*

Dar voces. *To cry. To shout.*

Corre la voz. *It's rumored. It's said.*

De viva voz. *By word of mouth.*

A voz en cuello. *In a very loud voice.*

En voz alta. *Aloud.*

En voz baja. *In a low tone.*

Estar en voz. *To be in voice.*

A una voz. *Unanimously. ("With one voice.")*

vuelco *m. overturning, tumble.*

vuelo *m. flight; distance flown; frill, ruffle; width, fullness (dress, skirt, etc.).*

Esta falda tiene mucho vuelo. *There's plenty of fullness in that skirt.*

Acaban de hacer un vuelo alrededor del mundo. *They have just made a flight around the world.*

Tomar vuelo. *To grow. To progress.*

Alzar (levantar) vuelo. *To fly off.*

A (al) vuelo. *Right away. In a jiffy. In passing. On the fly.*

Lo entendió al vuelo. *He caught on right away.*

De alto vuelo. *Of great importance. Of high*

standing.

VUELTA f. turn, turning; return; reverse; back (of a page); a walk; change (money).

Estar de vuelta. To be back. To know beforehand.

Me dijo que estaría de vuelta pronto. She told me she would be back soon.

Ya estoy de vuelta de lo que me dice. I already know what he's telling me.

Dar una vuelta. To take a walk.

¿Le gustaría dar una vuelta después de comer? Would you like to take a walk after dinner?

Dar vueltas. To turn. To walk back and forth. To keep thinking about the same thing. To hammer on a point.

Por más que doy vueltas, no acierto a comprenderlo. No matter how hard I think about it, I can't understand it.

Déme la vuelta. Give me the change.

Quédese con la vuelta. Keep the change.

Eso no tiene vuelta de hoja. There are no two ways about it.

Lo puso de vuelta y media. She gave him a good dressing-down.

Billete de ida y vuelta. Round-trip ticket.

Viaje de vuelta. Return trip.

A la vuelta de la esquina. Around the corner.

Dé la vuelta. Turn around.

Otra vuelta. Again. Once more.

¡Otra vuelta! Another round (of drinks)!

A vuelta(s) de. Around. Approximately.

A vueltas de Navidad. Around (about) Christmas.

A la vuelta. On the next page. Turn over. Carried over (bookkeeping).

De la vuelta. Continued. Brought forward (bookkeeping).

¡Media vuelta! Right about-face!

vuelto m. change, money returned (Amer.).

Guarde el vuelto. Keep the change.

VUESTRA (f. of vuestro) your, yours; pl. vuestras.

Vuestra madre. Your mother.

Vuestras hijas. Your daughters.

VUESTRO (pers. pron.) your, yours; pl. vuestros.

Vuestro amigo. Your friend.

Es un amigo vuestro. He's a friend of yours.

Vuestros amigos. Your friends.

vulcanizar to vulcanize.

vulgar adj. vulgar; common; ordinary.

vulgaridad f. vulgarity.

vulgarmente vulgarly; commonly.

vulgo m. the common people; populace; mob.

vulnerable adj. vulnerable.

W

whiskey m. whiskey.

X

x Most words originally written with x now have j. In Mexico, however, the words Méjico and Mejicano are still spelled with an x: México, Mexicano.

Rayos X. X-rays.

xenofobia f. hatred of foreigners.

Y

Y and.

Tú y yo. You and I.

Hoy y mañana. Today and tomorrow.

Pan y queso. Bread and cheese.

¿Y después? What next? What then?

¿Pero y ella? But what about her?

YA already; now; finally.

Tengo que irme ya. I have to go now.

Ya es tarde. It's late. It's late now.

Ya son las doce pasadas. It's after twelve now.

Es ya hora de levantarse. It's time to get up.

¡Ya voy! I'm coming.

Ya está el té. Tea is ready.

Ya no lo necesito. I no longer need it. I don't need it any more.

El niño ya puede andar. The child can walk now.

Lloverá pronto, ya está tronando. It will rain soon; it's thundering already.

Pasa ya de los cincuenta. She's over fifty.

¡Ya está! It's all done!

Ya no puedo más. I'm worn out. I can't stand it any longer.

Ya caigo en la cuenta. Now I see the point.

¡Ya me las pagará! I'll get even with him.

¡Ya lo haré! I'll do it in time. Certainly I'll do it.

¡Ya lo creo! I should think so! Of course! Certainly!

Ya lo creo que me acuerdo. Of course I remember (it).

¡Ya lo decía yo! Didn't I say so! I had a feeling that it might happen. I was sure of it.

¡Ya lo ves! See there! There you are! Now you see it!

¡Ya veremos! We'll see.

yacer to lie; to be lying (ill in bed); to be lying (in the grave).

yacimiento m. bed, layer, deposit (of ore); field (oil).

Yacimiento petrolífero. Oil field.

yanqui adj. and n. a native of the United States; Yankee.

yapa f. lagnappe, something extra given to a customer with a purchase. (See ñapa.)

yarda f. yard (a measure).

yate m. yacht.

yedra f. ivy.

yegua f. mare.

yema f. bud, shoot; yolk (of an egg); fingertip.

Me he lastimado la yema del dedo. *I hurt the tip of my finger.*

Este huevo tiene dos yemas. *This egg has two yolks.*

Hay muchas yemas en ese rosal. *There are a lot of buds on that rosebush.*

yerba f. herb; weed; grass; mate. (See hierba.)

Yerba mate. *Mate.*

Yerba buena. *Mint.*

yermo adj. waste, bare; m. desert, wilderness.

Tierra yerma. *Wasteland.*

yerno m. son-in-law.

yerro m. error, mistake, fault.

yerto adj. stiff; motionless.

yesca f. tinder.

yeso m. gypsum; plaster; cast (of plaster).

YO I.

Soy yo. *It's me (I).*

¡Soy yo mismo! *Yes, it's me. It's me in the flesh.*

Fuí yo el que telefoneó. *I was the one who phoned.*

Yo mismo se lo dí. *I gave it to him myself.*

Yo no sé. *I don't know.*

Yo no hablo español. *I don't speak Spanish.*

yodo m. iodine.

yodoformo m. iodoform.

yoduro m. iodine.

yuca f. yucca (a plant).

yugo m. yoke; bondage, slavery; marriage ties.

Sacudir el yugo. *To throw off the yoke. To free oneself. To become free.*

yunque m. anvil.

yunta f. yoke (of oxen, horses, etc.); couple, pair.

Una yunta de bueyes. *A yoke of oxen.*

yute m. jute.

yuxtaponer to juxtapose, to place side by side.

yuxtapuesto adj. juxtaposed, side by side.

Z

zacate m. grass; hay (Mex., Central America, the Philippines).

zafar to disembarrass; to lighten (a ship).

zafarse to get rid of; to escape, to get out of; to slip off, to come off; to break loose.

zafarrancho m. clearing for action (Navy); row, scuffle.

zafiro m. sapphire.

zafra f. sugar crop; crop of sugar cane.

zaga f. rear, back; load in the rear of a carriage, m. last player (at cards).

Ella no le va a la zaga. *She's quite as good as he. She's no worse than he is.*

Ir a la zaga. *To lag behind.*

Dejar en zaga. *To leave behind. To outstrip. To do better than.*

Quedarse en zaga. *To be left behind. To be outstripped.*

No ir en zaga. *To be as good as the next one.*

zagal m. lad, young man; young shepherd.

zaguán m. hall, foyer.

zaguero adj. laggard; m. backstop (in Basque ballgame).

zaherir to blame, to reproach.

zalamería f. flattery.

zalamero adj. flatterer.

Es una niña muy zalamera. *She's a flatterer.*

zamba f. popular South American dance.

zambo adj. bowlegged; m. mulatto.

zambullida f. dive, plunge.

zambullir to duck, to plunge.

zambullirse to dive, to plunge (into the water).

Se zambulló en el río. *He dived into the river.*

zampar to gulp, to swallow down; to conceal.

zamparse to rush in, to barge in.

Se zampó todo el pastel. *He gulped down the whole pie.*

Se zampó sin más ni más dentro de la casa. *He barged straight into the house.*

zanahoria f. carrot.

zanca f. shank; long leg.

zancada f. stride; long step.

De dos zancadas. *In a jiffy. In no time. ("In two jumps.")*

zanco m. stilt.

zancudo adj. long-legged; wading (bird); m. mosquito; waders, wading birds.

zángano m. drone; idler, lazy person.

zanja f. ditch.

zanjar to ditch, to dig a ditch; to settle in a friendly manner.

Hay que zanjar ese asunto. *We must settle that matter in a friendly way. That matter has to be settled amicably.*

zapa f. spade (tool); sap (trench).

Trabajo de zapa. *Underhanded work.*

zapatazo m. a blow with a shoe; stamping (with the feet).

Mandar a zapatazos. *To mistreat. To treat badly.*

zapateado m. Spanish tap dance.

zapatear to tap (with the feet).

Baile zapateado. *Tap dance.*

zapateo m. tapping; keeping time with the feet.

zapatería f. shoestore; shoemaker's; shoemaking.

zapatero adj. poorly cooked (vegetables); m. shoemaker; shoe dealer.

zapatilla f. slipper; pump (shoe); washer (ring of leather).

ZAPATO m. shoe.

Un par de zapatos. *A pair of shoes.*

¿Le lastiman los zapatos? *Do your shoes hurt (you)?*

Atese bien los zapatos. *Tie your shoelaces.*

Estos zapatos me vienen anchos. *These shoes are too wide for me.*

Estos zapatos me aprietan mucho. *These shoes are too tight.*

¿Quiere que le limpien los zapatos? *Would you like a shoeshine?*

Quiero que me compongan los zapatos. *I'd like to have my shoes repaired.*

Zapatos de charol. *Patent-leather shoes.*

Zapatos de cabritilla. *Kidskin shoes.*

Zapatos de goma. *Rubbers.*

Encontrarse uno con la horma de su zapato. *To find one's match.*

¡zape! *Scat!*

zaranda *f. screen, sieve (for sand, gravel, coal, etc.).*

zarandear *to sift; to winnow; to shake back and forth.*

zarcillo *m. earring.*

zarco *adj. of a light blue color.*

Ojos zarcos. *Light blue eyes.*

zarpa *f. claw; paw; weighing anchor.*

Echar la zarpa a. *To grab. To grasp.*

zarpar *to weigh anchor, to sail.*

Acaban de dar el último aviso, va a zarpar el barco. *They have just given the last signal. The boat is about to sail.*

zarpazo *m. pawing, stroke with a paw; thud, bang.*

zarrapastroso *adj. ragged, dirty, muddy.*

zarza *f. bramble; brier.*

zarzal *m. a place where there are many thorny bushes or bushes bearing berries.*

zarzamora *f. blackberry (fruit).*

zarzaparrilla *f. sarsaparilla.*

zarzuela *f. musical comedy, a typical Spanish operetta.*

¡zaz! *Smack! Slap! Bang!*

zeda *f. name of letter z.*

zigzag *m. zigzag.*

zinc *m. zinc.*

zócalo *m. pedestal, stand.*

zodíaco *m. zodiac.*

zonzo *adj. boresome; stupid; m. a bore; stupid person.*

zoología *f. zoology.*

zopenco *adj. dumbbell, blockhead.*

zoquete *m. block (of wood); morsel (of bread); boor; worm; little, ugly person.*

zorra *f. fox; vixen; streetwalker (coll.); drunkenness.*

zorro *m. fox (male); foxy (cunning, sly, crafty) person.*

zozobra *f. foundering, sinking; anguish, anxiety, worry.*

zozobrar *to be weatherbeaten; to capsize, to sink; to be in great danger; to grieve; to be afflicted.*

zueco *m. wooden shoe, clog.*

zumbar *to buzz; to ring (one's ears); to joke; to hit, to slap.*

El abejarrón zumba. *The bumblebee buzzes.*

Me zumban los oídos. *My ears are ringing.*

Le zumbó una bofetada. *He slapped him.*

zumbido *m. buzzing; ringing (in one's ear).*

zumo *m. juice; profit.*

Zumo de limón. *Lemon juice.*

Zumo de naranja. *Orange juice.*

zurcido *adj. darning; m. a place that has been darned.*

ZURCIR *to darn.*

¿Ha zurcido mis calcetines? *Have you darned my socks?*

zurdo *adj. left-handed.*

zurra *f. tanning (hide, skin); a beating, a whipping, a flogging.*

zurrar *to tan (hide, skin); to whip, to beat, to spank.*

Al llegar a casa su padre le zurró la badana. *When he came home his father gave him a (good) spanking.*

zutano *m. so-and-so; such a one. (See fulano.)*

¿Cómo se llama ese zutano? *What's that fellow's name?*

GLOSSARY OF PROPER NAMES

Alberto Albert.
Alejandro Alexander.
Alfonso Alphonse.
Alfredo Alfred.
Alicia Alice.
Ana Ann, Anne, Anna, Hannah.
Andrés Andrew.
Antonio Anthony.
Arturo Arthur.
Beatriz Beatrice.
Bernardo Bernard.
Carlos Charles.
Carlota Charlotte.
Diego James.
Dorotea Dorothy.
Eduardo Edward.
Elena Ellen, Helen.

Emilia Emily.
Enrique Henry.
Ernesto Ernest.
Ester Esther, Hester.
Eugenio Eugene.
Eva Eve.
Federico Frederic.
Felipe Philip.
Fernando Ferdinand.
Francisco Francis.
Gertrudis Gertrude.
Gustavo Gustavus.
Ignacio Ignatius.
Inés Agnes, Inez.
Isabel Elizabeth.
Javier Xavier.

Jesús Jesus.
Joaquín Joachim.
Jorge George.
José Joseph.
Josefa Josephine.
Josefina Josephine.
Juan John.
Juana Jane, Jennie, Jean, Joan, Joanna.
Julian Julian.
Julio Julius.
León Leo, Leon.
Leonor Eleanor.
Luis Louis.
Luisa Louise.
Manuel Emanuel.
Margarita Margaret.
María Mary, Maria, Miriam.
Marta Martha.

Miguel Michael.
Pablo Paul.
Pedro Peter.
Rafael Raphael.
Raimundo Raymond.
Ramón Raymond.
Ricardo Richard.
Roberto Robert.
Rosa Rose.
Rosalía Rosalie.
Rosario Rosary.
Santiago James.
Susana Susan.
Teresa Theresa.
Vicente Vincent.

GLOSSARY OF GEOGRAPHICAL NAMES

Alemania Germany.
Alpes Alps.
Alsacia Alsace.
Amberes Antwerp.
América del Norte North America.
América del Sur. South America.
América Española Spanish America.
Antillas Antilles, West Indies.
Aragón Aragon.
Argel Algiers.
Argentina Argentina.
Atenas Athens.
Atlántico Atlantic (Ocean).
Bayona Bayonne.
Bélgica Belgium.
Brasil Brazil.
Bolivia Bolivia.
Bretaña Bretagne. Brittany.
Bretaña (Gran) Great Britain.
Bruselas Brussels.
Castilla Castille.
Castilla la Nueva New Castile.
Castilla la Vieja Old Castile.
Cataluña Catalonia.
Chile Chile.
Colombia Colombia.
Costa Rica Costa Rica.
Cuba Cuba.
Ecuador Ecuador.
Egipto Egypt.
El Salvador El Salvador.
Escandinavia Scandinavia.
Escocia Scotland.
España Spain.
Estados Unidos de América United States
    of America.
Europa Europe.
Filipinas Philippines.
Finlandia Finland.
Flandes Flanders.
Francia France.
Génova Genoa.
Ginebra Geneva.
Gran Bretaña Great Britain.
Grecia Greece.
Guatemala Guatemala.
Habana Havana.
Hispano-América Spanish America.
Holanda Holland.
Honduras Honduras.
Hungría Hungary.
Inglaterra England.
Irlanda Ireland.
Italia Italy.
Japón Japan.
Lisboa Lisbon.

Londres London.
Madrid Madrid.
Marsella Marseilles.
Mediterráneo Mediterranean.
México Mexico.
Moscú Moscow.
Navarra Navarre.
Nicaragua Nicaragua.
Normandía Normandy.
Noruega Norway.
Nueva York. New York.
Nueva Zelandia New Zealand.
Oceanía Oceania, Oceanica.
Pacífico Pacific (Ocean).
Países Bajos Low Countries, Netherlands.
Paraguay Paraguay.
Perú Peru.
Pirineos Pyrenees.
Polonia Poland.
Portugal Portugal.
Prusia Prussia.
Puerto Rico Puerto Rico.
República Dominicana Dominican Republic.
Roma Rome.
Rumania Roumania.
Rusia Russia.
Sevilla Seville.
Sicilia Sicily.
Suecia Sweden.
Suiza Switzerland.
Sur-América South America.
Tejas Texas.
Tolosa Toulouse.
Turquía Turkey.
Uruguay Uruguay.
Valencia Valence (France); Valencia (Spain).
Venezuela Venezuela.
Viena Vienne (France); Vienna (Austria).

ENGLISH-SPANISH

A

a (an) un, uno, una.
able *adj.* capaz.
able (be) poder.
abolish abolir.
about cerca de; sobre; acerca; tocante a.
above sobre, encima de.
abroad fuera del país, extranjero.
absent ausente.
absolute absoluto.
absorb absorber.
absurd absurdo.
abundant abundante.
abuse abuso.
abuse (to) abusar, maltratar.
academy academia.
accent acento.
accent (to) acentuar.
accept aceptar.
acceptance aceptación.
accident accidente.
accommodate acomodar, ajustar.
accommodations acomodo, alojamiento.
accomplish efectuar, llevar a cabo.
according to según, conforme.
account cuenta; relación, narración.
accuracy exactitud.
accusative acusativo.
accuse acusar.
acid ácido (*noun and adj.*).
acquaintance conocido (person).
acre acre
across de través; a través de.
act acto, hecho, acción.
act (to) obrar (to work); conducirse (to behave)
    representar (theater).
active activo.
activity actividad.
actor actor, protagonista.
actual real, efectivo.
add añadir.
address dirección, señas.
address (to) dirigir (a letter).
adequate adecuado.
adjective adjetivo.
adjoining contiguo, inmediato.
administrative administrativo.
admiral almirante.
admiration admiración.
admire admirar.
admirer admirador.
admission admisión; entrada.
    Admission free. Entrada gratis.
admit admitir, confesar, reconocer.
admittance entrada.
    No admittance. Se prohibe la entrada.
admonish amonestar, exhortar.

adopt adoptar.
adoption adopción.
adult adulto.
advance *n.* anticipo; adelanto; avance.
advance (to) avanzar, adelantar.
advantage beneficio, provecho.
advantageous ventajoso.
adventure aventura.
adverb adverbio.
adversity adversidad.
advertise advertir, anunciar.
advertisement aviso, anuncio.
advice consejo.
advise aconsejar.
affected afectado.
affection afecto, cariño.
affectionate cariñoso, afectuoso.
    Affectionately yours. Afectuosamente.
affirm afirmar.
affirmative afirmativo.
afternoon tarde.
    Good afternoon! ¡Buenas tardes!
afterwards después.
again otra vez; de nuevo.
against contra.
age edad.
age (epoch) época.
age (to) envejecer.
agency agencia.
aggravate agravar.
aggressive agresivo.
ago
    a long time ago hace mucho tiempo.
    How long ago? ¿Cuánto tiempo hace?
agony angustia, agonía.
agree acordar, convenir en.
agreeable agradable.
agreed convenido.
agreement convenio, acuerdo.
agricultural agrícola.
agriculture agricultura.
air aire.
air mail correo aéro.
airplane aeroplano, avión.
aisle pasillo.
alarm alarma.
alarm (to) alarmar.
alarm clock despertador.
album álbum.
alcohol alcohol.
alight (to) apearse.
alike igual; semejante.
alive vivo.
all todo.
    all day todo el día.
    all right está bien, bueno.
    all the same igual, lo mismo.
allied aliado.

allow permitir.
    Allow me. Permítame.
allowed permitido.
ally aliado.
almond almendra.
almost casi.
alone solo.
along a lo largo de; al lado de.
    along with junto con, con.
    along the side al costado.
    all along siempre, constantemente.
    to get along hallarse, ir pasando.
    to go along with acompañar.
also también; además.
alternate (to) alternar.
alternately alternativamente.
although aunque, no obstante.
always siempre.
ambassador embajador.
amber ambar.
ambition ambición.
ambitious ambicioso.
amend enmendar.
amends compensación, satisfacción.
America América.
    North America América del Norte.
American americano, norteamericano.
among entre.
amount importe, cantidad, suma.
amount (to) montar, ascender, sumar.
ample amplio.
amuse divertir.
amusement diversión.
analyze analizar.
anchor ancla.
ancient antiguo.
and y.
anecdote anécdota.
angel ángel.
anger cólera, ira.
anger (to) enfadar.
angry enfadado, enojado.
    to get angry enfadarse.
animal animal.
animate animar.
annex anexo.
annex (to) anexionar, anexar.
anniversary aniversario.
annual anual.
anonymous anónimo.
another otro.
answer respuesta, contestación.
answer (to) responder, contestar.
anxious ansioso.
any cualquier, cualquiera, alguno, alguna.
anybody alguno, alguien, quienquiera.
anyhow de cualquier modo, de todos modos.
anyone cualquiera.

anything cualquier cosa, algo.
anyway como quiera, de cualquier modo.
anywhere en cualquier lugar, dondequiera.
apart aparte, separado.
apartment apartamento, piso.
apiece cada uno; por cabeza, por persona.
apologize disculpar; excusarse.
apology excusa, disculpa.
apparatus aparato.
appeal apelación (law); súplica (request); atrac-
    ción, simpatía (attraction).
appeal (to) apelar, recurrir; atraer, interesar,
    llamar la atención (to attract).
appear aparecer.
appetite apetito.
applaud aplaudir.
applause aplauso.
apple manzana.
applicable aplicable, extensivo.
applicant aspirante, candidato.
application aplicación; solicitud (petition).
apply (to) aplicar (put on).
    to apply for solicitar.
appreciate apreciar.
appreciation aprecio, reconocimiento.
approach acceso (access), táctica, manera de
    plantear un asunto o de acercarse a una
    persona.
approach (to) acercarse a (come near); aproxi-
    mar; abordar (a subject).
approval aprobación.
approve (to) aprobar.
April abril.
apron delantal.
arbitrary arbitrario.
arcade arcada.
architect arquitecto.
architecture arquitectura.
Argentina La Argentina.
Argentinian argentino.
argument argumento (to convince or persuade);
    disputa (dispute).
arid árido.
arm brazo (part of body).
arm (to) armar.
armpit axila.
army ejército.
around entorno de, al rededor.
    around here cerca de aquí.
arrangement disposición, arreglo.
arrival llegada.
arrive llegar.
article artículo.
artificial artificial.
artist artista.
artistic artístico.
as como.
    as . . . as . . .   tan . . . como . . .

as it were   por decirlo así.
as little as   tan poco como.
as long as   mientras, todo el tiempo que.
as much   tanto, tan.
as much as   tanto como.
ascertain   aseguarar; asegurarse.
ashes   ceniza.
aside   aparte; al lado.
ask   preguntar (a question); pedir (request).
asleep   dormido, durmiendo.
He's asleep.   Está durmiendo.
to fall asleep   dormirse, quedarse dormido.
aspire   aspirar.
assemble   reunir (to gather); montar, armar (a
      machine); juntar (collect).
assembly   asamblea.
assets   activo; capital; bienes.
assign   asignar.
assimilate   asimilar.
assist   ayudar, asistir.
assistance   asistencia, ayuda.
associate   asociado.
associate (to)   asociar, asociarse.
assume   asumir.
assumption   suposición.
assurance   seguridad, certeza.
assure   asegurar.
astonish   asombrar.
astounded   atónito.
astounding   asombroso, sorprendente.
at   a, en.
at all events   a todo trance.
at first   al principio.
at last   al fin, por fin.
at once   inmediatamente, al instante, de una
      vez.
at the same time   a la vez, a un tiempo.
at two o'clock   a las dos.
at that time   en aquel tiempo, entonces.
We were at John's.   Estábamos en la casa de
      Juan.
at work   trabajando.
athlete   atléta.
athletic   atlético.
athletics   atlético.
atmosphere   atmósfera, ambiente.
attach   prender, unir, adjuntar.
attack   ataque.
attack (to)   atacar.
attempt   intento, tentativa.
attempt (to)   intentar; tratar de; probar.
attend   acudir, asistir, prestar atención.
attention   atención.
attentive   atento.
attic   buhardilla, desván.
attitude   actitud.
attorney   abogado.
attract   atraer.

attraction   atracción.
attractive   atractivo.
audience   auditorio, público.
August   agosto.
aunt   tía.
author   autor.
authority   autoridad.
authorize   autorizar.
automobile   automóvil.
autumn   otoño.
avenue   avenida.
average   promedio.
on the average   por término medio.
avoid   evitar.
awake *adj.*   despierto.
awake (to)   despertar.
aware   enterado, consciente.
away   ausente, fuera, lejos.
to go away   marcharse.
awful   tremendo; horrible.
awkward   torpe; desmañado; embarazoso, difícil
      (embarrassing, difficult).
ax, axe   hacha.

B

babble   charlar, parlotear.
baby   nene, criatura, bebé.
bachelor   soltero.
back   espalda (of the body); posterior; atrás,
      detrás (behind); respaldo (of a chair).
behind one's back   a espaldas de uno.
back door   la puerta de atrás, puerta trasera.
to go back   volver.
to be back   estar de vuelta (regreso).
background   fondo (scenery, painting, etc.); edu-
      cación (education); antecedentes (of a
      person).
backward   atrasado; tardo; retrógrado.
to go backwards   andar de espaldas.
bacon   tocino.
bad   mal, malo.
badge   insignia; placa (of metal).
bag   saco; bolsa.
bait   cebo.
baker   panadero.
bakery   panadería.
balance   balanza (for weighing); equilibrio (equi-
      librium); balance (bookkeeping).
bald   calvo.
ball   bola.
balloon   globo.
banana   plátano.
band   banda.
bandage   venda.
banister   baranda, barandilla.
bank   banco; orilla, ribera (of river).
bank note   billete de banco.

bankruptcy quiebra.

baptize bautizar.

bar bar (where liquor is served); barra (of metal, etc.).

barber barbero.

barbershop barbería.

bare desnudo.

barefoot descalzo.

bargain trato, negociación; ganga (at a low price).

barge barcaza.

bark corteza (of a tree); ladrido (of a dog).

bark (to) ladrar.

barley cebada.

barn pajar, establo.

barrel barril.

barren estéril.

base base.

basin palangana (bowl).

basis base, fundamento.

basket cesta, canasto.

bath baño.

bathe (to) bañar, bañarse.

battle batalla.

be (to) ser; estar.
  to be hungry tener hambre.
  to be right tener razón.
  to be sleepy tener sueño.
  to be slow ser lento; atrasar, estar atrasado (of a watch).
  to be sorry sentir.
  to be thirsty tener sed.
  to be used to estar acostumbrado.
  to be wrong no tener razón.

beach playa.

beam n. viga, madero (of timber, etc.); rayo, destello (of light, etc.).

beaming radiante.

bean habichuela, judía, frijol, haba.

bear oso.

bear (to) aguantar, sobrellevar, sufrir (to endure, to suffer); soportar (to support); portar (to carry); tener (in mind); parir (children, etc.); producir (fruit, etc.).
  to bear a grudge guardar rencor.
  to bear in mind tener presente.

bearer portador.

beat (to) latir, palpitar (heart); golpear, pegar (strike); tocar (a drum); batir (eggs, etc.); ganar (in a game).

beating paliza, zurra (whipping); latido, pulsación (heart).

beautiful hermoso; bello.

beauty hermosura, belleza.

because porque.
  because of debido a; a causa de.

become llegar a ser, convertirse (to come to be); sentar, quedar bien (to be becoming).

becoming conveniente (appropriate); gracioso, mono, que sienta bien (speaking of a dress, hat, etc.).

bed cama.

bedclothes ropa de cama.

bedroom alcoba, dormitorio.

bee abeja.

beech haya.

beef carne de vaca (meat).

beehive colmena.

beer cerveza.

beet remolacha.

before antes, antes que; ante, delante de, enfrente de.

beforehand de antemano, previamente.

beg rogar.

beggar mendigo.

begin empezar; comenzar.

beginning principio, comienzo.

behind atrás; detrás.

Belgian belga, bélgico.

Belgium Bélgica.

belief creencia; opinión.

believe creer.

bell campana.

belong pertenecer.

below abajo, debajo; más abajo.

belt cinturón.

bench banco; tribunal (court).

bend doblar; inclinarse.

beneath debajo.

benefit beneficio.

benefit (to) beneficiar.

beside al lado de, contiguo.

besides además de, por otra parte.

best mejor.

bet apuesta.

bet (to) apostar.

better mejor; más bien.

between entre; en medio de.

beyond más allá.

bicycle bicicleta.

big grande.

bill cuenta (check, account); factura (invoice).
  bill of fare menú, lista de platos.

billion mil millones.

bind (to) atar, unir; encuadernar (a book).

binding encuadernación (book).

birch abedul.

bird pájaro, ave.

birth nacimiento.
  to give birth dar a luz.

birthday cumpleaños.

biscuit bizcocho.

bishop obispo.

bit (a) pizca, pedacito (small amount).

bite mordedura.

bite (to) morder.

bitter amargo.

bitterness amargura.
black negro.
blackbird mirlo.
blacken ennegrecer.
blame culpa.
blame (to) culpar.
blank (en) blanco.
blanket manta, frazada; cobija.
bless bendecir.
blessing bendición.
blind *adj.* ciego.
blind (to) cegar.
blindness ceguera.
blister ampolla.
block up obstruir.
blotter secante.
blouse blusa.
blow golpe.
blow (to) soplar.
blue azul.
blush rubor.
blush (to) ruborizarse.
board tabla (wood); pensión (food); cartón (pasteboard); junta, consejo (of directors, etc.); tablero (for chess, etc.).
   on board a bordo.
boarder pensionista.
boarding house pensión, casa de huéspedes.
boast jactancia.
boast (to) jactarse, hacer alarde.
boat bote, barca; barco, buque.
body cuerpo.
boil grano (on the body).
boil (to) hervir.
boiler caldera.
boiling *adj.* hirviendo.
bold audaz, temerario.
Bolivia Bolivia.
Bolivian boliviano.
bond bono (stocks).
bone hueso.
book libro.
bookseller librero.
bookshop librería.
boot bota.
border frontera; linde, límite (boundary); borde, ribete (edge).
bore (to) aburrir; taladrar, hacer agujeros (to make holes).
boring aburrido (dull).
born nacido.
born (be) nacer.
borrow tomar prestado.
both ambos.
bother molestia (trouble).
bother (to) molestar.
bottle botella.
bottom fondo.

bound atado, amarrado (tied).
bound for destinado; con rumbo a, con destino a.
boundless ilimitado.
bow saludo, reverencia (greeting); arco (weapon, bow of a violin); proa (ship).
bow (to) saludar, hacer reverencia (to bend in reverence); doblegarse, ceder, someterse (to submit or yield).
bowl escudilla, tazón.
box caja.
boy muchacho, niño; hijo varón (male child).
bracelet pulsera.
braid trenza.
brain cerebro.
brake freno. .
bran salvado, afrecho.
branch rama (of tree); ramal (railroad, etc.); sucursal (local office, etc.).
brand marca (of goods).
Brazil Brasil.
Brazilian brasileño.
bread pan.
break ruptura.
break (to) romper.
breakfast desayuno.
breakfast (to) desayunarse.
breaking rompimiento.
breath aliento.
breathe respirar.
breathing respiración.
breeze brisa.
bribe soborno.
bribe (to) sobornar.
bride novia.
bridegroom novio.
bridge puente.
brief breve, corto.
briefly brevemente.
bright claro (opposite of dark); radiante (radiant); inteligente (clever); vivo (lively).
brighten aclarar (to make clearer); alegrar, dar vida, avivarse (to make or become cheerful).
brilliant brillante, luminoso.
brim ala (hat).
bring traer.
   to bring together juntar, reunir.
   to bring toward acercar.
   to bring up educar, criar (to rear); traer a discusión (a matter, etc.); subir (upstairs).
bringing up educación.
Britain La Gran Bretaña.
British británico.
broad ancho.
broil asar (meat).
brook arroyo.
broom escoba.
brother hermano.
brother-in-law cuñado.

brotherly fraternal.

brown café; moreno.

bruise contusión.

bruise (to) magullar.

brush brocha, cepillo.

    clothesbrush cepillo para la ropa.

    toothbrush cepillo para los dientes.

brush (to) cepillar.

brushwood maleza, zarzal.

brute bruto.

bubble *n.* burbuja; pompa (soap).

buckle *n.* hebilla.

bud *n.* yema, botón, capullo.

buffet aparador (dresser); bufet (counter).

build construir.

building *n.* edificio.

bulb (electric) bombilla (eléctrica).

bull toro.

bull fighter torero.

bulletin boletín.

bundle atado; bulto.

burden carga; agobio.

bureau tocador (in a bedroom); oficina (an
    office) negocionado (a department).

burial entierro.

burn quemadura.

burn (to) quemar.

    to burn up quemarse, consumirse por com-
    pleto.

burst reventón, estallido.

burst (to) reventar, estallar.

    to burst out laughing soltar una carcajada.

bury enterrar.

bus autobús; camión (Mexico); guagua (Cuba).

bush arbusto.

bushel fanega.

business ocupación; negocio.

businessman comerciante.

busy ocupado.

but pero.

butcher carnicero.

butcher's (shop) carnicería.

butter mantequilla.

button botón.

buy comprar.

buyer comprador.

by por, a, en, de, para; junto a, cerca de (near).

    by and by poco a poco.

    by and large por lo general, de una manera
    general.

    by hand a mano.

    by reason of por razón de.

    by that time para entonces.

    by the way de paso.

    by then para entónces.

    by virtue of en virtud de.

    Finish it by Sunday. Termínelo para el do-
    mingo.

    Send it by airmail. Envíelo por correo aéreo.

C

cab taxi, coche de alquiler.

cabbage col, repollo.

cabinet gabinete.

cable *n.* cable.

cage jaula.

cake pastel, torta, pastilla (soap).

calendar calendario.

calf ternera.

call llamada (act of calling, a phone call, etc.);
    visita (visit).

call (to) llamar (in a loud voice); convocar (a
    meeting); citar (to summon); visitar (to call
    upon).

    to call back llamar, hacer volver.

    to call forth llamar a.

    to call out gritar.

calm *adj.* quieto, tranquilo.

calm *n.* calma, silencio.

camp campamento.

camp (to) acampar.

can *n.* lata, bote, tarro.

can poder (to be able); saber (to know how);
    envasar en lata (to put in a can).

canal canal.

candidate pretendiente, candidato.

candle vela, candela.

candy dulce, bombón.

cap gorra, gorro.

capital capital.

captain capitán.

capture (to) capturar.

car carro; automóvil, coche (passenger car).

card tarjeta; naipe, carta (playing card).

cardboard cartón.

care cuidado.

    to take care tener cuidado.

    to take care of cuidar de ocuparse de.

    in care of (c/o) al cuidado de (a/c).

care (to) importar, interesarse, tener cuídado.

    I don't care to go. No me interesa ir.

    He doesn't care a hang. No le importa nada.

    I don't care. No me importa.

    What do I care? ¿Qué me importa?

care about interersarse por, estimar.

    I don't care about him. Me tiene sin cuidado.
    No me importa.

    I don't care about it. Me tiene sin cuidado.
    No me importa.

    He cares about his appearance. Se cuida de
    su aspecto.

career carrera.

care for interesarse por, estimar, querer, gustar,
    desear.

    I don't care for it. No me interesa. No me

importa nada.

I don't care for wine.   No quiero vino. No me gusta el vino.

Would you care for some dessert?   ¿Le gustaría tomar algo de postre?

careful ciudadoso.

   Be careful! ¡Cuidado!

careless descuidado.

carpenter carpintero.

carpet alfombra.

carry llevar, conducir, portar.

   to carry away llevarse.

   to carry out llevar a cabo.

   to carry on continuar (continue), conducir, regentear (manage).

cart *n.* carreta, carretón.

carve tajar, trinchar (meat); esculpir, talar (marble, wood, etc.).

case caso (a particular instance; grammar, etc.); estuche (box for small articles); caja (case of wine, etc.).

   in case of en caso de.

cash dinero en efectivo, caja.

   cash on hand efectivo en caja.

   cash payment pago al contado.

cash (to) cobrar o hacer efectivo un cheque, etc.

cashier cajero.

cask tonel.

castle castillo.

casual casual.

casually casualmente.

cat gato.

catch (to) coger, agarrar.

   to catch cold resfriarse.

   to catch on caer en la cuenta, comprender.

   to catch (on) fire encenderse, prender.

   to catch up alcanzar (overtake).

catholic católico.

cattle ganado.

cause causa; razón; motivo.

cause (to) causar.

cavalry caballería.

ceiling techo, cielo raso.

celebrate celebrar.

celebration celebración, conmemoración.

celery apio.

cellar sótano.

cement cemento.

cemetery cementerio.

cent céntimo.

center centro.

century siglo.

ceremony ceremonia, formulismo, cumplido.

certain seguro; cierto, claro, evidente.

certainly ciertamente, sin duda, a buen seguro.

certificate certificado.

chain cadena.

chain (to) encadenar.

chair silla.

chairman presidente (of a meeting).

chalk tiza.

chance azar, acaso, casualidad (happening by chance); oportunidad (opportunity); probabilidad (probability); riesgo (risk).

   by chance por casualidad.

   to take a chance correr un riesgo, aventurarse.

chance (to) aventurar, arriesgar.

chances probabilidades.

change cambio (money).

change (to) cambiar.

chapel capilla.

character carácter.

characteristic *adj.* característico, típico.

charge carga (load; quantity of powder, electricity, fuel, etc.); orden, mandato (order); costo (price); cargo, acusación (accusation); carga, ataque (attack); partida cargada en cuenta (bookkeeping).

   in charge encargado; interino.

charge (to) cargar (a battery, etc.; to debit an account; to load; to attack); llevar, costar, cobrar (a price); acusar (to accuse).

   How much do you charge for this? ¿Cuánto cobra Ud. por esto?

charges gastos (expenses); partes (cost of carriage, freight, etc.); instrucciones (to a jury, etc.).

charitable caritativo.

charity caridad.

charm encanto.

charm (to) encantar.

charming encantador.

chart carta (for the use of navigators); mapa (outline, map); cuadro, gráfico (graph).

chase (to) perseguir.

chat (to) charlar.

cheap barato.

check cheque (banking); talón de reclamo, contraseña (slip of paper); cuenta (in a restaurant); jaque (chess); control, inspección (control); restricción (restraint); obstáculo, impedimento (hindrance); verificación, comprobación (verification).

check (to) examinar (to investigate); verificar (to verify); refrenar, reprimir (to curb, to restrain); facturar (baggage); dar a guardar, dejar (to leave for safekeeping); dar jaque (chess).

cheek mejilla (part of face).

cheer *n.* alegría, buen humor (gaiety); vivas, aplausos (applause).

cheerful alegre, animado.

cheer up animar; animarse, cobrar ánimo.

cheese queso.

chemical químico.

chemist químico.

cherish querer, estimar (to hold dear); acariciar, abrigar (a thought, etc.).

cherished estimado (dear); anhelado (longed for); caro (dear).

cherry cereza.

chest pecho (body); arca, cajón (box).

chestnut castaña.

chew (to) mascar.

chicken pollo.

chief *adj.* principal.

chief *n.* jefe.

child niño (*m.*); niña (*f*).

childhood infancia, niñez.

Chile Chile.

Chilean chileno.

chimney chimenea.

chin barba.

china porcelana, loza.

chocolate chocolate.

choice *adj.* selecto, escogido.

choice *n.* opción, elección.

choir coro.

choke sofocar, ahogar.

choose escoger; elegir.

chop chuleta (cut of meat).

chop (to) cortar (wood, etc.); picar carne (meat).

Christian cristiano.

Christmas Navidad.

church iglesia.

cider sidra.

cigar cigarro.

cigarette cigarrillo.

cigarette lighter encendedor.

cinnamon canela.

circle círculo.

circulation circulación.

citizen ciudadano.

city ciudad.

city hall ayuntamiento.

civil civil.

civilize civilizar.

claim demanda, petición (demand); pretensión (pretension); título, derecho (title, right).

claim (to) demandar (to demand); reclamar (to seek, to obtain); sostener, pretender (to assert as a fact).

clam almeja.

clamor clamor.

clap aplaudir.

class clase.

class (to) clasificar.

clause cláusula.

claw garra.

clay arcilla.

clean *adj.* limpio.

clean (to) limpiar.

cleanliness aseo, limpieza.

clear claro; neto (net).

clear (to) aclarar, despejar (to make clear); aclararse (to clear up); absolver (of blame, guilt); liquidar (to settle a debt, account, etc.); quitar la mesa (a table).

clearly claramente.

clerk dependiente; escribiente.

clever diestro, hábil; inteligente.

climate clima.

climb (to) trepar.

cloak capa, manto.

clock reloj.

close (near) cerca; junto a.
close by muy cerca.

close (to) cerrar (to shut, to shut down); terminar (a meeting, etc.); finiquitar, saldar (an account); cerrar (a deal).

closed cerrado.

closet ropero (clothes); alacena (cupboard, kitchen closet).

cloth tela, paño.

clothe (to) vestir.

clothes ropa.

clothesbrush cepillo para la ropa.

cloud nube.

cloudy nublado.

clover trébol.

club club, círculo (association); porra, garrote (stick).

coach coche.

coal carbón.

coast costa.

coat americana, saco; abrigo.

cocoa cacao.

coconut coco.

code código.

coffee café.

coffin ataúd.

coin moneda.

coincidence coincidencia.
by coincidence por casualidad.

cold frío.

coldness frialdad.

collaborate colaborar.

collar cuello.

collect (to) coleccionar; cobrar (money due).

collection colección.

collective colectivo.

college escuela de estudios universitarios (university); colegio (of cardinals, etc.).

Colombia Colombia.

Colombian colombiano.

colonial colonial.

colony colonia.

color color.

color (to) colorear.

colored de color.

colt potro.

column columna.
comb peine.
comb (to) peinar.
combination combinación.
combine combinar.
come venir.
    to come back volver.
    to come forward adelantar.
    to come across encontrarse con.
    to come for venir por.
    to come in entrar.
    to come down (stairs) bajar.
    to come up (stairs) subir.
    Come on! ¡Vamos! ¡Déjate de tonterías!
comedy comedia.
comet cometa.
comfort confort, comodidad; consuelo (consolation).
comfort (to) confortar, consolar.
comfortable cómodo.
    to be comfortable estar a gusto, estar bien.
comma coma.
command orden (order); mando, commando (authority to command).
command (to) mandar, ordenar.
commerce comercio.
commercial comercial.
commission comisión.
commit cometer.
common común.
communicate comunicar.
community comunidad.
companion compañero.
company compañía; huéspedes, visitas (guests).
compare comparar.
comparison comparación.
    by comparison en comparación.
compete with competir con.
competition concurso (contest); competencia (business).
complain quejarse.
complaint queja.
complete completo.
complete (to) completar, acabar.
complex complejo.
complexion cutis, tez (skin); aspecto (appearance).
complicate complicar.
complicated complicado.
complication complicación.
compliment cumplimiento, cumplido, galantería.
compliment (to) cumplimentar, gastar cumplimientos.
compose componer.
composition composición.
comprise comprender, abarcar.
compromise compromiso.

compromise (to) transigir (to settle by mutual concessions); arreglar, zanjar (a difference between parties); comprometer (to endanger life or reputation).
comrade camarada.
conceit presunción.
conceive (to) concebir.
concentrate (to) concentrar, reconcentrar.
concentration concentración.
concern asunto, negocio (business, affair); interés, incumbencia (interest); empresa, casa de comercio (a business organization); ansiedad, inquietud (worry).
concern (to) importar, concernir; interesarse, preocuparse (to be concerned).
concert concierto.
concrete *adj.* concreto.
concrete *n.* hormigón.
    reinforced concrete cemento armado.
condemn condenar.
condense condensar.
conduct conducta (behavior); manejo, dirección (direction).
conduct (to) conducir, manejar, guiar (to lead, to manage); portarse (to conduct oneself).
conductor conductor.
cone cono.
confer conferir (to grant); conferenciar (to hold a conference); tratar, consultar (to compare views).
confidence confianza (trust); confidencia (secret).
confident *adj.* seguro, cierto, confiado.
confidential confidencial, en confianza.
confirm confirmar, asegurar.
confirmation confirmación.
congeal helar.
congratulate felicitar.
congratulation enhorabuena, felicitación.
    Congratulations! ¡Felicitaciones! ¡La enhorabuena!
congress congreso.
conjunction conjunción.
connect conectar.
connection conexión; relación.
conquer conquistar.
conquest conquista.
conscience conciencia.
conscientious concienzudo, escrupuloso.
conscious consciente.
consent consentimiento, beneplácito.
consent (to) consentir.
consequence consecuencia.
consequently por consiguiente, en consecuencia, por lo tanto.
conservative conservador.
consider considerar.
considerable considerable.
consideration consideración.

consist (of) consistir, constar de, componerse de.
consistent consecuente (in ideas, etc.); congruente (congruous); consistente (solid).
consonant consonante.
constable alguacil, guardia rural.
constant constante.
constitution constitución.
constitutional constitucional.
consume consumir.
consumer consumidor.
consumption consumo (use of goods); consunción, tisis (med.).
contagion contagio.
contagious contagioso.
contain contener; abarcar.
container envase; recipiente.
contemplation contemplación.
contemporary contemporáneo.
contend sostener, afirmar (to assert, to maintain); contender, disputar, competir (to strive, to compete).
content *adj.* contento.
contents contenido.
continent continente.
continuation continuación.
continue (to) continuar.
contract contrato.
contract (to) contraer; contratar.
contractor contratista.
contradict contradecir.
contradiction contradicción.
contradictory contradictorio.
contrary contrario.
  on the contrary al contrario, por el contrario.
contrast contraste.
contrast (to) contrastar.
contribute contribuir.
contribution contribución.
control control, mando, dirección.
control (to) controlar, dominar, dirigir, verificar.
convenience conveniencia.
  at your convenience cuando le sea cómodo, cuando le venga bien.
convenient conveniente.
  if it's convenient to you si le viene bien.
convent convento.
convention convención, asamblea, junta, congreso.
conversation conversación.
converse (to) conversar.
convert (to) convertir.
conviction convicción.
convince convencer.
cook cocinero.
cook (to) cocinar.
cool fresco.
cool (to) enfriar.
cooperation cooperación.

cooperative cooperativa.
copy copia; ejemplar (of a book).
copy (to) copiar.
cordial cordial.
cork corcho; tapón (stopper).
corn maíz.
corner esquina (street); rincón (nook, corner of a room).
corporation corporación, sociedad anónima.
correct correcto.
correct (to) corregir.
correction corrección.
correspond corresponder.
correspondence correspondencia.
correspondent corresponsal.
corresponding correspondiente.
corrupt corrompido.
corrupt (to) corromper.
cost costo; precio.
cost (to) costar.
Costa Rica Costa Rica
Costa Rican costarricense, costarriqueño.
costume traje, vestido, indumentaria.
cottage hotel, casa de campo.
cotton algodón.
couch diván.
cough tos.
cough (to) toser.
council consejo, junta.
count conde (title).
count (to) contar.
counter mostrador (in a store).
countess condesa.
countless innumerable.
country país (nation); campo (opposed to city); patria (fatherland).
country house casa de campo.
countryman compatriota, paisano.
courage valor.
course curso; marcha (of events); estadio (grounds); plato (of a meal); rumbo (route).
court tribunal (law).
courteous cortés.
courtesy cortesía.
courtyard corral, patio.
cousin primo.
cover cubierta, tapa, tapadera.
cover (to) cubrir; tapar (to place a lid over, to conceal); recorrer (a distance); abarcar (to include).
cow vaca.
crab cangrejo.
crack hendidura, raja (split); chasquido (of a whip); chascarrillo (joke).
crack (to) hender (to split); chasquear (a whip).
cradle cuna.
cramp *n.* calambre.
crash estrépito, estruendo (noise); quiebra,

bancarrota (business); choque (collision).
crash (to)   romperse con estrépito (to break);
    estrellarse (a plane, etc.).
cream nata, crema.
create crear; ocasionar (to cause).
creation creación.
credit n.   crédito.
creditor acreedor.
cricket grillo (insect).
crime crimen, delito.
crisis crisis.
critic crítico.
criticism crítica.
criticize criticar.
crooked torcido (bent).
crop cosecha (harvest).
cross cruz (symbol).
cross (to)   cruzar, atravesar (a street); tachar,
    borrar (to cross out).
    to cross one's mind   ocurrírsele a uno, pasarle
      a uno por la imaginación.
    to cross over   cruzar, pasar al otro lado.
cross-examination interrogación.
cross-eyed bizco.
crossing cruce; travesía (sea); paso, vado (river).
crossroads encrucijada.
crouch (to)   agacharse, agazaparse.
crow cuervo.
crowd gentío, muchedumbre.
crowded apiñado, lleno.
crown corona.
crown (to)   coronar.
cruel cruel.
cruelty · crueldad.
crumb migaja (a small piece).
crumbling derrumbe.
cry grito; lloro (weeping).
cry (to)   gritar (shout); llorar (weep).
crystal cristal.
Cuba Cuba.
Cuban cubano.
cube cubo.
cucumber pepino.
cuff puño, bocamanga.
culture cultura.
cup taza.
cure cura.
cure (to)   curar.
curiosity curiosidad.
curious curioso.
curl rizo, bucle.
curl (to)   rizar.
current adj.   corriente.
current n.   corriente.
curtain cortina.
curve curva.
cushion cojín.
custard flan, natilla.

custom costumbre.
customer cliente.
customhouse aduana.
customhouse officer aduanero, vista.
customs (duties)   derechos de aduana.
cut corte.
cut (to)   cortar.

D

dagger puñal.
daily adj.   diario, cotidiano.
    daily newspaper   diario, periódico.
dainty delicado.
dairy lechería; quesería (cheese).
dam dique, presa de agua.
damage daño, perjuicio.
damage (to)   dañar, perjudicar.
damp húmedo.
dance baile.
dance (to)   bailar.
dancer bailarín m.; bailarina f.
danger peligro.

dangerous peligroso.
dare atreverse (venture); desafiar (challenge).
dark obscuro.
darkness obscuridad.
darling amado, querido.
darn zurcir.
date fecha (time); cita (rendezvous); dátil (fruit).
date (to)   datar, poner la fecha.
daughter hija.
dawn madrugada, alba, aurora.
    at dawn   de madrugada, al amanecer.
day día.
    day after tomorrow   pasado mañana.
    day before   víspera.
    day before yesterday   anteayer.
    every day   todos los días.
daze ofuscamiento, atontamiento, aturdimiento
dead muerto.
deadly mortal.
deaf sordo.
dealer vendedor; comerciante.
debatable discutible.
debate debate, discusión.
debate (to)   discutir.
debt deuda.
debtor deudor.
decade década.
decay decadencia (decadence); mengua (de-
    crease); podredumbre (rot).
decay (to)   decaer, declinar (decline); deterio-
    rarse (deteriorate); pudrirse, dañarse (fruit,
    etc.); picarse, cariarse (teeth).
deceit engaño.
deceive engañar.
December diciembre.

decency decencia.
decent decente.
decide decidir; resolver, terminar (a dispute, etc.).
decidedly decididamente.
decision decisión.
decisive decisivo.
declaration declaración.
declare declarar, manifestar.
decrease mengua, diminución.
decrease (to) disminuir, menguar.
decree n. decreto.
dedicate dedicar.
deduct deducir, descontar.
deduction deducción, descuento, rebaja.
deep hondo, profundo.
deeply profundamente.
defeat derrota.
defeat (to) derrotar.
defect defecto.
defective defectuoso.
defend defender.
defender defensor.
defense defensa.
defer diferir (to put off).
defiance desafío.
definite definido, preciso.
definition definición.
defy desafiar.
degenerate degenerar.
degree grado.
delay tardanza, demora, retardo.
delay (to) tardar, demorarse (to linger); retardar, diferir (to defer).
delegate delegado.
delegate (to) delegar.
delegation delegación.
deliberate adj. circunspecto, cauto (careful); pensado, premeditado (carefully thought out).
deliberate (to) deliberar.
delicacy delicadeza (finesse); golosina, bocado exquisito (food).
delicate delicado.
delicious delicioso.
delight deleite, encanto, gusto, placer.
delight (to) encantar, deleitar.
deliver entregar (hand over); librar de (delivery from); pronunciar (a speech).
delivery entrega (of goods); distribución, reparto (mail).
demand demanda.
demand (to) demandar, exigir.
democracy democracia.
demonstrate demostrar.
demonstration demostración, manifestación.
denial negativa, denegación.
denounce denunciar.

dense denso.
density densidad.
deny negar; rehusar (to refuse to grant).
depend (to) depender.
dependence dependencia.
dependent adj. dependiente, sujeto, pendiente.
dependent n. persona que depende de otra para su manutención.
deplore deplorar, lamentar.
deposit depósito.
deposit (to) depositar.
depth profundidad.
descend (to) descender, bajar.
descendant descendiente.
descent descenso.
describe describir.
description descripción.
desert desierto.
desert (to) desertar, abandonar.
deserve merecer.
desirable de desearse.
desire deseo.
desire (to) desear.
desirous deseoso.
desk escritorio.
desolation desolación.
despair desesperación.
despair (to) desesperar.
desperate desesperado.
despite a pesar de, a despecho de.
dessert postre.
destroy destruir.
destruction destrucción.
detach (to) separar, despegar, desprender (to separate or disunite); destacar (soldiers).
detain detener.
determination determinación.
determine determinar.
detour rodeo.
develop desarrollar; revelar (photography).
development desarrollo; revelamiento (photography).
devil demonio, diablo.
devilish diabólico, endiablado, satánico.
devote dedicar.
devotion devoción.
devour devorar, engullir.
dew sereno, rocío.
dial (clock) esfera.
dialogue diálogo.
diameter diámetro.
diamond diamante; oros (at cards).
dictionary diccionario.
die (to) morir.
diet dieta, régimen.
differ (from) diferenciarse (to stand apart); no estar de acuerdo (to disagree).
difference diferencia; distinción (of persons, etc.).

different diferente, distinto.
difficult difícil.
difficulty dificultad.
diffuse difundir.
dig cavar.
digest digerir.
digestion digestión.
dignity dignidad.
dim obscuro, poco claro, a media luz.
dimple hoyuelo.
dinner comida principal.
diplomacy diplomacia.
diplomat diplomático.
diplomatic diplomático.
direct directo (without deviation); en línea recta (straight line); derecho (straight forward).
direct (to) dirigir.
direction dirección.
directly directamente.
director director.
dirt mugre, suciedad.
dirty sucio.
disadvantage desventaja.
disappear desaparecer.
disappearance desaparición.
disappoint desengañar, desilusionar.
disappointment decepción, desengaño, chasco.
disapprove desaprobar.
disarm desarmar.
disaster desastre.
disastrous desastroso, funesto.
discipline n. disciplina.
discontent descontento.
discord discordia.
discourage desanimar, desalentar.
discouragement desaliento, desanimo.
discover descubrir.
discovery descubrimiento.
discreet discreto.
discretion discreción.
discuss discutir (to argue); tratar (to talk over).
discussion discusión.
disease enfermedad.
disgrace afrenta, deshonra.
disgrace (to) deshonrar.
disgust disgusto, asco.
disgust (to) disgustar, repugnar.
disgusting repugnante, odioso.
dish plato.
dishonest deshonesto.
disk disco.
dismal lúgubre, tétrico.
dismiss despedir.
disobey desobedecer.
disorder desorden.
disorder (to) desordenar.
dispatch despacho.
dispatch (to) despachar.

display despliegue (of troops); exhibición (show) alarde, ostentación.
display (to) desplegar; exhibir, mostrar (to show) lucir, hacer ostentación.
displease desagradar.
dispute disputa.
dispute (to) disputar, discutir.
dissolve disolver.
distance distancia.
distinct distinto, claro.
distinction distinción.
distinguish distinguir.
distinguished distinguido.
distort falsear, tergiversar.
distract distraer (divert).
distraction distracción.
distribute distribuir, repartir.
distribution reparto, distribución.
district distrito.
distrust desconfianza.
distrust (to) desconfiar.
disturb estorbar (to interfere with); turbar, inquieta (to disquiet); molestar (to put to inconvenience).
disturbance disturbio.
dive zambullida (into water); picado (a plane).
dive (to) zambullirse, sumergirse (into water), picar (aviation).
divide dividir.
dividend dividendo.
divine divino.
diving board trampolín.
division división.
divorce divorcio.
divorce (to) divorciar.
divorced (to be) divorciarse.
dizzy mareado, aturdido.
do hacer.
   How do you do? ¿Cómo le va? ¿Cómo está Ud.? ¿Qué tal?
   to do one's best hacer lo posible.
   to do without pasarse sin, prescindir de.
   to have to do with tener que ver con.
   That will do. Eso basta. Eso sirve.
   Do you believe it? ¿Lo cree Ud.?
   Do come. Venga sin falta.
dock (pier) muelle.
doctor doctor.
doctrine doctrina.
document documento.
dog perro.
dogma dogma.
dome cúpula.
domestic adj. doméstico (pertaining to the household); casero (homemade); del país, nacional (domestic trade, etc.).
Dominican Republic República Dominicana.
Dominican dominicano.

door puerta.
double doble.
doubt duda.
doubt (to) dudar.
doubtful dudoso.
doubtless sin duda.
dough masa, pasta.
down abajo; hacia abajo.
   to go down bajar.
   to come down bajar.
   Come down! ¡Baje!
downstairs abajo, en el piso de abajo.
downward descendente, hacia abajo.
dozen docena.
draft corriente de aire (air); letra de cambio,
   giro (bank); quinta, conscripcion (military);
   borrador, anteproyecto (sketch or outline).
draft (to) redactar, escribir (a document, etc.);
   hacer un borrador (a tentative outline).
drag arrastrar.
drama drama.
draw (to) dibujar (with a pencil); sacar (money,
   liquids, etc.); correr, descorrer (curtains).

   librar, girar (a bank draft); cobrar (a salary);
   tirar (to putt); redactar, escribir (to draw
   up); robar, tomar (a card); sortear (lottery,
   etc.).
   to draw back reintegrarse de (to get something back); retroceder (to go back).
drawer gaveta, cajón (of a desk, etc.).
drawing dibujo.
dread (to) temer.
dreaded temido.
dreadful horrible.
dream sueño.
dream (to) soñar.
dreamer soñador.
dress vestido, traje.
dress (to) vestirse (to get dressed); vendar (a
   wound).
dressmaker modista.
drink bebida (a beverage); trago, copa.
drink (to) beber, tomar.
drip (to) gotear.
drive paseo en coche (a ride in a car, etc.);
   paseo, calzada (a road); campaña (to raise
   money, etc.).
drive (to) conducir, guiar (a car, etc.); ir en coche
   (to take a ride); clavar (a nail); ahuyentar
   (to drive away).
driver chófer, conductor (of a car); maquinista (of
   an engine).
drop gota (of water, etc.); caída, baja (fall).
   cough drops pastillas para la tos.
drop (to) soltar, dejar caer (to release, to let
   fall); verter a gotas (fall in drops); abandonar, desistir de, dejar (to let go).
   to drop in on visitar.

   to drop a subject cambiar de tema.
drown ahogar.
drug droga.
druggist farmacéutico.
drugstore botica, farmacia.
drum tambor.
drunk borracho, ebrio.
drunkard borracho, borrachín.
drunkenness embriaguez, borrachera.
dry seco.
dry (to) secar.
dryness sequedad.
duchess duquesa.
due debido; pagadero (payable); vencido (at a
   given time).
duke duque.
dull opaco, muerto (color); pesado, oburrido, sin
   gracia (slow, boring); estúpido (stupid).
dumb mudo (deaf and dumb); estúpido (stupid).
durable duradero.
during durante, mientras.
dusk crepúsculo.
dust polvo.
dust (to) quitar el polvo.
dusty polvoriento.
duty deber.
dwelling habitación, morada.
dye tinte.
dye (to) teñir.

E

each cada.
   each one cada uno.
   each other mutuamente, el uno al otro, unos
   a otros.
eager ansioso.
eagle águila.
ear oído (the organ of hearing or the internal
   ear); oreja (the external ear); mazorca (of
   corn); espiga (of wheat, rye, etc.).
early temprano.
earn ganar.
earnest serio (serious); ansioso (eager).
   in earnest de buena fe, en serio.
earth tierra.
earthquake temblor de tierra, terremoto.
ease tranquilidad, alivio; facilidad (with ease);
   con desahogo, cómodamente (at ease).
ease (to) aliviar, mitigar.
easily fácilmente.
east este, oriente.
Easter Pascua florida.
eastern oriental.
easy fácil.
eat comer.
economic económico.
economy economía.

Ecuador Ecuador.

Ecuadorian ecuatoriano.

edge orilla, borde (of a stream, etc.), canto (of a table, a book); filo (of a blade).

edition edición.

editor redactor.

education educación.

eel anguila.

effect efecto.

effect (to) efectuar.

efficiency eficacia.

effort esfuerzo.

egg huevo.

eggplant berengena.

eggshell cáscara de huevo, cascarón.

egoism egoísmo.

eight ocho.

eighteen dieciocho.

eighteenth decimoctavo.

eighth octavo.

eighty ochenta.

either o, u (conj.); uno u otro, el uno o el otro, cualquiera de los dos, uno y otro, ambos (adj. and pron.).

   either one el uno o el otro, cualquiera de los dos.

elastic elástico.

elbow codo.

elder adj. mayor, de más edad.

elderly mayor, de edad.

elect (to) elegir.

elected electo, elegido.

election elección.

elector elector.

electric eléctrico.

electricity electricidad.

elegance elegancia.

elegant elegante.

element elemento.

elementary elemental.

elephant elefante.

elevation elevación; altura.

elevator ascensor.

eleven once.

eleventh undécimo, onzavo.

eliminate eliminar.

eloquence elocuencia.

eloquent elocuente.

else otro, más, además.

   nothing else nada más.

   something else algo más.

   or else o bien, o en su lugar, si no.

   nobody else ningún otro.

elsewhere en alguna otra parte, en otro lugar.

elude eludir, evitar.

embark embarcar.

embarrass embarazar, poner en aprieto.

embarrassing embarazoso.

in an embarrassing situation en una situación difícil, en un apuro, en un compromiso.

embassy embajada.

embody encarnar.

embrace abrazo.

embrace (to) abrazar.

embroidery bordado.

emerge surgir.

emergency emergencia, aprieto, apuro, necesidad urgente.

emigrant emigrante.

emigrate emigrar.

emigration emigración.

eminent eminente.

eminently eminentemente.

emotion emoción.

emphasis énfasis.

emphasize hacer hincapié; recalcar.

emphatic enfático, categórico.

empire imperio.

employ emplear.

employee empleado.

employer patrono, patrón.

employment empleo.

empty vacío.

empty (to) vaciar.

enclose (to) cercar (ground, etc.); incluir (in a letter, etc.).

enclosed adjunto.

encourage animar.

encouragement estímulo, aliento.

end fin; final (of a street); extremidad (tip).

end (to) acabar, terminar.

endeavor esfuerzo.

endeavor (to) esforzarse.

endorse endosar.

endow dotar.

endure soportar, resistir, aguantar.

enemy enemigo.

energetic enérgico.

energy energía.

enforce hacer cumplir, poner en vigor (a law); forzar, compeler (to compel).

engage ajustar (a servant); emplear (a clerk, etc.); alquilar (a room, etc.); trabar (in a conversation, etc.).

engagement compromiso, cita (date); promesa de matrimonio, compromiso (promise of marriage); contrato (employment for a stated time).

engineer ingeniero.

English inglés.

engrave grabar.

enjoy gozar, disfrutar.

   to enjoy oneself divertirse.

enjoyment goce.

enlarge aumentar, agrandar, ampliar.

enlargement ampliación.

enlist alistarse.
enlistment alistamiento, enganche.
enough bastante, suficiente.
enrich enriquecer.
entangle enredar, embrollar.
enter entrar (a house, etc.); anotar, registrar (in a register, etc.); entablar (into a conversation); ingresar, matricularse (a school); afiliarse (a society, etc.).
entertain tener invitados, agasajar (guests); conversar, entretener (to talk to); acariciar, abrigar (ideas); divertir (to amuse).
entertainment convite (for guests); entretenimiento, diversión (amusement).
enthusiasm entusiasmo.
enthusiastic entusiasta.
entire entero.
entitle titular, poner un título (title); autorizar, dar derecho a (right).
entrance entrada.
entrust confiar a.
entry entrada (entrance); asiento, íngreso (records, bookkeeping).
enumerate enumerar.
envelope n. sobre.
enviable envidiable.
envious envidioso.
envy envidia.
envy (to) envidiar.
episode episodio.
epoch época, era.
equal igual.
equal (to) igualar.
equality igualdad.
equator ecuador.
equilibrium equilibrio.
equip equipar, dotar de.
equipment equipo.
equity equidad.
era era, época.
erase borrar, raspar.
eraser goma de borrar.
err (to) errar, equivocarse.
errand recado, mandado.
error error.
escape fuga.
escape (to) escapar, escaparse de.
escort escolta (a body of soldiers, etc.); acompañante (an individual).
escort (to) escoltar, acompañar.
especially especialmente, particularmente.
essay ensayo; composición (school).
essence esencia.
essential esencial, indispensable.
establish establecer.
establishment establecimiento.
estate bienes, propiedades (properties, possessions); finca, hacienda (a country estate).

esteem estimación, aprecio.
esteem (to) estimar.
estimable estimable.
estimate presupuesto, cálculo.
estimate (to) tasar, calcular.
eternal eterno.
eternity eternidad.
ether eter.
evacuate evacuar.
even adj. par (not odd); parejo, llano, plano to be even with estar en paz con, estar mano a mano.
even adv. aun, hasta, no obstante.
    even as así como.
    even if aun cuando.
    even so aun así.
    even that hasta eso.
    not even that ni siquiera eso.
evening tarde.
    Good evening! ¡Buenas tardes!
    yesterday evening ayer por la tarde.
    tomorrow evening mañana por la tarde.
event suceso.
    in the event that en el caso de.
ever siempre (always); nunca (never).
    as ever como siempre.
    ever so much muy, mucho, muchísimo.
    ever since desde entonces.
    not . . . ever nunca.
    nor . . . ever ni nunca.
every cada.
    every bit enteramente.
    every day todos los días.
    every other day un día sí y otro no.
    every one cada uno, cada cual.
    every once in a while de cuando en cuando.
    every time cada vez.
everybody todos, todo el mundo.
everyone todos, todo el mundo.
everything todo.
everywhere en (por) todas partes.
evidence evidencia, prueba, testimonio.
    to give evidence dar testimonio, deponer.
evident evidente.
evil adj. malo.
evil n. mal.
evoke evocar.
exact preciso, exacto.
exaggerate exagerar.
exaggeration exageración.
exalt exaltar.
examination examinación.
examine examinar.
example ejemplo.
exasperate exasperar, irritar.
excavate excavar, cavar.
exceed exceder, sobrepujar.
excel sobresalir, descollar.

excellence   excelencia.
excellent   excelente.
except   excepto, menos; sino, a menos que.
except (to)   exceptuar, excluir.
exception   excepción.
    to make an exception   hacer una excepción.
exceptional   excepcional.
exceptionally   excepcionalmente.
excess   exceso.
excessive   excesivo.
exchange   cambio.
    in exchange for   a cambio de.
exchange (to)   cambiar.
excite   excitar.
    Don't get so excited. No se sofoque Ud.
excitement   excitación, conmoción.
exclaim   exclamar.
exclamation   exclamación.
exclude   excluir.
exclusive   exclusivo.
excursion   excursión.
excuse   excusa.
excuse (to)   excusar, dispensar, disculpar.
    Excuse me.   Dispense Ud.
execute   ejecutar.
executive   ejecutivo.
exempt   exentar, eximir.
exercise (to)   ejercer; hacer ejercicios (physical
      exercise); ejercitar (drill).
exhaust   agotar.
exhausted   agotado, exhausto.
exhausting   agotador.
exile adj.   exilado, desterrado.
exile   destierro, exilio.
exile (to)   desterrar.
exist   existir.
existence   existencia.
exit   salida.
expand   extender(se), ensanchar(se), dilatar(se),
      desarrollar(se).
expansion   expansión.
expansive   expansivo.
expect   esperar, aguardar.
expectation   expectativa, esperanza.
expel   expulsar.
expense   gasto, coste.
    at one's expense   a costa de uno.
expensive   caro, costoso.
experience   experiencia, práctica.
experience (to)   experimentar; pasar por (un-
      dergo).
experiment   experimento.
experiment (to)   experimentar.
experimental   experimental.
expert   experto.
expire   expirar.
explain   explicar.
explanation   explicación.

explanatory   explicativo.
explode   estallar.
exploit   hazaña, proeza.
exploit (to)   explotar, sacar partido.
exploration   exploración.
explore   explorar.
explorer   explorador.
explosion   explosión.
export   exportación.
export (to)   exportar.
expose   exponer.
express adj.   expreso.
express (to)   expresar.
expression   expresión.
expulsion   expulsión.
exquisite   exquisito.
extend   extender.
extensive   extensivo.
extent   extensión.
    to a certain extent   hasta cierto punto.
exterior   exterior.
exterminate   exterminar.
external   externo.
extinguish   extinguir.
extra   extra, extraordinario.
extract   extracto.
extract (to)   extraer.
extravagance   extravagancia.
extravagant   extravagante.
extreme   extremo.
extremity   extremidad.
eye   ojo.
eyebrow   ceja.
eye glasses   anteojos.
eyelash   pestaña.
eyelid   párpado.

F

fable   fábula, ficción.
fabulous   fabuloso.
face   cara.
fact   hecho.
    in fact   en realidad.
factory   fábrica.
faculty   facultad.
fade   decaer, marchitarse; desteñirse (color).
fail   omisión, falta.
    without fail   sin falta.
fail (to)   fracasar, no tener suerte (in an under-
      taking); salir mal (in an exam); decaer, ir a
      menos (health); faltar, dejar de (to do
      something).
    not to fail   no dejar de.
failure   fracaso; falta (fault, defect); quiebra
      (bankruptcy).
faint (to)   desmayarce, desfallecer.
fair adj.   rubio (hair); blanco (complexion); claro

(clear); justo, recto (just); regular, mediano
    (moderate); bonancible, buen (weather).
fair play juego limpio.
fair weather buen tiempo.
fair *n.* feria (exhibition, place for trade).
fairness justicia, equidad.
fairy tale cuento de hadas.
faith fe.
faithful fiel.
fall caída; otoño (autumn).
fall (to) caer; caerse (fall down).
false falso.
fame fama.
familiar familiar.
familiarity familiaridad, confianza.
family familia.
famine hambre.
famous famoso.
fan abanico; ventilador (electric fan).
fancy fantasía; capricho (whim).
fantastic fantástico.
far lejos.
    How far? ¿A qué distancia?
    far away muy lejos.
    so far hasta aquí, hasta ahora.
    As far as I'm concerned. En cuanto a mí
      toca.
    by far con mucho.
fare tarifa, pasaje.
farmer agricultor, labrador.
farming agricultura, cultivo de la tierra.
farther más lejos, más allá; además de.
fashion moda.
fashionable a la moda, de moda, elegante, de
    buen tono.
fast pronto, de prisa (quickly).
fasten trabar.
fat *adj.* gordo.
fat *n.* manteca, grasa.
fate destino, fatilidad.
father padre.
fatherhood paternidad.
father-in-law suegro.
fatten engordar.
faucet grifo, llave, canilla (Arg.).
fault falta.
favor favor, servicio.
favor (to) hacer un favor, favorecer.
favorite favorito.
fear miedo, temor.
fearless intrépido.
feast fiesta.
feather pluma.
feature rasgo, característica.
February febrero.
federal federal.
fee honorarios.
feeble débil, enfermizo.
feed alimentar, dar de comer.

feeding alimentación.
feel (to) sentir; tocar (touch).
feeling tacto (tact); sentimiento (sentiment);
    sensibilidad (sensitiveness).
fellow sujeto, individuo.
    fellow student condiscípulo.
    fellow traveler compañero de viaje.
    fellow worker colega, compañero de trabajo.
female hembra.
feminine femenino.
fence valla, cerca.
ferment fermentar.
fermentation fermentación.
ferry ferry, barca de transbordo.
fertile fecundo, fértil.
fertilize fertilizar, fecundar.
fertilizer abono.
fervent ferviente.
fervor fervor.
festival fiesta, festival.
fever fiebre.
feverish febriciente, febril.
few pocos.
    a few unos cuantos, unos pocos.
    a few days unos pocos días.
fewer menos.
fiber fibra.
fickle veleidoso, caprichoso.
fiction ficción; novela (story, novel).
field campo; campaña (military); ramo, espe-
    cialidad (specialty).
fierce feroz.
fiery vehemente, furibundo.
fifteenth decimoquinto.
fifth quinto.
fifty cincuenta.
fig higo.
    fig tree higuera.
fight riña, pelea, lucha, conflicto.
fight (to) pelear, luchar, combatir.
figure figura.
file lima (for nails, etc.); archivo, fichero (for
    papers, cards, etc.).
file (to) limar (with an instrument); archivar
    papers, etc.).
fill llenar.
film película.
filthy sucio, inmundo.
final final.
finally finalmente, por último.
finance hacienda, finanzas.
financial financiero.
find hallar, encontrar.
fine *adj.* fino, buen, magnífico, excelente.
    Fine! ¡Muy bien!
fine *n.* multa.
finger dedo.
finish (to) terminar; acabar.

fire fuego.

fire (to) incendiar (burn); disparar (a gun); despedir, dejar cesante (an employee).

firm *adj.* seguro, firme.

firm *n.* firma (business).

firmness firmeza.

first primero.

   at first al principio.

   at first glance a primera vista.

firstly primeramente.

fish pez (in the water), pescado (when caught).

fish (to) pescar.

fisherman pescador.

fishing pesca.

fist puño.

fit *adj.* apto, idóneo, adecuado, conveniente, a propósito.

   to see fit juzgar conveniente.

   If you think fit. Si a Ud. le parece.

fit (to) ajustar, adaptar; entallar (to fit a dress, etc.); caer bien, sentar bien (to have the right size or shape).

   to fit into encajar en.

   That would fit the case. Eso sería lo propio.

   The dress fits you well. El vestido le sienta a Ud. bien (le viene como pintado).

   It fits badly. Me sienta mal.

fitness aptitud.

fitting (be) sentar bien, venir bien.

five cinco.

fix (to) arreglar, componer, reparar (to repair).

flag bandera.

flagrant flagrante.

flame llama.

flannel franela.

flash *n.* destello (light); relámpago (lightning).

flashlight linterna.

flat plano, chato; insípido, soso (taste).

flatten aplastar, aplanar.

flatter adular.

flattery adulación, lisonja.

flavor sabor, gusto.

flavor (to) sazonar, condimentar.

flax lino.

flea pulga.

fleet flota, armada.

flesh carne; pulpa (fruit).

flexibility flexibilidad, docilidad.

flexible flexible.

flight vuelo (in the air); fuga (from jail, etc.).

flint pedernal; piedra de encendedor.

float flotar.

flood inundación.

flood (to) inundar.

floor piso.

flow (to) fluir, manar, correr.

flower flor.

flowery florido.

fluid flúido.

fly mosca.

fly (to) volar.

foam espuma.

foam (to) hacer espuma.

focus foco.

fog niebla, neblina.

fold pliegue, doblez.

fold (to) doblar, plegar.

foliage follaje.

follow seguir.

following siguiente.

food comida.

fool tonto, bobo.

foolish tonto, disparatado.

foolishness tontería.

foot pie.

   on foot a pie.

football futbol.

for para, por.

   This is for her. Esto es para ella.

   for example por ejemplo.

   for the first time por la primera vez.

   for the present por ahora.

   for the time being por de pronto.

forbid prohibir.

forbidden prohibido.

force fuerza.

force (to) forzar, obligar.

forced obligado.

ford vado.

ford (to) vadear.

forecast pronóstico, predicción.

forecast (to) pronosticar, vaticinar.

forehead frente.

foreign extraño, extranjero, ajeno.

foreigner extranjero.

foresee prever.

forest selva, monte.

forget olvidar.

forgetfulness olvido.

forgive perdonar.

forgiveness perdón.

fork tenedor.

form forma.

form (to) formar.

formal ceremonioso (ceremonial); oficial (official).

formality formalidad, ceremonia.

formation formación.

former previo, anterior.

former (the) aquél, aquélla, aquéllos, aquéllas, aquello.

formerly antiguamente, en otros tiempos.

formula fórmula.

forsake desamparar, abandonar.

fortunate afortunado.

fortunately afortunadamente.

fortune suerte, fortuna.
fortuneteller adivino.
fortunetelling buenaventura.
forty cuarenta.
forward *adv.* adelante, en adelante.
forward (to) remitir, reexpedir.
found encontrado.
found (to) fundar.
foundation fundación.
founder fundador.
fountain fuente.
fountain pen estilográfica, pluma fuente.
four cuatro.
fourteen catorce.
fourth cuarto.
fowl volatería, aves de corral.
fragment fragmento.
fragrance fragancia, aroma.
fragrant oloroso, fragante.
frail endeble, frágil.
frame marco (of a picture, door, etc.); armazón, entramado, estructura (structure).
    frame of mind estado de ánimo.
frame (to) encuadrar, poner en un marco (a picture, etc.).
France Francia.
frank franco, sincero.
frankness franqueza.
free *adj.* libre; gratis.
    free of charge gratis.
free (to) libertar, librar.
freeze helar, congelar.
freight carga; flete.
French francés.
frequent frecuente.
frequent (to) frecuentar.
frequently frecuentemente.
fresh fresco.
Friday viernes.
friend amigo.
friendly amistoso.
friendship amistad.
frighten asustar.
frightening espantoso.
frivolity frivolidad, trivialidad.
frivolous frívolo.
frog rana.
from de, desde.
    from a distance desde lejos.
    from memory de memoria.
front *adj.* anterior, delantero, de frente.
    front room cuarto que da a la calle.
    front view vista de frente.
front frente.
    in front of frente a.
frown ceño, entrecejo.
frown (to) fruncir el ceño.
fruit fruta.

fry freír.
frying pan sartén.
fuel combustible.
fugitive fugitivo
fulfill cumplir
full lleno.
fully plenamente, enteramente.
fun broma; diversión.
    to have fun divertirse, pasar un buen rato.
    to make fun of burlarse de.
funny divertido, cómico.
function función.
function (to) funcionar.
fundamental fundamental.
funds fondos.
funeral funeral, entierro.
fur piel(es).
furious furioso.
furnace horno.
furnish amueblar (a room, house, etc.); suplir (supply); proveer (provide).
furniture muebles.
furrow surco.
further *adv.* más lejos, más allá; además, aún.
    further on más adelante; y además de eso (in speech).
fury furor.
future futuro.
    in the future en lo sucesivo, en adelante, en lo futuro.

G

gaiety alegría, alborozo.
gain ganancia.
gain (to) ganar.
gamble (to) jugar por dinero.
game juego; partida, partido; caza (hunting).
    a game of chess una partida de ajedrez.
garage garage.
garden jardín.
gardener jardinero.
gargle (to) hacer gárgaras.
garlic ajo.
garment prenda de vestir, vestido.
garter liga.
gas gas; gasolina (gasoline).
    gas station puesto de gasolina.
gasoline gasolina.
    gasoline station puesto de gasolina.
gate puerta.
gather (to) reunir, juntar.
gay alegre.
gem piedra preciosa.
gender género.
general *adj.* general.
    in general en general, por lo general.
general general.

generality generalidad.
generalize generalizar.
generally generalmente, por lo general.
generation generación.
generosity generosidad.
generous generoso.
genius genio.
gentle suave; amable, delicado (of a person).
gentleman caballero.
    gentlemen señores; muy señores nuestros (in a letter).
gentleness ababilidad, delicadeza.
gently suavemente; amablemente.
genuine genuino, auténtico.
geographical geográfico.
geography geografía.
geometric geométrico.
geometry geometría.
germ germen; microbio.
German alemán.
Germany Alemania.
gesture n. gesto, ademán.
get (to) adquirir, obtener, conseguir, recibir.
    to get ahead adelantarse.
    to get away partir, marcharse; huir.
    to get back volver, regresar.
    to get home llegar a casa.
    to get in entrar.
    to get married casarse.
    to get off apearse, bajar.
    to get on montar, subir.
    to get out salir.
    to get up levantarse; subir.
giant gigante.
gift regalo, obsequio.
gifted agraciado.
ginger jengibre.
girl chica, niña, muchacha.
give (to) dar.
    to give in ceder, acceder.
    to give up desistir, darse por vencido.
    to give a gift regalar, hacer un regalo.
giver donante.
glad contento, feliz.
    to be glad alegrarse de, tener gusto en.
glance ojeada, vistazo.
glance (to) echar un vistazo, dar una ojeada.
    to glance at a book hojear un libro.
glass vidrio; vaso (for drinking).
    looking glass espejo.
    drinking glass vaso.
glimpse n. ojeada, vistazo.
glitter (to) brillar, resplandecer.
globe globo.
gloomy triste, sombrío.
glorious glorioso.
glory n. gloria.
glove guante.

glue n. cola.
go (to) ir.
    to go away irse, marcharse.
    to go back volverse atrás, retroceder; regresar, volver.
    to go down bajar.
    to go forward ir adelante, adelantarse.
    to go out salir; apagarse (a light, fire, etc.).
    to go up subir.
    to go with acompañar.
    to go without pasarse sin.
goal meta, objetivo, fin.
    to reach one's goal alcanzar el objetivo, llegar a la meta, obtener lo que uno se había propuesto.
God Dios.
godfather padrino.
godmother madrina.
gold oro.
golden de oro.
good buen(o).
    good morning buenos días.
    good evening buenas tardes.
    good night buenas noches.
good-by adiós.
goodness bondad.
    Goodness! (Goodness gracious!) ¡Válgame Dios! ¡María santísima!
    Goodness knows! ¡Quién sabe!
goods mercancías, géneros, efectos.
goodwill buena voluntad; nombre, reputación, traspaso (business).
goose ganso.
gossip chisme, chismografía, murmuración.
gossip (to) chismear, murmurar.
govern gobernar.
government gobierno.
governor gobernador.
gown vestido de mujer.
grab (to) agarrar, arrebatar.
grace n. gracia.
graceful gracioso.
gracious bondadoso, afable, cortés.
grade grado.
gradual gradual.
gradually gradualmente.
graduate (a) graduado, recibido de (doctor, etc.).
graduate (to) graduarse, recibir un título.
graduated (be) graduarse, recibirse.
grain grano.
grammar gramática.
grammatical gramatical.
grand gran, grandioso, magnífico, espléndido.
    Grand! ¡Estupendo! ¡Magnífico!
grandchild nieto.
granddaughter nieta.
grandfather abuelo.
grandmother abuela.

grandparents abuelos.

grandson nieto.

grant concesión.

grant (to) conceder, otorgar.
> to take for granted dar por sentado, presuponer.
> granting (granted) that supuesto que, concedido que.

grape uva.

grapefruit toronja.

grasp (to) empuñar, asir, agarrar; comprender, percibir.

grass hierba, pasto, césped.

grasshopper saltamontes.

grateful agradecido.

gratefully agradecidamente, gratamente.

gratis gratis, de balde.

gratitude agradecimiento.

grave *adj.* grave, serio.

grave *n.* sepultura, tumba.

gravel grava.

gravity gravedad, seriedad.

gravy salsa.

gray gris (color), cano (hair).
> gray-haired canoso.

grease grasa.

grease (to) engrasar.

great gran, grande.
> a great man un gran hombre.
> a great many muchos.
> a great deal mucho.
> Great! ¡Estupendo! ¡Magnífico!

Great Britain Gran Bretaña.

greatness grandeza, grandiosidad.

green verde.

greet saludar.

greeting saludo.

grief pesar, dolor, pena.

grieve (to) penar, afligirse.

grill (to) asar a la parrilla.

grind moler.

groan gemido.

groan (to) gemir.

grocer abacero; bodeguero (Cuba); abarrotero (Mex.).

groceries comestibles, abarrotes (Amer.).

grocery (store) ultramarinos, tienda de comestibles, abarrotes (Amer.).

groove ranura.

grope andar a tientas.

ground *n.* tierra, suelo, terreno.

group grupo.

group (to) agrupar.

grow (to) crecer.
> to grow old envejecer.
> to grow late hacerse tarde.
> to grow better ponerse mejor, mejorar.
> to grow worse ponerse peor, empeorar.

growth crecimiento.

grudge rencor.

gruff áspero, brusco.

grumble (to) refunfuñar, grunir.

guarantee garantía.

guarantee (to) garantir.

guard guardia; guarda; guardián.

guard (to) guardar, vigilar.
> to guard against guardarse de.

Guatemala Guatemala.

Guatemalan guatemalteco.

guess conjetura, suposición.

guess (to) adivinar, conjeturar.
> to guess right acertar.

guide guía.

guide (to) guiar.

guidebook guía de viajeros.

guilt culpa.

guilty culpable.

guitar guitarra.

gulf golfo.

gum encía (teeth).
> chewing gum chicle.

gun arma de fuego, cañón, fusil, revólver, escopeta.

gymnasium gimnasio.

gypsy gitano.

H

haberdashery camisería, mercería.

haberdashery store camisería.

habit costumbre, hábito.
> to be in the habit of estar acostumbrado.

habitual habitual.

habitually habitualmente.

hail granizo (during thunderstorm); viva, vitor (cheering, greeting).

hail (to) granizar (in a thunderstorm); vitorear (to cheer).

hair pelo, cabello.
> hairbrush cepillo para la cabeza.
> haircut corte de pelo.
> hairdye tintura para el pelo.
> hairpin horquilla.

half medio; mitad.
> half and half mitad y mitad.
> half past two las dos y media.
> half-hour media hora.
> half-year semestre.

half brother hermanastro.

half sister hermanastra.

halfway a medio camino, equidistante..

hall vestíbulo (entrance, foyer); salón (assembly room).

halt alto, parada.

halt (to) parar, detener.

> Halt ¡Alto!

ham jamón.
hammer martillo.
hammer (to) martillar.
   to hammer on a subject machacar.
hand mano; manecilla (of a watch).
   by hand a mano.
   in hand entre manos; (dinero) en mano.
   offhand improvisadamente, de repente; sin preparación.
   on hand disponible, a la mano.
   on the other hand por otra parte.
hand (to) pasar.
   to hand over entregar.
handbag maleta, bolsa.
handbook manual.
handful puñado.
handkerchief pañuelo.
handle mango, asa.
handle (to) manejar, manipular.
handmade hecho a mano.
handshake apretón de manos.
hang colgar.
hanger (clothes) gancho de ropa, colgador, colgadero, percha.
happen suceder, acontecer.
happening suceso, acontecimiento.
happiness dicha, felicidad.
happy feliz, contento.
harbor puerto.
hard duro; difícil.
   hard luck mala suerte.
   hard work trabajo difícil.
   to rain hard llover a cántaros.
   to work hard trabajar duro.
harden endurecer.
hardly apenas, difícilmente, escasamente.
hardness dureza.
hardware ferretería, quincalla.
hardware store ferretería.
hardy fuerte, robusto.
hare liebre.
harm n. mal, prejuicio, daño.
harmful nocivo, dañoso, dañino.
harmless inofensivo.
harmonious armonioso.
harmonize armonizar.
harmony armonía.
harness n. aparejo, arnés.
harsh áspero, tosco; desagradable.
harshness aspereza, rudeza.
harvest n. cosecha.
haste prisa.
   in haste de prisa.
hasten darse prisa, acelerar, apresurarse.
hastily apresuradamente, precipitadamente.
hasty apresurado.
hat sombrero.
hatch (to) empollar, incubar.

hatchet hacha pequeña.
hate odio.
hate (to) odiar, detestar.
hateful odioso.
hatred odio, aborrecimiento.
haughty soberbio.
have (to) tener (to possess); haber (auxiliary).
   to have in mind tener en cuenta.
   to have to tener que.
   to have a mind to querer, tener ganas de.
hay heno.
he él.
head cabeza, jefe (chief).
head (to) encabezar.

heading encabezamiento, título.
headache dolor de cabeza.
headline n. encabezamiento, titular.
headquarters cuartel general (Army); oficina principal (main office).
heal curar; recobrar la salud; cicatrizarse (a wound).
health salud.
   to be in good health estar bien de salud.
healthful saludable.
healthy sano.
heap n. montón.
   in heaps a montones.
heap (to) acumular, apilar.
hear (to) oír.
   to hear from saber de, tener noticias de.
heart corazón.
   heart and soul en cuerpo y alma.
   by heart de memoria.
   to have no heart no tener corazón.
   to take to heart tomar a pecho.
hearth hogar, fogón.
hearty cordial (warm); voraz (appetite).
heat calor.
heat (to) calentar.
heater calentador.
heating calefacción.
heaven cielo.
   Heavens! ¡Cielos!
heavy pesado.
   heavy rain lluvia fuerte, aguacero.
hedge seto.
heel talón (of foot); tacón (shoe).
height altura.
heir heredero.
hell infierno.
Hello! ¡Hola!
help ayuda; auxilio.
help (to) ayudar.
   to help oneself to servirse (comida).
helper asistente, ayudante.
helpful útil, provechoso.
hemisphere hemisferio.
hen gallina.

henceforth   de aquí en adelante, en adelante, en lo futuro.

her   la, le, ella, de ella, a ella, su.

herb   hierba, yerba.

here   aquí; acá.
     Here it is.   Aquí está.
     Come here.   Ven acá.
     around here   cerca de aquí, por aquí.
     near here   cerca de aquí.

hereabout   por aquí, por aquí cerca.

hereafter   en adelante.

herein   aquí dentro, adjunto.

herewith   con esto.

hero   héroe.

heroic   heroico.

heroine   heroína.

heroism   heroísmo.

herring   arenque.

hers   suyo, suya, de ella; el suyo, la suya, los suyos, las suyas.

herself   ella misma; sí misma; se, sí.
     by herself   sola; por sí, por su cuenta.
     she herself   ella misma, en persona.

hesitant   indeciso, vacilante.

hesitate   vacilar.

hesitation   vacilación, titubeo.

hidden   escondido.

hide (to)   esconder; esconderse.

hideous   horrible, espantoso.

high   alto, elevado; caro (price).
     to be high   tener de alto.
     It is five inches high.   Tiene cinco pulgadas de alto.

higher   más alto; superior.

highway   carretera.

hill   colina, cerro.

him   él, a él, le.

himself   el mismo; sí mismo, se, sí.
     by himself   solo; por sí, por su cuenta.
     he himself   él mismo, en persona.

hinder   impedir, estorbar.

hindrance   impedimento, estorbo, obstáculo.

hinge   gozne.

hint   insinuación, indirecta, alusión.

hint (to)   insinuar.
     to hint at   aludir a.

hip   cadera.

hire (to)   alquilar.

his   su, sus, suyo, suya, el suyo, la suya, los suyos, las suyas, de él.

hiss (to)   silbar, sisear.

historian   historiador.

historic   histórico.

history   historia.

hit   golpe.

hit (to)   golpear.
     to hit the mark   dar en el blanco.

hive   colmena.

hoarse   ronco.

hoe   azada, azadón.

hog   cerdo, puerco.

hold (to)   tener (in one's hands, arms, etc.); coger, agarrar, asir (to grasp); caber, contener (to contain, to have capacity for); tener, desempeñar (a job, etc.).
     to hold good   valer, ser válido.
     to hold a meeting   celebrar una reunión.
     to hold one's own   mantenerse firme, defenderse bien.
     to hold a conversation   sostener una conversación.

hole   agujero; hueco.

holiday   día festivo, día feriado.

holidays   vacaciones, asueto.

holy   santo.

homage   homenaje.

home   hogar, casa, domicilio.
     at home   en casa.
     home town   pueblo natal.

homely   feo.

homemade   casero, hecho en casa.

Honduras   Honduras.

Honduran   hondureño.

honest   honrado.

honesty   honradez.

honey   miel.

honor   honor.

honor (to)   honrar.

honorable   honroso; honorable.

hoof   casco, pezuña.

hook n.   gancho; anzuelo (for fishing).

hope   esperanza.

hope (to)   esperar.

hopeful   lleno de esperanzas, optimista.

hopeless   desahuciado, sin remedio.

horizon   horizonte.

horizontal   horizontal.

horn   cuerno (of animals); bocina (of car); corneta de caza (hunting).

horrible   horrible, terrible.

horror   horror.

horse   caballo.
     on horseback   a caballo.

hosiery   tienda de medias y calcetines (store); géneros de punto (goods knit).

hospitable   hospitalario.

hospital   hospital.

hospitality   hospitalidad.

host   anfitrión.

hostess   anfitriona.

hot   caliente.

hotel   hotel.

hour   hora.

house   casa.

household   familia (family); menaje de casa (furniture, etc.).

housekeeper ama (de llaves).
housemaid criada, sirvienta.
housewife ama de casa, madre de familia.
how cómo; qué, cuánto.
    How do you do? ¿Cómo le va? ¿Cómo está Ud.? ¿Qué tal?
    How many? ¿Cuántos?
    How much? ¿Cuánto?
    How far? ¿A qué distancia?
    How early? ¿Cuándo? ¿A qué hora?
    How late? ¿Hasta qué hora? ¿Cuando?
    How long? ¿Cuánto tiempo?
    How soon? ¿Cuándo a más tardar?
however sin embargo.
huge inmenso, enorme.
human humano.
    human race género humano.
humane humanitario, bienhechor.
humanity humanidad.
humble humilde.
humiliate humillar.
humiliation humillación.
humility humildad.
humor humor.
humorous humorista, chistoso, jocoso.
hundred cien, ciento.
hundredth centésimo.
hunger hambre.
hungry (be) tener hambre.
hunt caza.
hunt (to) cazar.
hunter cazador.
hunting caza.
hurry prisa.
    to be in a hurry tener prisa, estar de prisa.
hurry (to) apresurar.
    to hurry up darse prisa.
    Hurry up! ¡Date prisa! (familiar). ¡Dése prisa!
hurt (to) lastimar, herir; ofender (one's feelings).
husband esposo.
hydrant boca de riego.
hygiene higiene.
hyphen guión.
hypnotism hipnotismo.
hypnotize hipnotizar.
hypocrisy hipocresía.
hypocrite hipócrita.
hysteria histeria.
hysterical histérico.

I

I yo.
ice hielo, helado.
ice cream helado.
idea idea.
ideal ideal.
idealism idealismo.

idealist idealista.
identical idéntico.
identification identificación.
identify identificar.
identity identidad.
idiom modismo.
idiot idiota, imbécil.
idle ocioso.
idleness ocio.
if si.
    if not si no.
    even if aun cuando.
    If I may. Con su permiso. Si me permite.
ignorance ignorancia.
ignorant ignorante, inculto.
ignore ignorar, pasar por alto, no hacer caso.
ill enfermo (sick) mal, malo (wrong, bad).
    ill breeding malos modales.
    ill will mala voluntad.
illegal ilegal.
illegible ilegible.
illiteracy analfabetismo.
illiterate analfabeto.
illness enfermedad.
illogical ilógico.
illuminate illuminar, alumbrar.
illumination iluminación, alumbrado.
illusion ilusión.
illustrate ilustrar.
illustrated ilustrado.
illustration ilustración (picture, etc.); ejemplo (example).
image imagen.
imaginary imaginario.
imagination imaginación.
imaginative imaginativo.
imagine figurar, imaginar.
    Just imagine! ¡Imagínese!
imitate imitar.
imitation imitación.
immediate inmediato.
immediately inmediatamenta, en seguida, en el acto.
immense inmenso.
immigrant inmigrante.
immigrate inmigrar.
immigration inmigración.
imminent inminente.
immoderate inmoderado, excesivo.
immoral inmoral.
immorality inmoralidad.
immortal inmortal.
immortality inmortalidad.
impartial imparcial.
impatience impaciencia.
impatient impaciente.
imperative imperativo.
imperceptible imperceptible.

imperfect imperfecto, defectuoso.
impersonal impersonal.
impertinence impertinencia.
impertinent impertinente.
impetuous impetuoso, arrebatado.
implement herramienta, utensilio.
implied implícito.
imply implicar; querer decir, significar.
impolite descortés.
import (to) importar.
importance importancia.
important importante.
importation importación.
importer importador.
impose imponer; abusar de (impose upon).
imposing imponente; abusivo.

impossibility imposibilidad.
impossible imposible.
impress impresionar.
impression impresión.
   to have the impression tener la impresión.
impressive imponente, grandioso.
imprison encarcelar, aprisionar.
improbable improbable.
improper impropio.
improve mejorar, perfeccionar; adelantar, progresar; aliviarse, mejorarse (health).
improved mejorado, perfeccionado.
improvement mejora, adelanto, progreso, perfeccionamiento; alivio, mejoría (health).
improvise improvisar.
imprudence imprudencia.
imprudent imprudente.
impure impuro.
in en.
   in fact en efecto.
   in the morning por la mañana.
   in a week de aquí a una semana, dentro de una semana.
   to be in estar en (casa, en la oficina, etc.).
   in front enfrente, delante.
   in general en general, por lo general.
   in part en parte.
   in reality en realidad.
   in spite of a pesar de.
   in turn por turno.
   in vain en vano.
   in writing por escrito.
inability ineptitud, inhabilidad, incapacidad.
inaccessible inaccessible.
inaccuracy inexactitud.
inaccurate inexacto.
inactive inactivo.
inadequate inadecuado.
inaugurate inaugurar.
incapability incapacidad.
incapable incapaz.
incapacity incapacidad.

inch pulgada.
incident incidente.
inclination inclinación, propensión.
include incluir, comprender.
included inclusive, incluso, comprendido.
inclusive inclusivo.
incoherent incoherente.
income renta, ingreso.
incomparable incomparable.
incompatible incompatible.
incomprehensible incomprensible.
inconsistent inconsistente.
inconvenience inconveniencia; molestia.
inconvenience (to) incomodar, molestar.
inconvenient inconveniente; incómodo, molesto.
incorrect incorrecto.
increase aumento.
increase (to) aumentar.
incredible increíble.
incurable incurable.
indebted endeudado, entrampado, lleno de deudas; obligado, reconocido (under obligation).
indecent indecente.
indeed verdaderamente, realmente, de veras, a la verdad, sí, claro está.
   Indeed? ¿De veras?
   Yes indeed! ¡Claro que sí! ¡Claro está!
   No indeed! ¡Quiá! ¡De ninguna manera!
indefinite indefinido.
independence independencia.
independent independiente; acomodado, rentista (financially independent).
indescribable indescriptible.
index índice.
index finger índice.
indicate indicar.
indifference indiferencia.
indifferent indiferente.
indigestion indigestión.
indignant indignado.
indignation indignación.
indirect indirecto.
indiscreet indiscreto.
indispensable indispensable.
indisputable indisputable.
indistinct indistinto.
individual adj. individual, particular.
individual n. individuo.
individuality individualidad, personalidad.
individually individualmente.
indivisible indivisible.
indolence indolencia.
indolent indolente.
indoors dentro, en casa.
indorsement endoso.
indulge dar rienda suelta a, darse gusto; entregarse a (to indulge in).

indulgence   indulgencia; complacencia (self-
    indulgence).
indulgent   indulgente.
industrial   industrial.
industrious   diligente, trabajador.
industry   industria.
inefficient   ineficaz.
inequality   desigualdad.
inevitable   inevitable.
inexcusable   inexcusable, imperdonable.
inexhaustible   inagotable.
inexpensive   barato.
inexperience   inexperiencia.
inexperienced   sin experiencia, novel.
infallible   infalible.
infant   infante, niño.
infantry   infantería.
infection   infección.
infectious   infeccioso, contagioso.
infer   inferir; colegir.
inference   inferencia.
inferior   inferior.
inferiority   inferioridad.
infinite   infinito.
infinitive   infinitivo.
infinity   infinidad.
influence   influencia.
influence (to)   influir.
    to influence by suggestion   sugestionar.
influential   influyente.
influenza   influenza.
inform (to)   informar, hacer saber, poner al
    corriente.
information   información.
    information bureau   oficina de información.
infrequent   raro, no frecuente.
infrequently   raramente.
ingenious   ingenioso.
ingenuity   ingenio, talento.
ingratitude   ingratitud.
inhabit   habitar.
inhabitant   habitante.
inherit   heredar.
inheritance   herencia.
initial   inicial.
initiative   iniciativa.
injure   injuriar, agraviar (the feelings, reputa-
    tion, etc.); dañar, hacer daño, lastimar,
    (to damage).
injurious   nocivo, dañino, perjudicial.
injury   daño, avería; perjuicio, mal.
injustice   injusticia.
ink   tinta.
inkwell   tintero.
inland   interior, tierra adentro.
    inland navigation   navegación fluvial.
inn   posada, venta.
innate   innato.

inner   interior.
innkeeper   posadero, ventero.
innocence   inocencia.
innocent   inocente.
insane   loco, demente.
insanity   locura.
inscribe   inscribir.
inscription   inscripción.
insect   insecto.
insecticide   insecticida.
insecure   inseguro.
insecurity   inseguridad.
insensible   insensible.
inseparable   inseparable.
insert (to)   insertar, introducir.
insertion   inserción.
inside   dentro; interior.
    on the inside   por dentro.
    toward the inside   hacia dentro.
    inside out   al revés.
insignificance   insignificancia.
insignificant   insignificante.
insincere   falto de sinceridad, poco sincero.
insincerity   falta de sinceridad.
insist   insistir.
insistence   insistencia.
insolence   insolencia.
insolent   insolente.
inspect   inspeccionar, examinar.
inspection   inspección.
inspector   inspector.
inspiration   inspiración.
install   instalar, colocar.
installation   instalación.
instance   ejemplo; caso.
    for instance   por ejemplo.
    in this instance   en este caso.
instead of   en lugar de, en vez de.
instinct   instinto.
institute   instituto.
institute (to)   instituir.
institution   institución.
instruct   instruir, enseñar; dar instrucciones.
instruction   instrucción, enseñanza.
instructive   instructivo.
instructor   instructor.
instrument   instrumento.
insufficiency   insuficiencia.
insufficient   insuficiente.
insult   insulto.
insult (to)   insultar.
insulting   insultante.
insuperable   insuperable.
insurance   seguro.
intact   intacto.
integral   íntegro.
intellectual   intelectual.
intelligence   inteligencia.

intelligent inteligente.

intend intentar; tener intención de, proponerse (to have in mind).

   to be intended for   tener por objeto.

intense intenso.

intensity intensidad.

intention intención.

intentional intencional.

intentionally intencionalmente.

interest interés.

interest (to) interesar.

interested interesado.

interesting interesante.

interior interior, interno.

intermission intermisión, entreacto (theater).

internal interno.

international internacional.

interpose interponer.

interpret interpretar.

interpretation interpretación.

interpreter intérprete.

interrupt interrumpir.

interruption interrupción.

interval intervalo.

intervention intervención.

interview entrevista.

intestines intestinos.

intimacy intimidad.

intimate íntimo.

intimidate intimidar.

into en, dentro.

intonation entonación.

intoxicate embriagar; intoxicar (to poison).

intoxicated borracho.

intoxicating embriagante.

intoxication embriaguez; intoxicación (poison)

intricate intrincado, enredado, complicado.

intrigue intriga, trama.

intrinsic(al) intrínseco.

introduce introducir; presentar (a person).

   to introduce a person   presentar a una persona.

introduction introducción (book); presentación (person).

intruder intruso.

intuition intuición.

invade invadir.

invalid adj. inválido (person), nulo (void).

invalid n. inválido.

invasion invasión.

invent inventar.

invention invención.

inventor inventor.

invert invertir, volver al revés, trastocar.

invest invertir, colocar (money).

investigate investigar, inquirir.

investigation investigación.

investment inversión.

investor inversionista, persona que invierte dinero.

invisible invisible.

invitation invitación.

invite convidar, invitar.

invoice factura.

involuntary involuntario.

involve comprometer, implicar; enredar.

involved complicado.

iodine yodo.

iris iris.

iron hierro; plancha (for ironing).

iron (to) planchar (clothes).

ironical irónico.

ironing planchado.

irony ironía.

irregular irregular.

irresolute irresoluto.

irresponsible irresponsable.

irrigate regar, irrigar.

irrigation riego.

irritable irritable.

irritate irritar, exasperar.

irritation irritación.

island isla.

isolation aislamiento.

issue edición, tirada (books, etc.); asunto de que se trata.

issue (to) publicar, dar a luz (books, magazines, etc.).

it ello, el, ella; lo, la, le; esto, este, esta. ("It" is not translated in phrases like "it's raining" [llueve] "it's late" [es tarde], "it's two o'clock" [son las dos], etc.).

   I have it.   Lo masc. tengo.

   I have it.   La fem. tengo.

   I said it.   Yo lo dije.

   Isn't it?   ¿No es verdad?

   That's it.   Eso es.

Italian italiano.

Italy Italia.

itinerary itinerario.

its su, sus (de él, de ella, de ello, de ellos, de ellas).

itself sí, sí mismo.

   by itself   por sí.

ivory marfil.

ivy hiedra.

J

jack gato (tool).

jacket chaqueta (a short coat); camisa, cubierta (covering, casing).

jail cárcel.

jam compota, conserva (of fruit); apuro, aprieto (a fix).

janitor portero, conserje.

January   enero.

jar n.   tarro (for preserves).

jaw   quijada.

jealous   celoso.

jealousy   celos.

jelly   jalea.

jerk (to)   sacudir.

jest   broma.

jest (to)   bromear.

Jesuit   jesuita.

jewel   joya, alhaja.

jewelry   joyería.

jewelry shop   joyería.

job   empleo; tarea.

join   unir, juntar (to put together); unirse, asociarse (to unite); afiliarse, adherirse a, ingresar en (an organization).

joint   coyuntura, articulación (anatomical); empalme, junta, juntura, ensambladura (the place or part where two things are joined).

joke   broma.

joke (to)   bromear, embromar.

jolly adj.   alegre, divertido, jovial.

jostle   empellar, rempujar.

journal   diario.

journalist   periodista.

journalistic   periodístico.

journey   viaje.

journey (to)   viajar.

jovial   jovial.

joy   alegría, júbilo.

joyful   alegre, gozoso.

judge   juez.

judge (to)   juzgar.

judgment   juicio.

judicial   judicial.

juice   zumo, jugo.

juicy   jugoso.

July   julio.

jump   salto.

jump (to)   saltar.

June   junio.

junior adj.   más joven (younger); hijo (Jr. after a name).

junior partner   socio menos antiguo.

jurisprudence   jurisprudencia.

juror   jurado (individual).

jury   jurado.

just adj.   justo.

    It's not just.   No es justo.

just adv.   justamente, exactamente; solamente, simplemente, no más que.

    just as   al momento que, en el mismo instante en que; no bien.

    just as I came in   en el mismo instante en que entraba.

    just a moment   un momentito.

    just now   ahora mismo.

    I just wanted to   yo solamente quería.

    to have just   acabar de.

    I have just come.   Acabo de llegar.

    It is just two o'clock.   Son las dos en punto.

    Just as you please.   Como Ud. guste.

justice   justicia.

justifiable   justificable.

justification   justificación.

justify   justificar.

K

keen   agudo.

keep (to)   guardar.

    to keep away   mantener alejado; no dejar entrar.

    to keep back (retain)   detener, retener.

    to keep from   impedir (hinder); abstenerse (refrain).

    to keep quiet   callar.

    to keep house   tener casa puesta.

    to keep in mind   recordar, tener presente.

    to keep late hours   acostarse tarde.

    to keep one's hands off   no tocar, no meterse en.

    to keep one's word   tener palabra, cumplir su palabra.

    to keep track of   no perder de vista; tener en cuenta.

kernel   almendra, pepita.

kerosene   kerosen, kerosene, kerosina.

kettle   marmita, caldera.

key   llave; principal (main).

keyboard   teclado.

kick   puntapié; patada, coz.

kick (to)   patear; cocear.

kidney   riñón.

kill (to)   matar.

kind adj.   bueno, amable, bondadoso.

kind n.   clase, calidad.

    a kind of   una especie de.

    of the kind   semejante.

    nothing of the kind   no hay tal, nada de eso.

    of a kind   de una misma clase.

kindergarten   escuela de párvulos.

kindhearted   bondadoso.

kindly   bondadosamente; tenga la bondad, haga el favor, sírvase.

    Kindly do it.   Tenga la bondad de hacerlo.

kindness   bondad.

king   rey.

kingdom   reino.

kiss   beso.

kiss (to)   besar.

kitchen   cocina.

kite   cometa.

kitten   gatito.

knee   rodilla.

kneecap rótula.

kneel arrodillarse.

knife cuchillo.

knit tejer.

knock golpe (blow); llamada (on the door).

knock (to) golpear; tocar, llamar (on the door).

knot nudo.

know (to) saber; conocer (be acquainted with).

knowledge conocimiento.

to the best of my knowledge   según mi leal saber y entender.

known conocido.

knuckle coyuntura, nudillo.

kodak kodak.

L

label etiqueta.

labor trabajo.

laboratory laboratorio.

laborer jornalero, trabajador.

lace n. encaje.

lack falta, escasez, carencia, necesidad.

lack (to) carecer, faltar algo, necesitar.

lacking (be) hacer falta.

ladder escalera de mano.

lady señora.

Ladies. Señoras.

Ladies and gentlemen.   Señoras y caballeros.

lake lago.

lamb cordero.

lamb chops   chuletas de cordero.

lame cojo (limping); lisiado (crippled); defectuoso, inaceptable (unsatisfactory).

lame (be) cojear (to limp).

lameness cojera.

lament (to) lamentar.

lamentation lamento.

lamp lámpara.

land tierra (ground); terreno (terrain), país (country).

land (to) desembarcar (ship); aterrizar (plane).

landing n. desembarco (from a ship); aterrizaje (of an airplane); meseta, descanso (a staircase).

landlady propietaria, dueña, patrona.

landlord propietario, dueño, casero, patrón.

landscape paisaje, vista.

language lengua, idioma; lenguaje.

languid lánguido.

languish languidecer.

languor languidez.

lantern farol, linterna.

lap falda.

lard manteca, lardo.

large grande.

at large   en libertad, suelto (free, loose); extensamente, sin limitación (widespread); en general, en conjunto (in general).

large-scale en gran escala.

lark alondra.

larynx laringe.

last último; pasado.

lastly   al fin, finalmente, por último.

at last   al fin, al cabo, por fin.

last night   anoche.

last week   la semana pasada.

last year   el año pasado.

last (to) durar.

lasting duradero, durable.

latch aldaba, picaporte.

late adj. tarde.

to be late   llegar tarde.

late in the year   a fines de año.

How late?   ¿Hasta que hora?

lately poco ha, no ha mucho, recientemente, últimamente.

lateness tardanza.

later más tarde.

latest último.

latest style   última moda.

at the latest   a más tardar.

lather espuma de jabón, jabonadura.

Latin latino adj.; latín n.

latter (the) éste, último.

laudable laudable, loable.

laugh risa.

to make someone laugh   hacer reír.

laugh (to) reír.

laughable risible, que causa risa, divertido.

laughter risa.

launder lavar y planchar la ropa.

laundress lavandera.

laundry lavandería, establecimiento de la ropa; ropa sucia (clothes to be washed ropa lavada (washed clothes).

lavish pródigo, gastador.

lavish (to) prodigar.

law ley; jurisprudencia (legal science); derec (body of laws); código (code).

law school   escuela de derecho.

international law   derecho internacional.

lawful legal, conforme a la ley.

lawless ilegal.

lawn césped.

lawyer abogado.

laxative laxante.

lay (to) poner.

to lay away (aside, by)   poner a un lado, guar dar, ahorrar.

to lay hands on   sentar la mano a.

to lay hold of   asir, coger.

to lay off   quitarse de encima; despedir (to fire).

to lay the blame on   echar la culpa a.

laziness pereza.

lazy perezoso.

lead (metal) plomo.

lead (to) conducir, guiar.
    to lead the way mostrar el camino, ir delante.
    to lead up to conducir a.
leader líder, caudillo, conductor, jefe; guía
    (guide); director (band leader).
leadership dirección.
leading principal, capital.
    leading article editorial.
    leading man cabecilla, jefe.
leaf hoja.
lean (to) inclinar; apoyarse.
    to lean back retreparse, recostarse.
    to lean over reclinarse.
leaning inclinación, propensión, tendencia.
leap salto, brinco.
leap (to) saltar, brincar.
learn aprender (to acquire knowledge, skill); en-
    terarse de, tener noticia de, saber (to find
    out about).
learned sabio, docto, erudito.
learning saber, ciencia, erudición.
lease arriendo, contrato de arrendamiento.
lease (to) arrendar, dar en arriendo.
least mínimo, el mínimo, menos.
    at least a lo menos, por lo menos.
    not in the least de ninguna manera, bajo
    ningún concepto.
    the least possible lo menos posible.
    least of all lo de menos.
leather cuero.
leave (to) dejar (quit); abandonar (desert); salir
    (go out); irse (go away).
    to leave behind dejar atrás.
    to leave out omitir, excluir.
lecture n. conferencia; disertación (a discourse),
    regaño (a reprimand).
lecturer conferenciante.
left izquierdo.
    left hand mano izquierda.
    to the left a la izquierda.
    left-handed zurdo.
left (be) quedarse.
leg pierna; pata (of a chicken, etc.); pata, pie
    (of a table, etc.).
legal legal.
legend leyenda.
legible legible, que puede leerse.
legislation legislación.
legislator legislador.
legislature legislatura.
leisure ocio, holganza, comodidad.
lemon limón.
lemonade limonada.
lend (to) prestar, dar prestado.
    to lend an ear dar oídos, prestar atención.
    to lend a hand arrimar el hombro, dar una
    mano.
length largo, longitud.

    at length al fin, finalmente; detalladamente
    (with all the details).
    at full length a lo largo, a todo lo largo.
less menos.
    more or less más o menos.
    less and less cada vez menos.
lessen reducir, disminuir, disminuirse.
lesson lección.
let (to) lejar, permitir; arrendar, alquilar (to
    rent).
    Let's go. Vamos.
    Let her go que se vaya.
    Let's see Veamos.
    to let alone dejar en paz, no molestar.
    to let be no meterse con.
    to let go soltar.
    to let it go at that dejar pasar, no hacer o
    decir más.
    to let in dejar entrar, hacer pasar.
    to let know hacer saber, avisar.
letter carta; letra (of the alphabet).
lettuce lechuga.
level adj. plano, llano, igual, parejo nivelado,
    allanado.
    level crossing paso a nivel.
level nivel.
    to be on the level jugar limpio, ser honrado,
    no tener dolo.
level off (to) nivelar; planear (a plane).
liable sujeto, expuesto a (exposed to); propenso
    a, capaz de (liable to think, say, do).
liar embustero.
liberal liberal.
liberty libertad.
library biblioteca.
license licencia, permiso.
lick lamer.
lid tapa, tapadera.
lie mentira (falsehood).
lie (to) mentir (tell a falsehood) reposar, acos-
    tarse, echarse (lie down).
lieutenant teniente.
life vida.
    lifesaver salvavidas.
    lifeboat bote salvadidas.
    life insurance seguro sobre la vida.
lifetime toda la vida, duración de la vida.
lift alzar, levantar.
light luz; claridad.
    in the light of según, a la luz de.
    in this light desde este punto de vista.
light adj. liviano, ligero (in weight), claro
    (color).
    light complexion tez blanca.
    light reading lectura amena.
    light-headed ligero (alegre) de cascos.
light (to) encender (a match, etc.); alumbrar,
    iluminar (to illuminate).

lighten aligerar, quitar peso.
lighthouse faro.
lighting alumbrado, iluminación.
lightness ligereza.
lightning relámpago.
like parecido, semejante (similar).
   in like manner del mismo modo, análogamente.
   be like ser semejante, parecido.
like (to) querer, gustar, agradar.
   to like someone tener simpatía por.
   I like her very much. La quiero mucho.
   She doesn't like me. Ella no me quiere.
   As you like. Como Ud. quiera (guste).
   Do you like it? ¿Le gusta? ¿Le agrada?
   I like it. Me gusta.
   I don't like it. No me gusta.
likely probable; probablemente.
likeness semejanza.
likewise igualmente, asimismo.
liking afición; simpatía; gusto.
limb miembro.
lime cal.
limit límite.
limit (to) limitar.
limp (to) cojear.
line línea.
line (to) rayar, trazar líneas.
   to line up alinear, alinearse.
linen tela de hilo (goods, material); ropa blanca (bed linen, table linen, etc.).
lining forro.
link eslabón; enlace.
link (to) unir, enlazar, eslabonar, encadenar.
lip labio.
lipstick lápiz para los labios.
liquid líquido.
liquor licor.
lisp (to) cecear, balbucear.
list lista.
list (to) anotar, registrar, poner en lista.
listen escuchar.
literal literal, al pie de la letra.
literally literalmente.
literary literario.
literature literatura.
little pequeño.
   a little un poco, un poquito.
   very little muy poco.
   little boy chico, chiquillo.
   little girl chica, chiquilla.
   a little child un muchachito.
   a little dog un perrito.
   little by little poco a poco.
live *adj.* vivo.
live (to) vivir.
liver hígado.
living *adj.* viviente.

living *n.* vida; mantenimiento.
   to make a living ganarse la vida.
living room sala.
load carga.
load (to) cargar.
loaf pan, panecillo, hogaza (bread).
loan préstamo.
lobby vestíbulo.
lobster langosta.
local local.
locate situar.
located situado.
location sitio, localidad (place, locality); ubicación, situación, posición (site).
lock cerradura.
lock (to) cerrar con llave.
locomotive locomotora.
locust langosta.
log leño, tronco (wood).
   log book cuaderno de bitácora, diario de navegación.
logic lógica.
logical lógico.
lonely solitario, solo.
long *adj.* largo; de largo.
   It's five inches long. Tiene cinco pulgadas de largo.
   A long time ago. Hace mucho tiempo. Mucho tiempo atrás.
   long distance a large distancia (phone call).
long *adj.* a gran distancia; mucho, mucho tiempo.
   long ago mucho tiempo ha.
   all day long todo el santo día.
   not long ago no hace mucho.
   How long ago? ¿Cuánto tiempo hace?
   How long? ¿Cuánto tiempo?
   as long as mientras.
longer *adj.* más largo.
longer *adv.* más tiempo.
   How much longer? ¿Cuánto tiempo más?
   no longer ya no.
   to long for anhelar.
longing anhelo.
look cara, aspecto (appearance); mirada, ojeada (glance).
look (to) ver, mirar.
   Look! ¡Mire!
   Look in the mirror! ¡Mírate al espejo!
   to look for buscar; esperar.
   to look after cuidar.
   to look alike parecerse.
   to look forward to esperar.
   to look into examinar, estudiar.
   to look like snow parece que va a nevar.
   to look out tener cuidado (be careful).
   Look out! ¡Cuidado!
   to look over repasar, revisar.

loose suelto.
loosen (tc) desatar, soltar.
Lord Señor.
lose (to) perder.
loss pérdida.
     at a loss   perdiendo, con pérdida; perplejo (puzzled).
     to be at a loss   estar sin saber que hacer.
lot (a) mucho.
     a lot of money   mucho dinero.
loud ruidoso, fuerte.
     a loud laugh   risotada.
love amor, cariño.
     to be in love   estar enamorado.
love (to) amar, querer.
lovely encantador, precioso, bonito, hermoso.
low bajo.
lower más bajo, inferior.
     lower case   letras minúsculas.
lower (to) bajar; rebajar (price); arriar, abatir (a flag, etc.).
loyal leal.
loyalty fidelidad.
luck suerte, fortuna.
     good luck   buena suerte.
     to have luck   tener suerte.
luckily por fortuna, afortunadamente.
lucky afortunado.
     to be lucky   tener suerte.
luggage equipaje.
lukewarm tibio, templado.
lumber madera.
luminous luminoso.
lunch merienda, almuerzo.
lunch (to) almorzar, merendar.
     to have lunch   almorzar, merendar.
lung pulmón.
de luxe de lujo.
luxury lujo.
luxurious lujoso.

M

machine máquina.
machinery maquinaria.
mad loco.
     to go mad   volverse loco.
made hecho, fabricado.
madness locura.
magazine revista.
magic *adj.* mágico.
magic *n.* magia.
magistrate magistrado.
magnanimous magnánimo.
magnet imán.
magnetic magnético.
magnificent magnífico.
magnify aumentar.

magnifying glass lente (cristal) de aumento, lupa.
mail correo.
mailbox buzón.
mailman cartero.
main principal, esencial.
     the main floor   el principal.
     the main issue   la cuestión principal.
     main office   casa matriz.
     the main point   el punto esencial.
mainly principalmente, sobre todo.
maintain mantener, sostener, conservar.
maintenance matenimiento; conservación, entretenimiento, reparación (property, equipment).
majestic majestuoso.
majesty majestad.
major *adj.* mayor, más importante.
major *n.* mayor, comandante.
majority mayoría.
make (to) hacer; fabricar, producir.

     to make sad   poner triste, entristecer.
     to make happy   poner alegre, alegrar.
     to make a good salary   ganar un buen sueldo.
     to make a living   ganarse la vida.
     to make possible   hacer posible.
     to make ready   preparar.
     to make room   hacer lugar.
     to make known   dar a conocer.
     to make a hit   dar golpe, producir sensación.
     to make a mistake   equivocarse.
     to make a stop   detenerse.
     to make friends   granjearse amigos.
     to make fun of   burlarse de.
     to make haste   apurarse.
     to make headway   progresar, adelantar.
     to make into   convertir.
     to make for a place   dirigirse a un lugar, encaminarse hacia.
     to make no difference   ser indiferente, no importar.
     to make out   comprender, descifrar, sacar en limpio; salir bien o mal.
     to make sick   causar repugnancia, fastidiar (to annoy).
     to make the best of   sacar el mayor provecho de, sacar el mejor partido de.
     to make tired   cansar.
     to make one's mind up   decidirse, determinarse.
maker fabricante.
malady enfermedad.
malice malicia.
malicious malicioso.
man hombre.
     young man   joven.
     Men (*as a sign*). Señores.
manage (to) administrar; gestionar; arreglárselas.
management administración, dirección.

manager administrador, director, gerente.
manifest (to) manifestar.
mankind humanidad.
manly viril, varonil.
manner manera, modo.
manners crianza, modales.
mansion mansión.
manual manual.
manufacture (to) manufacturar, fabricar.
manufacturer fabricante.
manuscript manuscrito.
many muchos.
    many times muchas veces.
    as many otros tantos.
    as many as tantos como.
    How many? ¿Cuántos?
map mapa.
maple arce, meple.
marble mármol; canica, bolita (for children).
March marzo.
march marcha.
march (to) marchar.
margin margen.
marine adj. marino.
mark marca; seña, señal.
mark (to) señalar, marcar.
market mercado.
marriage matrimonio.
married casado.
    to get married casarse.
marrow meollo, tuétano.
marry casar; casarse.
marvel n. maravilla, prodigio.
marvel at (to) admirarse.
marvelous maravilloso.
marvelously maravillosamente.
mask máscara.
mason albañil.
mass masa; misa (religious).
massage masaje.
massage (to) dar masaje.
massive macizo, sólido.
mast mástil.
master amo, dueño.
masterpiece obra maestra.
mat estera (straw).
match fósforo, cerilla (to light with); partida,
    partido (sport); compañero, pareja (a pair);
    noviazgo, casamiento (marriage).
match (to) hacer juego (a vase, a picture, etc.);
    casar (colors).
material material.
maternal materno.
mathematical matemático.
mathematics matemáticas.
matinee matiné, función de tarde.
matter materia; cosa (thing); asunto, cuestión
    (question).

an important matter un asunto importante.
    What's the matter? ¿Qué pasa? ¿Qué ocurre?
    Nothing's the matter. No es nada.
matter (to) importar.
    It doesn't matter. No importa.
mattress colchón.
mature adj. maduro.
mature (to) madurar.
    to become mature madurar; alcanzar la
    edad madura.
maturity madurez.
maximum máximo.
    at the maximum a lo sumo.
May mayo.
may poder, ser posible.
    It may be. Puede ser.
    It may be true. Podrá ser verdad.
    May I? ¿Me permite Ud.? Si Ud. me per-
    mite. Con su permiso.
    May I come in? ¿Puedo entrar?
maybe acaso, quizás, tal vez.
mayonnaise mayonesa.
mayor alcalde.
maze laberinto.
    to be in a maze estar perplejo.
meadow prado.
meal comida.
mean adj. bajo, vil, despreciable.
mean (to) significar, querer decir, dar a entender.
    What do you mean? ¿Qué quiere Ud. decir?
meaning designio, intención (intent); sentido,
    significado (of a word, etc.).
means medio; medios, recursos.
    by all means sin falta.
    by no means de ningún modo.
    by some means de alguna manera.
    by this means por este medio.
meantime entretanto.
    in the meantime mientras tanto.
meanwhile mientras tanto, entretanto.
    in the meanwhile mientras tanto.
meanwhile n. ínterin.
measure medida.
    in a great measure en gran manera.
    in some measure en cierto modo, hasta cierto
    punto.
measure (to) medir.
    to measure up to ponerse a la altura de, ser
    igual.
measurement medición; medida.

meat carne.
mechanic mecánico.
mechanical mecánico.
mechanically mecánicamente.
mechanism mecanismo.
medal medalla.
meddle (to) intervenir, entremeterse.
mediate mediar.

medical médico.
   medical school   escuela de medicina.
medicine medicina.
medieval medieval.
meditate meditar.
meditation meditación.
Mediterranean Mediterráneo.
medium *adj.* mediano.
medium-sized de tamaño mediano.
meet (to)   encontrar, encontrarse (to come
   across); conocer (to know); pagar, honrar
   (a bill, etc.); hacer frente a (expenses, etc.);
   reunirse (to get together, assemble).
   to go to meet   salir al encuentro, ir a recibir.
   Glad to meet you.   Me alegro de conocerle.
   I hope to meet you again.   Espero tener el
     gusto de verle otra vez.
   Till we meet again.   Hasta más ver.
meeting *n.* mitin, reunión.
melancholy *adj.* melancólico.
melody melodía.
melon melón.
melt (to)   derretir, disolver; fundir (metals).
member miembro.
memorable memorable.
memorandum memorandum.
memory memoria.
mend remendar, componer; enmendarse, corre-
   girse (mend one's ways, etc.).
mental mental.
mention mención.
mention (to) mencionar.
menu menu, lista de platos.
merchandise mercancía.
merchant comerciante, negociante.
merciful misericordioso, compasivo.
merciless desapiadado, sin piedad.
mercury mercurio.
mercy misericordia.
mere mero, puro.
   by mere chance   de pura casualidad.
merely meramente, simplemente, puramente.
merit mérito.
merit (to) merecer.
merry alegre.
message mensaje, recado.
messenger mensajero.
metal *adj.* metálico.
metal *n.* metal.
meter metro (measurement); medidor, contador
   (for gas, electricity, etc.).
method método.
methodic(al) metódico.
methodically metódicamente.
metric métrico.
   metric system   sistema métrico.
metropolis metrópoli.
metropolitan metropolitano.

Mexican mejicano.
Mexico Méjico.
midday mediodía.
middle *adj.* medio.
   Middle Ages   Edad media.
   middle-aged   entrado en años.
   middle-class   clase media.
middle medio, centro.
   in the middle   en el centro.
   about the middle of March   a mediados de
     marzo.
midnight media noche.
might poder, fuerza.
mighty fuerte, potente.
mild suave (tobacco, etc.); moderado (moderate);
   leve, ligero (light); apacible, manso
   (character).
mile milla.
military militar.
milk leche.
milkman lechero.
mill molino; fábrica (factory).
miller molinero.
million millón.
millionaire millonario.
mind mente.
   to have in mind   pensar en, tener presente.
   to have on one's mind   tener en la mente,
     preocuparse por.
mine mío, el mío, lo mío.
   a friend of mine   un amigo mío.
   your friends and mine   sus amigos y los míos.
mine *n.* mina.
miner minero.
mineral mineral.
miniature miniatura.
minimum mínimo.
   at the minimum   lo menos, el mínimum.
minister ministro.
minor *adj.* menor; secundario.
minor *n.* menor (age).
minority minoría.
mint menta (plant); casa de la moneda (money).
minus menos.
minute minuto (time).
   minute hand   minutero.
   Just a minute, please.   Un minuto, por favor.
   any minute   de un momento a otro.
   Wait a minute!   ¡Aguarde un momento!
miracle milagro.
miraculous milagroso.
mirror espejo.
mirth júbilo, alegría.
misbehave portarse mal.
misbehavior mal comportamiento.
mischief travesura.
mischievous travieso.
miser avaro.

miserable miserable.

misery miseria.

misfortune desgracia.

Miss señorita (title).

miss (to) echar de menos (someone or something); perder (train, etc.); errar (mark, etc.).

    to miss the point desbarrar; no comprender el verdadero sentido.

mission misión.

missionary misionero.

mistake equivocación.

mistake (to) equivocar.

    to be mistaken equivocarse, estar equivocado.

mistrust desconfianza.

mistrust (to) desconfiar de.

misunderstand entender mal una cosa, tomar algo en sentido erróneo.

misunderstanding malentendido, concepto falso, error.

mix (to) mezclar.

mixture mezcla.

moan gemido.

moan (to) gemir.

mobilization movilización.

mobilize movilizar.

mock (to) burlar.

mockery burla.

mode modo.

model modelo.

moderate *adj.* moderado.

moderate (to) moderar.

moderately moderadamente; módicamente.

moderation moderación.

modern moderno.

modest modesto.

modesty modestia.

modify modificar.

moist húmedo, mojado.

moisten humedecer.

moisture humedad.

moment momento.

    Just a moment! ¡Un momento!

momentary momentáneo.

momentous trascendental, importante.

monarch monarca.

monarchy monarquía.

Monday lunes.

money dinero.

monk fraile, monje.

monkey mono.

monologue monólogo.

monopoly monopolio.

monosyllable monosílabo.

monotonous monótono.

monotony monotonía.

monster monstruo.

monstrous monstruoso, grotesco.

month mes.

monthly mensual.

monument monumento.

monumental monumental.

moon luna.

moonlight luz de la luna.

moral *adj.* ético, moral.

morale moral, estado de ánimo.

morals conducta, moralidad, ética.

morbid morboso.

more más.

    more or less más o menos.

    once more una vez más.

    no more no más.

    the more . . . the better cuanto más . . . tanto mejor.

moreover además.

morning mañana.

    Good morning! ¡Buenos días!

morsel bocado.

mortal mortal.

mortgage *n.* hipoteca.

mosquito mosquito.

moss musgo.

most lo más, los más, el mayor número, la mayor parte.

    at most a los más, a lo sumo.

    for the most part generalmente, en su mayor parte.

    most of us casi todos nosotros, la mayor parte de nosotros.

moth polilla.

mother madre.

mother-in-law suegra.

motion movimiento; moción.

motive motivo.

motor *n.* motor.

mount *n.* monte (hill); montaje, afuste (artillery); soporte, tripode (for instruments).

mount (to) montar.

mountain montaña.

mountainous montañoso.

mourn lamentar.

mournful triste, fúnebre.

mourning lamento.

    in mourning de luto.

mouse ratón.

mouth boca.

mouthful bocado.

movable móvil, movible.

move (to) mover, moverse (to set in motion), mudar de casa, mudarse (to another house), mudar, trasladar; poner en otro sitio (to change place, position).

movement movimiento.

movie cine, cinema.

moving *adj.* conmovedor (emotionally).

Mr. don, señor (abbre. Dn., Sr.).

Mrs. doña, señora, señora de.

much   mucho.
    as much   tanto.
    as much as   tanto . . . como.
    How much?   ¿Cuánto?
    too much   demasiado.
    much the same   casi lo mismo, más o menos
        lo mismo.
    this much more   esto más, tanto así más.
    much money   mucho dinero.
mud   barro, fango, lodo.
muddy   turbio.
mule   mula.
multiple   múltiple.
multiplication   multiplicación.
multiply   multiplicar, multiplicarse.
murder   asesinato, homicidio.
murder (to)   asesinar.
murderer   asesino.
murmur n.   murmuración.
muscle   músculo.
museum   museo.
music   música.
musical   musical.
musician   músico.
must   tener que, haber que, deber.
    I must go.   Tengo que irme.
    It must be.   Debe ser.
    It must be late.   Debe de ser tarde.
    I must confess.   Debo confesar. Debo reco-
        nocer.
mustache   bigotes, mostacho.
mustard   mostaza.
mutton   carnero.
mutual   mutuo, recíproco.
my   mi, mis.
myself   yo mismo; me, a mí, mí mismo.
mysterious   misterioso.
mystery   misterio.

N

nail   uña (finger nail); clavo (metal).
nail (to)   clavar.
naive   cándido, ingenuo.
naked   desnudo.
name   nombre.
    Christian name   nombre de pila.
    surname   apellido.
name (to)   nombrar, designar.
namely   es decir, a saber.
nap n.   siesta.
napkin   servilleta.

narration   narración.
narrative   relato.
narrow   estrecho, angosto.
nation   nación.
national   nacional.
nationality   nacionalidad.

nationalization   nacionalización.
nationalize   nacionalizar.
native adj.   nativo, oriundo.
    native country   país natal.
natural   natural.
naturalist   naturalista.
naturally   naturalmente.
naturalness   naturalidad.
nature   naturaleza; carácter, índole.
    good nature   buen humor.
    good-natured man   bonachón.
naughty   malo, granujillo, pilluelo.
naval   naval.
navigable   navegable.
navigator   navegante.
navy   armada, marina de guerra.
near   cerca de; cerca.
nearby   cerca, a la mano.
nearer   más cerca.
nearest   lo (el, la) más cerca.
nearly   casi, cerca de.
nearsighted   miope.
nearsighted person   miope.
neat   esmerado, pulcro (tidy); bonito, lindo (nice).
neatness   esmero, pulcritud.
necessarily   necesariamente, forzosamente, por
    necesidad.
necessary   necesario.
    to be necessary   hacer falta, ser necesario.
necessitate   necesitar.
necessity   necesidad.
    of necessity   por necesidad.
neck   cuello, garganta, pescuezo.
    neck and neck   parejos (in a race).
necklace   collar, gargantilla.
necktie   corbata.
need   necesidad.
need (to)   hacer falta, necesitar.
    to be in need of   tener necesidad de.
    to be in need   estar necesitado.
needle   aguja.
negative adj.   negativo.
    a negative answer   una respuesta negativa.
negative n.   negativa; negativo (photography).
neglect   descuido, negligencia.
neglect (to)   descuidar.
neighbor   vecino.
neither conj.   ni; adj. ningun, ninguno de los dos;
    pron. ninguno.
    neither . . . nor   ni . . . ni.
    neither this one nor that one   ni uno ni otro,
        ni éste ni aquél.
    neither one   ni el uno ni el otro.
nephew   sobrino.
nerve   nervio.
nervous   nervioso.
nest   nido.
net n.   red.

neuter neutro.
neutral neutral.
never jamás, nunca.
nevertheless no obstante, sin embargo, con todo.
new nuevo.
  new moon luna nueva.
  New Year año nuevo.
news noticia, noticias.
newsboy vendedor de periódicos.

newspaper diario, periódico.
newsstand puesto de periódicos.
next siguiente, próximo.
  the next day al día siguiente, al otro día.
  (the) next week la semana entrante.
  (the) next time la próxima vez, otra vez.
  next to al lado de, junto a.
  to be next seguir en turno.
  Who's next? ¿Quién sigue?
nice bonito, lindo; gentil, amable; simpático.
nickname apodo, mote.
niece sobrina.
night noche.
  by night de noche.
  good night buenas noches.
  last night anoche.
nightmare pesadilla.
nighttime noche.
nine nueve.
nineteen diez y nueve (diecinueve).
ninety noventa.
ninth noveno.
no no; ningún, ninguno, ninguna.
  no other ningún otro.
  no one nadie.
  no longer ya no.
  no more no más.
  no matter no importa.
  no matter how much por mucho que.
  by no means de ningún modo.
  No admittance. No se permite la entrada.
  No smoking. No se permite fumar.
nobility nobleza.
noble noble.
nobody nadie, ninguno.
  nobody else nadie más, ningún otro.
nod (to) mover, inclinar la cabeza en sentido
    afirmativo; cabecear (become sleepy).
noise ruido.
  to make noise hacer ruido.
noisy ruidoso, bullicioso.
none nadie, ninguno; nada.
  none of us ninguno de nosotros.
nonsense tontería, disparate.
noon mediodía.
nor ni.
  neither . . . nor . . . ni . . . ni . . .
normal normal.
north norte.

  North America. América del Norte.
northern del norte.
nose nariz.
nostril fosa nasal, ventana de la nariz.
not no; ni, ni siquiera.
  if not si no.
  not any ningún, ninguno.
  not one ni uno solo.
  not a word ni una palabra.
  not at all de ninguna manera.
  not even ni siquiera, ni aun.
notable notable.
note nota.
  bank note billete de banco.
note (to) notar.
notebook libreta, libro de apuntes.
nothing nada, ninguna cosa.
  nothing doing nada de eso.
  It's nothing. No es nada.
  nothing much poca cosa.
  for nothing de balde, gratis.
  That's nothing to me. Eso no me importa.
notice aviso.
  Notice to the public. Aviso al público.

notice (to) advertir, notar.
notwithstanding no obstante, a pesar de, aun
    cuando, aunque, si bien, sin embargo.
noun nombre, substantivo.
nourish alimentar.
nourishment alimento; nutrición.
novel novela.
novelist novelista.
novelty novedad.
November noviembre.
now ahora; ahora bien, ya.
  until now hasta ahora, hasta aquí.
  now and then de vez en cuando.
  Is it ready now? ¿Ya está hecho?
nowadays hoy día.
nowhere en ninguna parte.
number número.
number (to) numerar.
numerous numeroso.
nun monja.
nurse n. enfermera.
nursery cuarto de los niños (room).
nut nuez (for eating); tuerca (for a screw).

O

oak roble.
oar remo.
oat avena.
oath juramento.
obedience obediencia.
obedient obediente.
obey obedecer.
object objeto; complemento (grammar).

object (to) oponer.
objection objeción, reparo.
objective objetivo; acusativo (grammar).
obligation obligación.
oblique oblicuo.
obscure obscuro.
obscure (to) obscurecer.
observation observación.
observatory observatorio.
observe observar; notar.
observer observador.
observing observador, atento.
obstacle obstáculo.
obstinacy porfía, obstinación.
obstinate terco, porfiado.
obstruct obstruir.
obstruction obstrucción.
obtain obtener.
obvious obvio, evidente.
occasion ocasión, oportunidad.
occasional ocasional, accidental, casual (casual);
    poco frecuente (not frequent).
occasionally a veces, de vez en cuando.
occidental occidental.
occupation ocupación, empleo.
occupy ocupar; emplear (the time).
occur ocurrir, suceder.
occurrence suceso, acaecimiento.
ocean océano.
o'clock
    at nine o'clock a las nueve.
    It's ten o'clock. Son las diez.
October octubre.
oculist oculista.
odd impar (number); raro (strange); suelto, que
    no hace juego (an odd shoe, etc.).
of de, del
    to taste of saber a.
    to think of pensar en.

    of course naturalmente, por supuesto.
    of himself por sí mismo.
    It's ten of one. Faltan diez para la una.
    That's very kind of you. Ud. es muy amable.
off lejos, a distancia, fuera; cerca; quitado, sin;
    suspendido.
    off and on de vez en cuando.
    The meeting is off. Se ha suspendido la re-
    unión.
    The cover is off. Está destapado.
    off the coast cerca de la costa.
    ten miles off a diez millas de aquí.
    off the track despistado.
    a day off un día libre, un día de asueto.
    to be well off disfrutar de una posición desa-
    hogada.
    to take off quitar de; quitarse.
    Take it off the table. Quítelo de la mesa.
    Take your hat off. Descúbrase. Quítese el

    sombrero.
offend ofender.
offended (be) resentirse, enfadarse.
offense ofensa, agravio; delito.
offensive *adj.* ofensivo; desagradable (smell, etc.).
offensive *n.* ofensiva.
offer oferta, ofrecimiento, propuesta.
offer (to) ofrecer.
offering *n.* ofrenda (gift).
office oficina, despacho (a building, a room, etc.);
    juesto, cargo (position).
officer oficial.
official *adj.* oficial.
official *n.* funcionario.
often muchas veces, frecuentemente, a menudo,
    con frecuencia.
oil aceite.
    olive oil aceite de oliva.
    oil painting pintura al óleo.
ointment ungüento.
old viejo, antiguo.
    to be twenty years old tener veinte años.
    old man viejo.
    old age vejez.
    old maid solterona.
olive oliva.
    olive oil aceite de oliva.
    olive tree olivo.
omelette tortilla de huevos.
omission omisión.
omit omitir.
omnibus omníbus.
on sobre, encima de, en; a, al; con, bajo; por.
    on the table sobre la mesa.
    on the train en el tren.
    on that occasion en aquella ocasión.
    on the left a la izquierda
    on my arrival a mi llegada.
    on foot a pie.
    on credit al fiado.
    on time a tiempo, a la hora indicada.
    on my word bajo mi palabra.
    on my part por mi parte.
    on the (an) average por término medio.
    on the contrary por el contrario.
    on the whole en conjunto, en general, por lo
    general.
    on Saturday el sábado.
on *adv.* puesto; comenzado.
    with his hat on con el sombrero puesto.
    The show is on. Ya ha empezado la función.
    and so on y así sucesivamente, etcétera.
once una vez.
    once (and) for all una vez por todas.
    at once cuanto antes, en seguida.
    all at once de una vez, de seguida.
    once more otra vez más.
one (numeral) un, uno.

one se, uno.
    one by one uno a uno, uno por uno.
    one and the same idéntico.
    this one éste.
    the red one el rojo.
onion cebolla.
only *adj.* sólo, único.
only *adv.* solamente, únicamente.
    not only . . . but no sólo . . . sino.
opaque opaco.
open abierto.
open (to) abrir.
opening abertura.
opera ópera.
operate (to) operar; hacer funcionar (a machine, etc.).
    be operated on operarse.
operation operación.
    to have (undergo) an operation operarse.
opinion opinión.
    in my opinion a mi ver.
opponent antagonista, contendiente.
opportune oportuno.
opportunity oportunidad.
oppose oponer, resistir.
opposite opuesto.
opposition oposición.
oppress oprimir.
oppression opresión.
optic óptico.
optician óptico.
optimism optimismo.
optimistic optimista.
or o, u.
oracle oráculo.
oral oral, verbal.
orange naranja.
oratory oratoria.
orchard huerto.
orchestra orquesta.
order orden; pedido (of goods).
    in order that a fin de, para que.
order (to) ordenar (command); hacer un pedido (goods).
ordinarily ordinariamente.
ordinary ordinario, vulgar.
organ órgano.
organic orgánico.
organism organismo.
organization organización.
organize organizar.
organizer organizador.
orient oriente.
oriental oriental.
origin origen, principio.
original original.
originality originalidad.
originate (to) originarse.

ornament ornamento.
orphan huérfano.
ostentation ostentación.
other otro, otra, otros, otras.
    the other day el otro día, hace poco.
    the others los otros.
    Give me the other one. Déme el otro.
ought deber.
    I ought to Debo.
    you ought not to Ud. no debe.
ounce onza.
our(s) nuestro, nuestra, nuestros, nuestras.
out fuera, afuera.
    out of breath sin aliento.
    out of date anticuado.
    out of doors fuera de casa.
    out of order descompuesto.
    out of place fuera de lugar.
    out of print agotada (una edición).
    out of respect for por respeto a.
    out of season que no se da en una estación del año.
    out of style fuera de moda.
    out of the way donde no estorbe; apartado.
    out of work sin trabajo.
outcome resultado.
outdoor(s) fuera de casa; al aire libre, a la intemperie.
outline perfil, contorno; bosquejo, croquis.
outline (to) bosquejar, esbozar, delinear.
output producción, rendimiento.
outrage *n.* atropello, ultraje.
outrageous atroz.
outside externo, exterior; fuera, afuera; fuera de; ajeno.
outstanding sobresaliente, notable, extraordinario.
outward externo; aparente.
    outward bound de ida.
oven horno.
over sobre, encima; al otro lado de; más de; mientras, durante; por; en.
    over night durante la noche.
    to stay over the weekend pasar el fin de semana.
    to be over haber pasado; acabarse, terminarse.
    all over por todas partes.
    all the world over (over the whole world) por todo el mundo.
    over again otra vez.
    over and over repetidas veces.
overcoat gaban, sobretodo, abrigo.
overcome (to) vencer; superar.
overflow (to) rebosar.
overseas ultramar, de ultramar.
oversight inadvertencia, descuido.
overtake alcanzar.
overwhelm abrumar.

overwhelming abrumador, irresistible.
overwork trabajo excesivo.
overwork (to) trabajar demasiado.
owe deber, adeudar.
    owing to debido a.
owl buho, lechuza.
own propio, mismo.
    to write with one's own hand escribir con su
    propio puño.
    my own self yo mismo.
    This is your own. Esto es lo suyo.
own (to) poseer, ser dueño de, tener.
owner amo, dueño, propietario.
ox buey.
oxen bueyes.
oyster ostra.

P

pace paso; portante.
pack (to) empacar, empaquetar, hacer el baúl (la
    maleta), arreglar el equipaje.
package bulto, paquete.
packing n. embalaje.
paddle remo, zagual.
paddle (to) remar.

page página.
pail balde, cubo.
pain n. dolor, dolencia.
painful doloroso.
paint pintura.
paint (to) pintar.
painter pintor.
painting pintura, retrato, cuadro.
pair n. par; pareja.
pajamas pijamas.
palace palacio.
palate paladar.
pale adj. pálido.
    to turn pale palidecer.
paleness palidez.
palm palma (of the hand).
palm tree palmera.
pamphlet folleto.
pancake panqueque, panquec, tortilla hecha con
    harina y azúcar.
pane vidrio, cristal de la ventana (glass).
panel panel; painel.
panic pánico.
pant (to) jadear.
pantry despensa.
pants pantalones.
papa papá.
paper papel.
    writing paper papel de escribir.
    newspaper diario, periódico.
parade parada.
paradise paraíso.

paragraph párrafo, aparte.
parallel adj. paralelo.
paralysis parálisis.
paralyze paralizar.
parcel paquete.
    Send it parcel post. Mándelo como paquete
    postal. Envíelo por encomienda (South
    Amer.).
pardon perdón.
    I beg your pardon. Perdone Ud. ¡Dispense!
    ¡Perdón!
pardon (to) perdonar, dispensar.
    Pardon me. Perdone Ud. Perdóneme. Dis-
    pénseme.
parenthesis (parentheses) paréntesis.
parents padres.
parish parroquia.
park parque.
park (to) estacionar (cars).
parking estacionamiento (cars).
parliament parlamento.
parliamentary parlamentario.
parlor sala.
parrot loro.
parsley perejil.
part parte.
    a great (large) part of la mayor parte de.
    part of speech parte de la oración.
    for one's part por lo que a uno toca.
    to do one's part cumplir uno con su obliga-
    ción, hacer uno su parte, hacer lo que pueda.
partial parcial.
partially parcialmente.
participant participante, partícipe.
participle participio.
particular adj. particular.
particularly particularmente.
partly en parte, en cierto modo.
partner socio.
party partido; velada, fiesta (entertainment).
pass paso; pase (permit).
pass (to) pasar; ser aprobado (a student, a bill,
    etc.).
passage pasaje.
passenger pasajero, viajero.
passer-by transeúnte.
passion pasión.
passionate apasionado.
passive pasivo.
past prep. más allá de.
    past ten o'clock las diez dadas, más de la diez.
    half-past seven las siete y media.
past adj. pasado.
    the past year el año pasado.
past n. pasado.
    in the past en otros tiempos, anteriormente.
paste pasta.
pastime distracción, diversión, pasatiempo.

pastry pastelería, pasteles, pastas.
past tense pretérito.
patent patente.
paternal paternal.
path senda, sendero.
patience paciencia.
patient *adj.* paciente.
patient *n.* enfermo, paciente.
patriot patriota.
patriotic patriótico.
patriotism patriotismo.
pave pavimentar.
   to pave the way   preparar (allanar) el camino.
pavement pavimento.
pavilion pabellón.
paw pata.
pawn (to) empeñar.
pawnshop casa de préstamos (empeños), monte
   de piedad.
pay paga, sueldo, salario.
pay (to) pagar; prestar (attention); hacer (a visit).
   to pay attention   prestar atención.
   to pay a call   hacer una visita.
   to pay one's respects   presentar (ofrecer) sus
     respetos.
   to pay on account   pagar a cuenta.
   to pay cash (down)   pagar al contado.
   to pay dearly   costarle a uno caro.
payment pago, paga.
pea guisante; chícharo (Mex.); arveja (Arg., etc.).
peace paz.
peach melocotón, durazno (Amer.).
peanut cacahuate, maní.
pear pera.
pearl perla.
peasant campesino.
peculiar peculiar.
peddler buhonero, vendedor ambulante.
pedestal pedestal.
pedestrian transeúnte, caminante, peatón.
peel cáscara, corteza.
peel (to) pelar, mondar.
peg clavija, estaca.
pen pluma.
penalty pena; multa (fine).
pencil lápiz.
penetrate penetrar.
penetration penetración.
peninsula península.
pension pensión.
pensive pensativo.
people gente; pueblo.
   many people   mucha gente.
   the Spanish people   el pueblo español.
pepper pimienta.
perceive percibir.

per cent por ciento.
percentage porcentaje.

perfect *adj.* perfecto.
   Perfect!   ¡Muy bien!
perfection perfección.
perform ejecutar, poner por obra, llevar algo a
   cabo, desempeñar un cometido.
performance ejecución, actuación, funcionamiento, rendimiento (of a machine); representación, función (theater).
perfume perfume.
perfume (to) perfumar.
perhaps quizá, tal vez, acaso.
period período; punto final (punctuation).
periodical periódico.
perish perecer.
permanent permanente.
permanently permanentemente.
permission permiso.
permit (to) permitir.
perpendicular perpendicular.
perplex (to) confundir, dejar perplejo.
perplexed perplejo.
persecute perseguir.
persecution persecución.
persist persistir, empeñarse, obstinarse.
persistent persistente.
person persona.
personal personal.
personality personalidad.
personally personalmente.
personnel personal, empleados; tripulantes
   (crew).
persuade persuadir, inducir.
persuasion persuasión.
persuasive persuasivo.
pertaining perteneciente, concerniente, tocante,
   relativo.
pessimist pesimista.
pessimistic pesimista.
petal pétalo.
petition petición.
petroleum petróleo.
petty insignificante, trivial, sin importancia (trifling).
   petty thief   ladronzuelo.
   petty cash   dinero para gastos menudos,
     gastos menores de caja.
pharmacist farmacéutico.
pharmacy farmacia.
phase fase.
phenomenon fenómeno.
philosopher filósofo.
philosophical filosófico.
philosophy filosofía.
phone *n.* teléfono.
phone (to) telefonear.
phonograph fonógrafo, gramófono.
photograph fotografía.
photograph (to) fotografiar, retratar.

to be photographed retratarse.
physical físico.
physician médico.
physics física.
piano piano.
pick (to) escoger (choose).
    to pick up alzar, levantar (with the fingers),
      acelerar (speed); tomar incremento (busi-
      ness); restablecerse (to recover).
    to pick a quarrel buscar camorra.
    to have a bone to pick with habérselas con
      uno.
pickle encurtido, pepinillo.
picnic picnic, jira, partida de campo.
picture retrato, foto, cuadro, pintura, grabado.
    to be in the picture figurar en el asunto.
    to be out of the picture no figurar ya para
      nada.
picturesque pintoresco.
piece pedazo, trozo.
pier muelle.
pig puerco.
pigeon paloma.
pill píldora.
pillow almohada, almohadón, cojín.
pilot piloto.
pin *n.* alfiler.
pinch pellizcar.
pink rosado.
pipe pipa (smoking); tubo, caño, tubería, cañería
    (for water, etc.).
pistol pistola.
pitch pez, brea, alquitrán (tar); tono (music).
pitcher jarro, cántaro (for water, etc.); pitcher,
    lanzador (in baseball).
pitiful lastimoso.
pity lástima, piedad, compasión.
    It's a pity. Es lástima.
    What a pity! ¡Qué lástima!
    Out of pity. Por compasión.
    to have pity tener piedad.
pity (to) compadecer.
place lugar, sitio, parte, local.
    in the first place en primer lugar.
    in the next place luego, en segundo lugar.
    in place en su lugar.
    in place of en lugar de.
    out of place fuera de lugar (propósito).
    to take place tener lugar.
place (to) colocar, poner.
plain llano, simple, sencillo; franco.
    plain speaking hablando con franqueza.
    plain truth la pura verdad.
    plain food alimentos sencillos.
    a plain dress un vestido sencillo.
plan plan; plano (of a city, etc.).
plan (to) proyectar, hacer planes, pensar.

planet planeta.
plant planta.
plant (to) plantar, sembrar.
plantation plantación.
planter sembrador; colono, hacendado (owner of
    a plantation).
plaster yeso.
plastic plástico.
plate plato (food); plancha, lámina (metal in
    sheets); estereotipo, clisé (printing); placa
    (photography).
    a plate of soup un plato de sopa.
plateau meseta.
platform plataforma; andén (railroad station).
play juego (game); drama, representación, fun-
    ción (theater).
play (to) jugar; tocar (to play an instrument); dar,
    representar, poner en escena (in a theater).
    to play a part representar un papel.
    to play a game jugar una partida (un partido).
    to play a joke hacer una broma.
    to play a trick on someone hacer una mala
      jugada.
player jugador.
playful juguetón.
playground patio de recreo, campo de deportes.
plea ruego, súplica; alegato (law).
plead (to) rogar, suplicar; alegar, defender una
    causa (law).
pleasant agradable; grato; simpático (of a person).
please (to) gustar, agradar; complacer, dar gusto.
    I'm pleased. Estoy satisfecho. Estoy contento.
    It pleases me. Me place. Me agrada.
    It doesn't please me. No me agrada.
    He was quite pleased. Quedó bastante com-
      placido.
    please hágame el favor, por favor.
    Please tell me. Hágame el favor de decirme.
      Sírvase decirme.
    Pleased to meet you. Mucho gusto de cono-
      cerle.
pleasing agradable.
pleasure placer, gusto.
plenty abundancia.
plot *n.* complot, intriga (scheme); solar (of land);
    trama (of a novel, play, etc.).
plow arado.
plow (to) arar.
plug enchufe (electric plug).
plum ciruela.
plumber plomero.
plumbing plomería, instalación de cañerías.
plump gordo, rollizo.
plural plural.
plus más.
pocket bolsillo.
poem poema.
poetic poético.

poetry poesía.
point punto; punta (of a pin, etc.).
  point of view punto de vista.
  to the point al grano.
point (to) señalar.
  to point out indicar, señalar.
pointed puntiagudo; agudo.
poise porte; aplomo.
poison veneno.
poison (to) envenenar.
poisoning envenenamiento.
poisonous venenoso.
polar polar.
pole polo (north pole, etc.); poste, palo (of wood).
police policía.
policeman policía, agente de policía.
police station comisaría.
policy política (of government, etc.); norma,
  sistema, costumbre (a settled course);
  póliza (insurance).
  insurance policy póliza de seguro.
polish pulimento, lustre, pasta o líquido para
  sacar brillo.
  shoe polish betún.
polish (to) pulir, lustrar.
polished pulido.
polite cortés.
political político.
politician político.
politics política.
pond laguna, charca.
pool piscina (swimming pool).
poor pobre.
pope papa.
poppy adormidera, amapola.
popular popular.
popularity popularidad.
populate (to) poblar.
population población.
porch vestíbulo, portal, porche.
pore poro.
pork puerco, cerdo; carne de puerco (meat).
  pork chops chuletas de puerco.

port puerto (harbor).
portable portátil.
porter mozo; portero (building).
portion porción, parte.
portrait retrato.
  portrait painter retratista.
position posición.
positive positivo.
positively positivamente, ciertamente.
possess poseer.
possession posesión.
  to take possession of posesionarse de.
possessive posesivo.
possessor poseedor.
possibility posibilidad.

possible posible.
  as soon as possible cuanto antes.
possibly quizá, quizás, posiblemente.
post n. poste, pilar (pillar, etc.); correo (post
  office); puesto, guarnición (soldiers).
  post card tarjeta postal.
  post office correo, oficina (casa) de correos.
  post office box apartado de correos.
postage franqueo.
postage stamp sello (de correo), estampilla.
postal postal.
postal card tarjeta postal.
posterity posteridad.
postman cartero.
postscript posdata.
pot marmita, puchero, olla.
potato patata, papa (Amer.).
  fried potatoes patatas fritas.
  mashed potatoes puré de patatas (papas).
pound libra.
pour verter, vaciar; llover a cántaros (rain).
poverty pobreza.
powder polvo (for the face, teeth, etc.); pólvora
  (gunpowder).
  tooth powder polvo dentífrico.
  face powder polvos para la cara.
  powder box polvera.
power poder, fuerza, potencia, energía.
  electric power energía eléctrica.
  horse power caballo de fuerza.
  electromotive power fuerza motriz.
  the great powers las grandes potencias.
  power of attorney poder.
  to grant power of attorney dar poder.
  civil power autoridad civil.
powerful poderoso.
practicable practicable.
practical práctico.
practice práctica; regla, uso (usage); costumbre
  (habit); ejercicio (of a profession).
practice (to) practicar; ejercer (a profession).
praise alabanza, elogio.
praise (to) elogiar, alabar, encomiar.
prank travesura.
pray rezar, orar (to God).
prayer rezo, oración, plegaria.
precede (to) anteceder, preceder.
precedent precedente.
preceding precedente, anterior.
  preceding year el año anterior.
precept precepto.
precious precioso.
precipice precipicio.
precise preciso, exacto.
precisely precisamente, exactamente.
precision precisión.
precocious precoz.
predecessor predecesor.

predicament situación difícil, dificultad, apuro.
predict predecir.
prediction predicción.
predominant predominante.
preface preámbulo, prólogo.
prefer preferir.
preferable preferente, preferible.
preferably preferiblemente, preferentemente.
preference preferencia.
preferred preferente, preferido, predilecto.
prejudice *n.* prejuicio.
preliminary preliminar.
premature prematuro.
preparation preparación.
prepare preparar.
preposition preposición.
prescribe prescribir; recetar (medicine).
prescription prescripción, receta.
presence presencia.
present presente; regalo, obsequio (gift).
    at present   al presente, ahora.
    for the present   por ahora.
    in the present   al presente, actualmente.
    present participle   participio presente, gerundio.
    present-day   actual.
    the present month   el actual, el corriente.
    to give a present   hacer un regalo, regalar.
    to be present   asistir, estar presente.
present (to)   presentar, dar a conocer; dar un regalo, regalar (to make a gift).
presentation presentación.
presentiment presentimiento.
preservation preservación.
preserve preservar, conservar.
preside presidir.
president presidente.
press prensa (machine, daily press); imprenta (printing plant).
    the press   la prensa.
press (to)   apretar, prensar; planchar (clothes); apremiar, instar (to urge).
pressing urgente, apremiante.
pressure presión.
prestige prestigio.
presumable presumible.
presume presumir.
pretend pretender.
pretense pretensión, apariencia, disimulo.
    under pretense of   so pretexto de.
    under false pretenses   bajo falsas apariencias.
pretension pretensión.
preterite pretérito.
pretext pretexto.
pretty *adj.*   bello, bonito, lindo.
pretty *adv.*   algo, un poco, algún tanto; bastante.
    pretty tired   algo cansado.
    pretty good   bastante bueno.

pretty near   bastante cerca.
    pretty well   medianamente, así así.
    pretty much   casi (almost).
    pretty much the same   parecido, casi lo mismo.
prevail (to)   reinar, prevalecer, predominar.
    to prevail over   vencer, triunfar.
    to prevail upon   persuadir, convencer.
prevent prevenir, impedir.
prevention prevención.
previous previo.
    previous to   antes de.
    previous question   cuestión previa.
previously previamente, de antemano.
price precio.

pride orgullo.
    to take pride in   preciarse de.
priest sacerdote, cura.
primarily principalmente; en primer lugar.
primary primario, primero, principal (first, principal); elemental (elementary).
    primary color   color elemental.
    primary school   escuela primaria.
prince príncipe.
principal principal.
principally principalmente.
principle principio.
    in principle   en principio.
    as a matter of principle   como cuestión de principios, por principio.
    on general principles   por regla general, por sistema, por costumbre.
print (to)   imprimir.
printed impreso.
    printed matter   impresos.
printer impresor.
printing tipografía, imprenta; impresión.
prior *adj.*   anterior. precedente, previo.
    prior to   antes de.
prison cárcel, prisión.
prisoner preso; prisionero (of war).
private privado, particular, personal, confidencial, reservado, secreto.
    private affair   asunto de carácter privado.
    private hearing   audiencia secreta.
    private office   despacho particular.
    private secretary   secretario particular.
    in private   en secreto, confidencialmente.
privately en secreto, reservadamente.
privilege privilegio.
prize premio.
pro pro.
probability probabilidad.
probable probable.
probably probablemente.
problem problema.
procedure procedimiento, proceder.
proceed seguir, proseguir, proceder.

process procedimiento, método (method); proceso (of growth, etc.); curso (of time); causa, procedimiento (law).
　in the process of　en vía de, haciéndose.
　in the process of time　con el tiempo, en el curso del tiempo.
procession cortejo; procesión.
proclaim proclamar.
proclamation proclama, proclamación.
produce producir, rendir.
product producto.
production producción.
productive productivo.
profession profesión.
professional profesional.
professor profesor.
proficient proficiente, experto.
profile perfil.
profit beneficio, ganancia.
profit (to) sacar provecho, ganar.
　to profit by　sacar partido de, sacar provecho de, beneficiarse con.
profitable provechoso, útil, lucrativo.
program programa.
progress progreso, adelanto.
progress (to) progresar, adelantar, hacer progresos.
progressive progresivo.
prohibit prohibir.
prohibited prohibido.

　prohibited by law　prohibido por la ley.
prohibition prohibición.
project proyecto, plan.
project (to) proyectar.
prolong prolongar.
prominent prominente.
　to be prominent　sobresalir, ser prominente.
promise promesa.
promise (to) prometer.
promote promover, ascender (in grade); fomentar (industry, etc.).
promotion promoción, ascenso (in grade); fomento (of industry).
prompt pronto.
promptly pronto, prontamente.
promptness prontitud.
pronoun pronombre.
pronounce pronunciar.
pronunciation pronunciación.
proof prueba.
propaganda propaganda.
propeller hélice (of a ship, plane, etc.).
proper propio, conveniente, adecuado (right, fit); correcto, decoroso (correct).
properly propiamente, apropiadamente; correctamente.
property propiedad.
prophecy profecía.

prophesy (to) predecir, profetizar.
proportion proporción.
　in proportion　en proporción.
　out of proportion　desproporcionado.
proposal propuesta, proposición.
propose proponer.
proprietor dueño, propietario.
prosaic prosaico.
prose prosa.
prosper prosperar.
prosperity prosperidad.
prosperous próspero.
protect proteger.
protection protección.
protector protector.
protest protesta.
protest (to) protestar.
Protestant protestante.
proud orgulloso.
prove establecer, probar; resultar (to turn out).
proverb refrán, proverbio.
provide proveer.
　to provide oneself with　proveerse de.
　provided that　con tal que, a condición de que.
providence providencia.
province provincia.
provincial provinciano.
provisions provisiones, víveres, comestibles.
prudence prudencia.
prudent prudente.
prune ciruela pasa.
psychological psicológico.
psychology psicología.
public público
publication publicación.
publicity publicidad.
publish publicar.
publisher editor.
publishing house casa editorial, casa editora.
pudding pudín, budín.
pull (to) tirar de, tirar hacia, arrastrar.
　to pull in　tirar hacia uno.
　to pull out (off)　arrancar.
　to pull up　desarraigar.
　to pull apart　despedazar, hacer pedazos.

　to pull through　salir de un apuro.
pulpit púlpito.
pulse pulso.
pump bomba.
punctual puntual.
punctuate puntuar.
punctuation puntuación.
puncture n. pinchazo.
punish castigar.
punishment castigo.
pupil alumno (school); pupila (eye).
purchase compra.
purchase (to) comprar.

purchaser comprador.

pure puro.

purely puramente, meramente, simplemente.

purple púrpura, cárdeno.

purpose propósito, fin, objeto, intención.
 on purpose intencionadamente, de propósito.
 to no purpose inútilmente.
 for the purpose a propósito, al caso.
 With what purpose? ¿Con qué fin?

purse portamonedas (change purse).

pursue perseguir.

pursuit persecución.

push empujar.

put (to) poner, colocar.
 to put away poner aparte, apartar.
 to put in order arreglar, ordenar.
 to put off diferir, aplazar.
 to put up for sale poner en venta.
 to put up with tolerar, aguantar.
 to put on vestir, ponerse (clothes); ponerse gordo (weight).
 Put on your hat! ¡Cúbrase!
 to put on the spot poner en aprieto.
 to put out apagar (a light, etc.); publicar (a book, etc.).
 to put out of the way quitar, apartar, poner algo donde no estorbe.
 to put to bed acostar.
 to put to sleep hacer dormir.
 to put together juntar; armar (a machine, etc.).
 to put to a vote poner a votación.

puzzle n. enigma, rompecabezas (crossword, etc.).

puzzled (be) (estar) perplejo.

Q

quaint curioso, raro.

qualify calificar.

quality calidad; cualidad (of character).

quantity cantidad.

quart litro, cuarto de galón.

quarter cuarto (fourth).
 a quarter hour un cuarto de hora.

quarters alojamiento; cuartel (for soliders).

queen reina.

queer extraño, raro.
 a queer person un tipo raro.

quell reprimir, sofocar.

quench apagar.

question pregunta.
 to ask a question hacer una pregunta.
 to be a question of tratarse de.
 question mark signo de interrogación.
 What's the question? ¿De qué se trata?
 without any question sin duda.
 to be out of the question ser completamente ajeno al asunto, no haber ni que pensar.

questioning n. interrogatorio.

quick pronto, rápido, presto.

quickly prontamente, rápidamente, con presteza.
 Come quickly. Venga pronto.

quiet quieto, tranquilo.

quiet (to) calmar, tranquilizar.

quietly quietamente, tranquilamente.

quietness quietud, tranquilidad.

quilt edredón, cobertor, colcha.

quinine quinina.

quit dejar, parar, cesar de, desistir de.
 to quit work dejar de trabajar.

quite bastante, más bien; muy.
 quite good bastante bueno.
 quite soon bastante de prisa.
 quite difficult harto difícil.
 quite well done muy bien hecho.
 She seems quite different! ¡Parece otra!

quotation citación, cita, texto citado.
 quotation marks comillas.

quote (to) citar.

R

rabbit conejo.

race n. correra; raza (ethnic).

radiance brillo, esplendor.

radiant radiante, brillante.

radiator radiador

radio radio.

radio station radioemisora, emisora.

radish rábano.

rag trapo.

rage rabia, ira, cólera.

rage (to) rabiar, enfurecerse.

ragged andrajoso, harrapiento.

rail riel, rail (for vehicle).

railroad ferrocarril.
 by railroad por ferrocarril.

railway ferrocarril.

rain lluvia.

rain (to) llover.

rainbow arco iris.

raincoat impermeable.

rainfall cantidad de agua que cae durante un tiempo determinado.

rainy lluvioso.

raise aumento (salary).

raise (to) levantar, alzar, elevar; aumentar, subir (prices, salary); criar (animals); cultivar (a crop).
 to raise an objection objetar, poner una objeción.
 to raise a question suscitar una cuestión.
 to raise a row armar un alboroto, armar un lío.

to raise money   reunir dinero.
raisin   pasa.
rake   rastrillo.
rake (to)   rastrillar.
ranch   rancho, hacienda.
range   alcance (of a gun, of the voice, etc.); radio
  de acción (of a plane, etc.); cadena (of
  mountains).
  range of mountains   sierra, cordillera, cadena
  de montañas.
rank   grado (army, etc.); hilera (line of soldiers);
  posición (social rank).
  rank and file   la masa, la base; la tropa
  (military).
ransom   rescate.
rapid   rápido.
rapidity   rapidez.
rapidly   rápidamente.
rare   raro.
rarely   raramente.
rascal   granuja, pícaro, bribón.
rash *adj.*   arrebatado, temerario (reckless).
rash *n.*   sarpullido.
rat   rata.
rate   tarifa, precio.
  at the rate of   a razón de.
  rate of interest   tipo de interés.
  rate of exchange   tipo de cambio.
  at any rate   de todos modos, sea como fuere.
rather   más bien, un poco, algo.
  rather expensive   algo caro.
  rather than   más bien que, antes que.
ratio   proporción, razón.
ration   ración.
rational   racional.
rationing   racionamiento.
raw   crudo.
  in a raw state   en bruto.
  raw materials   materias primas.
ray   rayo.
rayon   rayón.
razor   navaja.
  razor blade   hoja de afeitar.
  safety razor   maquinilla de afeitar.
reach   alcance (range).
  beyond one's reach   fuera del alcance de uno.
  within one's reach   al alcance de uno, dentro
  del poder de uno.
reach (to)   alcanzar, llegar a, llegar hasta (arrive
  at).
  to reach the end   terminar, llegar al fin,
  lograr su objeto.
  to reach out one's hand   extender la mano.
react   reaccionar.
reaction   reacción.
reactionary   reaccionario.
read (to)   leer.
readable   legible.

reader   lector.
reading   lectura.
reading room   sala de lectura.
ready   listo.
ready-made   confeccionado, ya hecho.
ready-made clothes   ropa hecha.
real   real, verdadero.
  real estate   bienes raíces.
reality   realidad.
realization   realización; comprensión, conciencia
  cierta (understanding, awareness).
realize (to)   darse cuenta, hacerse cargo; llevar a
  cabo, realizar, obtener.
  to realize a danger   darse cuenta del peligro.
  to realize a project   llevar a cabo un proyecto.
  to realize a profit   obtener un beneficio,
  lograr un provecho.
really   en verdad, realmente, verdaderamente.
  Really!   ¡De veras!
reap   segar.
rear *adj.*   de atrás, trasero, posterior.
rear *n.*   parte posterior.
reason   razón, juicio, causa.
  by reason of   con motivo de, a causa de.
  for this reason   por esto.
  without reason   sin razón.
reason (to)   razonar, raciocinar.
reasonable   razonable; módico.
reasonably   razonablemente.
reasoning   razonamiento.
rebel   rebelde.
rebel (to)   rebelarse.
rebellion   rebelión.
rebellious   rebelde, refractario.
recall (to)   recordar (remember).
  to recall to mind   recapacitar.
receipt   recibo.
  to acknowledge receipt   acusar recibo.
receipts . ingresos.
receive   recibir.
receiver   receptor.
recent   reciente.
recently   recientemente.
reception   recepción, acogida.
recipe   receta de cocina.
recite   recitar.
reckless   temerario.
recklessly   temerariamente.
recline   reclinar.
recognition   reconocimiento.
recognize   reconocer.
recoil (to)   recular, retroceder.
recollect   recordar (to remember).
recollection   recuerdo, reminiscencia.
recommend   recomendar.
recommendation   recomendación.
reconcile   conciliar, reconciliar.
reconciliation   reconciliación.

record n. registro; acta; disco (phonograph); record (sports); constancia, comprobante (voucher, etc.).
    on record registrado, que consta, que hay o queda constancia.
records datos, memorias, archivo, anales.
recover recobrar.
    to recover one's health reponerse, recobrar la salud.
recovery restablecimiento (of health); recuperación (of money, etc.).
recreation recreación, recreo.
recuperate restablecerse, recuperarse.
red rojo, colorado.
reduce reducir, rebajar.
reduction reducción, rebaja.
refer referir; recurrir.
    to refer to recurrir a, acudir.
reference referencia.
    reference book libro de referencia, fuente de referencia.
referring referente.
refine refinar.
refinement cortesía, cultura, esmero.
reflect reflejar (light); reflexionar (think).
reflection reflejo (light); reflexión (thought).
reform reforma.
reform (to) reformar; reformarse.
refrain (from) refrenarse, abstenerse de.
refresh refrescar.
    to refresh one's memory recordar, refrescar la memoria.
    a refreshing drink refresco.
refreshment refresco.
refrigerator refrigeradora, nevera.
refuge refugio, asilo.
refugee refugiado, asilado.
refusal negativa.
refuse rehusar.
refute refutar, rebatir.
regard consideración, respeto.
    in regard to en cuanto a, respecto a, con respecto a.
    in this regard en este respecto.
    with regard to con respecto a, a propósito de.
    without any regard to sin miramientos de, sin hacer caso de.
regard (to) estimar, considerar, mirar.
regarding relativo a, respecto de, concirniente a.
regardless of a pesar de.
regards recuerdos, memorias, afectos.
    to give (send) one's regards dar memorias, dar recuerdos.
regime régimen.
regiment regimiento.
region región.
register registro.
register (to) inscribir, registrar.

    registered letter carta certificada.
regret pesar, pena, remordimiento.
regret (to) sentir, deplorar, lamentar.
    I regret it. Lo siento.
    I regret that. Siento que.
regular regular.
regularity regularidad.
regularly regularmente.
regulation reglamento, regla, regulación, reglamentación.
rehearsal ensayo.
rehearse ensayar (theater).
reign reinado.
reign (to) reinar.
reject rechazar, repeler, negar, desechar.
rejection rechazamiento, repudiación.
rejoice alegrar, regocijarse.
rejoicing regocijo.
relate relatar, contar (tell).
    to be related estar emparentado (kinship); relacionarse (be connected with).
    everything relating to cuanto se relaciona con.
relation relación; pariente (a relative).
relationship relación; parentesco (family).
relative adj. relativo.
relative pariente (family).
release (to) soltar; dar al público (release news); exonerar, descargar (from a debt, penalty, etc.).
reliability confianza.
reliable digno de confianza.
relief alivio (from pain); socorro (aid); relevo (of a sentry, etc.).
relieve aliviar (from pain); socorrer, axiliar (to aid); relevar (a sentry, etc.).
religion religión.
religious religioso.
relish (to) saborear; gustar de.
reluctance renuencia, mala gana, disgusto.
    with reluctance de mala gana.
reluctant reluctante, reacio.
reluctantly de mala gana.
rely on (to) confiar en, contar con.
remain quedar; quedarse, permanecer.
    to remain silent callar, guardar silencio.
    to remain undone quedar sin hacer.
remains restos, sobras.
remark observación, nota.
    to make a remark hacer una observación.
remark (to) observar, advertir, comentar, notar.
remarkable notable, interesante, extraordinario.
remarkably notablemente.
remedy remedio.
remedy (to) remediar.
remember recordar, acordarse.
    I don't remember. No me acuerdo.
    Remember me to him. Déle expresiones

mías.

remembrance memoria, recuerdo.

remind recordar.

reminder recordatorio, recuerdo; advertencia.

remit remitir.

remorse remordimiento.

removal remoción, acción de quitar; cesantía, deposición (from a position).

remove mudar, trasladar, cambiar (to take to another place); quitar (a stain, etc.); deponer, destituir, dejar cesante (from a job).

renew renovar; extender, prorrogar (to obtain an extension).

renewal renovación; prórroga (extension).

rent renta, alquiler.

    for rent   se alquila.

rent (to) alquilar, arrendar.

repair reparación, compostura, remiendo.

repair (to) reparar, componer.

repeal (to) derogar, revocar.

repeat repetir.

repeated repetido, reiterado.

repeatedly repetidamente, repetidas veces.

repetition repetición.

reply respuesta, contestación.

reply (to) contestar, responder.

report relación, informe, parte.

    to give a report   dar un informe.

report (to) informar, dar parte; denunciar (to the police).

    to report on the progress of   dar cuenta de la marcha de.

    it is reported   se dice, corre la voz.

represent representar.

representation representación.

representative representante, agente; diputado (to Congress, etc.).

reproach censura, reproche.

reproach (to) reprochar, censurar.

reproduce reproducir.

reproduction reproducción.

reptile reptil, lagarto.

republic república.

reputation reputación.

request ruego, petición.

request (to) pedir, rogar.

rescue rescate; salvamento.

rescue (to) rescatar; salvar, librar.

resemblance semejanza, parecido.

resemble (to) parecerse a.

    She resembles her mother.   Se parece a su madre.

resent resentirse de, ofenderse por.

reservation reservación.

    to make a reservation   mandar a reservar.

reserve reserva.

    without reserve   sin reserva; con toda franqueza.

    Speak without reserve.   Hable con franqueza.

reserve (to) reservar.

reside residir, morar.

residence residencia.

resident residente.

resign resignar, renunciar; resignarse (to resign oneself).

resignation resignación; renuncia (of a position, etc.).

resist resistir; rechazar, oponerse, negarse a (to repel, to refuse).

resistance resistencia.

resolute resuelto.

resolution resolución.

resolve resolver; resolverse.

resource recurso.

respect respecto; respeto (esteem, regard).

    in this respect   a este respecto.

    in some respect   en cierto sentido.

    in (with) respect to   tocante a, con respecto a.

    with due respect   con todo respeto.

    in all respects   en todo sentido, en todos sus aspectos.

    in every respect   en todo sentido.

respect (to) respetar.

respectable respetable.

respected considerado.

respectful respetuoso.

respective respectivo.

response respuesta.

responsibility responsabilidad.

    on your (own) responsibility   bajo su responsabilidad.

responsible responsable.

rest resto (what is left over), descanso, reposo (when tired).

rest (to) reposar, descansar.

restaurant restaurant.

restful sosegado, tranquilo.

restless inquieto.

restore restaurar, reponer.

result resultado, consecuencia.

result (to) resultar.

    to result in   venir a parar, acabar en, conducir a, causar.

retail venta al por menor.

retail (to) vender al por menor.

return vuelta.

    in return   a cambio.

    by return mail   a vuelta de correo.

    return trip   viaje de vuelta.

    Many happy returns!   ¡Feliz cumpleaños!

return (to) volver, regresar (to go or come back); devolver (to give back).

    to return a book   devolver un libro.

    to return a favor   corresponder a un favor.

    to return home   regresar a casa.

review revista; examen, análisis (examination);

revisión (law).
review (to) revisar; pasar revista, revistar (mil.).
revise revisar.
revision revisión.
revive hacer revivir, resucitar.
revolt rebelión.
revolt (to) rebelarse.
revolution revolución.
reward recompensa.
reward (to) recompensar.
rheumatism reuma, reumatismo.
rhyme rima.
rhythm ritmo.
rib costilla (anatomy).
ribbon cinta.
rice arroz.
   Chicken and rice. Arroz con pollo.
rich rico; muy sazonado, muy fuerte (food).
riches riqueza, riquezas.
riddle acertijo, adivinanza, enigma.
ride paseo en coche (in a car); paseo a caballo (on horseback).
ride (to) cabalgar, montar a caballo (on horseback); ir en coche, pasear en automóvil (in a car).
ridiculous ridículo.
rifle fusil.
right *adj.* derecho; recto, justo (just); correcto (correct); adecuado (fit).
   the right man el hombre, el hombre que se necesita, el hombre adecuado.
   right hand mano derecha.
   the right time la hora exacta, la hora justa.
   at the right time a buen tiempo, a su debido tiempo.
   right or wrong bueno o malo, con razón o sin ella.
   right side lado derecho.
   Is this right? ¿Está bien esto?
   It's right. Está bien. Es justo.
   It's not right. No es justo. No está bien.
   to be right tener razón.
right derecho.
   to be in the right tener razón.
   to the right a la derecha.
   to keep to the right seguir por la derecha.
   to have a right tener derecho.
   by rights de (por) derecho, con razón.
right *adv.* bien; rectamente, justamente, correctamente, perfectamente, propiamente; mismo.
   right here aquí mismo.
   right away inmediatamente, en seguida.
   right now ahora mismo, al instante.
   all right bien, está bien.
   Everything is all right. Todo va bien.
   Go right ahead. Siga todo derecho. Vaya todo seguido.
   right along sin cesar.

   right in the middle en plena actividad, en medio de.
   to know right well saber perfectamente bien.
ring anillo.
ring (to) tocar, sonar.
riot motín.
riot (to) amotinarse, armar motines.
ripe maduro.
ripen madurar.
rise *n.* subida; alza (prices).
   sunrise salida del sol.
rise (to) subir, ascender (to move upward); levantarse (to stand up, to get up); salir (the sun); sublevarse (to rebel); alzar (prices); aumentar (salary).
risk riesgo.
   to run the risk arriesgar, correr el riesgo.
risk (to) arriesgar.
river río.
road camino.
   main road camino principal.
roar rugido.
roar (to) rugir, bramar.
roast asado.
   roast chicken pollo asado.
roast (to) asar.
   roast beef rosbif, carne de vaca asada.
rob robar.
robber ladrón.
robbery robo.
rock roca, peña, peñasco.
rock (to) mecer.
rocking chair mecedora.
rocky rocoso, peñascoso, rocalloso.
roll rollo; panecillo (bread).
roll (to) rodar; arrollar, enrollar (to roll up).
romance romance; novela (novel).
romantic romántico.
roof techo.
room cuarto, pieza, habitación; lugar, sitio, espacio (space).
   inside room cuarto interior.
   to make room hacer lugar.
   There's not enough room. No hay suficiente sitio.
   There's not enough room in the trunk for all my clothes. No cabe toda mi ropa en el baúl.
   There's no room for doubt. No cabe duda.
rooster gallo.
root raíz.
rooted arraigado.
rope cuerda, cordel.
   to be at the end of one's rope estar sin recursos.
rose rosa.
rosebush rosal.
rotary giratorio, rotativo.
   rotary press rotativa.

rouge colorete.

rough áspero, rudo, tosco.

   rough draft borrador.

   rough sea mar alborotado (agitado).

   a rough guess a ojo, a ojo de buen cubero, aproximadamente.

   rough diamond diamante en bruto.

round *adj.* redondo.

   a round table una mesa redonda.

   round number número redondo.

   round sum suma redonda.

   round trip viaje de ida y vuelta; viaje redondo (Mex.).

   all year round todo el año, el año entero.

round tanda, vuelta (of drinks, etc.).

route ruta, vía, camino, curso, itinerario.

routine rutina.

row fila, hilera (rank, file); camorra, trifulca, riña (brawl).

row (to) remar.

rub (to) frotar.

rubber goma, caucho.

   rubber band goma, elástico.

   rubbers chanclos, zapatos de goma.

rude rudo, descortés, tosco, chabacano.

rudeness descortesía, grosería.

rug alfombra, tapete.

ruin ruina.

rule regla, norma; reinado, dominio (reign).

   as a rule por lo general, por regla general.

   to be the rule ser la regla, ser de reglamento.

rule (to) gobernar, mandar (to govern); rayar (to draw lines); disponer, determinar (court); establecer una regla (to establish a rule).

   to rule out descartar, excluir, no admitir.

   to rule over mandar, dominar.

ruler gobernante; regla (for drawing lines).

rumor rumor.

run correr; andar, funcionar (a watch, a machine, etc.).

   to run across tropezar con.

   to run into chocar con, topar con.

   to run away escapar, huir.

   to run the risk of correr el riesgo de, arriesgar.

   to run over derramarse, salirse (a liquid); atropellar (a car, etc.).

   to run up and down correr de una parte a otra.

   to run wild desenfrenarse.

rural rural.

rush prisa (haste).

   in a rush de prisa.

rush (to) ir de presa, apresurarse.

   to rush in entrar precipitadamente.

   to rush through ejecutar de prisa, hacer algo de prisa.

rust moho, herrumbre.

rust (to) enmohecer, enmohecerse, aherrumbrarse.

rusty mohoso, enmohecido, herrumbroso.

rye centeno.

S

Sabbath sábado, día de descanso.

sack saco.

sacred sagrado.

sacrifice sacrificio.

sacrifice (to) sacrificar.

sad triste.

saddle silla de montar.

saddle (to) ensillar.

sadly tristemente.

sadness tristeza.

safe caja fuerte, caja de caudales.

safe *adj.* seguro; salvo, ileso (unhurt); sin peligro (safe from danger); sin riesgo (safe from risk).

   safe and sound sano y salvo.

   Safe trip. Feliz viaje.

safely a salvo.

safety seguridad.

   safety razor maquinilla de afeitar.

   safety zone zona de seguridad.

   safety bolt cerrojo de seguridad.

sail vela; buque de vela, velero (boat).

sail (to) darse a la vela, zarpar; navegar.

saint santo.

   Saint Valentine's Day día de San Valentín.

sake causa, motivo, amor, bien, consideración.

   for your sake por Ud., por su bien; por consideración a Ud.

   for the sake of por causa de, por amor de, por, para mayor.

   for the sake of brevity por brevedad, para mayor brevedad.

   for mercy's sake por misericordia.

   for God's sake por Dios, por amor de Dios.

salad ensalada.

salary sueldo, salario.

sale venta.

   for sale de (en) venta.

salesclerk vendedor, dependiente.

salesgirl vendedora, dependiente.

salesman vendedor.

saleswoman vendedora.

salmon salmón.

salt sal.

salt (to) salar.

saltcellar salero.

salted salado.

same mismo, propio, igual.

   the same lo mismo, el mismo, los mismos; otro tanto.

   all the same todo es uno.

   It's all the same to me. Lo mismo me da, me es igual.

   if it's the same to you si le es a Ud. igual.

much the same   casi lo mismo.
the same as   lo mismo que, el mismo que, los mismos que.
sample   muestra.
sand   arena.
sandpaper   papel de lija.
sandwich   sandwich, emparedado.
sandy   arenoso.
sane   sano.
sanitarium   sanatorio.
sanitary   sanitario.
sanitation   saneamiento.
sanity   cordura, juicio sano.
sap   savia; zapa (trench).
sarcasm   sarcasmo.
sarcastic   sarcástico.
sardine   sardina.
satan   satanás.

satin   raso.
satire   sátira.
satisfaction   satisfacción.
satisfactorily   satisfactoriamente.
satisfactory   satisfactorio.
satisfied   satisfecho.
satisfy   satisfacer.
Saturday   sábado.
sauce   salsa.
saucer   platillo.
sausage   salchicha, chorizo.
savage   salvaje; silvestre (growing wild).
save *prep.*   salvo, excepto; *conj.* sino, a menos que, a no ser que.
save (to)   salvar, librar (a person); economizar, ahorrar (money).
to save appearances   salvar las apariencias.
savings   ahorros, economías.
savings bank   caja de ahorros.
saw   sierra; serrucho (handsaw).
say   decir.
that is to say   es decir, esto es.
it is said   se dice.
saying   dicho, proverbio, adagio, refrán.
as the saying goes   según el adagio, como dice el refrán.
scale *n.*   escala; platillo (the dish of a balance); balanza, báscula (for weights); escama (of fishes, etc.).
scales   peso, báscula.
scalp   cuero cabelludo.
scandal   escándalo.
scanty   escaso, escatimado.
scar *n.*   cicatriz.
scarce   raro, escaso.
scarcely   apenas, escasamente, con dificultad.
scarcity   escasez.
scarf   bufanda, chalina.
scarlet   escarlata.
scene   escena.

scenery   vista, paisaje; decoración (theater).
scent   aroma, olor.
schedule *n.*   programa, cuadro, lista; horario de trenes (train schedule).
scheme   plan, proyecto, designio; ardid, treta.
school   escuela.
schoolteacher   maestro de escuela.
schoolbook   texto de escuela.
schoolmate   condiscípulo.
schoolroom   aula.
science   ciencia.
scientific   científico.
scientist   hombre de ciencia.
scissors   tijeras.
scold   reñir, regañar.
scorn   desdén, desprecio.
scorn (to)   despreciar.
scornful   despreciativo, desdeñoso.
score   tantos (in games), partitura (music).
score (to)   marcar los tantos, llevar la cuenta (to keep a record in a game, etc.); apuntarse uno un tanto, ganar un tanto (to gain points, etc.).
to score a point   ganar un tanto.
scrape (to)   raspar (on a surface).
scratch   rasguño, arañazo (on the hand, etc.); raspadura, raya (on a table, etc.).
scratch (to)   rascar (from itching), rasguñar, arañar (to cause injury with the claws or nails); rayar (a glass, a table, etc.).
scream (to)   chillar, gritar.
screen *n.*   biombo, mampara (a portable partition); tela metálica, rejilla (for windows, etc.); pantalla, cine (movies); cortina (of smoke); barrera (of fire).
screw   tornillo; rosca (screw thread).
screw (to)   atornillar.
scruple   escrúpulo.
sculptor   escultor.
sculpture   escultura.
sea   mar, océano.
seal   sello; foca (animal).
seal (to)   sellar; lacrar (with wax).
seam   costura.
search   busca, búsqueda (act of looking for); pesquisa, investigación (scrutiny, investigation); registro (for concealed weapons, etc.).
in search of   en busca de.
search (to)   buscar (to search for); registrar (a house, etc.); explorar (to explore); indagar, inquirir, investigar (to inquire, to investigate).
to search after   indagar, preguntar por.
to search for   buscar, procurar.
seasick   mareado.
season   estación (of the year).
in season   en sazón.

out of season   fuera de sazón.

to be in season   ser de la estación, ser del tiempo.

season (to)   sazonar, condimentar (food).

seat n.   asiento.

to take a seat   tomar asiento, sentarse.

front seat   asiento delantero.

back seat   asiento trasero.

second   segundo.

second class   de segunda clase.

second year   el segundo año.

Wait a second!   ¡Espere un instante!

on second thought   después de pensarlo bien.

second to none   sin segundo, sin par.

secondary   secundario.

secondhand   de segunda mano, usado.

secondly   en segundo lugar.

secrecy   secreto, reserva.

secret   secreto.

in secret   en secreto.

secretary   secretario.

private secretary   secretario particular.

section   sección.

secure   seguro, firme.

secure (to)   asegurar; conseguir (obtain).

securely   seguramente, firmemente.

see (to)   ver.

See?   ¿Sabe? ¿Comprende?

Let's see.   A ver. Vamos a ver. Veamos.

to see about   averiguar.

to see someone off   ir a despedir a alguien.

to see someone home   acompañar a alguien a casa.

to see the point   caer en la cuenta, comprender el sentido de lo dicho.

to see a thing through   llevar uno hasta el cabo una cosa.

to see fit   creer conveniente.

to see one's way clear   ver el modo de hacer algo.

to see to   atender a, cuidarse de.

seed   semilla, simiente.

seeing   vista, ver.

seeing that   visto que, puesto que.

seek (to)   buscar.

to seek after   tratar de obtener, buscar.

seem (to)   parecer, figurarse.

it seems to me   me parece.

it seems   parece, a lo que parece.

seize   agarrar (to grasp); coger, prender (to apprehend); á poderarse de (to take possession of); darse cuenta de, comprender (to comprehend).

seldom   rara vez, raramente.

select adj.   selecto, escogido.

select (to)   elegir, escoger.

selection   selección.

self   mismo, por sí mismo; sí, se.

myself   yo mismo, me.

yourself   tu mismo, te.

himself   el mismo, se.

itself   ello mismo, se.

ourselves   nosotros mismos, nos.

yourselves   vosotros mismos, os.

themselves   ellos mismos, se.

oneself   uno mismo, se.

you yourself   tú mismo.

Wash yourself.   Lávate.

by himself   por sí mismo.

I shave myself.   Yo mismo me afeito.

self-conceited   presumido, presuntuoso.

self-confidence   confianza en sí mismo.

self-defense   defensa propia.

self-determination   autonomía, independencia.

self-evident   patente.

selfish   egoísta.

selfishness   egoísmo.

self-sufficient   que se basta a sí mismo.

sell (to)   vender.

senate   senado.

senator   senador.

send (to)   enviar, despachar, mandar, expedir.

to send away   despedir, echar a la calle.

to send word   mandar recado, avisar, enviar a decir.

to send back   devolver, enviar de vuelta.

to send in   hacer entrar.

to send for   enviar por, mandar a buscar.

sending   despacho.

senior   mayor, de mayor edad, más antiguo.

Suarez, Sr.   Suarez padre.

sense n.   sentido.

common sense   sentido común.

to be out of one's senses   haber perdido el juicio.

sensible   sensato, razonable.

sensibly   cuerdamente, sensatamente.

sentence   oración (grammar); sentencia (court).

sentence (to)   sentenciar, condenar.

sentiment   sentimiento.

sentimental   sentimental.

separate adj.   separado, aparte.

under separate cover   por separado.

separate (to)   apartar, separar.

separately   separadamente.

separation   separación.

September   septiembre.

serene   sereno.

sergeant   sargento.

serial adj.   de serie, de orden (a number, etc.); por partes, por entregas (publications); en episodios, en serie (a picture).

series   serie.

in series   en serie.

serious   serio; grave (grave).

seriously   seriamente.

seriousness   seriedad, gravedad.
sermon   sermón.
servant   criado, sirviente; criada, sirvienta (maid).
serve (to)   servir.
    to serve the purpose   venir al caso.
    to serve notice   notificar, hacer saber, dar aviso.
    It serves you right.   Bien se lo merece.
    to serve as   servir de.
service   servicio.
    at your service   servidor, a sus órdenes.
    to be of service   ser útil, servir.
session   sesión.
set adj.   fijo, establecido.
    set price   precio fijo.
set n.   juego.
    tea set   juego de té.
    set of dishes   vajilla.
set (to)   poner.
    to set aside   dar de mano, poner a un lado, apartar; ahorrar (money).
    to set back   atrasar.
    to set free   poner en libertad.
    to set in order   arreglar, poner en orden.
    to set on fire   pegar fuego a.
    to set to work   poner manos a la obra, poner (se) a trabajar.
settle   arreglar, ajustar, saldar (an account, a matter, etc.); instalarse, fijar su residencia, establecerse (to be established); posarse, asentarse (liquids).
    to settle an account   saldar una cuenta.
settlement   acuerdo, arreglo (adjustment of an account, etc.); colonia, caserío (a small village); colonización (colonization).
seven   siete.
seventeen   diecisiete.
seventh   séptimo.
seventy   setenta.
several   varios.
    several times   varias veces.
severe   severo.
severity   severidad.
sew   coser.
sewing   costura.
sewing machine   máquina de coser.
sex   sexo.
shade   sombra.
shade (to)   sombrear, dar sombra.
shadow   sombra.
shady   sombreado, umbroso.
shake   sacudida, temblor; apretón de manos (handshake).
shake (to)   sacudir; temblar (to tremble); estrechar, darse (shake hands); cabecear, mover (one's head).
    to shake one's head   mover la cabeza.
    to shake hands   darse la mano.

    to shake in one's shoes   temblar de miedo.
shall, will (auxiliary)   the future tense of the indicative is formed by adding -é, -ás, -á, -emos, -éis, and -án to the infinitive.
    I shall go   iré.
    you will go   irás.
    he will go   irá.
    we shall go   iremos.
    you will go   iréis.
    they will go   irán.
shame   vergüenza.
shame (to)   avergonzar.
shameful   vergonzóso.
shameless   desvergonzado, sin vergüenza.
shampoo   champú.
shampoo (to)   dar champú, lavar la cabeza.
shape   forma, figura.
shape (to)   formar, dar forma.
share   porción, parte; acción (stock).
share (to)   partir, repartir (to apportion); participar, tomar parte en (to share in).
    to share alike   tener una parte igual.
shareholder   accionista.
sharp   agudo; puntiagudo (sharp-pointed); afilado, cortante (sharp-edged).
    a sharp pain   un dolor punzante (agudo).
    a sharp answer   una respuesta tajante (áspera).
    a sharp curve   una curva muy pronunciada.
    sharp-witted   perspicaz, de ingenio agudo.
    at two o'clock sharp   a las dos en punto.
sharpen   afilar, aguzar; sacar punta a (a pencil).
shatter   destrozar, hacer pedazos, hacer añicos; romperse, hacerse añicos.
shave   afeitada.
shave (to)   afeitar, rasurar (someone); afeitarse, rasurarse (oneself).
shaving   afeitada.
    shaving cream   crema de afeitar.
    shaving brush   brocha de afeitar.
shawl   chal, mantón.
she   ella.
    she-cat   gata.
    she-goat   cabra.
shears   tijeras grandes, cizallas.
shed   cobertizo; cabaña, barraca (a hut).
shed (to)   verter, derramar (tears, etc.).
sheep   oveja(s).
sheet   sábana (bed); hoja, pliego (paper).
shelf   estante.
shell   concha (of mollusks); cáscara (of nuts, eggs, etc.); granada (artillery).
shelter   refugio, abrigo.
    to take shelter   refugiarse, guarecerse.
    to give shelter   albergar, dar albergue.
shelter (to)   guarecer, albergar, refugiar, poner al abrigo, poner a cubierto.
shepherd   pastor.
sheriff   jefe de policía de un condado.

sherry jerez.

shield escudo, resguardo, defensa.

shield (to) defender, amparar, resguardar.

shift cambio; tanda (work).

shift (to) cambiar (gears, etc.).

shine (to) brillar; limpiar, lustrar, dar lustre (to shine shoes).

shining brillante, radiante, reluciente.

shiny lustroso, brillante.

ship buque, barco, vapor.

   merchant ship buque mercante.

ship (to) embarcar; enviar, despachar (goods).

shipment embarque (act of shipping); envío, despacho (dispatch of goods); cargamento (goods shipped).

shipwreck naufragio.

shipyard astillero.

shirt camisa.

   shirt store camisería.

   sport shirt camisa de deporte.

shiver escalofrío, temblor.

shiver (to) tiritar.

shock choque; sacudida (shake); sobresalto, emoción (emotion).

shock (to) sacudir, dar una sacudida (to cause to shake); chocar, ofender (to offend); conmover (to move); escandalizar (to scandalize).

shoe zapato.

   shoe store zapatería.

   shoelaces cordones para los zapatos.

   shoe polish betún, crema para los zapatos.

shoehorn calzador.

shoemaker zapatero.

shoot (to) tirar, disparar.

shooting tiro.

shop tienda.

shop (to) hacer compras, ir de tiendas.

   to go shopping ir de compras.

shore costa.

short corto (not long); bajo, de escasa estatura (not tall); breve, conciso (brief); falto, escaso (of goods).

   short cut atajo.

   short circuit corto circuito.

   short story cuento corto.

   for short para abreviar, para mayor brevedad.

   in short en suma, en resumen.

   to be short estar escaso, andar escaso (of money, etc.).

   in a short while dentro de poco.

   a short time ago hace poco.

shorten (to) acortar, abreviar (to make short).

shorts calzoncillos.

shot tiro, disparo, balazo (of a gun).

should, would debe, deberá, debiera, debería.

   I should go. Yo debería ir.

   I would go yo iría.

   if I should go si yo fuese.

   The window should be left open. Debe dejarse abierta la ventana.

   Things are not as they should be. No están las cosas como debieran estar.

shoulder hombro.

   shoulder to shoulder hombro a hombro.

   shoulder blade omoplato.

shout grito.

shout (to) gritar, vocear.

shovel pala.

show exposición (exhibition); espectáculo (spectacle); función (theater); apariencia (appearance); ostentación, boato (ostentation).

   show window escaparate, vidriera (Amer.).

   showcase vitrina.

show (to) mostrar, enseñar; demostrar, probar.

   to show someone in hacer entrar.

   to show to the door acompañar a la puerta.

   to show off hacer alarde.

   to show up presentarse, parecer.

shower lluvia, chaparrón, chubasco; ducha (bath).

   to take a shower darse una ducha.

shrewd astuto, sagaz.

shrimp camarón.

shrink encogerse; mermar.

   to shrink from amilanarse, huir de, apartarse de.

shrub arbusto.

shut adj. cerrado.

shut (to) cerrar.

   to shut in encerrar.

   to shut out cerrar la puerta a uno; excluir.

   to shut up hacer callar, callarse (to be quiet).

shutter persiana (window); obturador (photography).

shy tímido, corto.

sick malo, enfermo.

   to feel sick sentirse enfermo.

sickness enfermedad.

   seasickness mareo.

side lado, costado.

   side by side lado a lado, hombro a hombro, juntos.

   on this side de (a, en, por) este lado.

   on that side de (a, en, por) ese lado.

   on the other side al otro lado, a la otra parte.

   (the) wrong side out al revés, del revés.

sidewalk acera, vereda (Arg.).

sieve cedazo, tamiz, criba.

sigh suspiro.

sigh (to) suspirar.

sight vista, aspecto.

   at first sight a primera vista.

   to be a sight parecer un adefesio.

   What a sight! ¡Qué espectáculo!

sight-seeing (to go) ver las cosas de interés, visitar los lugares notables.

sign seña, señal (mark); letrero, rótulo (over a shop); aviso (notice).
sign (to) firmar.
    to sign a check firmar un cheque.
signal señal, seña.
signal (to) hacer señas.
signature firma.
significance significación, importancia.
significant significativo, expresivo.
silence silencio.
silence (to) hacer callar.
silent silencioso, callado.
silently silenciosamente.
silk seda.
silly tonto, cándido.
silver plata; monedas de plata (silver money).
silverware vajilla de plata.
similar similar, semejante.
similarity semejanza.
simple simple, sencillo.
simplicity sencillez.
simplification simplificación.
simplify simplificar.
simply sencillamente, puramente, simplemente.
sin pecado.
sin (to) pecar.
since *adv.* desde entonces, hace.
    ever since desde entonces.
    not long since hace poco.
since *conj.* ya que, puesto que, pues que.
since *prep.* desde, después.
    since then desde entonces.
sincere sincero.
sincerely sinceramente.
    sincerely yours su seguro servidor (s.s.s.).
sincerity sinceridad.
sing cantar.
singer cantante, cantor, cantora.
single solo, sin compañero; soltero (unmarried).
    not a single word ni una sola palabra.
    single room habitación individual, habitación para uno.
singly individualmente, separadamente, de uno en uno.
singular singular.
sink lavabo (for washing); fregadero (kitchen sink).
sink (to) hundir, echar a pique, hundirse.
sinner pecador.
sip sorbo.
sip (to) tomar a sorbos.
sir señor, caballero.
    Dear Sir (My dear Sir): Muy señor mío:
siren sirena.
sister hermana.
sister-in-law cuñada.
sit sentar, sentarse.
    to sit down sentarse.

sitting room sala.
situated situado.
situation situación.
six seis.
sixteen dieciseis.
sixteenth décimo sexto.
sixth sexto.
sixty sesenta.
size tamaño, medida.
skate patín.
    ice skate patín de hielo.
    roller skate patín de ruedas.
skate (to) patinar.
skeleton esqueleto.
sketch bosquejo, dibujo.
sketch (to) bosquejar, esbozar.
skill destreza, habilidad.
skillful diestro, experto, hábil.
skin piel.
skinny flaco, macilento.
skirt falda.
skull cráneo.
sky cielo, firmamento.
    sky blue azul celeste.
slander calumnia.
slang caló, jerga.
slap bofetada.
slap (to) dar una bofetada.
slate pizarra.
slaughter *n.* matanza.
slave esclavo.
slavery esclavitud.
slay matar.
sleep sueño.
sleep (to) dormir.
    to go to sleep irse a dormir, acostarse.
sleepy soñoliento.
    to be sleepy tener sueño.
sleeve manga.
slender delgado, esbelto.
slice tajada, rebanada.
slice (to) rebanar, cortar en rebanadas.
slide resbalar, deslizarse.
slight *adj.* ligero, leve.
slight (to) despreciar.
slightly ligeramente.
slim delgado.
sling honda.
slip resbalón.
slip (to) resbalar, resbalarse.
    to slip one's mind irse de la memoria.
    to slip away escabullirse, deslizarse.
slippers zapatillas, babuchas.
slippery resbaladizo, resbaloso.
slope pendiente, declive.
slow lento, despacio.
    to be slow atrasar; ser lento.
slow down (to) reducir la marcha.

slowly lentamente, despacio.
    Drive slowly. Conduzca despacio.
    Go slowly. Vaya despacio.
slowness lentitud, tardanza.
slumber sueño ligero.
slumber (to) dormitar.
slums barrios bajos.
sly astuto.
small pequeño.
    small change suelto.
smallness pequeñez.
smart inteligente (clever).
smash (to) romper, quebrantar.
smell olor.
smell (to) oler.
smile sonrisa.
smile (to) sonreír.
smoke humo; cigarrillo (a cigarette).
    Have a smoke. Sírvase un cigarrillo.
smoke (to) humear; fumar (tobacco).
    No smoking. Se prohíbe fumar.
smoker fumador.
smooth liso, llano, suave.
    smooth wine vino suave.
    smooth surface superficie lisa.
snail caracol.
snake serpiente, culebra.
snatch (to) arrancar, arrebatar.
sneeze estornudo.
sneeze (to) estornudar.
snore (to) roncar.
snoring ronquido.
snow nieve.
snow (to) nevar.
snowflake copo.
snowy nevado.
so *adv.* así, tal; de modo que.
    That is so. Así es. Eso es.
    and so forth y así sucesivamente, etcétera.
    so and so fulano de tal.
    so much (many) tanto.
    at so much a yard a tanto la yarda.
    so that para que, de suerte que, de modo que.
    so then conque.
    so, so así, así; regular.
    if so si así es.
    Is that so? ¿De veras?
    I think so. Lo creo. Así lo creo.
    I hope so. Así lo espero.
    not so good as no tan bueno como.
    ten dollars or so cosa de diez dólares.
soak empapar.
soap jabón.
    cake of soap pastilla de jabón.
sob sollozo.
sob (to) sollozar.
sober sobrio.
sociable sociable.

social social.
socialism socialismo.
society sociedad.
socket portalámpara (for an electric bulb).
    eye socket órbita.
socks calcetines.
soda soda.
    soda water gaseosa; agua de Seltz (seltzer, carbonated water).
sofa sofá.
soft blando, suave.
    soft-boiled eggs huevos pasados por agua.
soften ablandar.
softness suavidad.
soil tierra (ground).
soil (to) ensuciar.
soiled sucio.
solar solar.
sold vendido.
    sold out agotado.
soldier soldado.
sole *adj.* único, solo.
sole *n.* suela (shoe); planta (foot).
solemn solemne.
solemnity solemnidad.
solid sólido.
    solid color color entero.
solidity solidez.
solidly sólidamente.
solitary solitario.
solitude soledad.
soluble soluble.
solution solución.
solve (to) resolver (a problem, etc.).
some algo de; un poco; alguno; unos; unos cuantos.
    Some (people) think so. Hay quienes piensan así.
    at some time or other un día u otro.
    Bring me some cigars. Tráigame unos puros.
    I have some left. Me sobra algo.
    some of his books algunos de sus libros.
    some two hundred unos dos cientos.
somebody alguien, alguno.
    somebody else algún otro.
somehow de algún modo.
something alguna cosa, algo.
    something else otra cosa, alguna otra cosa.
sometime algún día, en algún tiempo.
sometimes algunas veces, a veces.
somewhat algún tanto un poco.
    somewhat busy algo ocupado.
somewhere en alguna parte.
    somewhere else en alguna otra parte.
son hijo.
    son-in-law yerno.
song canto, canción.
soon presto, pronto, prontamente, a poco.
    as soon as tan pronto como, luego que, en

cuanto.

as soon as possible   lo más pronto posible.

sooner or later   (más) tarde o (más) temprano.

the sooner the better   mientras más pronto mejor.

How soon will you finish?   ¿Cuánto tiempo tardará Ud. en terminar?

soothe (to)   aliviar, calmar, tranquilizar.

sore *adj.*   dolorido, enconado; resentido (offended).

sore throat   dolor de garganta.

sore *n.*   llaga (on the body).

sorrow   pesar, tristeza.

sorry   triste, afligido.

to be sorry   sentir.

I'm very sorry.   Lo siento muchísimo.

sort   especie, clase, manera, suerte.

all sorts of people   toda clase de gentes.

a sort of   una especie de.

nothing of the sort   nada de eso.

What sort of person is he?   ¿Qué tal persona es?

soul   alma.

sound *adj.*   sano, robusto.

sound judgment   juicio cabal.

safe and sound   sano y salvo.

sound sleep   sueño profundo.

sound *n.*   sonido.

soup   sopa.

soup plate   sopero, plato hondo.

vegetable soup   sopa de legumbres.

sour   agrio, ácido.

source   fuente.

south   sur, sud.

South America   América del Sur. Sudamérica.

South American   sudamericano.

The South Pole   El polo sur.

southern   meridional.

sow (to)   sembrar.

sowing   siembra.

space   espacio.

spacious   espacioso, amplio, vasto.

spade   laya, pala.

Spain   España.

Spaniard   español.

Spanish   español.

Spanish America   Hispanoamérica.

Spanish American   Hispanoamericano.

Spanish language   Castellano.

spare *adj.*   disponible, sobrante; de respeto, de repuesto.

spare time   horas de ocio, ratos perdidos, tiempo desocupado.

spare money   dinero de reserva, ahorros.

spare room   cuarto para huéspedes, cuarto de sobra.

spare parts   repuestos, piezas de repuesto.

spare tire   neumático de repuesto.

spare (to)   ahorrar, economizar (to save); esca-

timar, ser frugal (to be sparing); perdonar (to forgive); ahorrarse trabajo, molestias (to spare oneself trouble, etc.).

They spared his life.   Le perdonaron la vida.

to have (money, time, etc.) to spare   tener (dinero, tiempo, etc.) de sobra.

I was spared the trouble of   me ahorré la molestia de.

sparingly   escasamente, parcamente, frugalmente; rara vez.

spark   chispa.

spark (to)   echar chispas, chispear.

sparrow   gorrión.

speak   hablar.

to speak for   hablar en favor de, hablar en nombre de.

to speak for itself   ser evidente, hablar por sí mismo.

to speak one's mind   decir uno lo que piensa.

to speak out   decir, hablar claro.

to speak to   hablar a.

to speak up   hablar, decir.

speaker   orador; presidente de (les cortes), la cámara de diputados (congress).

spear   lanza.

spearmint   hierbabuena, menta.

special   especial, particular.

special delivery   entrega inmediata.

special delivery stamp   sello de urgencia.

specialist   especialista.

specialize   especializar, especializarse; tener por especialidad, estar especializado (to be specialized).

specially   especialmente, particularmente, sobre todo.

specialty   especialidad.

specific   específico.

specifically   específicamente.

specify   especificar.

specimen   espécimen, muestra.

spectacle   espectáculo.

spectacles   anteojos, espejuelos, gafas.

spectator   espectador.

speculation   especulación.

speech   habla, palabra; discurso, disertación (address, discourse).

to make a speech   pronunciar un discurso.

speechless   mudo, sin habla.

speed   velocidad, rapidez.

at full speed   a toda velocidad, a todo correr.

speed limit   velocidad máxima, velocidad permitida.

speed (to)   acelerar, apresurar, dar prisa (to speed up); apresurarse, darse prisa (to hasten).

spell (to)   deletrear.

spelling   deletreo; otrografía (orthography).

spelling book   cartilla.

spend   gastar.

to spend time   emplear el tiempo, pasar un
tiempo.

to spend the night   pasar la noche, trasnochar.

I'll spend the winter in Florida.   Pasaré el
invierno en Florida.

spice n.   especia.

spicy   que tiene especias, picante.

spider   araña.

spin   giro, vuelta (motion); barrena (aviation).

spin (to)   hilar (thread, cotton, wool, etc.); girar,
dar vueltas (to turn, to revolve); tornear (on
a lathe, etc.).

spinach   espinaca.

spine   espinazo, espina dorsal (backbone).

spiral   espiral.

spirit   espíritu.

spiritual   espiritual.

spit   asador, espeto, espetón (for roasting).

spit (to)   escupir.

spite n.   rencor, despecho, malevolencia.

in spite of   a pesar de, a despecho de.

spiteful   rencoroso, vengativo.

splash   salpicadura, chapoteo.

splash (to)   salpicar, chapotear.

splendid   espléndido, magnífico.

Splendid!   ¡Espléndido!

splendor   esplendor.

split adj.   hendido, partido; dividido (divided).

split (to)   hender, partir, rajar; dividir (to divide).

to split the difference   partir la diferencia.

to split up   repartir, dividir.

to split hairs   pararse en pelillos.

to split one's sides with laughter   desternillarse
de risa.

spoil (to)   echar a perder, dañar, estropear (to
damage); estropearse, dañarse, echarse a
perder (to get spoiled); pudrirse (to rot).

to spoil a child   mimar demasiado a un niño.

spoiled   estropeado, dañado, echado a perder.

a spoiled child   un niño mimado.

spoke n.   rayo de la rueda (of a wheel); travesaño (rung, crossbar).

sponge   esponja.

sponsor   patrocinador; anunciante (radio sponsor).

sponsor (to)   patrocinar, fomentar, apadrinar;
costear un programa de radio (radio).

spontaneity   espontaneidad.

spontaneous   espontáneo.

spool   carrete, carretel.

spool of thread   carrete (carretel) de hilo.

spoon   cuchara.

teaspoon   cucharilla, cucharita.

tablespoon   cuchara.

soupspoon   cucharón (ladle).

spoonful   cucharada.

sport adj.   deportivo, de deporte.

sport shirt   camisa de deporte, camisa de

cuello abierto.

sports   deportes.

spot   mancha (stain); borron (of ink); sitio, lugar,
paraje (place); apuro, aprieto (fix, difficulty).

on the spot   alli mismo, en el mismo lugar; al
punto, inmediatamente (at once).

sprain   torcedura, distensión.

sprain (to)   torcerse, distenderse.

spray (to)   pulverizar, rociar.

sprayer   pulverizador.

spread   difusión.

spread (to)   propalar, difundir, divulgar (news,
etc.); esparcir, desparramar (to scatter);
tender, extender, desplegar, abrir (to stretch
out, to unfold, etc.), untar (butter).

spring   primavera (season); manantial, fuente
(water); salto (jump); resorte, muelle (of
wire, steel, etc.).

bed spring   sommier, resorte, colchón de
muelles.

spring (to)   saltar, brincar.

to spring at   lanzarse sobre, saltar.

sprinkle   rociar (liquid); polvorear (powder).

sprout   brotar.

spy   espía.

spy (to)   espiar.

squad   escuadra; pelotón (party).

squadron   escuadrón; escuadra, flotilla (Navy).

square   cuadrado; plaza (town).

squash n.   calabaza.

squeeze (to)   exprimir.

squirrel   ardilla.

stab   puñalada.

stab (to)   apuñalar, dar de puñaladas.

staff   palo, asta (pole); báculo, bastón (rod,
stick); bastón de mando (baton); jalón de
mira (for surveying); personal (personnel);
plana mayor, estado mayor (body of
officers).

office staff   personal de oficina.

editorial staff   cuerpo de redacción.

staff officer   oficial de estado mayor.

stage   etapa; escenario, tablas (theater).

by stages   por etapas.

stage (to)   representar, poner en escena (theater).

stain   mancha.

stain (to)   manchar.

stair   escalón, peldaño.

staircase   escalera.

stake   estaca, piquete (for driving into the ground).

at stake   comprometido, envuelto, en peligro.

His life is at stake.   En eso le va la vida. Su
vida está en peligro.

stake (to)   estacar, poner estacas; jugar, aventurar, arriesgar (to risk, to put at hazard).

to stake all   jugarse el todo por el todo, echar
el resto.

stammer   tartamudear.

stamp sello, estampilla (for letters); timbre (for documents).

postage stamp sello de correo.

stamp (to) estampar, sellar; poner un sello, poner los sellos (a letter).

stand n. puesto (stall); tribuna (platform); mesita, velador, estante, pedestal, soporte (a piece of furniture).

newsstand puesto de periódicos.

stand (to) poner derecho, colocar or poner de pie (to set something on end); ponerse or estar de pie (to take or keep an upright position); resistir, hacer frente (to resist); aguantar, sufrir (pain, etc.); pararse (to stop moving).

Stand back! ¡Atrás!

Stand up! ¡Levántese! ¡Póngase de pie!

I am standing. Estoy de pie.

I can't stand him. No lo puedo aguantar.

to stand a chance tener probabilidades.

to stand by estar listo (ready); estar cerca (near); estar de mirón (to be looking at); atenerse a, sujetarse a (to abide by).

to stand for estar por, ser partidario de, defender, mantener, aprobar, favorecer; querer decir, significar (to mean); tolerar, aguantar (to tolerate).

to stand in line hacer cola.

to stand in the way cerrar el paso, estorbar, ser un estorbo.

to stand off mantenerse a distancia.

to stand on one's feet valerse de sí mismo.

to stand one's ground resistir, mantenerse firme.

to stand out resaltar, sobresalir, destacarse (to be prominent, conspicuous).

to stand out of the way hacerse a un lado.

to stand still no moverse, estarse quieto.

to stand the test pasar, resistir la prueba.

to stand together mantenerse unidos, solidarizarse.

to stand up levantarse, ponerse de pie.

to stand up for sacar la cara por.

standard norma, tipo, pauta, patrón, standard; estandarte (flag).

standard of living nivel de vida.

gold standard patrón de oro.

standard price precio corriente.

standpoint punto de vista.

star estrella, astro.

starch almidón.

starch (to) almidonar.

start principio, comienzo (beginning); partida, salida (departure); arranque (of a car, an engine).

to get a start tomar la delantera.

start (to) comenzar, principiar (to begin); partir, salir, ponerse en marcha (to start out); poner en marcha, arrancar (an engine, etc.).

starvation hambre.

starve morir de hambre; matar de hambre (to cause to starve).

state n. estado, condición, situación.

state (to) decir, expresar, declarar, exponer, manifestar, afirmar.

statement declaración, manifestación, exposición, relación; informe, memoria (report); cuenta, estado de cuenta (of an account).

stateroom camarote.

statesman estadista, hombre de estado.

station estación.

railroad station estación de ferrocarril.

station master jefe de estación.

stationery papel para cartas, efectos de escritorio.

stationery store papelería.

statistical estadístico.

statistics estadística.

statue estatua.

statute estatuto.

stay estancia, permanencia, residencia (visit); suspensión temporal de un proceso (court).

stay (to) quedar, quedarse, parar, detenerse, hospedarse; aplazar, suspender (to put off).

to stay in quedarse en casa, no salir.

to stay in bed guardar cama.

to stay away estar ausente, no volver.

He's staying at the Waldorf Astoria. Para en el Waldorf Astoria.

steadily constantemente, invariablemente.

steady firme, fijo, estable, constante.

steak bistec, biftec.

steal robar.

They've stolen my watch. Me han robado el reloj.

steam vapor.

steamboat vapor.

steam engine máquina de vapor.

steamer buque de vapor.

steamship buque, vapor.

steamship line compañía de vapores, compañía de navegación.

steel acero.

steep empinado, escarpado.

steer (to) guiar, conducir, gobernar.

steering wheel volante.

stem tallo; raíz (grammar).

stenographer taquígrafo, estenógrafo.

stenography taquigrafía, estenografía.

step paso; escalón, peldaño (stair).

step by step paso a paso.

to be in step llevar el paso.

to be out of step no llevar el paso.

flight of steps tramo.

step (to) dar un paso, pisar, andar, caminar.

to step aside hacerse a un lado.

to step back retroceder.

to step down bajar, descender; disminuir (decrease).

to step in entrar, visitar; meterse, intervenir (take part).

to step on pisar, poner el pie sobre.

to step out salir.

stepbrother hermanastro, medio hermano.

stepchild hijastro.

stepdaughter hijastra.

stepfather padrastro.

stepmother madrastra.

stepsister hermanastra.

stepson hijastro.

stern *adj.* austero, severo.

stew guisado, estofado.

veal stew guisado de ternera.

steward camarero (on a ship).

stewardess camarera.

stick palo, garrote; bastón (cane).

stick (to) apuñalar (to stab); clavar, hincar (to thrust); pegar (to glue); fijar, prender (to fasten); perseverar (to keep on).

to stick by solidarizarse con, apoyar; mantenerse en.

to stick out sacar; asomar (one's head); perseverar hasta el fin (to put up with until the end).

to stick up atracar.

to stick up for defender, sacar la cara por.

to stick to atenerse a, perseverar, mantenerse en.

stiff tieso, duro, rígido; estirado, afectado (not natural in manners); ceremonioso (formal); fuerte (strong); caro (of prices).

stiff collar cuello duro, cuello planchado.

stiff neck tortícolis.

stiff-necked cuellierguido; terco, obstinado.

stiff resistance resistencia obstinada.

stiffen endurecer(se), atiesar(se), arreciar, enconarse, obstinarse.

stiffness rigidez, dureza.

still *adj.* quieto, inmóvil, tranquilo.

still water agua estancada.

to stand still estarse quieto.

still life naturaleza muerta.

Be still! ¡Cállate!

still *adv.* aun, aún, todavía, hasta ahora, no obstante.

She's still sleeping. Está durmiendo todavía.

stillness calma, quietud.

sting aguijón; picadura (wound).

sting (to) picar; pinchar (to prick).

stir (to) agitar; revolver.

to stir the fire atizar el fuego.

to stir up conmover, excitar, alborotar, despertar.

stirrup estribo.

stock surtido, existencias, mercancías (supply of goods); acción (share); valores, acciones (stocks); caja (of a rifle); raza (race).

stock market bolsa.

stock company sociedad anónima.

in stock en existencia.

out of stock agotado.

stockings medias.

stomach estómago.

stone piedra.

stool taburete, banqueta (seat).

stop parada (of streetcar, etc.).

stop (to) parar, pararse, detener, detenerse, hacer alto; quedarse (to stay).

to stop raining dejar (cesar) de llover.

Stop! ¡Alto!

Stop that now! ¡Basta!

Stop a minute. Deténgase un instante.

to stop talking dejar de hablar.

to stop working dejar de trabajar.

to stop payment suspender el pago.

to stop payments suspender pagos.

to stop at detenerse en, poner reparo.

to stop short parar en seco.

to stop over detenerse durante el viaje; quedarse.

store tienda (shop).

department store almacenes, tienda de variedades.

stork cigüeña.

storm tempestad, tormenta.

stormy tempestuoso, borrascoso.

story historia, cuento, historieta (tale); piso (building); cuento de viejas, embuste (falsehood).

short story cuento corto.

as the story goes según se dice, según cuenta la historia.

stout corpulento, gordo.

stove estufa.

straight derecho, recto.

straight line línea recta.

Go straight ahead. Vaya todo seguido.

straighten enderezar, poner en orden.

straightforward *adj.* derecho; recto; franco (frank); íntegro, honrado (honest).

strain tensión (tension); esfuerzo (effort).

strain (to) colar (through a strainer); cansar (the eyes, etc.); esforzarse (to make an effort).

Don't strain yourself. No se canse Ud.

to strain the voice forzar la voz.

strange extraño, raro (unusual); desconocido (not known).

strange face cara desconocida.

strangeness extrañeza, rareza.

stranger extraño, desconocido, extranjero (foreigner).

strap correa.

strategic estratégico.
strategy estrategia.
straw paja.
    straw hat sombrero de paja.
    the last straw el colmo, el acabose.
strawberry fresa.
stream n. corriente de agua, río, arroyo.
street calle.
    street crossing cruce de calle.
    street intersection bocacalle.
streetcar tranvía.
    streetcar conductor cobrador.
strength fuerza, vigor.
    to gain strength cobrar fuerzas.
    on the strength of fundándose en.
strengthen fortalecer(se), reforzar.
stress fuerza (force); esfuerzo (effort); tensión
      (strain); presión (pressure); acento (accent);
      énfasis, importancia (importance).
stress (to) acentuar, dar énfasis.
stretch (to) estirar, extender, ensanchar; dar de
      sí (to become longer or wider).
    to stretch oneself desperezarse.
    to stretch out estirar, alargar.
stretcher camilla.
strict estricto, riguroso, severo.
strike huelga (of workers).
strike (to) golpear, pegar, chocar.
    to strike at atacar, acometer.
    to strike a match encender un fósforo.
    to strike against chocar con.
    to strike back dar golpe por golpe.
    to strike home dar en el vivo.
    to strike out borrar, tachar (to cross out).
    to strike one as funny hacer gracia.
striking que sorprende, sorprendente; llamativo,
      que llama la atención (attracting attention).
stripe lista.
stroll paseo, vuelta.
    to go for a stroll dar una vuelta.
stroll (to) pasear(se).
strong fuerte, poderoso.
stronghold fortaleza, fuerte.
structure estructura.
struggle lucha.
struggle (to) luchar.
stubborn obstinado, terco.
student estudiante.
studious estudioso.
study estudio.
study (to) estudiar.
stuff n. tela, paño, género (cloth, material); cosa
      (thing), cachivaches, chismes, muebles
      (belongings, furniture).
stumble tropezar.
stump tocón, cepa (of tree).
stupid estúpido.
    to be stupid ser estúpido.

stupidity estupidez.
stupor estupefacción, estupor.
style estilo, modo; moda (fashion).
subdue subyugar.
subject sujeto; materia, asunto, tema (subject
      matter).
subject (to) sujetar, someter.
submarine submarino.
submission sumisión.
submit someter; someterse.
subordinate subordinado.
subscribe subscribir(se).
subscriber abonado, subscriptor.
subscription subscripción; cantidad subscrita
      (sum).
subsequent subsiguiente, ulterior.
subsequently posteriormente, subsiguiente-
      mente.
substance substancia.
substantial substancial.
substitute substituto.
substitute (to) substituir.
substitution substitución.
subtract quitar, restar, sustraer.
suburb suburbio, arrabal.
succeed salir bien, tener buen éxito (turn out
      well); suceder (come next after another).
success (buen) éxito, buen resultado.
successful próspero, afortunado.
successive sucesivo.
successor sucesor.
such tal, semejante.
    such as tal como.
    in such a way de tal modo.
    no such (a) thing no hay tal.
sudden adj. repentino, súbito.
    all of a sudden de repente.
suddenly repentinamente, de pronto, súbita-
      mente.
suffer (to) sufrir.
suffering adj. doliente.
suffering n. sufrimiento, padecimiento.
sugar azúcar.
    sugar bowl azucarero.
    sugar cane caña de azúcar.
    sugar mill ingenio.
suggest sugerir, proponer.
suggestion sugestión.
suicide suicidio.
    to commit suicide suicidarse.
suit traje (clothes); causa, pleito (court); palo (in
      cards).
    ready-made suit traje hecho.
    suit made to order traje a la medida.
    to bring suit entablar juicio.
suit (to) cuadrar, convenir, acomodar (to be
      suitable); venir or ir bien, sentar (to be
      becoming); satisfacer, agradar (to please,

to satisfy).
suitable adecuado, apropiado.
suitably adecuadamente, convenientemente.
sulphur azufre.
sum suma.
    in sum   en suma.
    sum total   suma total.
summary sumario.
summer verano.
    summer resort   lugar de veraneo.
summit cima, cumbre.
summon citar, emplazar, requerir, convocar.
summons citación, comparendo.
sum up (to) resumir, recapitular.
sun sol.
    sun bath   baño de sol.
    to take a sun bath   tomar un baño de sol.
sunbeam rayo de sol.
sunburn quemadura de sol.
sunburnt tostado por el sol.
    to get sunburnt   tostarse por el sol.
Sunday domingo.
sunlight luz del sol.
sunny de sol, asoleado; alegre, risueño (sunny disposition).
sunrise salida de sol, amanecer.
sunset puesta del sol.
sunshine luz solar.
    in the sunshine   al sol.
sunstroke insolación.
superb soberbio, grandioso.
superfluous superfluo.
superintendent superintendente.
superior superior.
superiority superioridad.
superstition superstición.
superstitious supersticioso.
supper cena.
    to have supper   cenar.
supplement suplemento.
supply abastecimiento; surtido (stock); oferta (business).
    supply and demand   oferta y demanda.
supply (to) abastecer, proveer, surtir.
support apoyo, sostén; sustento, manutención (act of providing for).
support (to) sostener, apoyar; mantener (to provide for).
suppose suponer.
supposition suposición, supuesto.
suppress suprimir.
suppression supresión.
supreme supremo, sumo.
    Supreme Court   Corte Suprema, Tribunal Supremo.
sure cierto, seguro.
    to be sure   estar seguro, sin duda, ya se ve.
    be sure to   no deje de, sin falta.

surely seguramente, ciertamente, indudablemente.
surface superficie.
surgeon cirujano.
surgery cirugía.
surname apellido.
surprise sorpresa, extrañeza.
surprise (to) sorprender.
surprising sorprendente.
surprisingly sorprendentemente.
surrender rendición, entrega.
surrender (to) rendir(se), entregar(se), ceder.
surround cercar, rodear.
surrounding circunvecino.
surroundings inmediaciones, alrededores; medio, ambiente (atmosphere).
survey examen, estudio; inspección (inspection); levantamiento de planos (surveying).
survey (to) examinar, estudiar; reconocer, inspeccionar (to inspect); levantar un plano (in surveying).
survival supervivencia.
survive sobrevivir.
survivor sobreviviente.
susceptible susceptible.
suspect n. persona sospechosa.
suspect (to) sospechar.
suspend suspender.
suspenders tirantes.
suspicion sospecha.
suspicious sospechoso, desconfiado, suspicaz.
swallow golondrina (bird).
swallow (to) tragar.
swamp pantano, ciénaga.
swan cisne.
swarm enjambre.
swarm (to) enjambrar, pulular, bullir, hormiguear.
swear jurar, tomar *or* prestar juramento.
    to swear by   jurar por, poner confianza implícita en.
sweat sudor.
sweat (to) sudar.
sweater sweter, chaqueta de punto.
sweep barrer.
sweet dulce.
    sweet apples   manzanas dulces.
    sweet potato   batata, patata dulce, boniato (Cuba), camote (Amer.).
    to have a sweet tooth   ser goloso.
    She's very sweet.   Ella es muy dulce.
sweetheart novio, novia.
sweetness dulzura.
swell adj. excelente, magnífico, estupendo.
swell (to) hinchar(se), subir, crecer (to rise above the level).
swelling hinchazón.
swift rápido, veloz.

swiftly velozmente, rápidamente.

swim (to) nadar.

My head's swimming. Se me va la cabeza.

swimmer nadador.

swimming pool piscina.

swing columpio (a seat hung from ropes), balanceo, oscilación (movement).

in full swing en pleno apogeo.

swing (to) columpiar, mecer; mover con soltura los brazos o el cuerpo al andar (to swing one's arms or body when walking).

switch la llave de la luz, el botón de la luz, interruptor, conmutador (electric switch); cambiavía, aguja de cambio (railroad); cambio (change, shift).

switch (to) dar vuelta la llave de la luz (to turn the switch); desviar, apartar (rails); cambiar (to change, to shift); azotar (to whip).

sword espada.

syllable sílaba.

symbol símbolo.

sympathetic afín, simpático, que simpatiza.

sympathize simpatizar.

sympathy simpatía.

symphony sinfonía.

symphony orchestra orquesta sinfónica.

symptom síntoma.

synthetic sintético.

syrup almíbar.

system sistema.

systematic metódico, sistemático.

T

table mesa; tabla (of measures, etc.).

to set the table poner la mesa.

tablecloth mantel.

tablespoon cuchara

tablet tableta, pastilla (of aspirin, etc.); bloc de papel (for writing); tabla, lápida (with an inscription).

tableware servicio de mesa.

tact tacto.

tactical táctico.

tactics táctica.

tactful cauto, atinado.

tactless falta.

tail cola.

tailor sastre.

take (to) tomar; coger (to grasp).

to take a bite comer algo.

to take a bath bañarse.

to take a picture sacar un retrato.

to take a walk dar un paseo.

to take a stroll dar una vuelta.

to take a nap tomar la siesta.

to take a look at echar un vistazo a, mirar.

to take a trip hacer un viaje.

to take an oath prestar juramento.

to take apart desarmar (a machine).

to take a step dar un paso.

to take away quitar, llevarse.

to take back retractarse, desdecirse de; devolver; tomar algo devuelto.

to take account of tomar en cuenta.

to take advantage of aprovecharse de, abusar de.

to take a fancy to prendarse de, simpatizar de.

to take a liking to coger (tomar) cariño a.

to take advice hacer caso, tomar consejo.

to take care tener cuidado.

to take care of cuidar de.

to take chances correr el riesgo, arriesgar.

to take down bajar, poner más bajo (to lower); tomar nota (to take note).

to take for granted tomar por sentado.

to take charge of encargarse de.

to take effect surtir efecto.

to take into consideration tener en cuenta.

to take to heart tomar pecho.

to take it easy no apurarse.

Take it or leave it. ¿Sí o no? Tómelo o déjelo.

to take from quitar de; restar de (to subtract).

to take leave despedirse.

to take note tomar nota.

to take notice advertir, observar, notar, percatarse de.

to take out sacar, quitar.

to take after salir a, parecerse, ser como.

to take it out on desquitarse con otro, hacer pagar el pato.

to take off despegar (a plane).

to take one's clothes off quitarse la ropa, desnudarse.

to take one's shoes off descalzarse.

Take your hat off. Descúbrase. Quítese el sombrero.

Take my word for it. Créame Ud. Bajo mi palabra.

to take pains cuidar.

to take part tomar parte.

to take place suceder, ocurrir.

to take possession of apoderarse.

to take refuge refugiarse.

to take time tomar tiempo.

to take one's time tomarse tiempo, no darse prisa.

to take up a subject abordar un tema.

to take up room ocupar espacio.

to take upon oneself encargarse de, asumir la responsabilidad, hacerse cargo de.

talcum talco.

talcum powder polvo de talco.

tale cuento; chisme (gossip).

talent talento.

talented talentoso.

talk conversación (conversation); charla (chat);

discurso (speech); comidilla (gossip); rumor
(rumor).
talk (to) hablar, conversar, charlar.
  to talk back replicar, responder irrespetuosa-
  mente.
  to talk over discutir, tratar acerca de.
  to talk to hablar a.
talkative locuaz.
tall alto.
tallness altura, estatura.
tame *adj.* domesticado, amansado, dócil.
tame (to) domar, domesticar.
tan *n.* color de canela, color café claro (color).
tan *adj.* atezado, tostado (skin); de color café
  claro, de color de canela.
tan (to) curtir; atezarse, tostarse (to become tan).
tank tanque, cisterna; tanque (mil.); depósito,
  tanque (for gasoline).
tape cinta, tira de tela, de papel o de metal.
  tape measure cinta para medir.
  adhesive tape esparadrapo.
tapestry tapiz, tapicería.
tar brea, alquitrán.
target blanco, objetivo.
  to hit the target dar en el blanco.
task tarea, feana, labor.
taste gusto.
  in bad taste de mal gusto.
  in good taste de buen gusto.
  to have a taste for tener gusto por.
taste (to) gustar, saborear, probar; saber a, tener
  gusto a (to have a flavor of).
  Taste it. Pruébelo.
  The soup tastes of onion. La sopa sabe a
  cebolla.
tavern taberna.
tax impuesto, contribución.
  income tax impuesto sobre la renta.
  tax collector exactor, recaudador de impuestos.
  tax rate tarifa de impuestos.
tax (to) cobrar impuestos, imponer contribu-
  ciones.
taxi taxi, coche de alquiler.
tea té.
teach enseñar.
teacher maestro.
teacup taza para té.
teakettle olla para calentar agua.
team pareja, tronco (horsés); equipo (sports).
  team work trabajo coordinado, esfuerzo
  aunado, actuación concertada.
teapot tetera.
tear lágrima.
  in tears llorando.
tear (to) desgarrar, rasgar, romper.
  to tear down demoler.
  to tear to pieces hacer añicos, despedazar.

  to tear one's hair arrancarse los cabellos.
tease tomar el pelo.
technical técnico.
technique técnica.
tedious aburrido, cansado.
teeth dientes.
  false teeth dientes postizos.
  set of teeth dentadura.
telegraph telégrafo.
telegraph (to) telegrafiar.
telephone teléfono.
  telephone booth cabina telefónica.
  telephone call llamada telefónica.
  telephone exchange central telefónica.
  telephone operator telefonista.
  telephone directory guía telefónica, lista de
  abonados, directorio telefónico.
telephone (to) telefonear.
telescope telescopio.
tell decir; contar, relatar, referir.
  to tell a story contar un cuento.
  Who told you so? ¿Quién se lo dijo?
  Tell it to him. Cuénteselo a él.
  Do what you are told. Haz lo que se te
  mande.
temper genio, carácter.
  bad temper mal genio.
  to lose one's temper enfadarse, perder la
  paciencia.
temperament temperamento.
tempest tempestad.
temple templo (for worship); sien (anatomy).
temporarily provisionalmente, temporalmente,
  transitoriamente.
temporary provisorio, temporal, interino.
temporize (to) contemporizar.
tempt tentar.
temptation tentación.
tempting tentador.
ten diez.
tenacious tenaz, porfiado.
tenant inquilino.
tendency tendencia.
tender *adj.* tierno.
  tender-hearted compasivo.
tennis tenis.
  tennis court cancha de tenis.
tense tenso.
tension tensión.
tent tienda de campaña.
tentative tentativa.
tenth décimo.
term término; plazo (period of time); especifica-
  ciones, condiciones (terms).
  in terms of en concepto de; en función de
  (math.).
  on no terms por ningún concepto.
  to be on good terms with estar en buenas

    relaciones con.

to come to terms   llegar a un acuerdo, convenir.

to bring to terms   imponer condiciones a, hacer arreglos con.

On what terms?   ¿En que términos?

terminal *adj.* terminal, final, último.

terminal término; estación terminal, final de trayecto (station, end of a line); terminal, borne (elec.).

terrace terraza.

terrible terrible, espantoso.

How terrible! ¡Qué espantoso!

terribly espantosamente, terriblemente.

territory territorio.

terror terror, espanto.

terse terso, sucinto, conçiso.

terseness concisión.

test prueba, ensayo, examen, análisis.

test (to) ensayar, probar, analisar.

testify atestiguar, testificar, declarar.

text texto.

textbook libro de texto.

than que.

more than that más que eso.

fewer than menos que.

She's older than I. Ella es mayor que yo.

thank (to) agradecer, dar las gracias.

Thank you. Gracias.

thankful agradecido.

thanks gracias.

thanks to. gracias a.

that ese, esa, eso, aquel, aquella, aquello (*dem. adj.*); ése, ésa, eso, aquél, aquélla, aquello (*dem. pron.*); que, quien, el cual, la cual, lo que, lo cual (*rel. pron.*).

that man ese hombre.

that woman esa mujer.

That's the one. Ese es.

That's it. Eso es.

That's to say. Es decir.

That may be. Es posible. Eso puede ser.

That's all. Eso es todo.

and all that y cosas por el estilo.

That way. Por allí. Por aquel camino.

that's how asi es como es, asi es como se hace.

That's that. Eso es lo que hay. No hay más que decir.

to let it go at that conformarse con eso, dejar correr.

that *adv.* tan, así de.

not that far no tan lejos.

that many tantos.

that much tanto.

that big así de grande.

that *conj.* que, para que.

so that de modo que, de suerte que, para que.

in order that para que, de modo que.

save that salvo que.

in that por cuanto, en que.

the el, la, lo; los, las.

the man el hombre.

the men. los hombres.

the woman la mujer.

the women las mujeres.

the sooner the better cuanto más pronto, tanto mejor.

the less . . . the better cuanto menos . . . tanto mejor.

theater teatro.

theatrical teatral.

their su, suyo, suya, de él, de ella; sus, suyos, suyas, de ellos, de ellas.

theirs el suyo, la suya, los suyos, las suyas, de ellos, de ellas.

them los, las, les; ellos, ellas.

theme tema, asunto.

themselves ellos mismos, ellas mismas; sí mismos.

then entonces, en aquel tiempo, a la sazón.

now and then de cuando en cuando, de vez en cuando.

but then si bien es cierto que, sin embargo.

and then y entonces.

just then entonces mismo, en aquel mismo momento.

by then para entonces.

And what then? ¡Y entonces! ¿Pues y qué? ¿Y que pasó después? (What happened then?) ¿Y que pasará después? (What will happen then?)

theoretical teórico.

theory teoría.

there allí, allá, ahí (near the person addressed).

Put it there. Ponlo ahí.

There she goes. Ahí va.

I was there. Yo estuve allí.

She lives there. Ella vive allí.

Go there. Vaya allá.

Over there. Por allí. Allá.

There in Spain. Allá en España.

There you are. Ahí tiene Ud. Para que vea. Eso es todo.

There! ¡Toma! ¡Vaya! ¡Mira!

there is hay.

thereabouts por ahí, por allí, cerca de allí.

thereafter después de eso; conforme.

there are hay.

There are many things. Hay muchas cosas.

thereby por medio de eso; con eso, con lo cual; de tal modo, así.

therefore por lo tanto, por esto, por esa razón; a consecuencia de eso, por consiguiente.

there is hay.

There's plenty (enough). Hay bastante.

thereupon en eso, sobre eso; por lo tanto; inmediatamente después, en seguida, luego.

thermometer termómetro.
these estos, estas; éstos, éstas.
thesis tesis.
they ellos, ellas.
thick espeso (like glue); tupido, denso (dense); grosor, grueso (not thin).
　three inches thick　tres pulgadas de espesor.
　thick-headed　torpe.
thickness grueso, espesor, grosor.
thief ladrón.
thigh muslo.
thimble dedal.
thin flaco (lean); delgado (not thick), delgado, esbelto (slender).
thing cosa, objeto.
　something　algo, alguna cosa.
　anything　cualquier cosa.
think (to) pensar; creer, opinar (believe).
　to think of　pensar en, reflexionar acerca de.
　to think well of　pensar bien de, tener buen concepto de.
　As you think fit.　Como Ud. quiera, como a Ud. le parezca mejor.
　to think it over　pensarlo, meditarlo.
　to think nothing of　no dar importancia a; tener en poco.
　to think twice　andar con tiento, pensarlo bien, reflexionar mucho.
　I don't think so.　Creo que no.
　I think so.　Creo que sí.
thinness delgadez, flacura.
third tercero.
　a third person　un tercero.
　thirdly　en tercer lugar.
thirst sed.
　to be thirsty　tener sed.
thirteen trece.
thirty treinta.
this este, esta; esto; éste, ésta.
　this man　este hombre.
　this woman　esta mujer.
　this morning　esta mañana.
　this one and that one　éste y aquél.
　this and that　esto y aquello.
thorn espina.
thorough adj. entero, cabal, minucioso, perfecto.
thoroughfare vía pública, calle, carretera.
　No thoroughfare.　Se prohibe el paso.
thoroughgoing cabal, completo, entero, hasta el final.
thoroughly enteramente, cabalmente.
those aquellos, aquellas.
though aunque, sin embargo, no obstante, si bien, bien que, aun cuando.
　as though　como si.
thought pensamiento.
　to give thought to　pensar en.
thoughtful pensativo, meditabundo; precavido

(careful); atento, considerado (considerate).
　It's very thoughtful of you.　Ud. es muy atento.
thoughtfully cuidadosamente, con precaución, con reflexión, con consideración.
thoughtfulness reflexión, meditación, atención, consideración, previsión.
thoughtless inconsiderado, descuidado, insensato.
thoughtlessly descuidadamente, sin reflexión, sin consideración.
thousand mil, millar.
thread hilo.
thread (to) enhebrar.
threat amenaza.
threaten amenazar.
three tres.
threefold triple.
threshold umbral.
thrift economía, frugalidad.
thrifty frugal, económico.
thrill emoción, estremecimiento.
thrill (to) emocionarse, estremecerse, temblar; causar una viva emoción.
throat garganta.
　sore throat　dolor (mal) de garganta.
　I have a sore throat.　Me duele la garganta.
throne trono.
through adj. continuo, directo.
　a through train from Barcelona to Valencia　un tren directo de Barcelona a Valencia.
through adv. a través, de parte en parte, de un lado a otro; enteramente, completamente.
　through and through　enteramente, hasta los tuétanos.
　I'm wet through and through.　Estoy mojado hasta los huesos. Estoy hecho una sopa.
　to be through　haber terminado.
　to be through with　no tener más que ver con, haber terminado, no ocuparse ya en.
through prep. por, por entre, a través, por medio de, por conducto de; mediante.
　through the door　por la puerta.
　through the strainer　a través del colador.
　through the trees　por entre los árboles.

　through his influence　mediante su influencia.
throughout prep. durante todo, en todo, a lo largo de, por todos lados; adv. de parte a parte, desde el principio hasta el fin, en todas partes.
throw echar; tirar (a ball, stone, etc.).
　to throw out　echar fuera, arrojar.
　to throw away　tirar, arrojar, botar (Amer.).
　to throw light on　esclarecer, aclarar.
thumb pulgar.
thumbtack chinche.
thunder trueno.
thunder (to) tronar.

It's thundering. Truena.

thunderbolt rayo, centella.

thunderclap tronada.

thundershower chubasco con truenos y relámpagos.

thunderstorm tronada.

Thursday jueves.

thus así, de este modo, en estos términos, como sigue.

thus far hasta aquí, hasta ahora.

thus much no más, basta, baste esto.

ticket billete, boleto (Amer.).

round-trip ticket billete de ida y vuelta.

season ticket abono, billete de temporada.

ticket window taquilla.

tickle (to) hacer cosquillas.

tickling cosquillas.

ticklish cosquilloso; quisquilloso.

tide marea.

high tide pleamar, plenamar.

low tide bajamar.

tie *n.* corbata (to wear); lazo (bond); atadura, nudo (a knot); traviesa, durmiente (railroad tie).

family ties lazos de familia.

tie (to) atar, amarrar.

tiger tigre.

tight apretado, muy ajustado, bien cerrado.

tighten apretar.

tile azulejo, losa, baldosa; teja (for roof).

tiling azulejos, tejas (tiles); tejado (roof covered with tiles).

till hasta; hasta que.

till now hasta ahora.

till further notice hasta nueva orden.

till (to) cultivar, laborar, labrar.

timber madera.

time tiempo; hora; vez; época; plazo.

What time is it? ¿Qué hora es?

the first time la primera vez.

on time a tiempo.

some time ago tiempo atrás.

a long time ago hace mucho tiempo.

at the proper time a su debido tiempo, en el momento oportuno.

at the same time al mismo tiempo.

any time a cualquier hora; cuando Ud. guste, cuando quiera.

at no time jamás.

one at a time uno a la vez.

at this time ahora, al presente.

at this time (of the day) a estas horas.

at times a veces.

for the time being por ahora, de momento.

time and again una y otra vez.

from time to time de vez en cuando.

in no time en un instante, en un abrir y cerrar de ojos.

in an hour's time en una hora.

Be on time. Sea puntual.

Have a good time! ¡Que se divierta!

We had a good time. Pasamos un buen rato.

to take time tomarse tiempo.

spare time tiempo desocupado, ratos de ocio.

timely oportunamente, a propósito (*adv.*); oportuno, a buen tiempo (*adj.*).

timid tímido.

timidity timidez.

tin lata.

tin can lata.

tin foil hoja de estaño.

tin plate hoja de lata.

tincture tintura.

tincture of iodine tintura de yodo.

tint tinte.

tip punta, extremidad, cabo (point, end); propina (gratuity); soplo, delación (secret information); advertencia (warning).

tip (to) ladear, inclinar (to slant); dar una propina (to give a tip); prevenir, precaver (to warn); delatar, soplar (to tip off).

tire neumático, llanta.

flat tire pinchazo, neumático desinflado.

tire (to) cansar; aburrir (to bore).

to tire out reventar de cansancio.

tired cansado.

tired out rendido de cansancio, agotado.

to become tired cansarse.

tiredness cansancio, fatiga.

tireless incansable, infatigable.

tissue tejido (a mass of cells, skin tissue, etc.); gasa, tisú (cloth).

tissue paper papel de seda.

title título.

title page portada.

to a, para, de, por, hasta, que.

to give to dar a.

to go to ir a.

to speak to hablar a.

ready to go listo para marcharse.

It's time to leave. Es hora de partir.

the road to Madrid la carretera de Madrid.

from house to house de casa en casa.

to be done por hacerse.

letters to be written cartas por escribir.

to this day hasta ahora.

in order to a fin de, para.

to and fro de un lado a otro, de acá para allá.

I have to go. Tengo que irme.

I have something to do. Tengo algo que hacer.

It's five (minutes) to three. Son las tres menos cinco.

toad sapo.

toast tostada.

toast (to) tostar.

toasted tostado.

toaster tostador, parrilla.

tobacco tabaco.

  tobacco shop   estanco (Spain) cigarrería, tabaquería (Amer.).

today hoy.

  a week from today   de hoy en ocho días.

toe dedo del pie.

together juntos; juntamente; a un tiempo, simultaneamente.

  Let's go together.   Vamos juntos.

  together with   junto con, en compañía de.

  to call together   reunir, congregar.

toil trabajo, pena, angustia, fatiga, afán.

toilet excusado, retrete, inodoro; tocado (combing the hair, bathing, etc.).

  toilet set   juego de tocador.

  toilet water   colonia, agua de colonia.

  toilet paper   papel higiénico.

tolerance tolerancia.

tolerant tolerante.

tolerate tolerar.

tomato tomate.

  tomato juice   jugo de tomate.

tomb tumba, sepulcro.

tomcat gato.

tomorrow mañana.

  day after tomorrow   pasado mañana.

  tomorrow morning   mañana por la mañana.

  tomorrow noon   mañana al mediodía.

  tomorrow afternoon   mañana por la tarde.

  tomorrow night   mañana por la noche.

ton tonelada.

tone tono.

tongs tenazas, alicates.

tongue lengua; espiga.

  to hold one's tongue   callarse.

tonic tónico.

tonight esta noche, a la noche.

tonsil amígdala.

tonsilitis amigdalitis.

too demasiado (too much), tambien (also).

  too much   demasiado, excesivo.

  too many   demasiados, muchos.

  It's too bad.   Es lástima.

  It's too early.   Es demasiado temprano.

  It's a little too early.   Es un poco temprano.

  That's too much.   Eso ya es demasiado. Es el colmo.

  You have gone a little too far.   Ud. se ha excedido un poco.

  He's too good.   Es muy bueno. Se pasa de bueno.

  none (not) too good   no muy bueno que digamos, malamente puede llamarse eso bueno.

  me (I) too   yo tambien.

  I am only too glad to do it.   Lo haré con muchísimo gusto.

  one dollar too much   un dollar de más.

  That's too little.   Eso es muy poco.

tool herramienta.

tooth diente.

  tooth powder   polvo dentífrico.

  toothache   dolor de muelas.

  toothbrush   cepillo de dientes.

  toothpaste   pasta dentífrica.

  toothpick   mondadientes, palillo.

top cima, cumbre (of a mountain); copa (of a tree); la parte superior, la parte de arriba, superficie (upper side); cabeza (head), pináculo (pinnacle); trompo (toy).

  the top of the mountain   la cumbre de la montaña.

  top hat   chistera, sombrero de copa.

  at top speed   a todo correr.

  at the top   a la cabeza, en la cumbre.

  from top to bottom   de arriba abajo.

  from top to toe   de pies a cabeza.

  on top of   encima de, sobre.

top (to) sobrepujar, aventajar, exceder, llegar a la cima.

  to top off   coronar, rematar, dar cima.

topcoat gabán de entretiempo.

torch antorcha.

torment tormento.

torrent torrente.

torrid tórrido.

  torrid zone   zona tórrida.

tortoise tortuga.

  tortoise shell   carey.

torture tortura, tormento.

torture (to) torturar, atormentar.

toss (to) tirar, lanzar.

  to toss aside   echar a un lado.

  to toss up   jugar a cara o cruz.

total total.

  sum total   suma total.

touch contacto.

  to be in touch with   estar en comunicación con, en relación con.

touch (to) tocar.

touching *adj.* patético, conmovedor.

touchy quisquilloso.

tough duro, fuerte; difícil, penoso (hard to bear).

toughen endurecer (se).

toughness endurecimiento, rigidez.

tour viaje, gira.

tour (to) recorrer, viajar por.

  touring turismo.

  touring agency   agencia de turismo.

  touring car   coche de turismo.

  touring guide   guía de turismo.

tourist turista.

tournament torneo.

tow (to) remolcar (a ship, etc.).

toward(s) hacia, para con, tocante a.
  to go towards (a place) ir hacia (un lugar).
  His attitude towards me. Su actitud para
    conmigo.
towel toalla.
  face towel toalla para la cara.
  hand towel toalla para las manos.
  bath towel toalla de baño.
tower torre.
town ciudad, pueblo.
  home town ciudad natal.
  town hall ayuntamiento.
toy juguete.
trace indicio, huella, pista.
trace (to) trazar (to mark out); seguir la pista
  (to follow).
track huella; vía, rieles (metal rails); andén (in a
  railroad station).
trade comercio.
  trade mark marca de fábrica.
  trade name razón social; nombre de fábrica
    (for products).
  trade union sindicato.
trading comercio.
tradition tradición.
traditional tradicional.
traffic circulación.
tragedy tragedia.
tragic trágico.
train tren.
  train conductor cobrador.
train (to) entrenar, adiestrar, instruir.
training preparación, entrenamiento.
traitor traidor.
tramp vago, vagabundo.
tranquil tranquilo.
transatlantic transatlántico.
transfer transferencia; traspaso (a store, a farm,
  etc.); transbordo (from one train, bus, etc.
  to another).
transfer (to) transferir (to change hands); transbordar (trains, busses, etc.); trasladar (from
  one place to another).
translate traducir.
translation traducción.
translator traductor.
transparent transparente.
transport transporte.
transport (to) transportar.
transportation transporte.
trap trampa.
trap (to) atrapar.
travel (to) viajar.
traveler viajero, viajante (salesman).
tray bandeja.
treacherous traidor, alevoso.
treachery traición.
tread pisada.

tread (to) pisar, písotear.
treason traición.
treasure tesoro.
treasure (to) atesorar, guardar.
treasurer tesorero.
treasury tesorería.
treat (to) tratar; convidar, invitar (with food,
  drinks, etc.).
  to treat a patient tratar a un enfermo.
  to treat well (badly) dar buen (mal) trato.
treatment trato; tratamiento (med.).
treaty tratado.
tree árbol.
tremble temblar.
trembling adj. trémulo, tembloroso.
trembling n. temblor.
tremendous tremendo, inmenso.
trench zanja; trinchera (fortification).
trend tendencia, giro, rumbo.
trial prueba, ensayo (test); juicio, vista de una
  causa (law).
triangle triángulo.
tribe tribu.
tribunal tribunal.
trick treta, artificio, jugada, artimaña; truco,
  juego de manos (with cards, etc.); maña,
  destreza (skill).
  to do the trick resolver el problema.
  He played a trick on me. Me hizo una juga-
    rreta.
trifle friolera, bagatela.
trim (to) adornar (a dress, etc.); podar (a tree);
  cortar ligeramente (the hair).
trimming adorno, decoración.
trinket dije, chuchería.
trip n. viaje (voyage); traspié, tropezón (stumble);
  zancadilla (act of catching a person's foot).
  one-way trip viaje de ida.
  round trip viaje de ida y vuelta.
trip (to) tropezar (to stumble); hacer una zancadilla, (to cause to stumble).
triple triple.
triumph triunfo.
triumph (to) triunfar.
triumphant triunfante.
trivial trivial.
trolley car tranvía.
troops tropas.
trophy trofeo.
tropic trópico.
tropic(al) adj. tropical.
trot (to) trotar.
trouble preocupación, pena (worry); dificultad
  (difficulty); molestia (bother); apuro, aprieto
  (distress); disgusto, desavenencia (disagreement) mal, enfermedad (sickness).
  to cause trouble causar molestia, dar que
    hacer.

to be in trouble   estar en apuro.

not to be worth the trouble   no valer la pena.

It's no trouble at all.   No es ninguna molestia.

stomach trouble   mal de estómago.

   I have stomach trouble.   Padezco del estómago.

trouble (to)   molestar, importunar.

   Don't trouble yourself.   No se moleste Ud.

troubled   preocupado, afligido.

   to be troubled with   padecer, sufrir de.

troublesome   molesto, embarazoso; importuno, alborotador (person).

trousers   pantalones.

trough   artesa, pila, cubeta, batea.

trout   trucha.

truck   camión.

true   cierto, exacto, verdadero, fiel.

   It's true.   Es verdad.

trunk   tronco (of a tree), cofre, baúl (for packing).

trust   confianza.

   on trust   al fiado.

   in trust   en depósito.

trust (to)   tener confianza, confiar, fiar.

   I trust him.   Le tengo confianza.

   I don't trust him.   No me fío de él.

trustworthy   digno de confianza.

truth   verdad.

truthful   verídico, veraz.

truthfulness   veracidad.

try (to)   probar, tratar de, esforzarse.

   to try on clothes   probarse ropa.

   Try to do it.   Trate de hacerlo.

   to try hard   hacer lo posible por.

tub   cuba, batea.

   bathtub   baño, bañera.

tube   tubo.

Tuesday   martes.

tune   tonada, tono, melodía.

   to be out of tune   desafinar.

tune (to)   afinar, entonar; sintonizar (radio).

   to tune in   sintonizar.

tunnel   túnel.

turkey   pavo.

turn   turno (time, order); vuelta, giro (motion); favor (favor).

   by turns   por turnos.

   in turn   a su turno, a su vez.

   to take turns   turnarse.

   It's my turn now.   Ahora me toca a mí.

turn (to)   dar vuelta; dar vueltas, girar (to revolve); volver, doblar, torcer (to change direction); ponerse, volverse (to become pale, etc.).

   to turn against   predisponer en contra, volverse en contra.

   to turn around   dar vuelta a.

   to turn down   rehusar, rechazar (to refuse).

   to turn into   convertir en, cambiar en.

   to turn off   cerrar la llave del (gas, steam, etc.).

   to turn off the light   apagar la luz.

   to turn off the water   cortar el agua; cerrar el grifo.

   to turn off the gas   apagar el gas.

   to turn on the light   encender la luz.

   to turn on the water   dejar correr el agua, abrir el grifo.

   to turn back   dar la vuelta, volverse, retroceder.

   to turn one's back on   voltear la espalda a.

   to turn out to be   resultar, venir a ser.

   to turn over   transferir (to transfer), entregar, dar (to hand over); volcar, tumbarse (to tumble); abuñuelar (eggs); dar vuelta, volver (to change in position).

   to turn sour   agriarse (milk, etc.).

   to turn to   recurrir a, acudir a; convertir en, convertirse en.

   to turn up   aparecer (to appear), poner más alto, levantar (to give upward turn to); volver (a card, etc.); resultar, acontecer, venir a ser (to occur).

   to turn a cold shoulder to   desairar.

   to turn upside down   poner patas arriba.

turnip   nabo.

turtle   tortuga.

twelfth   duodécimo, décimo segundo.

twelve   doce.

twentieth   vigésimo.

twenty   veinte.

twice   dos veces.

twilight   crepúsculo.

twin   mellizo, gemelo.

   twin brother   hermano gemelo.

   twin brothers   mellizos.

twist (to)   torcer, retorcer.

two   dos.

type   tipo.

typewrite (to)   escribir a máquina.

typewriter   máquina de escribir.

   portable typewriter   máquina de escribir portátil.

   typewriter ribbon   cinta para la máquina de escribir.

typical   típico.

typist   mecanógrafa.

tyrannical   tiránico.

tyranny   tiranía.

tyrant   irano.

U

ugliness   fealdad.

ugly   feo.

ulcer   úlcera.

umbrella   paraguas.

umbrella stand paragüero.
unable incapaz.
  I was unable to. No pude. Me fué imposible.
unanimous unánima.
unaware desprevenido, de sorpresa; inadverti-
    damente, sin pensar.
  to take someone unawares coger a uno de
    sorpresa.
unbearable insoportable.
unbutton desabrochar.
uncertain incierto.
uncertainty incertidumbre.
unchangeable inmutable.
uncle tío.
uncomfortable incómodo, molesto; indispuesto.
  to feel uncomfortable estar incomodo.
unconquered invicto.
undecided indeciso.
under bajo, debajo de, en; menos; en tiempos de.
    under the table debajo de la mesa.
    under consideration en consideración.
    under penalty of so pena de.
    under age menor de edad.
    under contract bajo contrato; conforme al
      contrato.
    under cover al abrigo, a cubierto; dentro de
      un sobre (in an envelope).
    under arms bajo las armas.
    under way en camino, andando, en marcha.
    under the circumstances en las circunstan-
      cias.
    under an obligation deber favores.
    under one's nose en las barbas de uno.
underclothes ropa interior.
undergo someterse a, pasar por, sufrir.
  to undergo an operation operarse.
underground subterráneo.
underline subrayar.
underneath bajo, debajo de.
understand comprender, entender; estar de
    acuerdo.
  Do you understand Spanish? ¿Entiende Ud.
    español?
  That's easy to understand. Eso se comprende.
understanding entendimiento, modo de ver;
    acuerdo, inteligencia (agreement).
  to come to an understanding llegar a una
    inteligencia.
understood entendido, sobreentendido, conve-
    nido.
  to be understood sobreentenderse.
  be it understood entiéndase bien.
  That's understood. Está entendido. Por
    supuesto. Estamos de acuerdo.
undertake emprender; comprometerse a.
undertaking empresa; compromiso, promesa
    (promise).
undo deshacer, desatar; anular.

undress desnudar (se).
uneasiness malestar, inquietud, desasosiego.
uneasy inquieto, molesto, incómodo, desasoseg-
    ado.
unequal desigual.
uneven desigual, irregular; non, impar (num-
    bers).
unexpected inesperado.
unfair injusto.
unfaithful infiel.
unfavorable desfavorable.
unfinished incompleto.
unfit inadecuado, impropio; inepto, incapaz de
    (unable).
unfold (to) desenvolver, desplegar; descubrir,
    revelar, mostrar (to reveal, to show).
unforeseen imprevisto, inesperado.
unforgettable inolvidable.
unfortunate desgraciado, desdichado.
unfortunately por desgracia, desgraciadamente.
unfurnished sin muebles, desamueblado, no
    amueblado.
  unfurnished apartment piso sin muebles.
ungrateful ingrato, desagradecido.
unhappy infeliz, desdichado.
unhealthy enfermizo, achacoso; malsano.
unheard of inaudito; que no se ha oído.
unhurt ileso, intacto.
uniform uniforme.
union unión.
unique único.
unit unidad.
unite unir (se).
united unido.
  United States Estados Unidos.
unity unidad.
universal universal.
universe universo.
university universidad.
unjust injusto.
unkind poco amable; despiadado (cruel); tosco,
    duro (harsh).
unknown desconocido.
unlawful ilegal, ilícito, ilegítimo.
unless a no ser que, a menos que, si no.
unlike diferente, desemejante.
unlikely improbable, inverosímil, inverisímil.
unload descargar.
unlucky desgraciado, desafortunado, de mala
    suerte.
unmarried soltero.
  unmarried man soltero.
  unmarried woman soltera.
unmoved impasible, inmutable, frío.
unnecessary innecesario.
unpaid sin pagar, no pagado.
unpleasant desagradable.
unquestionable indiscutible, indisputable.

unreasonable irrazonable, desatinado.

unruly ingobernable.

unsatisfactory que no satisface, inaceptable, poco satisfactorio.

unseen invisible; inadvertido.

unselfish desinteresado.

unsettled revuelto, turbio (liquid); variable, inestable (not stable); sin pagar, pendiente (a bill, etc.).

unsteady instable, inconstante, inseguro.

unsuccessful infructuoso, sin éxito; desafortunado.

unsuitable impropio, inadecuado.

until hasta.

untiring incansable, infatigable.

unusual extraordinario, poco común.

unwelcome mal acogido, malvenido.

unwilling maldispuesto.

    to be unwilling no estar dispuesto.

unwillingly de mala gana.

unwritten no escrito, en blanco.

unworthy indigno.

up arriba, en lo alto, hacia arriba; en pie, de pie.

    up and down arriba y abajo; de un lado a otro.

    to go up subir.

    to go upstairs subir.

    to walk up and down ir de un sitio para otro, dar vueltas.

    up the river río arriba.

    one flight up en el piso de arriba.

    Up there! ¡Alto ahí!

    to be up to one ser asunto de uno, ser cosa de uno.

    What's up? ¿Qué pasa? ¿De qué se trata?

    The time is up. Ya ha vencido el plazo. Ya es tiempo.

    She's not up yet. Todavía no se ha levantado.

    this side up arriba (on cases).

    up to hasta; capaz de (capable of doing); tramando (plotting).

    up to anything dispuesto a todo.

    up-to-date al día moderno.

    up to date hasta la fecha.

upon sobre, encima.

    upon my word bajo mi palabra.

    upon which sobre lo cual.

upper superior, alto.

    the upper floor el piso de arriba.

    upper lip labio superior.

upright vertical; derecho, recto, justo (character).

upset trastornar, perturbar, desarreglar.

upside

    upside down al revés, patas arriba; desconcierto.

upstairs arriba; en el piso de arriba.

    to go upstairs subir.

upstart *n.* advenedizo.

upwards hacia arriba.

urgency urgencia.

urgent urgente, apremiante.

use uso.

    to make use of utilizar.

    in use en uso.

    of no use inútil.

    to be of no use no servir.

    to have no use for no servirle a uno; no tener buena opinión de, tener en poco.

    It's no use. Es inútil.

    What's the use? ¿Para qué? Es inútil. ¿De qué sirve?

use (to) usar, servirse de, hacer uso de; soler, acostumbrer.

    to use one's own judgment obrar uno conforme le parezca.

    to use up gastar; agotar.

    I'm used to it. Estoy acostumbrado a ello.

    I used to see her every day. Solía verla todos los días.

used usado.

    used clothes ropa usada.

useful útil.

useless inútil, inservible.

usher acomodador.

usual usual; común, general, ordinario.

    as usual como de costumbre.

usually usualmente, ordinariamente, de costumbre, por lo común, por lo general, comunmente.

    I usually get up early. Por regla general me levanto temprano.

utensil utensilio.

    kitchen utensils batería de cocina.

utility utilidad.

utilize utilizar, emplear.

utmost extremo, sumo.

    to the utmost hasta no más.

    to do one's utmost hacer cuanto esté de la parte de uno, hacer uno cuanto pueda.

utterly enteramente, del todo.

V

vacancy vacante (unoccupied position); cuarto para alquilar (room); piso para alquilar (apartment).

vacant vacío, desocupado.

vacation vacaciones.

vaccinate vacunar.

vaccine vacuna (med.).

vacuum vacío.

vague vago.

vain vano.

    in vain en vano.

vainly vanamente.

valid válido.

valise maleta, saco de viaje.
valley valle.
valuable valioso.
value valor; justiprecio, valuación (estimated value); aprecio, estimación (regard).
value (to) valuar, tasar (to estimate the value); preciar, apreciar, tener en mucho (to think highly of).
valve válvula.
vanilla vainilla.
vanish desvanecerse, desaparecerse.
vanity vanidad.
variable variable.
variety variedad.
various varios; diverso.
varnish (to) barnizar.
vary variar.
vaseline vaselina.
vast vasto, inmenso, enorme, grandísimo.
veal ternera.
    veal cutlet chuleta de ternera.
vegetable vegetal, planta.
    vegetable man verdulero.
    vegetable soup menestra, sopa de legumbres.
vegetables legumbres, verduras, hortalizas.
vegetation vegetación.
vehement vehemente.
vehicle vehículo.
veil velo, mantilla.
vein vena.
velvet terciopelo.
ventilate ventilar.
ventilation ventilación.
verb verbo.
verdict veredicto, sentencia.
verse verso.
vertical vertical.
very muy, mucho, mucha.
    very much mucho, muchísimo.
    very many muchísimos, muchísimas.
    very much money mucho dinero.
    (Very) Much obliged. Muy agradecido.
    Very well, thank you. Muy bien, gracias.
    the very man el mismo hombre.
    the very thought el solo pensamiento.
vessel vasija, vaso (container); buque (ship).
vest chaleco.
veteran veterano.
veterinary veterinario.
vex molestar, enfadar.
vexation molestia, enfado.
vexing molesto, importuno.
vibration vibración.
vice vicio.
vice-president vicepresidente.
vice versa viceversa, al contrario.
vicinity vecindad, cercanía.
vicious malvado, depravado.

    vicious circle círculo vicioso.
victim víctima.
victor vencedor.
victorious victorioso.
victory victoria.
view vista, perspectiva, panorama.
    bird's eye view vista de pájaro.
    in view of en vista de.
    point of view punto de vista.
    What a view! ¡Que vista!
view (to) mirar, ver, contemplar.
vigil vigilia.
vigilant vigilante.
vigor brío, vigor.
vigorous vigoroso.
vile vil, bajo.
villa casa de campo.
village aldea, pueblo, pueblecito.
villager aldeano.
villain villano.
vine parra.
vinegar vinagre.
vineyard viña.
violate violar.
violation violación.
violence violencia.
violent furioso, violento.
violet violeta.
violin violín.
violinist violinista.
violoncello violoncelo.
virgin virgen.
virtue virtud.
virtuous virtuoso.
visa visto bueno, refrendo, visado.
visible visible.
vision visión.
visit visita.
    to pay a visit hacer una visita.
visit (to) visitar.
visitor visitante.
visual visual.
vital vital.
vitamin vitamina.
vivid vivo, vívido, gráfico.
vocal vocal.
    vocal cords cuerdas vocales.
voice voz.
void *adj.* vacío; nulo, inválido, sin valor ni fuerza (null).
void *n.* vacío.
volcano volcán.
volt voltio.
volume volumen; tomo (book).
voluntary voluntario.
volunteer voluntario.
vomit vómito.
vomit (to) vomitar.

vote voto, sufragio.

vote (to) votar.

voter votante.

vow voto.

vow (to) hacer promesa, hacer voto.

voyage viaje.

vulgar vulgar.

vulture buitre.

W

wade vadear.

   to wade through the mud andar por el barro.

wage(s) sueldo, paga, jornal.

   monthly wages sueldo mensual, salario.

   daily wages jornal.

   wage earner jornalero, trabajador, obrero.

wage (to) comprender.

   to wage war hacer guerra.

wager apuesta.

wager (to) apostar.

wagon carro; furgón (freight car).

wait (to) esperar, aguardar.

   Wait for me. Espéreme.

   to keep waiting hacer esperar.

   to wait on atender a, despachar (in a store, etc.); servir a (to serve).

waiter mozo, camarero.

waiting espera.

   waiting room sala de espera.

waitress camarera.

wake (to) despertar(se).

   to wake up despertar, llamar; despertarse.

   Wake me at seven. Despiérteme a las siete.

   I woke up at seven. Me desperté a las siete.

waken despertar.

walk paseo.

   to take a walk dar un paseo.

walk (to) andar, caminar.

   to walk away marcharse.

   to walk down bajar.

   to walk up subir.

   to walk out salir; declararse en huelga (to go on strike).

   to walk arm in arm ir del brazo.

   to walk up and down pasearse, ir y venir.

walking paseo, acción de pasear.

   to go walking ir de paseo; ir a pié.

   walking cane bastón.

wall muro, pared, muralla.

   wallpaper papel de empapelar.

walnut nuez (nut); nogal (tree).

waltz vals.

waltz (to) valsar.

wand vara, varita.

wander vagar; perderse, extraviarse (to go astray); divagar, delirar (of the mind).

want necesidad, falta, carencia.

   to be in want estar necesitado.

   for want of por falta de.

want (to) necesitar, tener necesidad de (to need); querer, desear (to desire).

   What do you want? ¿Qué quiere Ud.?

   Don't you want to come? ¿No quiere Ud. venir?

   Cook wanted. Se necesita una cocinera.

wanting defectuoso, deficiente; necesitado, escaso (lacking).

   to be wanting faltar.

war guerra.

   War Department Ministerio de la guerra.

   to wage war hacer la guerra.

ward sala, pabellón (in a hospital); barrio, distrito (of a city); pupilo, menor en tutela (person under the care of a guardian, etc.).

warden guardian, celador; carcelero (of a prison); director (of school, etc.).

ward off (to) parar, detener, desviar.

wardrobe guardarropa, armario, ropero.

   wardrobe trunk baúl ropero.

warehouse almacén, depósito.

wares mercancías, mercadería, géneros or artículos de comercio.

warfare guerra.

warlike belicoso.

warm caliente, cálido, caluroso.

   It's warm. Hace calor.

   I am warm. Tengo calor.

   warm water agua caliente.

warm (to) calentar.

   to warm up calentarse; acalorarse, tomar bríos.

warmly calurosamente, cordialmente.

warn advertir, prevenir, avisar.

warning advertencia, prevención, aviso; lección, escarmiento.

   to give warning prevenir, advertir.

warrant autorización; mandamiento, auto (a written order).

warrior guerrero.

wash lavado; ropa sucia (clothes to be washed); ropa lavada (clothes that have been washed).

   washbasin lavamanos, palangana.

   washing machine máquina de lavar, lavadora mecánica.

   washstand lavabo.

wash (to) lavar.

   to wash one's hands lavarse las manos.

waste despilfarro, derroche; desperdicio.

waste (to) malgastar, desperdiciar; perder, gastar.

   to waste one's time perder uno el tiempo.

wastebasket cesto de los papeles.

wastepaper papel de desecho.

watch reloj; guardia (guard).

wristwatch   reloj de pulsera.
to be on the watch   estar alerta, estar sobre sí.
to wind up a watch   dar cuerda a un reloj.
watch (to)   vigilar.
  to watch out   tener cuidado con.
  to watch over   guardar, vigilar.
  to watch one's step   tener cuidado; andarse
    con tiento.
watchful   alerta, vigilante, despierto.
watchmaker   relojero.
watchman   vigilante, sereno, guardián.
watchword   santo y seña; consigna, lema.
water   agua.
  fresh water   agua fresca.
  hot water   agua caliente.
  mineral water   agua mineral.
  running water   agua corriente.
  soft water   agua delgada.
  sea water   agua de mar.
  soda water   agua de seltz, soda.
  toilet water   colonia, agua de colonia.
  water faucet   grifo, grifo del agua.
  water front   litoral, tierras ribereñas; la sec-
    ción del puerto.
  water power   fuerza hidráulica.
  to make one's mouth water   hacer la boca
    agua.
  water bag   bolsa para agua, calientapiés.
water (to)   regar (to sprinkle); mojar, humedecer
  (to wet).
waterfall   cascada, catarata.
watermelon   sandía.
waterproof   impermeable.
wave   ola; onda (radio, etc.), ondulación (hair).
  short wave   onda corta.
  long wave   onda larga.
  sound wave   onda sonora.
  wave length   longitud de onda.
wave (to)   ondular; flotar (in the air); hacer señas
  (to signal by waving); agitar (a handkerchief, etc.).
  to wave one's hand   hacer señas con la mano.
waver (to)   vacilar, titubear; cejar, ceder (to give
  way).
wavering   irresoluto, vacilante.
waving n.   ondulación.
wavy   ondulado.
wax   cera.
  wax candle   vela de cera.
  wax paper   papel encerado.
wax (to)   encerar.
way   camino, vía, ruta; modo, manera (manner).
  way in   entrada.
  way off   muy lejos.
  way out   salida.
  by way of   por la vía de; pasando por.
  by the way   a propósito, dicho sea de paso.
  in such a way   de tal manera.

in this way   de este modo.
any way   de cualquier modo.
in no way   de ningún modo.
this way   así.
Go this way.   Vaya por aquí.
on the way   en ruta; de camino.
out of the way   fuera de camino; donde no
  estorbe.
across the way   al otro lado, en frente.
Which way?   ¿Por dónde?
Get out of the way!   ¡Atrás!
Step this way.   Venga Ud. acá.-
in some way or other   de un modo o de otro.
under way   en camino, en marcha.
to have (get) one's way   salirse con la suya.
the other way around   al contrario, al revés.
all the way   en todo el camino, durante el
  trayecto; del todo; hasta el fin.
to give way   ceder.
ways and means   medios y arbitrios.
we   nosotros, nosotras.
  we Americans   nosotros los norteamericanos.
weak   débil.
weaken   debilitar.
weakness   debilidad, flaqueza.
wealth   riqueza, bienes.
wealthy   rico, adinerado.
weapon   arma.
wear   uso, desgaste.
wear (to)   llevar, usar, llevar puesto, poner.
  to wear down   cansar, fastidiar (to tire,
    annoy); vencer (to overcome).
  to wear off   gastarse; borrarse (color).
  to wear out   gastarse, apurar mucho (a dress,
    etc.).
  to wear well   durar (to last).
  Which dress will you wear tonight?   ¿Qué
    vestido te vas a poner esta noche?
  I like the blouse she's wearing.   Me gusta la
    blusa que lleva puesta.
weariness   cansancio, hastío, aburrimiento.
wearing apparel   ropa, prenda de vestir.
weary adj.   cansado, hastiado, fastidiado.
weary (to)   cansar, hastiar, molestar.
weather   tiempo.
  bad weather   mal tiempo.
  nice weather   buen tiempo.
  The weather is fine.   Hace buen tiempo. Hace
    un tiempo muy bueno.
  weather conditions   condiciones meteorológi-
    cas.
  weather report   boletín meteorológico.
weave   tejer.
web   tela, tejido.
  spider web   tela de araña.
wedding   boda, nupcias.
  wedding dress   traje de boda.
  wedding present   regalo de boda.

wedge cuna.
Wednesday miércoles.
weed maleza, mala hierba.
week semana.
    weekday día de trabajo.
    last week la semana pasada.
    next week la semana que viene.
    a week from tomorrow de mañana en ocho
      días.
week end fin de semana.
weekly *adj.* semanario.
    weekly publication semanario.
weekly *adv.* semalmente, por semana.
weep llorar.
    to weep for llorar por, llorar de.
weigh pesar; levar (anchor).
weight peso.
    gross weight peso bruto.
    net weight peso neto.
    weights and measures pesos y medidas.
weighty de peso, ponderoso, serio, importante.
welcome *adj.* bienvenido.
    Welcome! ¡Bienvenido!
    You're welcome (answer to "Thank you.").
    De nada. No hay de qué.
welcome *n.* bienvenida.
welcome (to) dar la bienvenida.
welfare bienestar.
    welfare work obra de beneficiencia, labor
      social.
well pozo.
well *adj.* bueno, bien; *adv.* bien.
    to be well estar bien.
    very well muy bien.
    I am quite well. Estoy muy bien.
    I don't feel well. No me siento bien.
    to look well tener buena cara.
    well and good la enhorabuena, bien está.
    well-being bienestar.
    well-bred bien educado.
    well done bien hecho.
    well-to-do acomodado, rico.
    well-known bien conocido.
    well-timed oportuno.
    as well as así como, lo mismo que.
    well then con que.
    Well! ¡Cómo!
    Well, well! ¡Vaya! ¡Qué cosa!
    Very well! ¡Está bien!
west oeste, occidente.
western occidental.
wet *adj.* mojado; húmedo.
    to get wet mojarse.
wet (to) mojar.
whale ballena.
wharf muelle.
what qué.
    What's that? ¿Qué es eso?

What's the matter? ¿Qué pasa?
    What else? ¿Qué mas?
    What for? ¿Para qué?
    What about? ¿Qué le parece? ¿Que hay en
      cuanto a eso? ¿Qué diremos?
    What of (about) it? ¿Y eso qué importa?
    what if y si, qué será si, qué sucederá si, y
      qué importa que, aunque.
whatever cualquier cosa que, sea lo que fuere,
    lo que.
    whatever you like lo que Ud. quiera.
    whatever reasons he may have sean cuales
      fueren las razones que tenga.
wheat trigo.
wheel rueda.
    steering wheel volante.
    wheel chair silla de ruedas.
wheelbarrow carretilla.
when cuando.
    Since when? ¿Desde cuándo? ¿De cuándo
      acá?
whenever cuando quiera, siempre que, en cual-
    quier tiempo que sea.
    whenever you like cuando Ud. quiera.
where donde, dónde, adonde, en donde, por
    donde, de donde.
    Where are you from? ¿De dónde es Ud.?
    Where are you going? ¿Adónde va?
whereby por lo cual, por el que, por medio del
    cual, con lo cual.
wherever dondequiera que.
whether si, sea que, que.
    I doubt whether dudo que.
    whether he likes it or not que quiera, que no
      quiera.
which cual, que, el cual, la cual, lo cual.
    Which book? ¿Qué libro?
    Which way? ¿Por dónde? ¿Por qué camino?
    Which of these? ¿Cuál de éstos?
    all of which todo lo cual.
    both of which ambos.
whichever cualquiera.
while instante, momento, rato.
    a little while un ratito.
    a little while ago hace poco rato, no hace
      mucho.
    for a while por algún tiempo.
    once in a while de vez en cuando.
    to be worth while valer la pena.
while *conj.* mientras, mientras que, a la vez que.
whip látigo, azote.
whip (to) azotar, dar latigazos; batir (cream,
    eggs, etc.).
    whipped cream nata batida.
whirl giro, rotación.
whirl (to) dar vueltas, girar.
whirlpool remolino, vorágine.
whirlwind torbellino.

whisper cuchicheo.
whisper (to) cuchichear, decir al oído.
   to whisper in someone's ear decir al oído.
whistle silbido.
whistle (to) silbar.
white blanco.
   white of an egg clara de huevo.
   white lie mentirilla.
   White House Casa Blanca.
whiten (to) blanquear.
who quien, quienes, que, el que, la que, los que,
   las que; quien.
   Who is he? ¿Quién es?
whoever quienquiera, cualquiera.
   whoever it may be quienquiera que sea.
whole todo, entero, integral.
   the whole todo el.
   whole wheat bread pan integral.
   on the whole en conjunto, en general.
   whole number número entero.
wholehearted sincero, de todo corazón; enérgico, activo.
wholesale (al) por mayor.
wholesome sano.
   wholesome food alimento sano, alimento
   nutritivo.
wholly totalmente, enteramente.
whom a quien, a quienes.
whose cuyo, de quien.
why por qué.
   Why not? ¿Por qué no? ¿Pues y qué?
   the why and the wherefore el porqué y la
   razón.
wicked mala, malvado, perverso.
wickedness maldad, iniquidad.
wide ancho, vasto, extenso.
   two inches wide dos pulgadas de ancho.
   wide open abierto de par en par.
wide-awake muy despierto, alerta, vivo.
widely muy, mucho.
   widely different diametralmente opuesto,
   completamente diferente.
   widely used se usa mucho.
   widely known muy conocido.
widen ensanchar, extender, ampliar.
widespread divulgado, esparcido.
widow viuda.
widower viudo.
width ancho, anchura.
wife esposa, señora, mujer.
wig peluca.
wild salvaje (savage); silvestre (plants, flowers,
   etc.); atolondrado, descabellado, desenfrenado (of a person).
wilderness desierto.
will voluntad; testamento.
   at will a voluntad, a discreción.
   against one's will contra la voluntad de uno.

will (to) querer, desear; testar, hacer testamento
   (to make a will). (See also shall.)
   Will you tell me the time? ¿Me hace Ud.
   el favor de decirme la hora?
   Will you do me a favor? ¿Me quiere Ud.
   hacer un favor?
   I won't do it, but she will. Yo no lo haré,
   pero ella sí.
   Will you go? ¿Irá Ud.?
   I will not go. No iré. No quiero ir.
willing dispuesto, gustoso, pronto, inclinado.
   to be willing estar dispuesto, querer.
   God willing Dios mediante.
willingly de buena gana, gustosamente.
willingness buena voluntad, buena gana.
win (to) ganar, vencer, prevalecer, lograr.
   to win out salir bien, triunfar.
wind viento.
   wind instrument instrumento de viento.
wind (to) enrollar; dar cuerda (a watch).
windmill molino (de viento).
window ventana.
   windowpane vidrio (cristal) de la ventana.
   window shade transparente, visillo.
   window shutter postigo.
windshield parabrisas.
windy ventoso.
   to be windy hacer viento.
wine vino.
   red wine vino tinto.
   white wine vino blanco.
wing ala.
wink guiñada.
   not to sleep a wink no pegar los ojos.
wink (to) guiñar.
winner ganador.
winter invierno.
wintry invernal.
wipe (to) limpiar con un trapo, etc. (the floor,
   etc.); secar, enjugar (to dry).
   to wipe out arrasar, extirpar, destruir.
wire n. alambre (metal); telegrama (telegram).
   barbed wire alambre de púa.
wire (to) telegrafiar.
wisdom sabiduría, juicio; sentido común.
   wisdom tooth muela del juicio.
wise sabio; juicioso, prudente.
wish deseo.
wish (to) desear, querer.
   to make a wish concebir un deseo, pensar
   en algo que se quiere.
wit ingenio, agudeza, sal.
witch bruja.
witch hazel loción de carpe, hamamelis.
with con, en compañía de; a, contra, de, en,
   entre.
   coffee with milk café con leche.
   to speak with caution hablar con prudencia.

to touch with the hand   tocar con la mano.
She came with a friend.   Vino con un amigo.
identical with   idéntico a.
to struggle with   luchar contra.
to fill with   llenar de.
with the exception of   a excepción de.
with regard to   en cuanto a, con respecto a.
with the exception   a excepción de.
the girl with the red dress   la chica del
vestido rojo.
That always happens with friends.   Eso
ocurre siempre entre amigos.

withdraw (to)   retirar, retirarse, replegarse; retractarse (to retract).

withdrawal   retirada, repliegue.

within   dentro de; a poco de, cerca de.
within a short distance   a poca distancia.
within a week   dentro de una semana.
within one's reach   al alcance de uno.
from within   de adentro.

without   sin; *adv.* fuera, afuera, por fuera, de la
parte de afuera.
tea without sugar   té sin azúcar.
without fail   sin falta.
within and without   dentro y fuera.
without doubt   sin duda.
without noticing it   sin advertirlo.

witness   testigo.

witness (to)   presenciar, ver; declarar, atestiguar,
dar testimonio, servir de testigo (to act as
a witness).

witty   ingenioso, ocurrente, gracioso, salado.
a witty remark   una gracia, una agudeza.
She's very witty.   Es muy salada.

wolf   lobo.

woman   mujer.
young woman   joven.

wonder   maravilla.
No wonder.   No es extraño. No es para menos.

wonder (to)   admirarse, maravillarse de, preguntarse.
I wonder whether it's true.   Yo me pregunto
si será verdad.
I wonder what she wants.   ¿Qué querrá?
to wonder at   maravillarse de.
to wonder about   extrañarse, tener sus dudas
acerca de; tener curiosidad por.
I wonder why?   ¿Por qué será?
I wonder!   ¡Si será cierto!

wonderful   estupendo, admirable, maravilloso.

wood   madera (matinal); monte, bosque (woods).
firewood   leña.

woodwork   maderaje, maderamen.

wool   lana.

woolen   de lana.

word   palabra.
too funny for words   lo más gracioso del
mundo.
in so many words   en esas mismas palabras,

exactamente así, claramente, sin ambages.
word for word   palabra por palabra.
in other words   en otros términos.
by word of mouth   de palabra, verbalmente.
on my word   bajo mi palabra.
to leave word   dejar dicho, dejar recado.
to send word   mandar a decir.

work   trabajo, labor.
to be at work   estar en el trabajo; estar ocupado, estar trabajando.
out of work   sin trabajo.
work of art   objeto de arte, obra de arte.

work (to)   trabajar; funcionar (machine); explotar
(a mine); tallar (a stone); elaborar, fabricar.
to work out   resolver (a problem); llevar a
cabo (to carry out); salir bien, tener éxito
(to come out all right).
The machine doesn't work.   La máquina no
funciona.

worker   obrero, trabajador.

working   trabajo, funcionamiento.
working day   día de trabajo.

workman   obrero, trabajador.

workshop   taller.

world   mundo.
all over the world   por todo el mundo.
world-wide   mundial.
World War   Guerra mundial.

worm   gusano.

worn-out   rendido.
worn-out clothes   ropa usada.
I'm worn-out.   Estoy rendido.

worry   preocupación, cuidado ansiedad.

worry (to)   preocupar(se), inquietar(se).
Don't worry.   No se preocupe. No se apure.
to be worried   estar preocupado.

worse   peor.
to get worse   empeorarse.
so much the worse   tanto peor.
worse and worse   de mal en peor.
worse than ever   peor que nunca.
to take a turn for the worse   empeorar.

worship   culto, adoración.

worship (to)   adorar, venerar.

worst   pésimo, malísimo.
the worst   lo peor, lo más malo.
at the worst   en el peor de los casos.
if worst comes to the worst   si sucediera lo
peor.
to have the worst of it   salir perdiendo, llevar
la peor parte.

worth   valor, mérito.
What's it worth?   ¿Cuánto vale?
It's worth the money.   Eso vale su precio.
Es una buena compra.
He's worth a lot of money.   Tiene mucho
dinero.
to be worth while   valer la pena.

It's worth while trying.   Vale la pena intentarlo.

One dollar's worth in change.   Un dólar en calderilla.

worthless inútil, inservible, sin valor.

to be worthless   ser inútil.

worth-while que vale la pena.

worthy digno, meredor.

would querer. The future conditional is generally expressed by adding -ía, -ías, -ía, -íamos, -íais, -ían to the infinitive of the verb.

I would go.   iría.

I would like to go.   Quisiera ir.

I wouldn't go if I could.   No iría si pudiera.

She wouldn't come.   No quiso venir.

I wish she would come.   Querría que viniese. Ojalá que venga.

I would like to ask you a favor.   Quisiera pedirle un favor.

Would you do me a favor?   ¿Me haría Ud. un favor?

wound herida.

wound (to) herir.

wounded herido.

wrap (to) envolver (to wrap up).

wrapper envoltura.

wrapping adj. de envolver.

wrapping paper   papel de envolver.

wreath corona (of flowers, etc.).

wreck naufragio (shipwreck); ruina (ruin).

wreck (to) arruinar; hacer naufragar.

to be shipwrecked   irse a pique, naufragar.

wrench torcedura (wrenching), llave de tuercas, llave inglesa (tool).

wrench (to) torcer, dislocar, sacar de quicio.

to wrench one's foot   torcerse el pie.

wrestle luchar.

wrestler luchador.

wring torcer, retorcer, estrujar; escurrir (wet clothes, etc.).

to wring out   exprimir, escurrir.

wrinkle arruga.

wrinkle (to) arrugar.

wrist muñeca.

wristwatch   reloj de pulsera.

write (to) escribir.

to write down   poner por escrito, anotar.

writer escritor, autor.

writing escritura, escrito.

in writing   por escrito.

to put in writing   poner por escrito.

writing desk   escritorio.

writing paper   papel de escribir.

written escrito.

wrong n. mal; daño (harm); injuria, injusticia (injustice); agravio; adj. mal(o), incorrecto, falso, erróneo, injusto; adv. mal.

the knowledge of right and wrong   el conocimiento del bien y el mal.

to do wrong   hacer daño, obrar mal.

You are wrong.   Ud. no tiene razón. Ud. está equivocado.

to be wrong   no tener razón; estar mal hecho.

wrong side out   al revés.

That's wrong.   Eso está mal. Está mal dicho (said). Está mal escrito (written). Está mal hecho (done).

Something is wrong with the engine.   El motor no funciona bien.

Something is wrong with him.   Le pasa algo. Tiene algo raro.

I took the wrong road.   Erré el camino. Me equivoqué de camino.

X

X-rays rayos X.

Y

yard yarda, vara (measure); patio (court); corral (around a barn).

Navy yard   Arsenal.

yawn bostezo.

yawn (to) bostezar.

year año.

last year   el año pasado.

all year round   todo el año.

many years ago   hace muchos años.

yearbook anuario, anales.

yearly adj. anual.

yearly adv. anualmente, todos los años.

yeast levadura.

yell grito.

yell (to) gritar, chillar.

yellow amarillo.

yes sí.

yesterday ayer.

day before yesterday   anteayer.

yet adv. todavía, aún; conj. sin embargo, con todo.

not yet   aún no, todavía no.

as yet   hasta ahora, hasta aquí.

I don't know it yet.   Todavía no lo sé.

yield rendimiento, provecho.

yield (to) rendir, producir; ceder (to give in).

yoke yugo; yunta de bueyes (2 oxen).

yolk yema.

you tú (fam.); usted (polite).

young joven, mozo.

young man   joven.

young lady   señorita, joven.

young people   jóvenes.

to look young   verse joven, tener la traza de

joven, aparentar poca edad.

your   tú, tus, su, sus, vuestro(s), de usted(es).

yours   suyo(s), suya(s), tuyo(s), tuya(s), vuestro(s), vuestra(s), el suyo, la suya, el tuyo, la tuya, la vuestra, los (tuyos, suyos, vuestros), **las** (tuyas, suyas, vuestras), de (usted, ustedes).

This book is yours.   Este libro es tuyo (suyo, de usted, vuestro, de ustedes).

a friend of yours   un amigo tuyo (suyo, vuestro, de usted, de ustedes).

Yours sincerely   Su seguro servidor (S.S.S.), Su afectísimo y seguro servidor (Su afmo. y s.s.).

yourself   usted mismo, tú mismo.

Wash yourself.   Lávate. Lávese.

yourselves   ustedes mismos, vosotros mismos.

youth   juventud.

youthful   juvenil.

Z

zeal   celo, fervor.

zealous   celoso.

zero   cero.

zest   entusiasmo.

zigzag   zigzag.

zinc   zinc.

zone   zona.

zoo   jardín zoológico.

zoological   zoológico.

zoology   zoología.

GLOSSARY OF PROPER NAMES

Albert Alberto.
Alexander Alejandro.
Alfred Alfredo.
Alice Alicia.
Andrew Andrés.
Ann, Anna Ana.
Anthony Antonio.
Arthur Arturo.
Beatrice Beatriz.
Bernard Bernardo.
Catharine, Catherine Catalina.
Charles Carlos.
Charlotte Carlota.
Dorothy Dorotea.
Edward Eduardo.
Elizabeth Isabel.
Ellen Elena.
Emily Emilia.
Ernest Ernesto.
Esther Ester.
Eugene Eugenio.
Francis Francisco.
Frederic(k) Federico.
George Jorge.
Gertrude Gertrudis.
Helen Elena.
Henry Enrique.

Isabella Isabel.
James Jaime, Diego.
Joan, Joanna Juana.
John Juan.
Joseph José.
Josephine Josefina.
Juliet Julia.
Julius Julio.
Leo León.
Louis Luis.
Louise Luisa.
Margaret Margarita.
Martha Marta.
Mary María.
Michael Miguel.
Paul Pablo.
Peter Pedro.
Philip Felipe.
Raymond Raimundo, Ramón.
Richard Ricardo.
Robert Roberto.
Rose Rosa.
Susan Susana.
Theresa Teresa.
Thomas Tomas.
Vincent Vicente.
William Guillermo.

GLOSSARY OF GEOGRAPHICAL NAMES

Algiers Argel.
Alps Alpes.
Alsace Alsacia.
Andalusia Andalucía.
Antilles Antillas.
Antwerp Amberes.
Aragon Aragón.
Argentina Argentina.
Asturias Asturias.
Athens Atenas.
Atlantic Ocean Océano Atlántico.
Barcelona Barcelona.
Basque Provinces Provincias Vascongadas.
Bayonne Bayona.
Belgium Bélgica.
Bilboa Bilbao.
Biscay Vizcaya.
Bolivia Bolivia.
Brazil Brasil.
Brittany Bretaña.
Brussels Bruselas.
Buenos Aires Buenos Aires.
Castile Castilla.
Catalonia Cataluña.
Chile Chile.
China China.
Colombia Colombia.
Costa Rica Costa Rica.
Cuba Cuba.
Denmark Dinamarca.
Dominican Republic República Dominicana.
Ecuador Ecuador.
Egypt Egipto.
El Salvador El Salvador.
England Inglaterra.
Europe Europa.
Finland Finlandia.
Flanders Flandes.
Florence Florencia.
France Francia.
Galicia Galicia.
Geneva Ginebra.
Genoa Génova.
Germany Alemania.
Greece Grecia.
Guatemala Guatemala.
Havana Habana.
Holland Holanda.
Honduras Honduras.
Hungary Hungría.
Iceland Islandia.
Ireland Irlanda.

Italy Italia.
Japan Japón.
Lima Lima.
Lisbon Lisboa.
London Londres.
Madrid Madrid.
Marseilles Marsella.
Mediterranean Sea Mar Mediterráneo.
Mexico México.
Morocco Marruecos.
Moscow Moscú.
Naples Nápoles.
Navarre Navarra.
Netherlands Países Bajos, Holanda.
New York Nueva York.
New Zealand Nueva Zelandia.
Nicaragua Nicaragua.
Normandy Normandía.

North America América del Norte.
Norway Noruega.
Panama Panamá.
Paraguay Paraguay.
Pacific Ocean Océano Pacífico.
Peru Perú.
Poland Polonia.
Portugal Portugal.
Puerto Rico Puerto Rico.
Prussia Prusia.
Pyrenees Pirineos.
Rome Roma.
Roumania Rumania.
Russia Rusia.
Saragossa Zaragoza.
Scandinavia Escandinavia.
Scotland Escocia.
Seville Sevilla.
Sicily Sicilia.
Spain España.
Spanish America Hispanoamérica.
Sweden Suecia.
Switzerland Suiza.
Texas Tejas.
Toulouse Tolosa.
Turkey Turquía.
United States of America Estados Unidos de América.
Uruguay Uruguay.
Valencia Valencia.
Venezuela Venezuela.
Venice Venecia.
Vienna Viena.

Advanced ($14.95)	**Cassette**	**Record**
French	☐ 558866	☐ 558874
Spanish	☐ 558831	☐ 55884X

For Foreign-Speaking, Who Wish to Learn English ($17.95)

	Cassette	**Record**
English for French	☐ 50202X	☐ 508192
English for Spanish	☐ 558793	☐ 558807
English for Italian	☐ 513234	☐ 502003
English for German	☐ 513226	☐ 501996
English for Portuguese		☐ 508206
English for Chinese	☐ 508176	☐ 508184

Children's Courses ($17.95)

French	☐ 563290	☐ 563304
Spanish	☐ 563339	☐ 563347

Business Skills
Keyboard Typing
cassette $17.95	☐ 542536
record $17.95	☐ 010852
manual $3.00	☐ 512831

Shorthand
cassette $17.95	☐ 542528
record $17.95	☐ 010860
Book I $3.00	☐ 512718
Book II $3.00	☐ 512726

Better Speech
cassette $17.95	☐ 542455
record $17.95	☐ 001373
correct speech $3.00	☐ 512505
correct usage $3.00	☐ 512513

Living Language Videocassette Program ($29.95)

French (60 minutes)	☐ VHS	555549
	☐ Beta	555611
Spanish (77 minutes)	☐ VHS	555557
	☐ Beta	55562X
German	☐ VHS	560151
(90 minutes)	☐ Beta	560143

Order Here
LIVING LANGUAGE, Dept. 849
34 Engelhard Avenue, Avenel, N.J. 07001

YES—rush me the LIVING LANGUAGE COURSES® I've checked.

Name (Please Print) _____

Address _____

City _____ State _____ Zip _____

_____ Courses @ $17.95		
_____ Courses @ $14.95		
_____ Manuals/Dictionaries @ $3.95		
_____ Manuals/Dictionaries @ $4.95		
_____ Books @ $3.00		
_____ Videocassettes @ $29.95		
	N.Y. and N.J. Residents add Sales Tax	
	Shipping & Handling Charge _____ Items @ $2.60 Each	
TOTAL ITEMS ORDERED	**Total Amount Due**	

☐ Check or Money Order Enclosed Made Payable to Crown Publishers, Inc. (No cash or stamps, please)

Charge   ☐ MasterCard   ☐ Visa   ☐ American Express

Account Number (include all digits)

Card Expires   MO   YR

Signature _____